CW01336064

BIRD OBSERVATORIES
OF BRITAIN AND IRELAND

To all those who have contributed in any way to a bird observatory

Bird Observatories of Britain and Ireland

Edited by

Mike Archer, Mark Grantham,
Peter Howlett and Steven Stansfield

T & AD Poyser

London

Published 2010 by T & AD Poyser, an imprint of A&C Black Publishers Ltd, 36 Soho Square, London W1D 3QY

Copyright © 2010 text by Bird Observatories Council
Copyright © 2010 photographs by named photographers
Copyright © 2010 illustrations by Emma Stansfield (29, 81, 156, 205, 228, 372, 405); Simon Gillings (58, 128, 186, 303, 352, 426, 489); Pat McKee (101); Ray Scally (276, 460); Derek Robertson (325)

The right of the Bird Observatories Council to be identified as the author of this work has been asserted by it in accordance with the Copyright, Design and Patents Act 1988.

ISBN (print) 978-1-4081-1040-9
ISBN (e-pub) 978-1-4081-3906-6
ISBN (e-pdf) 978-1-4081-3905-9

A CIP catalogue record for this book is available from the British Library

All rights reserved. No part of this publication may be reproduced or used in any form or by any means – photographic, electronic or mechanical, including photocopying, recording, taping or information storage or retrieval systems – without permission of the publishers.

This book is produced using paper that is made from wood grown in managed sustainable forests. It is natural, renewable and recyclable. The logging and manufacturing processes conform to the environmental regulations of the country of origin.

Commissioning Editor: Nigel Redman
Project Editor: Jim Martin

Design by Mark Heslington Ltd, Scarborough, North Yorkshire
Printed in Spain by GraphyCems

10 9 8 7 6 5 4 3 2 1

Visit www.acblack.com/naturalhistory to find out more about our authors and their books. You will find extracts, author interviews and our blog, and you can sign up for newsletters to be the first to hear about our latest releases and special offers.

Contents

Accredited bird observatories in Britain and Ireland in 2010

Foreword

by Chris Packham

I'm afraid I only have somewhat hazy ideas about what the aura of bird observatories may have been like in the 1950s and 1960s. I imagine a very small guild of unfashionable geeks shivering or sweating in stale air and disintegrating sleeping bags, waking and walking in underpants to make formidably strong instant coffee before silently and religiously raising the nets or tramping off into the gloom. It's all a bit grey and green and World Service and definitely and perversely cliquey. If you were there, I'm sorry, but I wasn't. I was somewhere between an unfertilised ovum and thumbing my first Peterson. But, like so many, I am indebted to your frozen fumblings and all those mornings when your dedication was the only alarm clock required, to the hundreds of thousands of hours freely given, to all your ideas and inventions, to your collective imaginations and the intelligent developments which solidified the concept of the bird observatories, their *raison d'être* and their fabulous success.

My experience of 'obs' is all very bad-hair eighties, twitchy nineties and better hair and better-behaviour noughties. And recently it's been all very Portland, where the marvellous Martin Cade presides over a welcoming, clean, well-equipped centre of excellence. (I've not heard the World Service on there, they do have Earl Grey tea, and underpants have never been in evidence!). Of course, we have moved on, birding has broadened in its appeal and the number of visitors has vastly increased. What remains intact, however, is a meticulous attention to the welfare of the birds and to the quality of the data collected. And it is this unbroken continuum of comparable information which is so invaluable at a time when it is implicitly important to understand the movements, populations and ecologies of our birds. Only then will we stand a chance of being properly placed to effectively conserve any species, both in the UK and also overseas.

It's also about communicating what we now know, and to this end the accessibility of bird observatories, their staff and volunteers is equally vital – public relations, face-to-face dialogue and that irresistible elixir of boundless and effervescent enthusiasm should be mandatory. Not least because this scattered network of necessarily remote places now represents one of the few resources where young people, kids even, can get close, can touch, can truly engage with wildlife. Birds in the hand provide such a draw, it's impossible not be awed by the beauty of even everyday species, the big eye of a Robin, the exquisite delicacy of a Goldcrest, the stiff tail of a Treecreeper – and for all the science there is still something quite 'fairy tale' about fixing a little ring on these precious things and knowing that one day they may be found miles, perhaps thousands of miles away, and that they have become more than a bird, that they are an individual with the potential to tell us something we couldn't dare to guess at.

And despite all of the achievements to date, all our discoveries, our analysis and revelations, we are actually still guessing about aspects of the lives of birds which we 'take for granted' or think we know. For instance where are 'our' breeding Wheatears hanging out during winter? We know which route they take across Europe and into West Africa but have no recoveries in their final destination and they are a species in decline. New technologies may allow us to improve the pace and accuracy of gathering such data and the bird observatories will be at the fore-front of their implementation.

There is a synergy at hand too because it's not all about birds. Moth traps are active whenever possible at Portland, Martin is a 'moth-er' of repute, and due to the breadth of curiosity of the staff, visitors and volunteers, the flora and fauna of the entire immediate area are very well documented.

So, go, do, be inspired by the 21st century bird observatories, and if you can stay for the weekend all the better, and if you can take someone under twenty, do so; they might be inspired too.

Preface and acknowledgements

The credit for suggesting, several times, that this book should be written goes to Steve Wing, the warden at Cape Clear Bird Observatory. The decision to do so was taken at the Bird Observatories' Council AGM at Portland Bird Observatory in January 2006. Steve rightly commented that the first edition, Bird Observatories in Britain and Ireland (Durman 1976), was seriously out of date. The intention in this second edition is to record what has happened since then, and to introduce the new observatories.

The credit for writing the book goes solely to the observatories themselves. It could not have been accomplished without their enthusiasm, encouragement, effort and careful planning, backed by teams of writers, researchers and helpers of all descriptions whose numbers must run well into the hundreds. It has been written both for the observatories and their aficionados, and for a wider and more general readership.

As with the first edition, each observatory has prepared its own chapter and has contributed to the information in the appendices. This wide variety of authorship is reflected in the style, flavour and character of the writing. Whilst general structural guidelines were suggested, the emphasis varies from chapter to chapter, just as the subject matter reflects the wildlife and location of each observatory, its priorities and staff. Special mention must be made of Neville McKee and Keith Parkes, who have the distinction of being the only authors appearing in both editions of the book.

The text strikes a balance between the fun and excitement of birding at observatories, with some attention to rarities, and the more serious business of data-gathering to help drive advances in ornithology, conservation and environmental decision-making. On this basis, we hope that long-term data sets can provide answers to questions that have yet to be asked. For this reason, continuity of theme has been encouraged and the introduction and subsequent chapters take up the challenge of Bob Spencer's comment, in the first edition, namely that some of the opportunities for advancing our knowledge are 'gathering a thin film of dust in observatory files'. The important use of observatory data is described in many of the chapters.

The first edition contained two appendices: a checklist of bird species and a list of the non-avian species mentioned in the text. Whilst expanding the former to include the numbers of each species ringed at each observatory and retaining the latter, we have also included appendices listing the 56 new species of bird for Britain and Ireland found at the observatories, all present and past observatories, and also every warden and assistant to have worked at each of the currently accredited observatories since they were established. This latter is of interest, because well-known names from today's ornithological, scientific and conservation fields feature within the list as wardens and assistants of observatories long ago.

We have used the vernacular names for bird species in the text, but included a scientific name for races and for a few instances involving flora and non-avian fauna where there is no common name. Websites and e-mail addresses have been omitted as they are subject to change and are easily found elsewhere.

The observatories apart, many other people have helped considerably with the preparation of this book. Particular thanks are due to Professor Chris M. Perrins for his first draft of the Introduction and for stimulating its subsequent development, whilst John Marchant reviewed several of the chapters. His experience and advice were invaluable. To Stephen Message go sincere thanks for the cover illustrations, to the artists Simon Gillings, Emma Stansfield, Ray Scally, Pat McKee and Derek Robertson for preparing the vignettes, and to the photographers whose names are credited with their photographs in the text. Choosing the photographs has involved as much editorial discussion as any other aspect of the book. Excellent photos of 'rare birds of the moment' are instantly available on the web, in birding magazines and elsewhere, so the reader will find relatively few here. We chose instead to focus on high quality pictures of some of the common migrants that make up the 'bread and butter' of observatory work together with a sprinkling of historic and scarcer birds from the earlier days. Most of the other photographs have been chosen to illustrate and to complement the text in explaining the underlying objectives of observatory work.

Our very special thanks must go to Tony John, a good friend of Bardsey Bird and Field Observatory, who very gallantly undertook the mammoth, time-consuming and painstaking task of proof-reading the entire text.

We would also like to thank the many other people who have helped and encouraged us in many ways as the book has progressed including, but not exclusively, Nick Addey, Jed Andrews, Tim Bagworth, Ken Balkow, Dawn Balmer, Sophie Barker, Andy Bowler, Mick Briggs, Richard Brown, Rod Brown, Martin Cade, Niall Campbell, Val Clinging, Sal Cooke, Patrick Davies, Dan Dawson, Rufus Dawson, Tom Dawson, Alison Duncan, Peter Dunn, Richard Else, Christine and Ernest Evans, Pete Findley, David Foster, Roy Frost, Steve Gantlett, George Gregory, Kate Hawkins, John Hewitt, Stephen Hinde, John Hollyer, Jon Hornbuckle, Liz James, Joan James, Kelvin Jones, Jim Lennon, Lisa Lermon, Jim Martin, Neville McKee, Eric Meek, Geoff Neal, Bob and Alicia Normand, Bill Oddie, Nigel Odin, Dave Okill, David Parkin, Sian Parry-Jones, Colin Patrick, Roy Pearson, Steve, Jo, Rachel and Ben Porter, Trevor Poyser, Colin Raven, Sidney Renouf, Nigel Redman, Roger Riddington, Andy Roadhouse, Karen Rawlins, Gareth and Meriel Roberts, Sarah Sayburn, John Shaughenessy, Deryk Shaw, Carole Showell, Gwyn Stacey, Connor Stansfield, Denise Stansfield, Ian Tutt (Trinity House), Katrina van Grouw, David Walker, Derek Whiteley, Barrie Wilkinson, Chris Williams, Steve Williams, Kevin Wilson, Steve Wing and Ian Wright.

Finally, my own first contact with the bird observatories was years ago, when I attended a lecture by Ken Williamson, whom I approached afterwards. I gave him my name and address and he posted on a copy of a paper on the Yellow Wagtail, a small but unforgotten gesture. Sadly, I learned of his death shortly afterwards. The editors hope that they, too, have played a part in encouraging the next generation.

Mike Archer
on behalf of the editors

From the chair of the Bird Observatories Council

I have had the privilege of chairing the Bird Observatories Council (BOC) since 1994, and it has given me enormous pleasure to see the observatories' fortunes develop and evolve through what has been a challenging and turbulent time in ornithology. This period has seen the rise of the personal computer, the explosion of twitching with its focus on vagrants, and the realisation and final acceptance that climate change is real and is implicated in many of the dramatic changes that are taking place in bird populations and behaviour.

When I took over the chair vacated by Mick Rogers, the observatories were generally in good shape, most of them long-established with stable infrastructures, committees and supporters, and, if not well off, at least able to scrape by without fear of closing. The time was ripe to move into a new era of birding, data handling and environmental awareness. The mid-1990s saw wardens and other observatory aficionados up and down the country painstakingly extracting and transcribing data on a number of species from the hand-written logs. After two years of this exercise, it emerged that the data, when combined across the country, were sufficiently robust statistically to draw reliable conclusions on population changes, and that the data also offered enormous opportunities for further analysis in all sorts of unexplored contexts.

This reaffirmation of the value of the data has been a great boost to the observatories and the BOC, and has helped consolidate the observatories' position, with increased interest in the data, particularly for phenological studies. There have also been widespread improvements in observatory facilities with new buildings, extensions and renovations at many. Even the Isle of May are considering a flush toilet and abandoning 'Elsie'! Visitor numbers are good and new observatories have arisen or become re-established since the 1980s, most of which are still expanding and thriving.

The BOC continues to hold an annual weekend meeting when observatory representatives come together for an AGM with a packed and lively agenda. In February 1999 the weekend was spent defining a 'mission statement' which fined down and reconsidered exactly what the purpose of an observatory should be. It is interesting and gratifying in retrospect to see how closely this reflected the minute of the first meeting of the then 'Bird Observatories Sub-committee', fifty-three years earlier in February 1946, that consistency of activity at bird observatories is an essential basic criterion. Time is always given over to some socialising and birding, and once to cetacean watching, when the meeting was innovatively held on the Bilbao ferry. Of late, the meeting has been part-dominated by progressing this book, but the one recurring, unresolved aspiration is to get all the historic observatory data into digital format – a doorway to untold insights into the historical trends of behaviours and populations uniquely available from this data set. This remains the Holy Grail for the BOC, albeit a massive task.

What of the future? The key and unique feature of an observatory is that consistent and long-term coverage is maintained and recorded at a significant migration site. The records gathered in every additional year add progressively to the value of the data. Looking at a map of the current observatories, it is easy to see large gaps in coverage which might easily be filled. In fact during my time as chair I have had a number of informal enquiries about establishing new observatories and my response has been to encourage any sensible proposal, with the proviso that it must be considered a long term project. So, the future must be 'More of the same!', building on the consistency of the established and encouraging the development of the new.

Finally, I must acknowledge the vast army of people who give freely of their time to support the bird observatories, not least those who trek long distances from remote outposts to the meetings of the BOC. None of the following pages could have been written without everyone's help, from the novice visitor to the highly experienced and skilled observatory warden. A huge debt of gratitude is owed to the editors, the authors and all who helped them, and whose only reward will be the knowledge that they have contributed to a landmark publication in the history of the British and Irish bird observatories. Thank you.

Kevin Woodbridge
Twingness
North Ronaldsay

Introduction

by the editors and with contributions from
Professor Chris M. Perrins and Emma Stansfield

This book is a guide to the 18 accredited bird observatories scattered around the coast of Britain, Ireland and the Isle of Man.

The driving force behind this new edition is to increase awareness of the observatories and their work in the 21st century and to encourage more people to visit and become involved with them. It covers each in detail, from the history of their development to the birding and other highlights throughout the year, and includes information on how to visit them. The book also gives an insight into the daily and seasonal routines of the people who live and work at the observatories.

The bird observatory scene has changed, probably out of all recognition, since the first edition of this book was published in 1976. There were then 14 observatories, of which only Skokholm no longer has accredited status. Meanwhile, Filey, Flamborough, Hilbre, Landguard and North Ronaldsay are welcome newcomers. That the observatories are flourishing is evident from recent enthusiastic building, rebuilding and refurbishing activities, often at very considerable expense and with lots of help from volunteers. Visitor numbers are more than satisfactory.

Whilst still actively pursuing their original core activity of monitoring bird migration, many have broadened their focus to become involved with local nature reserves, conservation and education. The IT revolution has enabled lengthy and valuable data sets to be digitised, and finally made accessible and put to good use. Superb websites promote observatory activities as do wildlife television programmes. This introduction and the chapters that follow attempt to describe all this vitality and progress, and, of course, the birds and much other wildlife.

WHAT EXACTLY IS A BIRD OBSERVATORY?

To the uninitiated, the term 'bird observatory' evokes a picture of a building with a massive telescope, through which one looks at birds. The reality is at one and the same time less splendid, and infinitely more exciting.

This extract was taken from the first edition of this book, and it is as appropriate today as it was over 30 years ago. The basic concept behind an observatory is certainly the same now as it was then. Namely a 'bird migration and population monitoring station'; a field station established for the purpose of making and maintaining long-term observations on both migrant and local breeding birds, and for catching, examining and ringing them.

Naturalist and television presenter Iolo Williams (left) with Mike Archer, being filmed at Bardsey for a wildlife programme about the migration of birds and ringing (Steve Stansfield – www.wildlifeimages.eu).

The observatories are located around the coastline of Britain and Ireland at strategic sites on the flyways of migrant birds. Each operates within a defined recording area in which the migration of birds has been monitored consistently and in most cases for many decades. The majority of observatories have a paid full-time warden and a building where visitors can be accommodated.

As you can read later in the 'Daily life at an observatory' section, the primary role of the observatory is to undertake a daily census of the migrant birds within its recording area, that is, a count of all the birds there each day with particular emphasis on spring and autumn. This can be hard work, though an exciting and rewarding occupation for a keen birder. Other methods used to monitor migration include ringing, sea-watching and, at some sites, attending the attractions of birds to lighthouses. Other forms of wildlife, including invertebrates and marine life, are also monitored.

Bird observatories are found throughout the world. Some are government funded, but all those in Britain and Ireland are independent and run by small committees, and many have charitable status. Each observatory is specialised to the extent that it has adapted to its own locality and the problems and idiosyncrasies inherent within it. This very diversity gives each one an individual character, although the facilities outlined below are necessarily generalised.

Accommodation

Anyone can visit a bird observatory: you do not have to be a birdwatcher or a scientist, and many visitors arrive with only a minimal interest and background knowledge of birds. Although one of the aims is to provide accommodation for visiting naturalists and scientific researchers, a stay will appeal to anyone who enjoys an interest in wildlife. People wanting a change or a rest as well as artists, writers, archaeologists, walkers and photographers are just some of those to be found making use of the facilities.

The accommodation is reasonably priced, and varies from fairly basic, hostel-style self-catering with restricted use of electricity, to three-star, full-board guest house facilities. Of course, there have been considerable changes to observatory buildings since the 1970s. Modern, comfortably furnished and well-equipped facilities have replaced the cold, draughty and poorly-lit buildings and possibly primitive conditions of the early days. Some, such as North Ronaldsay, Sandwich Bay and Fair Isle are purpose-built, state of the art premises, built collectively at a cost of several million pounds, while others, like Bardsey, have undergone substantial renovation and modernisation.

The mainland observatories are the more accessible and usually have other good birding sites nearby. The island-based ones take somewhat longer to get to, which would usually mean a longer stay and the cost of getting to the islands, in the case of North Ronaldsay, Fair Isle and elsewhere, has to be borne in mind. However, the experience makes it well worth the effort. Details can be found in the relevant chapter for each observatory. The observatory staff members are dedicated individuals, and a great deal is owed to this small band whose enthusiasm and commitment has helped keep many observatories in operation. Most observatories also rely on the support of volunteers, who provide a significant amount of the manpower at each observatory. The expertise of skilled volunteers is always welcome, and practical skills such as building and maintenance, are particularly appreciated along with computer skills and, of course, any birding knowledge.

Ringing at observatories

Bird ringing is an integral part of observatory work and is undertaken within the national scheme run by the British Trust for Ornithology (BTO). Ringing at observatories helps support national and international projects such as the Seabird Monitoring Programme run by the Joint Nature Conservation Committee (JNCC) in the UK. Birds that are re-trapped are of particular interest, allowing a picture to be built up of the bird's life and its travels. In 2008, a Manx Shearwater was recaught on Bardsey which had been ringed as an adult in 1957, making it at least 56 years old (as young birds do not return to breed for several years). This is the oldest known living wild bird and has entered the Guinness Book of Records. All ringing data collected by the observatories are sent to the BTO and contribute to the huge database of information. Data from the BTO ringing scheme helps guide the conservation policies of such bodies as Natural England, the Countryside Council for Wales (CCW), Scottish Natural Heritage (SNH), Northern Ireland Environment Agency and the National Parks and Wildlife Service of the Department of the Environment for the Republic of Ireland (NPWS).

Education at observatories

Most bird observatories do all they can to inform and educate the general public, from creating an awareness of nature in the casual visitor with interpretive displays to providing training in more specialised areas such as ringing. They are places, too, where the public can often see ringing in action. There is usually a library, well-stocked with bird and natural history books, which is available for the use of visitors, and many have a shop selling relevant books and reports.

Observatory staff members are generally on hand to offer advice and information about the birds and the other wildlife of the area, the work of the observatory and the day's sightings. Visitors are able to learn about wildlife, birds and migration at educational talks and on guided walks (sometimes at night), by attending residential or day courses and by watching activities such as moth trapping and ringing. In addition to this, observatories such as Sandwich Bay run weekly clubs specialising in a wide variety of subjects including nature photography and bird or fungi identification.

Almost all observatories now have their own websites, which reach a far wider audience than could have been dreamt of 50 years ago. They are an exciting way of presenting daily sightings, photos and programmes of activities, the most popular having in the region of 2,000 hits a day.

Progress and advances in other technologies such as digital cameras, telescopes, computers, radio and satellite tracking, and data loggers are producing exciting, and previously untapped, information. Observatories are gaining in many ways from working with these technologies. For example, graphs charting the success of a species can be produced from over 50 years' worth of data within minutes, when they would previously have taken many hours to put together.

Bird observatories and conservation

The daily census of birds is a core task and forms the basis of the observatories contribution to scientific research. This method of monitoring migration, based on observation, has produced an impressive set of records spanning over 50 years. These daily counts of the migrant and breeding birds are in the main, these days, entered into a computer database whereas the records were entered into a paper log book in the pre-computer era. Bob Spencer wrote in his introduction over 30 years ago: 'The opportunities for advancing our knowledge of migration are enormous, and some of the clues, one may be certain, are already gathering a thin film of dust in observatory files.' In their paper form, these data are virtually inaccessible, but they represent a previously untapped goldmine of information, which holds untold benefit for birds and other wildlife.

Tackling this head-on has resulted in a gargantuan and ongoing project, namely the digitisation of all of the old dust-covered records in order to put them into a useable format. This will facilitate access and finally allow their analysis, as well as making them available for wider scientific study. This is a daunting task; as between all of the observatories there is something in the region of 750 years of data, and it would be easy to be intimidated by the sheer size of the job. However, North Ronaldsay and Bardsey now have all their data in electronic form, and Copeland, Gibraltar Point, the Isle of May and Landguard have the enterprise well underway. This milestone has only been achieved by the vision, patience and dedication of many staff and volunteers. The completion of the task will involve a great deal of coordination and manpower, and the next stage is to try and obtain funding to be able to complete the job, which is essential if the full value of the data is to be realised.

Observatories are concerned with the protection and conservation of wildlife at local and national levels. Part of the remit of observatories such as Filey, Holme and Sandwich Bay, is to provide protection for wildlife by way of the acquisition of land and creating and/or managing nature reserves. The recording areas of others, such as Bardsey and Fair Isle, contain seabird colonies of national importance, and they are instrumental in monitoring them and providing information to the national network run by the JNCC, as well as the CCW and SNH, the statutory national conservation bodies. The recording areas of Dungeness and Cape Clear, among others, are home to nationally scarce or rare species (avian or otherwise) and the observatories cooperate with conservation organisations to monitor populations. Some observatories also conduct biological research and surveys on behalf of local government, who occasionally approach the observatories for advice about the local area.

Conservation is a modern concept, little understood at the time when the observatories first started, and bird observatories owe a debt of gratitude to a few people who, many years ago, had the foresight to recognise that monitoring birds could be important in the future.

A BRIEF HISTORY OF THE OBSERVATORIES MOVEMENT

From the mid-nineteenth century, an artist and amateur ornithologist by the name of Heinrich Gätke spent some 50 years on the tiny coastal island of Heligolm, in the North Sea off the coast of Germany which was, and still is, an incredible place to witness bird migration. Here he pioneered the concept of the 'vogelwarte', which directly translates to mean ornithological station or bird observatory. Although mistaken in some of his beliefs about migration, he was keenly aware of the influence of the weather and, in his practice of making direct observations, he was ahead of his time. He was probably the inspiration that led to the foundation of some of the early British and Irish bird observatories, and doubtless many more worldwide.

The first bird observatory in the British Isles was set up in 1933 on the island of Skokholm, off the south-west coast of Wales, by the naturalist and author Ronald Lockley. He attracted much interest from ornithologists of the day, including Harry Witherby (one of the founders of the modern ringing scheme) and W. B.

Alexander (later the chairman of the Bird Observatories Sub-committee). Over the next few years, observatories were established on the Isle of May, on Fair Isle and subsequently at Spurn Point. More observatories followed soon after, constituting an exciting age of expansion and innovation. A sub-committee of the BTO was set up in 1946 to coordinate the work of all the observatories. Standardised recording methods were introduced in the 1950s, special log books were printed, routine duplication of records was instituted and training courses were set up for bird observatory workers. A bi-annual journal was also launched, under the name of *Bird Migration.*

In the late 1950s, however, the evolutionary biologist David Lack carried out a series of ground-breaking radar studies, the results of which changed some of the beliefs about migration that were previously held among ornithologists. This had a profound impact on bird studies in Britain and Ireland, and as a result, over the next 20 years or so, there was surprisingly little interest in bird migration. Despite this, the observatories persevered, continuing to record the day-to-day sightings at each site, and in 1971 the Bird Observatories Council was formed to ensure the continued coordination of all the observatories.

The 1980s and early 1990s saw a transformation in bird watching. Previously considered a specialist and somewhat unusual pastime, there was a new wave of interest. Improvements in transport, along with mobile telephones and pagers, lead to an increase in the number of people taking up 'twitching', whereby birders waited to see where rarities and scarce birds had been found before deciding where to go, rather than planning a stay at an observatory (or elsewhere) in the hope of finding a rare bird. This took many birders away from observatories in favour of 'ticking off' as many species as possible, and therefore had an impact on the number of people staying overnight, such that many observatories experienced financial concerns during these years. The new-found interest in birds, however, was an encouraging sign.

Since before the turn of the millennium, the observatories have expanded and broadened their horizons. They have opened their doors to more than the specialist birdwatching fraternity of the past, and are changing, adapting and evolving to embrace the modern world. The range of wildlife monitored now includes many branches of natural history, in particular moths and butterflies, dragonflies and cetaceans. Many also monitor seals, mammals, reptiles, amphibians and plants, and some have considerable datasets for these groups in addition to the birds. Although interest in chasing rarities is still high, there does recently seem to have been a renewed interest in counting birds. Several new projects run by the BTO have generated much interest, and the Watch Groups run by the various county Wildlife Trusts, which are encouraging younger people to make observations on their environments, have proved very popular. Fortunately, some birders are again learning to appreciate the joys of birding at 'local patch' level, and have developed an appreciation of species that are unusual to their particular locality. These birders, along with other naturalists with a wide variety of interests, represent a new breed of observatory-goers.

THE FUTURE

These are exciting times for the bird observatories which are ideally placed to provide the monitoring required to contribute to the protection and conservation of birds.

The primary aim of the observatories is the continuation of the census of migrating birds. As we look further into the future, one of the most obvious and immediate tasks is the completion of the digitisation of the historical datasets onto computerised databases and to continuing to improve on techniques of recording data, and annual report quality.

There are also opportunities for working alongside radar, satellite tracking and other methods that continue to help us understand more about the phenomenon of migration. Observatories would also like to encourage links with their European counterparts; it is not so far removed from reality to imagine web-based links between bird observatories worldwide, forming a phenomenal worldwide picture of live migration.

Observatories are undoubtedly playing a more direct part in conservation issues at local and national levels. Issues such as climate change and the damage humans are causing to the environment continue to make the headlines. The observatories are well placed to raise visitor awareness of these and other issues through the changes being seen at first hand in bird populations.

Observatories are keen to encourage capable and enthusiastic individuals as potential staff, visitors, volunteers and friends tomorrow and on into the future. They are also grateful for all the support and goodwill that has been given in the past and they would like to record their sincere thanks to all those who have helped, both physically and financially, over the last 60 years.

We hope the following chapters will inspire a visit.

THE BIRD OBSERVATORIES COUNCIL

At around the time that the first bird observatories were being set up in the 1930s, the importance of cooperative work in ornithology was starting to be fully appreciated. The BTO was founded in 1932, to support the work of the Oxford Census, one of the earliest coordinated census efforts. It grew quickly and was soon organising several national investigations into birds such as Swallow, Grey Heron and Woodcock (Fisher 1953). In 1938, the Edward Grey Institute of Field Ornithology (EGI) was formed, which also grew out of the Oxford Census. This was set up initially to promote the economic study of ornithology, particularly during the war years, but it soon expanded to encompass general research into field ornithology when the war was over. It seemed logical that these two organisations should take an interest in the blossoming network of observatories and ensure that the data they collected would be useful.

So in 1946 the two organisations established a body, named the Bird Observatories Sub-committee, to coordinate the work of the observatories and to ensure that they operated to appropriate standards. Some of the first members

The Bird Observatories Sub-committee, now the Bird Observatories Council, at Gibraltar Point on 30 September 1950 (Lincolnshire Wildlife Trust archive). Including W.B. Alexander (2nd from left), Richard Richardson (3rd from left), Ted Smith (4th from left with Mary Smith to his left), Ronald Lockley (behind Mary Smith), Peter Scott (front centre), Hugh Boyd (5th from right), George Ainsworth (4th from right), Ralph Chislett (3rd from right), Professor Harvey (front right), Peggy Hiold (far right).

included Ronald Lockley, W. B. Alexander, Richard Richardson, Ted Smith and Ralph Chislett. A representative from each observatory was elected to the committee as and when the observatory met the required standards.

As the BTO grew in size, the annual meetings of the committee gradually morphed into the annual ringing and migration conference (now the BTO conference) and the original Bird Observatories Sub-committee was disbanded in 1965. Coordination and monitoring of the work of the observatories was then given over to the BTO. The idea of an 'accredited' or 'official' status was maintained as it helped to distinguish the permanent observatories from other ephemeral sites. By 1965 a total of 23 observatories had achieved accredited status, 19 of which were still operating in 1965.

The objectives of the BTO included the promotion of networked research on birds, such as that carried out at the bird observatories, and the promotion of bird ringing for which the observatories provided important training facilities. It was not long, however, before most of the observatories realised that there was still a need for some coordination between them. As a result, in 1971 the Bird Observatories Council (BOC) came into being. A new operating agreement was drawn up between the BTO (as the body which licences and controls bird ringing in Britain and Ireland) and the BOC, laying down the guidelines to which an accredited observatory should operate. Any new observatory wishing to join the BOC must show it has been operating to these standards before it can gain accredited status.

Today the BOC holds one or two meetings a year, attended by members from

The Bird Observatories Council meeting at Portland in February 2006, when it was resolved to publish a second edition of the bird observatories book (Steve Stansfield – www.wildlifeimages.eu). Back row from the left: Jed Andrews, Peter Howlett, David Walker, Mike Swindells, Emma Stansfield, Kevin Woodbridge, Neville McKee, Mike Martin, Adrian Blackburn, Ed Bennett, Phil Knott, Martin Cade, Steve Wing. Front row from the left: Mark Grantham, John Walder, John McEachen, Alison Duncan, Adele Powell, Nigel Odin, Mike Archer, Steve Stansfield.

most of the currently accredited observatories and representatives from the BTO, and non-accredited observatories are also entitled to attend. It fosters professional standards and ensures that they are maintained and addresses issues raised by individual observatories. It provides support and a useful meeting place for wardens and associated people who so rarely get to speak to each other face to face and share expertise in every aspect of observatory work.

DAILY LIFE AT AN OBSERVATORY

The daily routine at most observatories is very similar. It generally revolves around getting up very early in the morning – particularly in spring, when migration can be over within a couple of hours of dawn, and counting birds within the recording area or trapping them for ringing. Now if you are the kind of person who only really wakes up at around 10 or 11 in the morning after a strong coffee, then this might not sound like your cup of tea. However, the excitement of waiting to see what the first net-rounds bring generally helps maintain the spirit, as does a walk around the census area looking for the occasional rare bird, with or without a spectacular sunrise. Just don't mention the mornings when there aren't any birds or it's cold and grey!

Staff

That then is the glamorous side to working at an observatory. The wardens, however, are also responsible for dealing with the day-to-day management and overall running of the observatory, its assistants, volunteers and visitors, ringing, data collation, writing the annual report and much more besides. The unpredictable nature of migration and life at an observatory means that there are constant demands on the staff for flexibility and adaptation, not only to the changing weather, phases of the moon and arrivals of birds but also the daily requirements of visitors. Due to the isolated nature of most observatories, many wardens are also called upon to 'become' plumbers, mechanics and roofers, or any number of other specialist occupations! Add this to the daily census round, and you will find committed and hard-working individuals who are working at ground level from day to day and developing an extraordinary and intimate knowledge of the natural world around them.

Staying at an observatory

The experience of visiting an observatory is not contrived; it can depend very much on the mood and mix of the other guests, the weather, the birds, ringing activity and how busy the staff are with their many other duties. However, a stay at any of the observatories can provide a very relaxed, enjoyable and informative experience. During a stay guests are likely to encounter a wide age range from young children to grey elders, like-minded and interesting people. Depending on the observatory, there may also be those working on scientific studies, specialists in marine life or other areas of natural history, and those who simply appreciate the special nature of the atmosphere and approach to life that is taken by many who spend their time at observatories. There is much ready comradeship when several strangers with common interests get together from different disciplines, from the fun of sharing food and drink, the give and take of a communal kitchen to the daily call over or log. Add to this the enjoyment of witnessing natural occurrences, such as an arrival of thousands of birds, usually in a very beautiful setting, and the combination of interaction and independence can lead to a sense of wonder, self-sufficiency and resourcefulness. At the right time of year you are also in with a chance to see rarities or big numbers of migrants and often both. Of course, there are significant differences between the observatories, not least of which is whether you are on an island or a short walk from civilisation (read pub) on the mainland. At the island observatories you have to make sure you have everything you need for your stay (with a bit extra in case your stay is extended by the weather), whereas at the mainland observatories you can come and go as you please.

   The character of each observatory varies enormously as well, from the wild heather-topped terrain and huge sea cliffs of Fair Isle, the wind-swept, marshy fields of Holme, the (often) calm tranquillity of Bardsey or the Calf of Man, to the beach-hut-studded fields adjoining the observatory at Portland. The individual character will come to the fore during a stay; first appearances can be very deceptive and should in some cases be ignored!

As will be clear from the individual chapters, the nature of each observatory also has an impact on the daily birding routine. Take Fair Isle, for instance. The island is unique amongst the observatories in that the weather and landscape have reduced the importance of mist-nets for trapping migrants to, almost, the incidental. The bulk of trapping is done using fixed Heligoland traps. So instead of the frequent net rounds of the other observatories, there are periodic drives of the traps. The remote location of Fair Isle also means that major arrivals tend to occur later in the day so that really early starts aren't necessary – probably just as well with dawn at around half-past three–four o'clock in May. At Dungeness, the public nature of the trapping area means mist-nets can't be left in place and have to be put up and taken down each day. The net round also involves a not-inconsiderable tramp over shingle, a stark contrast to the five-minute stroll around the permanently sited nets in the gardens at Portland, Bardsey and the Calf of Man.

In terms of daily censusing, each observatory has a defined recording area. In the case of the islands this tends to be the whole island, whereas for mainland observatories the boundary is usually a convenient feature such as a road, significant change in topography or some other geographical feature. Once again the differences between the observatories are also considerable and vary from the large recording areas of Sandwich Bay or North Ronaldsay, where two or three members of staff are required to get full coverage every day, to the more restricted recording areas of observatories such as Portland, Copeland and Landguard, where the recording area can be walked with ease. The vegetation in the recording area also has a significant impact on the ease, or otherwise, of counting birds. Finding and counting birds in the relatively tree and scrub-free recording areas of Copeland is a very different proposition to doing the same amongst the mass of Sea-buckthorn found at Gibraltar Point and Spurn.

THE SEASONS AT OBSERVATORIES

Winter

For many observatory wardens, the winter period is a time for taking holidays, being one of the few times of year when the observatory can be left without the fear of missing some migration. Once upon a time that break would have been any time between mid-November and March, but nowadays migration can still be significant at many observatories until the end of November and migrants start to return in mid-February, so the 'safe' period has shrunk to December–February. However, that's not to say there isn't anything going on. The recording areas of some of the mainland observatories encompass estuaries or marshes so that wintering wildfowl and waders can provide quite a spectacle. The sea can also be a source of interest, even in the winter months, with unseasonal movements of species such as auks, divers and gulls in response to severe winter storms. Out on the islands, things tend to be a little on the bleak side, with the sea generally not being as productive as mainland sites, and it is only hard-weather movements that are likely to provide the interest.

For the wardens of island observatories, the situation is slightly different in that the last visitors leave at the end of October and the first ones don't arrive until late March the following year – even though the wardens themselves may only be off the island for two–three months. Inevitably, given the exposed positions of the observatories, a considerable amount of work can be involved in readying them to receive visitors. Walls may need to be redecorated and, in extreme cases, repairs may be needed to the fabric of the building, such as replacing lost tiles or broken windows.

Even the permanently wardened mainland observatories will usually take down mist-nets for the winter period, there being little point in leaving the nets in place and furled, to be damaged by winter storms with little opportunity to use them. This means that net-rides need to be cleared and trimmed early in the year and sites generally prepared for the new season, although the net-ride trimming is an on-going battle with the surrounding cover, as growth kicks in during the spring and summer.

Spring

Early spring migration tends to be more of an event at the south and west coast observatories. The first Black Redstarts, Chiffchaffs and Wheatears are eagerly awaited in the hope they will be the harbingers of a good spring. On the east coast, early spring migration can be virtually non-existent – until May that is – when the roles can often be reversed, particularly for the observatories in northern England and Scotland. Everyone then is hoping for a breath of south-easterly wind to drift migrants, moving north over the near Continent, across the North Sea. Combine the wind with some drizzle or cloud along the coast and the number and variety of birds can be extraordinary – as you will find in some of the accounts.

Spring is also the time when birds from the south overshoot their breeding area and end up further north. The striking Hoopoe is a frequent spring visitor as are birds such as Red-backed and Woodchat Shrike, Wryneck and Bluethroat.

Summer

For some observatories it's questionable whether summer actually exists; no sooner have the last spring migrants left in mid-June than the first returning waders arrive in mid-July. Whether or not summer is another holiday opportunity for staff depends on whether there are breeding seabirds at the observatory. For those on the Scottish islands and for most of the observatories around the Irish Sea, there is no such chance. All have seabird colonies and all have long-term monitoring programmes that require considerable input from staff and researchers each summer. This monitoring has assumed ever greater importance over the past two decades as the breeding success of many species of seabird has been hard hit by the lack of suitable fish for food. There is growing evidence that many colonies of species such as Razorbill, Guillemot and Kittiwake could disappear altogether in the coming years. Away from the drama of the seabird colonies, the south and east coast observatories can generally look forward to a quiet couple of months before the autumn really kicks off in August.

Autumn

This is arguably the most exciting period for the observatories. The contrast with spring couldn't be greater, when the pace is hurried as birds rush back north, to their breeding grounds, and can pass through a recording area in minutes. If something unusual is found, the chances of it hanging around long enough to be seen by others tends to be low.

In autumn, the birds tend to be in less of a rush to head south and there are just far more of them, with all the juveniles of the year added to the adults from the spring. This means there is the potential for tremendous numbers to be seen if the weather conditions are right. High pressure and clear skies over Scandinavia with light north-easterly winds combined with low cloud sitting over the British Isles, particularly in October, add up to classic 'fall' conditions, a 'fall' here being birding-speak for a large arrival of birds – not the autumn! Birds most likely to be affected by these conditions are the thrushes and Goldcrests. It is not uncommon to see thousands and occasionally tens of thousands of Redwings or Fieldfares making landfall and once witnessed, it is a sight that will live in the memory.

Migration doesn't need to be that extreme to be memorable though. At some point in autumn, at every observatory, there will be a day (with luck it will be more than one!) when the weather conditions are right and the morning air is alive with flocks of birds – all heading into the wind, even if it is taking them north. Migration in action is a stirring sight and to see large flocks of Starlings and smaller flocks of finches, pipits or wagtails making their way past can be the high-light of the year. Such conditions also present a challenge for the birder, as it really tests your ability to identify birds by call. The individual accounts feature many such days, such is the thrill when they occur.

Autumn is also the time for the unusual. There will be very few keen birders who don't get a thrill from seeing something unusual on their local patch (despite protestations to the contrary) and observatory wardens are no different. Although rare birds are, quite frequently, doomed – in that they are unlikely to find their way to where they belong (particularly if it involves a trip back across the Atlantic) – there is no denying the excitement their finding causes. Sometimes though, the rare become less rare over the years and it turns out that we are probably witnessing some sort of range expansion. This is almost certainly the case with birds such as the Yellow-browed Warbler, which can now be seen in extraordinary numbers (49 on Fair Isle in one day in October 2008), compared to the numbers seen just a few years ago. Also, consider the change in status of species such as Red-flanked Bluetail which until a few years ago was a real 'mega' rarity. When you start getting almost double-figure totals in a year, you know something is happening to the range of that species.

Eventually though, the numbers of moving birds dwindle and thoughts turn to writing annual reports and tidying all the end-of-year paperwork – and another season draws to a close.

SCIENTIFIC RESEARCH AT THE OBSERVATORIES

The early years of the twenty-first century have seen a dramatic and welcome shift in the perceived value of the data collected by the observatories. For a time during the 1970s and 1980s there seemed to be very little external interest in bird migration, but increasing awareness of climate change has brought about a remarkable change. For example, the UK Government is now including migrant species such as Swallow in their 'quality of life' indicators (Cannell *et al.* 1999). The observatories are unique in that many have datasets for migrants stretching back over 50 years.

Perhaps their greatest strength is in the area of long-term studies. Observatories can run projects that need a lot of manpower or run for many years, and which could be potentially impossible to fund. Further, their geographic spread means they can shed light on species which other long-term schemes (such as the BTO/JNCC/RSPB Breeding Bird Survey) barely cover.

Whilst the observatories are able to provide information individually, their ability to provide data collated across the whole chain of observatories has considerably more potential, and can make important contributions to population studies such as those conducted by Sparks (1999) and Browne & Aebischer (2003). The establishment of a coordinated, all-embracing observatories database would further enhance the possibilities in this area.

An early example of the use of ongoing, long-term, observatory monitoring is the now classic case of the crash of Whitethroat numbers, where the combined observatory data showed that the Whitethroat population plunged some 70% between 1968 and 1969. Whilst the usual numbers of Whitethroats left the British Isles in the autumn of 1968, far fewer than expected returned the following spring – a clear case of greatly increased mortality in winter quarters (Winstanley *et al.* 1974).

Many bird species are declining in numbers and, sadly, only a few are increasing. The 40–50 years of daily counts of migrants held by the observatories provide a way of measuring these changes. They can, as with the Whitethroat, shed light on whereabouts a migrant species is in trouble. These long-term records are also valuable for studies into how birds are reacting to climate change as are the long-term data to be found in the ringing records. Indeed, some observatories have already 'blown away the dust' and digitised all or part of their daily count and ringing data, so that these are immediately accessible for research. All, hopefully, will do so before too long, although the task is, of course, considerable.

Migration count data is an asset that the observatories are well placed to utilise; there are a range of others. Firstly with ringing, observatories can obtain vastly greater knowledge from the bird in the hand at the time of trapping, than from ringing recoveries. Detective skills enabling the ringer to glean more from the bird in the hand have increased markedly in the last couple of decades. For example, the fuller understanding of the moult of each species has enabled us to determine more about the migratory behaviours of the different ages, sexes and populations of each species than we knew before.

One very promising development is the use of small feather samples to determine where the bird was when it grew the feather. The concentrations of a range of stable isotopes vary geographically and maps of these are being made. By comparing the concentrations in the feathers with these maps, it is beginning to become possible to say where a feather was grown or in the case of young birds, where they were hatched and fledged (e.g. Bearhop *et al.* 2005). This has implications for working out relationships between populations across Europe, such as in the Aquatic Warbler (Pain *et al.* 2004), whether the birds had wintered in the same habitat (Marra *et al.* 1998), whether the moult of individual feathers occurred in the same or different places (Neto *et al.* 2006) and where different populations of a species breed or winter. This technique has even been used to determine whether a Baikal Teal, found in Europe, was a genuine vagrant from the east or an escape from a collection in Europe (Fox *et al.* 2007) and so holds considerable promise for adjudicating on the provenance of other birds. This is an example of where cooperation between the observatories and academics will yield dividends. There are others. Observatories can provide a fund of ground-level knowledge of the birds, unknown to many academics studying molecular biology or diseases; they can also supply the birds! The academics can use their facilities to tell the observatories more about the birds.

One such potentially important new area for research concerns diseases, both those specific to birds and those that may be transmitted to other organisms, including humans. Interest in avian-borne diseases is again becoming strong; Avian influenza is high on the agenda, because it can be transmitted to humans or farmed animals. While the greatest spread of avian influenza is almost certainly through transport of domestic stock (Feare 2007, Gauthier-Clerc *et al.* 2007), the disease does occur in wild birds, and migrants may play an important part in its maintenance or spread. In the case of West Nile virus and some other insect-transmitted diseases, we still know very little about their importance, though they have been implicated in the decline of certain wild bird species in Austria. However, it has been shown that not only do they arrive on our shores in migrants, but also that antibodies to some of these exist in resident species, so that there must be transmission within this country (Buckley *et al.* 2003). Similarly, new techniques have made it possible to quantify the prevalence of many other diseases in wild birds, which may have important consequences for the birds themselves. Avian malaria is turning out to be more common than it was formerly known to be, and as yet we know little about the incidence in migrants versus residents (Pierce 1981). These are fields where the epidemiologist or microbiologist needs the help of expert ornithologists as well as the access to wild birds provided by the observatories.

Another area which has seen huge growth in the last few years is the use of satellite technology to track the movements of birds. The advantage this has over the metal rings is that the route the bird takes can be followed in almost real time. At the moment, the size of the transmitter and battery limit their use to birds about the size of a Manx Shearwater or Bar-tailed Godwit but advances are constantly reducing the size and weight, and it can only be a matter of time before much smaller birds can be tracked. Although observatories do not have the funding at the moment to undertake research programmes such as this, they can provide the base for the research to take place. Bardsey, for instance, provided the base, local knowledge and expertise to assist JNCC researchers in achieving the extension of the Special Protection Area around the island, through radio-tracking of Manx Shearwaters. These, and other projects, such as marking birds with plastic 'colour-rings' to monitor adult survival rates, help us to continue to understand more about the phenomenon of migration and weather.

The observatories do not necessarily have the skills to undertake all the analysis of the data and would benefit from links between observatories and academics, which unfortunately do not exist at present. It would be good if this book can go some way to introducing academics to the observatories. They are keen to encourage academics to make use of their data for research and their premises as a base.

Bird observatories are ideally placed to offer researchers a base for pursuing their studies, such as the radio-tracking of Manx Shearwaters at Bardsey (Steve Stansfield – www.wildlifeimages.eu).

Bardsey

by Steven Stansfield

BARDSEY

Ynys Enlli, the Welsh name for Bardsey (never 'Bardsey Island'), meaning 'the island in the currents', lies just three kilometres off the southern tip of the Llŷn (Lleyn) peninsula at the northern end of Cardigan Bay in North Wales. It is relatively small, being just 179 hectares (444 acres) in extent. It is separated from the mainland by the Bardsey Sound, a treacherous stretch of water with currents running up to nine knots when the spring tides are in full flood.

Bardsey's complicated geology forms part of the Precambrian sequence dating back some 580–610 million years and is similar in structure to that found in parts of Anglesey. It comprises mainly a matrix of slaty siltstone and mudstone with

Steve Stansfield began working at Sandwich Bay Bird Observatory in 1990 after finishing his 'A' levels. He planned to take a 'year out' before returning to college. In 1993 he moved from Sandwich Bay to North Ronaldsay Bird Observatory, where he stayed until 1997. In 1998 he took up the post of Warden at Bardsey Bird and Field Observatory and is now the observatory's longest-ever serving member of staff.

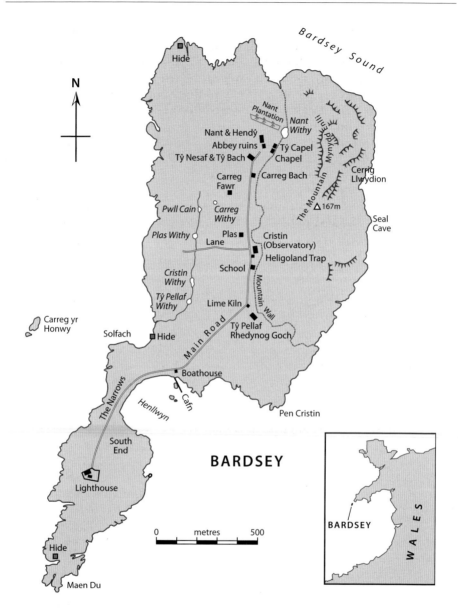

N

BARDSEY

0   metres   500

BARDSEY

W A L E S

innumerable inclusions of sandstone, limestone and quartzite, and there are a few igneous intrusions of olivine dolerite and numerous small-scale faults (Gibbons & McCarroll 1993). The likely opening of the Sound, probably at about 8,000–6,000 years before present, was summarised interestingly by Jones (1988), who also mentions several other visual features including the coastal erosion of a track in the west, a massive post-glacial (or possibly peri-glacial) rock fall on the east side of the island and tentative raised beach platforms around the Narrows.

Bardsey's natural history, and especially its birdlife, has been well described over the years: its wildlife by Roberts (1985) and Jones (1988), its flora by Bonner

& Jones (2002), and its archaeology and cultural history by Jones & Arnold (1996). The presence of many rare and scarce species and habitats has led to the island's designation as a National Nature Reserve (NNR), a Site of Special Scientific Interest (SSSI), a Special Protection Area (SPA), an Environmentally Sensitive Area (ESA) and an Area of Outstanding Natural Beauty. It is also part of the Pen Llŷn Heritage Coast and is covered by the Pen Llŷn a'r Sarnau Special Area of Conservation (SAC).

The observatory plays an important part in implementing the requirements of many of these designations, conducting much of the biological research and surveying required by the Countryside Council for Wales (CCW) and contributing to the island's management policy. The warden and several members of the observatory Council are also members of the island's joint scientific committee, the advisory body to the Bardsey Island Trust Limited (BITL), the island's current owner.

Arriving at the island

To reach the island, one passes the immense hills and mountains of Snowdonia and Snowdon itself. From the north, the route winds past the city of Bangor, along the Menai Straits to Caernarfon and onto the Llŷn following the pilgrims' trail of 1,500 years ago. Continuing to the end of the Llŷn, the small village of Aberdaron looks out across a long sandy beach to Ynysoedd Gwylan, the two small islands lying 1,500 metres offshore. These are home to up to 1,000 breeding pairs of Puffin, 300 pairs of Guillemot and several hundred pairs of large gulls; they also hosted the only Welsh breeding records of Whimbrel, in 1999 and 2000.

From the south, the route runs west from Porthmadog and past the castle at Criccieth to the port of Pwllheli, the last large town before entering rural Llŷn. Continuing west along the peninsula takes you through several small villages until Uwchmynydd, the south-western tip of the Llŷn, appears before you. From Mynydd Mawr, the hilltop of Uwchmynydd, the island can be seen across the Bardsey Sound. From here it looks strangely like a baseball cap. The steep east face of Mynydd Enlli (the Mountain) rises from the sea whilst the west side falls gently down to the northern lowlands, which reach out into the Irish Sea in the direction of Ireland.

From the car park at Cwrt Farm, just outside Aberdaron, the walk down the National Trust's wooded valley to the small cove at Porth Meudwy can give an exciting start to a birding trip. The valley can be almost as spectacular as Bardsey itself for passage migrants and large numbers of common migrants have been recorded here, as well as rarities such as Rüppell's Warbler and Lesser Grey Shrike.

The regular boat to the island usually sails from the sheltered commercial shellfishing cove of Porth Meudwy on Saturdays, but occasionally on weekdays by prior arrangement. As the name Ynys Enlli suggests, the boat journey out can be an adventure in itself. Adverse weather conditions and the treacherous currents mean the journey isn't always possible and visitors are sometimes delayed coming on or off the island. In the twenty-first century, when lives are dictated by the smallest detail, it can be one of the gifts of Bardsey that, for once, you are not in control, but are entirely dependent on the wind and tides. In the 1960s, when a much smaller boat was in use and powered by just a small outboard motor, there were tales of visitors, marooned on the island for several weeks due to the strong winds and rough seas, being reduced to eating gulls' egg omelettes with wild mushrooms after running out of food stocks. However, these stories were perhaps always the island equivalent of fishermen's tales. Now, with the presence of the observatory's small, but well-stocked, food shop, no recent visitors have gone hungry when delayed. The present boat is also much larger, is better equipped and makes the journey more regularly. A particularly good year was 2005 when, during the visitor season, crossings were not possible on only two Saturdays, and the boat arrived on the Sunday on both those weekends.

As the 12-passenger motorboat rounds the headland of Pen y Cil, the first views of the island are offered to the visitor; a large hump of 167 metres rising sharply from the sea, and looking rather inhospitable at first sight. All that can be seen are the rocky cliffs, bare scree and a large expanse of the sparsely grassed areas of the east side of Mynydd Enlli. Most of the island is hidden from view as the boat makes the 20-minute crossing. As the boat approaches the island the horizontally striped, red and white lighthouse comes into view and, in summer, the number of seabirds flying to and from the cliffs becomes apparent. The boat then docks in Cafn Enlli, a small and sheltered cove with a concrete slipway and gabion jetty. Once off the boat and at the top of the Cafn by the boat-house (Storws), with its associated small shellfishing vessels and tackle, the prospect of the walk to the observatory unfolds.

Looking south-west from the top of the Llŷn peninsula across the Sound towards Bardsey (Peter Howlett).

▲ In most years, the lighthouse on Bardsey attracts many thousands of migrant birds passing over the island after dark (Steve Stansfield – www.wildlifeimages.eu).

▼ At the foot of Bardsey mountain is the complex of former farm buildings known as Cristin, home to the observatory; the buildings of Plas are in the left foreground (Gwyn Stacey).

▲ The Calf of Man looking north-east, with the Isle of Man behind (photo courtesy of Manx National Heritage).

◀ Some of the best cover for migrant birds on the Calf of Man surrounds the observatory (photo courtesy of Manx National Heritage).

▼ The observatory on Cape Clear is by the harbour in the former Harbour House (centre) Mainland County Cork can be seen in the background across Roaringwater Bay (Peter Howlett).

◄ The Northern Waterthrush seen in 2008 on Cape Clear was the second record for both the Cape and Ireland; it often shared the bog with the Cape's second Solitary Sandpiper (Tom Shevlin).

▼ Black Guillemots, one of Copeland's specialities (Pat McKee).

◄ Observatory Island from Big (Copeland) Island (Neville McKee).

▲ The only area of standing water in the observatory recording area at Dungeness is the Long Pits (David Walker).

◄ The right-hand cottage of the former RNSSS buildings on the shingle spit at Dungeness is home to the bird observatory. The ARC pits and RSPB reserve can be seen in the distance (G. Hollamby).

▲ The new observatory building on Fair Isle, completed in 2010. Sheep Rock can be seen in the background (Deryk Shaw).

▼ The dramatic view looking along the west cliffs on Fair Isle. These are home to thousands of breeding seabirds (Deryk Shaw).

▲ *The view from Filey Brigg towards Carr Naze (Ian Robinson).*

▲ *Looking north from Filey Brigg towards Scarborough (Ian Robinson).*

▼ *Looking along Filey Brigg at low tide (Ian Robinson).*

▲ Flamborough Head juts out more than 11 kilometres into the North Sea and attracts many incoming migrants from mainland Europe (Andrew Lassey – PAL).

▼ One of the hedgerows on Flamborough Head along which many of the passage migrants can be found (Steve Stansfield – www.wildlifeimages.eu).

▲ The seasonal shorebird warden post has long been associated with the protection of the Little Tern colony Gibraltar Point (Steve Stansfield – www.wildlife images.eu).

◄ The Wash Study Centre provides accommodation for ringing course participants at Gibraltar Point (Barrie Wilkinson)

◄ Research on different races of migrant birds has been undertaken at the observatories over the years, including the Greenland Wheatears passing through Hilbre (Steve Stansfield – www.wildlife images.eu).

◄ The approach to Hilbre as seen from the north of Middle Island (Steve Williams).

◄ The Broadwater at Holme. Many of the mist-nets are sited within the bushes and trees on the right-hand bank (Peter Howlett).

◄ Volunteers are an essential part of any observatory; this group at Holme is helping prepare the observatory's newsletter for mailing to its members (Jed Andrews).

▲ The point at Landguard is sparsely vegetated, but it provides cover for many migrants that arrive in spring and autumn (www.mike-page.co.uk).

◄ The view from the fort at Landguard, looking toward the docks.

◄ The Low Light is the home of the observatory on the Isle of May (Margaret Thorne).

▲ *Looking north-west across the Isle of May in the Firth of Forth (Patricia & Angus Macdonald/Aerographica/SNH).*

◄ *Small numbers of Corncrakes can still be heard on North Ronaldsay during the spring (Peter Donnelly).*

▼ *Full-board accommodation is offered on a regular basis at only two observatories, one of which is based in the purpose-built, low-energy buildings at Twingness on North Ronaldsay (Kevin Woodbridge).*

◀ The garden at Portland (in the foreground) is one of the first areas of cover encountered by migrants arriving on the Bill (Martin Cade).

◀ Subalpine Warblers have been recorded at all bar one of the accredited observatories, and of 175 ringed in Britain and Ireland, 111 have been at bird observatories. This one, seen at Portland in May 2009, is of the much rarer eastern race Sylvia cantillans albistriata (Lee Fuller).

◀ A study at Sandwich Bay showed that the Snow Buntings present in mild winters are usually young Icelandic females, whereas in colder winters they tend to be young males, or adults of either sex (Tony Flashman).

◄ Observatories offer excellent educational opportunities for the general public, schools, and other groups such as the RSPB Wildlife Explorers, seen here being given first-hand experience of bird ringing with Pete Findley at one of the regular events organised by the observatory at Sandwich Bay (Margaret Douet).

◄ Birds travelling south along the Holderness coast are funnelled along the Spurn peninsula before crossing the mouth of the Humber to the Lincolnshire coast (Ian Glaves).

◄ Recording at bird observatories of migrants such as Chiffchaffs allows long-term population monitoring. Coastal migrants can occur away from their usual habitats, with birds such as warblers regularly seen on beaches and dunes (Steve Stansfield – www.wildlife images.eu).

▲ As a result of gravel extraction, South Walney has areas of shingle ridges and degraded sand dunes tha[t] shelter freshwater pools and brackish lagoons (Colin Raven).

▼ Walney Channel with Piel Castle in the left centre-ground and the hills of the Lake District beyond (Coli[n] Raven).

A wide range of wildlife is recorded and studied at bird observatories. Among many other forms of wildlife, the observatories keep records of cetaceans such as this Killer Whale at Fair Isle (Mark Breaks) and lepidopterans such as a Death's Head Hawkmoth at Bardsey (Steve Stansfield - www.wildlifeimages.eu).

Ringing at observatories is an aid to the monitoring of movements of a wide variety of migrant birds; here, Goldfinch is carefully ringed (Richard Brown).

▲ In the early years of bird observatories, the daily census data were recorded on to paper log forms (Hug Miles).

▼ The daily census continues to be a vital part of observatory work, but data are nowadays usual recorded directly onto a computerised database (Bardsey Bird and Field Observatory).

The island

Aligned roughly on a north–south axis, the island is almost three kilometres at its longest and one kilometre at its widest, and the irregular shape can be divided into two main areas. The South End is a low-lying roughly oval area of land, whilst the North End is roughly rectangular, consisting of lowland fields in the west and the Mountain in the east. These areas are joined by the Narrows, an isthmus which, at its narrowest, is less than 30 metres wide. Looking north and east from the boat-house, the gorse and bracken-covered west face of the Mountain can be seen. Due north are the fertile lowlands and grazing pasture, and to the south is the plateau of the South End.

The coastline, about 10 kilometres in length, comprises a mixture of high sea cliffs on the east, home to mixed seabird colonies, and lower cliffs and a more gentle, sloping, rocky coast on the north and west sides. The Narrows has, on its northern shore, the only sandy beach on the island, at Porth Solfach. It is here that many migrant waders, such as Dunlin, Sanderling, Turnstone and Ringed Plover, can be seen in spring and autumn from the small wooden hide situated on top of the beach, below a grassy bank. To the south of the Narrows is the wide bay of Henllwyn, the only real haven for visiting yachts and charter boats. The seaweed-covered rocks are home to up to 400 Grey Seals during the summer months, with numbers falling to about 150 during the winter. It is here that the larger waders are most frequently seen, with Oystercatchers and Curlew numbering into the hundreds during autumn and winter. Much of the southern coastline is bounded by fairly steep cliffs, rising to 30 metres above sea level. These are unsuitable for nesting seabirds and the very few ledges here are utilised by Ravens and Carrion Crows.

Towards the centre of the island, the only significant stream drains through the lowlands before flowing into the sea, just north of Solfach. It is along this stream that three of the island's four withy beds (small areas of willow trees) and the larger of the two established reed-beds are found. The withies were once coppiced for the production of lobster pots, but are now managed by the observatory for wildlife and are important ringing sites. At the top end of the stream, a small triangular reed bed borders one of the few permanent water bodies, Pwll Cain. This small pond was excavated in the early 1980s, though it has become much reduced in size and rather overgrown in recent years. There are several smaller ponds, wells and springs scattered throughout the island and many additional small streams and ponds form during the winter months.

The western side of the Mountain is now heavily covered in gorse and heather. Extensive areas of bracken are also found amongst some rather impressive lichen-covered rocky outcrops. The Mountain wall and main track provide a clear division between the declivitous hillside and the low-lying field systems. Along the track are 11 charming, white-fronted farmhouses (eight of them in pairs) and a Chapel, all of which were constructed in stone by order of Lord Newborough in the 1870s. A small and simple cottage, Carreg Bach, is described shortly. The Bardsey Island Trust leases three of these properties to tenants, including the observatory and the farm, retains one for its staff and rents out the remaining accommodation as self-catering holiday lets. The resident population on the island has varied from as high as 71 in 1871 to as low as six in 1981, and there are just eight today. However, this population is augmented by seasonal staff and volunteers, summer residents and weekly holidaymakers, so as many as 70 people may be on the island during the peak season, along with up to 100 day visitors who come ashore for just a few hours. Despite this, it is still possible to spend several days at a time during the early and late parts of the year without seeing anyone other than observatory staff.

At the north end of the island is the Nant plantation. Measuring 100 metres by 20 metres, this Sitka Spruce strip was planted in 1973 by the former owner, Michael Pearson. In 2005–06 it was extended to the north by the observatory. The extension comprises a mixture of native hardwoods with a sacrificial shelter belt of oriental pines (to be removed at a later date) to provide protection for the growing trees. Immediately south of the plantation, amongst a collection of buildings, is the Chapel, constructed in 1875. Nearby are the Abbey ruins, the graveyard and the largest cluster of houses on the island. There are the two pairs of houses, Nant and Hendŷ facing west and Tŷ Bach and Tŷ Nesaf facing south, the Chapel house (Tŷ Capel), and several yards and associated outbuildings. It is here, beside the Abbey ruins, that the cross and tomb of Lord Newborough (Sir Spencer Bulkeley Wynn) are situated.

Carreg Bach lies beside the track south of Tŷ Bach. It is the only remaining traditional 'crog lloft' dwelling on the island, a small and quaint cottage with its mezzanine floor bedroom, and was once the home of the 'King' of the island. Lower down the slope is Carreg Fawr, the former home of the artist and author Brenda Chamberlain; examples of her artistry are still to be found on several of the upper landing walls and are well worth an inspection. This was, until recently, a retreat house, run by the Carreg Trust on behalf of the Anglican Church in Wales.

Plas Bach lies just north of the observatory and is the largest single house on the island. Visible from the track is an ancient apple tree, trained to grow over part of its south-facing wall and so nearly two-dimensional in appearance. It is apparently of a unique variety, Afal Enlli (Bardsey Apple), unnoticed as such until very recently and unaffected by the subsequent media coverage. The pair of houses known as Cristin (Uchaf and Isaf), almost exactly in the centre of the island, is home to the Bardsey Bird and Field Observatory (BBFO). It is in the Cristin garden that the majority of the bird trapping and ringing of migrants takes place, and this is the site of the only Heligoland trap. The garden comprises a mixture of Damson and Willow trees as well as the largest Sycamore on the island. The former school building is just to the south of Cristin, and beyond this are the combined farmhouses of Tŷ Pellaf and Rhedynog Goch.

Much of the farmland is divided into about 120 fields, separated by low stone and earth walls, though some are rather dilapidated and damaged by livestock. The soils are rather variable but have supported a mixed cultivation of root crops and cereals over many years. However, the regime changed after the Second World War with the introduction of subsidies for sheep farmers and a much-reduced human population became the order of the day. A growing herd of pedigree Welsh Black cattle is now kept, along with the 450 sheep, and several fields at the north of the island are sown with arable crops to be used as fodder for the livestock. Jones (1993) compared a land management survey by Rees (1928) with his own studies in 1990 and reported that the use of the western lowlands of the island had changed dramatically from intensive mixed farming to almost pure sheep farming. Rabbits, extinct since late 1996, were a major part of the island's fauna for at least 500 years and had a major impact on the land.

No description of the island would be complete without hinting at the prospect of a particularly stirring view. From Tŷ Pellaf or from Nant, the visitor should take the ridge path to the summit of the Mountain on a fine morning and look to the north-east along the Llŷn peninsula, mystically studded with, perhaps, the stubs of several young volcanoes, whilst Snowdon lies to the right, as does Cader Idris and the Cardiganshire coast. Alternatively, nearer to home and in the evening, sit with friends on Cristin's front, in your hand a glass, and scan the peaceful Wicklow hills in distant Ireland, backlit by the setting sun.

Island history

Bardsey is a typical Celtic island and is now owned by the Bardsey Island Trust Limited (Ymddiriedolaeth Ynys Enlli Cyf). It was purchased in 1978 from the Right Honourable the fourth Viscount Cowdray, who had bought it from the Newborough family, in whose ownership it had been since the 1850s. It has weathered the evolution of a varied and rich history that includes periods of Mesolithic and Bronze Age occupation, a religious presence (interrupted only by the dissolution of the Augustinian monastery in 1537), piracy, subsistence farming and fishing, tenanted mixed farming, nature conservation and tourism. Man, therefore, has had a significant influence on the island for thousands of years. The earth banks edging the Narrows by Henllwyn were recently eroded to reveal evidence of ancient burials and numerous artefacts have been found. A variety of flint-work was recovered in a recent survey at the north end of the island (Dawson *et al.* 2002), including flakes, blades, cores and other debris. An initial assessment suggested that the bulk of the artefacts date from the Later Mesolithic (*c.*7,000–4,000 BC), a period in which pre-agricultural societies exploited what would today be regarded as wild resources, and the concentration of artefacts and waste flakes suggests that the collection area may have been a settlement or working area for a hunting and gathering community.

The island has been a place of pilgrimage since around the late sixth century, when St Cadfan established the first monastery here. Such was the importance of Bardsey as a pilgrimage site that early Christians believed that three pilgrimages to Bardsey were the equivalent of one to Rome. Human bones are found from time to time in the gardens throughout the island, lending some archaeological credence to the legend that the island is the last resting place of some 20,000 saints and martyrs who travelled here to die. There is also ancient documentary evidence that the bones of monks were transported to the island for burial. The ruins of a grand Augustinian abbey dating back to the late thirteenth century are all that now remain although the ancient religious links with the island are maintained and Carreg Fawr, already mentioned, until recently hosted those on retreat for spiritual renewal. Simple services are often held in the timeless atmosphere of the Chapel and these have included my own wedding, officiated by the Rt Revd David Hawkins, Bishop of Barking, in October 2007.

The island has six archaeological features that are considered nationally important and remain evident today; these are designated as Scheduled Ancient Monuments (SAMs). A further 11 features, the houses and buildings that remain in use today, are listed in the Sites and Monuments Record (SMR) maintained by the local archaeological trust. The SAMs include the Abbey Tower, several 'round houses' on the side of the Mountain and several presumed Viking 'rectangular houses' at the north end of the island. The Chapel houses the remains of a fifth century cross from the island and several other interesting features. The mortal remains of Lord Newborough lie beneath the Cross beside the ruined Abbey Tower and were brought to the island some 12 months after his death, on completion of the crypt.

THE OBSERVATORY

In 1951, Rupert Williams-Ellis invited representatives of the West Wales Field Society (WWFS) to his home on the Llŷn to discuss, amongst other things, the establishment of a bird observatory on Bardsey. Sadly, Ellis died soon after the meeting, and no further action was taken until mid-1952 when members of WWFS and Birmingham and West Midland Bird Club (WMBC) visited the island and met up with the lighthouse keeper Alan Till. Till had spent time as the lighthouse keeper on Skokholm and worked alongside Ronald Lockley where he learned much about the work of the observatory there. Till and others thus formed the committee of the observatory and on 7 March 1953 the observatory Council had its inaugural meeting. Present at this meeting were representatives from the island, Caernarfonshire, WWFS and WMBC. William Condry became the first secretary and his minutes of the meeting recorded that 'there would be a permanent observatory established on the island in order to study all aspects of natural history and it would be called the Bardsey Bird and Field Observatory'. The main objects of the observatory were the study of natural history, in particular to monitor birds and migration, and to help conserve the island's flora and fauna, and encourage an intelligent interest in nature, particularly amongst young people.

The observatory has been based at Cristin since 1953 and the buildings enjoy stunning views out over the Irish Sea and to the south end of the island. The house itself is a rather grand building and was once home to two of the island's families. It was inhabited by as many as 20 people, in the days when islanders had to row for up to five days to Liverpool to sell their produce and bring back essential supplies. The warden and his family are comfortably accommodated in an agreeable fully-converted byre and hayloft in the walled farmyard next to the observatory. The assistant wardens were accommodated for many years in the old keeper's cottages at the lighthouse. Although almost a mile from the main observatory buildings, it had the only flushing toilet on the island (the others being compost closets). Unfortunately, the lease of this accommodation expired at the end of 2007 and the assistants are being accommodated temporarily within the curtilage of the observatory, until alternative accommodation can be found.

THE BIRDS

Earlier records of wildlife

Records of the wildlife of Bardsey are available from many sources. There are early religious documents, from the thirteenth to the seventeenth centuries, containing occasional 'biological' allusions as an aside to the main purpose of the text. One example is the reference to 'herring' in a text of 1291, but only with regard to taxes levied by the Abbey on all catches at the time.

There are also a few ornithological notes from the eminent naturalist John Ray who visited in 1662 (Raven 1942) and Thomas Pennant who visited in 1778 (Pennant 1810). Eagle Clarke published the first detailed bird records for the island, collated from lighthouse keepers' notes between 1879 and 1887, and also used them in his general notes on bird migration ([in] Harvie-Brown *et al.* 1880–1890). It was not until 1902, however, that the first attempts were made at an annotated systematic list of birds. O. V. Aplin (1910) published details of a visit he made on 23 and 24 May 1901, and Ogilvie-Grant (1909–1914) collected records from lighthouse keepers in the same way as Eagle Clarke had done 30 years previously. It was the publication of his very detailed findings (which included records from many other light-stations around the country) that inspired N. F. Ticehurst to make two visits to the island in 1913. And it was Ticehurst's interest in the reports of birds found dead at the lighthouse that led to his first trip. From 12 to 25 June, he assessed the breeding populations on the island. His second trip, from 9 to 22 September, was made to investigate autumn migration and assess the impact of the lighthouse on the migrant birds. With the data he collected, he was able to publish the most comprehensive set of records of the day, in the journal *British Birds* in 1919 and 1920, forming the next major landmark in Bardsey's ornithological history.

Several other ornithologists visited the island, and some published their findings, but only Ronald Lockley visited outside the main migration periods. His three-week visit, in late November and early December 1934, was in order to record the birdlife at this ornithologically neglected time of year (Lockley 1938).

Moving on to the second half of the twentieth century, it is worth noting that the observatory's entire daily bird census data from 1953–1997 were digitised by Julia Davies, the assistant warden, in 2003 and 2004. This is now a particularly valuable resource as any question concerning past records can be promptly researched.

Breeding birds

A quick walk around the easily accessible part of the island on a spring morning gives a fairly good idea of the nesting land birds present on the island. There is birdsong everywhere. Wrens, making up for their diminutive size with their loud song, are scattered throughout the whole island. However, the population that peaked at over 100 pairs in 2003 has recently halved, following two consecutive cold spells during late winter. A handful of Dunnocks are found in the withies and gardens along with up to five pairs of Chaffinch, a very recent colonist. The songs of one or two Chiffchaffs, Willow Warblers and Whitethroats linger into the summer after the migrants have long since moved on to their own breeding grounds. Up to ten pairs of Stonechats give their scratchy song from atop the gorse, with Linnets twittering in a few small and loose colonies. Meadow Pipits sing from all over the island, and when the immigrants of winter and early spring have dispersed we are left with about 50 pairs rearing moderate numbers of young.

Skylarks were once numerous on the island, but were absent from 1977 to 2002. Up to five pairs have nested recently as the habitat alters again with the changes in agricultural use. The deep calls of Ravens echo over the hillside as they battle for territory; they are often harassed by the many Carrion Crows that nest in the withies and gardens. The ten pairs of Magpies can be seen scavenging in packs, moving from one compost heap to another, looking for food with which to feed their young, whilst the rasping calls of the Chough blast out from the sea caves on the west coast. On the shoreline, up to 90 pairs of Oystercatcher make themselves unpopular with visitors and their aggressive attacks during the summer are often a cause for complaint. The 25 or so pairs of Rock Pipits are not as obvious and keep to the rocky shore.

Shelduck and Mallard seem to lose at least as many young as they actually fledge, to the seals, gulls and corvids. Moorhen are generally found around the ponds and streams and the sink outlet from the observatory kitchen! Corncrake made a welcome return in 2004 and was present again in 2005, much to the annoyance of the farmer whose bedroom window was within a few metres of its territory. Whilst there was no definite evidence of breeding in either year, they were common breeders on the island before 1970 and perhaps they will breed again in years to come. Up to 25 pairs of Swallows nest in the many barns, sheds and outbuildings, and those that nest in the observatory's food store are regularly trapped in the warden's home. In the same outbuildings around the island breed ten pairs of Pied Wagtails, successfully so in most years.

There are several species that nest only occasionally and some that are less obvious than others. Little Owls nest in low numbers, though seeing them is not so easy until they have young. One or two pairs of Long-eared Owls have success-fully fledged young in most years between 1998 and 2007. Of the occasional breeders, some are Afro-Palearctic migrants, such as Sedge Warbler and Blackcap, whilst Goldfinch and Lesser Redpoll, both migrants, occasionally linger and breed.

Of the land birds, the Chough is the most important species of conservation concern and between four and seven pairs nest on the island in most years. One of the most concerning aspects, however, is that the non-breeding flock of immature birds, once resident on the island during the summer months, has been lost. One of the reasons for this loss is the change in land-use. The fields identified as important feeding sites for Chough by several authors, including Roberts (1983) and Gray (1995), were heavily grazed from 1974 to 1996, but reverted to hay meadows under the ESA agri-environmental scheme with a strictly controlled grazing regime in place. This type of conservation appears to improve scarce habitats (such as maritime heath and traditional hay meadows), but it has had an adverse effect on several species on the island. For example, breeding Wheatear numbers have decreased since the introduction of the ESA scheme. In the late 1980s and early 1990s, they peaked at about 35 pairs. However, from 1997 when the scheme started, the population plummeted to just three pairs in 2005 as the grazing changed and sward height over much of the island increased.

Managing the land is a 'balancing act' and not all species will benefit equally, but it does seem a shame to see one species suffer for the benefit of another. In 2007, David and Libby Barnden, the then tenant farmers on Bardsey, left the island. After much deliberation and discussion between the various parties, the Royal Society for the Protection of Birds (RSPB) became the tenant farmer and has a five-year farming business tenancy with BITL, contracting a local farmer to undertake the work on the ground. The RSPB involvement is on the basis of farming and managing the land for conservation, using its knowledge and experience and working with all of the interested parties to bring long-term stability to the conservation management of the island.

Over the years there have been many changes in the populations of land birds. In recent years the likes of Lapwing, Yellowhammer, House Sparrow and Starling have all become extinct as breeding species. This is probably due to changes in land use, but other factors may have had a part to play. Conversely, Shelduck, Puffin, Long-eared Owl and Goldcrest have been added to the breeding bird list since 1998. There are several other species, hitherto occasional breeders which now nest annually, for example, Whitethroat, Chiffchaff, Willow Warbler and Chaffinch. Blackbirds became extinct as Sparrowhawk numbers on the island increased. The last remnants of a fairly strong population, whose vocalisation was distinct and the subject of several studies, were annihilated by the nesting pair of Sparrowhawks in 1996 (Loxton & Silcocks 1997), though they started breeding again in 2006.

As well as the land birds, Bardsey is home to about 16,000 pairs of Manx Shearwaters (Leaper *et al.* 2005), including at least two individuals which are in their 50s. These two birds have been subject to much media attention, as one of them was the oldest known wild bird alive in the world at the time. The story made news on both sides of the Atlantic and was even mentioned in the *New York Times*. It also featured on the CNN News Channel and was included in the book *Guinness World Records 2007* (Glenday 2006). More than 36,000 Manx Shearwaters have been ringed on the island since 1953, and Bardsey now holds the largest known digitised dataset for shearwaters in the country and probably the world.

Manx Shearwaters apart, a moderately sized colony of seabirds nests on the steep slopes and cliffs on the eastern side of the island. Visitors are discouraged from going to this area nowadays. The disturbance of the seabirds has rightly become an issue, and the health and the safety of the visitors is also paramount. It was once part of the job of the observatory warden to take groups of visitors down the steep and dangerous grassy slopes, surrounded by hundreds of Razorbills and Herring Gulls, to Seal Cave, a rather spectacular and romantic, but almost inaccessible, sea-cave where Grey Seals swim within metres of the observer. For reasons of safety it is now thought not to be in the best interests of the visitor to take trips there, although it is a wonderful sight and many who have visited the area have fond memories.

Starting southwards from the north-east of the island, there are several small and mostly inaccessible seabird colonies, until the slope becomes slightly gentler (at about 60° to the horizontal), and it is possible to scramble down the grass towards some of the birds. As one approaches the area of Seal Cave, the Peregrines that nest on the crags high up on the east side circle overhead, screaming a warning to their chicks. The onomatopoeic calls of the Choughs are heard, as the pair that nests near Seal Cave begins alarming. Razorbills begin to pop out from under boulders and fly off onto the sea. Their grunting calls join the cacophony of the several hundred pairs of Herring Gulls and Lesser Black-backed Gulls and the colony of about 200 pairs of Kittiwakes that all nest nearby. Just north of the cave, there are a dozen or so pairs of Fulmars on the near-vertical grassy slopes above its entrance. It is a great pity that most visitors to the island never get to experience the sights, smells and sounds of a seabird colony.

However, regular and inexpensive boat trips go close inshore to see this spectacle and the Saturday boat often passes close by if conditions are favourable. Also in this area have been up to 110 breeding pairs of Storm Petrels whose colony has only recently been discovered. Whilst there were occasional records of churring from burrows or of a bird seen with eggs, back as far as the 1950s, it was not until the thorough surveys of all suitable areas in 2001 and 2002 that the best estimates so far were made for this notoriously difficult-to-find species. Above ground, on the ledges, are about 250 pairs of Guillemots balancing their bluish-green eggs on the ledges alongside the noisy Kittiwakes. There are also about 15 pairs of Puffins nesting in the area; presumably these are an overspill from the nearby Ynysoedd Gwylan population that has been thriving in recent years. Shags nest in loose colonies on some of the more inaccessible ledges and are best surveyed from the sea. On only one occasion has Cormorant been known to nest on Bardsey (in 2004), though a colony of about 60 pairs can be found on Ynysoedd Gwylan.

Migrant birds

Since Ticehurst published his notes on the birds of Bardsey (1919 and 1920), there has been an interest in the passage of birds through the island and since 1953 an almost constant record has been kept by the observatory during spring and autumn. Migrants can appear almost anywhere on the island. I am often asked 'Where is the best place to see birds on the island?'. My usual response is 'everywhere'. The habitats, as described earlier, play very little part in what species of migrants occur there. Indeed, whilst large numbers of Goldcrest are seen in the plantation at Nant, it is quite possible to see scores of them hopping about on the sandy beach of Solfach or feeding amongst the Welsh Black cattle in the lowland pastures. Pied Flycatchers are normally inhabitants of mature wood-lands, so seeing them fly-catching from barbed wire fences, rusty old gates, or even on washed-up car tyres on the beach can often surprise observers.

It is amongst these displaced migrants that scarcities can be found, and seeing a Great Spotted Woodpecker roosting on a rocky beach amongst Oystercatchers is quite a sight. Some migrants have sought shelter in man-made structures, for example, both Golden Oriole and Corncrake have been found sheltering in one of the three hides, a Long-eared Owl was discovered in the ladies' toilet, and a Grasshopper Warbler was found running around inside the assistant warden's bath. Most scarce migrants, however, such as Wryneck, Red-breasted Flycatcher and Yellow-browed Warbler are found in more typical habitat such as the withies and the gardens around the houses and are usually seen when many common migrants are present.

Bardsey regularly records large numbers of particular species. For example, Willow Warblers can often occur in their thousands and there have been many occasions when over 2,500 have been seen in a single day. Such events usually follow 'attraction-nights' when large numbers have been drawn to the lighthouse overnight. A species that also arrives on the island in large numbers following attractions is Grasshopper Warbler. On one day in May 2004, 362 were recorded on the island following a lighthouse attraction overnight. The whole island appeared to be covered with singing Grasshopper Warblers and 86 were trapped during the morning, including 20 in one drive of the Heligoland trap. Since 1979, whilst 189 have been killed at lighthouse attractions, a further 187 survived to be ringed.

Mid-summer migrants are scarce. Although there are occasional arrivals of Willow Warblers in early July, Starlings are usually the first migrants, arriving from the end of the first week of July. The autumn passage has become rather protracted recently, with warblers and waders beginning to arrive from mid-July and continuing until mid-November.

In autumn, a regular diurnal passage of finches is noted on Bardsey and in some years hundreds of Chaffinches and Bramblings are recorded moving south in the early mornings, often during specific atmospheric conditions, when the winds are fairly light and from the north-east, coupled with light cloud cover. These are usually augmented by lesser numbers of Greenfinch, Linnet, Siskin and Goldfinch. Such conditions are also good for the movement of large numbers of thrushes, and in October 1999 conditions were perfect for large movements of birds. On the 12th, a high pressure system was situated over northern Scotland and southern Scandinavia, whilst a weak low-pressure system was centred over the Midlands. This produced light north-easterly winds on Bardsey, favourable for birds continuing to migrate from further north. Large numbers of Greenfinches, Chaffinches, Goldfinches, Linnets, Fieldfares, Redwings and Song Thrushes were recorded moving through the island all morning, with smaller numbers of Blackbirds, Chiffchaffs and Goldcrests. At about 09:30 hrs an unusual thrush was extracted from a mist-net in the observatory garden. When it was handed to me in a bird bag as 'an unusual looking Redwing' I did not know quite what to expect. However, when the bird was removed from the bag and closely examined, it was clearly a first-winter Eyebrowed Thrush. The bird was the first record of this species in Wales and only the second to be ringed in Britain and Ireland.

Bardsey's reputation for rare birds may not quite match that of some observatories, but it is almost certainly the best site in Wales for rarities. A Blyth's Pipit in October 2005, a Red-flanked Bluetail in 2007 and a Paddyfield Warbler in 2008 are the latest additions and the island bird list now stands at 322 species.

The island has hosted two species that were new to the Western Palearctic. These were Summer Tanager in 1957 and Yellow Warbler in 1964. There have been several subsequent records elsewhere for Yellow Warbler in the British Isles but no others for Summer Tanager. Of the tanager, Reg Arthur wrote (Arthur, 1957, 1963):

At 07:20 hrs, on 11 September 1957 near the Cristin trap, Bardsey Island Caernarvonshire, R. Moss and R. Stjernstedt saw a bird resembling a large bright male Greenfinch Chloris chloris *without the wing and tail patches, as it left one bush and dived to cover a few feet ahead. Despite searching it was not seen again during the morning. At 12:15 hrs, J. D. Gay drove a similar bird into the Lane Trap. This was brought back to the laboratory for a detailed examination.*

First Impressions. An olive-above and deep yellow-below bird, smaller than song thrush with dark wing feathers. A heavy blunt bill; darkish legs, noticeably short for size of bird. Blunt tail extending well beyond wing tips; occasional reddish feathers. Weight 24.6gm. Release: It was released near the Cristin trap and immediately went to cover at the foot of the wall under brambles and a plum tree. It could be seen hopping around and pecking amongst fallen fruit and on the wall stones. It later flew to thick cover nearby. No attempt was made to flush it from the ripe blackberries. Details of Retrapping: taken in the Cristin trap on 15 September, weight 26.6gm. Coaxed into a nylon net on the 20th, weight 36.7gm. It was then obviously in very good condition. The main food was apparently blackberries. W. M. Condry saw it 'chewing' these and apparently only taking the juice, rejecting the remainder. On 13 September, it was seen to pick one, place it on a fence post and then to peck at the fruit. It passed seeds in the laboratory on 20 September. Seen to peck amongst fallen small plums several times and at a hanging plum on 19 September by M. P. M. Richards. W. M. Condry saw it take a small fly in the air and R.W.A and M.P.M.R also saw it make two flycatcher-like sallies from the laboratory chimney. It was seen to peck on stone walls as if seeking insects. Whilst in an examination cage on 11 September, it refused cut apple, elder berries and small plums.

George Evans wrote of the Yellow Warbler (Evans, 1964, 1965):

During the afternoon of 29 August 1964, at approximately 15:30 hrs, my newly arrived assistant H. Miles was conveying his belongings from the boathouse to the observatory on Bardsey Island, Caernarvonshire. Halfway between the boathouse and Tŷ Pellaf, his attention was drawn to a bird that appeared suddenly and briefly atop a hedgerow at close range. Only very general impressions were obtained, but the sheer vividness of its colouration rendered it quite unlike any species with which he was familiar. In his encumbered state, and lacking binoculars, H.M. made no attempt to pursue it. Though puzzled by its identity, he assumed it was probably a variant Willow Warbler Phylloscopus trochilus.*

Some two hours later a small party of visitors led by R.F. Durman left the observatory to undertake a short spell of mist-netting before the day's light faded. A net sited in Cristin withy bed was duly erected and the surrounding area driven. During this drive R.F.D observed what was manifestly the same bird seen by H.M. earlier in the day. I was summoned and obtained good, if fleeting, views with comparative ease.*

My first response was one of incredulity. Though palpably of warbler species, it possessed a vivid coloration quite different from anything I had seen before – the entire head, breast, belly and vent being a pure primrose-yellow. The mantle was very greenish and noticeably darker than the crown. The wing feathers were dark and prominently edged off-white. No superciliary could be discerned nor any sign of breast markings (though some faint reddish-brown streaks were seen on the breast when the bird was later in the hand). The bill was pale horn and the legs somewhat darker. Its demeanour was not strikingly different from that of a Phylloscopus. *When undisturbed it moved actively and usually at or just below canopy level, appearing in full view briefly before darting out of sight. Its movements were agile and fast. No fly-catching sallies were observed nor wing-flicking and it remained quite silent. There were no indications of nervousness or excessive timidity, but it was not confiding.*

The bird was caught just before dusk and as its identity had not been ascertained the decision was taken to roost it overnight. Unfortunately it did not survive the night and the skin was preserved by R.F.D. The carcass was examined and later dissected by P.M. Driver following his return to the mainland. He reported on the post-mortem inspection as follows.

'This bird had no observable signs of disease or parasitic infection, and seemed generally to be in good condition. There was, however, no sign of the usual fat deposits found in fall migrants – not even in the pelvic and pygidial regions or in the peritoneum – which suggests that it had recently exhausted its food stores. There was no obvious sign of muscle wastage. There was no sign of any food remains in the gut though this is to be expected in a small passerine after a night's rest from feeding. Features of interest concerning the viscera were well-developed gizzard and kidneys, and apparently normal liver and pancreas. The gut was approximately 12cm in length. With the aid of a 10× lens, a small pair of testes was obvious, in addition to the more diffuse and somewhat larger adrenal glands. The size of the testes suggests that the specimen was a bird of the year, rather than a breeding bird with post-breeding regressed sex organs. These immature male characteristics would seem to be borne out by the plumage features. The

condition of the bird would seem to support a supposition that it had reached this country by means of an "assisted passage". In the field and in the hand, it was quite active, suggesting, with the post-mortem conclusions, a healthy state. Yet there were no food stores. Such might well be the case with a bird which had crossed much of the Atlantic on board ship with a limited amount of insect food, and had recently arrived here – so recently that it had not been able to re-stock its food stores'.

On 3 September 1964, R.F.D. conveyed the skin to the British Museum (Natural History) where Derek Goodwin had no hesitation in confirming the identification as Dendroica petechia. *The species has a variety of races in America and a decision on the subspecies involved proved impossible. It was deemed to be in first-winter plumage.*

In conclusion, some remarks are warranted concerning the part played by the weather in this event, The report of P.M.D., though favouring the idea of assisted passage, certainly does not exclude the possibility that this mite crossed the Atlantic unaided except by the wind. If its first point of landfall was Bardsey, however, its weight on arrival would tend to suggest that perhaps it did not cross without some form of assistance and that it succeeded in obtaining meagre sustenance en route. It is very doubtful if it was on the island before the day on which it was first seen and caught. Furthermore, an examination of the Daily Weather Report covering the week prior to 29 August does not show weather situations likely to permit a bird of this size optimum conditions for drifting non-stop from America. On the day of its appearance on Bardsey an anticyclone was centred to the west of Ireland and a light north-westerly airstream affected all parts of Britain.

Nevertheless, the list of rarities recorded on Bardsey is rather impressive. It has a fine list of vagrants that have crossed the Atlantic, including American Bittern and Sora. There have been two records of Red-eyed Vireo (including one fatally attracted to the lighthouse) and two Blackpoll Warblers (including the second British record just days after the first on Scilly). A male Common Yellowthroat was seen in 1996, whilst records of Song Sparrow and White-throated Sparrow are much older and both Dark-eyed Junco and Rose-breasted Grosbeak have spent time in the observatory garden.

There have also been three records of Grey-cheeked Thrush, two being fatally attracted to the lighthouse. The bird killed on 10 October 1961 was thought at the time to belong to the form *bicknelli*, which was then just a race of Grey-cheeked Thrush but has since been elevated to full species status. Unfortunately, the skin cannot be traced, although the record is still accepted as Grey-cheeked Thrush.

The only other American thrush to have been recorded on the island was a stunning male American Robin in 2004. The excitement which followed is hopefully conveyed in these notes I made shortly after the event.

I had been told by one of the island residents that she had seen a 'female thrush' feeding in her garden, but I did not have time to go and look for it. I left the island later that day to attend an observatory council meeting the following weekend. The following morning David Barnden called me on my mobile just as I was eating breakfast at a local bed and breakfast. He said that he did not want to spoil my time off the island, but he had just seen an American Robin. I nearly choked on my sausage. Unfortunately the wind was too strong for boats to sail and therefore I could not return to the island. The forecast was still poor for the following day so my wife and I left North Wales and travelled to her parents in Lancashire. The following morning my telephone rang, and the farmer, Dave Barnden, told me the wind had dropped and the bird was still present. I phoned the boatman, put the news out to the bird information services, grabbed my wife and our two-year-old son and sped back to North Wales as fast as possible. Eventually 12 of us managed to get back to the island to see a very bright and richly coloured bird flying up and down the net rides in the plantation at Nant. We only had two hours on the island so we were unable to make any attempt to trap the bird, but at least we saw it.

To conclude, a number of American waders have also been recorded on Bardsey, with a Killdeer spending three days on the South End in 1982. Spotted Sandpiper and Baird's Sandpiper have both been trapped and ringed, and Lesser Yellowlegs and Buff-breasted Sandpiper have been recorded on just one occasion.

Eastern vagrants normally arrive with large numbers of commoner migrants from the east, and occasionally rare birds seem to outnumber common species. In October 2005 Blyth's Pipit, Red-throated Pipit, Pallas's Warbler and Red-breasted Flycatcher were all present and so close together that the observers could see them all from one spot; very little else was seen on the island all day. With three records to its credit, Bardsey is the best single site outside Shetland for Lanceolated Warbler, and it is perhaps surprising that there have not been more, considering the number of Grasshopper Warblers that occur here.

Seabird passage

Bardsey is not famed for rare seabirds, though the passage of common species on some days is tremendous. Vast numbers of Kittiwakes, Guillemots and Razorbills, too many for a single observer or even two observers to count accurately, pass south. With up to 15,000 Kittiwakes regularly seen in October and the same number of Black-headed Gulls, some scarcer species are inevitably found. Mediterranean Gull numbers have increased recently following the first record in 1964, to the extent that 93% of the 653 bird-days recorded to date have occurred since 2000. The discovery of a huge feeding flock of gulls (visible from the elevated position of the south hide) on the Bastram Shoal sandbanks about 1.5 kilometres east of the south end of the island, has certainly contributed.

As well as the gulls there are occasionally large movements of the more pelagic species (particularly skuas and petrels). Some of the most memorable sea passages have been when the sea has been so rough that observations had to cease as waves began to hit the hide. This particular cement and stone structure, at about 15 metres above the mean high water mark, was completely washed away in autumn 2001. One such day was in September 2002 when, after a prolonged period of strong south-westerlies, the winds switched to north-west mid-morning. Leach's Petrels began to move in reasonable numbers and in a two-hour period almost 80 birds had been recorded, along with four species of skua, thousands of Razorbills, and many hundreds of Fulmars and Gannets.

Imagine, also from the same hide, a 12 metre standing wave at the north-west corner of the island created as the sea, rushing through the Bardsey Sound, meets head on a force 8 to 9 autumnal gale. This is a spectacular sight in itself, but add to it several thousand seabirds and the event is unforgettable. There have been single records of Fea's/Zino's Petrel *Pterodroma feae/madeira*, Black-browed Albatross and Little Shearwater. Cory's Shearwater and Great Shearwater are both very rare too, but Sooty Shearwater and Balearic Shearwater are both recorded annually in moderate, and sometimes large, numbers.

Ringing activities

Since 1953 the observatory has ringed 248,686 birds of 190 species. The highest number ringed in a single year was in 1988, with a total of 11,301 of 93 species. The best year for diversity of species was 1987 when 98 species were ringed. There have been many days in the observatory's history when several hundred birds have been ringed in a day and in recent years there have been a few days when over 500 birds have been ringed. These high volume exercises have mostly involved breeding seabirds and particularly their young. For instance, on a day in June 2001, David Waddington, Rhys Dandy and I ringed 502 birds in a four-hour trip to Ynysoedd Gwylan and a two-hour excursion to the Razorbill colonies on the east side of the island. On 12 June 2002, I ringed 460 seabirds on the east side of the island and a further 563 just eight days later. Ringing birds in this volume is very exhausting on Bardsey. Many of the seabird colonies are separated by diffi-cult ground at sea level, so the ringer has to climb a hundred metres or so out of one colony and then descend again into the next. This, along with fitting several hundred large seabird rings, eventually takes its toll on the ringer, but it is all over in a few days each year. It should be mentioned that volume ringing of nestling (pullus) seabirds is considered desirable in terms of the recoveries generated. Nevertheless, it is the migrant passerines that occupy the bulk of the ringers' time, as may be seen from Table 1.

In 2008, over 80% of the full-grown passerines ringed on Bardsey were migrants, which emphasises the importance of ringing for migration studies.

The ringing details have been written on paper forms as the first point of record since the observatory opened. In 1998 the first attempts were also made to record the Bardsey data in electronic form. From the start of that year, all the ringing data were digitised from the hand-written 'field records' shortly after the

Table 1. Ringing totals for the 10 bird species
most frequently ringed on Bardsey (1953–2008)

Willow Warbler	46,652
Manx Shearwater	36,167
Goldcrest	27,257
Chiffchaff	14,723
Chaffinch	12,113
Sedge Warbler	10,110
Blackbird	9,207
Herring Gull	8,789
Whitethroat	6,145
Starling	5,484

birds had been ringed. Since then a major effort has been made to digitise the earlier 45 years of archival ringing data from 1953 to 1997. With the help of numerous volunteers and funding from the CCW and the Cheatle Trust, and not to mention a great deal of support from the staff of the BTO, the observatory has managed to digitise the entire ringing data, including all the retraps and recoveries. Whilst many papers have already been written, there should now be much scope for further analysis.

As with other observatories, BBFO has ringed many rare and scarce birds. Most notable in this context are Britain and Ireland's only Summer Tanager to be ringed, the first Sora and Blackpoll Warbler, the second Eyebrowed Thrush and Baird's Sandpiper and the third Sabine's Gull.

Retraps, recoveries and controls

As is well known, ringing produces a great deal of interesting information about the lives of birds, but space here is limited. Suffice to say that, in March 1999, the observatory published its Atlas of recoveries of birds ringed by Bardsey Bird and Field Observatory, 1953–1996 (Loxton *et al.* 1999), which is still available for purchase. This volume brought together all the re-traps, recoveries and controls of birds relating to Bardsey at the time, with summaries for each species ringed. Open the book at any page and there is a wealth of information. At pages 58 *et seq.*, for example, we learn that 2,562 Razorbills had been ringed up to 1996, and that only 3.9% (101) of these had been recovered off the island. The most distant recovery involved an individual ringed as a chick on 19 June 1987 and found dead in fishing net at Golfe de Tunis, Tunisia, on 2 February 1988. The longest-lived bird was ringed as a chick on 2 July 1962 and was reringed on 25 May 1979, having seriously worn its first ring. Following further encounters, it was most recently retrapped on 26 June 2004 some 41 years and 359 days after first being ringed. It is presently (in 2008) the oldest Razorbill known to the BTO Ringing Scheme.

Interestingly, Bardsey was also home to the ringing scheme's oldest known Wren; ringed as a juvenile on 22 July 1997, the bird was retrapped many times in

Scarce and rare birds are occasionally trapped at bird observatories. This Sabine's Gull (in October 2003) was only the third to be ringed in Britain and Ireland (Steve Stansfield – www.wildlifeimages.eu).

and around the observatory garden until 1 November 2004, seven years and 102 days later. The cold winter of 2004/2005 probably put an end to this tiny record breaker.

Manx Shearwaters winter off the coasts of Brazil, Uruguay and Argentina (Brooke 1990) and a number of Bardsey-ringed birds have been picked up as corpses along the coast of all three countries. There are also several recoveries from North America, perhaps unsurprisingly, as some of the one-year-old birds spend their summer off the coast of North America (Perrins *et al*, 1973), and a few of these shearwaters have bred there since the mid-1970s (Storey & Lien 1985).

Lighthouse attractions

Bardsey lighthouse is a notable feature of the island that dominates the south-ward view. It plays a considerable role in the life of the observatory, its staff and the numbers of migrant birds grounded on the island at certain times of the year. Its 30-metre tower was erected in 1821 and was initially powered by paraffin lamps. It is the taller of only two square lighthouse towers in the UK, the other being on Coquet Island in Northumberland. The Bardsey light was later magnified and projected by a series of prisms and lenses, to produce a 270,000 candela beam, officially visible for 43 kilometres. Its lantern is constructed so that the five continuously revolving beams appear to emit a series of five equally spaced flashes of 0.1 seconds over 15 seconds in every 30 seconds. On 26 March 1966 the light was electrified and now has a power of 693,000 candelas, extending its range to over 46 kilometres, which, perhaps surprisingly, did not have startling effects on the number of birds attracted.

The Bardsey light has long been known for its influence on bird migration. As early as 1909, Ogilvie Grant (1909–1914) noted that birds were attracted and killed there. Not all lighthouses attract birds, and it is fortunate that only a few have such devastating effects as the Bardsey light. It appears that birds are only attracted to white light coupled with a series of flashes created by a rotating prism. Thus, in general, a lighthouse with a permanently lit lantern attracts birds, whereas a tower where the bulb is periodically extinguished does not. Lighthouses on the mainland, where there are other artificial light sources nearby, e.g. streetlamps, also tend not to attract birds as the light from the other sources makes landmarks more visible to the migrating birds.

Whilst little is understood about the mechanics of lighthouse attractions, it appears that they usually occur under fairly specific conditions. Typically, birds are seldom attracted during full moon periods, even with full cloud cover, heavy rain or fog, as they are still able to navigate, using visible navigational cues. As a result, there are two weeks in each month when it is fairly safe to go to bed and sleep, as it can be fairly confidently predicted that no attraction of consequence will take place. During the new moon period however (usually up to one week either side of new moon), things are quite different. When the weather is conducive, some species begin their migration at dusk. If the weather ahead of the birds deteriorates, obscuring their navigational cues, they may be attracted to the lighthouse. It is significant that most attractions occur on occasions when the waxing moon sets below the horizon during the early part of the night, but has been visible since the fall of darkness (nautical darkness being when the moon is 12 degrees below the horizon and the sun's light is no longer visible). Birds begin to migrate when they can see the moon (even if small) and it provides enough light to illuminate geographical features. As it sets below the horizon, they no longer have their guiding light and the larger and more spectacular attractions take place.

Once attracted, birds usually fly continuously round the light until they find somewhere to land (and are possibly trapped by observatory staff), are killed or injured on collision with a solid structure or die of exhaustion. If the weather improves enough and the navigational cues become visible again, the birds will either continue with their migration or settle on the island until dawn. Some attractions can be enormous, involving many thousands of birds. The majority are typical nocturnal migrants, but several species that are considered to be diurnal migrants have occurred at attractions, including Swift, Swallow, Woodpigeon, Siskin, Chaffinch, Rock Pipit and Grey Wagtail. Many rare birds have also been attracted, including Grey-cheeked Thrush and Spotted Sandpiper from across the Atlantic, and Radde's Warbler, River Warbler and Booted Warbler from further east.

As early as the 1940s, Trinity House attempted to reduce the number of birds killed during spring and autumn migrations by erecting a system of ladder-like perches extending out from the balcony at the level of the light. Unfortunately, more birds struck the extensions (and were fatally injured) than actually perched on them. Later, in 1979, a gantry with two 500 watt lamps was erected to the east of the lighthouse. The floodlights illuminated the ground on that side, affording the birds a visible area on which to land. This single gantry was operated until 1998, when the use of lamps, mounted on three small, mobile gantries, was tried with very positive results.

The intention was to bring the birds down closer to the lighthouse tower and then to move the gantries to the side on which they appeared to be collecting. If, for example, the wind on a given night was from the south, the majority of the birds in the air would tend to be at the northern side of the tower. The gantries would therefore be moved to illuminate the ground on that side, immediately outside the lighthouse compound and ten metres from the tower. By the end of the season, there had been several large attractions, but fewer than usual casualties. At one of these, about 8,000 birds had been coaxed down to safety in the illuminated areas. This system is still in operation and seems to be working to good effect.

Bardsey's lighthouse appears to have been one of the most prolific killers of migrant birds in the UK. The numbers actually attracted to the light are not easy to quantify accurately, as the counting of thousands of 'twinkles' in the beams is rather subjective. We can, however, compare the number of birds killed with the number ringed. This assumes that the effort, both in capturing birds at attractions and in gathering up fatalities, has remained constant throughout, which is ensured by the various protocols that the observatory has in place.

The number of birds killed at the light varies considerably from year to year, with as few as 69 in one year but more than 1,900 in others. That 19,839 fatalities have been recorded between 1953 and 2008, gives some idea of the enormity of the problem over the years – although in reality this is a tiny number in comparison to those which die during migration, a number likely to be in the order of millions. This considerable figure covers 89 species ranging from birds as large as Grey Heron to those as small as Yellow-browed Warbler and from species as common as Chaffinch to those as rare as Grey-cheeked Thrush. The variety is perhaps unsurprising, given that so many species on the British and Irish lists engage in migrational and seasonal movements from the local to the most distant. It also serves to suggest just how many more birds pass over at night, unseen and unrecorded. That significantly fewer birds have been killed since the mobile gantry lights were first used in 1998, is apparent from Figure 1.

We know that the ringing effort has remained fairly constant over the period and there has been no change in the light signature throughout. Whilst it is possible that the numbers of those species most frequently and fatally attracted has substantially diminished over time, it seems more than likely that the gantry lights have played a significant part in reducing those fatalities.

The two largest attractions recorded on the island took place in autumn 2002 and are summarised here. The earlier attraction was on 4–5 November. The wind was from the north-east, cloud cover was complete, neither the outline of the Mountain nor the street lights on the Llŷn were visible, and the moon was new

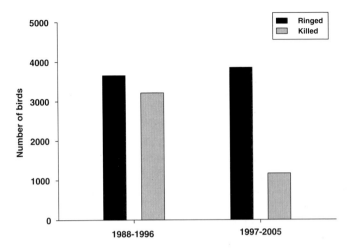

Figure 1. *Comparison of numbers of birds attracted (both ringed and killed) at Bardsey lighthouse in two nine-year periods between 1988 and 2005.*

(0.1% waning at sunset). The attraction began at about 21:00 hrs and was attended from 22:00 hrs until dawn. On arrival there were 40 Redwings, ten Song Thrushes, two Woodcocks, two Bar-tailed Godwits, a Ringed Plover and a Purple Sandpiper (dead). The gantry lights were placed facing south and Redwings began to drop into the illuminated area immediately. Their numbers slowly increased during the next two hours and by 01:20 hrs up to 600 were present, along with 100 Song Thrushes, ten Fieldfares, a Snipe, 16 Bar-tailed Godwits and 16 Lapwings. Redwing numbers increased steadily and by 05:00 hrs there were 7000 grounded and a further 2000 in the air. There were also 400 Song Thrushes, 100 Fieldfares and a Woodpigeon. At 06:00 hrs, 10,000 Redwings were present, with 8,000 grounded and a further 2,000 flying round in the beams of the light. Then, at dawn, birds were seen lifting off the ground and heading south. A total of 10,699 birds of 18 species had been recorded.

This, however, was to be totally overshadowed by events four days later, on the 9–10 November. The moon was five days old (28.6% waxing). There was full cloud cover with heavy and persistent rain and visibility was poor. Twilight had ended at 18:53 hrs, though the moon rose at 02:06 hrs. Birds were first seen in the light at 00:30 hrs and the attraction was attended from 01:00 hrs. Very large numbers of birds were already on the ground when observers arrived, with many fatalities. The gantry lights were set facing in a southerly direction, south of the tower, and the large number of birds dropping into the illuminated area was reminiscent of watching a blizzard. A decision was taken to collect only chilled and injured casualties due to the number of birds which were grounded, some as far north as the Narrows gate some 400 metres away. The area in front of the gantry resembled a bucket of maggots – shimmering and moving. The noise was tremendous. Numbers were estimated at 30,000 Redwings, 500 Fieldfares, 350 Blackbirds, 300 Song Thrushes, 350 Starlings, 30 Lapwings, nine Golden Plovers, 10 Woodcocks, seven Dunlins, seven Snipe, four Redshanks, two Blackcaps, two

Water Rails, a Storm Petrel and a Jack Snipe. In total 31,573 birds of 18 species were recorded with, surprisingly, only 249 fatalities.

The numbers of species most frequently killed and ringed respectively at lighthouse attractions are detailed in Tables 2 and 3.

Table 2. Bird species most frequently killed at lighthouse attractions at Bardsey from 1979 to 2005.

	1979–1996	*1997–2005*	*Total 1979–2005*
Redwing	3,640	421	4,061
Willow Warbler	698	169	867
Manx Shearwater	379	241	620
Sedge Warbler	338	157	495
Starling	441	23	464
Blackbird	203	20	223
Grasshopper Warbler	145	52	197
Song Thrush	126	31	157
Fieldfare	97	13	110
Whitethroat	72	35	107

Table 3. Bird species most frequently ringed at lighthouse attractions at Bardsey from 1979 to 2005.

	1979–1996	*1997–2005*	*Total 1979–2005*
Manx Shearwater	1,521	2,313	3,834
Redwing	1,557	93	1,650
Willow Warbler	624	197	821
Starling	432	22	454
Song Thrush	407	31	438
Blackbird	400	11	411
Sedge Warbler	183	131	314
Wheatear	186	52	238
Grasshopper Warbler	112	75	187
Goldcrest	133	15	148

All the corpses collected from the lighthouse are stored in a deep freezer and later sent to Amgueddfa Cymru – National Museum Wales in Cardiff. Some of these have been put to use in displays at the museum, whereas others have been used in studies of fat levels and body condition (Evans and Baggott 1970; Redfern *et al.* 2000).

OTHER FAUNA AND FLORA

Mammals

Bardsey's non-avian fauna have been very well documented by naturalists from all fields since the observatory opened over 50 years ago. Like its birdlife, the vertebrate and invertebrate fauna are well covered by many authors in the observatory reports and elsewhere. Nowadays, there are only two species of land mammal present on the island: the Common Shrew and the Wood Mouse. Both of these are recorded in small numbers, with the mouse populations fluctuating dramatically from year to year. The number of mice trapped during the winter months is a good indication of the health of the population.

Until 1996 there was a thriving population of Rabbits on the island. The exact date of their introduction is unknown, but from a survey of the Court of Augmentations in 1547, they were clearly of considerable ecological and agricultural significance (Jones 1988). So their extinction in 1996 had profound effects on the ecology of the island. With grazing pressure reduced, grasses and plants were able to thrive on the island for the first time in over 400 years.

As the human population decreased on the island, so also did the population of the House Mouse. In 1958 these mice were more prolific than the Wood Mice and were abundant in trappings during March and July, with numbers decreasing in September. In August 1962 Fullagar (1963) caught none in 663 trap-nights, though none of his traps were situated near buildings. Since then a single individual was trapped in an unspecified farm building on the island and one was found dead at Tŷ Pellaf (the farm) in 1982. There have been no records since.

One of the features of Bardsey's SSSI status is the Grey Seal population. In summer, up to 400 animals haul out in the bay of Henllwyn (Stansfield 2003). About 30 animals pup on the island each year at widespread locations, including several very close to the main haul-out site. Common Seal is seldom recorded and there are only about ten corroborated records.

The waters around Bardsey are thought to be an important area for Risso's Dolphin. Over the past few years the Whale and Dolphin Conservation Society (WDCS) have had a presence on the island each autumn and have been undertaking regular monitoring transects out to the south and west of the island. They have found many social groups of Risso's Dolphins using the waters here to feed and to give birth to their young. Several very small newborn calves have been seen and photographed in recent years. WDCS have also deployed a Train Porpoise Detector (T-POD) on the seabed off the island for several months at a time. This piece of modern technology can record the audible 'clicks' made by Harbour Porpoises and when the data are analysed the number of individual animals and their direction of travel can be assessed. This is very useful as the animals cannot be observed during hours of darkness or on windy days, and it gives a more detailed idea of what these animals are doing. Common Dolphin and Bottlenose Dolphin sightings are more frequent nowadays, though there have only been a scattering of records of the larger cetaceans such as Killer Whale, Sei Whale, Minke Whale and Long-finned Pilot Whale.

Amphibians, reptiles and invertebrates

The only representative of the Amphibia to be found is the Palmate Newt. Records of 'water-lizards' from the 1800s suggest that these newts have been on the island for some considerable time.

Only one reptile is known from the island, the Slow-worm. This lizard is known from various sites, though numbers found are never very high. In some years, as few as two animals are recorded, even though they are sought in their favoured sites, whereas in other years they are easily discovered under strategically placed slates and boulders in and around the observatory garden. There is a single record of Grass Snake on Bardsey, in 1958 or 1959. Jones (1988) suggested that it may have been regurgitated by a newly arrived Grey Heron, rather than arriving on the island by human agency, and that the identification was probably sound.

Loxton (2000) comprehensively described the invertebrate life of the island. The observatory keeps regular records of all freshwater and terrestrial invertebrates, and the common groups, such as Lepidoptera, Odonata and Diptera are given most attention. The common species of butterflies are regularly of interest to visitors and up to ten species can be seen on most days in the summer. A single Monarch was recorded in 2001, and the more regular migrants include Clouded Yellow, Painted Lady and Dark Green Fritillary, whereas Grayling, Common Blue and Small Copper are amongst the breeding species. There is, of course, a far greater diversity of moth species, the total of which presently stands at 320.

Flora

The flora of Bardsey has been well described over the years. A publication by Ian Bonner and Peter Hope Jones (2002) covers the flowering plants and ferns of the island's flora and is a detailed annotated systematic list of all the species recorded, giving the abundance and geographical location. Of the scarce and rare flora recorded on the island, four species are qualifying features of the Ynys Enlli SSSI. Small Adder's-tongue forms part of a qualifying assemblage of plants, whilst the other three species independently qualify the site's status.

The Small Adder's-tongue was first discovered in 1997, under bracken near the well above Nant. Up to 200 plants were counted and were thought to have been a mixture of both Adder's-tongue species *Ophioglossum vulgatum* and *O. azoricum*. Samples were taken for critical determination. Then, in 2000, an estimate of 500 fronds, mostly in pairs, was made from grassland near the withies and (a smaller number) from the south end of the island. Material from both these locations was collected and sent to the Natural History Museum (London) where Dr F. H. Rumsey confirmed that they were indeed *O. azoricum* based on morphological characters, and they were retained along with other Bardsey material for molecular analysis (Bonner & Jones, 2002).

The near-threatened Rock Sea-lavender was described as rare on the island in 1956 and again in 1986. Samples were taken for genetic analysis in 1990 and chromosome counts by Martin Ingrouille established it as *Limonium britannicum* subsp. *celticum* var. *pharense* (Bonner & Jones, 2002). The nationally scarce

Western Clover is recorded from a few sites on the island where it occurs on short species-rich turf. Sharp Rush is found very locally in two areas of low rocky cliffs with some seepage of fresh water. This impressive rush was first described from the island in the 1920s and is one of the island's special plants. It is very close here to its northern limit in the British Isles and is usually found growing in damp sand dunes (Bonner & Jones, 2002).

Generally, the island is covered at all times of the year with interesting flowers and plants. In spring, Bluebells give a splash of colour to the fields and are suggestive of a different habitat in earlier days. Later in the year, Common Spotted-orchid and Early Marsh-orchid can be found in the lowlands, along with Autumn Lady's-tresses (sometimes in their thousands) in the heavily grazed meadows from late August onwards. On many of the buildings and walls there is a good amount of Navelwort and stonecrop spp. amongst the grasses there. The withies support blooms of Marsh-marigolds, with the fragrant scent of Meadowsweet filling the air on damp August mornings.

Some of the lichen assemblages on the island are amongst the best in the UK. The rare Golden Hair Lichen can be found in patches along the ridge of the Mountain along with the equally rare Ciliate Strap-lichen. Both species are afforded special protection under the Wildlife and Countryside Act and are Red-listed on the EU list of rare lichens.

SOCIAL EVENTS

As with many bird observatories, Bardsey has a call-over or log each evening where both the serious birder and the casual holidaymaker are invited to contribute to the record of the day's sightings. Visitors staying at the observatory and at the other holiday homes on the island are often invited to join in the get-togethers, along with island residents and seasonal staff. The Old Schoolhouse is frequently the centre of entertainment in the evenings where various events are held, including illustrated slide shows, poetry readings, dances and art exhibitions. There are occasional barbeques to which observatory guests bring their own food, to be cooked, at times, by the observatory staff. In the past, as many as 100 people have been invited to barbeque parties on the beach at Solfach. Sporting events and games are usually organised during the summer months for the younger visitors, but typically most adults join in too. Nocturnal walks to watch observatory staff ringing Manx Shearwaters are always popular with the guests, as are the daytime trips to see the 'Manxie' chicks being taken from their underground burrows to be ringed, weighed and measured.

The island has a particularly relaxed atmosphere during school holidays in the summer months. Very few birdwatchers are found staying at the observatory during this time. This now seems to be in complete contrast to the Bardsey chapter in the first edition of this book in which Roger Durman (1976) wrote 'One week in July is usually set aside for families with young children, who would not normally be permitted to saty at the observatory at other times of the year. This event has been aptly named "potty week"!'. There are several weeks each year nowadays when the observatory is full of families, usually 60% of them children. September and October are still the busiest months of the year for visiting birders when the observatory is usually full, though the new moon periods in spring can also be attractive to both birders and ringers.

ACCESS AND ACCOMMODATION

Access to Bardsey is by boat from Porth Meudwy, with daily trips during the summer. There is a rail service as far as Pwllheli and buses run regularly (in the rural sense of the word) to Aberdaron, but these options would doubtless involve an overnight stay, at least on the outward journey.

The crossing takes about 20 minutes and it would be prudent to keep wet-weather gear to hand, just in case, although conditions are often calm and dry. Please keep your luggage to a minimum as the boat has limited hold capacity. Pack all parcels in small, easily handled loads (if the parcel is too heavy for you to handle then it will be too difficult to load onto the boat!), well-wrapped and securely tied. Luggage is taken up to the observatory by vehicle.

Visitors nowadays stay in considerably more comfort than hitherto and the observatory can sleep 12 guests in self-catering accommodation. On the first floor of each house are a single room, a double/family room, and a four-bedded room. Until the late 1990s the accommodation was rather 'rustic' with army-style bunk beds and old furniture that had been donated rather than thrown away. The rooms are now well furnished, clean and comfortable, as new carpets, rugs and furniture are regularly donated by Arighi Bianchi of Macclesfield. In 2002, another kind benefactor helped to finance the installation of a central heating system, which provides both background heating and hot running water. A shower was fitted into the washroom in 2008 to help make living at the observatory a much more pleasant experience. Water from the well on the mountainside above the observatory may run short towards the end of the summer season, but at least it now comes out of a tap and is no longer collected in buckets.

The observatory is open to visitors from about mid-March until mid-November and bookings are made with the bookings secretary whose details are posted on the observatory website. Further detailed arrangements will be e-mailed or posted on request and/or at the time of booking. The annual *Bardsey Bird and Field Observatory Report* can be obtained by post from the warden at the observatory. Records of birds and other sightings are always welcome from visitors to the island who are not able to attend the call over, and should be sent or passed on to the Warden at the observatory. Applications for membership of the Bardsey Bird and Field Observatory are warmly welcomed, please follow the directions set out on the Observatory website.

Observatory opened:	1953
Total number of bird species recorded at the observatory:	322
Best bird year:	2000
Number of species recorded:	201
Total of birds ringed at the observatory:	248,686
Number of species:	190
Best ringing year:	1988
Number ringed:	11,301
Number of species:	93
Maximum number of species ringed in any year:	98 in 1987

Calf of Man

by Kate Hawkins

THE ISLAND

Situated in the north of the Irish Sea and to the south-west of the Isle of Man, the Calf of Man is ideally placed on the bird migration routes over the western side of the British Isles. Its importance for migrating and breeding birds had been recognised long before the observatory was established in 1959, and local ornithologists played a large part in its designation and operation. The island, and the observatory once it was up and running, have been in the care of the Manx National Trust (now part of Manx National Heritage) since the organisation's founding in 1951. Wardens appointed by Manx National Heritage inhabit the island on a seasonal basis, usually between mid-March and mid-November (the season). Visitors can explore the Calf as day visitors or can stay in the hostel accommodation, which is shared with the wardens.

The Calf of Man is perhaps best known for its thriving resident population of Chough, and for its historical association with the Manx Shearwater. Though the once huge shearwater colony is long gone, through exploitation by people and

Kate Hawkins is curator of Natural History with Manx National Heritage, the organisation which owns the Calf of Man and is responsible for the operation and upkeep of the nature reserve and Calf of Man Bird Observatory.

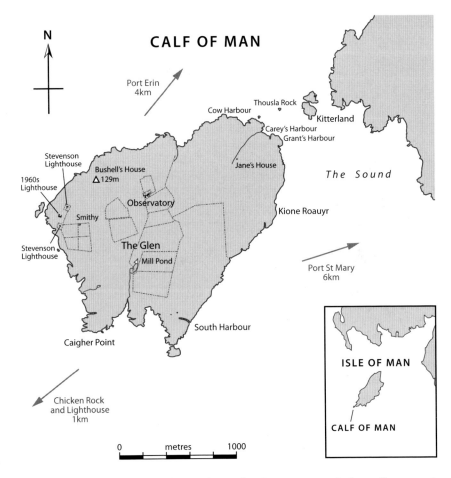

CALF OF MAN

N

Port Erin
4km

Cow Harbour
Thousla Rock
Carey's Harbour
Grant's Harbour
Kitterland

Stevenson
Lighthouse
Bushell's House
△129m
Jane's House

The Sound

1960s
Lighthouse

Observatory
Smithy
Kione Roauyr

Stevenson
Lighthouse
The Glen
Mill Pond

Port St Mary
6km

South Harbour

Caigher Point

Chicken Rock
and Lighthouse
1km

0   metres   1000

ISLE OF MAN

CALF OF MAN

predation by rats, there have been signs of a slow recovery in breeding numbers
in recent years. The cliffs and coastal turf support colonies of other seabirds, such
as Kittiwakes, Shags, auks and gulls. In the absence of mature woodland,
breeding birds are mostly ground or shrub-nesters, but the deficit in woodland
species is made up for by the number and variety of migrant birds visiting the
Calf.

Managed today as a nature reserve and observatory, the island bears plenty of
marks of past human activities in the buildings and field systems, perhaps
surprising, given its isolation and exposed position. Although only 500 metres off
the south-western tip of the Isle of Man ('the mainland' in this context), the Calf
is separated from the mainland by the tidal race of the Sound, a dangerous
stretch of water where tides can flow as fast as eight knots and test the most experienced of seamen. From the Sound café on the mainland side the Calf may look
tantalisingly close, but prospective visitors have to go to the village of Port Erin,
four kilometres north along the coast, or to Port St Mary, six kilometres to the
north-east, for a boat to take them there safely.

With an area of 250 hectares (616 acres), the Calf is approximately two and a half kilometres long and two kilometres across at its widest point. Its rocky coast is nearly eight kilometres long, and the land rises roughly from south-east to north-west to its highest point at 128 metres. The cliffs, rising to a maximum height of more than 100 metres, expose some of the Manx Group rocks, an enormous thickness of which underlies the Calf and three-quarters of the adjacent Isle of Man (Pickett 2001). These rocks, which over time were folded, tilted and changed by heat and pressure, have many faults and planes of weakness, along which crevices and blocky ledges have formed, providing ideal homes for cliff-nesting birds.

Inland, the landscape of the Calf of Man is largely heathland and rough pasture on acid soils, much like the coast of the adjacent mainland across the Sound. Bracken dominates some of the coastal slopes (or 'brooghs' as they are locally known) and threatens to invade grassland areas if not kept in check. A shallow valley known as 'the Glen' cuts north to south through the middle of the island and is drained by a stream which is the only permanently flowing water-course.

Along the Glen lies the old field system associated with the farming community which once subsisted on the Calf, the boundaries marked out by dry stone walls. Soils, derived from glacial drift deposits, are at their deepest here and were improved at some point by the addition of lime. Nowadays only sheep and rabbit dung add to the fertility, with bird guano locally affecting some of the coastal areas of vegetation. When the sun is low, its light sometimes picks out the old lazy beds, parallel mounds dug in small plots by past inhabitants to establish deeper soil.

An old mill pond is also located in the Glen and is kept clear of choking vegetation by the wardens and volunteers. At the northern end willows ('withies') have been planted as cover to attract migrating birds. At the head of the Glen is the observatory itself, which gleans its water from wells. Staff and visitors are heavily dependent on rainfall and acutely aware of the need for conservation of the supply. Boggy areas around springs, temporary streams and old peat workings add to wildlife habitat diversity.

There are other buildings on the Calf besides the observatory farmhouse and its outbuildings. Of considerable historical interest are the two older lighthouses situated on the western side of the island, built as a pair by Robert Stevenson and first lit in 1819. Working simultaneously, they warned passing ships of the treacherous submerged Chicken Rock, a tidal reef just over one kilometre off the south coast of the Calf. The crew of any vessel in the area would know that the ship was heading for the reef if the two lights appeared to coincide and that they should therefore take avoiding action. The upper lighthouse tower stands some 126 metres above high water and the lower tower at about 95 metres. Both have interesting architectural details, such as animal shapes in the cast ironwork around the balcony and lantern.

These lighthouses functioned until 1875, when a new lighthouse, built by the Northern Lighthouse Board, came into operation on Chicken Rock itself. The building of this 41 metre high granite sea tower must have been very difficult, as foundations had first to be laid five metres down into solid rock. The Chicken

Rock Lighthouse was manned until 1960, when a fire badly damaged the interior and the three keepers were only evacuated following a dangerous rescue operation. After that, the light and fog signal were made to run automatically. Nowadays a helicopter pad, built at the foot of the lighthouse, makes maintenance visits less hazardous and enables materials to be delivered more swiftly.

A fourth lighthouse, built on the Calf itself, was completed by the Board in 1968, and operated in place of the two Stevenson lighthouses. Until automation in 1995, the light was manned by up to four keepers who, on the cliff top at 100 metres above sea level, managed to live a civilised existence, cultivating a garden and even creating a golf course! The lure of electricity and associated television also provided a touch of civilisation for the observatory wardens. Watching a film or a football match made a welcome break from the Tilley lamps at the observatory. The extra hands also made light work of unloading supplies from the weekly boat. In 2007, this lighthouse too was finally closed down in favour of an upgraded light on the Chicken Rock, which now illuminates the land and seascape. A more detailed account can be found in *A Tour of Manx Lighthouses* (Hellowell 1998).

A group of small ruined buildings called 'the Smithy' lies on the track leading east from the lighthouses to the observatory and is associated with the Stevenson lighthouses. On a south-facing slope above Cow Harbour stands 'Jane's House', a small two-storey building constructed in about 1890 on the site marked on a 1771

The west coast of the Calf of Man showing the two Robert Stevenson lighthouses built in 1819, with the lighthouse of 1968 in between. The 'smithy' is just visible behind the lighthouse on the left (Courtesy of Manx National Heritage).

map as the 'Mansion House'. On the north coast, at the highest point of the island, are the ruins of 'Bushell's House', commonly connected with the seventeenth century fugitive-cum-hermit Thomas Bushell. This structure is something of an enigma, as it is very exposed to the elements and cannot have been much of a living space. All of these buildings on the Calf are maintained by Manx National Heritage, except the most modern lighthouse which remains the responsibility of the Northern Lighthouse Board.

Cow Harbour on the north-east coast is now the main landing point for visitors from Port Erin. In the early 1900s, cattle were obliged to swim across the Sound to and from this harbour, thus giving rise to its name. Equipment, supplies and staff for the observatory are brought over by boat from Port St Mary to South Harbour, on the other side of the island. A little to the south-east of Cow Harbour is Grant's Harbour ('the Dock'), which is used less regularly depending on the tides.

HISTORY

The early years

It is clear that the Calf of Man has been economically and strategically important for much of its history. Early evidence of occupation comes in the form of worked prehistoric flints and early Christian graves. When the fields were being set out in 1773, workers found part of a carved stone, believed to be from the front of the altar of an early Christian chapel or *keeill*. The carving, thought to date from the ninth century AD, depicts the crucifixion of Christ, with the spear bearer on one side. Known as the Calf Crucifixion Stone, this slab is recognised to be an outstanding example of the art of the time, and is now in the care of Manx National Heritage at the Manx Museum. Refuge for Christianity or not, the Calf in medieval times provided income both from lead mining and its wildlife, especially from the Manx Shearwaters which were harvested in their thousands for eating and for their oil and feathers.

For a time, the Isle of Man, including the Calf, was ruled by Norse, and later, Scottish kings. Such was the value of the shearwater harvest that the Calf most probably remained in royal ownership. In 1414 the Isle of Man came under English rule through the Stanleys, who were endowed with the title of Kings (and later Lords) of Mann. In 1644, James Stanley, the seventh Earl of Derby, claimed the Calf when military defences were necessarily prepared against potential attackers. Gun batteries were built and a garrison was maintained there during the English Civil War. The remains of one of these batteries are still visible as earth works just above Grant's Harbour. In 1651, three Parliamentary ships attacking the Calf were repelled by the defending forces. However, the pro-Royalist Stanleys were eventually defeated and the island passed into the control of the Commonwealth.

After the Restoration of the Monarchy and until 1736, the Isle of Man and Calf of Man were again held by the Earls of Derby, Lords of Mann. It is fairly certain that Rabbits were introduced during this time, to assist shearwater nesting by excavating burrows and as an additional source of revenue (Chiverrell *et al.* 2006). They were kept in cony warrens and collected mostly for the aristocracy as a delicacy. The Manx Shearwater colony was all but wiped out towards the end of the 1700s, but the Rabbits remained and provided nourishment and a source of income for the owners and tenants of the Calf right up to the founding of the observatory.

Several unsuccessful attempts were made by the Earls of Derby to establish Red Deer on the island. In 1736, the Dukes of Atholl succeeded the Earls of Derby as the Lords of Mann and took possession of the Calf. They exploited the shearwaters and Rabbits too, and also kept sheep on the island, tenanting it to John Quayle, amongst others, who made the first serious attempt at agricultural development in the 1770s. The lazy beds, still just visible today, are thought to date from this time.

Ownership of the Calf passed briefly to the British Crown in 1765, following the Act of Revestment, when the Crown purchased the Isle of Man from the Dukes of Atholl. It was then sold to the Drinkwater family, and by descent, came into the hands of Colonel George Carey who, in 1878, built the farmhouse and adjacent buildings, which today house the observatory. Subsequent owners built the silo near the farmhouse, widened the mill dam, and in the 1930s tried unsuccessfully to connect the Calf to the mainland by telephone. The attempt included laying an undersea cable across the treacherous Sound, but this was doomed to failure as the currents ripped the cable from the seabed.

Farming the Calf of Man was undoubtedly hard, and its occupants needed to be more or less self-sufficient. Nevertheless, the Calf continued to be farmed through the 1800s, and tenants supported themselves and their families by keeping cattle and sheep and growing arable crops. Rabbits were still a source of profit: one tenant, Mr Gourley, harvested 2,000 of them each year. Mr Gourley also supplemented his living by taking seabird eggs and, supposedly, Woodcock, though how many of the latter he was able to find on the by-then-deforested island is not clear. By 1851 there was a community of about 30, including the lighthouse keepers, and farm workers and their families.

Jack Maddrell, whose family looked after and farmed the Calf for 23 years in the early 1900s, wrote an account of life there. He told of how the farm kept animals for beef and mutton on 25 hectares, with 11 hectares of arable, much of it as fodder crop. Sheep were transported to the Calf by boat from Port St Mary on the mainland, while cows were swum across the Sound to Cow Harbour at slack water. They were reliant on the mainland only for the likes of fuel such as paraffin and coal. One poignant reminder of the harshness of life is a grave on the hillside near Bushell's House, thought to be the last resting place of a child from a lighthouse family who succumbed to scarlet fever.

In Victorian times the Isle of Man became a popular holiday destination; as a result the Calf started to attract visitors and became appreciated for its landscape and dramatic setting. In 1937 it was bought by F. J. Dickens, a distant relative of Charles Dickens, whose objective in doing so was to save it from a threatened tourism development. He promptly gave it to the National Trust for England and Wales 'to preserve its nature and beauty', a generous and wise move that eventually enabled the growing numbers of Manx birdwatchers to realise their dream of making the Calf of Man into a bird sanctuary.

The first warden and farm steward under the new regime was Robert Garrett, who stayed with his family until 1939, when the exigencies of raising small children persuaded them to leave such an isolated spot. The National Trust appointed the next warden, Robert Mitchell, who together with his family, stayed during the war years to look after the livestock, protect the breeding birds and prevent egg thefts. Summer visitors (thin on the ground anyway because of the war) were allowed, but not in the nesting season without special permission. The Mitchells' only means of communication was the postal service set up especially by the Isle of Man's Head Postmaster, with delivery by boat.

Since 1950

In 1951, the Calf of Man was leased to the Manx National Trust as land manager, shortly after its founding as the sister body to the Manx Museum. A Manx farmer, Fred Faragher took over as warden in 1952 and managed the Calf until 1954. He was followed by an ex-military man, Frank Williams, who by contrast had little experience of farming, and had to learn how to look after the livestock and crops. However, Williams and his wife managed to be self-sufficient by and large, although it seems that the Rabbits finally ceased to be profitable as a source of income, due to lack of help in trapping them and the arrival, in 1955, of myxomatosis. Life on the island was tough, but it took a dramatic turn when Mrs Williams went into labour during a November storm. Frantic attempts to alert the Chicken Rock Lighthouse keepers by flare and fire finally worked, and help was summoned by radio-telephone. Heavy seas foiled the lifeboats, so a helicopter was sent from Northern Ireland to airlift Mrs Williams to the maternity home on the mainland, where she gave birth to a daughter. After this fright the Calf wardens were provided with a radio-telephone of their own!

Frank Williams and his family stayed on the Calf until 1958, by which time farming had become uneconomic. This was a turning point for the Manx Museum and National Trust, later to become Manx National Heritage, which recognised the growing potential of the island as a nature reserve and place to study bird migration. With the help of a grant from the British Trust for Ornithology (BTO), the observatory was opened in 1959. Its first ornithological warden was the Norwegian Einar Brun who, with his wife, spent two seasons on the Calf ringing birds, conducting a census of the breeding birds and maintaining a migration log. In 1962, the observatory joined the growing network of officially recognised bird observatories around the British Isles. Since then, two wardens have been present on the Calf for nine to ten months of every year, and many volunteers and visiting ringing groups have aided the ringing effort and collection of data over the years. As a result there is now an unbroken record of migration and breeding productivity, stretching from 1962 to the present day, which makes a valuable contribution towards our understanding of bird behaviour, ecology and conservation.

In 1986, the National Trust for England, Wales and Northern Ireland at long last transferred inalienable ownership of the Calf to the Manx National Trust and, by extension, to the people of the Isle of Man.

Of the personalities that stand out in the story of the Calf of Man Bird Observatory, particular mention should be made of Ken Williamson who, in the 1930s and 1940s, was influential in establishing the bird observatory through his writings and contacts. Williamson was for a time the librarian at the Manx Museum, but his commitment to birds flourished into a career. After the war he went on to establish the observatory on Fair Isle and was a driving force in the development of the observatory network, before joining the BTO as an authority on bird population research. Part of his legacy is *Peregrine*, originally the journal of the Manx Field Club and now the journal of the Manx Ornithological Society. Many of the Society's members are still closely associated with birdwatching and research on the Calf, among them Pat Cullen, bird recorder for the Isle of Man and co-author of *Birds of the Isle of Man* (Cullen & Jennings 1986) and Anne Kaye, who has been very active in encouraging young people to take an interest in bird watching. A variety of additional background reading on the Calf can be found (Lockington Marshall 1978, Garrad 1986, Garrad 1990).

Life on the Calf of Man today

The ornithological warden, usually a licensed ringer, supervises the work of the observatory and submits annual reports. Duties of the estate warden vary according to skills, but usually involve some land management as directed by Manx National Heritage. Control of Common Rats (formerly known as Brown Rat and locally known as 'longtails') is unfortunately necessary on an almost annual basis in order to give the Manx Shearwaters and other ground-nesting birds a chance to build up their populations.

Between 2,000 and 4,000 people visit the Calf annually, including some from passing cruise ships. Efforts by the Manx Government to promote the Isle of Man as a tourist destination have had knock-on effects for the Calf in the form of visits by the media, including television companies. These can occupy quite a lot of the wardens' time in providing advice, demonstrations and interviews, but are well worth it for their educational value and in encouraging support.

People come to the Calf for a variety of reasons. Day visitors come over to watch birds, enjoy the landscape or just out of curiosity. Those who stay overnight are there to help out with the work at the observatory, or to 'get away from it all' and immerse themselves in the birds and other wildlife. One thing is certain; they do not come for luxury accommodation! Nightlife consists of conversation around a driftwood fire or ringing Storm Petrels out at the coast. If the weather suddenly deteriorates, a stay on the Calf can be longer than bargained for, and it is always wise to bring surplus food 'just in case'. The water supply can sometimes be a problem, especially in dry summers. One visiting musician must have felt such privations keenly, for he composed the 'Calf of Man Blues' as solace for others.

Groups such as the Manx Ornithological Society make regular pilgrimages, though it is not necessary to be enthusiastic about birds to make a contribution to the work of the observatory. On one occasion, the Territorial Army arrived for 'Operation Celtic Dig', the seriously messy task of clearing choking vegetation and sediment from the mill pond to make it more attractive to water birds. The ever-present possibility of being cut off from the mainland by bad weather makes the Calf a good candidate for practising rescue missions and the Coastguard regularly carry out exercises around the cliffs with assistance from the local lifeboat crews. Even the animals can benefit; one year a ram from the resident Loghtan flock was trapped down a cliff and had to be rescued by the Port Erin Coastguard Cliff Rescue and Port Erin Lifeboat.

Other groups visiting the Calf have added to the understanding of its natural history. A recent two-night stay by the Manx Geological Survey resulted in complete mapping of the geology of the island's coast, something of an achievement given the after-effects on the participants of the merry dinner party the previous evening. On the other hand, some groups value the peace and quiet of the Calf to concentrate on studying other subjects, such as alternative healing, and a local language group sometimes meets on the Calf to concentrate on improving their fluency in Manx Gaelic.

Calf wardens must be able to cope with isolation on an island for eight to nine months of the year, but the wardens of 2001, Tim Bagworth and Des Robinson, surely could not have expected to be as isolated as they were during the foot and mouth crisis. Neither the Isle of Man nor the Calf was infected with the disease but strict quarantine arrangements were in place to protect the stock. However, the near total absence of visitors may have given the birds a respite from human disturbance and Curlew tried to breed there for the first time in many years.

Bird ringing groups from Britain and further afield come to increase their experience of handling birds, and can be of considerable help at busy times, especially during large falls of migratory birds. Rye Meads Ringing Group once ringed nearly 1,000 birds in a single week. The Manx Bird Atlas project staff came to the Calf between 1998 and 2002 to conduct surveys during the breeding season, as an essential part of a five-year project to map the Isle of Man's breeding and wintering populations of birds. Atlas records were mapped at the one kilometre level, which is unprecedented for a county level avifauna.

THE BIRDS

There is much literature on the birds of the Calf of Man, particularly in locally based publications such as *Peregrine*. For a comprehensive and authoritative account of the avifauna, ten years on from the publication of the first edition of this book (Durman 1976), birdwatchers turn to the chapter on the Calf in *Birds of the Isle of Man* (Cullen & Jennings 1986). The Calf also features prominently in the *Manx Bird Atlas* (Sharpe 2007), the definitive account of the distribution of the Isle of Man's bird species. The annual reports are the best means of catching up on breeding productivity, ringing activity and migration highlights for those supporters of the observatory who cannot visit every year. As well as detailing species recorded and ringed at the observatory, the reports describe the many and various surveys to which the wardens contribute.

In recent years these have included British and international efforts, such as Seabird 2000, the North Atlantic Storm Petrel Study, International Chough Census (coordinated by the Manx Chough Project) (Moore 2004), the BTO's Nest Record Scheme and updates of migration and breeding bird atlases. More locally-based surveys, such as the Manx Bird Atlas and Manx Chough Project, are supported annually. Studies specific to the Calf are undertaken when the wardens and volunteers can fit them in between routine ornithological duties.

Of course the crux of the observatory's work is monitoring and ringing birds which breed on, or pass through, the Calf. At the time when the first edition was published there were 203 bird species on the Calf checklist, and 49,489 birds (of 123 species) had been ringed in the period of 15 years from 1959 to 1974. By the end of the 2008 season, the checklist total had risen to 269 species, with 220,047 birds of 154 species ringed. Between 4,000 and 5,000 birds are ringed annually.

At the heart of the ringing operation are the mist-nets and Heligoland traps around the observatory buildings, which are employed on a daily basis, as long as the weather is suitable. A crow trap on the land to the south-east of the observatory sometimes attracts Meadow Pipits, Pied Wagtails and White Wagtails *Motacilla alba alba*, although ironically, very rarely the species it is named after. Night-time trapping of Manx Shearwaters and Storm Petrels is conducted at South Harbour using, as a base, a storage shed furnished with an old picnic bench salvaged from the beach, a gas heater, camping lamps and a spirit of camaraderie. Many ground- or cliff-nesting birds are ringed as nestlings, though this can be a hazardous process when picking one's way down the rocks towards a colony, or fending off attacks from protective parent gulls. Only fit and experienced ringers are allowed to do this, and they have to be accompanied by a competent helper.

Breeding birds – seabirds

The cliff faces are occupied by colonies of Kittiwakes, Guillemots, Razorbills, Fulmars and Shags. Despite the Calf's generally mild maritime climate, the weather plays a big part in seabird breeding productivity, as the best nest-sites are mostly in the teeth of the prevailing south-westerly winds and accompanying rain. Cold, wet springs can badly affect gull colonies and exacerbate any shortages of food. In some years the colonies totally fail to rear young.

Kittiwake numbers on the Calf vary enormously, though this may be partly due to birds moving home to the mainland from time to time. Thus, colonies, mainly at Caigher on the south-west coast and at Kione Roauyr on the east coast, grew from 13 pairs in 1956 to 720 pairs in 1969, reducing to 175 in 1973 (Wright 1976). Cullen and Jennings (1986) reported an upward trend to more than 60 pairs, and by 1995 this had risen to 105 pairs. However, the count was back down to 71 pairs in 2005 and more recent reports suggest little improvement and poor breeding productivity.

Three other species of gulls breed on the Calf. Herring and Great Black-backed Gulls are resident all the year round, and their colonies tend to be amongst rocks above the tide line and on grassy cliff tops and slopes respectively.

Lesser Black-backed Gulls are summer visitors and are the least common of the breeding gulls, nesting mainly on the heath inland from the east coast. The number of breeding pairs has fluctuated considerably since the observatory opened, with peaks of 100 pairs in 1967 and 67 in 2002. There were only 14 pairs in 2005 and fledging success was very low, probably due to a combination of predation and very wet weather early in the season.

Auks are common around the Calf, and indeed around the Isle of Man as a whole. Whilst breeding numbers of Guillemots and Razorbills probably never exceed 200 pairs of each species, many more of these birds can be seen offshore as the season progresses. Black Guillemots are regularly noted in small numbers around the island in spring and a few pairs have nested in recent years. Puffins, otherwise known as 'sea parrots' or *Poltrag* in Manx, may once have nested on the Calf in reasonable numbers. Seen commonly around the Calf at the beginning of the twentieth century, numbers have decreased substantially. In the 1970s and 1980s, there were around 30 to 40 breeding pairs with fewer than five since the late 1980s, although evidence appears to have been limited to observing birds coming ashore with food. Nowadays, Puffins can, with luck, be spotted near the shore at the Lighthouses and sometimes in the Sound.

Amongst the most common seabirds are Shags, seen throughout the year around the Calf. Flocks, sometimes approaching 1,000 birds, gather in the Sound in the autumn. Up to several hundred pairs breed each year, nesting mainly among the massive boulders strewn along lower parts of the cliffs. Ringing recoveries suggest that the Calf and Isle of Man populations stay in the Irish Sea region, though one bird ringed on the Calf was recovered in the Netherlands in 2005. Recoveries of Calf-ringed Shags (sadly deceased) also confirm potential life-spans of over 22 years.

The first proven Manx breeding of Fulmars was on the Calf in 1936, at that time one of the most southerly known breeding stations in the British Isles, a distinction shared with a colony on the south-east coast of Yorkshire and six in Ireland (Fisher 1939). Numbers have continued to rise around the Isle of Man ever since, and the latest count of 64 occupied nests on the Calf in 2005 is probably an underestimate of the true population, because of the inaccessibility of some of the sites.

Of all the birds that frequent the Calf of Man, perhaps the most evocative of past treasures and future aspirations is the Manx Shearwater. Nowadays there are small breeding colonies around the island, a shadow of the once-vast population that must have been numbered in tens of thousands until the end of the eighteenth century. There are written references to the 'Mancks Puffin' as far back as the 1580s, and even before that (Brooke 1990). A description in one of the Norse sagas, of a nocturnal cacophony of bird calls over the Sound, most likely describes Manx Shearwaters returning to their colony on the Calf. The Viking chieftain who heard them in 1014 took this as an ill omen, sailing very shortly afterwards to his defeat at the Battle of Clontarf in Ireland.

Francis Willoughby, in 1676, was the first to describe Calf specimens systematically using the name Manx Shearwater (Ray 1676, 1678), thereby distinguishing the species from the bird we now know as the Puffin. In those times, many thousands of young birds, plump and downy, were taken from their burrows with an iron hook and killed for food or oil. They were eaten fresh or preserved, and were supposed to have had a fishy taste, such that they could be eaten during Lent. Their oil had various applications, particularly to prevent armour from rusting, for treating wool and for lighting. The trade was valuable to the Lord of Mann, who even had enough Mancks Puffins to export them through Liverpool. Culling was merciless, and the colony must have been huge to sustain such losses. However, in the end it seems to have been rats, shipwrecked from a Russian vessel in the 1780s, which all but wiped out the Calf shearwaters by the beginning of the nineteenth century.

Since the opening of the observatory, successive wardens have been alert to the possibility that the Manx Shearwater might return as a breeding species as they continued to be abundant around the Calf in summer and September movements of up to 30,000 birds were recorded. The Calf of Man Bird Observatory's annual reports made regular mention of shearwaters calling at night over the Calf itself and searches by the wardens for evidence of breeding yielded convincing signs on several occasions.

The first serious attempt to eliminate the rats on the island was made in 1979, and since then the evidence that shearwaters are returning to breed has been building up. In 1982, Jennings (1983) announced that a small colony of about 20 breeding pairs had been found. In the 1990s the warden, Norman McCanch, reported calls from burrows, and found down and feather sheathing in debris excavated from a number of them (C. Sharpe, pers. comm.).

Then in 2000 the Manx Bird Atlas surveyors and Calf wardens found definitive proof of breeding. Tape luring techniques (using recordings of the call of the male bird) established the presence of three occupied burrows in the breeding season. Two young birds were found in their burrows later that summer and ringed. Since then, and with refinement of searching methods, the Manx Bird Atlas team and Calf wardens confirmed that there were at least five breeding colonies on the north, south and east coasts. Whilst a total of 104 occupied burrows was located in 2005 (Cope and Pimm 2006) there were responses to recorded calls from 84 out of the 124 marked and monitored burrows in 2008. Provided systematic control of the rats continues, it looks as though the Manx Shearwater might hold its own as a breeding species.

When conditions are suitable in the summer, the wardens undertake night-time catching and ringing of birds by a combination of tape-luring, dazzling and mist-netting. Most Manx Shearwaters and Storm Petrels are trapped this way as they fly ashore under cover of darkness. Large numbers of Storm Petrels may be ringed in a season (372 were ringed in 2005), and useful information gained about their movements and survival. Within the area of Britain and Ireland, recoveries and controls frequently feature Sanda Island, Lunga (Treshnish Isles) and Ailsa Craig, all in west Scottish waters. Petrels are also regularly picked up at, or come from Copeland, the Isle of May, Bardsey, Flamborough and North Sands (Hartlepool). Calf-ringed petrels have also been recovered in the Faeroes, France (Finistere), Norway and the Algarve in Portugal. Storm Petrels are suspected of breeding on the Calf, as the muddy feet of birds retrapped on the island would suggest, possibly in rock cavities or dry stone walls, although definite proof has yet to be found.

Breeding birds – waders and waterfowl

The rocky coast is attractive to Oystercatchers and around 10–20 pairs breed annually, representing the only remaining breeding wader species. Curlew, Snipe and Lapwing once bred, but no longer do so, the latter unfortunately reflecting the downward population trend in the UK.

Two species of duck breed regularly on the Calf, although productivity depends on how well the parents can hide their offspring from the gulls. Eiders have been extending their breeding range southwards within the British Isles lately and have been seen in increasing numbers around the Manx coast. The first breeding pair was recorded in 1992, and since then nesting has increased with at least 12 recorded attempts in 2008. The ducklings have a hard time avoiding predation, but some survive, though not in every year. A few Mallard also regularly attempt to breed, bringing their young to the mill pond. Though numbers are low, Shelduck are often seen on the coast and probably breed.

The mill pond is also home to one or two pairs of Moorhens, and Water Rails often lurk around the pond and withy as they pass through. The latter bred in the 1990s, but may have been displaced when the Moorhens moved in (J. Thorpe pers. comm.).

Breeding birds – raptors

The 1980s and 1990s saw the welcome return of several raptor species as breeders with Peregrines returning in 1980, after an absence of 30 years or more. At least one pair now regularly nests on a cliff ledge. Furthermore, it has been especially gratifying for wardens to witness Hen Harriers nesting regularly on the Calf heathland since 1991. The Isle of Man is now well known for supporting a relatively large population of this species, which is threatened in the UK. Here, in the absence of extensive grouse moors, the harriers are not persecuted. Though they will take young ground-nesting birds, they seem to thrive mostly on Rabbits, of which there is no shortage on the Calf. Noted as 'uncommon' in the species check-list, they are in fact one of the bird species most frequently encountered by visitors to the Calf because of their characteristic gliding flight, low over the hillsides and heath. In addition to the breeding birds, up to 20 Hen Harriers were formerly recorded roosting on the Calf in the autumn, although numbers have been much lower in recent years.

Breeding birds – the crows

That most flamboyant member of the crow family, the Chough, is a spectacular success story in the Isle of Man, thanks to a group of people dedicated to monitoring its population, understanding its needs and encouraging conservation management (Bullock and del-Nevo 1983, Moore 2004). The Manx Chough

Project has been instrumental in this work, for example, organising the ten-yearly Chough Censuses. On the Calf in 2002, 14 pairs raised 30 young, a very respectable figure for such a small area.

Choughs do so well on the Calf, as on the adjacent mainland, because they have access to a wide range of feeding opportunities, and because the mild, generally wet weather allows them to forage all year round. The old field system and coastal grasslands on the Calf are grazed short by Rabbits and Loghtan sheep, enabling Choughs to probe the soil for invertebrates. Non-breeding flocks often fly between the Calf and the mainland to forage in pastures or at the strandline on beaches.

Another member of the crow family, the Raven, is associated with myth and legend in the Isle of Man. Ravens were believed by the Vikings to accompany the Norse god Odin who sent them out to gather knowledge about the world. One or two pairs usually nest on the Calf, and non-breeding birds often wander across from the mainland. Much more common, and more of a problem for other nesting birds, are the Hooded Crows. Only small numbers breed on the Calf, but they are joined by birds coming across the Sound in search of food or a place to roost.

Breeding birds – passerines

Typical of the heath and grassland are some of the smaller birds of open country. Most common are Meadow Pipits, both as residents and as migrants. The breeding population currently stands at about 60 to 70 pairs, but movements of several hundred migrants can be recorded in spring and autumn. Rock Pipits are familiar residents all around the coast and large family parties of up to 30 can be observed. The sentinel-like behaviour of Stonechats makes them easy to find on rougher ground, and both males and females are seen throughout the season on wall-top lookouts. Twelve breeding pairs were recorded in 2005.

The population of Wheatears breeding on the Calf has fluctuated around eight pairs in recent years. Spring migrations include individuals of the larger Greenland race *Oenanthe oenanthe leucorhoa* on their way north-west. The remarkable ringing recovery of a Wheatear which was re-trapped on the Calf seven years after ringing shows that these birds can be quite long-lived. Linnets are characteristic inhabitants of the heathy parts of the Calf, forming large feeding flocks in the summer after breeding.

A number of species nest around the observatory and other buildings, encouraged by the planting of trees and shrubs in the garden. The resident Pied Wagtails are joined by migrants in spring and autumn, and by White Wagtails of European origin which can out-number the Pieds on autumn passage. Grey Wagtails can be numerous on autumn passage, but there is no recent confirmation of breeding.

Birds which are normally common residents in urban gardens can occur only sporadically on the Calf, such as the one or two pairs of Blackbirds and Robins which usually try to nest. Greenfinches and Chaffinches have bred only occasionally. Swallows are regular summer visitors to the observatory and lighthouse buildings and have been successful in raising young recently. In 2007, as many as eight pairs nested, three with double broods, and managed to rear a total of 33 young. Wrens can nest almost anywhere on the Calf, including around the observatory, but their numbers are difficult to census.

Breeding birds – recent additions and losses

Some of the gratifying additions to the Calf's list of breeding species since the first edition was published have already been mentioned. Unfortunately there have been some losses too, such as Grey Partridge and (until very recently) Short-eared Owl, both of which used to breed regularly. The decline in Grey Partridge, originally an introduced species, is no doubt part of a wider population trend, but the specific reasons for its departure from the Calf in the late 1970s are hard to pin down. Theories range from the ending of farming and a series of wet breeding seasons to predation by Hen Harriers (Cullen and Jennings 1986). Short-eared Owls do breed across on the mainland but might no longer be able to find enough food for dependent young on the Calf, now that the rat population is closely controlled (J. Thorpe, pers. comm.).

Migration – waterfowl and waders

Bird migration through the Calf is monitored by the wardens whilst they are on the island between March and November. Weather conditions are of course the main factor in dictating movements and a spell of fog or rain can ground large numbers of birds for a day or so. Sea-watching is usually most productive in the autumn, especially when the wind turns north-westerly after south-westerly gales, when birds pushed off course by the conditions are making their way south again.

Whooper and Bewick's Swans are seen occasionally along with White-fronted, Pink-footed, Greylag and Canada Geese. Both Dark-bellied *Branta bernicla bernicla* and Pale-bellied *B. b. hrota* forms of the Brent Goose have been seen.

Among the waders, Curlews can be seen heading north in February and March, and their return passage in July and August (often at night) is joined by small numbers of Whimbrels, Common and Purple Sandpipers, and Greenshanks. Green and Wood Sandpipers occur rarely, usually as individuals or in small groups. Lapwings are regularly recorded during migration, as are Turnstones, Golden Plover and Snipe. Grey Plovers come through a little later than the other waders, in April and September.

Migration – raptors and owls

Birds of prey can provide excitement during migration periods and some stay around for a time to take advantage of the flocks of small birds making landfall on the Calf. Sparrowhawks, Kestrels and Merlins appear fairly reliably each year. Some Merlins are thought to overwinter here and there can be daily sightings in October. Hobbies appear rather sporadically. The larger raptors tend not to linger over the Calf, although in 2005 an Osprey proved to be more obliging by landing for a while and allowing birdwatchers some good views. There have been some 13 records of Ospreys between 2000 and 2007, and it is tempting to assume that they are part of the growing Scottish population.

There seems to have been a recent upsurge in records of Marsh Harriers, with one or two recorded every year since 1998, mirroring the increasing breeding population in the rest of the UK. The burgeoning population in Wales could also be responsible for the four Red Kites recorded in 2004, following only six earlier observatory records. Buzzards appear occasionally in October or November. Of the owls, Short-eared is seen most frequently, although it is always worth keeping an eye on the conifers at the back of the observatory garden as the occasional Long-eared Owl also passes through. Barn Owls are rare; only two have appeared in the last five years.

Migration – near-passerines

Cuckoos still seem to be appearing as expected, despite declining numbers elsewhere in the UK. There were three records of Nightjars between 1995 and 2005, a species which had not been recorded on the Calf before. The Isle of Man is notable in lacking breeding populations of any of the woodpeckers, a legacy of early deforestation. However, a few Green Woodpeckers and Great Spotted Woodpeckers have passed though the Calf on migration, and Wrynecks are seen regularly.

Migration – passerines

It is always good to see Sand Martins returning to the Calf in spring, some of them hopefully on their way to nest on the north coast of the Isle of Man. House Martins and Swallows also pass through; the former had an exceptional year in 2005, with maximum counts well into the hundreds in both directions. Swifts are among the latest of the spring migrants to arrive, though they are still earlier than the stragglers, such as Spotted Flycatchers, which may linger in the observatory garden for a few days during June to feed up on insects.

Fieldfares, Redwings, Blackbirds, Robins and Song Thrushes can all occur in good numbers, especially on autumn passage, and many are ringed. Recoveries and controls of Blackbirds show migration movements predominantly to and from Scandinavia and over eastern and north-eastern Britain. One or two Ring Ouzels can be present in almost any month of the season, though fewer seem to have been coming through in recent years, mirroring a decline in the British population.

A scattering of Whinchats is usually seen each year through April and May and then again in August and September. Although they had a reasonable season in 2005, Redstarts have been recorded in decreasing numbers on the Calf for a while, as have Pied Flycatchers and Wood Warblers. These three species typically nest in sessile oak woodlands on the western side of Britain, and are giving particular cause for concern amongst ornithologists (J. Thorpe pers. comm.). About 15 Black Redstarts were recorded in 2005, a welcome upsurge after a period of decline since the mid-1990s.

Willow Warbler is usually the commonest warbler recorded; sometimes hundreds can be seen on good fall days. Through the season, you can also expect to see Chiffchaffs, Sedge Warblers, Whitethroats, Garden Warblers, Grasshopper Warblers and Blackcaps, often in good numbers. The Reed Warbler and Lesser Whitethroat are still unusual on the Calf, being on the north-west edge of their range here. Rarities and vagrants amongst the warblers also provide challenges for the keen-eyed birdwatcher; for example, Barred Warbler, Yellow-browed Warbler, Melodious Warbler and Icterine Warbler have all been recorded in recent years.

Goldcrests can be abundant during spring and autumn migration and are among the birds most frequently ringed. However they are very susceptible to harsh winters and every now and then a population crash will be detected by a huge reduction in numbers. In 1991, the passage was down by as much as 96% on the previous year. It is worth checking the Goldcrests carefully as Firecrests have been seen in most years recently.

Lacking woodland, the Calf does not support resident populations of tits, but small flocks of Long-tailed Tits and a few Great Tits, Blue Tits and Coal Tits can be seen during the autumn. House Sparrows now only visit in small numbers, though they were probably resident on the Calf when it was actively farmed. Tree Sparrows fared quite well in the 2005 season when the wardens reported the best year since the mid-1980s, and a flock of 12 was present in mid-October. In 2007, 22 of these birds were recorded in small groups or as individuals around the island.

Among the finches, Linnets, Greenfinches and Chaffinches tend to dominate the large autumn movements, with maximum counts of several hundred birds being not unusual. Siskins can be recorded in every month of the season and, although none breed on the Calf, up to 100 can move through in September and October. In most years there will be a few Bramblings, reaching double figures from time to time. The early 1990s saw the first occurrence of Serin and there have been four records since then. The vast majority of the redpolls ringed since the taxonomic split in 2000 have been Lesser Redpolls. In most years, a few Common Crossbills can be expected, but rarer finches such as Hawfinch are more sporadic in occurrence. Common Rosefinch, though still irregular, has been seen more often on the Calf in the last 15 years or so, reflecting a pattern emerging in Britain (J. Thorpe pers. comm.).

There are generally few buntings; Reed Buntings are the most frequent. They are usually present throughout the season in small numbers and, in addition to those birds passing through, several pairs may breed. One or two Yellowhammers are recorded in most years along with occasional Lapland Buntings, whilst Ortolan, Snow and Little Buntings may also put in an appearance from time to time.

Migration – rarities

For the connoisseur, the rarities and vagrants which have visited the Calf since the observatory opened will be apparent from the full checklist in the appendices of this book and a perusal of back-copies of *Peregrine* (Bagworth 2000, Bishop 2000 and Bagworth 2003). Of the major rarities, the occurrence in 1989 of a Mourning Dove (a new species for the Western Palearctic), and in 1983 the first record of White-throated Robin for the British Isles, are particularly noteworthy. A Pechora Pipit caused excitement in 1991 and a Sardinian Warbler in 1995.

Recent records of scarce migrants include Hoopoe, Golden Oriole, Rose-coloured Starling, Red-backed Shrike, Marsh Warbler, Waxwing, Purple Heron and Bittern. A species that has not been seen on the Calf lately, but which is a distinct possibility, is the Corncrake. Calling males have occasionally been heard on the mainland, and at least two young broods have been sighted, raising hopes

This striking Hoopoe is amongst an impressive list of scarce migrants that have been seen on the Calf of Man (Tim Bagworth).

that these threatened birds will become regular summer visitors to the Isle of Man in the future and will drop in on the Calf when passing.

Migration – sea-watching

Favoured spots for sea-watching on the Calf are the Cow Harbour area on the north-east coast and the west coast between the lighthouses and Caigher Point. Amongst the passing Manx Shearwaters are small numbers of Sooty and Balearic Shearwaters while fortunate observers may occasionally pick up a Great or a Cory's Shearwater. Arctic and Great Skuas are regularly seen, while Pomarine and Long-tailed Skuas occur more erratically. Unusual gulls also occur, such as Little, Sabine's and Iceland Gull. Gannets can be present at any time during the season, fishing in Manx waters or on their way to and from their breeding sites in Scotland. Among the terns, Sandwich are probably the most commonly seen, but Arctic and Common Terns are also recorded. Little Terns are rarely seen, even though there is a breeding colony on the north coast of the Isle of Man. Ducks can include Pintail, Shoveler, Pochard, Common and Velvet Scoters, Goldeneye and Red-breasted Merganser. Divers are recorded annually off the coast, most usually Great Northern and Red-throated, though Black-throated Divers are not unknown.

OTHER FAUNA AND FLORA

Mammals and other vertebrates

Visitors to the Calf soon become aware of the flourishing population of Rabbits, whose burrows honeycomb parts of the island. Unoccupied burrows are used by Manx Shearwaters while the Rabbits themselves are a food source for gulls and Hen Harriers. Turf kept short by Rabbits allows Choughs access to soil-dwelling invertebrates. Rabbit droppings, together with those of the sheep, manure the ground and encourage dung beetles and their larvae, which in turn are prey for birds. Despite ever-present myxomatosis, the number of Rabbits remains relatively stable from year to year, and includes a few black individuals. Common Rats are of great significance to the functioning of the Calf's breeding bird colonies, though in a very unwelcome way. Keeping these animals at bay is a constant battle, but one which must be won if there is to be any future for the Calf's ground-nesting birds. The Wood Mouse is the only other rodent species recorded and has not been seen for many years. It is thought to be extinct due to the rodent baiting. The insectivorous Pygmy Shrews are frequently seen and are often partial to a digestive biscuit in the wardens' lounge. Bats are sometimes recorded around the observatory buildings.

Loghtan sheep have been part of the Calf scene since they were first brought to the island in 1969. Elsewhere, this breed of small, hardy, long-legged sheep was for a while in trouble (Bazin 1984, Wade-Martins 1990). Numbers dwindled from the mid-eighteenth century onwards following lack of demand for their dark-coloured fleece, which is more suited to hand spinning than commercial spinning and weaving. The breed declined until a small group of concerned individuals in the Isle of Man took up the cause. The Manx Museum and National Trust (now Manx National Heritage) played a key role in rescuing Loghtans from extinction, taking on responsibility for one of the remaining flocks which was gifted to the Trust in 1953. Initially consisting of three ewes, a lamb and a ram, the Calf flock has grown considerably, so that between 50 and 60 animals are now kept on the island over the winter. They are a characteristic sight for visitors, especially when the four-horned rams are brought over for breeding purposes. The lambs' fleece is chocolate brown and becomes a lighter brown as they grow. The name 'Loghtan' comes from the Manx Gaelic for 'mouse-brown', which is an appropriate description of the fleece colour after the sun has bleached it a little. Nowadays the sheep are an important component of the management strategy for Choughs. Their dung encourages the presence of soil-living invertebrates and their grazing helps keep the turf short, giving the birds easy access to their food.

Seals frequent the well known haul-out places on the Calf coast, and at Kitterland and Thousla Rock in the Sound. Grey Seal numbers have grown in past decades to between 100 and 200 adults, with 20 to 30 pups usually recorded in September and October. Common Seals have also become a regular sight recently and ones and twos may be seen, often in the vicinity of Cow Harbour. Assiduous sea-watching also produces records of passing cetaceans. Most commonly seen are Harbour Porpoises but Common, Risso's and Bottlenose Dolphins are also recorded. A lucky observer might also catch a glimpse of Killer Whale or Minke Whale. Basking Sharks are attracted to the plankton swarms around the south and west coasts of the Isle of Man, and there can be several of these huge beasts in view off the Calf coast on calm days in summer.

The only reptile species on the Calf, and indeed in the Isle of Man, is the Common or Viviparous Lizard. Individuals are best found as they bask in the early morning sun on dry stone walls or on stones by the side of the main tracks.

Invertebrates

Growing interest in the dragonflies and damselflies that are drawn to the mill pond has produced a list of at least six species, including Migrant Hawker and Emperor Dragonfly in the last three years. This latter species has not been recorded from the mainland but is a recent colonist of southern Ireland, so the Calf may be its first landfall in the Isle of Man.

Wardens and volunteers have maintained a light trap for some years and have built up a respectable list of more than 200 species of macro and micro-moths. The fauna broadly reflects the range of available habitats, with a smattering of occasional immigrants, such as the day-flying Hummingbird Hawkmoth. Heathland species include True Lover's Knot and Emperor Moth. Specialities of the coast include Thrift Clearwing and the Grey *Hadena caesia mananii*, a Red Data Book species (Shirt ed. 1987) which is protected in the Isle of Man.

Fifteen species of butterfly are regularly recorded on the Calf. Since 1996 the wardens and volunteers have walked a weekly transect throughout the season and have built up a substantial body of data on the island's butterfly populations.

These include the typically coastal butterflies, Grayling and Dark Green Fritillary. Colonies of the latter species favour bracken covered slopes where their larval food plants (violets) grow.

As relatively little is known of the other terrestrial invertebrates, there are many interesting opportunities here for further investigation. What information there is comes mostly from small pitfall trapping exercises and there are lists for ground beetles (mostly Carabidae), dung beetles (*Aphodius* spp.), ants, spiders, woodlice and millipedes. More obvious to the casual observer are the jewel-like, Green Tiger Beetles, which are active in sunny weather in late spring, the large clumsy Minotaur Beetles, which clear up the rabbit dung, and Mottled Grasshoppers, which are common in the coastal turf in late summer.

Flora

Visiting botanists may wish to dip into *A Preliminary Review of the Calf of Man Flora* (Aspey and Fairhurst 1995) and will not be disappointed by a walk around the Calf of Man, though some species may have to be searched for in places out of the reach of hungry sheep and Rabbits.

In May, the bracken slopes are carpeted in Bluebells and the coastal turf is dotted with Spring Squill. In May and June, rocky outcrops above the tide line support scurvygrass, sea-spurreys, Thrift, Sea Campion and English Stonecrop. Heathers dominate the heathland areas but, perhaps surprisingly, Western Gorse, which is interspersed with heather on heathland across the Sound, is comparatively rare on the Calf.

In the boggy areas and wet flushes Round-leaved Sundew, Marsh St John's-wort and Ragged-Robin appear. *Sphagnum* mosses occupy an area of permanent bog above Jane's House, where Creeping Willow is also found. Wetter areas of pasture support spring-flowering Cuckooflower.

Five species of orchids have been recorded, including Early Marsh-orchid around the mill pond. In the mill pond itself are pondweeds and an introduced white water lily. Marsh Pennywort borders the water's edge. The old dry stone walls support a good lichen flora, including the bushy *Ramalina siliquosa*, and this is also the usual habitat of Navelwort. Ferns grow on shadier walls behind the observatory buildings.

Marine life

The waters around the Calf support an exceptionally rich marine fauna and flora and provide some of the best sites for diving in the British Isles (Sanderson *et al.* 1994). Strong tidal currents sweep nutrients over prolific bedrock, boulder and coarse sediment communities, and the clear sea allows luxurious growth of marine algae. Rare species are present, such as the bryozoan Ross Coral *Pentapora foliacea* and there is a particularly high diversity of sea-slugs (Nudibranchia).

ACCESS AND ACCOMMODATION

Ferries to the Isle of Man run twice in any 24 hours from Heysham, near Lancaster. The crossing normally takes three and three-quarter hours. A fast-craft service operates in summer from Liverpool, and takes two and three-quarter hours. Flights to Ronaldsway Airport in the Isle of Man operate from a number of airports around Britain and Ireland. Local boat services to the Calf from Port Erin can be reached by the No.1 bus from Douglas, which also calls by the airport on the way. From the nearest bus stop to the ferry port to Port Erin village takes about 50 minutes.

The boat from Port Erin breakwater goes to the Calf (Cow Harbour) roughly twice a day and takes 15–20 minutes. Whilst weather and tide dependent, the first boat usually leaves at about 10:00 hrs. However, it is best to check in advance through Manx National Heritage or the local Tourist Information Office, although times can also be checked at the harbour jetty. The observatory's service boat departs weekly from Port St Mary on the south coast of the Isle of Man, docking at South Harbour on the Calf to deliver supplies, maintenance staff and post. This boat may take other visitors by prior special arrangement.

Wardens are present from March until November, and will be pleased to offer advice and assistance to day visitors and those wishing to stay overnight. There may be restricted access to some areas, and the wardens will provide guidance on where visitors can go safely. Please note that there are no toilet facilities for day visitors. Basic, self-catering accommodation is available at the Calf of Man Bird Observatory for eight people, and group bookings can be made on application to Manx National Heritage. Those wishing to stay must bring all their food supplies, warm and waterproof outdoor clothing and sleeping bags. It is essential to remember that the Calf is effectively remote and changing weather conditions may delay return to the mainland, so enough supplies should be brought to cover this eventuality. Visitors are reminded of the need to conserve the water supply if intending to stay overnight. Medical help on the Calf is very limited, but the wardens can call for urgent assistance if there is an emergency.

Enquiries and bookings should be directed to Manx National Heritage, The Manx Museum, Douglas, Isle of Man, IM1 3LY, telephone + 44 (0) 1624 648000. Check the web for an up-to-date e-mail address. Copies of the Calf of Man Bird Observatory annual reports can also be obtained from Manx National Heritage. Visitors' records of bird and other sightings are very useful and they are asked to pass records on to the observatory wardens or, if the wardens are temporarily unavailable, to Manx National Heritage headquarters at the Manx Museum.

Acknowledgements

Since the first edition was published there have been 42 Wardens. Their work is summarised in the Calf of Man Bird Observatory annual reports, as are the contributions of the many volunteers who have supported the observatory and increased our knowledge of birds on the island, for which Manx National Heritage is most grateful. Thanks are also due to the boatmen (and especially the current one, Juan Clague) who have kept the Calf occupants supplied, brought over visitors and maintained the island's communication with the outside world.

No account of the observatory's supporters would be complete without mention of Chris Sharpe and the Manx Bird Atlas team, who devoted much time to searching for conclusive proof of breeding Manx Shearwaters. Thanks are also due to the late Gordon Craine who assisted the wardens in the early years and continued to support the observatory. John Thorpe, a Director of Manx Bird Atlas and great friend of the Calf for many years, has been a welcome source of help and advice with this chapter, as has Ben Jones, one time Countryside Warden for Manx National Heritage.

Observatory opened:	1959
Total number of bird species recorded at the observatory:	269
Best bird year:	1997
Number of species recorded:	171
Total of birds ringed at the observatory:	220,047
Number of species:	154
Best ringing year:	1989
Number ringed:	10,891
Number of species:	88

Cape Clear

by Steve Wing

THE ISLAND

The island of Cape Clear, or Oileán Chléire, is the most southerly inhabited piece of land in Ireland, lying just less than eight kilometres from the nearest mainland harbour of Baltimore in County Cork. Some five kilometres to the south lies the Fastnet Lighthouse, of yacht-racing fame and 20 kilometres to the west, across Roaringwater Bay, lies the Mizen Head. Cape Clear, Sherkin Island (sitting between Cape and the mainland) and Roaringwater Bay now form 'The Roaringwater Bay Special Area of Conservation' under the European Habitats Directive.

Cape Clear is five kilometres long, up to two kilometres wide and covers an area of some 640 hectares with a variety of habitats ranging from barren moorland to mature gardens. The highest point on the island is Knockcaranteen, which rises

Steve Wing developed an interest in birds whilst working on Lundy in the 1970s and has been warden of Cape Clear Bird Observatory since 1998.

CAPE CLEAR ISLAND

163 metres above sea level and has a disused wind generator marking the peak. The climate is very mild with a mean temperature range of only 8°C (from 7°C in January to 15°C in July). Frosts are very rare and snow is even rarer whilst lying snow is only present a few days each century and, despite its exposed position, the average rainfall is much lower than on the nearby mainland. However, as with many islands, Cape often has its own microclimate – sunny here while all around are suffering heavy rain or vice-versa! The exposed position also means any trees that find enough shelter from the ever-present wind remain stunted, except in the most secluded gardens.

The rugged coastline is typically 'West Cork', full of deep inlets, coves and high cliffs but sadly lacking in sandy beaches. As you sit in the observatory on a stormy day and watch the sea spume flying past the window, it is easy to understand how the island has been shaped – almost cut in two between the North and South Harbours. The underlying rock of the island is Old Red Sandstone of the Devonian age (*c.* 350 million years ago) that has been folded through the ages into fantastic sea-arches and near vertical strata making it unsuitable for large breeding seabird colonies. The Irish language has given incredibly descriptive names to many of the natural features around the coast, such as Carrignashoggee (Rock of the Shags), Coosaneska (Cove of the Running Water), Coosfoilaskehaun (Cove of the Cliff of Wings) and Coosnaganoge (Cove of the Puffins). The latter, sadly, no longer breed on the island.

Cape Clear lies on a north-east–south-west axis with a narrow waist – ironically called The Waist – roughly a third of the way up the island from the south-western end. The islanders call the north-eastern end 'up east' while most birders call it 'up north'. The smaller, south-western, end is named Ballyieragh and is fortunately where many of the rarity 'hotspots' are and is fairly easily covered by a single observer in a day.

A century ago there were over 1,200 inhabitants on the island, but today the figure is closer to 120 and this large fall is reflected in the manner in which many of the fields are now overgrown with Bramble and Bracken. The bird observatory has always had a very good relationship with the islanders, and we receive a warm and open welcome all over the island. While access to gardens is usually granted, it is always appreciated if you ask, and often involves stopping for a cup of tea and a piece of cake.

The ferry lands its passengers in North Harbour, which is the hub of island life. The fishing industry was once the backbone of the island's economy, and it is said that you could walk right across the harbour, stepping from boat to boat, without getting wet feet. Nowadays, there is only a full-time trawler and a small fleet of long-liners and crabbers in a harbour more used by pleasure craft. The road leads from the harbour up past Cotter's Garden, which is probably the best known garden in Ireland and has seen many rarities. Blue-winged Warbler and Red-eyed Vireo have been seen feeding together here. The Waist, which is just 100 metres away, has recently had a small plantation of Willow and Alder planted and alongside Cotter's is where the majority of the ringing takes place.

To cover Ballyieragh from here, it is best to take the High Road. Check the gardens and hedges, until you reach Lough Errul, a 4.5 hectare freshwater lake, lined with small sandy shores on two sides and evidence of the stones used by ladies from nearby cottages when washing clothes (washing stones) on the other two sides. The small outfall from the lake runs over the cliff and on many days is blown straight back over the lake in the form of spray. Beyond the lake lies the West Bog, a reed-filled hollow at the bottom of a natural amphitheatre, which stares out at the Fastnet Lighthouse. Many local birders consider this area to be the arrival point for most rarities and to back this up Bobolink, Richard's Pipit and Sardinian Warbler have all been recorded there. The collection of small paddocks, ditches and stone walls in this area seem to be a magnet for Wrynecks and Red-backed Shrikes in both spring and autumn. Wheatears are regular migrants in this spot and also breed in the walls and rabbit burrows. The land then rises up to the coastal heathland that overlooks Blannan and is a favourite spot for the fine weather sea-watchers and whale and dolphin-watchers to gather. Across the mouth of South Harbour lies the third sea-watch point, Pontabullig – a rugged headland used by many hundred Fulmars and Herring Gulls.

Heading back towards the Waist, you pass the East Bog, where Sedge Warblers and Reed Buntings breed, and then on to the Low Road and the Central Bog. This used to hold a large area of open water but was drained in the 1960s to improve grazing. Although the loss of open water was lamented at the time, the

The renowned garden beyond Cotter's Bar has played host to many Nearctic and Asiatic vagrants (Peter Howlett).

ditch and associated boggy areas have provided another habitat equally as profitable. Just before reaching the Waist, there is a large garden set below the level of the road and therefore very easy to cover. This area was planted specifically with birds in mind but despite the many trees and shrubs, has yet to produce the goods. Below the Waist is a small beach where Ireland's first recorded Black-and-white Warbler was found in 1978, feeding amongst the seaweed. When, in 2005, a Yellow-rumped Warbler disappeared from Cotter's Garden after a very brief visit, the finder guessed, correctly, that it would turn up on the same beach. The Youth Hostel Garden has lost a little of its charm over the years but is still the favoured spot for Common Rosefinch, Red-breasted Flycatcher and Pallas's Warbler.

The island's farms, of which there are many, consist of numerous small fields surrounded by dry stone walls, covered in carpets of lichen. Looking down from the windmill, or from the now defunct lighthouse, the walls form an intricate mosaic, providing plenty of shelter for both animals and birds. The number of trees on the island is increasing rapidly, with a plethora of plantations springing up in the eastern half of Cape, and the Mass Track area is now being treated as a tree nursery – adding to the already huge amount of cover. The gardens at this end of the island have hosted many major rarities such as Yellow-rumped Warbler, Little Bunting and Eastern Olivaceous Warbler. The general lack of manpower means that this area is vastly under-watched and one can only guess at what is missed.

The small slipway at the eastern end is a good spot to look for Grey Seals, and Minke Whales have been seen less than fifty metres from shore. The low cliffs to the west are well suited to Wheatears and Rock Pipits, and there have been many sightings of Otters.

HISTORY

In the early days of 1959, J. T. R. Sharrock was advised by Ken Williamson to go to Cape Clear in the autumn and when four pupils from Leighton Park School, Reading, were given the same advice a few months later, the five met and the seeds of Cape Clear Bird Observatory were sown. So, on 19 August 1959, Lin Cornwallis, Brian Dickinson, Humphrey Dobinson and Mike Seddon arrived on Cape Clear armed with not only food and clothing, but ringing equipment and a collection of (bird) skins on loan from the British Trust for Ornithology.

A large building in South Harbour, which is now used as the Youth Hostel, was rented for the sum of five shillings – or 25 pence – a week. The house is set in a superb position, at the head of a large inlet, roughly in the centre of the island and had the benefit of an excellent garden for ringing and finding migrants. In that first season of the Cape Clear Bird Observatory, 17 species regarded as major Irish rarities were recorded in just eleven weeks. The original committee must have been gutted when, after just one season, they were informed that the building was being put up for sale. In fairness, they were offered first refusal for the now paltry sum of £300 but were unable to raise the 'vast sum' of money (you would not even raise an eyebrow if you were to offer £300,000 currently) and the building was sold to An Oige (the Irish Youth Hostel Association).

The observatory was then homeless until the building called Stroma was offered to them. Stroma could not be more different from the South Harbour site if it tried, but it was a base. Set at the top of the A1, some 100 metres above the North Harbour, Stroma was an experience that most would like to forget. It was just too far from the major birding areas to cover them more than once a day, although it did offer superb views across Roaringwater Bay.

During 1961 and 1962 the observatory began negotiations for the purchase of Harbour House in North Harbour – a mere 100 metres from the ferry berth. With the help of an anonymous donation and free legal services, the committee was successful in the purchase, taking possession of the building on 22 March 1963 and the observatory has been there ever since. As with many observatories in the early years of their existence, lack of funds made it impossible to employ a full-time warden and Cape Clear had to rely heavily on the voluntary services of visiting birders to keep the place going. For a short time there were four observatories in Ireland, all on islands; Cape Clear in the south-west, Tory Island in the north-west, Copeland Island in the north-east and Great Saltee Island in the south-east. Of these, only Cape Clear is manned full-time, whilst Copeland is manned part-time and the other two are no longer in existence.

In 1999, at the request of the current committee, Birdwatch Ireland took over the running of the observatory and, in the process, secured its future. Major renovations were undertaken in 1999 and 2000 and now the building provides very comfortable accommodation for up to seven guests on a self-catering, hostel-type basis. The observatory now has the benefit of central heating and indoor facilities – a shower in the autumn or a night-time visit to the 'bathroom' at the back of the obs, as recently as 2000, was an experience never to be forgotten!

THE BIRDS

Cape Clear Bird Observatory has become famous over the years for two reasons: the large number of rare migrant birds seen on the island and more importantly, as one of Europe's foremost sea-watching sites.

The experience of clambering out to the very tip of Blannan is, in the right conditions, both terrifying and mind-blowing. The right conditions are, of course, about as inclement as you could imagine. A south-westerly gale with heavy showers, frequent if possible, mist or fog a few hundred metres offshore and all just after dawn are the best and the most dangerous. The rocks are sharp and extremely slippery, just right for sitting on for two or three hours, and the waves are a constant niggling thought as you concentrate on the birds passing by. The plus side to all this is that the birds will pass at point-blank range, sometimes above your head or even behind you. It really is awe-inspiring to see the tens of thousands of Manx Shearwaters and auks, thousands of Gannets, Fulmars and Kittiwakes, hundreds of Sooty, Great and Cory's Shearwaters, Storm Petrels, skuas and, if you are very lucky, the odd Wilson's Petrel, Fea's/Zino's Petrel *Pterodroma feae/madeira* or Leach's Petrel, practically at touching distance.

No-one is naïve enough to believe that this happens all the time, nor every time the weather conditions happen to be perfect, but it does happen and fairly regularly. The following passage is taken directly from *The Natural History of Cape Clear Island*, a book edited by J. T. R. Sharrock (1973) that summarises the first 11 years of the observatory:

Through the night the wind and rain beat on the walls and windows of the observatory. Alarm clocks go off an hour before dawn and reluctant observers stagger out of bed and snatch a hasty breakfast, brew up flasks of tea and coffee and don oilskins whilst listening to the uninviting gale blowing outside. It is still almost dark, the mooring ropes of the fishing boats still a hazard on the harbour wall and the roads slippery under foot, as the sea-watchers leave the observatory. The hill to Cummer seems steeper than ever in the dark with the wind and rain blowing from straight ahead. Half an hour later, as East Bog is reached, the decision has to be taken. Is it a day for Pontabullaun or a day for Blannan? Blannan it is, and another 30 minutes will be spent climbing over the slippery and highly dangerous rocks, some razor-sharp, with the sea crashing below. The air is filled with rain and salt-spray, often blowing vertically upwards, the sea is foam-covered and the occasional large wave crashes through a gap in the rocks. Some sea-watchers brave the climb above it; others take the easier route below, risking a thorough soaking if the next large wave comes as they pass the gap.

On reaching the tip, each observer lies on sea-drenched rocks, trying to find that seemingly impossible combination – comfortable position and a degree of shelter. This is the moment when anticipation is keenest. Was the entire expedition a ghastly mistake or is this going to be one of those really memorable birdwatching experiences – a good sea-watch? The next few minutes will tell. Sea-watching in these conditions is never mediocre. There is either virtually no passage of birds or a large and impressive movement. A Great Skua is always a good sign – they are seldom seen unless a good passage is taking place. If one appears, it may be only a few yards away, beating laboriously into the wind.

Then Storm Petrels flicker low over the water, a flock of Manx Shearwaters cruises past and a little knot of Kittiwakes, their cries of 'Kitti-wa-ak' snatched away but audible despite the gale, so close do they pass. A flock of auks appears, each one flapping madly but hardly progressing, and as they reach the tip they meet the full force of the wind, fly backwards for a moment before giving up the struggle and settle on the water. More Great Skuas and a string of Gannets, some so close that their eye colour can be seen – they turn their heads as they pass, to stare at Homo sapiens. Next some large shearwaters, looking languid and relaxed, fly effortlessly past – far out, perhaps at 60 metres! The sea-watchers sheltering under an umbrella can identify them as Greats but the others are busy cursing at the raindrops and salt spray on their binocular lenses.

An hour later a stop is called and the tally in a sodden notebook is totted up. Two, three or four thousand birds, perhaps of ten or twenty species. But that is not the point. The figures may have some scientific value and be analysed by someone one day, producing histograms and graphs, but how can that compare with the spectacle of those oceanic birds all passing within a couple of hundred metres? Guillemots fly with their bills parted but Razorbills and Puffins do not; Kittiwakes are noisy migrants; Great Shearwaters have dark shoulder marks like autumn Black Terns. At no other time can such a variety of seabirds be seen in their natural element at such close range. It may be madness to go to such a place at such a time but every birdwatcher ought to visit Blannan tip on a day like this at least once in his lifetime.

Wow! It may have been written 40-odd years ago but add a few more species to the list and it's as true now as it was then.

The sheer size of the island makes it very difficult for a single observer to cover adequately so that the hotspots are given priority and ringing is very often not possible. It would appear from comments from other observatories that this is not just a problem on Cape Clear. The geographical location of Cape Clear does not lend itself to be in the mainstream migration routes of most common European passerines, and this is reflected in the comparatively low totals of birds ringed. This makes any fall that much more special and whereas seeing 30 Pied Flycatchers or ringing 100 Goldcrests in one day may not raise too many eyebrows in the UK, they are both major events on Cape, or indeed in Ireland.

Despite a significant drop in observer numbers, the observatory continues to be the best place in Ireland to see uncommon Irish species such as Wood Warbler,

Pied Flycatcher and Redstart. For some inexplicable reason, the month of September is always vastly undermanned on Cape when the seabird passage is still running and the autumn migration is well under way. The sea-watchers are here in August, the twitchers in October and only a few regular visitors in between. Taking just the last ten years, 23 species have been recorded during September that are considered as Irish rarities, some of them almost annually. The general lack of birders on the island makes Cape a perfect place to add rare or uncommon species to your 'finders list'. It is rare that more than ten birders are on the island on any day of the year and very often there are only one or two, so the potential for finding 'something good' is considerably higher than, for example, on the Isles of Scilly.

One of the hidden delights of Cape in springtime is sitting out at the base of the Bill, watching the Black Guillemots displaying; the male swimming just under the surface, showing off his white wing flashes and bright red feet to his mate on the surface or the pair swimming around in circles squeaking at each other, showing their velvety red mouths. Later in the year, as the ferries and pleasure craft steam in and out of North Harbour, the Black Guillemots there carry out their feeding duties, flying back and forth all day with Butterfish or Lesser Sandeels, hardly noticed by the human visitors present.

Best birds

The first president of Cape Clear Bird Observatory, Major R. F. Ruttledge MC wrote in his forward to *The Natural History of Cape Clear Island* (Sharrock 1973) 'Heaven forbid that visits should be made merely to 'rarity-hunt', but even this frivolous pastime has some value in the long run'. How birding has changed in a few short years! If the 'rarity-hunters' were to go elsewhere then Cape would be almost devoid of birders in the peak periods, but luckily, they pay no heed to the Major's comments.

In recent years the observatory has had more than its fair share of luck and the 'best' bird has to be the first Blue-winged Warbler for the Western Palearctic, found on 4 October 2000 in Cotter's Garden. The day before had been spent hiding indoors from the horrendous conditions that Hurricane Isaac brought across the Atlantic, dreaming of all the American migrants falling from the sky.

On 13 October 1968, while two birders were checking the Central Bog, a warbler-type bird was seen fly-catching from nearby brambles. Upon further checking, this turned out to be Ireland's first American Redstart and the second for Britain and Ireland.

While watching a collection of Swallows, a House Martin and Swifts, J. T. R. Sharrock was lucky to spot a smaller swift amongst the feeding party and identified the bird as Britain and Ireland's first Little Swift. Not a bad reward for relaxing in the warm evening sunshine on Cape in June 1967.

The first Irish and European record of Rose-breasted Grosbeak occurred on 7 October 1962 in a bush in North Harbour. Incredibly, also in that same small clump of bushes, at the same time, were a Subalpine Warbler and a Red-backed Shrike – at times it's almost too easy!

The Fan-tailed Warbler found near the East Bog on 23 April 1962 constituted the first for Britain and Ireland. Cape's second record of this species turned up remarkably close to the original's spring date on 18 April 1985, this time in the West Bog.

The Bulwer's Petrel seen flying past Blannan on 3 August 1975 is the only accepted record for Britain and Ireland.

On the almost treeless ground along the Low Road one of the last species you might expect to see would be a woodpecker and an American woodpecker would be even further from your mind. The Yellow-bellied Sapsucker that was flushed from there on 16 October 1988 and into Cotter's Garden was the first Irish and the second record for Britain and Ireland.

In 1986, a Grey Catbird was heard calling in the Coastguards' Garden but could not be located and was not seen. Late the following day, a single birder was passing the garden when the bird popped out of a bush, sat out for a moment and then flew out through South Harbour and off the island.

Best days

Finding a Chimney Swift, Ireland's first record, while looking for an elusive Little Bunting or going up to the lake to check an 'odd looking' Pochard – itself a third record for Cape – and realizing that we were looking at a Redhead, another first for Ireland, both rate fairly high as best days, but there are many more. Obviously, finding an American species ranks high on anyone's 'best day' list and Cape has an impressive list on that score. Rather than comment on each individual, it is easier and clearer to show them all in one small table (Table 1).

On 8 October 1990, a visiting birder looked down on the Post Office area, and noted that the warden was staring intently at a particular stretch of stone wall. He was later to find out that the warden had been watching a Swainson's Thrush sitting there. The bird dropped into the undergrowth, never to be seen again, but while trying to relocate it, a Pallas's Grasshopper Warbler was disturbed from the same field – east meets west in spectacular style.

Then there are the days that just catch you unawares, completely by surprise. 11 September 2000 dawned bright, sunny and with little wind, just right for a bit of ringing in Cotter's. After an hour or so it became apparent that 'it was not happening' in Cotter's and that a change of plan was needed. A walk around the Bogs to check for migrants was the next choice and after a relaxed cup of coffee, off I set along the low road. Reaching the corner in the road where you can check the seabird passage, if any, I raised my bins, more because I should do, rather than in hope, and was staggered at what was happening. Over a flat calm blue sea a passage of birds was indeed taking place and seemingly of just one species – Great Shearwaters! By the hundred! Close in! Even at this distance I could make out the dark belly patch and the shoulder markings. I started running and did not stop until I reached the rocks at Blannan, where caution took over and I slowed to a speedy jog.

Arriving at the tip, I prepared myself for an hour's count as the birds were still passing at an amazing rate, out with the clicker, pad ready, set watch, Go! There were times when my fingers could not click fast enough so that a mental running total was kept until the passage slowed briefly enough for me to scribble figures down on paper. Eventually the alarm went off. The end of an hour, check the figures and … just over 5,000! I was stunned. What was happening? Why now on a quiet sunny day when every book says that you need strong winds and rain? Who can I tell!

Leaving my gear at the tip, I legged it off the rock and up to the top of the cliffs into cell phone reception where I called the Irish Birdline and tried to call one of the birding islander's message machines. 'Get up and get out here!' or words to that effect were screamed at the machine and I ran back down to the rock where I met the same birding islander on his way out, having seen the event from his kitchen window. Returning to the tip, we settled down for an amazing day's sea-watching and saw another 150 birds; then someone turned the tap off. Everything just disappeared and the sea returned to exactly how you would expect it to be on a calm sunny day in September – empty. The weather patterns before or after the 11th did nothing to explain the extraordinary passage that day when Great Shearwaters outnumbered Manx Shearwaters by more than 20 to 1 and Gannets by 30 to 1!

Autumn 2005

After what was arguably the worst summer of sea-watching records since the observatory began in 1959, the autumn needed to be something special to keep Cape 'on the map'. During discussions with the Sherkin Island Marine Station on the lack of sea passage it was revealed that their sampling had shown a 50% drop

Table 1. North American rarities recorded on Cape Clear up to December 2008.

Species	Total	Species	Total
Red-eyed Vireo	13	Northern Waterthrush	2
Yellow-rumped Warbler	9	American Redstart	1
Pectoral Sandpiper	5	American Goshawk	1
Grey-cheeked Thrush	5	Taiga Merlin	1
Buff-breasted Sandpiper	4	Ring-necked Duck	1
Rose-breasted Grosbeak	4	Baltimore Oriole	1
Blackpoll Warbler	3	Blue-winged Teal	1
Bobolink	2	Black-and-white Warbler	1
Spotted Sandpiper	3	Blue-winged Warbler	1
Chimney Swift	2	Hermit Thrush	1
Lesser Yellowlegs	2	Grey Catbird	1
Swainson's Thrush	2	Indigo Bunting	1
American Golden Plover	2	Killdeer	1
Solitary Sandpiper	2	Redhead	1
White-rumped Sandpiper	2	Wilson's Phalarope	1
White-throated Sparrow	2	Yellow-bellied Sapsucker	1
Yellow-billed Cuckoo	2	Yellow Warbler	1
Ring-billed Gull	2		

in plankton levels in the area south of Cape Clear (pers. comm.). Hopefully this will prove to be a blip and not a permanent feature.

September started with the year's highest count of Sooty Shearwaters (42), a feat topped on the 21st with 54 birds but apart from a single Cory's Shearwater on the 21st, a Great Shearwater on the 5th and a Red-throated Diver on the 10th, there were few seabird records to raise any excitement. However, the arrival of the Birdwatch Ireland Seabird and Migration Course heralded the start of the best autumn's birding I have experienced anywhere.

A Melodious Warbler was found in Cotter's Garden early on the 4th, eclipsed by the discovery of a Western Bonelli's Warbler, same place, same day. This little gem stayed in the garden for 13 days giving excellent, if brief, views for its many admirers. A Wryneck found in the West Bog and a Wood Warbler in Cotter's, both on the 6th, rounded off an excellent start to the month. The arrival of a Greenish Warbler brought about the bizarre scenario of me saying things like 'Is that the Bonelli's or the Greenish?' – not often heard in an Irish garden. Two lucky birders, along with two very lucky islanders, were fortunate to see a Lesser Grey Shrike that visited the Youth Hostel area on the 18th, the first record for Cape. The second Wryneck for the month showed well at the eastern end of the island on the 19th and 20th, heralding a welcome quiet period – welcome because I was on holiday on Lundy. Upon my return a second Greenish Warbler was found, again in Cotter's Garden, this bird being the last highlight of September. What a month!

October started very quietly, with few birds and even fewer birders. However, that was all about to change, with a Barred Warbler and a Lapland Bunting found on the 3rd. The Barred Warbler stayed around the Bogs for four days giving unusually good views. To help it feel at home during its stay, the island hosted two Red-breasted Flycatchers (on the 4th and 5th) and two Firecrests on the 4th. An amazing total of 33 Firecrests on the 5th were joined that day by 11 Yellow-browed Warblers, two more Lapland Buntings, a fly-past Richard's Pipit, five Lesser Whitethroats, four Pied Flycatchers, eight Spotted Flycatchers, two Redstarts and a Yellow Wagtail – now, that's a fall.

A group of five Whinchats on the 6th and a sprinkling of Redstarts and Black Redstarts were joined by a Common Rosefinch at the eastern end, which remained until the 11th, making this the quietest period of the month.

The 11th also saw a major twitch from Cape when the seven birders present boarded a local fishing boat and set sail for Schull harbour, across Roaringwater Bay, to see Ireland's first Green Heron – pure magic! It was argued, unsuccessfully, that as we had not set foot on land, it was technically a pelagic and, therefore, monies should be paid to the observatory 'tick jar'. On the same day two Snow Buntings were located, frequenting their favoured spot at the Bill and another Lapland Bunting was found near the Old Lighthouse on the 12th. While doing a bit of late night fishing on the 13th, a Waterford birder was lucky to see both Long-eared Owl and a Barn Owl, a Cape rarity. During the daylight hours of the 13th, a large pod of cetaceans were found off the Bill which included three Minke Whales, one Fin Whale, ten unidentified large whales and three Bottlenose Dolphins.

The 15th saw the start of an incredible two weeks, when several flocks of up to 150 Siskins were moving through the island – most of them very weak and feeding furiously. While we were checking the east end, which was awash with Chaffinches, two Hawfinches popped into view and as we watched these spectacular birds, two more joined them. An incredible fall of Robins (a conservative estimate of 1,200) on the 16th was joined by more Chiffchaffs, three Ring Ouzels, more Chaffinches and a flock of 30 Snipe over West Bog. Cotter's Garden hosted an incredible ten Hawfinches on the 18th when a Great Northern Diver was seen flying over the garden. A total of nine Ring Ouzels was in the Glen, presumably avoiding the four Merlins seen over the Bill. Also on the 18th, at least 25 Hummingbird Hawkmoths and many Silver Y moths were recorded.

The 19th saw a little respite but we were back in gear on the 20th with half a dozen Common Crossbills seen along the Low Road, a Long-eared Owl on the Mass Track, only seven Hawfinches in Cotter's and a Little Auk close to the shore in South Harbour. On the 21st an Icterine Warbler arrived, staying until the 24th. The list for the 22nd included a Dotterel flying around the island, Hen Harrier, Icterine Warbler, Melodious Warbler, Barred Warbler, six Mute Swans, four Ring Ouzels, two Hawfinches, two Yellow-browed Warblers and two Lesser White-throats. It rained hard on the 23rd so we all had a rest, which lasted for four days, although we did manage to add another Little Auk and a Sabine's Gull on 24th.

Then came the long holiday weekend. A new Barred Warbler was found in Cotter's Garden on the morning of the 28th and a Radde's Warbler was seen near the lake later that afternoon – a star bird and possibly the bird of the weekend? No.

The following morning, after a wet and windy night, the first two birders out found a Grey-cheeked Thrush feeding on newly disturbed ground next to the shop. Completely out of character, the bird was feeding in the open giving stunning views of a normally skulking species and continued to do so well into November. Later that day, a smallish swift was seen flying over the lake and was subsequently identified as a Chimney Swift, coinciding with two or three Chimney Swifts seen on Sherkin Island later that day. The 30th dawned with the thrush still outside the shop and, strangely, the second rarest bird of the weekend, a Little Egret seen flying through North Harbour. While admiring the Grey-cheeked Thrush again, news broke of a Yellow-rumped Warbler next door in Cotter's, another long distance twitch. Initially, only three birders saw this bird as it whizzed about the garden before disappearing. It was relocated, by the original finder, on the beach below the Waist, where all of the birders present on the island caught up with it. While watching this little American gem, a Grey Phalarope was located just offshore giving superb views. Then came news from one of the islanders that a Chimney Swift had just flown over her head whilst working at the Abalone Farm! Just how many places in Europe can boast three American passerines or near passerines in one day?

The month came to an end with the Yellow-rumped Warbler seen briefly as it fed alongside the Grey-cheeked Thrush outside the shop – how bizarre is that?

Table 2 shows a selection of what was on the island during the months of September and October.

August 2008

One day that will be remembered forever in Cape's birding history will be 27 August 2008 when, most remarkably, three American rarities were present on the island within 200 metres of each other! The first, a first-winter female Yellow Warbler, had been seen briefly, but not identified, near the lake on the 24th. It was relocated two days later in the same place, with the same horribly brief views. But it was positively identified. The news was released and birders arrived the following day for the tick! While getting more brief views of the warbler in terrible, foggy conditions, a wader was seen flying overhead, giving the four birders a predicament. 'Do we chase what we think is a Solitary Sandpiper or do we stay and watch the Yellow Warbler?' I never thought I would be asking that question! We 'chased' the wader, splitting up into two groups to cover more ground and checking every wet spot we knew of and for an hour we were unsuccessful. Then one lucky individual noticed a movement alongside a flooded tractor track, got good binocular views and shouted at the others to get down to his location. Ten seconds and a hundred metres later, we were asking 'Where's the Solitary Sand?' and receiving an answer somewhere along the lines of 'It's a Waterthrush! It's only a Waterthrush!' An absolutely stunning surprise and it quickly got even better; the Solitary Sandpiper casually waded into the same telescope view while we were watching the Northern Waterthrush feeding! Days like this do not happen very often, but Cape Clear has now had two days with three American rarities in the four years to 2008!

Table 2. Selected bird species present on Cape Clear in September and October 2005.

Species	Bird days	Species	Bird days
Dotterel	1	Little Auk	2
Turtle Dove	7	Barn Owl	1
Long-eared Owl	5	Chimney Swift	2
Wryneck	4	Richard's Pipit	1
Black Redstart	60	Redstart	11
Whinchat	40	Grey-cheeked Thrush	3
Ring Ouzel	40	Reed Warbler	27
Icterine Warbler	3	Melodious Warbler	5
Barred Warbler	7	Lesser Whitethroat	53
Garden Warbler	10	Blackcap	243
Greenish Warbler	3	Yellow-browed Warbler	71
Radde's Warbler	1	Western Bonelli's Warbler	14
Wood Warbler	1	Firecrest	96
Spotted Flycatcher	95	Red-breasted Flycatcher	2
Pied Flycatcher	52	Lesser Grey Shrike	1
Brambling	59	Common Rosefinch	4
Hawfinch	41	Yellow-rumped Warbler	2
Lapland Bunting	7	Snow Bunting	8

Ringing

Ringing on the island is mainly carried out in Cotter's Garden or the Waist and occasionally in West Bog for Meadow Pipits or the odd night trip to the cliffs for Storm Petrels and Manx Shearwaters.

As stated before, Cape Clear is never going to get huge falls of migrants so the relatively low ringing total of 32,169 birds since 1959 is not surprising (and over 13,000 of those are Storm Petrels). The species total stands at a healthy 124 with plenty of scope to improve and as such Cape is an ideal place for a ringer to boost his or her species total. The experience of island ringing is completely different from that of any mainland site, especially in the migration periods. You really have no idea what to expect – if anything at all! On a quiet September day in 2004, I was closing the nets after a two hour session had produced absolutely nothing when, in the last net I saw a Red-eyed Vireo, lying in the middle shelf alongside a Great Tit – the only two birds of the day! This also turned out to be the earliest Irish record for this American visitor.

You also have to be aware that many of the regular non-birding visitors to Cape Clear have a casual interest and that you should listen to what they say. A few years ago we were going through the process of ageing a Wren when the trainee's niece, aged four and a half, came running up to tell us of 'an owl in the net'! After a few questions we decided that it was probably a Song Thrush, but a while later she pointed to a Little Owl in the books saying it looked like that and three hours later, we caught a Scops Owl in the same garden.

The joy of Storm Petrel ringing cannot really be expressed in words alone. It is a mixture of sight, sound, smell and a sense of atmosphere all in one. When you arrive at the cliffs after a sometimes hairy walk in the dark and wait for the nets to be opened, the peace is almost overwhelming; people whispering in the dark, the gentle lapping of the waves on the rocks below and the soft breeze rustling the grasses.

Then, the tape-lure is switched on and all peace is lost as the recording blasts into full voice (if you listen to the song, they say 'Conas atá tú? Ha, ha, ha!' which is Gaelic for 'How are you?'). Within seconds the air can be filled with hundreds of little dark shapes, fluttering like butterflies all around you, some of which get caught in the nets. The first Storm Petrel you ever see in the hand will present an image that remains with you for ever, the 'smallness' of it, the tiny matchstick legs and the fantastically delicate webbed feet. It really is amazing how such a small bird can survive the Atlantic storms. Then you have the sense of smell, the unique earthy aroma and the pungent smell of shrimp oil that they regurgitate into your hands as you extract them from the nets. The latter takes days to wear off, despite constant washing and can remain on your clothes for years. Then, when the tape is turned off, the birds disappear and peace returns as you pack up and head for home, exhausted but exhilarated.

Looking south over Ballyieragh with the Blannan in the left background (Peter Howlett).

Data

Thanks to funding from the Heritage Council of Ireland, all of the observatory's bird and mammal records have been digitised, providing instant keyboard access to the records of countless staff, visitors and local naturalists, gathered over some 50 years. The ringing data from 1970 have also been digitised and plans are in hand to enter the remaining earlier data.

OTHER FAUNA AND FLORA

Mammals

The two common mammals most frequently seen by visitors to Cape are Rabbits and Grey Seals, although a more problematical and increasingly regular candidate is the Feral Cat. It is now difficult to take a morning walk without seeing at least one Feral Cat hunting along a hedgerow or sitting patiently above the mouth of a rabbit burrow. Over the years, Rabbit numbers have fluctuated dramatically as a direct result of the arrival of myxomatosis in 1963. This terrible disease seems to keep their numbers down without ever completely exterminating them. At present, the population appears to be stable and fairly widespread, particularly around the lake and the western cliffs where the erosion they cause is becoming a slight problem.

Although the Common Rat was very common in the early years of the observatory, numbers have dropped considerably and only 22 were recorded in 2005. The Pygmy Shrew, however, is seen regularly, as are the Wood Mouse and the House Mouse. A more welcome, if infrequent, visitor is the Otter which can be seen or heard at any time of the year. They are far less common now than they were even ten years ago and any lucky observer should consider themselves very privileged.

American Mink were recorded first in 1996 and seen on the island in thankfully small numbers until 2002. The island of Sherkin is less than half a mile from Cape and a shorter distance from Baltimore so it is not inconceivable that the first American Mink arrived on Cape by swimming across the two short stretches of open sea. Alternatively, Cape is visited by many boats, both working and pleasure, during the year and these could quite easily have had a American Mink stowaway – they are quite commonly seen in fishing ports along the West Cork coast scavenging for fish on moored trawlers. They have also been recorded on uninhabited offshore islands along the west coast of Ireland, prompting fears for the local seabird breeding colonies.

The study of the bat population on Cape is negligible, but records show that at least three species are fairly regular visitors, Common Pipistrelles being the commonest.

Marine life

The waters around Cape Clear are a haven for divers, with two very rare red seaweeds *Pterosiphonia complanata* and *Grateloupia filicina* present. Grey Seals can be seen almost anywhere around the coast of Cape but are usually recorded from one of the sea-watch sites – reflecting observer effort rather than particularly favourable habitats for the seals. Seals are incredibly curious creatures and, although they have a healthy respect for humans, the animals will approach remarkably close, staring back at you with unblinking eyes before snorting loudly and disappearing beneath the waves. They have been recorded in every month but are much more common in the latter half of the year. The Common Seal is far more irregular and, normally, only single animals are recorded, in either the spring or autumn periods. On only three occasions have more than two been recorded on the same day, a good indication of its status here on the island, although they are not uncommon in Roaringwater Bay.

One of the obvious by-products of watching and counting seabird movements is that you are also going to see cetaceans and from Cape you see a lot of cetaceans. On one recent whale and dolphin watching weekend organised by the Irish Whale and Dolphin Group, seven species of cetacean were seen, a feat unlikely to be paralleled anywhere in Europe. The most commonly seen are the Harbour Porpoise and Common Dolphin, usually on a sea-watch in autumn. Probably the most common 'large' cetacean recorded from Cape is the Minke Whale which has been seen in most months of the year but in direct association with the sea-watch effort and usually between July and October. Humpback Whale, Fin Whale and Killer Whale are also relatively frequent although not of annual occurrence. In the early days of the observatory Northern Bottlenose

Whales were regularly recorded, with up to 30 records by 1967, but sightings have dwindled since then and the last two individuals were noted in 1989.

Basking Sharks can be seen occasionally and Sunfish are a common sight from the tip of Blannan or Pontabullig from May to October. One of the most sought after views, however, is the sudden appearance of a Leatherback Turtle on its slow-motion hunt for jellyfish. Since 1971 there have been 239 records, almost always of a single creature, so imagine the excitement on the 15 August 1993 when an amazing total of 30 were seen passing Blannan!

Butterflies and moths

The Lepidoptera on Cape Clear have been relatively neglected and the 140 species seen so far is far lower than would be expected. The Monarch butterfly is the obvious highlight and has been recorded on 15 occasions, all in late September or October. Clouded Yellows are almost annual and the rarer Pale Clouded Yellow has been seen in six years.

Flora

The plants and other non-avian fauna of the island in the early days of the obser-vatory were described by Sharrock (1973) and summarised in the first edition of this book. Since then, encouraged by earlier surveys of the area by Oleg Polunin (1950) and by additions made by visitors to the observatory, the flora of the entire bay was surveyed by botanists from the Sherkin Marine Station and the impressive results of this survey have been published (Akeroyd, 1996). In this recent flora, the whole bay is described as a 'botanical hot-spot' rivalling the well-known plant areas of Ireland, such as the Burren and Connemara. Cape Clear is part of this hot-spot with many rare plants but also a wealth of more common species which are becoming less common on the mainland. On the island itself, 382 flowering plants and ferns have now been recorded, which is very impressive for such a rela-tively small area with many habitat types absent. Much of the following is based on this excellent survey.

The flora of the island has changed relatively little since the 1960s. Some species, such as aquatics like the White Water-Lily, have been lost since the draining of central bog in the 1960s. However, new species have appeared, mostly as garden introductions, but some as perfectly natural arrivals such as the small Holly bushes, which have been found, always near Hawthorns. It is interesting to think of flocks of thrushes arriving in the winter and feeding on the Hawthorns, yet depositing seeds of Holly following a previous meal on the mainland. Other species found recently, such as Barren Strawberry, may simply have been overlooked before-hand.

The island's mild winter climate, where frosts are rare, means that plants normally found in more southern areas can survive here. Examples include rare 'southern' species on the northern edge of their range such as Hairy Bird's-foot-trefoil and Chaffweed, and so-called 'Lusitanian' species, which have a range restricted to south-west Ireland, south-west England, Brittany and north-west

Spain, such as Irish Spurge and Pale Butterwort. Then there are the introduced garden species that thrive in the south-west of Ireland and form a characteristic part of the flora such as Fuchsia which has been given an Irish name (deora Dé , or 'God's teardrop') and is now the symbol used by West Cork Tourism, as well as Escallonia, Monbretia and Hooker's Hebe.

Weathering of the Old Red Sandstone of the island and its covering of glacial till together with leaching of the soil due to high rainfall produces a slightly acid soil, which favours the dominant gorse and heathers of parts of the island. However, much of the island is covered in bare rock or very thin soils which favour a lot of the rarer species, e.g. Hairy Bird's-foot-trefoil, Bird's-foot and Yellow Centaury which would otherwise be out-competed by plants requiring deeper soils. Salt spray allows other more lime-loving plants, such as Kidney Vetch, to flourish along the coastlines, where other coastal species such as Sea Stork's-bill, Rock Samphire, Tree-mallow, Sea Campion and Sea Plantain can be found.

Fewer arable crops are now grown on the island and some parts have reverted to Bracken and Brambles, which nevertheless provide good habitat for birds. Some of the best bird habitats away from the cover provided by gardens are the natural tangled patches of Ivy, Honeysuckle and Bramble that all provide an abundance of food for both insects and birds. The island is less intensively farmed than many parts of the mainland and many plants associated with the old farming methods such as Corn Marigold, Corn Spurrey, Yellow Bartsia, Field Woundwort and fumitories still survive. Some plants are associated with present day farming such as Marsh Cudweed, Swine-cress, Allseed and Ivy-leaved Crowfoot which are found in water-logged areas trampled by cattle.

The island has been occupied, at least at times, perhaps since the Neolithic period (4000–2000 BC) and was very important in early Christian times as it was the birth place of Saint Ciarán. Some species that still survive are plants that were introduced for medicinal reasons; Marsh-mallow, Elecampane and Wormwood. Others are naturalised from old gardens, such as Dame's-violet, Altar Lily and Pink-sorrel. In addition to these are the rich wet areas with Royal Fern and majestic Western Marsh-orchids sometimes referred to as the 'West Cork Orchid' *Dactylorhiza majalis* ssp. *occidentalis*. The dry stone walls provide a home for ferns, Navelwort and English (known in Ireland as 'white') Stonecrop and other plants associated with grassland, scrub and heath.

Not only is the flora of the island rich and diverse but one of the things that visitors notice most are the dramatic colours from the hazy blues and yellow/greens of the bluebells and Irish Spurge in the spring to the gold and purple of the gorse and heathers in late summer, described at one time by a journalist as 'Cape in the Archbishop's cloak'. And many of the common plants have unusual colour variations, such as white heathers and Foxglove, pink Kidney Vetch and Scarlet Pimpernel appearing as scarlet, pink and blue variants.

When the birding is dull, there is much else to look for. Many rare plants have been recorded on neighbouring islands, especially on Sherkin, which have not been found on Cape, and at present there is an on-going competition to win a pint of Guinness by finding a plant species not recorded by the Sherkin survey. The only pints the warden has tried to claim so far have been for plants that have appeared where he has been spreading bird seed, which obviously do not count, but the offer is still open.

ACCESS AND ACCOMMODATION

The transport system in Ireland has improved vastly over the past 20 years and getting to Cape Clear by public transport is now very easy. The International Airport at Cork, accessible from pretty well every British airport, is only a 15-minute taxi ride away from the city bus station from where you can get an express coach direct to Skibbereen and then on to Baltimore. Alternatively, the airport has a selection of car hire companies vying for your business and Baltimore is only an hour and a half's journey from the airport, providing you do not go into the city. Cork can also be reached by train from Dublin. If a short ferry trip appeals then regular services also run from Fishguard and Pembroke Dock, both landing at Rosslare and taking around four hours. This option would allow you to visit two Irish birding hotspots, Wexford Slobs and Tacumshin, en-route.

The *Naomh Ciarán II* ferry between Baltimore and Cape takes roughly 40 minutes on a good day and up to an hour on a bad one and runs twice a day in winter and up to four times a day in the peak summer months. It is very rare that the boat cannot make at least a single trip and this happens only once or twice a year. During the summer months, a ferry also runs a regular daily service from Schull, a small village on the Mizen Peninsula.

The observatory's Harbour House has in the past held up to 25 paying guests but now numbers are restricted to a more manageable seven people. The accommodation is arranged in three bedrooms, a single, a twin and a room with four divans. There is a fully equipped kitchen, a dining room and a well-stocked library. Bed linen in the form of duvets, duvet covers, blankets, sheets and pillow cases are provided, but visitors should remember to bring towels. Booking is essential to guarantee a place and this is done through Birdwatch Ireland.

Birdwatch Ireland organizes a number of courses during the year on a variety of subjects from 'Beginner Birding' to 'Birds, Bees and Flowers' and 'Migration and Sea-watching'. The courses are aimed at all levels of age and experience and are designed to be an enjoyable experience rather than a return to school. Full details and costs of the courses are available on the Birdwatch Ireland website. There is now a seasonal warden present at the observatory from March until early November who will take the daily log, and, if necessary, delegate household chores if these are not carried out voluntarily.

There is a popular restaurant at the island shop, which is just across the harbour and carries a large selection of fresh vegetables and dry food. During the summer months there are three bars on the island providing a wide variety of food, atmosphere and frequent live music. There is a wealth of private accommodation on the island in the form of the An Oige Youth Hostel, self-catering cottages and bed and breakfasts, for all of which details can be found on the Cape Clear Co-operative, or the Comharchumann Chléire Teo, website. The current timetable for the Naomh Ciarán II can also be accessed from there as well as special Bank Holiday sailings which differ from the norm. A point worth noting is that Irish Bank Holidays are on different days from the UK and accommodation can be very difficult to obtain over these periods.

Observatory opened:	19 August 1959
Number of bird species recorded at the observatory:	308
Best bird year(s):	1968 and 1990
Number of species recorded:	172
Total of birds ringed at the observatory:	32,169
Number of species:	124
Best ringing year:	1983
Number ringed:	3,499
Number of species:	42
Best passerine ringing year:	1999
Number ringed:	940
Number of species:	45

Copeland

by Neville McKee

THE ISLAND

The three Copeland Islands lie on the south side of the entrance to Belfast Lough, Northern Ireland, which runs westwards from the North Channel for about 24 kilometres to the city. The Observatory Island, as I shall call it, is the central island of the three, just 100 metres west of Mew Island where the lighthouse now stands, and over a kilometre north of Big Copeland. The nearest part of the County Down coast is Orlock Head, almost five kilometres to the west, while that of County Antrim is 12 kilometres away to the north-west at Whitehead. Portpatrick, on the outer Galloway coast, is the nearest part of Scotland and only 24 kilometres away. The all-round views from the observatory roof are a pleasant surprise to newcomers. At just 15 kilometres to the south, is Burial Island, off the village of Ballyhalbert, which is the most easterly part of Ireland. Moving anticlockwise, after a short stretch of sea, one's eyes come in turn to the Calf of Man, the Isle of Man, the Galloway coast (to the east), the Ayrshire coast, Ailsa Craig, Arran Island in the Clyde, Kintyre (due north), the Antrim coast, Belfast and its Lough (to the west), and finally the Ards coast of north-east County Down.

Big, Main or Great Copeland, nearly two kilometres off Donaghadee, is nearly 150 hectares in area. The Big Isle, as it is often known in local parlance, is not part of the observatory's daily recording domain, but its breeding populations are monitored annually and pulli seabirds are ringed, mainly gulls and terns. The island's last inhabitants left in 1946 but it is still accessible to the public.

Neville McKee was a founder member of the observatory and has been active on the island every year since.

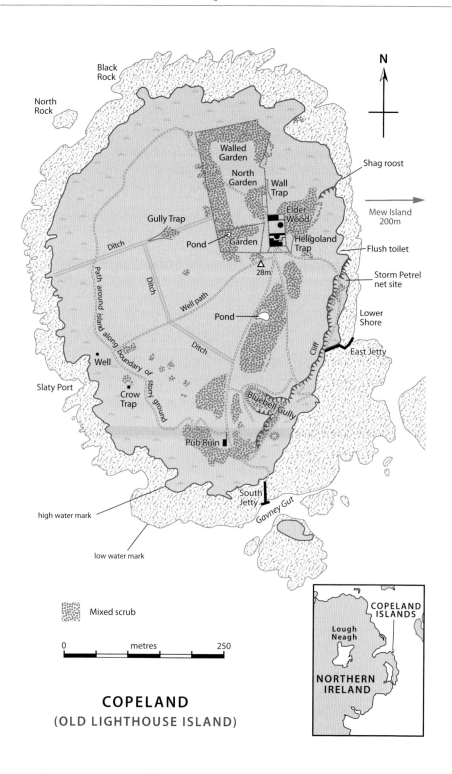

N

Black
Rock

North
Rock

Walled
Garden

North
Garden

Wall
Trap

Shag roost

Gully Trap

Elder
Wood

Mew Island
200m

Ditch

Pond

Garden

Heligoland
Trap

Flush toilet

Ditch

△
28m

Storm Petrel
net site

Well path

Pond

Lower
Shore

Path around island along boundary of storn ground

Ditch

Cliff

East Jetty

Well

Slaty Port

Crow
Trap

Bluebell Gully

Pub Ruin

South
Jetty

Gavney Gut

high water mark

low water mark

Mixed scrub

0   metres   250

COPELAND
ISLANDS

Lough
Neagh

NORTHERN
IRELAND

COPELAND
(OLD LIGHTHOUSE ISLAND)

The next island is Observatory Island which is a mere 16 hectares in area. Its buildings stand at the highest point, at about 36 metres above sea level, and well to the north-east of the centre. There is a central 'plateau' from which the ground slopes gently away to the sea on the whole of the western half of the island. A 20-metre cliff runs from the south round to the north-east, below which are a sloping scree and a narrow cleft cave running in for about 17 metres. Continuing round to the north, the cliff gives way to steeply sloping rocks which plunge straight into the sea. There are two good jetties which were built by members of the observatory over the years. These are quite sheltered and allow landing at any tide.

Though the island's soil is mainly a deep dry loam, there are some small damp flushes and winter pools. A walled garden of just over two hectares is situated to the west and north-west of the buildings. There is an indentation in the south-east cliff due to the former quarrying of the island's rough Ordovician slate, which provided the stone for the walled garden, finished in 1816. It goes inland for about 50 metres and is just 12 metres wide and eight metres deep. Nowadays it is known as Bluebell Gully though Bluebells actually turn most of the island blue in spring. The vegetation is quite mixed depending on the topography but was dominated in the 1950s by fescues and Yorkshire-fog on the open sward with a good mix of marine sward species. The area of sward declined considerably after the crash in the Rabbit population from 1956 when myxomatosis arrived. Recent management has been directed at reversing this change. Other extensive areas are dominated by bracken. There are smaller zones of Red Campion, Sea Campion, and Hogweed, and variable amounts from year to year of thistles, nettles and ragwort, the latter seeming to cover the whole island in some years.

Mew Island, the third in the group, is rocky, very low-lying and dissected at high tide into six islets by narrow muddy creeks which are, sadly, too small to support more than a few passing waders. It has always been part of the observatory's recording area as much of it can be viewed easily, particularly by telescope, from the top of Observatory Island. The total area is about 14 hectares. Much of the main islet, although formerly grassy, has been completely overrun by Bracken and Bramble, though this process is now being reversed. Mew Island's lighthouse is nearly 650 metres east of the observatory buildings. It is very tall and bright, but the flash duration is comparatively short so that the light is not a serious attraction for migrating birds.

THE ISLAND'S HISTORY

Observatory Island has had a variety of names over the years. Currently it is often referred to, in the nearby port of Donaghadee, as the Bird Isle (where the mad birdwatchers go!), but its Ordnance Survey name is still Lighthouse Island which is a bit odd, as the lighthouse was abandoned in 1884. Most shipping and boating people call it Old Lighthouse Island. In former times it was referred to as John's Island, after a miscreant monk, who refused to leave when Bangor Abbey Monastery closed its island retreat some 400 years ago. He lived out his life there as a hermit.

To conclude, some old maps use the name Lesser Copeland whilst many years ago it was also known as Cross Island. There is said to have been a large cross on top of the island but whether it had ecclesiastical or navigational significance in olden times is not known. In the days before roads, most goods were moved in small boats and the island was strategically situated for such traffic. It was also a trading island where passing boats could buy, sell and barter goods and this commercial status is thought to have survived into the early eighteenth century, by which time a coal-burning lighthouse had been established. A brief upgrade to paraffin burning was followed by closure just four years later as a new lighthouse had been constructed on Mew Island, the most easterly of the Copeland group, which was closer to the shipping lanes.

Very little is known of what happened on the island from 1884 to 1941. It is said that a woman lived alone, at least towards the end of this period, and survived on Rabbits which she shot. It is probable that the Rabbits were only introduced after 1884 as the lighthouse keepers were always keen gardeners. The walled garden, which was built between 1812 and 1816 by two stone masons (who carved their names on the wall of the cave under the east cliff), was erected on the surface of the ground without foundations and it is inconceivable that this would have been done if Rabbits were already present. In more recent times, the wall has been undermined by Rabbits, causing several gaps to open. Folklore says that during the nineteenth century, the walled garden contained a very fine canker-free orchard of both apple and pear trees. Since Rabbits appear to have been extant on the island for only just over 100 years, it can be surmised that the shearwater colony is even younger than that.

After 1920, the island became a popular place for a day out for folk from Belfast. They came on the railway to Donaghadee (now long-closed) and then out by open passenger boat, of which there were many serving all three islands. Picnics were popular, as was egg-collecting in season. Gulls and terns were probably the main targets. Unfortunately a combination of 'normal' vandalism (even in the 1930s) and some organized commandeering of building materials, particularly slates and fireplaces, left the buildings in ruins, though with substantial walls, which were eventually the starting point for the current observatory buildings.

The first recorded ornithological visit, in 1939, was made by local leading ornithologist C. Douglas Deane, known to all as Jimmy. In the manner of the time, he dug out a breeding burrow, complete with egg (now in the Ulster Museum), to prove that Manx Shearwater bred on the island. The first fully documented bird survey was carried out on a short visit by a group of four servicemen in June 1941 (Williamson *et al.* 1941). They found very large populations of four species of terns but surprisingly few gulls. Perhaps their eggs had been collected preferentially. Interestingly, one of these men was Ken Williamson who largely inspired the establishment of the British Bird Observatories' network. Subsequently he visited Copeland (which should be taken to mean the observatory from here on) on at least two occasions in his role as Migration Officer of the British Trust for Ornithology (BTO). Ken's quiet expertise was an inspiration for me as a teenager, training to ring birds and to operate a migration study station.

THE OBSERVATORY

Another leading local ornithologist of the time, Arnold Benington, brought out parties of enthusiasts on at least three occasions after the war between 1947 and 1953 to evaluate the island as a site for migration watching and to ring a few Manx Shearwaters. He concluded that it might be suitable and worth a try. His last group, in 1953, was a class of Workers Educational Association adult students. They decided to set up the observatory as an organization, each taking on a role in its administration and Arnold was accorded the job of Director. In this role, he had a strong and benign influence as leader and teacher, as well as trainer of many new ringers. He was a biology teacher and a devout Quaker who had a strong conviction about Sunday observance.

The next lines are taken directly from the first Copeland Annual Report (1954):

> *During the winter of 1953–54 much preliminary work was done. A Committee was appointed and a Charter drawn up. Then detailed plans were made, portable traps constructed and equipment collected.*
>
> *At last the great day arrived, when we were to go and take over the island. The 27th February, 1954 dawned cold and clear and by 10.30 am quite a number of members had collected on the pier at Donaghadee. Half an hour later our loaded lorry arrived and we proceeded to unpack it and stow all kinds of gear into Andy White's motorboat.*
>
> *In a short time Andy cast off and we were away. Across a cold green sea the Mull of Galloway gleamed white under a mantle of snow, and to some it seemed too early in the season for this kind of undertaking. However the weather was kind to us and in about half an hour the first working party landed safely on the island. We unloaded the boat, and before work began we collected at the South landing and committed ourselves into the care and keeping of our Heavenly Father who giveth us richly all things to enjoy.*

Thus began Copeland Bird Observatory, with a singular lack of formality. The owner of Observatory Island, Captain Ker of Portavo, had agreed to let the island for a 'peppercorn' rent of one shilling. In 1967, he leased the island to the National Trust for 999 years on the understanding that the observatory could continue as tenants as long as the organization existed. The observatory's infrastructure was quickly built up, three Heligoland traps were constructed, accommodation was secured within the derelict lighthouse buildings and the BTO sanctioned accreditation in 1956.

At first, visits were made from Friday at 18:00 hrs until Saturday afternoon. Sundays were not manned. This matched the general custom of Sunday observance in Northern Ireland at the time. However, many of the new committee felt that Sundays should be manned, as it was not 'work'. Arnold agreed to Sunday operation in 1956 on condition that no 'work' was done other than observing and ringing but he soon became unhappy with the Sunday operation and withdrew.

Jack Gray was appointed the new director but he soon abolished the post, resulting in the very democratic administration that has continued until the present time. As time went by, Arnold became reconciled to the changed ways and he returned to the observatory in the mid-1970s for a very enjoyable final weekend reunion with all the old guard. From my point of view, in the 1950s, and scarcely more than a child, Arnold was a most likeable person and inspired me to become a biologist, a teacher and a bird ringer. He left me with a love of Copeland as my single-site birding home, luckily shared by my wife and children. My wife Pat has been of great importance in the running of the observatory over the past 45 years in very many ways – as committee member, keeping me organized, and producing our children, both of whom have played major roles too.

Jack Gray and Joe Mitchell were the people who carried the ornithology forward in the early days. Jack was a bird-catcher and ringer par excellence and the ringing ancestor of nearly all the present-day Copeland ringers, including the present-day younger ones. Joe, as ringing secretary, was a meticulous documenter who kept discipline among the ringers by gently informing them of their mistakes and educating them in how to improve every aspect of their ringing. Chris Acheson, who followed him in the job, has also continued in the same inspirational and kindly mode. In 52 years, only two have held the post, which demonstrates the long-term continuity that is typical of the modus operandi of Copeland.

The reconstruction of the fabric of the buildings played a major part in the early success and continuing prospects of the observatory. Of the founding fathers, as we affectionately refer to them, John Wilson and Jack Loftus were very important as skilled DIY people who literally could turn their hand to anything. As money was only available for basics, such as the boat, John and Jack built window frames, flooring, tables and eventually, an entire new laboratory, from driftwood and retrieved bricks and tiles from the ruins of the old lighthouse complex. Driftwood was particularly abundant in the 1950s and 1960s because the Belfast shipyard was still busy and each launch brought piles of good timber to our western shores. But the work was not without its dramatic moments, on one occasion Jack Gray, re-tarring the roof, put his foot on a wet bit and slid down the tarry roof on his bottom and over the edge, to land on his feet about four metres below. He walked away unscathed, to no surprise of the onlookers as this was typical of the good fortune which accompanied his active birding life.

During the Second World War, a giant radar screen had been built just north of the buildings. It was about 20 metres high and made of heavy girders and thick weld mesh. It roared in any strong wind. By 1959, it occurred to the DIY brigade that it might not stand for ever and would be best cut down. This job was undertaken by Jack Loftus, John Wilson and Dan Hayman, whose wife Margaret was our first and best botanist. It took many hours to saw through the eight legs; but the plan to fell it south-eastwards failed and the entire structure fell the other way, completely destroying the northernmost Heligoland trap! During 1962, work began on roofing the west side of the southern single-storey derelict buildings. This meant that we had a big kitchen, a cosy common room and two dorms. By the late 1980s leaks became so serious that an appeal was launched by our then secretary Peter Munro for £3,000 which the members raised in two weeks. A new modern steel cladding roof was then attached over the old one and there have been no drips on heads or sleeping bags since!

It is interesting that, though the gender balance of early visitors was strongly tilted in favour of males, there were several female Duty Officers. Edith Addy was a local art teacher whose gentle but skilful handling of birds trapped at the nets was a fine example for all. Marion Macmillan was Northern Ireland's first police-woman, rising to the rank of Woman District Inspector (Superintendent), and combined formidable efficiency with great kindness in her role as Duty Officer. By 1975, the observatory committee still consisted of a majority of the founders. A very important meeting was one in which Jack Gray suggested that we should think of upgrading the facilities by conforming to modern building standards and that we should find the money to buy new materials instead of making do with found or used material. Work was started on a programme of improvements involving many people and particular mention must be made of George Thomson, Sandy McWilliams, Larry Donnelly, Jim Megarry, Stephen Allen and Terry Paton.

Some members of the local Lisburn Members' Group of the Royal Society for the Protection of Birds (RSPB) volunteered to get the work under way. One was an architect and the other three were skilled builders. Two weekends saw the structural work nearly finished and the rest was subsequently completed by members. It was estimated that 20 tons of building material were shipped out and wheel-barrowed nearly a kilometre up the island for this project, entirely by volunteer members.

Further work resulted in a new ladies dorm and a grand common room or lounge with a view over Mew towards Scotland. Many consequential improvements followed: a small dorm with a double bed, another dorm with a double bed and three bunks suitable for families, new washrooms (cold water only) for men and women, more water storage tanks, a cold water tap in the kitchen and significantly, a new flush toilet, built in a small tin hut below the cliff, about three minutes' walk from the buildings. This peculiar place was chosen because of a well in a small open cave just uphill. Oddly enough, the water was unusable for drinking because it smelled of hydrogen sulphide. This can come as a surprise during flushing. However, the most remarkable feature of this WC is the half door. Not only is this good for ventilation, but it also allows the occupant to use binoculars or even a telescope, whilst leaning on the top of the door, with a fine view eastwards over and beyond Mew Island towards Scotland.

It is worth putting on record that chemical toilets were the only ones available for visitors for the first 25 years. These had to be emptied in pits dug in the garden. Nowadays, the contents of the flush toilet pass harmlessly into the sea at a deep point in the Mew Sound and local fishermen say that the lobsters below the outfall are among the biggest in the area. Tin cans, bottles and glass have also been dumped in the sea in the same place. Local divers have assured us that they break down quickly and disintegrate. Recently, however, most of this type of rubbish has been taken home by visitors for recycling. Nevertheless, the biggest problem is the debris from elsewhere that washes up on the beach. Each spring lately, a collection has produced up to 1,200 plastic bottles for destruction.

Additional improvements in recent years include the building of a glass-fronted porch over the front entrance to reduce draughts and warm the building by collecting heat from the sun. Another flush toilet close to the back of the buildings has very recently been up-graded to a low-volume flush type. Lighting was originally by hurricane lamps which were superseded by butane gas mantles. Solar electric (photovoltaic) panels were installed in 2000, to charge the big storage batteries which power a 24-volt low energy lighting system throughout the buildings. A solar water heating system was installed in 2006 and the gas bill for boiling dish-washing water has been considerably reduced. The solar panels for both these systems have recently been doubled in capacity. Gas cookers replaced the original Primus stoves long ago. The kitchen sink now boasts a hot water tap! Altogether, these improvements have made the island seem unimaginably luxurious considering that none of the usual utilities are available.

Some of the trees planted over 30 years ago are now being felled or coppiced on rotation and the original plan to make the island self-sufficient for heating fuel is at last coming to fruition. The accommodation is to be improved so that there should soon be five dorms or bedrooms, so that visitors can have more privacy, although, the number of beds is not to be increased. All the windows and doors have been replaced with double-glazed draught-free units. A new lab has been constructed and one of the three Heligoland traps has been replaced with a timber frame.

In 2008 Kerry Leonard, one of our members, commendably completed the digitisation of the observatories' entire bird sight-records, the details of which date back to 1956. Much detailed analysis will now be possible. It will undoubtedly be the single most important inventory of bird records, especially of migrants, in Northern Ireland and this project is the very welcome culmination of 55 years of enthusiastic voluntary recording on the island.

Who runs the observatory and its funding?

The observatory is run on communal lines which is not a bad thing in that it greatly improves efficiency and consistency. It has resulted in an active membership that is made up of many very long-term members. I was a founder member in 1954 and Chris Acheson is only the second ringing secretary, and has been in post for 37 years. Similarly, Peter Munro has been a member for nearly 50 years and is the second long-term general secretary in the post, following Chris Bailey, who had a steadying elder-statesman-like influence over the observatory's affairs for many of the early years. John Lyons, treasurer for 27 years, retired recently and was replaced by Fiona McCrory, both my daughter and grand-daughter of the first treasurer, Hugh McKee. Of the committee members of the last six years, all but one have been members for over 20 years. The longest family lineage at the present time consists of Iain, Philip and Erin Galbraith who are the great-grand children of John Wilson, a founder and DIY expert.

John Stewart was our editor for many years and was also editor of the Northern Ireland Bird Report. He modernized the presentation of the report, later improved and brightened with colour photographs by Shane Wolsey. A perpetual problem, however, is that while so much useful data have been collected, those who could write up scientific papers are very busy people. Regrettably from Copeland's point of view, John Stewart has recently left for New Zealand to pursue his enthusiasm with the Procellariiformes.

A Community Award grant, from BT, to buy a computer, made a big change to how the observatory communicates with members and with other organisations. E-mail news for members and friends has transformed communication but has also meant that one member has had to spend a lot of time preparing and e-mailing the news. This has raised awareness of survey and ringing activities and therefore general enthusiasm and participation. The introduction of e-mail has also allowed the committee to transfer information, discuss matters and make decisions, if necessary between formal meetings, thus saving travelling.

Personal Millennium Awards were obtained by three members for various projects. Pat McKee was able to produce a set of 12 fine wall charts, which are now hanging on the walls of the common room and have been a great educational asset. They depict all the seasons, wildlife and island activities and have been much appreciated and admired. She also produced advertising literature including a brochure, a poster and various types of stationery. Jim Megarry obtained a grant for the installation of solar panels to power the 24-volt electric lighting system and spent a week learning about the technology at Machynlleth. I used my grant to visit other island reserves to study their methods of land and visitor management. An 'Awards for All' grant helped us to make great improvements to the south jetty and install interpretive display panels.

Since the millennium, Copeland has obtained further grants for a wide range of improvements. The biggest problem with these is finding the manpower to do the work and meet time deadlines set for completion. Even the logistics of obtaining and transporting materials to the island are not easy. The observatory has been fortunate to obtain substantial grant aid from the Northern Ireland Environment and Heritage Service which has helped to fund important visits early and late in the migration seasons, other surveys, and all the environmental projects already mentioned.

A small team of experts in the methodology of grant applications, consisting of Ian Humphreys, Fiona McCrory, John Stewart and Shane Wolsey, has done invaluable work and put the observatory on a pathway of modernisation as a result. Fund-raising, two anniversary dinners and individually sponsored efforts by our fund-raising champion Shane Wolsey have added thousands of pounds to the funds.

The membership

There is a core of active people who are occasional or regular committee members. To become one of this core requires a mixture of abilities and enthusiasms over a long period of apprenticeship, especially if the person is to become a ringer too. Copeland has been very lucky over the years in that there has been very little controversy or dissent. Indeed, there is a tradition of not having votes on the committee. Decisions are made by discussion, persuasion and eventual unanimous agreement. The committee and office bearers are elected at the AGM and there is a planned rotation to ensure a turnover in the committee.

When new prospective lead members appear, they are given every encouragement. If they can cope with boats, the isolation, the island life and routine, the others already there, and the recording and ringing systems and find that it is to their liking, nothing will stop them from becoming 'proper' islanders. It is just as much about island living as it is about wildlife and ornithology and the committee has recently drawn up a programme for newcomers to clarify the necessary knowledge and skills required to be a Duty Officer (DO). Two categories of DO have been established. The full DO is also ringer-in-charge, but a restricted DO status has been established so that a non-ringer can keep the sightings records and can also take charge of the island and operate the facilities when other projects are undertaken, such as maintenance work and habitat management. Whilst ringing training happens mostly on the island, the observatory has recently promoted a programme of ringing courses on the mainland.

Apart from the need to recruit new DOs, there are other types of valued member. Some go to the island simply because they like it. They often give much needed backup to the DOs and generally do much of the work required to maintain or improve the facilities. Some people have great DIY skills and find the island ideal for their hobby with plenty of opportunities. Others are purely observers and make an important contribution to the recording and the census work. Yet others seem to do nothing tangible on the island but if they enjoy going, they are welcome simply as visitors contributing to the costs and the daily chores. Of the members who visit the island, everyone can find their own level of participation, and all are valued. There are in fact many appreciated long-term members who almost never come out to the island, but who support us with their annual subscription. Their existence has raised our total membership to around 300 and their support and subscriptions have been very important in recent times in helping us to obtain grant aid from various sources, where numbers can be important and matching a percentage of the grant is usually a requirement. Interestingly, the membership is drawn from a wide range of people from all walks of life, a significant number of whom live in the Republic of Ireland, Scotland and England.

The observatory has a Forward Plan covering all aspects of organisation and future projects, including plans to increase the number of breeding bird species. Shane Wolsey led the planning project, using his professional business management skills, and has been very successful in keeping the work focused. Plans for closer cooperation with Queen's University, Belfast are currently progressing.

THE BIRDS

Compared with other observatories around the periphery of Britain and Ireland, it has to be conceded that Copeland is in a relative backwater for rarities. The east coast of Northern Ireland is in a migration shadow, protected on all sides by big land masses. Thus migrants from the east and North America reach Copeland infrequently. Even by Northern Ireland's standards, the absolute numbers of migrants pausing at or passing the island is a bit limited, though there have been some big arrivals and fall events. Nevertheless, the regulars all feel well rewarded with the good days that they have had.

As a rough guide, only about one day in four has significant migration during the main seasons. It is therefore occasionally quite possible to go for a weekend without seeing any migrants. As against that, the good days can be overwhelming for a single ringer. Unfortunately, these days are unpredictable so there are many tales of really big days when far more birds could have been ringed than were. The best example was a big Chaffinch day on 18 October 1995 when 2,000 descended on the island. The sole ringer furled the nets as he extracted and planned to re-open when he'd ringed the first catch of 44, only to find that they all had gone. A lovely male Merlin in the lab also delayed the proceedings. Outdoors, two Red Kites passed by. Even worse was on 13 May 1956, the first ever big day in the history of the observatory when an estimated 1,500 Whitethroats swarmed over the island. So unexpected was this that there were only about 60 size 1 rings in store, so after ringing 57, the rest of the day was spent driving Whitethroats out from the ramp end of the main Heligoland trap and using the last few rings on some specials. This story is still distressing to relate, especially because nothing like it has happened since.

An average sort of day would see 30 migrants ringed but there are a few days in most years when 100 or more are ringed. Species of which more than 100 individuals have been ringed in one day include: Meadow Pipit, Swallow, House Martin, Willow Warbler, Goldcrest and Lesser Redpoll. As well as these, several migrants occur in sufficiently good numbers for an index of abundance over time to be developed, Chiffchaff being the most important. Many other species occur in rather lower numbers but there is a surprising consistency in their occurrence. In our analysis of trends over the years, it has been convenient to analyse these in five-year blocks. The resulting histograms smooth out annual fluctuations and mostly reflect the trends produced by the various BTO surveys.

There seem to be two types of falls of migrants on the island. When the wind is a typical south-west or westerly, light to fresh, there is usually a steady movement of the regular species on what looks like normal coastal migration, in which the passing birds feed briefly before they move on. The other type is the fall due to adverse conditions, usually poor visibility. This most often happens in spring when the wind is in the southerly sector. Autumn falls are less pronounced but can happen in nearly any wind direction. In both seasons, north to north-west winds, clear skies and good visibility mean few to no arrivals. Whilst it can be presumed that the summer migrants are travelling to and from the western side of Scotland and the northern third of Ireland, winter visitors could be coming from any areas of northern Britain or Europe.

Traps and trapping techniques

In 1954, the Heligoland trap and some cage traps of the crow or pipit type were the only ones available for catching migrants. The first mist-net was brought to Northern Ireland in 1956 after a meeting of the Bird Observatories Sub-committee at the Edward Grey Institute in Oxford. The net was a six-metre Japanese nylon type and the first bird caught was a Goldcrest. I eventually extracted it (although only 11 years old at the time) after the others had given up! Subsequently, the use of nets has become the primary method of catching migrants.

Surprising numbers of migrant species were caught in the first 15 years of the observatory, with some really large falls of Willow Warblers and Whitethroats occurring. However, bird totals were recorded very cautiously by the early observers and were undoubtedly underestimated. Even so, it soon became clear that the passerine numbers were very low compared with most other observatories. When they pass or pause on Copeland, migrants are near the end of their journey. Unless they are in real trouble, they can see the mainland beyond and continue on their way. That this is true is shown by the big arrivals in poor visibility. Another indication is the big drop in the numbers of Blackbirds and Song Thrushes arriving in October. Whereas 1,235 Blackbirds were ringed in the ten years up to 1965, only 2,058 have been ringed in the 40 years since (Table 1), coinciding with the installation of ever-brighter street lights in the conurbations of Belfast and Bangor on the mainland in full view of the island. Even the coast road along the nearby mainland of north-east County Down had bright street lights installed. It can also be surmised that other species are being similarly encouraged towards the mainland.

Table 1. Numbers of Blackbirds at Copeland at ten-year intervals from 1956 to 2005.

Decade	1956–1965	1966–1975	1976–1985	1986–1995	1996–2005
Blackbirds ringed	1,235	996	499	343	220

Birds of prey travelling between Ireland and Scotland tend to cross the island in preference to open sea. Twelve species have been recorded, of which Kestrel and Merlin numbers have remained steady. Buzzard and Peregrine have increased around ten-fold, but Hen Harrier has shown the greatest increase, commensurate with becoming a widespread breeder in Northern Ireland (Table 2). Nearly all the sightings are outside the breeding season.

Table 2. Numbers of Hen Harriers at Copeland at ten-year intervals from 1956 to 2005.

Decade	1956–1965	1966–1975	1976–1985	1986–1995	1996–2005
Numbers	0	2	7	28	113

Copeland sightings in the Northern Ireland context

Nowhere else in Northern Ireland has such a set of ornithological records been kept for such a long period of time. Despite arguably being in a migration backwater, there have been many first records for Northern Ireland, mainly of passerines, and those marked with an asterisk below have been Northern Ireland's only records.

At least 50% of Northern Ireland's records of the following species in the last 50 years have been recorded on Copeland: Wryneck, Tree Pipit, Red-throated Pipit*, Yellow Wagtail, Nightingale*, Bluethroat, Redstart, White's Thrush*, Icterine Warbler*, Melodious Warbler*, Subalpine Warbler*, Barred Warbler*, Lesser Whitethroat (on passage), Yellow-browed Warbler, Red-breasted Flycatcher*, Pied Flycatcher (on passage), Red-backed Shrike (just 33%), Woodchat Shrike*, Common Rosefinch*, Scarlet Tanager*, and Fox Sparrow*. Copeland has also produced a significant percentage (but less than 50%) of Northern Ireland's sightings of Sooty and Balearic Shearwaters, Red Kite, Marsh Harrier, Rough-legged Buzzard and Red-footed Falcon. Most of the passerine records refer to birds that were ringed. Other species which are rarely ringed in Northern Ireland have been caught on Copeland, notably singles of Quail and Corncrake.

Very small numbers of Whinchat, Ring Ouzel, Garden Warbler and Wood Warbler breed in Northern Ireland, but the bulk of the passage records of these species, presumably travelling to and from western Scotland, are from Copeland. There are marked fluctuations in the occurrence of some of Copeland's regular migrants. Other species such as Willow Warbler, Chiffchaff and Swallow are relatively regular. Even though Blackcap occurs in only small numbers, it is consistently recorded in the range of five to twelve annually and it has increased as breeding numbers in Northern Ireland have increased. Goldcrest numbers fluctuate hugely from year to year. In some autumns, Meadow Pipits are scarce, which could be because they are moving down the west side of Ireland in those years. Generally, the nomadic finches, especially Lesser Redpoll, have all increased in recent years. Of the few tits that show up, mainly in October, the Coal Tit is by far the most regular and increasing. Many of the Coal Tits handled are considered to be of the British *Periparus ater britannicus*, not the Irish race *P. a. hibernicus*, but the north-eastern Irish birds are of somewhat intermediate plumage characteristics and it is therefore hard to be certain of the origin of all Copeland Coal Tits.

Special experiences on the island

A lengthy association with one particular place inevitably generates a kaleidoscope of affectionate memories, both the general and the specific, and a few of these follow in a loosely structured format.

It seems that the weather on Friday evenings is often calm, perhaps reflecting the end of the working week. The sea and the island are peaceful and nothing beats sitting by the front door and looking back at 'civilization', but not hearing it. The silence is broken only by the lapping of the sea, the murmuring of the gulls, the toots of the Oystercatchers, an occasional scream from a Water Rail and flapping sounds from the shearwater rafts. It is also hard to beat sitting above the cliff in the early morning, watching and listening to dozens of Eiders oo-ee-oo-ing and up to 100 Black Guillemots squeaking in the channel just 15 metres below and sunning themselves on the jetty.

On a calm summer evening, many islanders like to relax by watching the gathering rafts of shearwaters, swept along by the incoming tide and occasionally rising with a whirring sound to fly back and regain their original positions. But the best island sound is the shearwater colony on a foggy night as they swirl around the island and over the buildings. It is an essential ornithological experience. The daytime flocks of Manx Shearwaters, terns and Gannets diving and gulls dipping and diving on offshore shoals of fry also has an excitement of its own as does a big Swallow and House Martin day when they hunt low over the island, sometimes landing on the roof to sunbathe, preen and chatter.

Some remarkable cooking and fine dining goes on, especially on communal work weekends. There is no better way to spend a long October evening than sitting in the Common Room in front of a roaring fire. After dark comes dinner and the bird list, then everyone puts their feet up and enjoys the fireside chat known on Copeland as 'good crack'. Traditionally, little alcohol is consumed on the island because there is ringing to be done outdoors after dark on most nights – shearwaters, Storm Petrels and sometimes a few waders in autumn. The sight of the shearwaters coming in over the cliff at barely 30cm from the ground is easily obtained by sitting comfortably on the cliff steps looking westwards against the glow of the bright city lights. After going to bed, one is lulled to sleep by the cacophony of calling birds.

On some spring mornings, a fall of Willow Warblers can actually be seen arriving at the south-east end and then within minutes they advance north-west across the island like a tumbling, rolling wave sweeping from bush to bush. On a crisp October morning one can really feel the excitement of the birds themselves as they arrive on the island. The diurnal migration of hundreds of larks, up to a thousand pipits and hundreds of finches of many species can be a really amazing spectacle. However, the favourite for some is the swishing of flocks of thousands of Starlings as they cross the island, heading to Ireland for the winter.

Razorbills pass in big numbers every October but on one particular day the estimate for birds heading into the Irish Sea was 48,000; there are, however, too many other sea-watching events to detail, although the days when we see Sabine's Gulls, Leach's Petrels, Mediterranean Shearwaters, Sooty Shearwaters and lots of skuas are always with us.

Particular rarities stick in the mind such as the Quail which was processed with 40 day-trippers watching and photographing the bird. Likewise the day in May 1965 when four Turtle Doves arrived and two were ringed, which is unimaginable now and none has been seen since 1985. My wife and I spent the second half of our honeymoon on the island and the highlight of our stay was the catching of a lovely dreamy juvenile Long-eared Owl. Chris Acheson, our Ringing Secretary, will never forget the first drive of the main Heligoland Trap one October weekend when two Long-eared Owls ended up in the catching box. We celebrated our first wedding anniversary by catching a Woodchat Shrike!

Many ringers have a special place in their memory for a bird that they have caught without the use of catching aids. Jack Gray once plucked a Swallow safely out of the air as it passed him and there were many witnesses for Shane Wolsey's special and equally spectacular catch. A party of people were walking down the north garden when a Long-eared Owl was spotted sitting on the west wall with an elder bush just behind it. Shane back-tracked and went round behind the bird, while the rest of us froze. Kerry Leonard was nearest to the owl and he stared at it, and it stared at him. After several minutes, Shane's hands erupted out of the bush and over the wall to neatly grasp the bird, to a big cheer and round of applause! It would have made a great bit of movie footage, but camcorders had not reached Copeland at that time.

Our only Hoopoe, Wryneck and Great Spotted Woodpecker were also significant as none of these has been ringed elsewhere in Northern Ireland. Another great day was the catching of an Ashy-headed Wagtail *Motacilla flava cinereocapilla*, the race breeding in Italy and Istria, which had arrived with a Blue-headed Wagtail *M. f. flava*. Next day an Ashy-headed Wagtail, bearing a fresh new ring, was recorded at the RSPB Belfast Lough Reserve about 24 kilometres to the west.

The catching of the White's Thrush was tinged with just a little disappointment because a Short-eared Owl just missed the same net on the same drive. The next few days were chaotic as several hundred birders came to the island to 'tick' it. After 21 Ring Ouzels ringed in the first 30 years, David Galbraith's famous luck brought him the only one since, in April 2006. My own favourite day was 13 October 1974, when a misty, nearly calm, morning brought down 100 Fieldfares, dozens of Redwings and Goldcrests, and my only Yellow-browed Warbler. The Grasshopper Warbler occurs in very small numbers each spring and only 33 had been ringed from 1954 to 1969. However, 43 were ringed in 1970, 36 of them on 2 May, out of an estimated 40 on the island. Reed Warbler has become a regular if still scarce breeder in Northern Ireland in recent years. Only five have ever been

The White's Thrush on Copeland in April 1993 was the first Irish record in modern times (Pat McKee).

caught on Copeland but one of these was a control – ringed just 16 days previously in Jutland, Denmark in September 1998.

Our view of the best ringing days would be unimpressive for eastern or southern observatories, as many of England's common species are very rare or absent in Northern Ireland. One of Kerry Leonard's weekends in 1989 was memorable for floods of Willow Warblers, accompanied by five other warbler species, two Redstarts, a Yellow Wagtail and a Tree Pipit. This is the stuff of our dreams. There have been many days when over 100 Willow Warblers have been ringed, but they are not often accompanied by 'specials'.

Breeding birds

The first record of gull numbers is in the account of 1941 by Williamson, Jones, Rankin & Rankin. At that time 300 Herring Gulls were breeding on Observatory Island. By 1960, this number had risen to 1,000 and the first birds had started breeding on nearby Mew Island. The populations peaked in 1982, by which time 6,500 pairs were breeding on the two islands. However, nearly 100 adults died in the first year of botulism in 1983 and the population then crashed to around 120 pairs on the two islands over the next ten years. Lesser Black-backed Gulls were scarcely affected by botulism and their numbers rose from 200 pairs to nearly 400 by 1990, but have declined since to just over 200 pairs again. Botulism has clearly become a problem for them, too, in recent years.

The rise in gull numbers was accompanied by a decline in many other breeding species, such as Red-breasted Merganser, Mallard, Shelduck, Lapwing and Ringed Plover. Eider could have been expected to increase from the three pairs of the 1950s but did not really expand their population significantly until the late 1970s. A project to ring nesting females was started in 2004 and approximately 50 birds are handled each year. In 2008 Mew Island was estimated to have over 100 pairs – having never been counted before the surveyors expected 20 nests and were somewhat surprised!

Now that gull numbers are low again, most of the lost species have returned. Over the period of the observatory's custodianship of the island, there have been quite remarkable increases in the breeding strength of many important species. Thirty pairs of Oystercatchers now breed on Observatory Island, and over 150 pairs breed over the three islands. Manx Shearwater numbers are always difficult to estimate but were thought to be around 200 pairs in the mid-1950s and are now estimated, by the play-back technique, to be around 3,500 pairs. Fulmars first flew along the cliff looking interested in landing in 1956, but did not actually land until 1982. The first egg was laid in 1983. Soon three young were being reared annually and recently up to eight are produced. Similarly on Big Copeland, the simultaneous colonisation has progressed to an annual productivity of up to 19 young.

On Big Copeland, the gull collapse was accelerated by one of the cottage owners, the late Ronnie Ramm, who was originally from Norfolk. He was an enthusiastic shooter and decided to remove all the large gulls from the south-western half of the Big Island. By 1987, not only had he succeeded, but four pairs of Arctic Terns bred for the first time in 25 years. Ronnie couldn't grasp the idea of preserving gulls while terns were in trouble everywhere else. He lived to see the numbers reaching about 300 and it's a pity he didn't survive to see the 1,000 pairs there now.

Black Guillemots are a very special breeding species on the island. I was just starting on my ringing career as a very skinny teenager, when the first pair bred in 1959, so my long arm was selected to reach down into the nest under a huge slab to lift out the chick. Ken Williamson happened to be visiting the island, accompanied by his daughter Herver. She was further into her ringing career than me then and she was accorded the honour of ringing the first chick. I have to admit to a feeling of disappointment at the time, but I have fully recovered since and we now ring around 30 annually! It was also on this weekend that the first Storm Petrel was trapped, but that story comes later.

A pair of Mediterranean Gulls settled on Big Copeland in 2002 and successfully nested in Northern Ireland for the first time. The ringing of the single chick was naturally a big event, but not nearly as exciting as the news in 2006, that it was alive and well in Belgium. As has often been said – if you want a good recovery, ring just one! Well, we ringed another one in 2006 and have our fingers crossed!

The Manx Shearwater study

The first nineteen Manx Shearwaters were ringed in 1952. Increasing numbers have been ringed annually since and this reflects the steady increase in the size of the colony over the period of our stewardship. With considerable foresight, Joe Mitchell developed a large ledger book system for recording all the ringing and re-trapping details. Currently we are on the fifth volume and a considerable number of the birds recorded in the first volume are still alive. The most famous one, which hit the news headlines, was the adult ringed in July 1953 and re-trapped by George Thomson in June 2003, at which time it had survived for 49 years, 11 months and 4 days since it was originally ringed. It had been re-trapped 15 times previously and was carrying its fifth ring, number EJ14240, the earlier worn ones having been replaced. Interestingly, only 25 shearwaters were ringed on Copeland in 1953 and it is really remarkable that one of them survived so long. Unfortunately, the exact location of its burrow is not known, though its re-trapping location is known to within about 50 metres. Bardsey have a bird ringed in 1957 for which they do know the approximate nest location, and their elderly bird was able to exceed our bird's long-held longevity record in 2008. But for a while, the Copeland bird was the oldest known ringed bird in the BTO scheme and even the northern Hemisphere. It was only beaten by a Northern Royal Albatross *Diomedea sanfordi* which carried a ring for 52 years but is now thought to be dead.

In the early 1970s it was decided to put the shearwater and Storm Petrel ringing on a more scientific footing. Rather than compete with or duplicate the studies already underway on the Welsh Islands, it was decided that the requirements of the new approach to the shearwater study should be undemanding, allowing the catching to remain enjoyable, so that everyone would help. It was decided simply to record the position of catching of all handled birds. About 20 sub-colonies were designated. The recording of all retraps, of which there were many, became obligatory. At some stages in the year, such as early spring, the proportion of the total catch to retraps can approach 100%. Tony Irwin, Peter Munro, David McAllister and I planned the new recording system.

The Manx Shearwater colony on Copeland is probably the brightest lit colony in the world. A great glow from the Greater Belfast conurbation illuminates the island, especially the densely occupied western slopes. Anyone who has not experienced a shearwater colony at night should consider visiting Copeland. It is surprisingly easy to get to from any part of Britain or Ireland. In 2007, the Manx Shearwater colonies on Observatory Island and on nearby Big Copeland were fully surveyed. There has been a slight increase on Observatory Island although statistically not significant. However, there has been a statistically significant decrease on Big Copeland. Overall the population across the two islands has remained stable.

The first GPS tracking experiments were started on our Manx Shearwaters under the direction of Professor Tim Guilford of Oxford University after the installation of 80 study burrows in early 2006 and another 40 in 2007. Tracking studies are only possible with study burrows which allow quick and easy access to the nest and the birds. It is hoped to trace where the adults forage during incubation and also when they are feeding their chicks. This follows on from studies by Tim on Skomer using geolocators to track shearwater migration routes and shed more light on where the birds actually spend the winter. The results show that birds migrate south down the east side of the Atlantic before crossing to the west, south of the equator. The birds then go as far south as the Falklands shelf, where they seem to spend most of the winter. For the northward journey, they stay on the west side of the Atlantic to about 30°N before following the Gulf Stream east back to their nesting islands (Guilford *et al.* 2009). More birds have been tagged since the initial study and further results are awaited with interest. The recent designations of Observatory Island as an Area of Special Scientific Interest (ASSI) and as a Special Protection Area (SPA) are because of the shearwater colony and have led to many opportunities for seeking funding.

The catching of shearwaters on Copeland

In the early days, caught birds were brought up to the buildings for processing in good light as torches at the time were very primitive. The Eveready rubber torch was a great innovation. Eventually we agreed to process the birds at the catching site which would clearly cause far less disruption to the birds' lives. The modern ringer uses a powerful hand lamp and usually also an LED head lamp and appreciates being accompanied by a good scribe.

When the observatory opens at the end of March, prospecting and cleaning out of burrows is underway. The dead vegetation allows the catchers to roam over every part of the island, unlike later in the season. Coinciding with egg-laying, the vegetation starts to grow rapidly. A closed season has been observed for many years from mid-April to the end of May, to avoid disturbing the shearwaters during egg-laying. This is also in the interests of other nesting birds which might be co-incidentally disturbed.

Nearly all the birds breed in just 3.5 hectares of the island's total of 16 hectares. It is estimated that 55% of the burrows are occupied by shearwaters which breed most densely in areas that have easy places from which to take-off. The summer growth of thistles and Indian balsam, ragworts, nettles and bracken becomes a major obstacle to access and especially the departure from the nest burrows. The rampant vegetation becomes 1–2 metres tall and a vegetation management programme was initiated in 1982. In the main shearwater areas, mowing equipment has been used to cut two-metre-wide tracks through the bracken in June and July. The shearwaters find them easily and walk out of the dense cover to take off from these 'runways'. Access for the ringers has also been improved. The colony was estimated to be only around 200 pairs in 1954, compared with 2,800 pairs in 2000 and the increasing number of pulli ringed each autumn is now around 1,000.

The annual peak of ringing activity in late July is also the best time for first-time visiting birdwatchers to visit the colony as the prospecting adolescents are very noisy. Catching of adults, mainly retraps, continues from June to August and by 20 August, our attention switches to ringing the chicks which will shortly depart. The shearwater ringing and retrapping can only be undertaken by ringers who are fully familiar with every part of the island and know which sub-colony they are in, even in the dark. Some visitors wait up for the departure of the adults just before dawn in July and it is possible to hide beside the bottom of the well path and watch and hear the shearwaters taking off. They move out on to the runway for take-off, thundering down the path and heading towards the glow of light from the Greater Belfast area and pass any well-placed observer at less than a metre above ground level at a rate of at least two per minute.

The colony has extremely low predation levels, although Great Black-backed Gulls were formerly a minor problem and Otters have caused a few deaths in the colony recently. In other colonies, such as on Rum, shearwaters dig their own burrows, but much of Copeland's soil is heavy and they use rabbit burrows. Shearwaters might not have bred on Copeland until Rabbits had created some burrows. Hence, the current management of the colony takes into account the necessity for the maintenance of good sward conditions for the Rabbit population. Unfortunately the Rabbit population is regularly and increasingly knocked back by bursts of myxomatosis, viral haemorrhagic disease, and even by liver flukes. Without such events, the mowing effort would not have to be as intense. In view of the known history of the island, we estimate that the colony has risen from zero to almost 3,000 pairs in approximately 100 years.

If the Copeland colony is little more than 100 years old, it is possible that the origin of the colonisers might be identified by genetic testing. In 1977, in the days before DNA 'fingerprinting', David Whitehouse and David Parkin from Nottingham University visited Copeland to sample blood plasma proteins. One hundred and twenty birds with retrap histories and known to be of breeding age were analysed using protein electrophoresis to examine genetic variation in a group of proteins involved in the immune response system. The results indicated that the Copeland birds were slightly different when compared with those breeding on Skokholm or Skomer, suggesting either that the colonists came from a different sub-population, or that a small founding population had originated on one of these islands, but subsequently diverged rather rapidly.

Perhaps surprisingly, the catching technique has a big effect on the age profile of the catch. There are two such techniques. One is 'hunting' where the catching ringers simply walk around with torches and pick up the dazzled birds that present themselves. The other is the 'lying-in-wait' method, where the catchers lie on the ground in the dark and pounce on any bird that lands nearby. In trials, the mean age of retraps caught by hunting is around eight years while the lying-in-wait method produces a mean retrap age of 15 years. If this turns out to be substantiated in further trials, it will have interesting implications on how catching for population estimation might be conducted elsewhere. The biggest problem with the lying-in-wait system is that it is relatively less productive and rather boring! However, a considerable annual effort has been made to ring pulli, particularly since 1973. Fewer than a hundred were ringed each year until 1970, but numbers then increased and passed 200 in 1973, 400 in 1984, and 700 in 1996, before reaching 1,136 in 2005.

Foreign recoveries

There have been a good number of overseas shearwater recoveries. They include one from Spain, 17 from Brazil, two from Uruguay, four from Argentina, one from South Africa, one from Angola, one from the USA (Florida) and two from Canada. Interestingly, only one of the Brazilian recoveries involved a bird that survived as long as six years and therefore was old enough to be a breeder, so Copeland recoveries have not been able to shed any light on where adult mortality occurs in the winter.

There have been three atypical recoveries. Two were of freshly fledged birds to Denmark and Switzerland. They followed the pattern of some others on their first flights, recovered in many locations in Britain and Ireland, save that these two went rather further. Local recoveries and controls of fledglings, apparently on their first flight, are not uncommon and many are quite far inland which begs the question of whether it is normal for our birds to cross Ireland south-westwards on their way to the South Atlantic. Some of these birds, often described as sick, but nevertheless released, eventually reappear on Copeland to breed. The most remarkable example was a bird which became grounded in the centre of Belfast, over 30 kilometres away. It was picked up by a shipyard fitter on his way to night shift and taken to the docks where it was thrown into the sea from the gang plank. Three years later, it was back prospecting on Copeland. Thirdly, the recovery of a Copeland shearwater from the shore of Lake Huron, Michigan, U.S.A. on 19 August 2000, was interesting in that it was ringed on 7 September 1991 and had not been handled on Copeland thereafter and it was clearly of breeding age in 2000.

Retrap histories

The chance of a ringed breeding Copeland shearwater being recaught with some frequency is quite high. The likelihood of a bird being re-trapped depends on the location of the breeding burrow and the age of the bird. Birds in burrows well away from the main tracks or in less frequently worked sub-colonies are less frequently caught and birds with burrows near an easy take-off point tend to evade recapture. Older birds also become good at spotting the ringers coming and take off immediately, or go down a burrow.

The retrap histories of ringed shearwaters follow several patterns. Birds ringed as chicks have a reappearance rate of only around 12%. Many birds will have died between fledging and the age they would normally return to the colony. Some could have settled in another colony. Re-trappings of birds ringed as chicks begin mainly in years 3 and 4 with several handlings in the subsequent two or three years. They then follow the retrapping pattern of adults with long intervals between handlings.

An amazing 45% of birds ringed as adults are never re-trapped. Of the 55% that develop retrap histories, most are retrapped initially quite frequently for two or three years during, it is suspected, the period in which they prospect for a mate and a burrow. Most such birds are presumed to have been reared as chicks on Copeland but not intercepted for ringing at the time of fledging. A small proportion will be immigrants, reared elsewhere, settling on Copeland to breed. The frequency of re-trapping of such apparently prospecting birds usually falls away quickly and thereafter they are only re-trapped infrequently. Though the interval between re-trappings is rather variable, the most frequent (modal value) would be around eight years. Some older birds develop a burst of re-trappings within a one–three year period and then revert again to long retrap intervals. It is thought that these birds may have lost mates and are temporarily prospecting or courting again.

The progress of the study

The total number of shearwaters now ringed on Copeland is 28,353. The ringing and retrap histories of every bird handled have been recorded, starting in 1952. Since 1973, the catching location has also been recorded. Despite the best intentions of many involved, it was not until 1995 that Fiona McCrory analysed the dates of first return of birds ringed as pulli. This was followed later by the First International Manx Shearwater Workshop on Madeira in 2000 (Zonfrillo 2001). Eight members attended this workshop and it turned out to be a most inspiring event. Presentations were made on the Copeland study by me (McKee, 2001) and by John Stewart (Stewart, 2001). The workshop demonstrated how our data was of real importance because of its long-term continuity and uniqueness. Further work is now under way, mainly as a result of the very successful Second International Workshop held in Belfast in 2005. This was the most important event in the observatory's history, and was organized by Kerry Leonard (by this time our specialist shearwater secretary), John Stewart and Fiona McCrory. Eighty delegates attended from all over the world and the presentations and discussions were inspirational.

Study burrows were not considered useful for our study until the Workshop in 2005 when it was realised that a number of important questions could be resolved by having them, so 80 were set up later that year. Of these, 48 were occupied in

2006, so success with this new aspect of the study seems to be assured. From 40 burrows with young chicks in early July, 39 eventually fledged by October. By 2007, a total of 120 study burrows had been created.

Storm Petrels on Copeland

The first Storm Petrel was caught accidentally, on a late May night in 1959 in an unfurled mist-net, as nets were often left open in those early days. This happened on a four-day 'Ken Williamson inspection'. Ken decided that it would be safe to box the bird until the morning so that the 'young lad' could ring it. That lad was me and ringing that bird marked the beginning of an enthusiasm for petrels that has lasted a lifetime of ringing. In 1967, an attempt to catch more was made by setting nets around the perimeter of the island, mainly under the cliff. Seventeen were caught that summer and subsequent efforts narrowed down the best catching sites to just two places, which have been used ever since, to catch between 50 and 200 in most summers.

Just what these birds were doing on Copeland was the subject of considerable debate. By the late 1970s many regular Copelanders had been on expeditions to both our adopted colonies (Inishglora and Roaninish on Ireland's west coast) and were completely familiar with the signs and sounds of a breeding colony, but no Storm Petrel has ever been heard 'singing' on Copeland. Other researchers had been pioneering Storm Petrel studies elsewhere, so their wandering behaviour was understood and well-described by Scott (1970). Mainwood (1976) was able to shed more light on the phenomenon as the recoveries and controls accumulated. It seems that young Storm Petrels, up to around six years old, wander widely over the north-eastern Atlantic and regularly visit coastlines at night, perhaps to get used to the different turbulence that occurs over land and at the colonies.

To establish the breeding status of the birds visiting Copeland, we developed a method of recording the state of the brood patch which develops well in breeders and is bare for at least two months. However, it is smaller and the duration of the nearly bare period is of shorter duration in non-breeders. The situation is also complicated as the effect varies over time with latitude. The brood patch classification used on Copeland and at our study colonies is based on D. A. Scott's (1970), but slightly modified. Whilst not perfectly precise, it is clear that the proportion of non-breeders to breeders is quite small at large colonies such as Inishglora, whereas breeders are often out-numbered by non-breeders at a small colony such as Roaninish (McKee 1982).

It is hoped that it will soon be possible to produce suitable correction factors to allow a calculation of colony size based on mark-recapture methods (comparing the number of birds recaptured with the number originally ringed). Even if this can only be done as an 'order of magnitude' estimate, it could still be of value in comparing colonies, in detecting changes in colony size over time and in augmenting the other well-known censusing techniques. We have discovered that the best time of year to distinguish breeders from non-breeders on brood patch (and weight) is from mid-August. All the visits to the two study colonies since 1976 have been made in mid-August, which has the extra advantage that it does not interfere with other breeding species. In this context, we were rather horrified to find, in July 1974, that terns (including Little Terns) were widespread on Inishglora.

The thrust of the studies has been to compare a large colony (Inishglora, c. 10,000 pairs) with a medium-sized colony (Roaninish, 100–1,000 pairs) and a non-breeding catching site (Copeland, no pairs). The ringing at the three sites has generated an enormous number of controls, both outwards and inwards, from the entire European coastline from Portugal to Norway. By far the greatest numbers have been to or from Scotland, of which about two-thirds have been between the observatory and Sanda, which has been well-worked over many years and is both a colony and a site that is often visited by non-breeding wanderers. Recoveries elsewhere of Inishglora-ringed birds (going outwards) until 2005 totalled 48, while 50 controls of birds ringed elsewhere (coming inwards) were trapped out of a total catch of 20,000. This contrasts markedly with nearly 50 years ringing at the observatory where just over 300 recoveries and 300 controls have arisen from a total catch of just 4,000 birds, approximately 30 times more than for Inishglora. The most distant recoveries have been from Cape Province (South Africa), Namibia (two) and Mauritania.

Mark and recapture studies by the observatory at Copeland and elsewhere are directed towards gaining a better understanding of Storm Petrel movements and breeding populations respectively (Steve Stansfield – www.wildlifeimages.eu).

OTHER FAUNA AND FLORA

Mammals

There are no rats, mice, voles or shrews on the island and the Rabbits have already been mentioned extensively.

The many sightings of cetaceans leave a lasting impression. Many of the sightings are to the east of Mew Island or north of the Observatory Island at a distance of around one kilometre. Therefore a telescope is essential to see them at all well. There have been rare sightings of Killer Whales, Common Dolphins, Minke Whales and Risso's Dolphins. Bottlenose Dolphins pass by almost annually, but Harbour Porpoises are frequently seen from July to October in numbers up to 250 on flat-calm days.

Around 30 Grey and two Common Seal pups are born each year around the island. It is possible to get quite close to young Grey Seal pups in October and to watch them dabbling in shallow water as they practise swimming. One can be lulled to sleep at any time of the year by the moaning of the adults as they lie on the rocks of Mew Island, only 300 metres from the dormitory window. Otters are not often seen, but patient and lucky observers have had some very close encounters.

Invertebrates

The island has a very rich fauna of insects, including moths. The unfertilised, unenriched coastal grassland habitat ensures that huge numbers of moths can be caught in mid-summer. However, the history of moth trapping on the island is patchy. Whilst Ernie Donaldson, among others, carried out some work in the 1970s and 1980s, there was practically no trapping in the 1990s. However, there has been a renewed interest since 2000, largely the work of Kerry Leonard, and many more new moth species have been recorded. The total presently stands at over 140 and rising. Many of these may now find the island hospitable because of the tree planting programme and species more usually associated with woodland, such as Green Arches, have recently been recorded. However, the island is most important for species associated with coastal grassland and rocky shores. These include a number that are scarce and rarely recorded elsewhere in Northern Ireland, such as Crescent Dart, Square-spot Dart and Feathered Ranunculus. The island is the only site in Northern Ireland where Netted Pug has been recorded in the last 35 years. Sandy Carpet is also scarce in Northern Ireland but is abundant on the island, which is also a good site for migrants, particularly in September, and these have included Pearly Underwing, White-speck, Convolvulus Hawkmoth and Dark Sword-grass. Micromoths, however, are poorly recorded.

The island is also a staging post for migrant butterflies. At times, there are vast numbers of Red Admirals, Small Tortoiseshells, Peacocks and Painted Ladies whilst Silver Y moths also abound briefly on occasion. Clouded Yellows, however, are very rare on Copeland.

Plants

Recent pond creation, coppicing of willow plantations and mowing of wildflower swards by a team of dedicated people have made a very important contribution to the island's current and much-improved environment. In the early days of the observatory, the only bush cover on the island was scattered Elder. Most were in front of the Heligoland and wall traps. In 1974, a pioneering effort was made to establish a plantation in the north garden. Sitka Spruce was recommended by the Forest Service, but of 500 planted, only nine survived. After careful study, it was decided to plant native trees of the types that occur naturally on nearby coasts and two members developed small tree nurseries to supply the young plants. Nevertheless, the difficulties of trying to grow young plants on a windswept offshore island were considerable. Strong, dry, north winds in the late spring would burn off the tender new leaves, but Rabbits were the worst problem, jumping fences 'beyond their capabilities'. Barely one-tenth of all planted trees have survived.

By 1988, my son, Ian McKee, had organized three wire exclosures, to keep Rabbits out of proposed planting areas from the centre to the south side of the island. A mixture of Willows, Alders, Birch and a few other native trees were planted, and these have grown very successfully to the stage where they now are regularly coppiced. This improves their insect life, their health, their lifespan and the density of their branches. It also keeps them low enough to be perfect for mist-netting rides. All the areas selected for planting are well away from shearwater zones and any sensitive plants.

The most recent major planting was of 500 trees in the Millennium Wood, sponsored by Bass Ireland, at the exposed north end of the north garden. This project was also organised by Ian McKee, now a forester by profession. After 25 years of steady progress, a narrow ribbon of over 1,000 scrubby trees and shrubs, 30 metres at its widest and over two hectares in area, meanders across the middle of the island from south to north. There has been a noticeable increase in invertebrates and insect-eating migrant birds now spend longer on the island. An increase in weight, rather than a decline, is now the norm. The planting plan was intended to provide additional sheltered net sites and this has been a great success. The new north garden site is so successful that it now catches about 75% of all mist-netted birds. Meanwhile, other sites, including the main Heligoland trap, have become less successful. An interesting side effect of the planting work has been an increase in both the variety and numbers of breeding birds of which Reed Bunting and Sedge Warbler have been particular beneficiaries.

Herbaceous plants and management

The vegetation on the island in the early 1950s was quite grassy with areas of nettles, thistles, Bracken, Ragwort, Red Campion, Hogweed, Yellow Iris and the alien Indian Balsam. After myxomatosis in 1955, the grassland gradually contracted and the other species spread rampantly, fertilised by increasing gull populations. By 1982, many wildflowers such as Selfheal, Common Centaury, Eyebright and Brookweed, in the wetter areas, had almost disappeared. It was realised that hand scythes were ineffective so an old, powered Allen Scythe was tried out on a small scale. A grant for the purchase of a modern type of recipro-cating blade cutter and a lawn mower later allowed a small team of very dedicated mowing enthusiasts, again headed by Ian McKee, to re-establish the marine sward. Additional equipment has recently been obtained and all the access paths have now been opened up and restored to grass by regular mowing and removal of the cuttings. This has effectively reduced the nutrient levels and promoted permanent slow growing rabbit pasture, so very suitable for migrant pipits, larks and finches.

Another effect of the mowing regimes has been to encourage orchids, of which there is only one common species – the Northern Marsh-orchid. Flowering heads had appeared sporadically in about six places, but rarely more than 50 in any one year. However, once the mowing and lifting of a large area of the north garden had reduced nutrient levels significantly, the vegetation became noticeably trans-formed and orchid numbers rapidly increased. In July 2005, it was estimated that over 600 flowering heads and 2,000 vegetative plants were growing in an area just 60 metres by 20 metres. This was a stunning sight by any standard. The current management involves heavy close mowing in October (after the seeds have dispersed) and more mowing from March to early May. While few of these plants seem to be of direct use to migrant birds, they are a very welcome addition to the island's biodiversity.

ACCESS AND ACCOMMODATION

Visiting is surprisingly easy nowadays, even from London. In terms of travel time, Copeland is the nearest shearwater colony to London and indeed almost any airport with flights to Belfast. Buses travel frequently between Belfast International Airport, The George Best City Airport, Belfast City Centre and Donaghadee.

Most visitors come for a weekend from Friday at 18:00 hrs to Sunday at 17:00 hrs. There is sleeping accommodation for 20 people but 12 is a more comfortable number in the kitchen and common room. The Bookings Secretary arranges the boat times with the boatman, Philip McNamara, who is also the coxswain of the Donaghadee Lifeboat. Bookings can be made by telephone (at 0044 (0) 28 9443 3068) or by e-mail, to the Bookings Secretary, Neville McKee. Further updated information is available on the observatory website.

Advice on what is needed for a visit and what to expect is sent by e-mail or post. Overnight visitors should bring their own sleeping bag, pillow case, towel, torch, food and clothing for every eventuality. Self-catering is usual though some small groups may join together. There is a large kitchen with three full-sized gas cookers. There are two large dormitories for seven to nine people and two small rooms for families. Communal chores involve dish-washing, carrying water and collecting firewood, though many bring a sack of coal as an easier option.

The observatory opens at the end of March and closes at the end of October. Midweek stays are also possible occasionally, but are not recommended for a first visit. When planning a visit, most folk will be aware that the spring migrants pass through during April and the first half of May. Day visits are arranged on some Saturdays in May and June. Ringing trips to the other islands for small gulls and terns during June and July are set up by e-mail just before each visit. The Black Guillemot young are ringed on a day trip in July. Shearwaters and Storm Petrels are at their best from mid-July to mid-August. The shearwater chick ringing runs from 20 August to 20 September. Good numbers of autumn migrants are ringed from mid-September to the end of October. Sea-watching (for both birds and cetaceans) is best from July to October. There are two sea-watching hides. One is at the top corner of the North Garden and the Chris Bailey Hide is on the eastern slopes with a view over Mew Island to Scotland.

Getting to and from the island is never guaranteed due to the weather. It has to be admitted that nearly half the planned weekends in October fail to start and of those that do, the return journey can be on Monday or on Tuesday! Most October regulars plan to stay a week and simply accept that their journeys will take place when the weather allows. Crossings are rarely disrupted from May to August. Details of membership and current charges are available from the Bookings Secretary and on the website.

Observatory opened:	1954
Total number of bird species recorded at the observatory:	207
Best bird year:	2001
Number of species recorded:	116
Total of birds ringed at the observatory:	101,717
Number of species:	138
Best ringing year:	2006
Number ringed:	3,416
Number of species:	47

Dungeness

by David Walker

INTRODUCTION

Dungeness Bird Observatory is situated on the eastern extremity of a huge shingle promontory jutting out into the English Channel. It is the largest expanse of shingle in Britain and is composed of a complex series of ridges laid down over a period of around 4,000 years. Historically, the beach would grow outwards in an easterly direction as a result of longshore drift, but in recent times this has been prevented because of the need to protect the nuclear power station complex from the sea.

Shingle is an important commercial product and has been extracted in years gone by leaving an area of open water known as the Long Pits and a less deeply excavated area supporting extensive Willow carr and Bramble which is now becoming drier. In addition, Dungeness Point has long been occupied and the activities of the inhabitants have resulted in numerous small gardens. The terrace of houses, which includes the observatory, is surrounded by a raised bank and a

David Walker has been warden of Dungeness Bird Observatory since 1989.

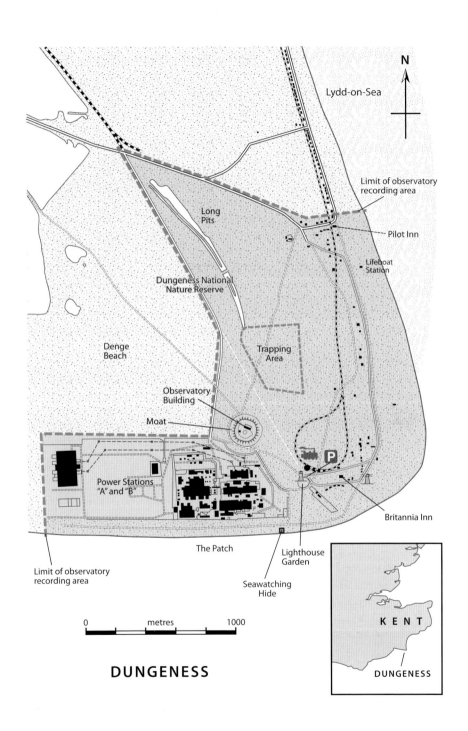

Lydd-on-Sea

N

Limit of observatory
recording area

Long
Pits

Pilot Inn

Lifeboat
Station

Dungeness National
Nature Reserve

Denge
Beach

Trapping
Area

Observatory
Building

Moat

Power Stations
"A" and "B"

Britannia Inn

The Patch

Lighthouse
Garden

Limit of observatory
recording area

Seawatching
Hide

0   metres   1000

DUNGENESS

KENT

DUNGENESS

shallow depression known as the Moat. This is a reference to the not too distant past when the area was subject to regular winter flooding and there could, indeed, be a moat around the observatory. The proximity of these areas to the Channel coast and the lack of large areas of bushes, in the 1950s and 1960s at least, meant that any small area of vegetation was very attractive to migrant birds passing through.

HISTORY

On 30 March 1952 following a meeting of interested parties led by Denby Wilkinson and including members of the Kent Ornithological Society, London Natural History Society, Hastings Natural History Society, the then Nature Conservancy and the Royal Society for the Protection of Birds (RSPB), a committee was organized with the aim of establishing a bird observatory at Dungeness to be in place by the following autumn. Accommodation was found in the Watch House at the Royal Naval Shore Signal Station (RNSSS) at a rent of five shillings a week and H. E. Axell was appointed as warden. On 25 October 1952, at the annual meeting of the Bird Observatories Sub-committee at Monks House, Seahouses, Dungeness Bird Observatory was elected to membership. In 1953 the observatory moved into No.1 RNSSS and in 1957 into its current accommodation in No.11 RNSSS.

From the outset it was clear that Dungeness Bird Observatory was well placed for the monitoring and study of migration. Since the start of operations in 1952, great emphasis has been placed on this work and a full-time warden has been employed since 1960. In the early years a steady stream of youngsters, keen to make their way in the ornithological world, would spend several months at a time working as voluntary wardens. More recently this aspect has been put on a more permanent footing with the observatory employing an assistant warden throughout the main migration periods.

One of the great strengths of the data collected is the length of the data run, now over 50 years. There may, inevitably, be slight differences in the manner of the bird recording as the various full-time wardens have changed. Having said that, several of the wardens have actually spent very long periods in their position, so lack of complete continuity should only be a very minor issue.

Ideally, there would also have been consistency in the recording area too, but in reality there have been several changes to the area that need to be taken into account when analysing the data. The boundary of the recording area has, however, remained consistent, with the power station access road furnishing the western border whilst the northern boundary lies along the section of public road from the junction with the power station to the coast at the Pilot Inn.

The most obvious change to the site has been the establishment of two nuclear power stations resulting in a large loss of habitat, extra traffic and human distur-bance and much more light at night. One major side effect was the replacement of the lighthouse (which had revolving beams) with one with an occulting beam and there was an immediate and noticeable decline in the concentration of migrants on 'lighthouse nights'. Work on the foundations of Dungeness A Power Station began in 1960 and it first came on line in September 1965. Work on Dungeness B began in 1965 and it came on line in April 1983.

One other significant change occurred in the area following the construction of the power stations. This was the creation of disturbed areas of sea water some 50–100 metres offshore caused by the cooling water outflows and which have become known collectively as 'the Patch'. The presence of this was first noted in April 1963 when, amongst other species, a Gull-billed Tern was seen feeding over the disturbance. It now attracts large numbers of gulls and terns along with the occasional attendant skuas, and an Osprey has been seen fishing over it on at least one occasion.

It is also clear from conversations with people who were here when the observatory opened that there have been considerable changes to the vegetation of the area. The areas of Bramble and Willow scrub are now much more extensive and this is reflected in the way birds are caught for ringing. In 1952 the observatory operated nine Heligoland Traps, the functioning of which relied on discrete areas of vegetation to be covered by the structure of the trap. Presently, we operate just one such trap, near to the observatory. Mist-netting began in 1956 and now provides most of the birds we catch for ringing. A so-called 'Crow Trap', although it rarely catches corvids, is also operated near the observatory. With water as its main attraction, it can catch very useful numbers of Meadow Pipits and Wheatears, and the occasional Yellow Wagtail, Whinchat and Stonechat. The changes over time are basically beyond the observatory's control and include the abstraction of water for drinking and the departure of the goats and cattle with a consequent loss of grazing pressure and also, in recent years, a general decline in the annual level of rainfall.

In 1996 various parcels of land were granted improved conservation status when the area was designated as a National Nature Reserve. This has allowed some restrictions on the use of the land to be put in place, for instance a ban on driving four-wheel drive vehicles on the fragile shingle habitat. Another benefit is easier access to National Heritage Lottery money, for example, to fund various visitor channelling projects such as boardwalks and car parking.

THE BIRDS

Spring migration

Dungeness enjoys long and varied migration seasons, the first signs of spring movement often occurring in February with movements of Brent Geese and ducks east through the Channel. The first passerine migrants usually appear by mid-March and typically include Wheatears, Black Redstarts and Chiffchaffs. By the end of the month the first Willow Warblers have usually arrived and Firecrests and Ring Ouzels are increasing in number. Migrants increase through April with most of the commoner species making their first appearances during the month and passage at sea can be impressive with ducks, waders, skuas and terns all moving through in large numbers if conditions are suitable. In the past, late April and early May was often considered to be the best time for large arrivals of land migrants, but these are now infrequent and more emphasis has been placed on watching the sea with Pomarine Skuas, in particular, being sought. May and early June are the months for overshooting vagrants and large numbers of Mediterranean Gulls can be seen at the Patch.

Early in the spring the chance of a rarity is quite small, although Night-heron, Red-rumped Swallow, Subalpine Warbler and Short-toed Treecreeper have all been seen at this time over the years, but as the volume of birds passing through begins to fall away so the possibility of a rarity appearing increases. In recent springs notable birds have included a singing Blyth's Reed Warbler on 31 May 1999, Subalpine Warbler, Sardinian Warbler, Greenish Warbler, a singing Iberian Chiffchaff in April 2001, several Woodchat Shrikes (including a bird of the Balearic race *Lanius senator badius*), Common Rosefinch and Trumpeter Finch. Late spring is also the best time for a Golden Oriole to appear or, perhaps more correctly, to be heard.

Summer is a very short period in the birding year, in fact from the bird-watcher's point of view it is debatable whether it even exists. No sooner have the last of the spring migrants passed through Dungeness than other migrants begin to move south again.

Autumn migration

A trickle of Sand Martins passing overhead and a few waders herald the begin-ning of autumn migration, often as early as the middle of July. Then from late July Cuckoos and the first few Willow Warblers begin to appear in the bushes. Autumn migration often has a much less urgent feel to it than that of spring with arrivals in August being less dependent on weather conditions and even calm weather will produce birds. Early in August a few Redstarts and Pied Flycatchers might be seen or perhaps a Wood Warbler or two. Reed and Sedge Warblers also move through, but remarkably few are seen in the recording area. Ringing operations in the reed beds on the nearby RSPB Reserve suggest that much larger numbers pause there. By late August the number of Whinchats, Lesser Whitethroats and Garden Warblers increase and Spotted Flycatchers start to appear.

By September Chiffchaffs begin to take over from Willow Warblers as the domi-nant *Phylloscopus* and Robins and Goldcrests also start to move through. Numbers of the latter can vary enormously. A series of mild winters can result in large numbers, while a hard winter can decimate the population. Large numbers are also associated with the presence of easterly winds which push birds over from the Continent. If populations are high the passage can continue well into November. Fine days in September can also bring spectacular movements of Swallows and House Martins with every telegraph wire bowing under the weight of birds resting on them. Rarities which can turn up at this time of year include Melodious and Icterine Warblers, the occasional Red-backed Shrike or Wryneck, or even rarer birds such as Western Bonelli's Warbler and Isabelline Shrike.

October sees increasing numbers of thrushes arriving, mainly Blackbirds and in most years small numbers of Ring Ouzels. In October 1998, however, weather conditions conspired to produce spectacular numbers of Ring Ouzels. Fine weather and easterly winds on the Continent encouraged large numbers of birds to depart northern Europe. These birds were then caught up in gloomy, cloudy weather across the south-eastern corner of Britain, which resulted in the grounding of large numbers. On 4 October, there were 215 Ring Ouzels, along with 150 Chiffchaffs, 30 Blackcaps and a Red-backed Shrike. More birds then arrived daily with the 7th producing another 360 Ring Ouzels, 80 Mistle Thrushes and 150 Chiffchaffs and on the 9th there were 60 Ring Ouzels and 75 Tree Pipits, 150 Robins, seven Redstarts, 200 Chiffchaffs, 110 Bramblings, 5,500 Linnets and a Yellow-browed Warbler.

Large numbers of Goldcrests sometimes bring with them another Dungeness speciality in the form of the Firecrest, although they can also appear without Goldcrests being present, clearly reflecting differences in their origins. Strong south-easterly winds, often with heavy cloud, can bring large numbers, as in 2003 when 450 bird-days were recorded with highest day counts of 30 on 15 October and 27 on 21 October. If it is a mild winter, one or two birds will often stay throughout the season, favouring either the moat or the bushes around the banks of the Long Pits.

Late October and early November is the best time for Pallas's Warbler, which breeds in southern Siberia and Asia. During the autumn the population usually moves south to wintering grounds in south-eastern China and northern Indo-China. Prior to the mid-1990s this bird was a considerable rarity in Britain, but since then the status has changed dramatically to the extent that it no longer even needs a formal description to be submitted to county level for acceptance. Nevertheless, this is still an eagerly sought-after bird in late autumn and always causes excitement when one is found. Single birds are the norm as would be expected, but there are occasional multiple occurrences, usually following south-east or north-east winds. One memorable day was 15 November 2002 when at least three birds were present in the area. There is also always the possibility of a Dusky Warbler at this time of year. Most of the rarer birds that turn up at Dungeness reflect our position in Britain, being generally eastern in origin, but we have not missed out totally on North American birds as a Red-eyed Vireo was trapped on 7 October 1986.

Visible migration

In both seasons large numbers of migrants can be seen on 'visible migration'. Numbers are generally fairly small in spring, unless it is a Woodpigeon year, but birds of prey are a feature at this time with perhaps a Montagu's Harrier or a Honey-buzzard passing through. Swallows are also present in some numbers and occasionally a Bee-eater or a Red-rumped Swallow might be seen with them. However, it is in autumn that numbers can be really impressive. The main species involved in August are likely to be Sand Martins and Yellow Wagtail, but unfortunately the latter has shown a steep drop in numbers in recent years (Figure 1).

The first half of September sees numbers dominated by Swallows and as the

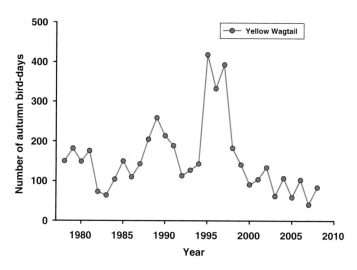

Figure 1. *Autumn bird-day numbers of Yellow Wagtails at Dungeness 1978–2008.*

month progresses by increasing numbers of House Martins. This is the best time for us to attempt to catch a sample for ringing. A tape recording of their calls is played to attract them to within range of the nets and the effect can be quite dramatic. Swallows are always slower to react and numbers build up gradually, making many passes of the nets before a few birds start to get caught. The conditions need to be perfectly calm as their eyesight is so good that they can easily see the nets and sweep up and over or around them with ease.

House Martins behave very differently. All that may be heard at first is a few calls from a handful of birds passing high overhead, but play the tape of their calls and within a few minutes there can be hundreds of birds flying around the observatory. The flock then sweeps around the Moat gradually getting lower and lower, until eventually one bird makes a mistake and is caught. This changes the behaviour of the flock, as they seem to investigate the misfortune of that first bird and within minutes there can be 20 or 30 birds in the nets and hundreds perching along the shelf strings, thus preventing any more from being caught. As we remove the birds the rest of the flock just look on, some even entering the net as you stand there. For no obvious reason, and almost as quickly as numbers build up, the birds suddenly seem to decide that enough is enough and will rise up high into the sky and head off to the south. Only 278 House Martins had been ringed here prior to 1989, but since then a total of 3,900 have been caught. The best day's ringing total was 267 on 19 September 1998, which also contributed to the best annual total of 644 birds ringed. Recoveries and controls of these birds shows they are most likely to be British birds from further north, but it is still not known where the main wintering areas are located.

Watching for visible migration can be carried out from anywhere on the Point, but there are several particularly favoured locations. The bank outside the observatory is one such site and has the advantage of a slightly elevated position coupled with access to the facilities of the observatory, ensuring a steady supply of cups of tea and coffee. The beach itself is also a good place to watch from, but the exact spot varies depending on wind conditions. A good knowledge of calls is essential as many of the birds are flying overhead at some height and reveal little in the way of plumage features. The beach also has the advantage that the sea can be watched, but wave action on the shingle can create a distracting background noise.

As the autumn progresses into October, the number of hirundines passing through falls away to be replaced by large numbers of Skylarks, pipits and finches. The actual direction of any movement will be determined by the wind direction with the majority flying into the breeze. Meadow Pipits can occasionally number in the thousands and are frequently seen from first light. However, it is often mid-morning before Skylarks and Chaffinches appear which may suggest a Continental origin, the time lag being due to the time it takes to cross the Channel after an early morning departure from the French coast. Goldfinch numbers can be spectacular and in 2005 a record total of just over 37,000 birds were noted, including a single day total of 12,400 birds on 14 October. Redpolls and Tree Sparrows used to occur in large numbers, but passage in recent years has shown a dramatic decline reflecting the national picture. By late October huge numbers of Starlings can be seen, usually arriving in big flocks low across the sea before climbing higher and heading rapidly inland. This is also the best time for seeing the occasional Snow or Lapland Bunting and on more than one occasion a Penduline Tit has occurred, although familiarity with its thin, high call is an essential factor in identifying this species. Passage continues well into November or even longer in some autumns.

Raptors are always exciting to see and the best conditions are often in light north-west winds. These usually bring clear skies and brilliant visibility when Merlins and especially Sparrowhawks can be seen arriving from the south and east, low over the coast, before climbing high on the warm air above the heat-reflecting shingle and heading off inland. The autumn of 2000 was particularly memorable for a massive arrival of Honey-buzzards from northern Europe. Their passage was tracked across the country and although most of the birds were recorded departing via Beachy Head or Portland Bill, we still recorded a total of 26 individuals between 27 August and 4 October. The occasional Osprey also passes through and on at least one occasion a bird has stopped to fish at the Long Pits.

Irruptive species

Whilst the overall species component of a typical spring or autumn season is relatively predictable, there are some species which are best described as irruptive. These are not usually great rarities, but occur from time to time in unexpected, and often large, numbers. Species occurring at Dungeness for which this term could be applied include Coal Tit, Nutcracker, Jay, Siskin, Common Crossbill and redpolls and it might be argued that Pallas's Warbler, in recent years, could also be placed in this group. These irruptions are usually correlated with high population levels and low food supplies in their normal breeding areas.

Coal Tits normally arrive in very small numbers in both spring and autumn (Figure 2), but in autumn 1996 over 759 individuals were noted and these birds also provided a small spring peak the following year. A similar, though smaller, irruption occurred in 2005. Observations in the field, backed up by detailed examination of birds caught for ringing, confirmed that all these birds were of the Continental race *Periparus ater ater* rather than our own *P. a. britannicus*. Further evidence of a Continental origin for the 1996 influx came from a bird we caught which had been ringed in May of the same year as a nestling in a nest box near Düsseldorf, Germany. Another bird caught and ringed at Dungeness during this irruption was subsequently found in deepest Surrey and thus provided that county with its first record of this subspecies.

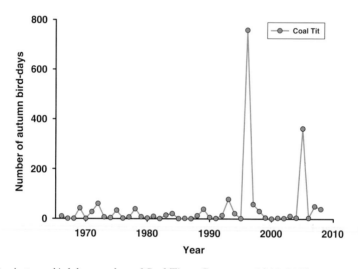

Figure 2. *Autumn bird-day numbers of Coal Tits at Dungeness 1966–2008.*

Some crow species are often associated with irruptive behaviour, including the Jay (Figure 3). Although not recorded in some years, there are sudden peaks in others, notably in 1965, 1983 and 1997, the latter being the best year so far. However, 1997 was unusual, in that birds arrived in the spring rather than the more usual autumn, and were seen on 30 days between 11 April and 8 July and with a highest day count of 38 on 26 May. The smaller peak in 1955 actually produced the only recovery of a British-ringed Jay abroad, in Zeeland, the Netherlands, in June of the following year. Another crow species, the Nutcracker, last reached our shores in large numbers way back in 1968 when the only records for the observatory occurred.

As a family, the finches often show irruptive behaviour, with Siskin, Common Redpoll and Common Crossbills all showing almost cyclical irruptions, related to cycles in the seed production of their favoured trees. Irruptions of Common Crossbills often occur surprisingly early in the summer with birds starting to appear from July. Siskin movements occur much later, but are often in huge numbers (Figure 4).

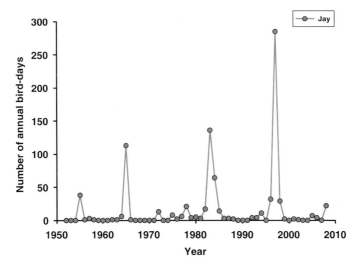

Figure 3. *Annual bird-day numbers of Jays at Dungeness 1952–2008.*

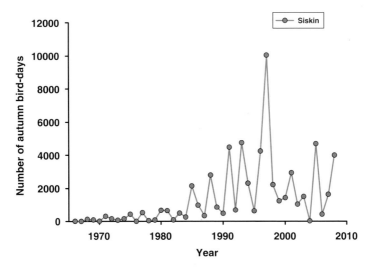

Figure 4. *Autumn bird-day numbers of Siskins at Dungeness 1966–2008.*

Our sea-watching records also show cycles, in particular, the numbers of high-Arctic species' whose breeding success is related to the lemming cycle. In 'lemming years' predators, such as Arctic Fox, feed more on young lemmings, with consequently higher breeding success for ground-nesting birds. These so-called 'lemming years' often see a significant increase in the numbers of young Pomarine and Long-tailed Skuas moving south in the autumn.

Breeding birds

Dungeness is not only an important site for migrants; it also holds several interesting breeding species, the most important of which are the small populations of Wheatears and Black Redstarts. The former, a rare breeding bird in southern Britain, can be found over the whole of the peninsula where it typically nests in old rabbit burrows or amongst piles of rubble. Numbers have varied between six and 20 pairs. Many of the adult birds are ringed and some of them survive and breed here for several years. The latter breed within the power station complex and can often be heard singing from the observatory. In most years, 2–3 pairs breed and the young often move into the Moat after fledging, where they can then be caught for ringing.

When the observatory was first established, Stone-curlews used to breed in small numbers on the open shingle. However, the population was already decreasing and, sadly, the main part of their breeding area was lost with the building of the power stations; they were last known to breed here in 1965. Little Terns bred until 1978, but increased disturbance also resulted in their demise as a breeding species, although they do breed at the nearby Rye Harbour Nature Reserve and are often seen feeding offshore during the summer.

Reference has already been made to the fact that the observatory recording area was much wetter in the observatory's early years and some breeding species have been lost with the drying of the area. Lapwings peaked at 20 pairs in 1960, but have not bred here since 1978 (with the exception of a pair in 1990), and up to three pairs of Redshank bred until 1961. In addition, Little Grebe bred in the area until 1972 and Great Crested Grebe has bred in two years.

A total of 62 species have bred in the observatory recording area. Amongst the less regular are Nightingale in 1981 and 1982, Lesser Whitethroat, Blackcap, Garden Warbler in 2005, Willow Warbler and Chiffchaff. Gadwall bred in 2001

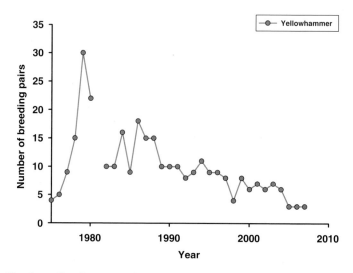

Figure 5. *Numbers of breeding pairs of Yellowhammers at Dungeness 1975–2008.*

after a now rare wet winter. It is also surprising to note that likely breeding species such as Wren, Song Thrush and Robin only occasionally do so. This is particularly significant as the absence of these species as residents makes it easier to detect the arrivals of migrant individuals.

The Stonechat has not been a regular breeding bird, but following a series of warm winters and resultant high winter survival rates, one or two pairs have bred in recent years. Interestingly, close study of the plumage of these breeding birds suggests that they are of the Continental race *Saxicola torquatus rubicola,* rather than the more expected British race, *S. t. hibernans.*

Yellowhammer first bred in the area in 1975 and reached a peak population of around 30 pairs in 1979. Numbers then dropped, stabilising at between 10 and 15 pairs during the 1970s and 1980s; Figure 5 shows how they have since declined further to just three pairs in 2005 and none in 2008. Whilst this is clearly corre-lated with population changes at the national level, other factors are likely to be involved, including simply the changing habitat in the recording area.

As the area of willow scrub has grown and aged it has become able, since 2001, to sustain a pair of Green Woodpeckers, although it should be added that they have actually nested in telegraph poles at some expense to British Telecom.

Sea-watching

One of the most popular birdwatching pursuits at Dungeness is that of sea-watching. This typically involves the often uncomfortable challenge of looking out to sea for many hours in the hope of seeing birds moving up or down-Channel. The peak time for this activity is during the spring, with the best chance of seeing birds when the wind is blowing onshore, but other times of year can be equally interesting. In spring, the beach on the south side of the power station is the best place to watch from. However, sea-watching in autumn tends to require poorer weather conditions for success.

Spring sea-watching

Passage usually begins in late February with small numbers of Brent Geese begin-ning to move eastwards and this usually peaks in mid-March. There have been some spectacular movements, with large flocks pouring eastwards all day long and giving day totals of, for instance, 7,000 on 9 March 1993 and 10,080 on 13 March 2006. During the course of a whole spring, up to 46,000 individuals have been recorded (Figure 6).

Large movements are likely to occur in south-westerly winds, but as March progresses other wildfowl begin to appear and the ideal conditions begin to change so that the best weather is in light south to south-easterly winds. Species recorded may include large numbers of Pintail (860 on 13 March 2006), Shoveler (1,324 on 1 April 2004) and Teal (576 on 31 March 1971).

By the end of March Sandwich Tern passage is usually in full swing and the first Common Terns are beginning to appear. There is an almost daily passage of Common Scoters throughout the spring with overall totals of up to 51,000 birds,

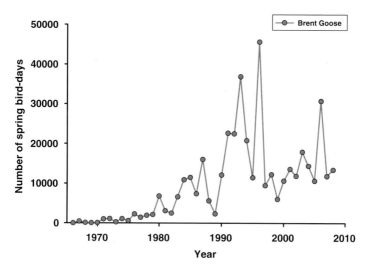

Figure 6. *Spring bird-day numbers of Brent Geese at Dungeness 1966–2008.*

including some very large movements. One particular day that lives in the memory of those who were there was a movement of 27,000 birds on 8 April 1979 when at least one flock was described as extending right across the visible field of view from east to west.

April is often the best time to see Garganey and they seem to have become more regular in recent years, with a record count of 39 on 2 April 2005. As April progresses the number of skuas begins to increase, with both Great and Arctic Skuas peaking between 16 and 24 April. This period also sees large numbers of terns, including good numbers of Little Terns. Little Gulls also pass through at this time. The passage of waders on their way to high arctic breeding grounds really gets underway in the last third of April and continues well into May. Flocks of brightly coloured Bar-tailed Godwits pour through, calling excitedly as they go, along with smaller flocks of Grey Plover, Knot and Sanderling, the majority of which are in breeding plumage. The first third of May sometimes sees a movement of Black Terns, all in beautiful black breeding plumage and frequently passing through very close inshore.

However, the first half of May is now best known and eagerly awaited for the passage offshore of Pomarine Skuas. At this time of year there will invariably be a large gathering of birdwatchers hoping to see a flock or two. Unlike the two commoner skua species which usually move through singly or in pairs, these birds migrate in tight flocks which means that a long session may be necessary. The best weather conditions are usually in light south-easterly or stronger north-easterly winds, and often in bright but very hazy weather, so sitting out on the beach is not too great a hardship. Large numbers usually occur on just one or two days during a spring, with the record day count of 151 on 7 May 1981 and the general pattern of occurrence (at five-day intervals) is clear from Figure 7. The highest spring total is of 306 birds in 2004 and Figure 8 illustrates how the annual counts have varied since 1952.

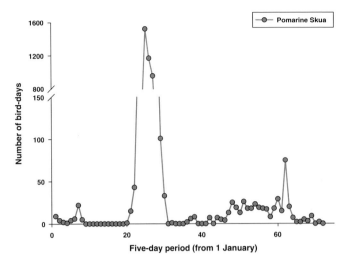

Figure 7. *Pattern of occurrence – bird-day numbers of Pomarine Skuas at Dungeness at five-day intervals 1966–2008.*

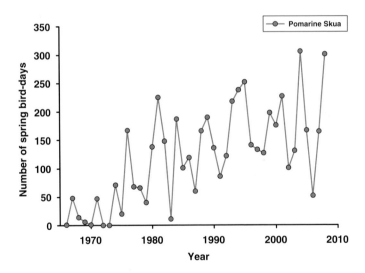

Figure 8. *Spring bird-day numbers of Pomarine Skuas at Dungeness 1966–2008.*

There is always a chance of a real rarity when birds are on the move and in recent years these have included several White-billed Divers, Cory's Shearwater, and most memorable of all to those who were there, a Black-browed Albatross which lingered for 40 minutes on 4 May 2001. Passage usually comes to an end by mid-May and it is then fairly quiet through the summer until the return passage in autumn, except for the occasional summer storms which may bring a few Manx Shearwaters close inshore.

Autumn sea-watching

Autumn movements begin in early August, but unlike the spring, the best area to watch from is along the eastern shore, although shelter is much harder to come by and generally speaking the worse the weather the better the watching. Terns and skuas are the first to appear and there is always the chance of a Long-tailed Skua or maybe a Sabine's Gull mixed in with the flocks of terns passing through.

One of my most memorable days was 6 September 1992. Conditions must have been perfect for a massive emigration of Black Terns from their staging areas in the Netherlands and with fresh south-easterly winds many birds were pushed onto our side of the English Channel. During the morning over 10,000 Black Terns passed through, in long lines, with one flock taking over half an hour to stream by. Other species of tern and skuas were also in evidence, with 1,900 'Commic' (unidentified Common or Arctic) Terns and 132 Little Terns as well as 94 Arctic, 20 Great and two Pomarine Skuas.

As the autumn progresses the chance of shearwaters, especially Sooty Shearwater, increases with occasional very large numbers. The period from 7 to 10 October 1987 was one very notable occasion with the 9th being the best day. The wind was SW force 5 backing S-SE force 6 with frontal rain and produced 408 Sooty Shearwaters, 241 Manx Shearwaters, one Storm and two Leach's Petrels, two Pomarine Skuas, 22 Great Skuas and two Sabine's Gulls and the bird of the day, the first county record of Macaronesian Shearwater. The following day produced another 143 Sooty Shearwaters, 67 Manx Shearwaters, a Balearic Shearwater, 11 Leach's Petrels, three Pomarine Skuas, 37 Great Skuas, 406 Little Gulls and 540 Kittiwakes.

Later still, in October and early November, there is always the chance of a Leach's Petrel or two (Storm Petrel is a very rare bird off here) and maybe a few Little Auks if the wind is from the north or north-east. On two occasions there have been very large movements of Little Auks, both more or less unexpected, showing that you can never take anything for granted. The first of these was during December 1990, in south-west winds, with numbers peaking at 105 birds on 28 December. The second was on 2 November 1995 when 168 flew west close inshore in a fresh north-west wind. A large passage of 485 Little Gulls on 2 January 2003 offers further proof that sea passage is anything but predictable. Normally, however, autumn passage has come to an end by mid-November and for the following three months any sea-watching is usually as a result of very stormy weather when large numbers of gulls and auks, mainly Guillemots, can appear.

To aid our sea-watching efforts, a number of hides have been built on the beach overlooking the sea and the Patch. Unfortunately the original hides were lost in the October 1987 hurricane, but these were subsequently replaced by the then Central Electricity Generating Board and are currently still in use.

The Patch

In addition to sea-watching, the Patch is worth a visit at any time of year for close views of gulls and terns. At times, thousands of birds can be seen here as they feed over the disturbed waters and then gather on the beach to rest. They can be quite approachable and there are great opportunities to study the various plumages of the gulls and terns of all ages that gather here. During the winter there may be a Glaucous Gull or an Iceland Gull amongst the many Herring Gulls. There are also nationally important numbers of Great Black-backed Gulls, with regular counts of up to 2,000 birds, and at most times of year there are usually a few Yellow-legged Gulls to be seen. Recently, as our knowledge of its field characters has become better understood, this site has proved to be a good place to find Caspian Gull.

Since 2003 there has been a significant passage of Mediterranean Gulls between late May and early July. The highest day-count so far is 150 birds on 25 June 2003. If the viewing conditions are good it is well worth checking for colour-rings, which can be seen on a high proportion of the birds. The majority have been ringed at breeding sites on the near Continent, between Boulogne and Amsterdam, but ringed birds from Poland, the Czech Republic and Hungary have also been present. One of the Polish-ringed birds has been seen in consecutive summers and long and interesting life-histories unfold from these colour-ringing programmes. Many of the birds then move south and spend the winter months on the south-western coast of France and the northern coast of Spain.

During spring migration many terns linger on their way north, especially if a very strong north-easterly is blowing and Arctic Terns can be picked out among the more abundant Common Terns. There are often a few Black Terns as well

The cooling-water outflows from the nuclear power station at Dungeness create an unsettled area of water known as 'the Patch' which, at its busiest, is a spectacular sight, attracting many hundreds of gulls and terns (David Walker).

and, if you are lucky, maybe a Roseate Tern. Terns are present throughout the summer, but numbers increase greatly from mid-July as family parties start returning south. The young often allow quite close approach, but at the risk of attack from the adults. Rarer terns sometimes appear, with a Caspian Tern on 15 July 1990 and White-winged Black Terns in many years, although they have become much less regular recently. Rarer gulls have included two Slender-billed, a couple of Bonaparte's and a Laughing Gull but, perhaps surprisingly, Ring-billed Gull has never been seen here.

Memorable days

Migration during spring, or at least the observation of it, is very often weather dependent. Radar studies have shown that large numbers of birds pass over the coast in fine and clear conditions at night without making landfall and head straight inland to their breeding sites, but if there is calm weather and an increasingly cloudy sky, ideally with some rain, then large arrivals (or falls) of migrants can occur. There are spectacular accounts of such events during the early years and one often quoted day was 5 May 1957. The diary entry for this day reads:

> *After a fine evening, the wind veered unexpectedly to the south by midnight and the sky became overcast by 02:00 hrs; rain began at about 02:30 hrs and the wind continued to veer. By dawn at 03:30 hrs it was west by north, force 3 and the rain was thinning off. These conditions had brought a good many small passerines to the light – about 25 could be seen at once – usually Whitethroats and a few Redstarts, Wheatears and Willow Warblers. Whimbrel, godwits and Dunlin were also heard. Small birds continued to arrive on the light winds until about 30 minutes before dawn. Fifteen birds were caught at the light and the first drive of the Wheatear trap resulted in a record bag of 65 birds and... with the last drive at 19:00 hrs new birds were still being caught in quantity. A fairly strong wind for most of the day kept birds down well until they were driven and even then seemed to be a help rather than a hindrance when the driving was against the wind. Throughout the day the moat was full of birds and went on producing good totals. There was little time at all for observation, apart from trapping, and little in consequence was seen. The only birds of interest seen but not trapped were a Ring Ouzel, a Whimbrel, a Turtle Dove and the first Swifts. The ringing total for this day was 689 birds including 496 Whitethroats, 114 Willow Warblers, 39 Redstarts, seven Garden Warblers, four Whinchats, two Pied Flycatchers and a Cuckoo.*

During my time at the observatory major spring arrivals have been very scarce and usually dominated by Willow Warblers in terms of numbers, but several occasions stand out in my memory. The first was on 7–8 April 1996 when thick, damp cloud overnight produced a huge movement of birds. Many birds could be seen in the light from the lighthouse and what sounded like discrete flocks of waders were streaming through. The following estimates of birds during the night include some 40 flocks of Bar-tailed Godwits, thousands of Redwings and Blackbirds, 200 groups of Fieldfares and oddities including at least six Grey Herons, 15 Coot, several Moorhens, a Little Ringed Plover, a Greenshank, three Green Sandpipers and four Ring Ouzels. Thrushes were still much in evidence the following morning, including 500 Fieldfares and 1,350 Redwings, and other migrants included 250 Meadow Pipits, 15 Black Redstarts, 45 Wheatears, 20 Chiffchaffs and a Short-eared Owl.

Another notable day was on 28 March 1998 when in light south to south-easterly winds and cloudy skies an excellent fall of migrants occurred. Black Redstarts were a particular feature on this day, with at least 55 birds being seen on the Point. These were part of an arrival of this species all along the Kent coast involving a minimum of 305 birds. Other migrants also arrived in good numbers including two Ring Ouzels, 60 Wheatears, 120 Chiffchaffs, 250 Goldcrests and 12 Firecrests. As with any such arrival of birds there is often an occasional rarity or two to be seen and on this day a Hoopoe came in off the sea from the south and a Serin was also noted.

A third particularly memorable date was on 21 May 1991, in part because of the lateness of the fall. The spring had seemed over for numbers of migrants when a calm and misty morning suddenly produced at least 200 Willow Warblers along with eight Redstarts, 20 Whinchats, 35 Wheatears, 12 Sedge Warblers, 75 Whitethroats, 15 Garden Warblers, ten Blackcaps, two Wood Warblers and 12 Spotted Flycatchers. There are also very rare occasions where the fall involves only small numbers of birds but the 'quality' can be very high. In this category was a spell in mid-May 1996 when on 19 May two Melodious Warblers were found in the trapping area. This was followed the next day by an incredible ten birds and another three new birds on 21 May. There were hardly any other migrants to be found; indeed Melodious Warbler was the commonest migrant on 20 May.

Rarities

Of course, in the current world of birdwatching, rarities play an important part in the birdwatcher's year and it is impossible not to mention a few of those seen at Dungeness. Pride of place probably goes to the second-summer Audouin's Gull which was found on 4 May 2003. Initially seen briefly, there was a tense hour or so before it was relocated. The species had been expected to turn up somewhere in Britain sooner or later and as this individual had been seen in the Netherlands a few days earlier, it was not a total surprise. It arrived on a Bank Holiday Monday and so was bound to attract a huge crowd of observers; within minutes of news being put out there was an ever-increasing crowd of birdwatchers, many with tales of birders hurrying here before it flew off. In the event it stayed for three days and gave excellent views throughout its stay.

For sheer excitement there is probably no better example than the sighting of a Black-browed Albatross which appeared in the middle of a very quiet seawatch on 4 May 2001 in the least likely conditions for a seabird at Dungeness, namely a strong and cold north-westerly wind. Some visitors to the observatory were even

Bird observatories have hosted many additions to the avifauna of Britain and Ireland, including this Audouin's Gull, found by David Walker at Dungeness in May 2003 (Nigel Blake).

in bed at the moment of its discovery, but not for long, as colleagues went to rouse them, waking up most of the human residents of Dungeness in the process. One observer drove down from Greatstone-on-Sea. After running to the hide, his binoculars steamed up from his exertions and he had to wait an anxious few minutes until he had cooled down enough to see the bird. Yet another observer arrived still wearing his slippers, having driven from Hythe, just in time to see the bird before it took off and flew steadily out of sight to the west.

All rarities seem to have their tales of misfortune as well. For example, on 6 May 1989, a Lesser Crested Tern flew east close inshore, just minutes after one observer had gone home for a belated breakfast at 16:00 hrs, having previously sat in the hide all day from first light! Or my own incredible misfortune on missing both Slender-billed Gull and Trumpeter Finch, and hearing of the latter by text message half way up a mountain in Slovenia! But of all the major rarities, Dungeness has become *the* place in Britain to see Short-toed Treecreeper. There are currently 22 accepted British records and 11 of these have been seen at Dungeness. Difficult to identify in the field, the most reliable feature is the call. However, it was the ring on its left leg in the case of the first really twitchable bird in 1990.

Finally, on the rarity theme, it is always worth remembering that you never know what is lurking around the next corner or in the next bush, whatever the weather or time of year. July is not normally reckoned to be a great time for birds and certainly not for rarities. So it was that on 8 July 1989 I decided to check the Long Pits for dragonflies. I was not even really birding. I had crossed the path between the two Long Pits when suddenly perching in front of me was a stunning juvenile Great Spotted Cuckoo which is still one of my most memorable moments for instant surprise and delight.

Population trends in some common migrants

The continuing daily monitoring of numbers and the ringing of migrants in the area over such a long time scale allow us to look at the trends in overall numbers and also at the pattern of occurrence of our commoner migrant species. Many of these species' population trends are reflected in the national picture. There are in fact good indications that observatory data will signal population changes before they are noted in more national and widespread breeding bird surveys. Whilst the local conditions have changed over the years, it is clear that many of the fluctuations are independent of such local effects. The following species are some of those which, passing through Dungeness both in spring and autumn, show dramatic changes in numbers, and currently give great cause for concern about our breeding bird populations.

Willow Warbler numbers in both spring and autumn have shown a dramatic decline since the high numbers in the late 1970s, peaking at just under 3,000 birds in spring 1980 and just over 7,000 in autumn 1978. The decline has been very steady to the extent that passage totals are now about 12% of those recorded at their peak (Figure 9). National surveys show that numbers, particularly in the south-east, have declined at an equally alarming rate.

Garden Warblers are a typical migrant of late April and early May, but numbers have declined (Figure 10), whilst Turtle Dove and Spotted Flycatcher numbers have now become so low (Figures 11 and 12) that they might be classed as scarce migrants.

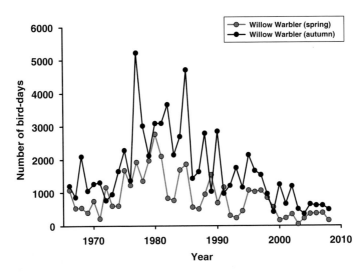

Figure 9. *Spring and autumn bird-day numbers of Willow Warblers at Dungeness 1966–2008.*

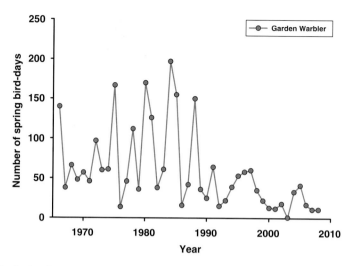

Figure 10. *Spring bird-day numbers of Garden Warblers at Dungeness 1966–2008.*

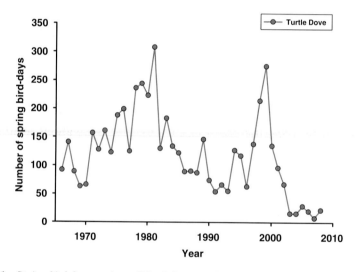

Figure 11. *Spring bird-day numbers of Turtle Doves at Dungeness 1966–2008.*

The Whitethroat is one species that actually appears to buck this trend, but is not without its own history of dramatic ups and downs. The accuracy of counts is slightly clouded by the presence of a breeding population, but in fact both sets of data mirror the national trend. Prior to 1969 this species was one of the commonest migrants at Dungeness, but in 1969 a sudden fall in Whitethroat numbers was noticed, both passing through migration sites and arriving at breeding grounds. Studies were made at the time and it was shown that the decline in returning birds was due to a long period of drought in the Sahel region of West Africa. Further studies have shown that this period of drought affected a

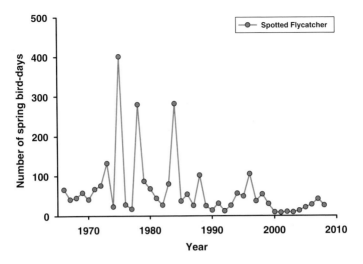

Figure 12. *Spring bird-day numbers of Spotted Flycatchers at Dungeness 1966–2008.*

wide range of other species, including Sedge Warblers and Redstarts, and numbers recorded at Dungeness clearly showed parallels with the national picture. However, Whitethroat numbers have bounced back and, helped by semi-natural changes in the habitat of the recording area, breeding numbers are now actually higher than they were before the crash. The breeding population peaked at 100 pairs in 1996 and it is still the commonest breeding bird in the area (Figure 13).

Not only is it worrying that many of our own bird populations seem to be in continuous decline, but it is becoming clear that these changes are also being felt

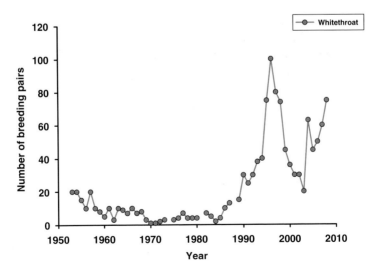

Figure 13. *Numbers of breeding pairs of Whitethroats at Dungeness 1953–2008.*

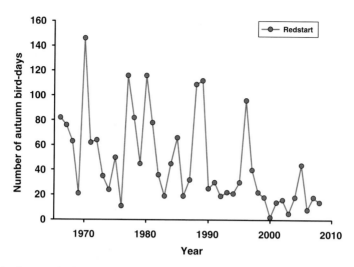

Figure 14. *Autumn bird-day numbers of Redstarts at Dungeness 1966–2008.*

across wide areas of Europe. Even though numbers have never been large, it is sobering to study the old logs and read of multiple arrivals of species such as Wryneck and Bluethroat. Presently, any more than a single Wryneck in a day would be quite an event and only one Bluethroat has been recorded since 1989. Even so-called common Continental migrants, such as Redstarts, are in serious decline (Figure 14).

OTHER FAUNA AND FLORA

Over the years, the observatory has branched out from just recording birds into many other areas of natural history. The mainly shingle habitat has long been known to support an unusually rich flora and this, allied to its position so close to the Continent, has resulted in a rich invertebrate fauna.

Mammals, reptiles and amphibians

As with most locations on the British mainland, the land mammals recorded at Dungeness are not particularly exciting, although Stoat and to a lesser extent Weasel provide some entertainment, but species such as Hedgehog and Badger are surprisingly rare. With many hours spent looking at the sea for birds it is perhaps surprising that whales and dolphins are not recorded more frequently, but this is probably a genuine reflection of the unsuitability of the waters off Dungeness. By far the commonest species seen is the Harbour Porpoise and there are occasional sightings of Bottlenose Dolphin, Long-finned Pilot Whale and Risso's Dolphin. On one memorable day, 8 December 2004, a party of seven White-beaked Dolphins spent the afternoon and evening feeding offshore, spectacularly leaping completely out of the water on several occasions.

Of the reptiles and amphibians, Marsh Frog, Common Lizard and Grass Snake are all very common and, in the case of the frog, very noisy. Smaller numbers of Common Frog, Common Toad, Common Newt and Slow-worm can sometimes be found.

Moths and butterflies

The moths are very well studied, with the observatory, along with other local and visiting lepidopterists, running light traps for most of the year. The whole area can be well lit up on suitable nights. There are numerous species which are more or less restricted within Britain to the Dungeness peninsula. These include the Sussex Emerald, the White Spot, the micro-moth *Ethmia bipunctella* and various other species which are nationally scarce. Several species exist in forms peculiar to Dungeness including Pale Grass Eggar *Lasiocampa trifolii* f. *flava* and Pigmy Footman *Eilema pygmaeola pallifrons*.

As with birds though, it is the unusual that we are all hoping for and over the years the observatory has built up a spectacular list of very rare moths including Dusky Peacock, Spurge, Striped and Death's Head Hawkmoths, Oak Processionary, Great Dart, Dewick's Plusia and Golden Twin-spot. In 1996 we added a new species to the British list when a Pale-shouldered Cloud was found in one of the traps.

Counts are made of all the macro-moths and many of the pyralid species caught. These provide a picture of long-term trends in many of our common species. Whilst the larger 'macro-moth' fauna is pretty well known, there are still additions to the list each year and we are now working towards improving our knowledge of the less popular 'micro-moths'. The attraction of the light is not limited to moths. A variety of other insects are also seen, including the occasional butterfly and dragonfly. In 2005 a number of Harlequin Ladybirds were recorded. Even more surprisingly, on 2 September 1998, an Ant-lion was seen in the garden, one of the few British records of a migrant individual of this large and unusual insect. The garden also attracts insects in its own right and three Violet Carpenter Bees have been seen; one on 12 July 1996 and singles on 8 and 20 June 2005.

The butterfly fauna is not as spectacular in terms of species, but this is more than made up for by the sometimes huge numbers of individuals that can be seen. The typical grassland species are particularly abundant, with counts of 1,000 or more Meadow Browns and hundreds of Gatekeepers not being unusual, whilst populations of Common Blues and Small Coppers are often very high. One of the scarcer butterflies to be seen regularly is the Grizzled Skipper, although numbers are always small. In recent years Marbled White, Brown Argus and Speckled Wood have all colonised the area and in good years Holly Blue can sometimes be found. On the debit side the Small Tortoiseshell, Comma and Wall Brown populations currently seem to be declining rapidly. As with the moths, we are well placed to receive migrant butterflies and there are recent records of Swallowtail, Camberwell Beauty and Large Tortoiseshell, and even a record of a Monarch on 13 October 2001.

Dragonflies

Dragonflies are also a feature of the recording area, with the Long Pits providing fantastic opportunities for observing several species. Hairy Dragonfly is amongst the first to be seen in spring and by early June Black-tailed Skimmers and Four-spotted Chasers (these often being hunted by Hobbies) can be very abundant along with smaller numbers of Emperor Dragonfly and, later in the year, Brown Hawkers. The smaller species are particularly abundant and careful searching amongst these occasionally reveals a Variable Damselfly, whilst Red-eyed Damselfly was first seen here in 1996 and is now a very common insect. Very small numbers of the Small Red-eyed Damselfly, a recent colonist into Britain, have been seen in the last two years, and there are also several records of Lesser Emperor from the area.

One of the more spectacular dragonfly events was in early August 1996 when there was a massive invasion of *Sympetrum* species into Britain, with eight individuals of the Vagrant Darter, over 300 of the scarce Yellow-winged Darter and several Black Darters being found amongst the thousands of Common Darters. Perhaps surprisingly, no Red-veined Darters were seen at this time, but occasional individuals are seen at the Long Pits.

Grasshoppers

In late summer grasshoppers and crickets can be seen in huge numbers. The Grey Bush Cricket is one species which has a range restricted mainly to south-east England, but is quite easy to see here. Perhaps reflecting the recent trend towards warmer and drier summers, the Long-winged Conehead was first found in the area in 1999. It has now spread into almost all the suitable habitat. A careful search of the damp, vegetated margins of the Long Pits can sometime reveal Cepero's Groundhopper alongside the commoner Slender Groundhopper.

Flowering plants

The flora of the recording area is very rich and varied with large numbers of nectar-bearing plants providing feeding opportunities for many insects, including the aforementioned butterflies and also day-flying moths. Hummingbird Hawkmoth is frequently seen feeding at clumps of Red Valerian. Some of the more important plants in this respect are Sea-kale, Common Bird's-foot-trefoil, Weld, Wild Mignonette and Red Valerian, whilst from a botanist's point of view, some of the less common plants include Greater Spearwort, Small-flowered Buttercup, Spring Vetch, Yellow-vetch, Bur Medick, Lesser Water-plantain, Red Hemp-nettle, Early Spider-orchid and Autumn Lady's-tresses. Dungeness used to be the only British station for Stinking Hawk's-beard, but this was last seen growing in a wild state in 1981 and is now the subject of an ongoing re-introduction programme.

Data recording

All our rare birds are fully described, with records submitted to both the Kent Ornithological Society and, when relevant, to the British Birds Rarities Committee. Copies of our log data are also provided to the British Trust for Ornithology (BTO) and the Bird Observatories Council and all our records are available to the Kent Ornithological Society. All ringing work is carried out under licence from the BTO who receive details of every bird handled. Nick Riddiford (1991) analysed the data for the period 1953–1977 for a Master's Degree and a copy of the resulting two-volume tome is kept at the observatory. Moth records are sent to Kent Lepidopterists Group and Butterfly Conservation (along with our butterfly records) and summaries of the rarer migrants appear in the magazine *Atropos* and in the British Entomological Society publications. Copies of our Annual Report are lodged with the BTO, Natural England, RSPB and Edward Grey Institute for Ornithology at Oxford University, and summaries of our work are given to the two power stations. Mammal records are given to the Kent Mammal Group and records of cetaceans are also given to the Sea Watch Foundation.

Our data have also been used by the Centre for Ecology and Hydrology at Monks Wood, particularly in relation to first arrival dates of spring migrants and as a measure of global warming. Recent studies of the population dynamics of various species including Turtle Dove, Yellow Wagtail, Ring Ouzel, Sedge Warbler and Willow Warbler also use observatory data. Notes and papers on rarities, aspects of identification and phenology have also appeared from time to time in *British Birds* and *Birding World*. Data gathered by the observatory may also play a part in the current evaluation of planned developments at Lydd Airport and have already played a significant part in Impact Assessment and Mitigation with regards to the decommissioning of Dungeness 'A' Power Station. They may well be important when or if Dungeness 'C' becomes a serious proposition. The observatory has also, on occasion, helped to fund original studies of some of the rarer insects found in the area.

The future

So, what of the future? As already described, one of the strengths of the observatory and the data it records is the constancy of the data series. Birds have been counted on a more or less daily basis since 1952. Moths, butterflies and dragonflies are all systematically recorded and these can provide important insights and even early warning signs into the changing populations of many species.

The observatory has always considered that one of its important functions is the provision of training of ringers to the high standards required by the BTO. Despite the steady decline in overall numbers of birds ringed, this is still the case today.

The current energy policies of the government may well have an effect on our work. A new Dungeness 'C' power station may be built and if this comes about it could well have serious consequences for the observatory. Dungeness 'A' ceased generation and began decommissioning at the end of 2006, which will reduce the

Patch to just one disturbed water outlet. Current plans are to make the ground of 'A' station available for future use by around 2031 – though just what that use might be remains to be seen. The upgrading of many parcels of land to National Nature Reserve status has helped to maintain the area in favour of wildlife, but pressures on the area increase as more and more people live in the southeast of England.

ACCOMMODATION AND OTHER INFORMATION

In addition to the observatory recording area covered here, the observatory provides an excellent base from which to explore the local area. A short distance away is the Dungeness RSPB Reserve with a fine Visitor Centre, hides and nature trails. The Reserve, Lade and Scotney Gravel Pits and also Lade Sands are excellent locations for waders in spring and autumn. Slightly further away (about a 40 minute drive) is the Rye Harbour Nature Reserve with large numbers of breeding seabirds. Extensive woodlands are easily accessible around Hamstreet, with breeding Nightingales amongst other typical woodland birds if a change of scenery is required.

The observatory employs a warden throughout the year and an assistant warden, currently for around ten months of the year. Inexpensive hostel-type accommodation is available for most of the year with beds for up to ten visitors in two rooms. There are full facilities with a bathroom, central heating and double glazing. Electric cookers and a microwave are provided along with all cooking utensils, crockery and cutlery, and there is a small deep freeze. Blankets and pillows are provided, but visitors must bring their own sheets or sleeping bag and pillow cases. Gone are the days of old when an entry in the log for 10 January 1963 (the famous cold winter) read: 'the observer did not attempt to travel further afield apart from a quick visit to the shore to collect firewood' whilst for the next day: 'the bitter freezing weather continues and all houses in the road are frozen, except the warden's (!) which is the only one with running water. The observatory retains eight dust-bins full of water as emergency supplies'.

Meals can also be obtained at two local hostelries within walking distance of the observatory or further afield in Lydd and New Romney. For those without their own transport there are frequent rail services to Rye and Folkestone and a bus service from both which stops close by (ask for the Pilot Inn stop). Anyone with any interest in natural history, and not just birds, may stay at the observatory and accommodation can be booked via the phone or through e-mail.

Annual Reports are produced, following reinstatement as part of our work in 1989, and there is an almost daily update of events on our website which gives lots of additional information about the observatory. A membership scheme is operated, the 'Friends of Dungeness Bird Observatory'. Members pay a small annual subscription and for this they can make use of the facilities. They also benefit from reduced accommodation charges and receive a copy of the Annual Report and Autumn Bulletin. Annual Reports can also be purchased from the observatory.

Observatory elected to Bird Observatory Council 25 October 1952 and fully wardened since 1960

Total number of bird species recorded at the observatory: 319

Total of birds ringed at the observatory: 270,286

Number of species: 208

Best ringing year: 1977

Number ringed: 10,057

Number of species: 106

Fair Isle

by David Okill and Deryk Shaw

THE ISLAND

Fair Isle lies about halfway between Shetland and Orkney. Sumburgh Head, at 39 kilometres to the north-east, is slightly closer than North Ronaldsay, in Orkney, to the south. Positioned at 59°32'N, 01°37'W, it is almost as far north as the southern tip of Greenland and further east into the North Sea than most people realise. It is Britain's remotest inhabited island and, because of that, transport to and from the isle has always been an issue. The island is relatively small, being just five kilometres long and three kilometres wide, but the coastline, cut by numerous geos (rocky gullies) and bays, is disproportionately long.

Consisting mainly of Old Red (Devonian) Sandstone overlain with boulder-

David Okill is the vice-chairman of Fair Isle Bird Observatory Trust and first visited Fair Isle in the early 1970s. A long-term ringer, he has collaborated on a number of papers and is one of the authors of *The Birds of Shetland* (Pennington *et al.* 2004).

Deryk Shaw spent three years (1989–1992) as assistant at Sandwich Bay Bird Observatory. He graduated in Zoology from Newcastle University in 1996 and has been the observatory warden since 1999.

N

Kirk Stack
Inner Stack
Wester Lother
Easter Lother
Lericum
North Lighthouse
Dronger
Kim O' Skroo
Easter Lother Water
Mopul
North Felsigeo
Wirvie
Golden Water
Toor o' da Ward Hill
Guidicum
Ward Hill
△217m
Communication Mast
Lerness
Swey
Bird Observatory & Toilet
North Naaversgil
Mire o' Vatnagaard
Furse
North Haven
North Gavel
Burrista
Roskilie
South Naaversgil
Eas Brecks
Buness
Troili Geo
Holmisdale
South Haven
Gunnawark
Burrashield
Sukka Mire
Airstrip & Toilet
South Gavel
Dutfield
Landberg
Hoini
Vaadal
Plantation
Finniquoy
Mavers Geo
Tarryfield
Hill Dyke
Gilseller
North Park
Hjon Park
Pund
Gilly
Johnny Arcus Pk
Bulls Pk
Vaasetter
Goom
The Raevas
Hjukni Geo
Hesswalls
Sheep Rock
Steensi Geo
Linni Geo
Shop & Toilets
Taing
Sma Trinket Geo
Boini Mire
Da Water
Klingers Geo
Malcom's Head
Meadow Burn
Rippack
The Holms
Hegri Burn
Walli
Swarzie Geo
Busta Brecks
Hesti Geo
South Lighthouse
South Harbour
Meoness
Da Burrian
Muckle Uri Geo
Skadan
Da Keels
Da Skerry

0   metres   1000

FAIR ISLE

Shetland Islands

FAIR ISLE

Orkney Islands

studded peat, the island is nearly surrounded by cliffs: these are highest on the north and west coasts. The coastal scenery is spectacular and varied and the cliffs are highly indented with geos and enhanced with stacks, blowholes, boulder screes and caves, which together provide many nesting places for seabirds and feeding areas for migrants. The distinctive grass-topped stack of Sheep Rock (or Sheep Craig), accessible only by rope or a stout chain, was traditionally a grazing area for some of the island sheep, but has fallen out of use recently. The sloping top of the stack is also a breeding area for Great Black-backed Gulls, whose numbers have tumbled in recent years, and a variety of other seabirds which nest on its steep southern cliff face, including a small but increasing colony of Gannets. The steep geos, with their remote beaches, provide safety for an expanding Grey Seal population – around a hundred pups are born each autumn.

In the north-east, a short isthmus connects Buness with the main island and this provides the base for the road which leads to the pier. The two bays, North and South Havens, form sheltered areas depending on the wind direction, and the pier at North Haven, with its man-made breakwater and ferry-ramp for the *Good Shepherd*, provides a mooring place for visiting fishing boats and pleasure yachts. North Haven also has a fine sandy beach, affording a feeding focus for migrant waders. The beach on the south side of the isthmus is shingle, often with a strand-line of seaweed.

In the south of the island is another low rocky area, stretching from Hesti Geo at the foot of Malcolm's Head and around past the South Light to South Harbour, where low seaweed-covered rocks provide feeding areas for Turnstones and Purple Sandpipers as well as haul-out areas for seals. The kirkyard is situated next the sea, as are so many in Shetland. In South Harbour, the islanders' yoals were traditionally and safely stored in noosts, cut-out hollows in the banks into which the yoals neatly fit. These small clinker-built fishing boats, said to be based on a Viking design and powered by oars or a simple sail, were used for fishing to vary an otherwise monotonous diet and also to trade with passing ships.

The highest hills are Ward Hill (217 metres), Burrashield (150 metres), Malcolm's Head (107 metres) and Vaasetter (100 metres). The island is divided in two by the Hill Dyke (a dry stone wall), which keeps the island's flock of hill sheep on the rough moorland grazing and out of the crofting area in the south of the island. On 'the hill' to the north of Hill Dyke, the Shetland sheep roam freely, fending largely for themselves on the heather moor, the rough grassland and the short maritime heath around the coast. To the south of the Hill Dyke lie the crofts, with better-quality land surrounding the 20 or so croft houses, the school, the kirk, the chapel and the shop.

From the observatory, the single-track road goes north as far as North Light and also down to the pier and North Haven. Running south, a spur leads off and up to the air strip and the main road later divides, and loops around the south, passing each of the croft houses and the other buildings, and off which run further spurs; one to South Light, and another along to five of the croft houses and the Brecks aero generator.

Administratively, Fair Isle is part of the Shetland Isles and is within the area of the Shetland Islands Council (SIC) which provides the ferry service and subsidises the air service, presently run by Directflight but for 35 years previously by Loganair. SIC is also responsible for a variety of other services such as the school, piers, road repairs and the refuse collection, together with some recycling facilities. The island's children are educated at the primary school until the age of 12 when they move to the secondary school in Lerwick as boarders, returning every third weekend. The mains water is supplied by Scottish Water from bore holes and a small dam on the Gilsetter Burn at the Vaadal. Health services are provided by the Shetland NHS Board, which employs a nurse on the island and coordinates the Air Ambulance Service. A doctor visits for a day every six weeks. Post arrives and leaves on the mail boat, the *Good Shepherd* and on the Islander plane.

The agricultural regime is one of crofting, typical of the north and west of Scotland. The land is owned by a laird – since 1954 the National Trust for Scotland (NTS). Each croft has an area of in-bye land (the arable and better grazing where sheep cannot roam free) that was traditionally used to supply the crofters with much of their basic food. The small fields and rigs would be worked for hay and to provide other animal feed and vegetables for the home. A rig is a strip of arable land, perhaps five metres wide and 30 metres long and was worked in rotation, for growing the likes of tatties (potatoes), neeps (turnips), kale (cabbage), and oats, followed by a fallow year. Most crofts would have at least one cow, overwintering in a byre. Some would support larger cross-bred sheep and perhaps one of the small Shetland ponies used as pack animals for transporting goods and peat, cut from the hill. Fair Isle, however, is not particularly rich in peat and only a small amount is cut each year, from the banks on the north side of Ward Hill.

This traditional agricultural scene has changed in recent years and little arable land is cultivated. Nowadays it is only sheep, a few cows, the occasional pig, and chickens and ducks that are kept and the majority of croft land is used for grazing and haylage whilst vegetables are grown in the occasional 'tattie' rig and else-where. Importantly, the change in land use has had a major impact on the amount of cover and food available for migrant birds, which the observatory has tried to counter in recent years by fencing off field corners and small areas and planting trees and bushes to provide cover. Other areas have been ploughed to grow low-maintenance mixed crops. Minimal upkeep also has the advantage of encouraging bird-friendly weeds and these areas now provide a significant food supply for autumn passerine migrants. The crofting area is also criss-crossed by numerous dykes, ditches and fences, and all are used by migrants. Finally, some of the crofts have well-cultivated gardens, providing vegetables for the kitchen and further cover for migrants.

The hill land or scattald is grazed communally with each croft having a share of the grazing rights. The flock is worked cooperatively by all the islanders, together with their dogs, and involves caaing the hill (rounding up the sheep) four or five times a year, a major social event at which visitors are welcome to lend a hand. The hill sheep are of the small Shetland breed, very resilient to the weather and able to survive on the poor grazing. They are traditionally of different colours;

black, white, grey and moorit (a dark, gingery-brown colour). These natural colours are spun and mixed to give the colours for the knitting wool used in the production of the distinctive Fair Isle knitwear. Other traditional island crafts and industries include making straw-backed chairs and spinning wheels, and boat-building.

There are currently 70 people living on the island, forming one of the most active island communities in Shetland. The good fortunes of both the isle and the observatory have gone hand in hand for many years, and it is likely that this inter-dependence will continue for many years into the future.

HISTORY

Fair Isle was recognised as a remarkable place for birds from the early 1900s, when the study of migration was in its infancy. William Eagle Clarke of the then Royal Scottish Museum (RSM) had visited a number of offshore islands and light-houses to which he knew night-migrants were often attracted, his studies into bird migration being instigated by the British Association for the Advancement of Science (recently renamed the British Science Association). He visited the island eight times between 1905 and 1911 to cover the spring and autumn migra-tions and recorded 207 species, then half the total on the British list, and he trained Jerome Wilson of Springfield to hunt and work with him and to collect specimens when he was away from the isle.

His visits were soon followed by others and Mary, Duchess of Bedford, who visited Shetland in her yacht *Sapphire*, stayed at Pund on several occasions between 1910 and 1914. On Clarke's last visit, in 1921, he was accompanied by a younger man, Rear Admiral James Hutton Stenhouse, who was, effectively, to warden the island for the next decade. They stayed at Pund and George Stout was said to comment that 'They lived on bad food and good whisky for a fortnight'. Stenhouse was able, in turn, to pass on the enthusiasm to George Waterston.

George Waterston met Stenhouse as a schoolboy at the RSM and, being a member of the Midlothian Ornithological Club, knew the Misses Baxter and Rintoul. The club had already set up the Isle of May Bird Observatory in 1934, a year after the establishment of Skokholm by Ronald Lockley. Waterston first visited Fair Isle in 1935 and returned annually until the start of the Second World War, sometimes staying with Fieldy – George Stout – on his croft, where the first thoughts of a bird observatory were born.

In June 1941, Waterston was captured in Crete and was a prisoner of war in Germany for the next two and a half years. Amazingly, he found a fellow prisoner with whom to discuss his ideas for the bird observatory on Fair Isle in the shape of Ian Pitman. In October 1943, due to ill health and thanks to the Red Cross, he was invalided out and sent home via Gothenburg. On that journey an epoch-making moment occurred when, amazingly, his first sighting of British soil happened to be Sheep Rock with Fair Isle behind it.

In 1948, Waterston bought the island from Robert Bruce of Sumburgh and the Fair Isle Bird Observatory (FIBO) was launched as a public trust. George was secretary, Ian Pitman treasurer and Sir Arthur Duncan chairman. Ken Williamson was appointed as director and with his wife, Esther, organised the conversion of the old Naval Headquarters at North Haven into the observatory, hostel and laboratory. He set up the scientific programme and constructed the Heligoland traps so that birds could be trapped, ringed and examined in a systematic way. Williamson stayed on the island until 1956 when he left to join the staff of the British Trust for Ornithology (BTO) and was followed by Peter Davis and, later, by Roy Dennis, who oversaw the construction of a new purpose-built observatory in nearby Maver's Cup in 1969.

It was on Fair Isle that Williamson developed his theories of drift migration. It was already known that big falls of migrants could occur in association with south-easterly winds and he went on to examine the weather systems that led to his theories, publishing his work in *Fair Isle and its Birds* (Williamson 1965) and in earlier scientific papers in *British Birds* and elsewhere (e.g. Williamson 1955). The observatory has been fortunate over the years in gaining the support of many notable ornithologists, amongst them Richard Richardson from Norfolk, who saw the island as his second home. He drew many of the vignettes which appeared in the FIBO annual reports and also the one of displaying Arctic Skuas which is used as the symbol of the observatory.

THE OBSERVATORY AND ITS STAFF

The observatory is overseen by Fair Isle Bird Observatory Trust (FIBOT), a charitable trust whose chairman, vice-chairman, finance director and ten directors manage its strategy and direction. Directors' meetings are held at least twice a year, in Edinburgh in the winter and on the island in late spring. The make-up of the board of trustees has varied greatly over the years, with members bringing in various skills and differing areas of expertise. It has recently included an NTS representative and an islander, and it is the trustees who appoint the warden and administrator.

The observatory, a wooden building erected in 1969 and reinforced in block-work in 1989, served its purpose well with comfortable accommodation, a large dining room and a homely lounge. However, 40 years of Fair Isle's climate has taken its toll on the fabric of the structure and in 2008 the Trustees embarked on an ambitious plan to replace it with a modern eco-friendly building with comfortable single, twin and family en-suite bedrooms, a spacious lounge bar, an interpretive centre, conference facilities, shop, ringing room, and increased space and facilities for researchers. The new building, costing over four million pounds, opened in spring 2010. The setting is spectacular, with views out to Sheep Rock and down to the Havens; outside, new pools and sheltered areas have been created, viewable from the lounge. Power is provided by photovoltaic cells on the roof as well as diesel generators located in the old garage near to North Haven, where there is also space for a small workshop, the observatory vehicle, a boat and general storage.

The observatory employs two full-time members of staff: the warden who oversees the ornithological and scientific work of the observatory and the administrator who is responsible for the domestic accommodation and the running of the Lodge. Seasonal ornithological members of staff include an assistant warden, a seabird monitoring officer and a Ranger, this last post being supported by Scottish Natural Heritage as part of their Ranger Service. Seasonal domestic members of staff comprise a cook, an assistant cook and as many as three domestic assistants.

The John Harrison Memorial Fund, set up by the late Richard Richardson, is available to grant-aid working visits by young people to the observatory. An educational scholarship is also offered by FIBOT to selected students to encourage academic research and volunteers are welcome to help out with the observatory work.

Members of staff have their interesting moments, as Deryk Shaw recalls:

> *17 September 1999: I had been called to Gilsetter to look at 'a possible Great Snipe' and was standing with a small crowd peering through a 'scope at a Snipe's head in the long grass. Alex Wood drove up in the obs van, screeched to a halt, wound down the window and yelled 'Deryk, Hollie's waters have broken! The afternoon plane is due in any minute!!' It was approaching 15:00 hrs. My wife was already in Mainland Shetland awaiting the birth of our second child. I told the bemused group they'd have to sort it (the Snipe) out themselves and 'legged' it towards the van, leaving behind mutterings of 'Priorities!' I stood in the obs flat somewhat stunned as Alex packed me a bag, bundled me back into the van and sped to the airstrip where the plane was already waiting. Just over three hours later I was (still stunned) holding a wee baby boy in my arms! We all returned to the isle the following morning! At five days old Fyntan Merlin Shaw scored his first BB 'rare' when his eyes were prised open to look at a Paddyfield Warbler in the ringing room!*

Observatory recording area

The recording area covers the whole of the island, which is divided into three parts for the daily census and surveyed every day from mid-April until spring migration ends in mid-June when seabird work becomes the overriding priority. The daily census begins again in late July and finishes when the warden's assistants depart in early November. Detailed sightings of sea-watches are recorded as are reports of birds seen from the *Good Shepherd* on the 'Fair Isle half' of the ferry-crossing between the island and Mainland Shetland. A daily log is called in the evening, when records of all the sightings are coordinated and this is used to compile the annual Bird Report. Highlights are included in the Friends of Fair Isle Newsletter, whilst records and other information are regularly posted on the observatory's website.

THE BIRDS

From the earliest days, Fair Isle was noted for its breeding seabirds and its large numbers of migrants. Not least, it was recognised as a place where rarities could be found. There can be no place of similar size that has recorded more 'firsts' for the Western Palearctic, Britain, Scotland and the county – and Fair Isle has added no fewer than 27 species to the British List. But, despite having such an impressive list, new species are being added all the time – for example, no fewer than five were added to the island list in a year as recently as 2008. Almost anything can turn up at any time and often does. It is one of the magical things about the place that you don't know what is around the corner, or what will fly past next and the tales of finding rarities are legion.

However, a number of species are missing from the county list because of Shetland's geographical position. Nick Riddiford, ex-warden, recalls being asked:

What is the best bird you saw during your time at the observatory? This question, sometimes framed as 'What is the rarest bird' is one of the most frequent fired at me by birders wherever I am in the world – and, let's face it, Fair Isle's reputation goes worldwide amongst the birding community. My answer usually disappoints, whichever question is posed, even though it is true. My mind drifts back to 22 April 1987. I was on a round of the traps before heading south. A steady east wind was enough to heighten expectation and quicken the step. I was given little time to dwell on the implications of an empty first trap because my attention was diverted to a biggish black and white bird taking off from the wall beyond. My first thought was "that Oystercatcher's got a long tail". Deployment of the binoculars soon resolved that one: a Magpie. Very well, so the Magpie is not Britain's rarest bird, but in the Fair Isle context... it shares the 'one Fair Isle record' tag with the likes of Great Bustard and Dusky Thrush but in many ways was even less expected.

I could hardly contain my excitement at the time, and on reflection it was the total surprise as much as the (local) rarity value that made the moment so thrilling. It all goes to show that rarity, as defined by the birder, is relative. The story has a coda. At lunchtime, I received a phone call from a very excited islander: "You'll never guess what's sitting on my wall" she said. The falling tone of her voice told that she was crushed by my answer. It's not just birders who want to be first to the bird. But despite its extreme rarity, no-one asked me to write a description. Just as well; likening it to an Oystercatcher might have seriously undermined my credibility! The 1987 Magpie is still the only Shetland record.

Winter

Shetland winters are long and dark, often with poor weather. Short days allow only a few hours for feeding at these northern latitudes and many species have to leave for the winter, whilst the resident Rock Doves, Rock Pipits, Wrens, corvids, Starlings and House Sparrows remain. Occasionally a handful of migrant Robins, thrushes, finches or Snow Buntings, left over from the autumn, attempt to spend the winter, plus the odd Water Rail, Merlin or Long-eared Owl. A few waders also hang on, the Turnstones and Purple Sandpipers around the coast and Snipe, Jack Snipe and a few Curlews and Redshanks in the fields, but the depths of winter generally see few birds in any numbers. However, cold-weather movements on the Continent can result in flocks of Lapwings or Golden Plovers turning up, or perhaps a skein of geese or Whooper Swans flying through, and winter gales can bring large roosts of storm-bound Herring and Great Black-backed Gulls, often with Glaucous or Iceland Gulls mixed in. These Herring Gulls frequently have darker upper wings and mantle, indicating a more easterly origin.

Most seabirds also depart, and even some of the (otherwise) resident Shags and Tysties (Black Guillemots) leave the isle for more sheltered waters where juvenile birds can get some protection from the winter storms. Little Auks can sometimes be seen in numbers offshore and a few Long-tailed Ducks, Red-breasted Mergansers or Goldeneyes join the resident Eiders. However, even winter can produce surprises such as the Great Bustard which arrived in January 1970. It was captured and fed on a diet of cabbages until April when it was transported to Wiltshire as part of a reintroduction scheme. Harlequin Duck, Gyr Falcon, Ivory Gull, Black-bellied Dipper *Cinclus cinclus cinclus* and Black-throated Thrush have all been discovered in December or January.

In late January or early February the first of the Oystercatchers will be heard, 'kleeping' their eagerness to return to their breeding grounds. Subsequently there are small influxes of Curlew and Ringed Plover and then Skylarks and Meadow Pipits move slowly north onto nesting areas. But even in winter there can be the odd good day, although the weather suggests otherwise. Deryk Shaw recounts such a moment on 3 February 2000:

A slight reprieve from the howling north-westerly wind and driving sleet allowed for a walk around the south of the isle. I ventured down the east side and got as far as the Haa without having seen very much. I was scanning out to sea following a flock of Whooper Swans when a large bird rose up from below the cliff in South Harbour. It hung in the wind and, to my amazement, I saw it was a white-

Gordon Barnes with the Great Bustard which arrived on Fair Isle in January 1970, a welcome surprise in mid-winter. (Photo: Dennis Coutts)

morph Gyr Falcon. It sank out of view and I ran to the edge of the cliff in time to see it rise up again and hang just a few feet overhead; an absolutely unforgettable moment.

It then drifted a short way inland and pounced on a Starling at Skerryholm before gathering it up in one foot and powering its way towards Malcolm's Head. It spent the next fortnight near the airstrip, usually sitting quietly on a rock, but from time to time it would give a marvellous aerial display as it chased Ravens, Starlings, pigeons and rabbits around the south of the isle. Virtually every islander made the effort to see it during this time and I received many excited phone calls over the two weeks from people regaling me with their experiences with this magnificent raptor. It still ranks as the best bird I have ever had the good fortune to spend time with on Fair Isle.

Spring migration and exceptional days

Spring arrives late in the Northern Isles. It can be well into March or even April before the first 'proper' migrants begin to appear, but eventually, with the lengthening days, they come. The first are often thrushes and early finches and species such as Stonechat and Goldcrest. Numbers can be impressive, as in early April 1984, when 3,000 Blackbirds descended on the isle, the vast majority of which headed off in an easterly to north-easterly direction as dusk approached, one or two at a time and calling as they went. Deryk Shaw remembers another 'big' day on 30 March 2001:

My new assistant warden, Paul French, had arrived the previous day and the plan was to show him the census routes. However, as soon as we stepped outside it became apparent there had been a very large fall. We trapped 30 Blackbirds on the way out and processed them in the ringing hut as fast as we could before venturing further south. It was incredible; the fields were carpeted with Blackbirds, akin to a recently ploughed field covered in Rooks in rural England. There were several hundred other thrushes mixed in and a similar number of Robins – a 'tic-tic' could be heard around every corner. By the evening, Paul's head was spinning. Final totals for the day were a Garganey, 50 Woodcock, 100 Skylark, 400 Robin, 2,500 Blackbird, 500 Fieldfare, 650 Song Thrush, 380 Redwing, 40 Chiffchaff, 73 Chaffinch and three White-spotted Bluethroats Luscinia svecica cyanecula. *The lack of manpower and daylight meant that only the south of the island was censused so who knows how many Blackbirds (or whatever else) the north may have held. I assured Paul that it was not like this every day on Fair Isle!*

Depending on the weather conditions, and especially the wind direction, migrant numbers increase through April both in terms of the range of species and the numbers of birds. Many are in full breeding plumage and males will sometimes give quick bursts of song. However, it is generally in May when there is the best chance of a spectacular arrival, particularly if the wind is in the east or south-east. The falls can be memorable on suitable days as Roy Dennis, the then warden, found on 3 May 1969.

The day started off quietly and only a Redwing and a Blackbird were caught on the first round of the traps, nothing in fact to predict one of Fair Isle's most outstanding falls of migrants. The wind was east to north-east and force 3–4, the skies were overcast all day but the drizzle cleared at mid-day.

At midday six Tree Pipits arrived at the observatory and very soon it was obvious that many migrants were coming in –a short walk to South Haven beach yielded 12 Tree Pipits, a Black Redstart, two Whinchats and an Ortolan Bunting. A round of the traps after lunch found that birds were streaming onto the isle, especially Tree Pipits, and Gilsetter was full of them. On a walk up past Setter to Gunnawark there were Tree Pipits everywhere, and they were very much in evidence along the west cliffs with flocks of up to 30 and 40 coming in from the north and coasting down to the crofting land. The air was full of their cries – a thrilling spectacle. Small numbers of other species were mixed up in these flocks and included Redstarts, Whinchats, Pied Flycatchers and Bramblings. In the sheltered hollows many very tired Willow Warblers were searching for insects, and virtually formed a moving carpet on the wet ground above Troili Geo, flicking away as you walked along. There were fewer birds on the north cliffs but very large numbers at the south end of the island.

Such was the excitement that the evening meal was a brief affair before everyone headed back south to have a look at the crofting land. A field of new-sown oats at Stackhoull held four Ortolan Buntings feeding together, but this record was short-lived because there were no fewer than 14 feeding on the Shirva croft, most of them superbly-plumaged males. Spurred on, every croft had been searched for migrants before dusk and the tally was exceptional.

A total of 77 species was recorded on the island during the day, the numbers of Tree Pipits being outstanding and very difficult to estimate. The following migrants were observed (the numbers for the common species are certainly an absolute minimum and the numbers actually present were probably a good deal more): one Wood Sandpiper, five Common Sandpipers, Cuckoo, 45 Wrynecks, House Martin, in excess of 1,500 Tree Pipits, three male Grey-headed Wagtails of the race *Motacilla flava thunbergi,* one male Yellow Wagtail *Motacilla flava flavissima,* 75 Robins, Bluethroat, Black Redstart, 75 Redstarts, 130 Whinchats, many Wheatears, 300 Ring Ouzels, 35 Blackbirds, 250 Fieldfares, 150 Song Thrushes, two Grasshopper Warblers, Blackcap, Whitethroat, six Chiffchaffs, 400 Willow Warblers, 25 Pied Flycatchers, two Great Grey Shrikes, 20 Chaffinches, 500 Bramblings, Siskin, three Bullfinches, two Lapland Buntings, 32 Ortolan Buntings and 80 Reed Buntings. This still ranks as one of the best days ever known on Fair Isle and the numbers of Wrynecks, Tree Pipits, Ring Ouzels and Ortolan Buntings are all record day-totals.

More exceptional spring days

Early May 1970 saw another exceptional few days when 107 species were recorded and numbers rivalled the fall of the previous year. On the 7th the wind was south-easterly and force 5 just after dawn but decreased quickly, giving way to a fine sunny day. A few captures on the early trap-round suggested an arrival of migrants overnight and a good selection of newly arrived birds were found on the morning search of the croft-land. However, most of the day's excitements occurred after lunch. The 'best' bird was a superb male Black-headed Wagtail *Motacilla flava feldegg* at Easter Lother Water and the totals for other migrants included: Quail, 12 Wrynecks, 100 Tree Pipits, three Blue-headed Wagtails *M. f. flava* and two Grey-headed Wagtails *M. f. thunbergi*, two Bluethroats, eight Black Redstarts (then a record day-total), 30 Redstarts, 33 Whinchats, 10 Grasshopper Warblers, 19 Lesser Whitethroats, Wood Warbler, 100 Willow Warblers, 11 Pied Flycatchers, 14 Tree Sparrows, 22 Bramblings and two Ortolan Buntings. A total of 37 birds was ringed.

On the 8th the wind backed around to the east with a few showers before break-fast, and with increasing clouds and a shower at dusk, on what was otherwise a fine sunny day. The numbers of migrants had increased considerably, especially Willow Warblers, Whinchats and Redstarts while, unlike the previous May, Tree Pipits were less plentiful and Ring Ouzels were scarce. The rarest bird of the day was a Thrush Nightingale trapped in the morning at Setter. With the wind fresh for most of the day, large numbers of birds were sheltering in the north and west cliffs. The numbers seen on a walk in the afternoon from Gunnawark to the North Light staggered the senses; Lerness was alive with small passerines and the slopes actually appeared to be moving. The sheer numbers made for a very long and complicated roll-call that evening and the final totals were: Tufted Duck, Coot, eight Common Sandpipers, two Cuckoos, Short-eared Owl, 15 Wrynecks, two Shore Larks, 350 Tree Pipits, 10 Dunnocks, 66 Robins, nine Bluethroats, 300 Redstarts, 350 Whinchats, 15 Ring Ouzels, 34 Fieldfares, 49 Song Thrushes, eight Blackcaps, 13 Whitethroats, 50 Chiffchaffs, 1,000 Willow Warblers, 35 Pied Flycatchers, five Red-backed Shrikes, two Ortolan Buntings and 140 Reed Buntings. One hundred and thirty birds were ringed; six of the species were new for the year and a Dutch-ringed Redstart was caught in the afternoon.

The wind backed further to north-east on the 9th and the day was bright and sunny. The island was still alive with passerines and some species had increased further overnight, especially Redstarts. A new Thrush Nightingale was discovered at Hesti Geo at midday and trapped a little later. The island was again very well covered by observers who found that most species were either present in the same strength or that numbers had increased. Redstart numbers rose from 300 to 700, Wrynecks had increased to 35 and there were 31 Bluethroats. Other totals were 100 or more Robins, 500 Tree Pipits, 45 Whitethroats, 120 Pied Flycatchers, 14 Red-backed Shrikes, 21 Tree Sparrows, 35 Bramblings, and eight Ortolan Buntings. A wonderful mixture of *flava* wagtails included three Blue-heads *M. f. flava*, four Grey-heads *M. f. thunbergi* and a Yellow *M. f. flavissima* as well as the Black-head *M. f. feldegg*, which had moved to Byerwall. In total, 199 birds of 25

Great Skuas nest in good numbers on the hill, with most returning from their pelagic wintering areas by early April (Rebecca Nason – www.rebeccanason.com).

species were ringed during the day; the higher totals including 54 Redstarts, 31 Willow Warblers, 27 Robins, 14 Whitethroats, five Wrynecks and five Bluethroats.

As May comes to an end, the commoner species decline and scarcer species such as Marsh Warbler, Red-backed Shrike and Rustic Bunting are frequently recorded. Rarities are expected at the end of May and into June and exotic species such as Black-eared Wheatear, River and Savi's Warblers, Lesser Grey Shrike, White-crowned Sparrow, Serin, Citril Finch and Cretzschmar's Bunting have all been found at this time of year.

Late spring though can also be a time of amazing arrivals, such as 27 May 1992. Spotted Flycatchers were everywhere, with a record-breaking 350 logged. Twelve Wood Warblers and no fewer than 11 Icterine Warblers also represented record-breaking counts. Two Subalpine Warblers appeared, whilst Red-backed Shrikes numbered 20 and Bluethroats eight; there was barely time to double-check a couple of Nightingales. A Shore Lark was found on the Houll, whilst searching for a possible Bonelli's Warbler. Three Red-throated Pipits and four Common Rosefinches were also found, whilst a Sandwich Tern was new for the year. As for common migrants, the most notable counts were: 12 Lesser Whitethroats and 30 Whitethroats, 60 Garden and eight Sedge Warblers. The evening produced two Marsh Warblers and a superb Honey-buzzard, the latter pausing briefly before continuing north. It was approaching midnight before the log was completed – with an incredible 94 species recorded!

The 28th was not quite as spectacular but still very impressive. Although Spotted Flycatchers again numbered 350, ringing activities indicated there had been a considerable turnover of birds. A new male Subalpine Warbler, showing characters of the eastern race *Sylvia cantillans albistriata*, was found at the top of Ward Hill and there were two new Marsh Warblers and another Nightingale. The five Common Rosefinches included two red males and a record 15 Wood Warblers were found along with six Grey-headed Wagtails *M. f. thunbergi*, eight Bluethroats, nine Icterine Warblers and 20 Red-backed Shrikes. In the evening, the now regular raptor chase occurred, this time the target being the spring's first Hobby.

The wind remained a gentle easterly and there were more surprises in store on the 29th. The seventh Red-throated Pipit of the spring was found at Busta and there were two new Red-footed Falcons, another first-summer male and a stunning female. Among the common migrants there were increases in Redstart (15), Whinchat (12) and Willow Warbler (40). Incredibly, there were still 350 Spotted Flycatchers on the island. A second Hobby, this time an adult, three Sandwich Terns, two Marsh Warblers and six Common Rosefinches were found on the 30th, but bird of the day was undoubtedly a singing Greenish Warbler. Almost inevitably, the 31st was duller, but it still produced the eighth and ninth Red-throated Pipits of the spring, along with 280 Spotted Flycatchers and a record nine Common Rosefinches. Most observers fortunate enough to have been present during the last week of May that year agreed that it ranked as one of the best week's birdwatching they had experienced anywhere in the world!

Breeding birds

Gannets and Fulmars can be seen on any fine winter's day and return early to their nest sites and Guillemots and Razorbills often repair to their ledges on fine days in early March. The first Puffins are back on their grassy slopes and Bonxies (Great Skuas) have returned to the hill by early April. Arctic Skuas have taken up territories by early May when the first Tirricks – the Shetland Arctic Terns – appear, often rapidly building up to thousands of birds on some days.

As summer sets in, the emphasis of the work shifts to ringing and monitoring programmes. Seabird populations in Shetland expanded rapidly during the 1970s and early 1980s, but many species have declined since the early 1990s – often dramatically. A shortage of sandeels, their main food, appears to be the main reason. Our regular seabird studies are carried out under contract to the Joint Nature Conservation Committee (JNCC) to help ascertain the health of Britain's seabirds as a whole (Fair Isle being one of their four 'key sites') and it was here that the current seabird/sandeel crisis was first noticed.

During the late 1980s, feeding watches of species such as Puffin, Razorbill and Guillemot, where it is very obvious what the adults are bringing back, showed they were starting to feed their chicks on the fry of fish belonging to the Gadidae – the family of fish which includes many of our common fish such as Whiting, Cod, Haddock and Pollack. Unfortunately for the chicks, the fry of these fish are far less nutritious than sandeels and consequently fewer chicks were surviving to fledging.

These observations are backed up with data we collect through our ringing activities. Measurements are taken to monitor the growth of chicks and both adults and chicks are ringed to monitor survival. Whilst in the colonies we also collect diet samples which are analysed to identify which species of fish are being brought in by the adults. From these data, survival estimates are calculated.

For the really numerous species such as Fulmar, Guillemot, Puffin and Razorbill, populations are monitored annually from counts of study plots, as it is impractical to count them all every year when you have a population of 50,000–100,000 birds! The study plot is a defined sub-area of a colony, carefully mapped out on an image of the cliff so that counts can be replicated from year to year. To supplement these annual counts, complete island censuses are undertaken as part of a rolling programme. For less numerous species such as the skuas, terns and Gannet, whole island counts are carried out each year.

Tables 1 and 2 illustrate how the populations of some of the seabird species have changed since 1969 and 1987 respectively. It is all too easy to see that if the current rate of decline in species like Kittiwake and Puffin continues then they may not be breeding on the island in the near future. These changes in population and the continued threats of overfishing and climate change ensure that this monitoring will remain a vital part of the observatory's work in the future.

Guillemot, Razorbill and Shag colonies are reached either by descents (drops) from the cliff-top or by use of the observatory's inflatable Zodiac boat. Puffins, being burrow nesters, present their own problems – finding short burrows is important as the birds move out of range in the longer ones. The Ranger's 'Puffin-walks' are always popular with visitors who adore their bright bills and shuffling gait, only to discover at Roskilie that they are most definitely not that cute when taken in the hand for ringing.

Tysties nest in nooks and crannies on various cliffs from easily accessible to the steepest geos. When searching out Tystie nests, breeding Rock Doves are frequently encountered at the back of some of the deeper caves. Gannets first nested in 1974, with successful breeding confirmed in the following years; they have expanded rapidly on the west cliffs and have now colonised Sheep Rock. Bonxies and Arctic Skuas nest on the hill and both are well known for their extremely aggressive defence of their nests; the monitoring visits invariably involve being clipped, rather painfully, around the ear or back of the head by their feet.

Arctic Terns, interspersed with a few pairs of Common Terns, breed on some of the flatter areas of low heath. It appears that if birds fail in one year they may move elsewhere the following year. This is almost certainly why the Fair Isle population rose from 83 pairs in 1986 to a peak of 2,836 in 2001. However, productivity has always been patchy and no young were fledged during 2000–2005. By 2004 the population had declined to 11 pairs. This trend was briefly reversed in 2006 when 800 pairs fledged over 300 chicks, but 2007 saw a return to poor form when 208 pairs failed to raise any young and the colonies were deserted by mid-June. Despite *c.*400 prospecting in mid-May, no birds nested in 2008.

Small numbers of Storm Petrels breed around the precipitous cliffs and for many years they have been ringed at night on the cliff tops near to their nesting areas. More effort has gone into the nocturnal trapping of these seabirds since

Table 1. *Changes in whole-island counts of seabird populations on Fair Isle 1969–2008.*

Fair Isle whole island counts

	Fulmar	Gannet	Shag	Kittiwake	Arctic Tern	Great Skua	Arctic Skua	Guillemot	Razorbill	Puffin	Black Guillemot
1969	16,264	0				8		10,000			
1975	25,674	17				21	135	19,000			
1986		258	1,099	19,075		84	115	33,607	3,882	20,224	367
1987		304				72	95	32,437			
1988		488		19,340	211	78	78		5,114		
1989		676			345	72	114	32,321		23,050	345
1990		643			283	75	105				
1991	35,213	687	1,073		400	79	99				
1992		781			650	110	109				
1993		764	646	18,159	1,100	101	107		4,130		280
1994		825			808	101	93				304
1995		965			615	130	87			17,386	277
1996	43,178	1,090			1,200	120	86				
1997		1,116		11,650	1,250	152	98				
1998		1,118	556		1,730	79	67		3,296		206
1999		1,123			1,249	132	69	39,257			230
2000	20,424	1,162		8,175	562	135	65		3,599	15,118	
2001		1,406	663	8,204	1,251	143	78			13,507	
2002		1,585			2,836	133	60				
2003		1,866	732		115	145	55				
2004		1,875			80	96	33				
2005	27,896	1,817		5,399	11	144	71	27,320	3,421		
2006		2,145			47	189	105			6,915	
2007		1,957			818	224	68				
2008		2,488	235	2,688	208	294	37				

Table 2. *Changes in plot counts of seabird populations on Fair Isle 1987–2008.*

	Fulmar	Shag	Kittiwake	Guillemot	Black Guillemot
Plot counts of Fair Isle's seabirds					
1987	439	240	1,446	3,278	220
1988	398	221	1,406	2,388	253
1989	419	241	1,427	2,475	286
1990	423	202	1,363	1,757	263
1991	401	198	1,253	2,551	241
1992	469	175	1,230	3,161	215
1993	361	174	997	3,045	190
1994	373	171	975	2,934	240
1995	387	160	917	2,675	216
1996	431	206	924	2,703	224
1997	400	163	885	2,926	254
1998	379	135	765	–	160
1999	339	96	751	2,658	144
2000	404	155	716	3,174	173
2001	364	149	695	2,446	139
2002	358	135	441	2,489	124
2003	337	119	463	2,022	157
2004	160	122	273	1,496	115
2005	266	97	391	2,030	144
2006	314	137	349	2,116	151
2007	278	131	283	1,429	164
2008	300	55	137	980	144

the late 1970s, when it was realised that non-breeding birds could be tape-lured at suitable sites around the coast. This usually takes place near to South Haven on suitably calm nights during July and August, and it is the highlight of many a visitor's holiday to see and touch one of the world's smallest seabird species. There is also the possible bonus of seeing one of the small number of Leach's Petrels that are caught every year.

Away from the cliffs the few passerine species to breed regularly are Skylark, Meadow and Rock Pipits, an endemic race of Wren *Troglodytes troglodytes fridariensis* known as the Fair Isle Wren, Wheatear, Hooded Crow, Raven, the endemic Shetland race of Starling *Sturnus vulgaris zetlandicus,* House Sparrow and Twite. Of these, the well-studied Starlings are the most numerous and seem to be nesting every few metres along some of the stone dykes. By mid-June, the first broods have fledged and form noisy flocks, following the adults about and begging for food. The Fair Isle Wren population has also been the subject of an annual census for many years. The numbers of this cliff-dwelling endemic have fluctuated, reaching a peak of 52 territories in 1964 and falling to a low of 10 in 1981, but stabilising in the past 20 years at around 30–40.

On the wetter areas Lapwings, Snipe and Curlew all nest and Oystercatchers are common, nesting on any patch of gravel and occasionally by the side of the road. Ringed Plovers can also be found nesting in the drier areas. A few pairs of Common Gulls have a colony on Buness and the larger gulls, Herring, Lesser Black-backed and Great Black-backed, breed in small numbers around the coast.

Observatory work involves more than just the study of migrants. The Fair Isle Wren, Troglodytes troglodytes fridariensis, is a race endemic to the island and has been the subject of various research projects since it was first described by Ken Williamson in 1951 (Rebecca Nason – www.rebeccanason. com).

Eiders can be encountered nesting almost anywhere amongst the heather in the north of the island, and the females sit so tight you can touch them.

Migrants will stay to breed in some years. Byres are occasionally used by Swallows, a few pairs of *alba* wagtails nest in tussocky cliffs and even Grey and two races of Yellow Wagtails have bred near streams. In eruption years it is in the summer that the first flocks of Common Crossbills arrive and on Fair Isle they tend to feed on thrift and heather. Several species, unfortunately, no longer breed, including White-tailed Eagle, Corncrake, House Martin, Robin, Blackbird and Corn Bunting. An attempt was made to reintroduce 'sea-eagles' in 1968, but this was unsuccessful, not least because the released birds became contaminated with Fulmar oil. Three young birds from Norway were held in release cages on the hill to acclimatise before being given their freedom and, although the attempt failed, it did pave the way for successful introductions in the west of Scotland in later years. Peregrines nested successfully again in 2008, for the first time since 1969.

Seabirds apart, the *zetlandicus* race of Starling has been the subject of the longest study on the isle. Peter Evans commenced a study into the breeding biology and population genetics of this isolated population in 1980 and he and Jane Reid (with the aid of a number of PhD/MSc students) continue it to this day. The native Fair Isle Starlings differ genetically from those from the Shetland mainland and both are distinct from mainland Starlings in being larger and having darker-plumaged juveniles. Away from the cliffs, all of the breeding pairs in the middle of the island are part of this long-term research project, which targets those nesting in dykes and piles of stones. The sites are visited each year and records are kept of timing of breeding, clutch size and hatching and fledging success as well as nestling growth rates and adult measurements. Many of the chicks are individually colour-ringed, which enables their subsequent return and breeding activities to be monitored closely.

Whilst the adult Starlings remain throughout the year, the juveniles leave for their first winter, with most going south rather than north to Shetland, and a few penetrating even as far as southern Britain. However, many of them return for the next breeding season and set up territory very close to or in the same site as where they fledged. Most females nest in their first summer (being the first summer after the one in which they fledged) whilst males tend to start breeding in their second summer. Between 150 and 250 pairs of Starlings now nest on the island and, although the breeding numbers vary from year to year, the overall population is healthy and, unlike some parts of Europe, is slowly increasing.

FIBOT are always keen to encourage research on the island and this is often into breeding birds. An educational scholarship scheme is in place to help support approved students to carry out such academic research.

Autumn migration

Autumn migration can begin as early as mid-June when waders that have failed to breed begin heading south. Curlew, Lapwing and Golden Plover are generally the most numerous, and Sanderling, Ruff and Knot can appear in small numbers, especially in years when the season has been poor in the far north. Oystercatchers also start heading for their wintering quarters and Whimbrels are regularly heard migrating overhead in July, after leaving their breeding grounds in Shetland, the Faeroes and Iceland.

Passerine migration doesn't usually start until August and even then can be slow, although the best dates for Aquatic Warbler happen to be around the 12th. Warblers become a daily feature from then on with Barred and Icterines occurring together with flycatchers and species such as Wryneck and Common Rosefinch arriving. By the end of the month large flocks of Meadow Pipits, wagtails and Wheatears are moving south and warblers such as Greenish and Arctic may well appear. The flocks of pipits are often chased by Merlins and ringing has shown that many of these small raptors are Shetland-bred birds and not from Iceland as Williamson (1965) suggested. The traditional time for rarities is from September through to the last week in October and a series of notables are found in every year. Fair Isle specialities include Yellow-breasted Bunting (103 records up to the end of 2008), Lanceolated Warbler (79 records), Olive-backed Pipit (76 records), Citrine Wagtail (60 records), Pechora Pipit (41 records) and Pallas's Grasshopper Warbler (20 records). Many even rarer species from the east and west have also been discovered in this period, including, in more recent times: Siberian Rubythroat (1975, 2003, 2005), Eyebrowed Thrush (1987, 1992), Baillon's Crake (1991), Blackpoll Warbler (1991), Solitary Sandpiper (1992), Hermit Thrush (1995), Harlequin Duck (1999), Brown Shrike (2000), Pallid Swift and Black-faced Bunting (2001),

The first Citrine Wagtail recorded in Britain and Ireland was caught in the Gully trap on Fair Isle as recently as 1954. There have been a further 231 records since, inclusing 59 on Fair Isle (Rebecca Nason – www.rebeccanason.com).

Buff-bellied Pipit and Grey-cheeked Thrush (2007) and Siberian Thrush and Asian Brown Flycatcher (2008).

From the last week in September impressive skeins of geese are a feature as they head south. Odd parties occasionally stop and it is quite a sight to see a flock of Barnacle or Pink-footed Geese quietly feeding amongst the migrant thrushes. Whooper Swans from Iceland regularly fly through, again stopping only occasionally. Slightly later can come large falls of Fieldfares and other Scandinavian migrants, not least of which are Woodcock and Lapland Buntings.

October can be even better than September both in terms of numbers and the quality of rarities. One such occasion was from 14 to19 October 2003. A streaky brown bunting-type bird at Neder Taft on the 14th was, after a couple of hours of deliberation, confirmed as Britain's third (Fair Isle's second) Savannah Sparrow and sparked one of the biggest mass twitches to Fair Isle. Over the course of the next few days, planes and boats arrived from as far south as the Isles of Scilly. Those landing at the airstrip on the 17th were greeted with the now legendary line: 'So lads, what do you want to see first – the Savannah Sparrow or the Siberian Rubythroat?' The latter had been found during morning census, sparking further pandemonium. The visiting birders were airborne at the time the news broke and were blissfully unaware there were now two extremely good birds on Fair Isle, one from each side of the world. Their faces must have been a picture! Around 150 people travelled north to see the birds and some even made the long journey from the Isles of Scilly to Fair Isle twice in a few days! Fair Isle airstrip recorded more traffic than Sumburgh during the period and the FIBO tick tin raised £900.

As is often the case with Fair Isle though, just when you think things couldn't possibly get better, along comes another autumn to prove you very, very wrong. This time it was October 2004 with not one but two firsts for the Western Palearctic – in the space of seven days!

First, on the 16th, a puzzling bunting in the bird-cover crop at Skadan was giving only fleeting views and appeared to show some features of many species but never wholly fitted any one in particular. A net was erected and it was trapped but that didn't help either. It really was a mystery. It was eventually identified back in the ringing room when a copy of *Birding World* (2001) was found with a picture of the mystery bird along with the caption: '...Chestnut-eared Buntings breed in north-east China and Korea and are middle to long-distance migrants to their wintering grounds in south-east Asia. This species has not been recorded in Western Europe, but a bit of blind optimism never hurts...!'

News was released on the grapevines and this sparked off another major twitch to Fair Isle (akin to 2003) with many familiar faces returning to 'tick' it. As the warden Deryk Shaw waved off the Shetland birding crew, who had made the trip in a boat, he assured them 'You'll all be back again next week for the real biggie!' Never a truer word spoken ...

On 23 October FIBOT finance director Mike Wood was strolling to Stackhoull Stores (the island's shop) with his family when he found what looked like a young Robin. Realising this was perhaps unlikely in October he grabbed the nearest (and only) birder he could find, Mark Newell. Deryk was on Ward Hill and they informed him there was a *Catharus* thrush at Bulls Park. By the time he arrived it had been identified as Veery, but Deryk wasn't totally convinced. For although the breast markings were good for Veery, the reddish tail contrast with the more olive-brown upperparts was more like Hermit Thrush.

Tentative news was put out, but no-one was entirely happy with the identification. It was over lunch and with the aid of literature and the internet that the true identity was discovered. Deryk was staring in disbelief at a Rufous-tailed Robin on the computer screen when Alan Bull burst into the office with a picture he'd found of the same species in a journal. Unbelievably it was another first for the Western Palearctic! Stunned, they returned to the scene and informed Mark Newell who had been left on watch. He was quite pleased! Deryk then phoned Paul Harvey who was on a boat with the Shetland crew, zooming their way towards Fair Isle and not knowing if they were coming to see a Veery or a Hermit Thrush. Phone reception was poor but he managed to get the words 'Rufous-tailed Robin!' across before he lost signal. The atmosphere on that boat must have been electric! Unfortunately for others, they were the only off-island birders to see it, as it departed overnight.

October 2008

Just as the 1970s saw a run of phenomenal falls in spring, so the 2000s have in the autumn. The theme continues with late September and early October 2008 going down as one of the best autumn periods on record for scarce and rare migrants. It all started on 23 September with a Buff-breasted Sandpiper at North Light before breakfast, followed by an extremely obliging Lanceolated Warbler in Bulls' Park mid-morning. After lunch, a Red-throated Pipit was discovered in Boini Mire and half-an-hour later one of the assistant wardens, Simon Davies, rang to say a Pectoral Sandpiper had just dropped in by the Haa. Just minutes later he rang again to say he had found a Pallas's Grasshopper Warbler at Busta Geo. Everyone headed for the south-east corner of the isle and after a few tense moments the bird showed itself (albeit rather obscurely on the stony beach at the base of the cliff) resulting in many big smiles and pats on the back for the finder. Whilst on the way home for tea, the day was rounded off with another Lanceolated Warbler in Gilsetter – found by Micky Maher, who had also found the first one that day – it was a lively bar and bird log that evening!

The following day it was Deryk Shaw's turn to grab the limelight. Whilst following a flock of ten Yellow-browed Warblers up Ward Hill he glimpsed a dumpy flycatcher near the top, but unfortunately there was no sign of it by the time he arrived. However, a brief sighting as he headed towards the peat cuttings suggested it might be something 'better' than just a Spotted, Pied or Red-breasted Flycatcher. It took another half-an-hour to track it down at the communications mast where, to his relief and exhilaration, he was able to confirm it as a first-winter Asian Brown Flycatcher. It showed well to all-comers throughout the day and there was a steady procession of islanders, coming in their cars to see what everyone was so excited about. Luckily the track to the mast had just been resurfaced following tremendous rainfall on 10 August when 100 millimetres fell in one day and washed away the surface! Then, as the light was fading the other assistant, Mark Breaks, got in on the action with a nice Red-flanked Bluetail at Kenaby. A record total of 45 Yellow-browed Warblers plus Pectoral Sandpiper and Corncrake, with a nice variety of common migrants meant the log that evening took far longer than usual – but nobody minded!

It got better the following morning. A Honey-buzzard flew over prior to break-fast and an unstreaked *Acrocephalus* warbler set pulses racing for a while before it was trapped and identified as a Reed Warbler. After breakfast, Deryk was searching for the flycatcher as there was a group of twitchers sitting at Tingwall airport awaiting news of the bird, when he stumbled upon a stunning first-winter male Siberian Thrush in Guidicum. This was special: he'd found two major rarities in two days and although this one was not as rare as the first (it was the eighth for Britain and Ireland), it somehow felt more worthy – one of those dream birds that every birder hopes to find! Shaking and barely able to press the digits on his phone he put out news of the latest find. Unsurprisingly, despite the negative news on the flycatcher, the charter plane came in! To add to the sense of occasion an Arctic Warbler, Red-breasted Flycatcher, three Bluethroats, two Common Rosefinches and a Little Bunting were also found that afternoon. Yellow-browed Warblers had dropped to a disappointing 32!

The next few days continued in a similar vein with a nice scattering of scarce and common migrants, but there was a lull in the arrival of rarities with the best new bird being a Siberian Stonechat *Saxicola torquata maura/stejnegeri*. As

September gave way to October the flow picked up once again and an Arctic Redpoll of the nominate race *Carduelis hornemanni hornemanni* at Setter after breakfast on the 1st was quickly followed with a Sabine's Gull floating through and barely an hour later the second Pallas's Grasshopper Warbler of the autumn was discovered near Springfield – unlike the first this one was extremely obliging, creeping around in rough grass, allowing excellent views and some stunning photographs to be taken. To cap the morning off there was still time for a fleeting White's Thrush before lunch, although the majority of people had to wait until the afternoon to catch up with this enigmatic bird. As if having one White's Thrush on the island wasn't good enough, it turned out there were in fact two birds – one at Swatzi Geo and the other (another feather in Deryk's cap) at Sma Trinket Geo! Amazingly, and perhaps a sign of how the status of this species has changed in the last few years, a third bird arrived a week later!

Commoner autumn migrants

September and October are also the months when there can be huge falls of common migrants, with warblers and flycatchers predominant around the middle of September. Once into October, the most numerous migrants become the thrushes, Goldcrests and finches, notably Chaffinch, Brambling and Siskin. Under the right weather conditions the numbers of thrushes can almost be uncountable – the hill land often occupied by flock after flock of Redwings, with Blackbirds all the way along every dyke. Such a day was 14 October 1979 when a staggering 65,000 Redwings were estimated, along with 2,000 Fieldfare but, perhaps surprisingly, only 300 Blackbirds. It seems to be a rare event to get large numbers of all the thrush species at the same time. Woodcock, usually a difficult-to-see species, can be a real feature of October on Fair Isle and occasionally they can occur in large numbers. On 27 October 1976 there were at least 1,000 present on the island and days where more than 100 have been seen are numerous. Some of the expected and more abundant scarce migrants are species such as Short-toed Lark, Richard's Pipit, Yellow-browed Warbler and Little Bunting.

   November still sees significant numbers of migrants, typically species like Long-eared Owls, Great Grey Shrikes, Waxwings, Woodcock and Snipe. There will still be flocks of thrushes and finches, but not in the same huge numbers as in September and October, although some large movements of Fieldfare do occur (3,000, for example, on 2 November 2002), but by the end of the month the numbers and range of species have fallen dramatically as most species move on to avoid the short Shetland winter days. However, although the weather can be inclement (to put it mildly) and the days very short, a few notable discoveries have been made in November over the years, for example Black Duck (2006), Little Bustard (1994), American Golden Plover (2003), White-rumped Sandpiper (1972), Little Swift (1991), Black-bellied Dipper *C. c. cinclus* (2001), several Olive-backed Pipits, Rock Thrush (1931), White's Thrush (1948, 1958), Dusky Warblers (1986, 1987), Hume's Warbler (2003), Arctic Redpoll (1995, 2001) and Pine Bunting (1994, 1995).

   There isn't the space to cover all the excellent days that have occurred over the years – it would take a book in itself – but there are very few other places in Europe that can match Fair Isle for the range and number of species which can be seen in a good autumn.

Ringing

Ringing has always been an integral part of the work of the observatory. There are currently nine Heligoland traps, as well as a crow trap – called the Axell Trap, as it was originally built by Bert Axell.

Most of the traps were originally constructed in the days of Ken Williamson and some are regarded as classics of Heligoland design. Three traps are built over dykes, with the Double Dyke trap being designed with entrances and catching boxes at each end so that it can be driven from either direction. The Plantation trap is built over the small plantation trees, which include willows and Sitka Spruce, planted in the shelter of the small valley draining down from Sukka Mire and the airstrip. Behind the plantation is the Vaadal which bridges the narrow steep-sided valley. This is very useful for trapping, amongst other things, any Long-eared Owls flushed out of the plantation. On one occasion, three Long-eared Owls avoided the plantation trap but were gathered up in the Vaadal – although one escaped as a Goldeneye, flushed from the stream, took precedence for the assistant warden driving the trap.

The observatory trap, originally at the rear of the building, was very usefully sited as ringers passed it on a regular basis. It has been removed to make way for the larger new observatory building and will probably be rebuilt over the Observatory Plantation in the near future. The most famous, however, is the gully trap, a classic and unique trap design. The gully itself drains the marshy area of Gilsetter and forms a sheltered valley, beloved of migrants, at the upper end of the gully. The trap, cleverly constructed with wires and beams, spans one arm of the upper valley and is driven from the mouth of the gully. The drive proceeds past a tiny patch of bushes, up a ladder beside the burn, onwards under the roof of the trap and up to the catching end, which can be closed off by a rope closing a door, isolating birds in the catching end.

Most of the catching boxes are equipped with carefully weighted tipping plates, designed so that the birds can trap themselves. These are useful devices, but it does mean the traps need to be checked regularly when the plates are set. However, the device has resulted in the catching of a stunning array of birds including Rock Thrush, Great Reed Warbler, Great Grey Shrike, and Little Bunting, not to mention many Merlins and Sparrowhawks.

In the windy climate of Fair Isle mist-nets cannot always be used, but on the rare suitable days they are used to catch migrants down the isle and after dark during the summer to catch Storm Petrels using play-back of their song. Another side effect of the windy climate is that a wide range of additional trapping methods have been used over the years – to greater or lesser effect. These include drop traps, walk-in, wader and duck traps, and even whoosh nets and fleyg nets (for catching seabirds). Dazzling can be effective on dark winter nights and has resulted in good catches of storm-driven gulls, including Glaucous and Iceland

Gulls and other difficult-to-catch species such as Short-eared Owls, herons, geese, ducks and waders.

The summer seabird work is an aspect of wardening on Fair Isle which is fondly remembered by many former members of staff. It occupies virtually the entire period between the tail-end of the spring and the first signs of autumn (at least in the years when Shetland's seabirds are doing well); the days of high summer when the daylight seems to extend for ever and – when the sun shines – the island is at its best. Many factors combine to make these days so vivid: the almost overwhelming noise and smell of the big Guillemot colonies; the majesty of the Gannets, precarious on the island's spectacular north-western extremities; the stench and squalor of the Lericum Shag cave; the immaculate Razorbills that will so easily lacerate your hands if concentration slips and, most elegant of all of Fair Isle's seabirds, the Arctic Terns, which breed so abundantly in some years, on Tarryfield and Eas Brecks. Nor would the season be complete without experiencing the exuberant nest-defence of the two skua species; or enjoying every visitor's favourite, the comical but feisty Puffin.

Seabird teamwork makes for great camaraderie. There is tremendous variety to the work and nervous energy to heighten the senses – care with handling the birds, the discipline of checking and securing the ropes used to descend into the colonies, and the concentration needed to negotiate steep sheep-tracks before reaching the rope-off points at Gunnawark and Guidicum.

For some, one of the most enjoyable aspects is piloting the observatory Zodiac to drop off teams at some of the more inaccessible colonies. With the team ashore the pilot has the opportunity to marvel at the spectacle of Guillemot chicks fledging. The chicks leave the colony when only three weeks old and, though little more than a third of the weight of the adults, they are able to dive almost immediately. They swim out to sea with their male parent, where they continue to grow, less vulnerable to gulls and skuas than on their precarious nursery ledges. The chicks are extremely vocal close to the colony and their piercing, high-pitched calls so distinctive, but are seemingly less so further out to sea. Watching Guillemot chicks fledging in the twilight of a late June evening can make for a vivid Fair Isle memory.

If time and sea allow, there is also the chance of a sea-ramble along Fair Isle's rugged west coast, where the towering cliffs plunge to a turbulent sea. If the waters are calm enough – a rare event, given the almost constant swell washing in from the Atlantic – it is possible to explore the more remote nooks and crannies that are so often out of reach when the weather is less than clement. Discover then the magical places with mystical names: pass under the big arch into North Felsigeo, penetrate the Naversgils, both North and South and marvel at the amphitheatre of Troili Geo.

OTHER FAUNA AND FLORA

Mammals and amphibians

The two smallest land mammals are House Mouse and Field Mouse (the latter described as a separate race, endemic to the isle) and both introduced by man. There is, in the museum, an ancient wooden mousetrap, designed to try to control these pests of stored food. Rabbits (whose population is also of pest proportions) are ubiquitous and coloured ones are common, presumably indicating their domestic origins and the interbreeding of a closed population. Feral Cats are encountered frequently along the cliffs, but the population size and their effect on the local breeding birds is currently unknown.

Grey Seals are resident and best seen on the rocks and inlets in the south of the isle. Around 100 pups are born along shingle beaches below the steep west cliffs during the late autumn and a small number of Common Seals can sometimes be seen hauled up on the beach at South Harbour.

Offshore, there are sightings of cetaceans and a number of species are fairly regular. Most frequently encountered is the White-beaked Dolphin, seen occasionally from the island but much more regularly from the *Good Shepherd* as she crosses between Mainland Shetland and the island. Risso's Dolphin, Atlantic White-sided Dolphin, Harbour Porpoise and Long-finned Pilot Whale can also be encountered. Of the larger whales, Minke Whale is most often seen and, in line with an increasing number of sightings around the Northern Isles, there have been several sightings of Humpback Whale in recent years. There is also a single record of Sperm Whale as a pod of six bulls was seen loafing around off the South End in November 1988.

For sheer spectacle, however, the prize must go to the Killer Whale (or Orca). The frequency of sightings seems to have increased in the last few years and they are now more than annual. The excitement of seeing these animals is well captured by Deryk Shaw:

> *21 June 1999: My first sight of Killer Whales. We were all seated in the obs dining room, tucking into another tasty meal when someone mentioned there were dolphins close inshore in Finniquoy Bay. I stood up and looked out the window just in time to see a huge dorsal fin break the surface of the water. 'That's not dolphins, it's Killer Whales!!' I exclaimed. That was it! Pandemonium ensued as everyone rushed out of the dining room window, climbed over the garden fence and rushed, in socks, to the edge of the cliff. We all watched in awe as a pod of 10 Killer Whales cruised around the bay, hugging the shoreline, before disappearing around the edge of Sheep Rock. It got better – everyone then grabbed shoes, binoculars and cameras and bundled into the obs van; we set off in pursuit and caught up with them at Busta Geo in the south-east corner of the isle. We all sat on the edge of the cliff opposite Da Burrian as this group of magnificent beasts circled around the rocks below us. A cry of mixed emotions went up when an immature grey seal was tossed out of the water, then silence, when a few seconds later the water turned red for a moment, before the blood dissipated. We then had to leave*

the Killer Whales on their quest for seal meat as we were hosting a live music evening at the obs.

I've had many, many views of Killer Whales since then but none came close as a spectacle – until 11 June 2005, when a pod of four came almost within touching distance at Head o' Tind near South Light and when, two years to the day later, a pod of three cruised around North Haven, even nosing our Zodiac tied up at the pier!

Common Frogs have been introduced and survive in small numbers, spawning in the ditches around Pund, the Parks and in Golden Water.

Invertebrates

Moths are trapped regularly during the summer and autumn and are detailed in the annual reports for the year. The species list is not as extensive as in other parts of Britain, but many of the local resident species are of a local (and usually dark) variant. A few migrant species occur each year, including Hummingbird and Convolvulus Hawkmoths, and there are additions to the list in most years, including the most northerly British records for some species. A recent feature has been an annual influx of Magpie moths, including over 100 in 2007, being unknown on the isle before the late 1990s. The number of regular butterfly species, however, can be counted on one hand, but Swallowtail, Meadow Brown and Small Heath have also occurred.

Pride of place among other invertebrate groups goes to the water bug *Corixa iberica*. Described as new to science as recently as the 1980s and still known only from a small scatter of localities along the Atlantic coastal fringe from Portugal to Shetland, it is abundant in all standing water on the isle. This relict species survives in places like Fair Isle because of its unpolluted waters coupled with reduced competition from more dominant sibling species and the general absence of predators. Ward Hill rises to only 217 metres above sea level, but experiences some of the most extreme conditions in Britain, particularly on its northern flank. The area, where 14 obligate or facultative montane spider species bear witness to its highland characteristics, remains to be fully investigated.

Insect migrants are not restricted to butterflies and moths. There are frequent influxes of hoverflies, including Britain's second record of *Eupeodes lundbecki* in 1982, and lacewings, beetles and bugs are turning up with increasing frequency. Indeed, Fair Isle may be well placed to register the impact of climate change on insect populations. The first-ever wasp, a drone of the Norwegian Wasp *Dolichovespula norvegica*, was found in 1991 and the previously unknown Sexton Beetle *Necrophorus humator* is now commonly seen at bird and mammal carcasses. In most years there is something unexpected and new, including a Birch Shieldbug in 2006 and two species of brown lacewing in 2008.

Flora

Scott (1972) recorded 238 species of plants on Fair Isle and Duncan (1963) listed 107 lichens for the island, whilst Professor Roy Watling and colleagues (1992, 2001) have undertaken some investigations of the fungi.

The island is home to several species of nationally and locally rare plants including Oysterplant, Frog Orchid, Lesser Twayblade, Lesser Marshwort, Bog Pimpernel, Small Adder's-tongue and Wilson's Filmy-fern. Its lichens include a far-flung population of *Anaptychia ciliaris mamillata*, otherwise known from the central belt of Scotland. *Lecanora straminea* found in 1961 was new to Britain. The expression 'First for Britain' extends to the fungi too, in the form of *Russula medullata* on Dwarf Willow at the top of Ward Hill. This important plant community also supports the attractive *Lactarius lanceolatus*, elsewhere in Britain reported only from Foula. Ward Hill is home to arctic–alpine plants such as Alpine Bistort and Stiff Sedge, whilst Mountain Everlasting occurs almost to sea level.

A feature of many of the habitats is the strong populations of species which were once widespread but have been in dramatic decline elsewhere in the face of changes in water quality and chemicals and modern practices such as improved drainage and intensive agriculture. The isle has been largely spared and supports good populations of a range of maritime, marsh and montane species such as Greater and Lesser Sea-spurrey, Sea Spleenwort, Moonwort, Allseed, Lousewort, Few-flowered Spike-rush and much more. Even the common flowers benefit, and the fields and cliffs of Fair Isle are a riot of colour throughout the summer months.

The arable areas also provide habitat for an exciting array of species for visiting botanists; half are now hard to find in Britain and some of the others are northern species with which southern botanists may not be familiar. Whilst the amount of land turned over to arable has been in steady decline in recent years, the observatory is leading a campaign to reverse this by encouraging the planting of arable cover. Arable rigs not only benefit the birds, but also provide refuge for some of our special plants.

THE FUTURE

The FIBOT committee is very keen to encourage serious students to carry out work from the observatory and has awarded grants to assist with costs and accommodation and it is likely this initiative will be expanded in the future. The regular work of the observatory staff will continue and it is likely the seabird work will become even more crucial as the nation's populations come under more pressure. Thought will be given on how to collate, analyse and publish more of the long-term data sets that the observatory holds and add to countless papers already written on aspects of the breeding biology of a variety of seabirds, migration and on passerines including Starling, Fair Isle Wren and Wheatear.

It is certain that the future will bring an expansion of the educational side of the observatory work. Whilst this has a good grounding through the Ranger Service, better facilities will encourage development of various projects.

During 2009 the Trust replaced the observatory building, which had virtually come to the end of its life, with a new one, sitting in the same footprint. This whole operation cost over four million pounds and involved closing to visitors for the 2009 season. Scientific work continued uninterrupted, however, with staff housed down the island for the season. The observatory is such an integral and vital part of the Fair Isle economy and way of life that FIBOT and the island community are determined to secure the future of this famous institution and the island for the next 50 years and beyond.

ACCESS AND ACCOMMODATION

Access to Fair Isle is usually via Shetland Mainland. Travel to Shetland is by a variety of ferry or air services. There are daily overnight ferries from Aberdeen to Lerwick, which connect three times a week through Orkney, operated by NorthLink. During the summer, there are occasional ferries and flights from Shetland to Norway.

There are direct flights, currently operated by Flybe, to Sumburgh airport in the south of Mainland Shetland from Edinburgh, Wick, Inverness, Glasgow and Orkney and at least four flights a day from Aberdeen, where there are connecting flights to London and other major European airports. There are summer flights direct to Stansted and the Faeroe Islands. From Shetland, sea travel is by the *Good Shepherd*, the island-based ferry which, in summer, operates three days a week to Grutness in the south Mainland and once a fortnight direct to Lerwick. There are flights by Directflight's Islander aircraft on four days per week to Tingwall airstrip near Lerwick, with a flight to Sumburgh from the island on a Saturday. In addition, in some years there is an Islander service from Kirkwall in Orkney operated by Loganair.

For parties, it may be possible to charter either boats or planes. It is possible to 'day-trip' the island from Shetland on some days. At times of extremely rare birds, charters take place from Shetland Mainland and from as far away as England when twitchers fly up from their local airport direct to the island for the day. Cruise liners have become a feature of the summer when large numbers of people can be disgorged onto the island to be shown the observatory's work, meet some Puffins and perhaps purchase a piece of Fair Isle knitwear, but occasionally the weather is too poor for landing and they have to sail on.

Access to the hill and around the island is generally free and open. Stiles have been provided for fence crossing and these should be used. Birders should keep out of gardens, crops and other private areas, but islanders are always happy to pass the time of day with visitors. Stock should be avoided at all times and special care should be taken near ewes at lambing time.

Accommodation in the observatory is available from April to October on a full-board basis, in a variety of single, twin and family rooms. There may be special offers during quiet periods and visitors should check with the administrator or the website. There are information boards and leaflets plus a Ranger Service which provides guided walks and local information. Guests receive a welcome talk on arrival and in the evening there are often illustrated talks from the staff or visiting naturalists.

Contact with the observatory may be made by post to Fair Isle Bird Observatory, Fair Isle, Shetland, ZE2 9JU or by phone – 01595 760 258 or by fax – 01595 760 258.

Membership of the *Friends of Fair Isle is* open to anyone with an interest in the work of the observatory. For a very reasonable subscription, Friends receive two newsletters and an illustrated annual report and they also get a discount on bookings in certain months. Details of joining can be found on the observatory website.

Observatory opened:	1948
Total number of bird species recorded at the observatory:	374
Best bird year:	1992
Number of species recorded:	216
Total of birds ringed at the observatory:	350,190
Number of species:	271
Best ringing year:	1998
Number ringed:	11,965
Number of species:	125

Filey

by Peter J. Dunn, Ian Robinson and David Williams

SG 10

INTRODUCTION

Filey is situated on the east coast of North Yorkshire between Scarborough and Bridlington. Filey Brigg is the peninsula of rock and clay jutting out into the North Sea to the north of Filey and to the south of Scarborough. The headland forms a natural breakwater and the northern boundary for Filey Bay, which is also protected to the south by the white cliffs of Flamborough Head.

About 40 million years ago the earth's crust experienced an orogenesis, or large-scale movement, which forced up mountain ranges such as the Alps. These forces also caused sedimentary rocks in the area to rise above their natural level,

Peter Dunn was a founder member of Filey Brigg Ornithological Group and, later, the bird observatory. He was the recorder for ten years from 1980–1990 and has been the ringing officer since 1983. He is currently the chair of the observatory directors and has taken over the recorder's position again from 2009.

Ian Robinson joined the group in 1987. He served as secretary for 12 years and chairman from 2000 to 2008. He is a director of FBOG and has been site manager of Parish Wood and the Old Tip Nature Reserve since day one. Ian also started his second term as chairman in 2010

David Williams has been a member of the group for 30 years. He was the recorder for two years and is the author of the book *Bird-Watching in Filey*.

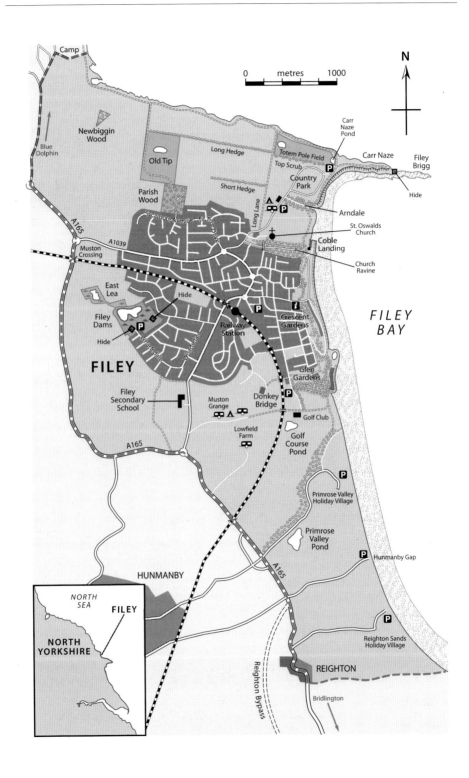

Camp

Newbiggin Wood

Blue Dolphin

Old Tip

Long Hedge

Carr Naze Pond

Totem Pole Field

Top Scrub

Carr Naze

Filey Brigg

Hide

Parish Wood

Short Hedge

Country Park

Arndale

A165

A1039

Sycamore Avenue

Muston Crossing

St. Oswalds Church

Coble Landing

Church Ravine

East Lea

Hide

Filey Dams

Hide

Railway Station

Crescent Gardens

FILEY

Glen Gardens

FILEY BAY

Filey Secondary School

Muston Grange

Donkey Bridge

Golf Club

Lowfield Farm

Golf Course Pond

A165

Primrose Valley Holiday Village

Primrose Valley Pond

Hunmanby Gap

HUNMANBY

NORTH SEA

FILEY

NORTH YORKSHIRE

A165

Reighton Sands Holiday Village

REIGHTON

Reighton Bypass

Bridlington

N

0   metres   1000

forming hills. The high point of one of these hills runs out into the sea near Ravenscar to the north of Scarborough and slopes down on either side, eventually disappearing below sea level. Filey Brigg is part of the southern edge of this hill, at the point where it dips down into the sea, its structure being evident from the way the flat Brigg rocks incline to the south as they disappear into the bay.

Some 10,000 years ago the whole area was covered with a layer of boulder clay, a deposit left under a glacier moving south. The sea eroded away all those clay deposits which were not protected by flat underlying sedimentary rock and Filey Bay was formed. The flat rock is a hard middle-calcareous gritstone of the Upper Jurassic geological epoch and is much resistant to the destructive actions of the waves, although deposits of softer material within the rock have been worn away to leave gullies and pits. The rock at the Brigg forms a natural, but uneven, promenade on which the adventurous can walk out to sea for about half a mile at low tide. It is also an SSSI on account of its geological interest.

The flat-topped headland of boulder clay, above and to the west of the rocky Brigg, is known as Carr Naze and has been a useful spot for a lookout post as far back as the fourth century AD, when the Romans positioned a signal station there as part of the local coastal defence system. In more recent times, it has been used as the site of the coastguard watch post.

The deposits of boulder clay on top of the underlying rock at Carr Naze have been eroded over the years by wind, rain and frost to form deep gullies and sharp ridges, known geologically as 'badlands topography'. Even to this day, the contours of the clay are changed by these natural forces and new landslips are evident after each winter. To the north of the Brigg the cliffs afford quarters to many nesting seabirds. Because of the angle and composition of the rock, the sea has been able to cut into the cliff face to form the holes and shallow caves known locally as 'doodles'.

South of the Brigg and the Carr Naze, and protected by them, is Filey Bay, an expansive, gently sloping embayment. The wide sandy shore of the bay extends to the south of the Brigg for several miles until it meets the white chalk of the cliffs leading to Flamborough Head. Nestling in the northern lee of Filey Bay is the town of Filey, benefiting not only from the shelter offered by the Brigg, but owing its very presence to it. Filey has been there since at least the fourteenth century, when it was known as Fyvely or Filo. Documentary evidence suggests that an ancient pier of Roman origin graced the waterfront of the bay, probably at or near Filey Brigg, but there is no harbour here now nor anywhere else in the bay. Nevertheless, a small fleet of fishing cobles has worked from the town for generations, as it still does today, with vessels formerly launched across the expanse of sandy beach, with or without draught animals, but more lately using tractors.

HISTORY

An observatory-style recording regime has operated at Filey since the formation of the Filey Brigg Ornithological Group (FBOG) in late 1976. It was in January 1999 that Filey became an accredited bird observatory, operated by the group under the umbrella of the Bird Observatories Council. The full title is Filey Brigg Ornithological Group and Bird Observatory, but it is also shortened to Filey Bird Observatory for ease of use.

Membership of the Group had risen to almost the hundred mark by 2006; that, and the Group's recent land ownership and increased management responsibilities prompted FBOG to look at becoming a limited company, and it was on 12 January 2007 that we were incorporated into a company limited by guarantee.

It was the bird collectors in the late 1800s that first discovered the ornithological riches of Filey Brigg. With their eagerness to 'bag' a rarity for the taxidermist's shop, they came to the Brigg in the hope of finding unusual migrants resting in the area. The first rare-bird records for Filey, such as Britain and Ireland's Steller's Eider shot there in 1845, came as a result of this activity. But with the passing of legislation and the passage of time, the bird collector was replaced by the birdwatchers or birders of today.

In the early days, the birdwatchers would only record the rare or unusual species and, unsurprisingly, very few records were published. The earliest reference to birds at Filey was by Thomas Allis in 1844, when he wrote of Purple Sandpipers on the Brigg: 'A. Strickland observes that this bird generally confines itself to rocky or stony parts of the shore, and is seldom found on the sand and is met with at Filey and other parts of the coast.'

Some of the cheerful and enthusiastic founding members of the Filey Brigg Ornithological Group by the sea-watching hide in 1977 (Scarborough Evening News). Back row (from the left): Walter Clark, Terry Hobson, Frank Thompson, David Small. Front row from the left: Steve Race, Terry England, Peter Dunn, Peter Chambers.

Birdwatchers visited the Brigg on day-trips or on holidays to the seaside towns of Filey and Scarborough during the summer and autumn, but no-one recorded there throughout the year until the late 1940s when H. J. R. Pease kept regular watch at the site and noted many birds which, up until then, had never been associated with the Brigg. In 1948 A. J. Wallis's name appeared in Yorkshire Naturalists' Union bird reports alongside Filey records, and he was the most regular recorder of the bird life until R. H. Appleby was introduced to the area in 1952.

Before the creation of the North Cliff Country Park in the early 1970s, the area above and inland from Filey Brigg was farmland and was not developed in any commercial way. An account of Filey Brigg by Ron Appleby, another of its first regular watchers, in *The Birds of Yorkshire* (Mather 1986), described it in the period from 1952 to 1970 as 'a wild and lonely place' and spoke of spending whole days there alone.

It is to Ron Appleby that the observatory is particularly indebted for the systematic recording of Filey birds. He mentions a log book started in 1960, with a list of 194 species recorded over the next 15 years, including Shore Lark, Lapland Bunting, Red-necked Grebe and Slavonian Grebe. With a prophetic hint of things to come, he also speaks of using the hut on the Brigg, kindly made available by the lessee, for sea-watching in bad weather. He was joined by F. J. Thompson in 1965 and together they increased the species list for the area.

One of the saddest notes in his diary, for 28 October 1967, reveals that shooting had not been entirely left behind in the nineteenth century. He recorded that '57 Common Terns and three Arctic Terns were found shot dead. All had obviously been shot at point blank range while roosting'. Fortunately, this unhappy incident caused a huge outcry in the press and elsewhere. In *The Birds of Yorkshire*, Ron Appleby gives 27 September 1975 as the date of his last regular visit. It was in September 1976 that the first stirrings of activity took place to lead, that year, to the founding of FBOG. As it happened, more birdwatchers were beginning to come to Filey in the early 1970s, some from Scarborough and York and others from the Hull area (who doubtless decided to travel north rather than follow the well-trodden path to Spurn). All these people would meet more or less informally at the Brigg. In the summer of 1976, having realised in the course of sea-watching that the hut on the Brigg had not been used as a café for at least a year, they decided to approach Scarborough Council's Tourism and Amenities Department to see if they could take it over for use as an observation hide. Permission was refused. However, the autumn of 1976 was so rewarding in terms of the species recorded (including 54 Sooty Shearwaters in three hours, and Wryneck, Bluethroat, Barred Warbler and Greenish Warbler) that they decided to try again and were successful. The hut was taken over by the recently formed FBOG on 1 August 1977 and Andy Paterson kept the first log of birds recorded by the group.

FBOG originally recorded the bird life found in a defined area to the north of Filey, which was expanded in 1981 to cover the ten kilometre square TA18 in order to take part more usefully in national surveys organised by the British Trust for Ornithology. Exploration of the additional area led to the discovery of Filey

Dams, a summer-meadow grazed by the local dairy herd and susceptible to flooding in the winter. The subsequent acquisition of this land was an important milestone in FBOG history and is described later.

The sea-watch hide on the Brigg

In 1990, the Yorkshire coast was pounded by the worst storms for many years and considerable damage was done to buildings locally on the night of 7/8 December. The following morning the sea-watch hide, which had stood at the base of the Brigg since 1941, was spotted briefly floating in the bay. A local fisherman questioned wryly whether the birdwatching group had had planning permission to move it out there.

Like many a structure beforehand, it was washed into the bay and smashed to pieces on the rocks. Minds turned at once to thoughts of a replacement. It soon became clear it would be sensible to think in terms of a permanent stone construction, built on proper foundations; not only would this withstand the might of similar storms, but planning permission was unlikely to be forthcoming for a wooden building. The disadvantage was that building a stone structure on a larger scale would be a daunting project and much more expensive. Nevertheless, a start was made on two fronts in the New Year of 1991 being driven by Ian Robinson; preliminary drawings were prepared and fund raising commenced.

Both these activities took time, and it was to be 19 months before a new, purpose-built stone hide was completed on the spot from which the old hide had been swept away. This meant that sea-watching had to be endured for two winters without the benefit of any shelter, and the group was made aware of the value of a hide in the most dramatic fashion. Inevitably, sea-watching became impossible in the very worst weather and records for the winters of 1990/1 and 1991/2 certainly suffered from reduced coverage on the Brigg.

All thoughts of blizzards, biting winds and frozen fingers were banished as soon as the spring of 1992 arrived. The plans were ready, donations had been received both from individuals and interested bodies and substantial grants had been promised by the councils of Filey and Scarborough. A builder had also been engaged and work was ready to begin. Now, however, a whole new set of problems had to be faced. We will draw a kindly veil over the arrangements for moving some 30 tons of building material, including fresh water, save to say that the problem was partly solved when RAF Leconfield kindly agreed to deliver the bulk of the material from the Country Park to the base of the Brigg as a helicopter training exercise. It is difficult to see how we would have coped without their help.

The credit for masterminding the project and seeing it through, down to the last detail, must go to the group's secretary, Ian Robinson, who maintained a cheerful optimism throughout the 18 months of planning and building. He never fell prey to panic, even during the darkest moments, or, if he did, he never said so! The only hint that it had not been a time of uninterrupted pleasure and satisfaction for him was when he was heard to mutter darkly that this hut had better not get swept away because he wasn't going through all that again! The new hide was duly opened by Mrs Wendy Hudghton, the Filey Town Clerk, on 2 August 1992 amid much consumption of wine and cheese and the clicking of cameras. She had been an enthusiastic supporter of the project throughout.

Serious sea-watching began again immediately and before the end of the month a new species for Filey was recorded when a couple of Gull-billed Terns fed off the Brigg on the evening of 18 August.

Filey Dams Nature Reserve

When FBOG was founded in 1976, what is now the Filey Dams Nature Reserve was an area of marshy grass and juncus owned by Scarborough Borough Council and tending to flood in winter. FBOG members discovered it when the recording area was extended inland from the Country Park in 1981. Although little frequented by birds, it soon became apparent that Common (Smooth) and Great Crested Newts and a healthy population of Water Shrew were present along with a wide variety of marshland plants, including the comparatively rare Adder's-tongue and Nodding Bur-marigold.

By the autumn of 1981, Jack Whitehead had realised the importance of the dams as the last remaining wetland in the Filey area, and he registered it with the Yorkshire Wildlife Trust (YWT) as interesting habitat in the local context. However, the real spur to action came in January 1984, when Scarborough Borough Council's Housing Services Committee agreed to hand over the 40 acre Pastures site – including the dams area and the large field to the north-east – to the Land Sub-Committee for sale for residential development.

A first letter, expressing interest in the fate of the marshy area, was sent to the council by Jack Whitehead, as secretary of FBOG. In early March, Stephen Warburton wrote on behalf of YWT, asking for the marshland area to be reserved from any building proposals. In October 1984, Jack Whitehead briefed the Nature Conservancy Council (NCC) on the importance of the area, who, in turn, advised the Scarborough Borough Council of the wildlife interest. Following a planning application to develop the whole area, the council asked for observations from FBOG, who responded, suggesting a 4.9 hectares nature reserve. A few days later Philip Horton of the NCC submitted a proposal suggesting that 12 acres of the marshy area be excluded from the building plan and retained as a nature reserve, to be owned by YWT and managed on their behalf by FBOG.

On 20 November, the vital decision was made. Scarborough Borough Council's Development Services Committee accepted the development plan for the area, but with provision for a nature reserve of at least 4 hectares, and on 25 November Jack Whitehead wrote to YWT formally asking for the adoption of the site as a reserve. Agreement had been won for its retention as a nature reserve exactly three years after the area had been registered with the YWT as interesting habitat. The first hurdles had been successfully negotiated.

A management committee, made up of FBOG and YWT representatives, met in 1985 and throughout the year the proposed area for the reserve was thoroughly investigated, with results that served only to emphasise its importance.

Nocturnal surveys of amphibians took place on several nights in April and May and produced interesting results, with maximum counts of 152 Great Crested Newts and 209 Common (Smooth) Newts. On 11 and 12 May, a Rustic Bunting paused at the site and became the first rare bird on the Filey Dams' list. It also put the area on the map for visiting birdwatchers. In June, over 50 Adder's-tongue were discovered nearby, and the first mammal trapping session in August identified the dams as one of the most important sites in the county for the scarce Water Shrew, with a count of 15 animals.

Permission was given to start the management work, which proceeded throughout 1986, funded in part by donations and by group fund-raising including a 'bird race'. The new hide was open for the first time on 24 January 1987 and generous grants from the NCC and Filey Town Council made it possible for screens, handrails and paths to be added, giving the site an air of real quality. On Easter Saturday, 18 April 1987, the reserve recorded its second rare bird, a Purple Heron, which arrived late in the afternoon. It roosted overnight and was seen again next morning before flying off. The following Saturday, 25 April, the reserve and the new hide were officially opened, very appropriately, by Councillor A. G. Riley, Mayor of Filey, given the interest and support that he and his Council had shown. There was plenty of activity on the reserve throughout 1987. Surveys of arachnids and other invertebrates and of plants were effected, and a further mammal trapping session took place in August, when increased numbers of the regular species were caught, including 25 Water Shrews. Cattle were brought on for the first time to graze the grass, an experiment which has worked successfully every summer since, to the mutual benefit of the reserve and a local farmer. By the end of the year, the reserve was so well known that the provision of a car park became a priority. This was completed on 14 July, funded partly by a welcome grant of £475 from the Countryside Commission. Numerous other enterprises of improvement and extension followed, including levelling, digger work at the main pool, attention to footpaths and tree planting. In spring 1989 another landmark event occurred when Scarborough Borough Council agreed to allow a further area of wetland to be incorporated into it to the east of the reserve, ideal for the creation of an additional pool. More trees were planted and a second hide overlooking the new pool was officially opened on 3 August 1993 by Lord Peel, President of the YWT, who visited the reserve with other YWT officials.

In summary, the reserve now comprises four pools and two hides with supporting infrastructure and has been managed for the many species of wildlife that inhabit the only piece of wetland habitat within the observatory area. It has proved its worth many times over, adding new species to the Filey lists on a regular basis.

The achievements of the past 20 years are there for all to see, and the Filey Dams Reserve stands as a tribute to the initial vision and determination of Jack Whitehead, without whom the area would now, very likely, either be developed or abandoned. Scarborough and Filey Councils, YWT, NCC and members of FBOG, along with numerous others, have played a significant part in the enterprise, which is an excellent example of what can be achieved by a few people with imagination and foresight.

Spurred on by its considerable success at the Filey Dams Reserve and the building of the new sea-watch hide, the group then looked into the possibility of purchasing some local land to develop into small reserves within the recording area.

Parish Wood and Old Tip Nature Reserves

Development of the wood now known as Parish Wood began in 1996, when part of Filey's redundant refuse tip was reclaimed as a nature reserve following 20 years spent lying fallow as rough pasture. In a joint venture, FBOG and Filey Town Council planted over 3,000 native trees and shrubs during the winter months on the six acre site which was divided into two parts: a public area with paths and seating and a private fenced area reserved for Filey's wildlife. Later, in 2003, FBOG negotiated a 30-year lease of the site with Filey Town Council and are now responsible for its upkeep and management.

More than a decade has passed since the wood was planted and growth has been relatively slow. A thin layer of soil and an open aspect close to North Cliff seem to be responsible. However, at least 95% of the trees have survived, and we will soon have to remove some to allow others to develop fully. The reserve is situated off Sycamore Avenue, Filey, and forms part of a circular walk from North Cliff Country Park, passing through Parish Wood and continuing along part of the coastal path section of the Cleveland Way.

The remainder of the tip, comprising about six hectares, together with 2.5 hectares of agricultural land adjoining Parish Wood to the north, was purchased by the group in November 2000. The prime object was to create wintering areas for seed-eating birds, with the provision of breeding habitat for declining farmland species as a secondary consideration, and the area is now known as Old Tip.

The field has been divided into three management units; the first, of 0.8 hectares, is a flower meadow, cut in late summer and the second central part of about five hectares has been stock-fenced and is grazed by cattle during the summer months. The 2.5 hectares of agricultural land closest to the cliffs is the most interesting and has been ploughed in strips between two and four metres wide, alternating with similar fallow strips. A number of game-cover and 'super-bird' seed-mixes have been sown. From the outset we decided to grow crops without using pesticides or herbicides, but only time will tell whether this will be successful. Results will be monitored with bird counts and we will experiment with different planting and cropping regimes. Some crops may need to be cut annually; whilst others, such as kale, are more productive in their second year. Yet others may be best left standing. However, our experimental strip crop programme hasn't been going entirely to plan, with wild oats, thistles, slugs and long periods of drought giving us quite a few headaches. Nevertheless, good numbers of Reed Buntings and Yellowhammers assemble during February and March and 750 Skylarks were counted on one occasion. Corn Buntings are seen occasionally, but have yet to re-establish themselves, although Grey Partridge have returned to breed, with several young birds seen feeding in the crop field.

Nine species of buntings, including Rustic, Pine and Little were recorded here during 2001, so we couldn't have wished for a better start.

Totem Pole Field

The field which borders the Country Park scrub and the North Cliff is locally known as the 'Totem Pole Field' because of the white 'totem pole' situated in the middle. The local farmer's lease expired in 2000 and he decided not to renew it, so FBOG approached the owners, Scarborough Borough Council, and took on a new lease with the help of grants and subsidies from DEFRA. The 'totem pole' is in fact a 'rocket pole', formerly used for firing rockets during coastguard training exercises and simulated rescues from ships. It was restored and painted by FBOG as a term of the acquisition.

This 17-acre site is split into two, with one part being used as a grazing meadow in the summer whilst the other is seeded every two years with six recommended grass species under a DEFRA Arable Reversion Scheme. Some remnant species cling to the ditch sides within the field, including Lady's Bedstraw, Harebell and Common Knapweed, and it is ideal habitat for breeding species such as Skylark, Meadow Pipit and Grey Partridge. The Totem Pole Field, the Top Scrub area of the Country Park and Carr Naze are shortly to be amalgamated to form the first Local Nature Reserve (LNR) for the Scarborough Borough Council area, which will be managed on behalf of the Council by FBOG Bird Observatory.

East Lea Nature Reserve

Collecting thousands of newts from the Pastures building site was an important part of fulfilling the purpose of the new East Lea Local Nature Reserve. More than 1,700 Great Crested Newts and 3,000 Common (Smooth) Newts, together with 17 Common Lizards and numerous frogs and toads, were caught on the site by pit-fall trapping and carried to the dam-side of a newt-proof barrier to prevent them returning to their former haunts. Syd Cochrane, Mick Butt and other observatory members toiled on just over 100 trapping days to complete this vital work.

Following initial survey work undertaken by Andrew McCarthy Associates of Sheffield, a European Protected Species Licence (EPSL) was obtained to legally move the newts. As part of the EPSL, steps were taken both to rescue and move the newts and to obtain and enhance new newt habitat, to compensate for the habitat lost to development. As a consequence, David Wilson Homes made £42,000 available to FBOG for the purchase and ongoing management of East Lea. Major earthworks transformed the 3.6 hectares of improved grassland to an area of low-level grazing with an extensive and newly created area of water and pools, newt hibernacula banks and areas of rough grass. Six Temminck's Stints arrived as the work was completed. East Lea lies to the north-west of Filey Dams. There is no public access at present but negotiations are ongoing. The assistance of David Wilson Homes throughout is gratefully acknowledged.

THE BIRDS

Winter

The link between weather conditions and the arrival of birds is at best only partially understood. Many are the days on which birdwatchers have trekked down to the Brigg or around the Country Park and the top fields in supposedly ideal conditions, only to discover that there is not a bird to be seen. However, certain trends and patterns have been noted over the years and these are worth recording.

When the near continent is dominated by high pressure and subsequent low temperatures, an influx of wildfowl, seabirds, gulls and waders can be expected. January 1987 began with cold northerlies, before easterlies set in from the 10th, and the temperatures fell further at the month end. The weather was even more inclement over the Baltic and all four species of diver were noted at Filey, together with several Glaucous Gulls, Red-necked Grebes, Brent Geese and Little Auk. In the absence of such conditions recently, influxes like these remain ever more distant memories. However, mid-winter Great Northern Diver and Slavonian Grebe records have increased over the last decade, whilst a decline has been apparent in their close relatives. The immediate coastal area can often remain ice free, whilst fields on the Wolds' edge, only a kilometre away, remain snowbound. During such spells, Filey often witnesses an influx of winter thrushes, Lapwing, Golden Plover and farmland passerines. Counts can be spectacular with several hundred Yellowhammer and Skylarks appearing overnight. For example, a mixed wintering passerine population barely into double figures was bolstered overnight to 1,500 birds during a cold snap on 1 February 2003. However, the birding can be very disappointing in either winter period if conditions remain mild with south-westerly winds holding sway.

Spring

From early March, it is the light winds from the south-west to the south-east that bring the first migrants. Scandinavian Rock Pipits *Anthus petrosus littoralis* often feature, together with the first Wheatears, Sand Martins and Common Chiffchaff. If the winds feature an easterly component then White Wagtail *Motacilla alba alba* and Firecrest are a possibility. However, recent years have witnessed a trend to cool northerlies during the early spring period. The turnover of birds during such spells is very limited and most attention is focussed on the ever-burgeoning gull roosts, as Common and Black-headed Gulls head north towards their breeding grounds. Mediterranean Gulls often feature, as do Iceland Gulls in early spring, particularly if the northerly winds have been preceded by westerlies pushing the birds into the North Sea.

Late April and early May often bring significant falls of common passerines such as Wheatear and Willow Warbler; light, warm, south-westerlies and overnight rain are the most conducive conditions. However, from the second week of May attention focuses on the synoptic charts, the most cherished conditions being those associated with low-pressure systems tracking well to the south bringing north-easterlies and rain. However, high-pressure systems dominating over the Continent can also produce light drift from the east. Whilst such conditions may not produce large numbers of migrants, the best rarities are often associated with these weather systems. This was the case during May 1992 when an anti-cyclone over Northern Europe brought easterly winds from the 14th. Over the next two weeks a Short-toed Lark, two Red-footed Falcons, a Bee-eater and Britain's first ever Spectacled Warbler were discovered.

The first half of June can be productive for late spring migrants bound for Scandinavia, but only if the winds have an easterly vector. During such conditions Marsh and Icterine Warblers, Red-backed Shrike and Common Rosefinch are typical. However, if winds remain stubbornly in the west then spring is effectively over.

Summer

Summer is traditionally a quiet time, with breeding in full swing at Filey Dams and on the cliffs. There have been some surprises, such as a summer-plumaged Red-throated Pipit and a territory-holding male Sardinian Warbler. The first returning waders tend to be logged from the last few days of June and south-westerly winds tend to be the best conditions. Highest numbers tend to be seen passing south over the sea, although small numbers of freshwater waders are attracted to Filey Dams. Waders reappear on the Brigg during late July, and the first Purple Sandpipers return, after the briefest of absences.

It is perhaps worth noting that the last two weeks of July and the first few days of August are the prime time for the tape-luring and ringing of Storm Petrels on the Brigg. This concerted ringing effort has become part of the Filey calendar in recent years, with over 700 birds trapped in the last decade. Considerable excitement was generated on 27 July 2003 when a Leach's Petrel was netted. This bird, the first for the observatory, had been ringed eight days previously on the island of Sule Skerry, to the west of Orkney and 596 kilometres away.

Autumn

Undoubtedly the best time for both passerines and seabirds, autumn is the season for the unexpected. Whilst it is customary for Willow Warblers to pass through in large numbers from early August, suitable conditions can prompt the arrival of Pied Flycatchers, Redstarts and Whinchats from across the North Sea. North-easterly winds in late August and September can produce dramatic falls of warblers and chats, with Barred Warblers, Greenish Warblers, and Red-backed Shrikes appearing regularly. Yellow-browed Warblers are annual, with double-figures most years between mid-September and the end of October. The latter month can produce almost anything, with annual Pallas's Warblers vying for attention amongst the rarest Siberian vagrants; Pechora Pipit, Lanceolated Warbler and Yellow-breasted Bunting were recorded in 1994 alone.

From the end of August through to mid-November, most attention is focussed on passerine migration with the weather, as always, playing a considerable part. Falls tend to occur in most years, those on a smaller scale often resulting from high pressure drift across the North Sea on light easterly winds. Less frequently, low pressures produce classic conditions, when heavy rain and stronger easterlies ground hundreds of migrants. On 26 August 1986 over 100 Garden Warblers arrived at Filey in such conditions (the remnants of Hurricane Charley), together with a Temminck's Stint, several Wrynecks and three Ortolan Buntings. However, high pressures can also trigger massive arrivals. For example, a high pressure system was centred over the country in mid-October 2005. With calm, anticyclonic weather also nudging into Scandinavia, the wind switched to the east. Immediately, large numbers of Goldcrests started to arrive, with 2,000 logged on the 15th, undoubtedly an underestimate of the huge numbers making landfall and then quietly filtering in flocks down the hedgerows! Eleven Yellow-browed Warblers, 2,000 Redwing, seven Ring Ouzels and a Red-breasted Flycatcher were also present and an unprecedented 499 birds were trapped by the ringing team.

The pattern for passerines in November and December tends to be much the same as for January, February and March. These last two months of the year are variable, with November being either an extension of an exciting autumn or ushering in a relatively quiet early winter period, depending on weather conditions. For instance 8 November 2000 saw high pressure over Scandinavia, with associated clear skies, cold temperatures and light easterly winds. A low-pressure system to the south of the UK tracked up the Channel before entering the North Sea. Local weather conditions at Filey were extreme, with flooding and heavy rain borne on strong north-easterlies. Despite the late date a large arrival ensued: of most interest was a Hume's Warbler, but five Pallas's Warblers, four Firecrests, a Hawfinch and a Richard's Pipit. 300 Robins, 350 Goldcrests, 1,000 Redwings, 1,500 Blackbirds and 1,000 Fieldfares also enlivened proceedings.

Sea-watching

Sea-watching is also very worthwhile in autumn and begins in earnest in early July. Large numbers of Sprats and Herring can appear offshore with a resultant and spectacular increase in seabirds and cetaceans. Flocks of terns increase, to peak in the last two weeks of August when counts of over 2,000 Common Terns have been recorded, with smaller numbers of Arctic Terns and as many as 29 Roseate Terns. Careful scrutiny will often be rewarded with the sighting of small numbers of Black Terns and past gems have included Lesser Crested, White-winged Black and Gull-billed Terns.

North-westerly winds can furnish dramatic sea-watches throughout the season, from large numbers of Manx Shearwaters, Arctic and Long-tailed Skuas in August through to Sooty Shearwaters and Pomarine Skuas in September and October, whilst winds with a more easterly component can often produce Sabine's Gull and Leach's Petrels.

Two strong northerlies on 1 September and 3 October 1994 produced 334 Arctic Skuas, 93 Great Skuas and 27 Pomarine Skuas, and 11 Long-tailed Skuas, 37 Pomarine Skuas and a Sabine's Gull, respectively. Although numbers of Arctic and Great Skuas have declined appreciably over recent years, strong northerlies can still induce spectacular movements of other species. For example, a weather system which produced force 6 north-westerly winds on 22 September 2002 triggered a northerly movement of 1,706 Sooty Shearwaters.

Strong northerlies in the first half of November can also provide spectacular sea-watching, as occurred in the first week of November 1986 with 12 Great Northern Divers, 29 Pomarine Skuas and 133 Great Skuas on the 1st, and 116 Little Auks tracking back north the next day.

Late autumn will often witness the movement of divers, geese and ducks past the Brigg. Winter waders arrive and are best watched there and also at the Country Park at high tide. Although now in much smaller numbers than previously, Purple Sandpipers are ever-present and are joined by Knot, Dunlin, Sanderling and Turnstone.

Gull numbers at Filey appear to be in decline, presumably due to the demise of the fishing industry and the ban on the discharge of raw sewage into the sea. Glaucous Gulls seem to be scarcer than Icelands nowadays, although both are now very scarce in the depths of winter.

Divers tend to move south in November, and then north in late February, although Red-throated Diver and, lately, Great Northern Diver, have begun to winter within the bay in small numbers. The latter location has also hosted five White-billed Divers over the years, while more regular visitors include Long-tailed Duck, Red-necked and Slavonian Grebes. The Brigg was formerly one of the best areas in the country for Grey Phalarope, even in the middle of winter, but they no longer stay more than a day or two, following the clean-up of sewage discharge over the past 15 years.

Ringing

Another important change – or innovation to be more exact – has been the gradual and increasing involvement of the group in the trapping and ringing of birds. Ringing started fairly tentatively in 1983 (although a visiting ringer did trap and ring a number of birds in Arndale in 1977) and has gone from strength to strength under the leadership of Peter J. Dunn.

Since 1983, some 26,232 birds of 110 species have been ringed in the top scrub and Arndale areas of the Country Park, including a good number of rarities and semi-rarities.

Ringing is an important part of the work of the observatory, particularly as the information about bird movements and populations can be used in scientifically structured projects. It is also a valuable tool in positive identification: the description of the Spectacled Warbler while in the hand in May 1992 doubtless helped in the confirmation of the record and led to its speedy acceptance by the British Birds Rarities Committee and the British Ornithologists' Union as the first record for Britain. The Spectacled Warbler was discovered on the Long Hedge by Craig Thomas and Richard Harbird during the morning of 24 May 1992, after a period of anticyclonic easterly winds. Their initial views of the blackish lores, salmon-pink underparts and rufous wings were enough to summon Peter Dunn

(PJD) from his ringing site some 450 metres way. The bird was trapped on the first attempt, along with a Whitethroat, and the enormity of the discovery became evident. Fearful of getting it wrong, full biometrics were taken, proving the identity, but PJD forgot to ring the bird before it was released into Arndale some 30 minutes later. Unfortunately, it failed to 'show' to the gathering birders over the rest of that day, but then performed extremely well back on its original hedge to the well-organised masses for the next five days. It was the first accepted British record following the rejection of three earlier claims.

In July 1990, the ringing team experimented with tape-luring Storm Petrels. Prior to that date, Storm Petrels were rarely seen from the Brigg (there was in fact only a single sight record at that point), but encouraged by the success of the Tyneside ringers, nets were set on the flat rocks of the Brigg. It was an immediate success and the numbers caught indicated just how many birds use this part of the North Sea. With the nearest breeding populations in the far north of Scotland, it

Four Collared Flycatchers have been ringed in Britain, three of them at bird observatories, including this one at Filey in 1995 (John Harwood).

was apparent from recovery data that the birds were moving north and that some individuals regularly passed the area. Sessions are usually held during July and early August, but specific weather conditions are necessary, with west to south-west winds to carry the sound of the tape-lures out to sea. From 1990 to 2008, the group has ringed 732 Storm Petrels and 42 others have been controlled from elsewhere.

Birds ringed at Filey have been recovered from as far afield as Syria and Morocco, Sweden, Denmark and France. Birds ringed elsewhere and recovered at Filey, being either trapped or found as corpses, have come from similar distances, including Germany, Norway, Estonia, Lithuania and Russia. The Russian recovery was of a Pied Flycatcher, ringed as a pullus (a nestling) on 28 June 1996, in Tomsk, in south-western Siberia, north of eastern Kazakhstan and very much at the eastern extremity of its breeding range (Cramp & Perrins 1993). It was recaught at Filey on 16 September 1996, some 80 days later, having travelled at least 5,382 kilometres. Interestingly, Pied Flycatchers are long-distance migrants wintering in West Africa, south of the Sahara, and many stop over to fatten up in Iberia on their autumn migration. This bird's journey may have been typical, save that it failed to travel sufficiently to the south, and its recapture demonstrates the value of ringing in improving our general understanding of long-distance migration.

Apparently, there is a tendency towards greyish plumage in eastern Pied Flycatchers, so if *Ficedula hypoleuca sibirica* (birds from east of the Urals) are passing through Western Europe, it could explain some of the occasional greyer Pied Flycatchers that turn up in eastern Britain.

In 1993, the Filey ringers, who up till then had worked alone, joined up with those from Flamborough and Hornsea, to form the East Yorkshire Ringing Group (EYRG), whose area stretches from Cowden (near Hornsea) north to Scarborough and west to the North Yorkshire forests. EYRG produces its own occasional report and specialist papers, but the FBOG report continues to publish the annual Filey totals.

Best ringing (2005)

Over the past ten years EYRG has organised what is locally known as the 'Ringing Week' at Filey, where both local and visiting ringers maintain a constant ringing effort from dawn to dusk when weather permits. This is mainly to help trainee ringers learn more about the ageing and sexing of migrants and for 'inland' ringers to brush-up on their techniques by working at a coastal ringing site during autumn migration. In 2005, the Ringing Week coincided with a fall of migrants for the first time. A minimum of four ringers was present throughout the week. As can be seen from Table 1, a record 1,195 new birds were ringed during the week with 1,084 birds ringed in the first four days alone, of which 806 were Goldcrests.

Visiting ringers are always welcome to join ringing sessions at the observatory, especially during Ringing Week, when there is a good chance of connecting with 'fall conditions' and seeing plenty of migrants.

Recording data

The observatory does not employ a warden and observatory duties and activities are carried out by the members of FBOG and, in particular, by the chairman, secretary, treasurer, recorders and ringing officer. The recorders collect, maintain and deal with all the records on behalf of the observatory and all the daily log sighting records since 2005 have been computerised using Wildlife Recorder. Furthermore, the ringing data have already been computerised back to 1993 and similar work is proceeding on the data gathered between 1983 and 1993.

The observatory's recording area includes the Ordnance Survey ten-kilometre square TA18 and is bounded by the A165 Scarborough to Bridlington Road on the western side, the road to the Blue Dolphin holiday camp to the north and the chalk escarpment on its southern edge, just to the south of Reighton Holiday Camp. The map depicts the recording area, which includes the freshwater nature reserve at Filey Dams, the reclaimed and planted tip at Parish Wood, the Country Park caravan site bordered to the north by the 'Top Scrub' (which is the main ringing site), East Lea Nature Reserve, the seawatch hide on the Brigg and the whole of Filey Bay as far south as Speeton.

Table 1. *Numbers of birds ringed at Filey during the Ringing Week in October 2005.*

Species	Totals
Sparrowhawk	1
Woodcock	1
Woodpigeon	1
Long-eared Owl	1
Meadow Pipit	3
Wren	1
Dunnock	7
Robin	56
Ring Ouzel	1
Blackbird	67
Song Thrush	18
Redwing	36
Blackcap	31
Pallas's Warbler	1
Yellow-browed Warbler	1
Chiffchaff	4
Willow Warbler	1
Goldcrest	825
Blue Tit	4
Great Tit	3
Tree Sparrow	2
Chaffinch	7
Brambling	19
Greenfinch	98
Goldfinch	1
Lesser Redpoll	1
Common Redpoll	4
	1,195

A record book or 'log' is kept in the Country Park Café from Easter to November, where keys for the seawatch hide can be rented. At the time of writing, the café proprietor is a member of the group and a daily sightings board is maintained inside the café. Details of recent sightings and information concerning events together with contact details for the recorders can be found on the group website. Visitors are encouraged to leave their records in the café or at the seawatch or Dams hides, or to send them to the recorder. The first Filey Bird Report, running to 28 pages, appeared in 1977 and was produced in black & white by 13 of the members –the latest (in 2008) was a full colour affair with 128 pages covering many aspects of wildlife recording, including butterflies, moths, dragonflies and cetaceans.

FLORA AND NON-AVIAN FAUNA

Initially, the focus at Filey was on the birds. Following the founding of the observatory, the group began to record all forms of wildlife, including the special flora of the area, and since accreditation a recorder has been appointed for each of the important taxa, reports on which have started to appear in the Filey Bird Report.

Attention turns to dragonflies and butterflies during the summer months when birding can be slow. The additional water-bodies, including the excellent ponds in the newly extended observatory area at Reighton, have seen increased records of Red-veined, Yellow-winged and Black Darters, and Southern Hawker have established small populations there in recent years. With changes in climate and the presence of open water, additional butterfly species have established themselves. Speckled Wood and Comma were almost 'twitchable' in the early years but now have established populations, mainly around the Country Park. Clouded Yellow is recorded as a fairly regular migrant, feeding alongside Hummingbird Hawkmoth on the cliff sides. In recent years, with the expansion of the observatory area, colonies of Marbled White and Dingy Skipper have been found at Reighton.

Moth trapping is carried out by members within the Filey recording area, successfully adding new species to the Filey list each year. Several Yorkshire rarities, including Golden Twin-spot, White-line Dart and Death's Head Hawkmoth, have been recorded.

The additional presence of Great Crested Newts and Water Shrew was important when establishing the Filey Dams reserve and now that the former are thriving, they also appear in the ponds on Carr Naze, Top Scrub and The Tip where other newt species are also noted. Another success story at Filey Dams has been the return of the Water Vole, while evidence of Harvest Mouse nests has been found in the regenerated Totem Pole field where one was trapped during a mammal trapping session in October 2008.

Sea-watchers have regularly reported sightings of cetaceans, mainly of Harbour Porpoise, but also, over the years, of White-beaked and Bottlenose Dolphins. Spectacularly, up to seven Minke Whales were seen feeding off the Brigg in 2006.

The notable plants were also an asset when seeking to set up some of the reserves in the early years, with the presence of Nodding Bur-marigold and Adder's-tongue helping to establish the Filey Dams Reserve in the early 1980s. The Tip, Parish Wood and North Cliff Reserves all hold several orchid species including Bee, Fragrant and Pyramidal.

ACCESS, ACCOMMODATION AND ACKNOWLEDGEMENTS

Access by road from the north and south is along the coastal A165 road and by way of the A64 and A1039 from the direction of York. There are car parks at the Country Park, Church Ravine, and Filey Bus Station where there are also public toilets. A car park can also be found in the southern end of the town at West Avenue and there is a small car park at Filey Dams. Filey is also accessible by rail and bus, following which a walk of about 20 minutes will take a visitor to the nearest reserve at Filey Dams. The Country Park and access to the Brigg can be reached in approximately 25 minutes. The Filey Dams and Parish Wood reserves are accessible by wheelchair.

   The observatory is a 'virtual' observatory in the sense that there are no observatory buildings or accommodation at the present time. However, a wide range of accommodation can be arranged through the Filey & District Tourism Association and Filey Tourist Information Centre. The members of FBOG are particularly grateful to Filey Town Council and Scarborough Borough Council for their help and support in setting up and maintaining the reserves mentioned in this chapter and to a local farmer Derek Megginson, Eastburn, Driffield for generous access over his land.

Operational on unaccredited observatory lines from 1976 and accredited in 1999	
Total number of bird species recorded at the observatory:	320
Best bird year:	1994
Number of species recorded:	226
Total of birds ringed at the observatory:	26,232
Number of species:	110
Best ringing year:	2005
Number ringed:	2,440
Number of species:	51

Flamborough

by D.I.M. Wallace and members of
Flamborough Bird Observatory

THE HEAD

I never before saw Flamborough look to such perfection as it did this morning; the grand range of cliffs on our left rising perpendicularly from the water, their tops still circled by their gorse-like wreaths of mist. Seen through the medium of this light transparent veil they loomed gigantic. Filey Bay in the distance was enveloped in the same thin veil, with the famous 'Brig' showing low down on the water as a darker shade. While far out to seaward the horizon was shut in by a rich purple haze. The sea was not rough, but a long unbroken swell was rolling in. As our light boat rose like a sea-gull on the summit of these long rolling swells far out to our right we saw 'wold' beyond 'wold' of green water heaving gently upwards and then sinking again; floating on the green ocean fields, as far as the eye could reach, were innumerable Kittiwakes and Herring Gulls, Black and

---

Ian Wallace is a well-known ornithologist and writer, *Beguiled by Birds* being his latest book, and his artwork is legendary. He is also honorary life president of the Flamborough Bird Observatory.

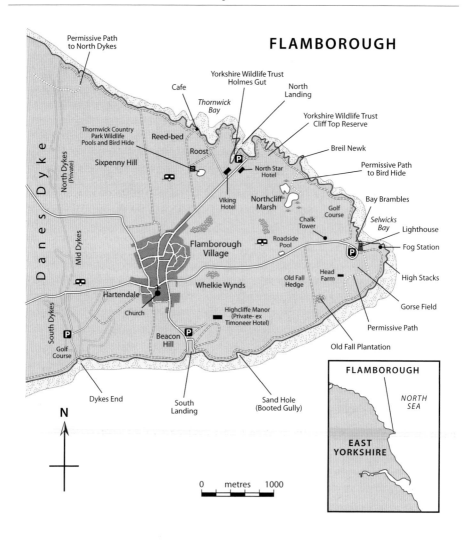

White Razorbills and Guillemots, dotted about on the waters like flowers in the inland meadows.

John Cordeaux (25th April 1865a).

Flamborough Head is a great white cape sticking out into the North Sea near Bridlington in East Yorkshire, 55°07′N, 0°05′W. Although the author always thinks of it as 'the cape', it is more popularly known as 'the Head', which is the name used throughout the chapter. Its abrupt interruption of the low-lying coast-line of Holderness to the south might be taken as a major geological feature, but the Head and its surroundings are actually part of the same post-Jurassic chalk deposit. The thrust of the original scarp around the North Wolds still shows in the eastwards runs and heights of the Head's cliffs: to the north, up to 100 metres at Danes Dyke and 11 kilometres long, and to the south, up to 76 metres and six and a half kilometres long. Although not eroding as fast as the Holderness coastal deposits, the retreat of the cliffs is nevertheless obvious at spring tides when many caves and an extensive rock skirt are exposed. In most years, exceptional rainfall and later run-off lead to increasing faults along the edges of the Head's tilted plateau and occasionally to chalk falls. For this reason, the edges of the Head are very dangerous and this must always be remembered.

Historically, the main land use on the Head's plateau was agricultural, centred on the village of Flamborough. As coastal areas became increasingly accessible, this has been much interrupted by the artefacts of seasonal tourism, noticeably in the development of two caravan sites, a second golf course, a complete coastal path system and two nature trails. Nearly all of these rights of way are situated eastwards from Danes Dyke and at peak times bring numbers onto 10–15% of the area. In recent decades, the stocking of farm animals has changed from cattle to sheep and the general field aspect is now of seed crop rotation, modified by the taking up of Environmental Stewardship Schemes and 'set aside' (a scheme now sadly redundant). New hedge plantings have also been encouraged under heritage coast and new stewardship schemes, ably encouraged by Richard Baines, conservation officer of the observatory.

The most mature woodlands are those of Danes Dyke, which have filled in the depths of the ancient earthwork for nearly five kilometres, and six much smaller patches around Micklemires, Flatmere, Syke's Plantation (all three private), South Landing, Whelkie Wynds and Old Fall Plantation. The ancient field system is mostly delineated by long thorny hedges. These link to tangles or tumbles of scrub and weeds, particularly at Hartendale, along the South Cliffs and in Selwicks and Thornwick Bays, and North Landing. Gorse has established itself as a major community at Head Farm, Holmes Gut and in Selwicks Bay, and two small, but dense reed-beds have grown up in run-off sumps in Thornwick Bay.

The advance of Bramble and willowherb has been inexorable since the mid-1980s (reducing the already small area of glades in the woodlands almost to nothing) and the huge growth of tree canopy in some areas, e.g. at Dykes End and in South Landing, has been another significant change (not least in success-fully hiding birds!).

> *The old trench and embankment called the Dyke, now covered with gorse and bracken, runs completely across the promontory, here about three miles from the sea to sea. Popular tradition ascribes it to the Danes, although it is probably of much older date. Even now, after the lapse of so many centuries, the work remains in a wonderful state of preservation, and will well repay exploring from end to end.*
>
> John Cordeaux (24th April 1865b)

In spite of its extension into the North Sea, Flamborough Head is often starved of any form of precipitation. Apart from the streams at Hartendale, Thornwick Bay and North Landing, which are used to channel treated sewage, no water course runs permanently and even the largest of farm ponds can dry out. Following torrential rain, temporary flashes can be extensive, but none has ever persisted through a sustained drought. Conversely, the littoral habitats along the cliff base have been remarkably stable. Along the southern skirt, judging by the distribution of feeding birds, they evidently support a wide range of tidal organisms.

Offshore, the sea is unusually shallow to the south, but deep to the north, combined with the confluence of waters a kilometre south-east of the Head's end creates, in almost any wind, an area of noticeable turbulence, making the area particularly attractive to seabirds. The main ecological attribute of the sea off the Head, though, is the strong extension of a southbound cool and food-rich current, flowing down the east coast from as far as the Northern Isles (Wallace & Bourne 1981).

Within the four square kilometres of the Head, the Flamborough Ornithological Group (formalised in 1982), now the Flamborough Bird Observatory (FBO), uses as its recording area only what is commonly called the 'Outer Head'. This part of the Head encompasses the woods at Danes Dyke (including the westward spurs and golf course ponds) and all of the plateau habitats, cliffs, skirt and offshore waters to the east. Not all observers confine themselves to this restricted patch, but it is the geographical fundament of the ornithological records presented later in this account. Other bird observations (e.g. from the Bempton Cliffs Reserve operated by the Royal Society for the Protection of Birds (RSPB) are not included here, but can be traced in the annual Yorkshire Naturalists' Union (YNU) reports, and Flamborough and Bempton Seabird Colony Census data now available through the observatory.

MAN AND BIRDS AT FLAMBOROUGH HEAD

To the twentieth century

Three meetings of man and bird dominate the early history of the Head's ornithology. These are the exploitation of the eggs of breeding seabirds by 'climming' the north cliffs, the periodic slaughter of Kittiwakes and other marine species for so-called 'sport' or plumage and the occasional glimpse of the ancient bird community characteristic of the chalkland areas. The most evocative of this 'lost paradise' of chalkland birds is the certain presence from at least the seventeenth century to 1830 of Great Bustards. Breeding regularly, parties of up to 15 were also encountered in journeys from Bridlington Town to Flamborough Village. More surprisingly, in the winter of 1814/15, one of two Little Bustards was shot. Other victims of the gun in this era included many Dotterels annually – hence the aptly named 'Dotterel Inn' at Reighton – and further records include the 1791 observation that they were 'stupid birds easily enticed into a net'. Their passage was, however, mainly an inland one with few reaching the Outer Head (as is still the case).

The realisation that the Head had a magnetic effect on seabirds appears to have gained favour at the beginning of the 1840s, but with many specimen clues (to be later repeated by modern discoveries) also secured from sailboats in the 1880s. Thus the occasional multitude of tubenoses, the passing of all four skuas and even titbits such as King Eider at Bridlington in 1846 and a White-winged Black Tern off the Head in 1867, were all demonstrated before 1900, but without any sense of scale or pattern of occurrence.

One reason for the erratic interpretation of the Head's early records was the preoccupation of local people and visiting 'sportsmen' with the harvesting for consumption, profit and 'sport' of the breeding seabirds. This remarkable exploitation lasted, in various fashions from, certainly, the late eighteenth century to the last 'climming' in 1953. Climming lacks a completely definitive account, but it is well covered by Mather (1986) and Vaughan (1998). Intriguingly, the 'sporting' slaughter of Kittiwakes and other seabirds provoked one of the earliest English initiatives in bird conservation, culminating in the passing of the Sea Bird Preservation Act in 1869.

'One of these would-be sportsmen laid a wager that he would shoot eighty sea-birds within an hour, and he had the discredit and disgrace of having succeeded in doing so. In fact, the very tameness of the birds, through the unwanted protection extended to them for the summer months, proved in the end an element of danger to them. "They trust in our humanity, and suffer in consequence." I went three or four years ago from Bridlington to Scarborough for the day on a steamboat, and one of these cheap excursionists employed himself for the whole of the way back in shooting at every unfortunate seabird which the vessel came near … the tameness of the birds kept them without fear in the track; and these, of course, as there could be no stopping to pick them up, could only be left on the sea, to die, maimed and mangled, utterly useless to the wretched shooter himself or any one else; a painful and pitiable sight.'

The Reverend F.O. Morris fulminating against the slaughter
of Kittiwakes and other seabirds in The Times (1874).

Ornithological records in the nineteenth century were also driven by the economic forces of the collectors' marketplace. Specimens were sold at prices that offered substantial profit to the gunner or middle-handler. Accordingly, the countryside was full of sharp eyes and Flamborough Head provided many targets. Overall, the list of migrants and vagrants produced by John Cordeaux (the father of British migration studies) and Matthew Bailey (the then Bridlington taxidermist) in 1894 set the stage for the future 'miracles' of east coast watches. Not all their claims have stood the test of time, but they did include a Red-footed Falcon at Bempton on 10 July 1869, 'many thousands' of Little Auks in December 1894 and January 1895, a Snowy Owl on the Head on 14 October 1867, a Tengmalm's Owl on 1 October 1863 and a 'vagrant' Little Owl in 1860. Add to this numerous Shore Larks, 'Scandinavian' Rock Pipits and Waxwings, an immigration of Jays in 1882, a Two-barred Crossbill in 1898 and Lapland Buntings in both spring and autumn 1893 in a period when the number of Snow Buntings was described as 'immense'. Even one of Heinrich Gätke's Christmas wishes to John Cordeaux (they were great friends) was fulfilled on 24 May 1888 when a flock of 50–60 Pallas's Sandgrouse came in.

Comparable records of breeding birds and common migrants from the nine-teenth century are infuriatingly scant, but both the runs of cliffs were tenanted not just by seabirds, but also by Stock Doves (until 1890), Swifts and House Martins (the latter only just surviving today), Chough (to 1861), Ravens (to 1894) and even Tree Sparrows. For other species of the fields and trees, the record is harder to interpret. The introduction of Red-legged Partridges in 1892 appears to have depressed the population of Greys. Snipe were regular in winter, after 'many' in autumn, Skylarks occurred in 'enormous numbers' in autumn and Dunnocks swarmed everywhere in early September 1882. Both Wheatears and Whinchats bred and Black Redstarts came on easterly winds, often in 'consider-able numbers' in May, but curiously there was not one old record of Bluethroat. Rooks came in 'immense immigrations from the Continent' and amazingly Hooded Crows (now a scarce bird) bred irregularly from 1871 to 1891. In addi-tion to the resident Starlings, 'vast arrivals' of 'purple-headed' birds came in winter, and where Lesser Redpoll were truly resident the Common was a 'some-what irregular October immigrant', but formed an 'enormous' flock in January 1907.

Overall, the historical ornithology of the Head is a remarkable testament to the enthusiasm and application of its then very few collectors and observers. So it is astonishing that from the first decade of the twentieth century the trail of the Head's birds was almost entirely lost for half a century.

After the war

After the Second World War, the Head attracted small but growing numbers of birdwatchers, but their normally late arrivals (on most days not before 11:00 hrs) clearly obscured the true scale of seabird passage. What was certainly an albatross was not claimed and even the occurrences of Sooty Shearwaters remained rather clouded. 'If you want to see such, you really ought to go to Filey Brigg' was the atti-tude of Henry Bunce, who led the four visiting observers of the YNU. It was a strange statement because Geoff Brown of Bridlington already knew of summer evening flypasts of Manx Shearwaters. Regrettably, the two communicated little and there was no repeat of the Cordeaux-Bailey cooperation, in fact rather the opposite. Even so, the Flamborough list began to grow again in the 1960s, partic-ularly given the early ringing efforts of Alan Walker, who travelled determinedly from Knaresborough.

The Head's first Icterine Warbler, on 30 August 1942, was the only wartime delight, but in the 1950s three new species were found, while in the 1960s 11 more appeared. These included some remarkable waders including a Stone-curlew on 1 October 1960, a Red-necked Phalarope for two days in May 1962 (found by current stalwart Brett Richards, then a youthful teenager), a Temminck's Stint for four days in May 1963 and an Avocet on 23 April 1968. Also in 1963, up to 15 Wood Sandpipers appeared in late June and early August, and they have never come back again in such numbers. At long last, at the end of the 1960s a few observers and ringers demonstrated that the Head could actually pull down uncommon passer-ines. Spurn Point's then virtual monopoly of such delights was broken by an

Ortolan Bunting on 8 September 1968, a Pallas's Warbler on 27 October of that year and a Yellow-browed Warbler on 5 October 1969.

Of breeding birds, there was little real information: the slow recovery of the Kittiwakes peaked in the 1950s; Collared Doves bred first in 1961. For wintering species, the 1960s saw proof of the residence of Purple Sandpipers along the rock skirt and at Bridlington Harbour, and following an arrival of up to 40 Shore Larks in October 1961, 24 wintered. A new decade opened with a Red-throated Pipit on 10 May 1970 and a huge arrival of Waxwings on 7 November, but it was not just the birds that changed in the 1970s.

From ornithological group to bird observatory, 1972–2008

From August 1972, a new group of enthusiastic and organised observers emerged. First Ian Wallace, then Andrew Lassey, Irene Smith, Andrew Grieve, Dave Hobson, Andrew Allport and finally John Harriman appeared and took on the Head's dual challenge of sea-watching and landbird hunting, the latter now without the gun. From the beginning of this era, Andrew Lassey ensured a personal daily log was maintained, the data of which the observatory has access to. History has a habit of repeating itself, and following the big, diverse falls in August 1972 (and a stunning Rufous Bush Chat found in Selwicks Bay by a lucky Keith Allsopp on a day trip on 5 October 1972), Flamborough Head quickly gained a raised profile in county and national ornithology. 'You lot are definitely putting the Head on the map', commented John Mather as the flow of records to the YNU grew and grew. Spurn and Filey had a rival at long last!

It is worth repeating that the more recent observers on the Head, and particularly the Outer Head, owe their introduction to the marvellous birds of Flamborough Head to that earlier group of observers along with Henry Bunce, Bill Curtis (another stalwart of the YNU) and Geoff Brown (the most caring local inheritor of the Head's traditions). But for their help in the early and mid-1970s, the nascent Flamborough Ornithological Group (FOG) might not have developed. As it was, their experience and guidance was instrumental in the development and discipline of new observers coming to the Head. As a result of the work of these stalwarts of Flamborough, the possibility of observatory status was discussed as a new objective for the Head, in the late 1990s.

Following a period of intense activity by a small band of dedicated people, lead principally by Jenny and Paul Butterworth, FBO was finally accredited in January 2002. After its first few years, the observatory was successful in persuading Peter Pearson (already heavily involved in the successful acquisition of reserves for the Wildlife Trust movement in both Yorkshire and Lancashire) to take on the role of chair. Under Peter's leadership, the observatory started to chart a new course at Flamborough. However, it is still important to recognise that the traditions and successes of the Head are bound up inextricably with the dedicated band of observers who came to explore 'the Cape' in the 1970s.

THE BIRDS

Breeding birds

The mapping discipline of the first two British Trust for Ornithology (BTO) Breeding Bird Atlases places the Head plateau within three ten-kilometre Ordnance Survey squares, namely TA72, TA73 and TA63. Awkwardly, the group's selection of the Outer Head as its recording area means that all of TA72 and the inner (westward) parts of TA73 and TA63 (about 1.6 kilometres wide) are not searched. Accordingly, relating the overall modern record of breeding bird diversity on the Head to that of the Outer Head alone is not easy.

It appears, however, that from a maximal presence of 99 potentially breeding species registered from the Head during the two Atlas periods (1968–1972 and 1988–1991), 86 were proved to have bred successfully. Intriguingly, from 1988–1991, the overall diversity in the inner square was no higher than that in the outer two, with 84 species in each area, giving the lie to the long-cherished idea that the Outer Head had something of an impoverished 'island community' of breeding

Table 1. *Breeding birds of Flamborough Head cliffs (including the Bempton seabird colony counts).*

Species	History	Recent counts
Fulmar	First bred 1922	725 pairs (1985–88)
Gannet	First chick 1938	2,552 nests (1999)
Cormorant	Extinct by 1880s	1 or 2 pairs erratically
Shag	Re-colonised 1957	32 pairs (1998–2002)
Peregrine	Extinct in 1879 and again in 1920	1 pair (2004—2006)
Herring Gull		1,250 pairs
Kittiwake		85,095 pairs (1998–2002)
Guillemot		46,685 birds (1998–2002)
Razorbill		8,539 birds (1998—2002)
Black Guillemot		Extinct after 1838, single pair in 1938
Puffin		2,615 pairs (1998–2002)
Rock Dove/ Feral Pigeon	Long the largest British colony	70% pure in the 1960s, 60% in the 1980s, with 5,000 mixed birds in the 1980s
Swift	Entered cliffs in 19th century	<10 pairs nest in Flamborough village regularly
Sand Martin	Large colonies in sand veins of the south cliffs in 19th century	c.150 pairs (1985)
House Martin	Sizeable numbers in 19th century	c.150 pairs (1985)
Rock Pipit		20 pairs (1985)
Black Redstart		1 pair, latterly in 1994
Chough	Extinct in the 19th century	
Raven	Extinct in 1894	

birds. If it has any merit, it is in the marked and understandable restriction of woodland species east of Danes Dyke.

The observatory's records from the Outer Head have added six species to the 86 proven breeding birds; the most remarkable being the 'invasion' of Common Rosefinches in 1992 and a pair of Marsh Warblers in 2001. These most recent additions bring the overall total for the recording area to 92 species. No true measure of the total number of breeding birds on the Head has been attempted. Any total would be dominated by the hordes of cliff-nesting seabirds whose fortunes have been most recently summarised by Brown and Grice (2004).

Counts and estimates of the scarcer species of the Outer Head can be found in the observatory's annual reports. Many farmland bird species such as the Yellowhammer breed and winter in locally significant numbers and the Corn Bunting, which is now reduced to a mere handful of pairs where there were once scores. Conversely though, the local Tree Sparrows ride on and in 2005 it was a double delight to welcome back the Peregrine and the Reed Warbler. Currently our most threatened breeding birds may be Garden Warbler and Spotted Flycatcher, going or gone the same way as Willow Tit and Lesser Redpoll, but only reflecting national trends.

Wintering birds

Fieldwork for the BTO Winter Atlas ran its course for three winters from 1981/82 to 1983/84 and in the same three ten-kilometre squares a total of 121 species were recorded, a figure exceeding the breeding species by 48%. Over the same period, all these species were registered within the Outer Head recording area, and at least 11 others can be added to give a grand total of 132 species that have occurred in winter. Furthermore, a variety of the commoner wintering species have occurred in substantial numbers (Table 2).

The early 1980s saw two major changes in the species mix in winter: the almost complete withdrawal of summer visitors, with only the odd 'replacement' Blackcap and Chiffchaff fitfully present, and the hard weather passage of northerly breeding birds, with the variety of divers, grebes, wildfowl, birds of prey, waders, gulls, thrushes, finches and buntings noticeably increased.

Table 2. *Peak one-day counts of commoner wintering species 1976–2008.*

Species	Count	Month
Purple Sandpiper	83	December
Dunlin	611	December
Redshank	177	February
Turnstone	273	December
Skylark	970	December
Shore Lark	92	December
Rock Pipit	75	December
Twite	85	December
Lapland Bunting	416	November
Snow Bunting	192	November
Corn Bunting	191	December

In the last two decades, however, the winter bird community has become much thinner and more unstable. The factors formerly affecting the arrival of wintering birds have become less regular and predictable, most notably the less severe winter weather both here and on the near Continent and, in particular, the collapse in fish landings by near-water trawlers in to Bridlington. Dramatic decreases in the records of Red-throated Diver, Great Crested Grebe, Shag, 'grey geese', sea-ducks, Golden Plover, Lapwing, Snipe, Herring Gull, both 'white-winged' gulls and Skylark, Shore Lark and Snow Bunting have led to a marked reduction in the winter diversity of birds, both at sea and in the fields. Other species in decline are Woodcock, Long-eared Owl, winter thrushes, Starling and Reed Bunting. All this means that the woods and other dense cover are emptier than they used to be in the dark months. However, recent habitat creation by the Stewardship schemes is close to achieving the once three-figure flock of Corn Buntings wintering on the Outer Head, with the 80 birds counted in the winter of 2007/08.

> *After a quiet first half, February became Flamborough's best ever time for wild geese 'on the deck', Northcliff Marsh did not pull down the ten Brents of the 13th, but from the next day until the 23rd, it became tenanted by six, later 21 Barnacles, one, later 21 Russian Whitefronts and best of all, for six days a majestic rossicus Bean.*
>
> (Newsome & Willoughby 1993)

> *1996 started with only average counts of Red-throated Divers, the January peak being 115 on the 8th, but numbers noticeably increased in early February, with 245 on the 4th, 270 on the 11th and 363 on the 18th. A notable movement of 603 occurred on the 23rd, but this was smartly and totally eclipsed on the 24th with another 1040 south and in a demonstration of their unusual displacement 341 north at the same time. After another 605 on the 25th, the all time record dispersal – equivalent to 20 to 30% of the British winter population – ceased, but was also noted off East Kent where day counts exceeded 200.*
>
> (Lassey 1996)

Migrant birds

Since the status of many breeding and wintering species off or on the Head is complex, where they often present themselves as migrants, it is difficult to describe succinctly the classes and numbers of migrants seen at Flamborough Head. What is clear is that the promise of the nineteenth century observations and those of the post-war era had been more than kept by modern observers. The record of migration has also been remarkably diversified, not least by the Head's most dedicated watcher, Andrew Lassey, who became resident in Flamborough in 1978 and has recorded almost daily since then.

As with many birding hotspots (and Flamborough Head is no different), birders tend to visit the known key areas with the hope of a find. However, the dedicated group of regular observers on the Head have, over the years, deployed all techniques open to them. This ranges from netting down 'Old Fall', all day sea-watches (particularly by Brett Richards and the late Dave Beaumont), deep-wood and other hotspot searches, further dedicated netting (operated by East Yorkshire Ringing Group), hedge-walks, stubble-sweeps, raptor-scans, beach and rock-checks, roost-inspections, indeed any ploy that would increase the sampling of all habitats and so uncover the full mix of migrants. Few stratagems remain untried, including initiating the first tape-luring of petrels in Yorkshire by Andrew Lassey, Mike Pearson, Mark Newsome and Paul Willoughby, and we may yet add fixed nets in the two reed-beds.

Over the past 30 years, since the first year of substantial cover in 1976, Flamborough Head has delivered to Yorkshire ornithology many records of passerine migrants that were once thought to be the prerogative of Spurn and the other northern and eastern bird observatories. Although in a way plagued by too much cover – good for birds, but frustratingly less so for observers – the observatory has logged an impressive overall record of landbird migration. Thus while diurnal overhead passage is not pronounced – the Head offers no major leading line and actually interrupts coasting birds – nocturnal and diurnal falls can be quite dramatic and occasionally huge (exceeding 30,000 birds). The visibility to migrants of the Head's bulk, with its white sides or brilliant light, no doubt contributes to its avian magnetism. One example from October 2005:

> *Things started to happen in 'the bushes' in the late afternoon on the 14th with a Long-eared Owl and 540 Goldcrests the forerunners of an enormous influx on the 15th. On that day the birds were 'carpeted' across the Head, being led by 9,500 Goldcrests, 27,000 Redwings, 650 Bramblings, 31 Ring Ouzels and 24 Stonechats. Quality came in the way of two Pallas's Warblers, 15 Yellow-browed Warblers, two Richard's Pipits, two Northern Bullfinches, a Hawfinch, a Crossbill and six [Common] Redpolls. On the 16th, a Marsh Tit was moving inland from Selwicks Bay – our first ever migrant of that species relegating an Olive-backed Pipit to an also-ran.*

(Marshall 2005).

The other result inexorably came as, sitting on average ten kilometres out to sea, the observatory's sea-watchers rewrote, piece by piece, virtually the entire

Table 3. *Peak one-day passage counts of commoner waterfowl 1976–2008.*

Species	Count	Month
Red-throated Diver	1,040	February
Whooper Swan	52	November
Pink-footed Goose	4,837	November
Wigeon	1,128	October
Teal	651	November
Eider	1,473	November
Common Scoter	1,630	October
Goldeneye	112	November
Red-breasted Merganser	52	November

ornithology of the western North Sea. Hopefully the ghosts of the pioneers and collectors of the late nineteenth century will have smiled.

An early indication of what the observatory has contributed to east coast perceptions was given by Wallace and Bourne (1981), already referred to, but it bears repeating that our 'at sea' location and all out effort has delivered the longest series of records, and many of the highest land-based counts, for the North Sea, of the three commoner divers, Fulmar (both light and blue morph), Great and Cory's Shearwater, Sooty and Manx Shearwater, Balearic (and possibly Yelkouan) Shearwater, all the skuas (with Long-tailed never a rarity), Little Gull, terns and auks, most notably Little Auk (not just in wrecks, but in 'return movements' in the thousands). Table 4 gives a flavour of some of the counts. Dropped chins and rubbed eyes have long been dispensed with, particularly given a northerly blow and cloud cover to mask the glare of the sunrise. The seabird pageants off the Head are truly phenomenal. Always note, though, that at Flamborough Head, the sky can be as full of birds as the surface of the sea, as in big movements divers pass at up to 90 metres above sea level!

We have yet to calculate long-term trends for most of our migrants, but there is little doubt that both 'at sea' and 'in the bushes', many of the recent spring and autumn movements have been far less substantial than those of the 1970s and early 1980s. For passerines, this clearly stems from the reductions in western European populations and, particularly for our veterans, it is sad to note today's paltry counts of Red-throated Diver, Shag, Teal, Golden and Grey Plovers, Jack Snipe, Arctic and Great Skuas, Turtle Dove (with no autumn birds in 2005!) and Cuckoo.

For the passerines 'in the bushes', the vagaries of long distance migration, local fall conditions and changes in the growth of cover obscure species trends more

Table 4. *Peak one-day passage counts of commoner seabirds 1976–2008.*

Species	Count	Month
Fulmar	19,300	February
Sooty Shearwater	2,721	September
Manx Shearwater	2,658	September
Gannet	7,390	September
Cormorant	240	October
Shag	1,379	January
Pomarine Skua	330	November
Arctic Skua	1,056	August
Long-tailed Skua	485	October
Great Skua	266	August
Little Gull	8,034	September
Herring Gull	1,700	February
Kittiwake	156,000	July
Sandwich Tern	2,134	August
Common Tern	3,800	September
Guillemot	94,700	June
Razorbill	32,700	April
Puffin	37,800	June
Little Auk	10,947	January

than those of the marine birds. Again, there can be no doubt that the migrations of many are now only shades of what once reached the Head, with the most obvious long-term reductions being in Skylark, Tree Pipit, Yellow Wagtails (of several races), White Wagtail *Motacilla alba alba,* Redstart, Whinchat, Bluethroat, Ring Ouzel, Grasshopper Warbler, Sedge Warbler, Garden Warbler, Willow Warbler, Spotted and Pied Flycatchers, Red-backed Shrike, Hooded Crow (now a true rarity; what would Gätke and Cordeaux have made of that?), Starling, Chaffinch (outnumbered by Brambling in 2005) and Reed Bunting.

Conversely, some irruptive and 'reversed' migrants have recently been recorded in surprising numbers. Thus some solace to the oft-heard 'general lack in birds' has been provided by persistent Northern Great Spotted Woodpeckers *Dendrocopos major major* (and Treecreeper), Dunnock, Stonechat (of some intriguing plumage variations), Pallas's and Yellow-browed Warbler (both outnumbering Chiffchaff on some autumn days!), Siskin, Common Redpoll, Crossbill and one of the Head's annual specialities – Northern Bullfinch *Pyrrhula pyrrhula pyrrhula.* Young observers, please note, it isn't all 'doom and gloom'.

> *It was a superb year for Northern Bullfinches in Britain. 22 arrived on the 17th October, beating the 1994 peak count by three, and were followed by other birds or small parties of up to three on nine days up to the 7th November. Intriguingly, other Bullfinches were also on the move in the same period with up to three initially, but no less than eight on 14th November and six on the 20th.*
>
> (Marshall 2004).

Rare birds

The Head's almost marine location and food source is unique; its second light-house (the first being Britain's oldest, a chalk tower dating back to 1674) blasts out a beam visible in nearly all directions for 32 kilometres and more, and once reached, its habitats offer nourishment and shelter to exhausted vagrants. Bar

Table 5. *Maximum daily counts of commoner landbird migrants 1976–2008.*

Species	Count	Month
Skylark	880	October
Meadow Pipit	2,100	September
Robin	1,200	October
Blackbird	7,800	November
Fieldfare	24,000	October
Song Thrush	6,000	October
Redwing	27,000	October
Goldcrest	9,500	October
Starling	25,000	January
Brambling	650	October
Siskin	1,000	October

the lack of a leading line for diurnal strays, the Head and (especially) the Outer Head, present a rare bird viewpoint cum platform par excellence.

From a storm-twisted bush near the lighthouse a redbreast, the 'messenger of calm decay', was pouring forth its sweet and lonely song, while overhead the bright scarlet and white rays from the highly polished reflectors were projected, like the spread of a gigantic fan, far into the gathering gloom. Various species of migratory birds have from time to time been picked up outside the lantern; attracted by the glare they fly like moths against the glass, and are killed; about the middle of October, last year a woodcock dashed right through the glass, which is a quarter of an inch in thickness, and was picked up mutilated and dead from amongst the lamps.

John Cordeaux (16th October 1865c)

The usual October contrasts showed in the third week. On the 20th, a Long-tailed Duck stopped off, not on the sea, but at the unlikely venue of Old Fall Flash. The immature Saker [Falco cherrug] whizzed through for a second time on the 22nd, but the real shaker on that day was our second-ever Yank [North American] passerine, an adult White-throated Sparrow – not so likely to have been helped by the wind as by a passing ship. The crowds searching for it on the 23rd came up with the added prize of two Bearded Tits.

(Marshall 2002).

Table 6. *Peak one-day counts of scarcer landbird migrants 1976–2008.*

Species	Count	Month
Wryneck	23	May
Wheatear	205	September
'Greenland' Wheatear	113	May
Bluethroat	10	May
Tree Pipit	65	September
Black Redstart	19	October
Redstart	263	September
Whinchat	90	September
Ring Ouzel	61	October
Icterine Warbler	14	August
Barred Warbler	6	August
Pallas's Warbler	6	October
Yellow-browed Warbler	28	October
Firecrest	26	October
Pied Flycatcher	150	August
Red-breasted Flycatcher	7	September
Red-backed Shrike	25	August
Common Rosefinch	7	June
Lapland Bunting	416	October

Racial attributions

About 20 subspecies are mentioned regularly in county bird reports, but given our wealth of Palearctic experience, we look for more than the normal or expected. We feel that careful assignation to subspecies, summed over long periods of time, can make for real advances in ornithological knowledge. Our detailed observations, often coupled with in-hand examination, have featured numerous races from fascinating species complexes that are sadly all too often ignored in today's rush for more species. Passerine examples encompass two Continental forms of Song Thrush (occurring annually), Asian Lesser Whitethroat (from 1977), Northern and European Long-tailed Tits, and Northern Treecreeper (almost annual) whilst, most resembling a minefield, are intergrading hybrid Pine Buntings and Yellowhammers! We are eager to cooperate with other bodies interested in racial attribution, as a huge source of dispersal data is going begging.

Best year and best days

One of the things about purposeful birdwatching is that every year brings its triumphs (and the odd disaster) but, if a long list is the criterion, Flamborough Head's best year has to be 1995. With 42 observers including experienced sea-watchers and ringers contributing records, 245 species found their way into the annual report. This total beat the previous record, from 1993, by two and was 26 more than our most recent nadir score of 219 in 2004. It may be some time before the observatory beats this record.

For best days, we are spoilt for choice. From the early years, we could look at the spring 'rush' of 1 May 1978, starring Red-footed Falcon and Siberian Stonechat *Saxicola torquata maura* (Wallace 1979), or the amazingly diverse seabird passage of 1 October in the same year, both of which stand out. More recently, even one of our most ardent observers, Brett Richards, was ecstatic over Britain's first Taiga Flycatcher found at Flamborough by Andrew Lassey on 26 April 2003, and the record avalanche of 27,000 Redwings and 9,500 Goldcrests on 15 October 2005 show how either just one bird or many thousands can equally thrill.

Sea-watching

The biggest, most diverse offshore passages or 'compressions' occur in periods of strong north-west to north-east winds and are most easily watched in 'grey light', i.e. with good cloud cover. These are viewed from the Fog Station, or in the shelter of the southern wall of the Fog Station buildings and on the cliff rim south of the stack. The cliffs can be very dangerous and it is important to state the observatory cannot be held responsible for anyone not following safety procedures.

After, or during, easterly blows, many birds also come out of the 'seabird trap' of Bridlington Bay and form an eastward procession along the south cliffs. The best spots in such conditions are at the mouth of South Landing or a suitable perch on the south-west-facing cliff to the east of South Landing. These movements allow closer views than the former, but the winds that provoke it blow less regularly.

In favourable weather conditions, Little Auks can pass the Head in their hundreds and can occasionally be seen sitting on the sea at South Landing (Ian Robinson).

Occasionally, when the north-easterlies are strong, birds are also blown into Filey Bay against the north cliffs. They then make their way back out to sea in another eastward procession This is best seen from the Fog Station.

In normal autumn weather, there is a marked southward drift and occasional strong passage of birds. To see this, the Fog Station is, again, recommended. Indeed, an evening sea-watching from here, with the birds over the sea bathed in perfect light, can be bliss!

Ringing

Ringing activities on Flamborough Head are carried out under the auspices of the East Yorkshire Ringing Group. Tactics range from the sampling of large migrant falls to the regular netting of woodland birds at Danes Dyke and the tape-luring of Storm Petrels at Thornwick Bay. The most productive sites are at Danes Dyke South, Thornwick and Selwicks Bay and along Old Fall Hedge and Old Fall Plantation.

The unusual balance of ringing catches is clearly visible in the total numbers presented in the observatory's systematic list. We are particularly proud, both of the Storm Petrel captures, which have demonstrated a remarkable range of origins, due in no small part to Andrew Lassey and Mike Pearson's hard work over many years and the diversity of our migrant samples ringing, continually supported by Ian Marshall. The grand total for the last 30 years is 36,554 birds of 147 species ringed, representing no mean effort (and investment) from our handful of voluntary part-time ringers. Whatever the fun in catching and ringing birds, the real discoveries come from the subsequent recoveries.

OTHER FAUNA AND FLORA

The mammals of Flamborough Head

We are not aware of any systematic mammal survey of the Head and our own records have all been incidental to the main bird studies. Nevertheless at least ten species of cetaceans have been recorded from the Head and the most notable observations have been of a Harp Seal in February 1983 and a small black whale that was probably a False Killer Whale in 1980. After rodents, the most visible land mammals are the small parties of European Roe Deer that appeared in the late 1970s and survive in our sparse woodland and Danes Dyke. An annotated list of 34 species, by Mark Newsome, was published in the 1994 Annual Report and the lowly Bank Vole is the only recent addition.

The larger insects of Flamborough Head

For well over 25 years through the work of Andrew Allport (in the main) and Ian Marshall (latterly), we have attempted to keep more than a considered eye on butterflies, dragonflies and damselflies, and our embryonic lists now contain 26 butterflies and 18 dragonflies and damselflies, details of which are in our annual report.

Mike Pearson had the luck to photograph one great rarity, a Camberwell Beauty, on 14 August 2002, when it conveniently alighted beside him. The second and third records of this species occurred in August 2006, and another butterfly to venture onto the Head for the first time in that year was Marbled White.

Whilst Camberwell Beauty is probably the best example of a Continental vagrant, the Head regularly attracts commoner migrants such as both Large and Small White. Naturally, numbers vary from year to year, but their occurrences can only increase if forecasts of a warming climate are to be believed. Painted Lady is a visitor from afar that can also be numerous; their ranks are thought to be swelled by butterflies emanating from Saharan Africa. An immigrant that is by no means annual is Clouded Yellow, and even in good years double-figure counts are unheard of, though there have been invasions on occasions. There is nothing more rewarding on a walk around the Outer Head on a sunny day in late summer than the sighting of a Clouded Yellow.

In recent years, Brown Argus and Comma have become established at Flamborough, while Speckled Wood has enjoyed a meteoric rise. First seen in 2003, it is now a familiar fixture, especially in autumn. With just six records so far, it is also likely that Gatekeeper will gain a foothold on the Head in the coming years as the butterfly is slowly spreading north in Britain.

One former resident worthy of mention is the Grizzled Skipper, which frequented just one acidic field close to Danes Dyke until the mid-1970s. It is sadly now thought to be extinct in Yorkshire, and it seems quite possible that the Flamborough colony post-dated others in the county by a couple of years. If the butterfly shows any signs of a northward shift again in the future, we could be a prime candidate for its return.

During the past decade, far more attention has been paid to dragonflies and damselflies than previously. Since the start of the millennium, eight species have been added to the Flamborough list, mirroring a theme encountered across much of the country. As other Odonata continue to expand their ranges, further wanderers can be expected, even though they have a distinct lack of suitable habitat to settle in.

In the 1990s, Migrant Hawker first reached the Head and August and September now see them omnipresent. Common Darter lives up to its name and is by far the most numerous of the family, with peak counts into four figures and crops such as wheat and barley the favoured locality.

Incomers from the Continent have put in numerous appearances, especially in 2004, when the first records of both Lesser Emperor and Yellow-winged Darter were made on the same day. The former was found in Selwicks Bay by visitors watching a Greenish Warbler that had arrived a few hours earlier! More recently, 2006 saw a huge influx of Red-veined Darters into Britain and Flamborough did not miss out, with totals of 25 or 30 being far in excess of any that had gone before.

Black Darter has been noted occasionally towards the end of this dragonfly's flight period, while a major surprise in the 1970s was a Golden-ringed Dragonfly hunting the same field that was so liked by Grizzled Skipper.

The moths of Flamborough Head

There has been sporadic light trapping on the Head since the late nineteenth century when a flame was used. However, the advent of more advanced equipment and techniques in the 1970s caused local naturalists to visit the Head a few times each year. The results obtained were encouraging and both the YNU recorder, Philip Winter, and Tony Ezard, recorded periodical successes at Flamborough.

Since 2003, much more attention has been paid to moths at Flamborough. The use of light traps to attract the insects has revealed previously untold secrets. Richard Baines has worked on the Outer Head with a mercury vapour (MV) lamp and Mike Pearson has used an actinic light in the village on a nightly basis outside the winter months. They are joined at weekends by Ian Marshall, who has introduced a second actinic trap in the village. Several forays with a mobile MV lamp have been made to the more diverse habitats within the recording area, such as Danes Dyke, South Landing and Thornwick Bay. An annual event has been arranged in recent years, usually at Thornwick, where the public can enjoy the spectacle of several hundred moths being drawn to a bright, powerful light.

Flamborough is famous for migrant birds and has proved to be equally so for migrant moths. Bedstraw Hawkmoth and Convolvulus Hawkmoth are two of the spectacular larger species to have been found here. 2006 saw an unprecedented influx of vagrant moths into the country and Flamborough was able to contribute in no small part. Although the sheer scale is unlikely to be repeated, 2008 also reaped rewards in terms of the quality of the immigrants, when Yorkshire's first Flame Wainscot and second Pigmy Footman were captured. The former is resident in the fens of Cambridgeshire, whereas the latter's British population is in Kent. We believe, though, that both were probably of Continental origin. In addition, the third Yorkshire record of the moth *Cydia amplana*, was seen. Emanating from Europe, it rarely ventures far away from the south coast. Given our geographical location, these incomers are hardly surprising, and the Head is now firmly on the 'mothing' map. As our experience grows, we also hope to concentrate more on 'micro-moths'.

The Head's woodlands have a wealth of resident moths that only occasionally venture into the village. Of the moths thought to be breeding at Flamborough, the chalk grassland on the cliff tops holds the species of most significance. Brindled Ochre, Confused and Annulet are three that occupy this habitat, along with healthy populations of Antler Moth and three-day fliers, namely Six-spot Burnet, Narrow-bordered Five-spot Burnet and Chimney Sweeper. We are delighted that they can be encountered here. Unfortunately, mirroring the whole country, the very small population of the rare Chalk Carpet has not been sighted since the 1990s. Contrastingly, the nationally scarce day-flying Marsh Pug has taken a particular liking to one stretch of grassland and appears to be doing extremely well. The observatory recognises the importance of Lepidoptera and also that there is still much to do regarding the moths of Flamborough Head.

THE OBSERVATORY

Although the observatory is proficient in its recording and ringing activities, it is not able to offer a daytime, let alone a night-time, base to visitors. However, being within an area which is dominated by tourism, there is no shortage of local accommodation. Given the laudable initiatives of the Butterworths, who were instrumental with Andrew Lassey in securing our observatory status, the lack of the usual 'observatory welcome' is regretted. Whilst we may never see an observatory building and a warden, we are, however, committed to working continually with other organisations with regard to the funding of further developments and the maintenance work of the Northcliff Marsh.

Although the observatory has no land of its own, we should not fail to recognise the important role that FBO played in the establishment, in 2000, of the Flamborough Cliffs Nature Reserve, owned and managed by Yorkshire Wildlife Trust. Part of the land is a designated SSSI, with the ultimate responsibility for its management resting with Natural England. It includes Holmes Gut at North Landing, and the cliffs and their border for one and a half kilometres to the east. The first management plan for the site ran until 2005 and has seen new fencing and conservation-friendly hay-making and grazing. The aim is to recreate the original coastal chalkland ecosystem and we have been contributing to the ongoing recording of its use by birds.

In 2006, an opportunity arose, with the arrival of funds through Natural England's Higher Level Stewardship scheme, to restore the once-famous Northcliff Marsh and Simon and Peter Waines, the landowners/farmers, were also keen to re-establish a thriving habitat for birds. In August 2007, after design and help from Wold Ecology Ltd, the RSPB, Steve Wadsworth representing FBO and many others, a relatively large area of wetland pools was created. The excavation work was expertly carried out by Beverley farmer Chris Freer. Shortly afterwards, a permissive access path was established and a small group of local birders built a screen from which to watch the site. Within the first two months, only the second Pectoral Sandpiper for the FBO recording area made landfall, along with Little Stint. The main target birds were also starting to use the area, particularly 20 Snipe and over 30 Teal. Records since then have shown the site to be most attractive to migrant waders and wildfowl as a resting and refuelling site on their long migrations. Whilst stop-off can be brief, as with the Avocet and the two small groups of Spoonbill sighted in 2008, the second-ever Bittern recorded by FBO spent a day on the marsh in March 2008!

These activities chime well with one of the primary objectives discussed when setting up the observatory, namely to become more involved with bird conservation on the Head. FBO have since established strong positions on management committees and with consultation groups. Management meetings are conducted with a range of bodies, including East Riding of Yorkshire Council (ERYC) (responsible for three Local Nature Reserves at South Landing, Danes Dyke and the Outer Head), Simon and Peter Waines owners of Northcliff Marsh, and Yorkshire Wildlife Trust (YWT). These links have proved instrumental in achieving visible habitat enhancement for birds and a higher profile for FBO, which is recognised as an important participant on the Head. It also plays a full role in the many jointly run projects, in particular with seabird monitoring with the RSPB and the BTO, and with the major research projects on migration through the North Sea. Finally, FBO awarded a grant to Northcliff Marsh nature reserve in 2008 and this is now regarded as an annual commitment by the observatory.

In 2007 and 2008, the arrival of the Brown Flycatcher and Brown Shrike provided a great opportunity to raise funds for local charities including FBO. Over £2,000 was collected in a car park opened by the Waines family and run by them and FBO members over the duration of the birds' stays. Head Farm is now a thriving business closely connected with bird conservation and education. Richard Baines leads tours around the farm for the farmer and FBO, and visitors can discover the rich bird life and history of the farm where breeding seabirds live cheek to beak with migrant birds!

Another subsidiary group activity has been in following many of the Head's specialities back to their home ranges. To this end, both individual members and full expeditions have ranged east to Siberia, Mongolia, Ussuriland (from 1980) and Kazakhstan (from 1987), south-east to the United Arab Emirates, Oman and Egypt (from 1988), south to Morocco (from 1982), and even to the Atlantic isles

The arrival of this Brown Flycatcher at Flamborough on 3 October 2007, the second record for Britain, enabled the observatory to raise funds for local charities (Josh Jones).

of magic tubenoses (in 2006). Taking our wits, nets and optics to such places, we have studied our vagrant species as few other groups have, and it was good to see such a formidable reach recognised in the appointment of Andrew Lassey to the British Ornithologists' Union Records Committee in 2005. Even our honorary life president, Ian Wallace, still helps that body and the British Birds Rarities Committee on occasion. Meanwhile, at a more local level, we regularly send out bird news and give as much field assistance as our small team can manage. The main conduits for more information are the observatory's website, via e-mail and via our annual report which is available from the secretary.

GETTING TO FLAMBOROUGH HEAD

Road

From Flamborough village, follow the signs to the Lighthouse along the B1259 to the car park area at the end. Those approaching via the A166 or the A614, should note that these are heavy with tourist traffic in summer.

Rail

Local trains run from Bridlington to Scarborough with a stop at Bempton, but this still leaves a further eight kilometres to the Head.

PLACES TO STAY

There is a range of options for accommodation at Flamborough: the North Star and Flaneburg Hotels, Thornwick and Sea Farm Holiday camps for caravans or camping all offer competitively-priced comfortable accommodation and are renowned for the quality of meals that include a wide range of local produce.

FINDING BIRDS AT FLAMBOROUGH

To visitors, the Head looks impressive and above all big. Where to start for a good bird of your own? Regrettably, we have to stress that much of the farmland on Flamborough Head is strictly private and that access to many areas is restricted. But never fear, several of the 'hottest spots' for uncommon birds are nowadays on or alongside official and permissive paths and the road.

For your first trip, we recommend you choose a day with easterly wind after rain and this route:

1. Drive all the way to the Lighthouse car park, pay for two or three hours and decide on either a sea-watch or a search of the bushes.
2. For a sea-watch, walk east past the Lighthouse and down to the Fog Station. Choose a safe watch point and look out scanning first the south-east sector of the sea.
3. For birds in the bushes, walk back from the Lighthouse, west along the rim of Selwicks Bay, up the road past the café, through the cottages and past the chalk tower (the original lighthouse), checking all cover and inside the 'walled garden' before the tower.
4. Once past the last of the small wooden cottages to the north of the road, turn left down the steps and path that lead south along Old Fall Hedge to Old Fall Plantation. As you do so, you will begin the most dependable kilometre for uncommon birds on the whole cape, so check anything that moves!
5. At Old Fall Plantation, you can either circle the wood or use the fenced path. The trick is to watch the tree and bush canopies as that is where the birds will be feeding. Be patient, there is nearly always an interesting bird, but you may have to wait and see.
6. Continue south from Old Fall Plantation to the South Cliffs, scanning the sea for ducks (they often flock offshore) and passing seabirds.

Now the choice is yours. Turn left to get back to the Lighthouse, via the cliff path or the new one that takes a northerly dog-leg through Head Farm. Or, turn right and check out more of the South Cliffs, the gullies and eventually South Landing. The latter route will nearly double your walk's distance, but it will also increase the chance of a successful hunt. If you choose the shorter return, your total distance will be about 3.7 kilometres, and the time taken will depend on the birds that show!

Other site guides which were published in the Flamborough Ornithological

Group Report, including a short index of 11 hot spots (1994, reprinted 1995) and more detailed descriptions of the Fog Station sea-watch area (Lassey 1993), the outermost head containing the Gorse Field, Selwicks Bay, the Golf Course and the south-east cliff top (Willoughby 1994), South Landing, the boundary of Highcliffe Manor, formerly the Timoneer Hotel, and Booted Gully (Newsome 1995), and Danes Dyke South and Beacon Hill (Newsome 1996).

The site descriptions included range scale maps and precise advice on which pieces of cover or sea sections are most likely to be harbouring birds and this information is now transposed onto the observatory website.

Although run independently of the observatory, the RSPB Seabird Cruises on the *Yorkshire Belle* from Bridlington take both members and others out into the waters off the Head. The prizes in recent years have included Fin Whale, other cetaceans and many seabirds. To share the elements with shearwaters, skuas and auks is a great experience.

For details of the cruises, please telephone RSPB Bempton Office 01262 850959 or see the East Yorkshire RSPB Local Group's website.

Flamborough Ornithological Group was formalised in 1982, becoming Flamborough Bird Observatory, which was founded in 2001 and accredited in January 2002.

Total number of bird species recorded at the observatory:	346
Best bird year:	1995
Number of species recorded:	245
Total of birds ringed at the Observatory:	36,554
Number of species:	147
Best ringing year:	2002
Number ringed:	2,715
Number of species:	69

Gibraltar Point

by Kevin Wilson, Michael Briggs, Roy Pearson,
Ted Smith and Barrie Wilkinson

Kevin Wilson is the site manager at Gibraltar Point National Nature Reserve for the Lincolnshire Wildlife Trust with responsibility for the bird observatory management and wildlife recording for the whole site.

Michael (Mick) Briggs has ringed at Gibraltar Point since the mid-1990s and is now the ringer in charge and observatory secretary.

Roy Pearson is a retired headmaster, who first visited Gibraltar Point in 1966. He commenced ringing in 1967 and gained an 'A' Permit two years later. From 2001 he has been a member of the observatory team.

A. E. (Ted) Smith was co-founder of Gibraltar Point Bird Observatory in 1948/9 with C. L. Ottoway, founder and honorary secretary of the Lincolnshire Wildlife Trust 1948–1969, chairman 1969–98 and president from 1998. He was a member of the Nature Conservancy/NCC 1956–78 and chairman of the Committee for England from 1971–78, receiving an OBE for services to nature conservation in 1963 which was advanced to CBE in 1998.

Barrie Wilkinson first became involved with Gibraltar Point when he got on his bike and cycled over to Gib soon after his fifteenth birthday in 1952, becoming ringer in charge at the observatory from 1955 to 1958 and again from 1964 to 1976. He worked in the main for the then Lincolnshire Trust for Nature Conservation, ultimately becoming reserves manager with responsibility for coordinating the management of 100 reserves.

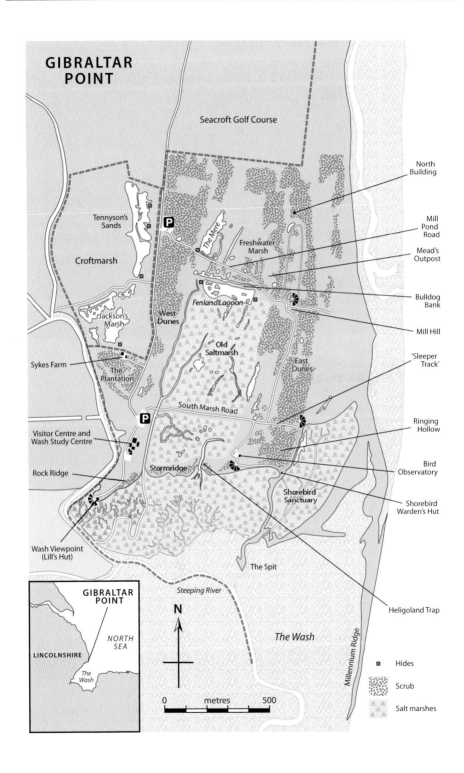

GIBRALTAR
POINT

Seacroft Golf Course

North
Building

Tennyson's
Sands

P

The Mere

Freshwater
Marsh

Mill
Pond
Road

Mead's
Outpost

Croftmarsh

Bulldog
Bank

Fenland Lagoon

Jackson's
Marsh

West
Dunes

Mill Hill

Sykes Farm

Old
Saltmarsh

East
Dunes

'Sleeper
Track'

The
Plantation

South Marsh Road

Ringing
Hollow

P

Visitor Centre and
Wash Study Centre

Bird
Observatory

Rock Ridge

Stormridge

Shorebird
Sanctuary

Shorebird
Warden's Hut

Wash Viewpoint
(Lill's Hut)

The Spit

Heligoland Trap

GIBRALTAR
POINT

Steeping River

N

NORTH
SEA

LINCOLNSHIRE

The
Wash

The Wash

Millennium Ridge

0   metres   500

Hides

Scrub

Salt marshes

INTRODUCTION

The exposed central section of the Lincolnshire coast has been subject to erosion since the Middle Ages, and is now protected by massive sea walls. Within the shelter of this coastal bulge, however, the coastline turns gradually westwards, and sand and shingle accretion forms a broad promontory at the north-western corner of the Wash. This was the 'ness' of the village of Skegness. In the more sheltered conditions prevailing in the Roman period, a ferry across the Wash from hereabouts connected the end of the road from Lincoln with the start of the Peddars Way at Brancaster on the north Norfolk coast.

Accretion continued southwards in the form of a massive sand-dune system (the West Dunes), which ends in the new promontory known as Gibraltar Point where the coast turns south-westwards to form the western shore of the Wash. This process also diverted the outfall of the River Lymn (or Steeping River) further south into the Wash. Salt marshes, which developed in the shelter of this dune system, were progressively reclaimed for agriculture, a process completed by the early nineteenth century with the creation of Sykes Farm.

At the southern end of these dunes by the estuary of the river, a small settlement grew up with the name of Gibraltar which, significantly perhaps, is first mentioned in documents in the 1770s not long after the British capture of the more famous rock of the same name. An inn known as the Ship Inn was built at the end of the dune ridge and no doubt attracted custom from sea and river trade. In later years it became a private house and was eventually demolished in 1939. Meantime, in 1859, a coastguard station with a small tower was built on what was then the edge of the sea. The coastguards left in 1925 and the building became a holiday home until its acquisition as a field station in 1958. It still forms the core of the Wash Study Centre.

Although less than five kilometres from Skegness, Gibraltar was still relatively remote. It was reached from near the outskirts of the town by a sandy track along the landward edge of the dunes, which was converted to a tarmac road only during the Second World War when Gibraltar Point was under military occupation for artillery training and coastal defence. The accessibility of the place, however, was to change dramatically once the war was over and car ownership vastly increased.

During the nineteenth century a ridge and runnel beach – dune ridges interspersed with strips of salt marsh – developed to the east of the West Dunes. One of these ridges, 500 metres to the east of the West Dunes, accreted more strongly than the others and built up into a line of higher dunes (the East Dunes), leaving a large expanse of salt marsh, the Old Marsh, flooding only at the highest spring tides. This marsh was almost entirely cut off from the sea by a surge tide in the 1920s, which threw up a bank of sand and shingle – still known as the Storm Beach – from the base of the East Dunes across the southern end of the marsh leaving only a single creek open to the sea.

At an earlier date the upper part of the Old Marsh had been entirely enclosed from the sea by the building of an earth bank known as Bulldog Bank to create an area of pasture for cattle grazing. The Freshwater Marsh, as it became known, developed a rich and varied flora and provided the site for the one and a half hectare Mere, which was excavated in 1972–73 and which has proved to be a major bird attraction throughout the seasons. The Freshwater Marsh also has several smaller ponds that are important for invertebrates. On the southern side of Bulldog Bank is the Fenland Lagoon, excavated in 1991 and named after its sponsors, Fenland Laundries of Skegness. Water levels are controlled by a sluice, and islands provide nest and roost sites for waders and gulls.

The East Dunes continued to grow southwards, initially in the shape of a shingle spit (the Spit), which through the second half of the last century provided the main nesting site for Little Terns and Ringed Plovers and a high tide roost for waders. This eventually developed into a sand dune ridge, the distal end curving westwards before decaying. In its shelter a salt marsh, the New Marsh, developed and in its early stages of vegetation succession provided an important feeding area for waders and seed-eating passerines. The pattern of ridge and salt marsh development has continued to seaward, culminating in the development of the Millennium Ridge.

A BRIEF HISTORY OF GIBRALTAR POINT
NATIONAL NATURE RESERVE

In 1937 Lindsey County Council purchased 76 hectares of the East and West Dunes in order to preserve it as an Open Space. In 1948, after wartime military occupation, the County Council and the newly founded Lincolnshire Naturalists' Trust (now the Lincolnshire Wildlife Trust and from here on referred to as the Trust) agreed that the area should be managed under lease, as a nature reserve, by the Trust. The Council then acquired a further 28 hectares to add to the reserve, including land on which the old coastguard house stood. Leases of the foreshores were also secured, and the Skegness Urban District Council (now East Lindsey District Council) agreed in 1955 that 80 hectares of its adjoining sand-hills property should also be managed as part of the reserve. The status of the reserve, already an SSSI, was strengthened in 1953 when the County Council became the first Local Authority in England to declare a nature reserve under the provisions of the National Parks and Access to the Countryside Act of 1949. The national status of the whole reserve was formally recognised by the Nature Conservancy Council in 1984. It is also a Natura 2000 site under the EC Birds and Habitat Directives and a Ramsar site.

Shortly after the 1953 declaration, however, a new threat arose to the reserve in the shape of a large caravan camp project in the home paddock of Sykes Farm (the farmhouse had been destroyed by fire in 1947) immediately adjoining the southern end of the reserve. After a major public enquiry the Council acquired the land through a Compulsory Purchase Order and the field became part of the reserve. It was planted as a wood – the Plantation – in 1966, adding a new habitat to the reserve that is especially valuable for birds. The site of the house and the farmyard were purchased by the Trust in 1977, the three-bay cart shed and barn being splendidly converted into the office and management base for the reserve with a flat for the assistant warden. In 1995 and 2000 the arable fields to the north covering some 32 hectares were also purchased by the Trust for reversion to pasture with extensive lagoons, which have now produced a rich bird habitat. Four hides now overlook this area known as Jackson's Marsh and Tennyson's Sands or collectively Croft Marsh.

The popular concept of a nature reserve in 1949 was still one of a closely guarded place where the public were not welcomed and probably excluded. Gibraltar Point had to be different. There was open access for the public and the Trust had to adapt management practices accordingly. In doing so it pioneered some of the now familiar means of reconciling access with conservation: a good footpath system including a sleeper track through the East Dunes to the seashore; hides for birdwatching at strategic points; and a voluntary wardening system to reinforce staff, including a full-time seashore watch to protect the Little Tern and Ringed Plover colonies. However, perhaps most important was the creation of an information kiosk on the main car park – believed to be the first of its kind on any nature reserve in England – that displayed pictorial notices and guides on the reserve and its wildlife. This was replaced in 1974 by a visitor centre adjacent to the residential field station, which itself underwent a major expansion and refurbishment and reopened in 2006 as the Wash Study Centre. The later development of the field station is more fully described by Ted Smith (2007). The centre is available for use by schools, colleges and universities and amateur naturalist groups. By such means it has been possible to protect the wildlife and natural features of this popular reserve which is visited now by some 200,000 people each year.

THE DEVELOPMENT OF THE BIRD OBSERVATORY

The establishment of the Gibraltar Point Bird Observatory was an integral element in the creation of the nature reserve. Although Gibraltar Point was not as well known to migration watchers as some of the other early observatories like Skokholm, Fair Isle or Spurn, it had attracted local interest in the immediate post-war years, and evidence of its ornithological importance gave added impetus to the nature reserve negotiations. Action to set up the observatory came initially in 1947 from county ornithologists Lenten Ottoway and Ted Smith, the latter the prospective honorary secretary of the Trust. Both had become familiar with Gibraltar Point and its birds and had identified the most promising site for a Heligoland trap near the southern end of the East Dunes. Fortuitously a small brick building, a relict of war-time army occupation, had been left at the same site and was adopted as the observatory. It was door-less and window-less and, until permission for its use had been obtained and repairs carried out, the two pioneers spent weekends camped out in the building. Even after renovation, conditions were extremely cramped with accommodation for only two or three visitors, a desk for ringing and cupboards for storage of rings and records.

Other local volunteers soon appeared, including local builder Frank Bean who was invaluable in repairing the building and constructing the main trap. Others, like local garage owner Ken Green and building trade operators Philip and Douglas Lill, gave invaluable local support and acted as the first voluntary wardens of the nature reserve. Dick Cornwallis, an ornithologist of national repute, also became closely associated with the observatory and, until his untimely death in 1968, played a leading role in the Trust, the British Trust for Ornithology (BTO), and in the Society for the Promotion of Nature Reserves, which had become the County Trusts' national association. Two young bird enthusiasts also appeared on the scene. One of them, Dennis Hill, became a professional biologist and university teacher. For the other, Barrie Wilkinson, the observatory was the beginning of a lifetime's attachment to the Trust, first as a volunteer in charge of the observatory for a time, and later as a member of the Trust's staff where he eventually became the reserves manager.

In May 1948 Ottoway and Smith visited the observatory on Skokholm, to gain experience of operating a Heligoland trap and of observatory routine generally. By the time the nature reserve agreement between the Trust and the County Council was signed in December 1948 work on the building and trap was well underway and the observatory was opened on 11 April 1949. The confidence of its founders was amply justified in that first year when 1,564 birds of 61 species were ringed. In the same year, following a visit by W. B. Alexander, chairman of the Bird Observatories Sub-committee, the observatory achieved accredited status and, in 1950, the Sub-committee met there for their autumn meeting.

The new observatory soon attracted ornithologists (and ringers) from other parts of the East Midlands and from natural history and ornithological societies such as the Sorby Natural History Society from Sheffield and the Leicestershire & Rutland Ornithological Society whose Honorary Secretary Ronald Hickling, a nationally important figure in ornithology, served for many years as the Chairman of the Gibraltar Point Bird Observatory Committee. Visitors to the reserve were also encouraged to see the work of the observatory and in that first year more than 600 took advantage of that opportunity. Such encouragement of popular interest was amply rewarded by the volume of support which the Trust was able to muster in favour of the County Council's opposition to the establishment of the caravan site in 1953.

Some extra accommodation for those manning the observatory was provided in 1952, when the Trust purchased a caravan sited by the main car park known as 'Fred's Place' after the old sailor who had lived there for many years. Then in 1958, the acquisition of the old Coastguard House and its conversion into a field station with a self-catering annex enabled ornithologists manning the observatory to be accommodated in more salubrious surroundings. A major expansion a few years later provided excellent facilities for research and education and, in 1974, the information kiosk on the car park was replaced by a new visitor centre adjoining the Field Station. The first administrator and manager of the new complex was, appropriately in view of its origins, an ornithologist, George Evans, who had been warden of Bardsey Bird Observatory. An outstanding field ornithologist, George was the author of the Gibraltar Point chapter in the first edition of this book.

Since the founding of the observatory there had always been a Ringing Committee. This committee has been chaired by various people through the years, but in 1990 was finally dissolved when the then chairman Ron Hickling retired from the committee. The observatory managed to continue without a formal committee, until in 1994 Mark Grantham breathed new life into the ringing effort on the reserve, followed a year later by Michael Briggs. These two, along with the reserve warden Kevin Wilson, reformed the Observatory Ringing Committee, this time in the form of an observatory team. Several ringers, whom they knew, had a close association with the reserve and were invited to the first team meeting in 1995. Held four times a year, they have continued ever since. Since then and to comply with the BTO/Bird Observatories Council agreement on running an accredited observatory, the team has adopted the BTO-recognised positions of a ringer in charge and an observatory secretary.

One of the difficulties Gibraltar Point has, compared to many other observatories, is that the reserve warden is employed by the Trust and that job does not include being the observatory warden. Gibraltar Point NNR is so large that their time is completely taken up with managing the reserve and it is unlikely the two posts will ever come together again. At the time of writing, the observatory is manned by the ringer in charge on a purely voluntary basis and the observatory team is keen to encourage other ringers to use the facilities; they may be basic but the wealth of birdlife more than makes up for this. Gibraltar Point is big, it is unique and it is under-recorded, there is great potential and ringers who have the time and inclination to exploit this will find they are more than welcome.

BIRD RECORDING AT GIBRALTAR POINT

The recording area

The Gibraltar Point National Nature Reserve covers about five kilometres of coastline stretching from the Wash to the extreme south of Skegness, bounded by the Seacroft Golf Course to the north and west and Steeping River to the south. This tract of land covers some 600 hectares (at low tide) and would be an impossible area to cover adequately in terms of regular bird counts. Thus, the main census area for ringing, migrant counts and the common bird census is limited to the habitats south of the northern boundary of the Freshwater Marsh, taking a line out to the tideline from here, about 60% of the nature reserve area. To the north, an area of contiguous dune and marsh, known as Seacroft, generally receives only casual attention, save for observations of breeding shorebirds.

There have, however, been changes within the recording area since 1949. The creation of the Freshwater Mere in 1973 offered a previously unavailable habitat of open water, muddy islands and reed fringe which naturally gave rise to an increase in records of various breeding, passage and wintering waterbirds. In more recent times, the reserve has also been extended through the purchase of former arable land for habitat creation. Brackish lagoons and pasture, now established, have greatly added to the attraction of waterbirds to the area. From a recording perspective, discrete subsites are maintained where new features have been created or the site has been 'expanded'. This will always enable direct comparison with the original habitat/recording area of the early days. The scale of the whole reserve and its diversity of habitats ensure its use by a wide variety of bird species, and when passage is fully underway in spring and autumn, it is possible to record over 100 species in a day.

Recording and coverage

Trust staff have been employed primarily to meet the management needs of a demanding nature reserve and its increasing visitor numbers. There is no regime that enables the daily walking and recording of a transect or a daily ringing programme, although staff have, of course, made major contributions to both the ringing and field recording, in a voluntary capacity. Additionally, the data collation and reporting schedules have generally been maintained by staff. However, as with so much of the Trust's work, the contribution and involvement by volunteers has always been significant. Since the establishment of the observatory, volunteers have played a major role in the ringing scheme and the field recording.

Full counts of the recording area are made on a fortnightly basis to provide an index during the breeding season and winter and more regularly to record the turnover of birds during passage periods. In most years, some 15,000–20,000 individual records are added to the database (in addition to the annual ringing data). It is estimated that more than 75% of the records have been submitted by fewer than 5% of contributors over the past 60 years. In 2008 observatory data was used in the environmental impact assessment prior to the establishment of an offshore windfarm. Following this, funding was secured from Centrica to start safeguarding this data through storage on an electronic database. Enormous credit goes to the small number of people who have diligently collated, processed and entered records onto the paper logs over the years. Much credit likewise goes to Mick Briggs who has already digitised virtually all of the archival ringing data, thus placing the observatory ahead of most in this context.

The dense scrub habitat and the low level of observer coverage also has a serious impact on the number of scarce and rare migrants found on the site; undoubtedly many more pass through than are found. Of those that are, many are often more obvious and showy species such as Pied Wheatear or Terek Sandpiper, or more obscure species delivering distinctive calls or song such as Thrush Nightingale and River Warbler, or rarities that drop into mist-nets for ringing such as Blyth's Reed Warbler or Northern Waterthrush.

Perhaps the best illustration of this concerns two records of Sardinian Warbler. The first was trapped on 30 June 1979; it remained in the vicinity until 15 September, but was recorded on only seven dates in between. Remarkably, another long-staying individual was found (by way of a mist-net) on 6 July 1986 and was not seen again until 24 August. The first of these was the first record for Lincolnshire, the seventh for Britain and a precursor to an unusual grouping of records of male and females of this species around the Wash in later years.

Table 1. *The occurrence of firsts for Lincolnshire at Gibraltar Point and their finders.*

Species	Year	Date	Recorder(s)
Pectoral Sandpiper	1948	12 Oct	Unknown
Mediterranean Gull	1950	6 Aug	L. Ottoway, D. Hill, H. A. Hems
Woodchat Shrike	1960	7 Jun	D. Hill
Lesser Grey Shrike	1960	11 Oct	N. J. P. Wadley
Serin	1961	16 May	A. D. Townsend
Balearic Shearwater	1963	5 Oct	K. Atkin, G. Bundy
Roseate Tern (2)	1964	29 May	D. Holyoak
Black-winged Stilt	1965	26 Apr	J. C. Sillitoe, J. A. Ewan
Gull-billed Tern	1967	30 Aug	M.C. Chambers, D. Elias
Pallas's Warbler	1968	19 Oct	Roy Pearson
Short-toed Lark	1971	18 Sept	R.B. Wilkinson, E.J. Mackrill, R. L. Swann
Yellow-breasted Bunting	1977	15 May	R. Burton, S. E. Crooks, R. Lambert
Red-rumped Swallow	1977	29 Oct	R. Thompson
Sardinian Warbler	1979	30 Jun	R. Lambert
American Redstart	1982	7 Nov	R. K. Watson, K. W. Winfield
Citrine Wagtail	1983	4 Sept	R. K. Watson, K. W. Winfield
Green-winged Teal	1984	11 Nov	A. C. Simms, D. J. Jenkins
Northern Waterthrush	1988	22 Oct	I. Hartley, K. W. Winfield
Pine Bunting	1995	29 Mar	N. A. Lound
River Warbler	1998	29 May	K. D. Durose
Pied Wheatear	2000	18 Nov	S. Pettifer, G. W. Allison, K. M. Wilson
Hume's Warbler	2003	23 Oct	R. Cosgrove, K. M. Wilson, P. M. Troake
Terek Sandpiper	2005	18 Jul	G. Garner
Sora	2006	5 Mar	T. Bagworth, P. M. Troake
Greater Yellowlegs	2007	30 May	J. P. Shaughnessy

Besides the Sardinian Warbler, Gibraltar Point has produced a good number of county firsts, which are detailed with their finders in Table 1.

Perhaps the site's most well known rarity and some may say, its most memorable bird, was an American Redstart in November 1982. Its protracted stay really put Gibraltar Point on the birding map. Found on 7 November, the daily account reads:

> *The bird of the day, year and probably of the 33 years of the observatory's existence was found by Rob Watson and Ken Winfield in the hawthorn patch along the edge of the Plantation. It was identified as an American Redstart and was seen at 10:30 hrs by Dick Lambert. It was tentatively sexed as a male due to the orange tinge in the flank patches and is a bird of the year.*

Next day's log reports:

> *The American Redstart was located at 07:00 hrs, in exactly the same site and seen by some 200 observers through the day, remaining in the same general area all day. A single net put up at 10:00 hrs caught the bird within two minutes. It weighed 10 grams (spring weight = c. 6 grams) so it had evidently been in Europe for some time and was in excellent condition – an amazing bird!*

The long-staying American Redstart in November 1982 was seen by over 1,500 visitors and put Gibraltar Point firmly on the birding map (Dick Lambert).

The bird remained visible for the crowds over the next few days, ultimately staying until 5 December by which time it was estimated that over 1,500 people had been to see it.

More recently, the occurrence of a Red-flanked Bluetail in the Ringing Hollow in November 2002 was likewise expected to attract a large-scale twitch the following morning, a Saturday, but a mere handful of birders were on site to see it during the first hour of light. However, the following day it is estimated that 500 birders dropped by – the bird having departed overnight! Then in 2006, when news of a Sora, an even rarer bird, was provided to Birdline, it was met with only two birders the following morning – the furthest travelled from Boston some 26 miles away.

Migration hotspots

In contrast to some other observatories that have a lighthouse or other nearby nocturnal illuminations, such as a container port, there are no lights to attract migrants. However, this does ensure that the Field Centre remains a popular base for astronomical societies and courses, which have developed here since the 1990s. Thus migrants can occur evenly along the whole stretch of coast, although, there are some 'hotspots' that deserve immediate attention during good fall conditions.

The south-facing dune ridge between the observatory building and the shore-bird warden's hut is one such area. Angled sufficiently to avoid the full force of a migrant-yielding north-easterly, but also to receive the early morning sun, it can be buzzing with chats, flycatchers, warblers and thrushes feeding along the edge of the dune scrub and saltings after an overnight arrival. However, a popular visitor route passes along the length of this feature and the birds generally move deeper into cover as walkers pass by later in the morning. So, local birders appreciate the need to cover this area early on, before moving north to more secluded zones, for example at Shoveler's Pool where a watch point provides good views over a sheltered pool and a large clump of sallows, a good spot for warblers, Goldcrests and other migrants.

Moving east, the outer ridges can harbour some very interesting migrants, desperate to make landfall during the most extreme conditions. The series of ridges stretch from the mouth of the Wash northward to the limit of the SSSI. The Millennium Ridge resembles a condensed version of Blakeney Point, but probably receives less attention from visiting birders. It is indeed remote, but on occasion 'expeditions' to this new peninsula have been undertaken during migration periods and birds such as Robin, Blackcap, Goldcrest and Woodcock have been found newly arrived here, sheltering in small clumps of Marram grass hundreds of metres from any appreciable scrub cover. To the north, the Polypody Ridge – named after the locally rare dune fern – has hosted Wryneck, Nightingale and other migrants.

Further inland, there are large, dense, scrubby areas that are only surveyed during breeding bird census or ringing operations. One such area is accessible via a large open grazing enclosure, where scrub was cleared in 1971. This open area became the favoured site for the ringing base during the BTO ringing courses run by Chris Mead and soon became known as Mead's Outpost.

Visible migration

One of the key features of the site given its geographical position is the volume of visible migration. Generally commencing in March with the first corvids, finches and thrushes on the move, spring migration continues with wagtails, hirundines, Swifts, pipits and others going through until late May. Surprisingly, the bulk of spring migrants are heading south (theoretically demonstrating the reorientation of overshooting migrants) and largest movements are stimulated by a south-westerly wind. The migration takes place over a broad front stretching from the West Dunes to out over the sea.

The majority funnel over the East Dunes, and Mill Hill is certainly the place to be if a Crane or Red-rumped Swallow is reported flying south off Spurn, the former taking up to four hours to materialize with the swallow making it in half that time. Despite the best efforts of observers, Pacific Swift and Chimney Swift could not be picked up here after leaving Spurn. It is suspected that many migrants leave the Spurn peninsula and make for the Norfolk coast rather than skirting the Lincolnshire coast. Autumn passage sees significantly larger numbers of birds involved in the southward passage from the first hirundines in August to the last Rock Pipits, Woodpigeons and finches well into November. Each of the seasons has something to offer the visiting birder as the following accounts will show.

Winter

An early morning stroll on site during the thick of winter can be a lonely experience. It is at this time of day and time of year that the reserve appears most akin to a bleak wilderness. There is something almost eerie about leaving the vehicle in an otherwise empty car park and heading off down the South Marsh Road through salt marsh and dune to the estuary. Along the salt marsh trail, Redshanks typically rise up from the creeks and pools giving shrill alarm calls. Rock Pipits are the dominant passerine in the marsh at this time, but they are seldom seen on the ground, only taking flight if flushed by a passing Hen Harrier or Merlin. The pipits eke out a winter existence foraging for invertebrates and probably seeds in the clumps of the Sea-purslane. Experienced ears are needed to separate their flight calls from the few wintering Meadow Pipits and occasional Water Pipits. It seems an unusual phenomenon that such a dense breeding population of Meadow Pipits is almost entirely replaced by Rock Pipits in the marshes over winter.

Looking back through the records, there are impressive counts of 1,000 Tree Sparrows, 1,000 House Sparrows and 900 Greenfinches in the winters 1962–65. At that time, there are log entries reporting sizeable sparrow flocks being attracted to 'freshly nipped chaff' in the farmyard at Sykes Farm long before the Trust ever dreamt of purchasing the holding. Up to 250 Yellowhammers, 250 Reed Buntings and 400 Corn Buntings could be seen in the winter of 1970/71. Twite numbers were highest from 1970 to 1977, with up to 1,000 in some years. Sadly such numbers are now largely a thing of the past, although a flock of Corn Buntings, albeit reduced to just 40 or so birds, have remained a feature of the Old Salt Marsh. During the late afternoon they conveniently settle in the lone sycamore adjacent to the Visitor Centre Car Park before going to roost.

Brent Geese are often prominent in the winter soundscape, their 'chuntering' being audible from some distance. Very few were recorded until the 1960s when numbers built up to the first four-figure count in 1979. Some 2,000 birds now regularly winter here, with peak numbers in January and February when up to 4,500 have been seen. In most years, a good flock use such an area in quite close proximity to the South Marsh Road where a good view can be obtained. Often, the Brent flock drops in to the lagoons on Croftmarsh for bathing whilst commuting between the estuary and winter wheat fields inland. This offers the best chance of locating any Pale-bellied Brent *Branta bernicla hrota* or Black Brant *B. b. nigricans.*

Pink-footed Geese used the area extensively in the past as a feeding ground and roost, and Peter Scott and his team from the Severn Wildfowl Trust made study visits in the early 1950s. At this time potatoes were a principal crop locally and discards were available as fodder. However, this practice dwindled during the 1960s, and in combination with increased disturbance from the Wainfleet bombing range, it was inevitable that the geese should look for pastures new. The last big flock occurred over the 1966/67 winter and today they rarely pause whilst en route from the west coast to the north Norfolk coast. Cold weather on the Continent in February 1993 brought a most unexpected crop of grey geese to the reserve in the form of 208 White-fronted and 27 Bean Geese. Other east coast sites also became hosts to such flocks that had presumably left a frozen Dutch landscape. Otherwise these species are irregular visitors to Gibraltar Point.

A modest flock of Wigeon also winter in the area and commute between the estuary and the grassy banks of the Steeping River channel to the west of the reserve. Numbering up to 3,000 as recently as the early 1990s (with circa 500 Mallard and 1,800 Teal), the morning and evening flights were an attractive stake-out for local wildfowlers, but 20 years on less than half of this number is to be expected. The cessation of cattle-grazing on the adjacent Steeping River banks and washlands will certainly have resulted in degradation of feeding areas, and it is hoped that in future the re-created grazing marsh on Croftmarsh will prove attractive. Other waterfowl important in the context of the Wash include the Shelduck, here reliant upon sieving tiny salt marsh snails on the estuary during the winter months.

The estuary can be scanned from the Wash Viewpoint or more cautiously from the end of the Spit, beyond the shorebird warden's hut. Waders and wildfowl can be numerous here, particularly on the ebbing tide, but they are easily disturbed and will quickly move south across the Steeping River Haven and deeper into the Wash. Low tide yields anything up to a kilometre of invertebrate-rich mudflat between the tideline and the green marsh frontage. Scanning deep into the Wash, waders can be seen spread out across the mudflats and although many are distant, the sheer scale of numbers can be appreciated. Dunlin, Knot, Grey Plover, Oystercatcher, Redshank, Bar-tailed Godwit and Curlew are usually all well represented. One can easily lose a couple of hours here with a telescope.

Extrapolation from this local view can reconcile the figure of 350,000 wintering waterbirds on the Wash as a whole. However, smaller numbers of waders are recorded during the winter than during passage periods. Different geographical populations of each of the key species are involved. Studies carried out by the Wash Wader Ringing Group have identified that the wintering population of Knot breeds in Greenland and Arctic Canada and three populations of Dunlin use the Wash at varying times of year – *Calidris alpina alpina* being represented principally in winter. Numbers may be lower than in autumn but can still be very impressive, with Knot always comprising the greater percentage of overall totals – some 5,000–10,000 during winter roosts.

Results from ringing suggest that some 50% of the wintering Redshank are Icelandic and, whilst here, rarely stray from their salt marsh and higher estuarine niche. Because of their reluctance to leave the marsh, they are not easily counted at high tide – preferring to wait out the high water in small groups clinging onto Sea-purslane clumps rather than joining the main roosts. As the tide ebbs and mud becomes exposed Redshanks materialise again, apparently from nowhere. However, their reliance upon this upper zone of the system does make them more susceptible to cold weather periods as these areas are likely to freeze harder and longer, so denying the birds access to food. The consequences of hard weather could be seen in January–February 1963. Rick Pilcher carried out a tide-line survey of bird corpses from Friskney to Freiston during this period and found a total of 603. The most numerous were Redshanks (144), Knot (104) and Shelduck (58). Surviving Redshanks were seen in poor condition and apparently very tame. In addition, various auks, divers and scoter were found to be oiled to varying degrees.

The combination of hard weather and lack of food is an even worse scenario for birds. Oystercatchers were very badly affected during the winter of 1991/92 when shellfish populations had crashed disastrously. Driven by starvation and weather, emaciated Oystercatchers were forced to leave the environs of the Wash in a struggle to find worms in parks, gardens and even on the roundabouts of local roads, a tragic situation that resulted in the death of many birds and was followed by significantly depleted Oystercatcher roosts for the following decade before numbers built up again.

The extension of habitats over Croftmarsh has helped to consolidate the wintering status of both Lapwing and Golden Plover locally, with winter flocks into four figures of each, roving between the newly created grazing marsh, local arable and the estuary, mostly for the evening roost. Cold weather can push vast numbers to the coast – up to several thousand of each. In addition to the diurnal waders, Woodcock move out of adjacent dune scrub at dusk to feed on the damp grassland. Another bird to take advantage of these new habitats is Little Egret. They tend to accumulate on Jackson's Marsh before flying to roost in the late afternoon. In 2008 the winter roost contained up to 50 birds. The brackish lagoons provide an excellent refuge for dabbling duck, particularly Mallard, Wigeon and Teal, with a scattering of Gadwall and Shoveler, and the minimal reed fringing has on occasion harboured a Bittern. More likely, though, is a chorus of squealing Water Rails and a roost of *alba* wagtails at dusk.

Raptors are another draw for birders. As well as the harriers, Merlin is a daily winter occurrence and if not seen pursuing small waders on the estuary or passerines over the salt marsh one should try scanning the outer ridges and beach for any irregular blob perched on the ground. Failing this, find a hunting Hen Harrier and it may have a lingering Merlin in attendance picking up on any pipits and others flushed by the former. Peregrine sightings have become more numerous since Golden Plover numbers have built on the estuary and surrounding hinterland. A good strategy for those hoping to see raptors but not wishing to venture out into the cold is to watch the Old Salt Marsh during the late afternoon from the comfort of the car. Short-eared and Barn Owls regularly hunt here and Merlin, Sparrowhawk and Hen Harrier often pass over on their way to roost. Close views can be obtained of the owls and the Short-eared was at one time guaranteed to put in an appearance – regularly up to three and as many as seven in February 1993.

The occurrence of a wintering Snowy Owl south of the Point was reported to site wardens by a Wainfleet farmer in December 1990. It was duly checked out and confirmed with some degree of amazement! Naturally it aroused a fair amount of interest from birders and photographers during its stay and, having been inadvertently flushed, it flew north to add itself to the observatory list. Unfortunately, it spent most of the time out of view on the wrong side of the sea bank, its presence being confirmed by up to three Short-eared Owls rising and dropping to harass it.

Lapland Buntings are undoubtedly present in most winters in ones and twos, but are secreted in deeply vegetated salt marsh and only given away on call when flushed. They are near impossible to see well on the ground – one member of the staff team who has recorded them annually over more than a decade has never seen one on the ground! Snow Buntings can still be encountered in small numbers along the beach and shingle ridges, but in the past it was possible to see flocks of 400–500. The site has also been one of a few reliable wintering venues for Shore Lark in Britain. However, numbers have fluctuated wildly from over a 100 in 1972 to just a handful through the 1980s, followed by a resurgence bringing 60–90 again in the mid-1990s, before dropping back to much smaller numbers today.

Offshore, the immediate marine environment is favoured by wintering Red-throated Divers, but the majority are distant on the shallow shelving seabed. Daily north and south movements seem more attributable to sea-state rather than to any passage, but these movements do enable local numbers to be ascertained. During the latter part of the winter, large numbers can build up, involving hundreds of birds. It is likely that a significant proportion of the southern North Sea population assemble here before departing north. Up to 1,500 have been seen in a day. Confirmed sightings of Black-throated and Great Northern Diver are scarce, but recent windfarm surveys show that they are present in small numbers in the deeper water further out. Also, these surveys have detected much pelagic activity by Little Gulls during the winter months.

Northerly or easterly gales may bring such birds into view and often produce significant movements of Kittiwakes and Fulmars (including occasional blue morph birds) and maybe the odd skua or Little Auk. Occasionally sea-duck are blown onto waterbodies such as the Fenland Lagoon, which has hosted Common Scoter, Long-tailed Duck, Smew and Slavonian Grebe.

Sea-duck are generally unpredictable, with regular small numbers of Eiders and Red-breasted Mergansers. In some years a wintering flock of Common Scoters has become established offshore with over 1,000 birds involved and up to 60 Velvet Scoters too. This occurrence is thought to be dependent on the health of the local shellfish colonies.

The latter part of winter is marked by movements of Pink-footed Geese. Regular skeins move to the west coast from north Norfolk on the first leg of their journey to Iceland. On the shore, Ringed Plovers reappear from late February and Meadow Pipits arrive back on salt marsh territory.

Spring

Other than those avian signals already mentioned, to those who are very familiar with the site other subtle occurrences in early March can be taken as indicative of the onset of spring migration. These may include the occasional Lesser Black-backed Gull floating through or an errant Rook, calling as it passes over. In the dunes and the Plantation at this time, there may be a light build-up of winter visitors preparing for departure, such as Robin, Song Thrush, Redwing, Starling or Goldcrest.

Visible migration gathers pace during March and most prominent can be the passage of Continental finches – particularly Chaffinches, and with them, often Brambling. Such movements were quickly appreciated by the early recorders and a movement of 2,000 Chaffinches on 21 March 1954 still holds as one of the largest for spring. A larger Chaffinch movement on 10 March 1991 involved 2,125 birds heading south in two hours. Meadow Pipits and Redwings were also prominent migrants that morning and single Woodlark, Common Crossbill and two Lapland Buntings also joined the flocks.

Corvids can also be prominent in spring movements. On 19 March 1950 a massive movement included 500 Jackdaws and also 1,000 Rooks. Migrant Jackdaws tend to excite their local relatives, which may become airborne and start heading off south, before giving up the idea and returning back to the Plantation. A corvid movement in 2008 provided the reserve's first record of a Raven which paused briefly on the Freshwater Marsh before heading over the Wash to Norfolk. This was also the first record for coastal Lincolnshire since 1980. Had it not been calling loudly, it might have been overlooked completely.

Returning to the cycle of routine migration, the classic sign of spring here is the trio of Stonechat, Black Redstart and Wheatear in mid-March. Up to six Black Redstarts have occurred in a day, mostly female or immature birds. It is easy to assume that if two birds are seen on one day and two birds the next that they are the same, but this may not necessarily be the case. Detailed field observations and targeted trapping/ringing one spring revealed the turnover of birds was in the order of 11 individuals between late March and mid-April. Casual field observa-

Early spring is not the classic time of year for North American vagrants, so this Sora, the 18th for Britain and Ireland, was an unexpected find on 5 March 2006 (Graham Catley).

tions alone would have proven only half this number. Typically, this migrant trio frequent the area around the field station and the 'Rock Ridge' heading down to the Wash Viewpoint and are usually first encountered by staff and volunteers going out to the Meteorological Station to take the daily readings.

Since the 1990s, passage Woodlark have become expected during the early spring. Although most pass straight through, sometimes they may pause a few days and even deliver full song – looking very much at home in the closely grazed sandy environment. Although around in March, April is the best month for Firecrests and there have been up to six in a day. Records in spring and autumn have generally increased since the 1980s, but this is no reflection on the hearing of earlier staff!

Late April and May is the period when there is most likely to be a 'fall' of migrants, although they seem to occur less regularly now than they did in the early days of the observatory. These 'falls' can include warblers, wagtails and chats in particular. Wheatears and wagtails are immediately attracted to the strip saltings between the East Dunes and the outer dunes. Small parties of pipits may be present with the wagtails and may provide an opportunity to identify Scandinavian Rock Pipits *Anthus petrosus littoralis*. In addition, spring Tawny Pipits have occurred on the saltings on at least two occasions, similarly Stone-curlew, Dotterel and even Hoopoe. On the dunes and freshwater marsh, pipits and wagtails may be attracted to feed around the cattle or sheep. A flock of *flava* and *alba* wagtails on Jackson's Marsh in April 2006 amounted to 60 birds and included 35 Yellow Wagtails, three Blue-headed Wagtails, one 'Channel' Wagtail (*Motacilla flava flava* × *M. f. flavissima* intergrade), a bird showing some features of Citrine Wagtail and up to seven White Wagtails all showing at close range in front of the hide.

The scrub along the seaward margins of the East Dunes is a very productive area for newly arrived migrants where it catches the early morning sun and provides plenty of insect activity. In addition to the common warblers, signs of a good migrant arrival could include Wood Warbler, Firecrest, Redstart, Whinchat and Pied Flycatcher. It quite often pays to find a sheltered, sunny spot and see what appears in front of you: hungry warblers will often appear, even leaving the protective scrub to pick flies out of the strandline below.

As with other east coast sites, a spell of easterly winds in May can produce displaced Scandinavian-bound migrants. There is the possibility of encountering a scarce species such as Bluethroat, Icterine Warbler, Wryneck, Red-backed Shrike, Marsh Warbler, Common Rosefinch or Golden Oriole. The latter three are perhaps more likely these days and, in most springs at least, one of the trio will be recorded. Clearly they are far easier to find, as most are detected by song initially. Rosefinch is still a well sought after bird in Lincolnshire and up to 2008, the majority of county records had come from Gibraltar Point.

An even rarer Scandinavian migrant, Thrush Nightingale, has also been found on two occasions by its song. The first, in May 2001, was found in pouring rain when it and a male Firecrest were the only birds singing on the East Dunes, and the other, in May 2003, was also on the East Dunes. The second bird remained for a week and could be heard from Aylmer Avenue on a still night, in combination with the evening chorus of Natterjack Toads, despite being halfway down the East Dunes. In between, the spring of 2002 was most unusual in that three Nightingales arrived in early May. They were first detected when site staff were leading a dawn chorus event for visitors – probably the most productive event of its kind for birdsong here and certainly providing a record day count for Nightingale. Two territories were held subsequently and breeding may have occurred. Continuing the theme of nocturnal birds, Nightjars have been seen on five occasions, four of which have been between 20 and 22 May.

In some years, spring has provided even rarer and more unexpected species. A male Yellow-breasted Bunting on 15 May 1977 was an exceptional find and is more normally associated with the northern isles in autumn. Paradoxically, it was found by Stuart Crooks whilst leading a 'Birds for Beginners' course based at the centre. A pristine individual in full colour, the complete antithesis to pretty much all other British records, the bird fed on short turf along the salt marsh edge close to the observatory and often at close range. The Leicestershire & Rutland Ornithological Society, present on a day visit, must have been praising their events organiser that day!

Then on 8 May 1993, a fine male Rustic Bunting was found, obviously exhausted and feeding on the path just seaward of the observatory. As is often the case, the bird arrived late in the day on a busy Sunday when all the birdwatchers had gone home! A male Bluethroat was within 100 metres and, as if this was not enough, another male Bluethroat was found further up the East Dunes. Typically these celebrities were enjoyed by a very small number of local birders and there was a supporting cast of a Montagu's Harrier, two Black Redstarts, three Redstarts, five Pied Flycatchers, three Whinchats, three Ring Ouzels and seven Wheatears – quite good for a spring fall.

A singing River Warbler, on 29 May 1998, was also a more notable record from a national perspective. Aside from one well-watched bird in mainland Scotland, this species has remained generally an exclusively island visitor in recent years. The bird was found by renowned rarity-finder Kevin Durose (having found Lincolnshire's first Franklin's Gull and second Lesser Scaup the previous week) on a one-off visit to the little-watched outer dunes at the reserve's northern boundary. Having calmly alerted site staff to the bird's presence and double-checked the song on CD, he led a small group from the observatory back up to the site. Fortunately, the distinctive reeling song was delivered for all to hear, although no-one managed to see the bird, other than the finder, save for a few fleeting glimpses. Unfortunately for everyone else, it departed overnight.

Although the easterlies are eagerly anticipated during late spring, southerly airstreams encourage pioneering migrants (or hapless youngsters?) to overshoot from breeding grounds in southern Europe. Over the years, these have included Serin, Bee-eater, Alpine Swift, Night-heron, Woodchat Shrike and a Subalpine Warbler. After a series of strong south-westerly winds in May 1976 an itinerant Glossy Ibis arrived on 16th – the first record for the site. What may be even more remarkable is the note in the log relating to five unidentified flamingos which flew north-east over the field station the previous day!

The Croftmarsh lagoons are visible from a series of hides and there is a good turnover of migrating waterbirds. Spring highlights have included a small number of Water Pipits (up to seven) that appear in late March or early April, fairly regular Garganey and local rarities such as Black-necked Grebe. Passage waders include small numbers of Greenshanks, Black-tailed Godwits and Common Sandpipers, but Temminck's Stints and Wood Sandpipers have also been regular since these lagoons have been created. The most unexpected visitor was identified in late May 2007 – a Greater Yellowlegs – another county first.

Numbers of waders on the lagoons and on the estuary during spring clearly do not compare to the autumn arrival, but the high tide roosts can still bring some spectacular sights of Arctic waders in full breeding plumage, particularly Knot, Grey Plover and Dunlin through April and May (see Table 2). Sanderling are the last to pass through, with their peak numbers in the latter part of May. Close scrutiny of the 'small wader' flocks usually reveals Curlew Sandpiper or Little Stint. Also obvious are the parties of calling Whimbrel moving north and over 100 have passed through on several dates.

Visible migration overland has a very different theme during the late spring. Finches are represented mostly by passing Goldfinches and Linnets. Flocks of the latter have been known to harbour the occasional Serin. Swifts and hirundines can pour though in good numbers and increased scrutiny of these has detected Red-rumped Swallows in many years since the late 1990s. On one remarkable day, 29 April 2003, a single Red-rumped Swallow had arrived during the morning and showed itself well over the West Dunes with a small group of Swallows and martins. It later moved to the Mere where it was joined by a second bird. As hirundines continued to pass through during the afternoon, observers realised that a third bird had arrived and into the early evening a fourth! At the time, a spring group of four Red-rumped Swallows in Britain was believed to have been a record.

Table 2. *Peak monthly counts of key waders at Gibraltar Point 1996–2007.*

	January	February	March	April	May	June
Grey Plover	2,800	5,050	9,000	6,460	2,640	300
Knot	20,000	30,000	35,240	34,430	3,800	3,000
Sanderling	300	300	1,000	800	3,100	1,600
Dunlin	4,010	5,000	9,150	10,100	4,000	500
Bar-tailed Godwit	1,920	1,400	7,000	3,750	600	385
Ringed Plover	37	85	130	137	255	200
Curlew	465	800	450	250	151	450
Oystercatcher	3,805	2,400	6,780	3,000	1,100	1,102

	July	August	September	October	November	December
Grey Plover	1,004	4,200	7,500	9,500	3,800	5,000
Knot	16,264	76,000	90,000	122,000	40,000	10,000
Sanderling	4,070	2,880	1,700	1,010	430	600
Dunlin	9,282	7,165	8,000	13,500	4,350	5,040
Bar-tailed Godwit	1,200	4,200	8,000	6,600	3,400	1,680
Ringed Plover	200	544	500	307	40	31
Curlew	802	700	504	352	1,030	410
Oystercatcher	412	7,930	8,100	9,050	6,000	2,580

Gibraltar Point has gained a reputation, in Britain, as a great site to watch migrating raptors. Hobbies are routinely expected with hirundine migration and there are those warm spring days when everything can happen at once, often late morning or early afternoon, when large soaring birds appear simultaneously. Marsh Harrier, Buzzard, Honey-buzzard, Montagu's Harrier, Osprey and Red Kites have become pretty much annual spring visitors since the 1990s and could occur in such a situation. For example, on 30 May 1995, Osprey, Honey-buzzard and Hobby were all passing over the car park at the same time. April 1996 saw the passage of eight Buzzards and two Rough-legged Buzzards, whilst on 15 May 2007 raptor movement involved eight southbound Marsh Harriers. Red-footed Falcons have paused briefly on three occasions and there are three accepted records of Black Kite.

Although White Storks have passed on several occasions, Cranes are now to be expected drifting over in spring, and small parties have involved up to nine birds. March 2002 saw a good series of records, with one north-west on 9th, three moving south on 16th and then seven heading south on 19th, followed later by two more. When such movements are taking place, many birders have had great views of migrating raptors and large soaring birds moving over the car park and Visitor Centre, but things happen very quickly and 'good' birds are easily missed.

Spotted Flycatcher and Turtle Dove are amongst the last migrants to arrive. Counts of the latter rarely get above 50 nowadays and it is difficult to imagine some of the large-scale movements that used to occur, such as the 800 flying south on 26 May 1972, 500 on 8 June 1983, some 455 during 22–28 May 1985 and 268 as recently as 20 May 1996. There seems no limit to the species that may show strong migrational tendencies, despite being thought of as fairly sedentary in Britain and Ireland. It is often no surprise to find a Jay or two in late spring and in 1984 there was a major movement; 30 flew north and 46 flew south on 30 May and later, on 13 June, another 35 moved south. It seems no coincidence that there had been a large influx of Jays the previous autumn. This was surpassed in 1997 though, when a movement commenced with 35 on 29 April, followed by 34 next day, 84 on 3 May and 77 on 9 May!

Summer

Summer is generally the term associated with the breeding season for resident and migrant species in the northern hemisphere. To the layman, migration has long ceased at this time. However, in practice, observations show spring migration for some species continues well into June, long after many resident species have raised their first brood. Spring migration can almost overlap with the first signs of return migration. This is well demonstrated by waders such as the Sanderling. It is one of the last species to assemble on the Wash, still journeying north to Greenland's arctic tundra from winter quarters in West Africa. Well over 1,000 can still be this far south in early June. It is difficult to imagine a species with a more condensed breeding period, as birds are back in significant numbers by early August.

Breeding birds

The diversity of habitats ensures a broad range of breeding birds. Altogether 86 species have bred on the reserve, 72 are, or have been, regular breeding species and another 14 have bred on isolated occasions.

In 1965, the aim of quantifying the populations of all the species in the various habitats was achieved through the initiation of the Common Bird Census (CBC). A field course led by Ken Williamson covered almost all of the census area described earlier and was followed up by R. A. Morgan who repeated the survey in 1974. Full surveys thereafter were only completed in 1983 and 1988 before efforts to record annually from 1990 onwards were conducted on a slightly expanded area.

Interestingly, as part of the study, other areas were also included in the survey. They included the grass paddock at Sykes Farm (now the Plantation woodland) and the arable field to the north (now Jackson's Marsh), although fallow in that year. The beach, outer dunes and extensive areas of salt marsh and strip saltings were surveyed, thus incorporating the populations of Little Tern and Ringed Plover. The habitat descriptions alone provide a valuable record of the coverage at the time and serve to illustrate how rapidly the scrub was colonising even the youngest dunes as they stabilised.

Although carried out late in the season (June) the number of observers involved and the intensive nature of the 1965 study meant that confirmation of breeding of various species could be established through nest-finding, as well as the more usual methods of plotting singing males, territorial disputes and birds carrying nest material or food. Analysis of the fieldwork determined a total of 586 pairs of 35 species across the area.

The dunes and dune scrub

The study recorded Whitethroat as the dominant species with circa 47 pairs per 40 hectares in the dune scrub, and despite some low ebbs this still holds true today. It is difficult for some visitors to comprehend that a trans-Saharan migrant is our commonest breeding bird over and above perceived residents such as Blackbird, Chaffinch, Robin and Dunnock, although Dunnock, Linnet and Reed Bunting were the co-dominant species in the dune scrub in the first survey. Whilst recorded only as probably breeding in 1965, there were four pairs of Willow Warblers by the time of the 1974 survey. From then on, they became a significant part of the dune scrub assemblage and reached a peak of 58 territories by 1998 before a decline set in. Unexpectedly, as with Reed Bunting, Sedge Warblers were prominent in the dry dune scrub during the 1960s and 1970s. However, popula-tions have since contracted to optimum habitat. Colonies of Linnets were commonplace on the East and West Dunes in the early surveys. The total of 119 pairs in 1974 is actually the highest number of territories recorded for any species during the history of the survey, here a successful species, able to exploit a variety of dune and marsh micro-habitats in the 'days of plenty'.

The accolade for the most volatile breeding population must surely go to the Lesser Redpoll. It was basically a passage migrant at Gibraltar Point during the first census period. However, there followed a large-scale range expansion and the Gibraltar Point dunes were duly colonised. A remarkable 62 pairs were recorded during the 1974 survey, but unfortunately, and in line with its decline nationally, this bird was lost completely as a breeding species by 2004.

Even by the time of the first survey, it is likely that some stands of scrub were already beginning to senesce. The die-back of elders provided a very important dead wood habitat for hole-nesting tits and maybe Tree Sparrows. Great Tit was not recorded breeding on the first survey and Blue Tit has been the commoner for the most part, although the population gap has shown signs of closing due to a steady increase in Great and decline in Blue. Willow Tit used to be annual and may also have bred on occasion, but today it appears less frequently in the annual report than Pallas's Warbler!

In the first edition of this book, George Evans stated Turtle Doves were plentiful and breeding (1973). The 1974 survey showed the population had almost doubled since 1965 on the East Dunes, presumably as the habitat matured. Unfortunately, the survey has served only to plot the demise of this charismatic species since the turn of the 1990s. Only four pairs remained on census plots by the turn of the following decade. Besides blaming the well-documented local and international factors, their chosen nest sites may bring them into conflict with a massively expanding population of Woodpigeons.

Most of the species mentioned so far in the dune habitat have some connection with the scrub. However, one of the most obscure of the dune species is the Shelduck which is reliant upon the availability of unused rabbit burrows in which to nest. Small groups of Shelduck look very unusual waddling around the dune landscape prospecting for nesting sites. Historically recorded as using hay ricks on bordering farmland, the species has probably always suffered a degree of fox predation. Nonetheless, crèches of youngsters are moved out of the dune environment during the late summer in most years, to feed on the salt marsh and mudflats.

Salt marsh

The salt marsh provides a distinctly contrasting environment to the dunes and a much lower species diversity. However, of those species that do breed, Skylark and Meadow Pipit density rivals some of the species in the dune scrub. On a still summer's day Skylarks, Meadow Pipits and Redshanks can be displaying all around and at close quarters. The 1965 CBC revealed that Skylark breeding density in the salt marsh, at 44 pairs per 40 hectares, was higher than any other recorded population in Britain at that time. What makes this even more amazing is that it is likely that Skylarks were still recovering from the harsh winter of 1962/63, because Morgan's study in 1974 showed an increase to an even higher density of 57 pairs per 40 hectares. Given good weather, the resulting chorus of Skylark song over the marsh is positively therapeutic!

The male Reed Bunting makes its own nonchalant contribution to the soundscape, but what it lacks in melody, it makes up for in plumage and obliging views – often singing from the clumps of Sea-purslane or Sea Couch grass. During the 1965 survey, surprise was expressed at this species' connection with 'dry' habitats on the dunes where 29 pairs contrasted with only 23 in the salt marsh and salt-ings. However, a decline in overall numbers has culminated in a consolidation of the salt marsh population with few remaining in dune scrub.

The clumps of couch and purslane are the favoured nesting sites of the Redshank, although nests are remarkably hard to find. Despite requiring fairly large territories, Redshanks are a very prominent component of the marsh, partic-ularly when vociferously defending young from human approach or raptors.

Short-eared Owls have nested on or close to the reserve in a couple of years and rely heavily on the Old Salt Marsh for hunting. This mature marsh with extensive areas of tall couch can provide plentiful Field Voles. Any 'eared' owl should be thoroughly checked, though, for Long-eared Owls are prone to regular day-hunting when there are hungry young to feed. Both species seem comically oblivious to human presence when intent on hunting. Barn Owls also make daily sorties to this marsh.

Wetlands

With the inclusion of the Croftmarsh land, the whole site now provides a range of fresh and brackish water ponds, lagoons and ditches. Little of this network was established at the time of the first CBC, but over the years, an assemblage of common waterbirds has become established from Reed Warblers to Mute Swan. In addition to the swamping by seawater in storm flood events the shallow dune water tables have also been influenced by the extremes of precipitation events, not least the lack of it.

One of the most charismatic and important birds of the Freshwater Marsh was the Lapwing, up to three pairs breeding in occasional years and with three broods of young reared as recently as 1984. However, the three prospecting pairs in 1989 did not breed – presumably due to the dry conditions. This was the first of the three notorious drought summers experienced in the region. The 1991 annual report stated:

> For the third consecutive year, well below average rainfall caused a dramatic lowering of the water table and consequently, the pools and Mere have held little water for most of the summer. Indeed it is feared that the quality of the Mere as a freshwater habitat may have declined markedly with no successful breeding of waterbirds.

During these summers, the Mere was reduced to a couple of puddles out of which Herons were seen plundering some sizeable eels. Fortunately, the water tables were restored by 1993, after heavy winter rains, and successful breeding was apparent for many waterbirds, but Lapwing were never to return. They had been chosen as the emblem of the Trust as symbolic of a typical and charismatic bird widespread in the county, so it should come as no surprise that it was a target bird when the lagoons and grazing marsh were created on Croftmarsh. The scheme has slowly attracted nesting pairs back to the area and fledged chicks were again to be seen during the late 2000s.

Another success story concerns Avocets which quickly colonised the newly created lagoons. A pair, which made a nesting attempt here in 2000, represented the first nesting on the Lincolnshire mainland since 1837, but chicks were not successfully raised to fledging until 2004. In the years following the first breeding, a modest colony has developed. The Avocet parents have to be the most protective and resilient of any of the shorebirds – their aggression even extending to innocuous small waders. On the mix of mud and shingle islands, small numbers of Common Terns and occasional Little Ringed Plover and Oystercatcher are accepted as bona fide companions by the Avocets, whilst many of the vegetated islands are covered in breeding Black-headed Gulls. The developing reed fringes of the lagoons have seen increased numbers of breeding duck, including Tufted Duck, Gadwall and Ruddy Duck, whilst Reed Warblers are common.

From their previous position in the dry dune scrub community (which harboured nearly 70% of the 1965 territories), Sedge Warblers now show a more defined niche – along the fringes of the Freshwater Marsh where there is a matrix of small wetland features with margins of Sea Club-rush, dense beds of Greater Pond-sedge and Great Willowherb and pockets of scrub. The Mill Pond Road borders this habitat and visitors can be shouted at by up to nine territorial males as they pass. This area is also the stronghold of the Grasshopper Warbler. Up to seven reeling males have arrived on spring migration and usually result in up to three breeding pairs. It has been known as a breeding bird here since 1979, when a nest was found near Bulldog Bank, with seven chicks, some of which were seen fledged by 17 June.

Woodland

The old Sykes Farm compound was bordered by a fringe of mature elms which succumbed to Dutch Elm disease by the 1970s. In their prime, they held a thriving rookery. Latterly, the few substantial dead wood stumps remaining have harboured regular Tawny Owl, Stock Dove and Jackdaw, along with isolated successful breeding by Treecreeper and Great Spotted Woodpecker. The grounds of the original farmhouse are marked today with large Sycamores and Beech and there is a small orchard which is well maintained. Contiguous with this area, the Plantation now provides a valuable woodland habitat of some two and a half hectares, planted in 1966 predominantly with a mix of Ash and pines (Scots, Lodgepole and Corsican). Many of the trees had matured by the 1990s and the Trust's active management of the 'wood' involved thinning out the non-native pines, coppicing some of the Ash and underplanting with a range of native broadleaf shrubs and trees (Field Maple, Willow, Hawthorn, Hazel and Spindle) to diversify the species and canopy structure.

It is clear that some birds are almost exclusively tied to the woodland – Chiffchaff, Blackcap and Tawny Owl for example – but for some more widespread species, the CBC has demonstrated that woodland is the preferred habitat when compared with dune scrub. Some milder winters in the early 1990s may have assisted the two pairs of Long-tailed Tits and the first ever breeding Goldcrests. The loss of breeding Spotted Flycatcher is disappointing when suitable habitat remains, particularly as the last recorded pair in 2001 successfully reared three young. One species that did make a comeback, though, was the Sparrowhawk. A pair that nested in the Plantation in 1987 provided the first confirmed breeding on the reserve for 30 years.

Breeding shorebirds

The most important nesting species on site relies upon what is seemingly the most inhospitable, barren, windswept and tide-shaped landscape – the shingle ridges. Wintering off the West African coast, a population of Little Terns returns to the Lincolnshire coast every April. Pair-bonding takes place quickly and the accompanying aerial courtship involves a spectacularly choreographed tandem display flight – followed by the ritual presentation of food from the male to the female. The frenzy of Little Tern display activity is one of the ornithological highlights of the year.

At one time (1971) 131 pairs nested at seven sites along the Lincolnshire coast. Four colonies were extant through the 1980s, but Gibraltar Point was the only one remaining by 2008, despite habitat remaining suitable on at least two other sites. The precarious nature of the national population was recognised and the species became a priority for protection. In contrast to other breeding terns, the nature of the Little Tern 'colony' is positively dispersed as some 30 pairs may be scattered along a kilometre of coast. Whilst the birds may perceive advantages to this strategy, there are distinct management complications!

The earliest reference to the Gibraltar Point Little Terns was published by Blathwayt (1915), referring to a colony of some 20 pairs in 1914 nesting on the old sand and shingle spit which extended southwards from the Coastguard House (now the Wash Study Centre) to the Haven, although it states that the colony had probably been in existence for much longer. Subsequently, the colony moved to the beach with up to 127 pairs in 1927 and still 80 in 1933. There followed a gap in recording until post-war observations in 1945 and 1946 revealed up to 40 pairs nesting in the old minefields (possibly one of the species' most successful strategies at the time in view of the threat of egg collectors and the increasing pressure of holidaymaker footfall along the coastal fringe!).

Through the 1950s it became evident that the birds were suffering damage and disturbance from human visitors and their canine associates as well as predators. From 1965–1967 Barrie Wilkinson undertook detailed nest records of the shorebird colony and concluded that 70–80% of tern clutches were lost to fox predation and 7.5% to human interference. The latter covered deliberate collection of the eggs through to indiscriminate trampling – and this is possibly a conservative figure as in some years up to 19% of nest failures could not be positively determined. The survey revealed that Ringed Plovers suffered even greater losses through trampling. During this period the fencing off of colony areas was practised for the first time and explanatory signs were provided to request people to keep out of the exclosures.

The first full-time shorebird warden, Kevin Woodbridge, took up his post in 1976 and established a management base – essentially a tent – at the base of the

Spit where the colony could be kept in view and visitors intercepted before they entered the exclosure. A 24-hour watch was maintained with help from reserve staff and a loyal band of local volunteers. Much diplomatic work was carried out in relation to the public, and zoning the beach area, previously a 'free for all', to a shorebird sanctuary, discrete from the broader area of open access, also helped matters. That year, 14 juvenile Little Terns fledged.

Today, the sanctuary areas are largely respected by visitors, egg collecting is no longer a casual pastime and the main causes of failure are deemed to be natural: predation, weather and tides. Predation by foxes and corvids is perhaps the main factor limiting productivity and some control measures have been put in place over the years. Electric fencing and wire guards have yielded success in some years. Typically though, as soon as eggs have hatched, the parents lead the chicks away from these protected environments. There is also a limit to the amount of intervention possible when the colony is under siege from raptors, and through the early 1990s the annual arrival of a large female Merlin was feared by the wardening team. This bird took a good number of chicks over four seasons. The combined mobbing of the Little Terns and local Oystercatchers may have reduced this predation somewhat, but a 'ringtail' Montagu's Harrier took absolutely no notice of the pandemonium as it went from clutch to clutch eating eggs in 2008. There have also been concerns over food availability, both early in the season (e.g. 2005) when incubating birds just deserted the colony for no other apparent reason, and later in the season when chicks have starved during periods of good weather.

The Trust continues to invest heavily in the shorebird protection scheme, but volunteer input has always been vital to the protection of the colony and managing and informing visitors. Despite this input, the colony has suffered lean years interspersed with occasional good years, most notable being 34 young fledged in 1999 and 30 in 2006. The 1999 total represented 30% of all chicks fledged in the north-east region that year and the highest productivity of 0.9 chicks per pair.

The shorebird sanctuary has had to be expanded through the years to encompass new areas of shingle as they become favoured as nesting sites by the terns and plovers. The sanctuary also envelopes a considerable area of salt marsh, affording protection to nesting Redshank, Reed Bunting, Linnet and Skylark. It also protects the best example of a Sea-holly colony in the county and allows undisturbed feeding and roosting for passage waders and terns.

Around 30 pairs of Ringed Plover breed annually on the reserve, making this a nationally important colony as well. As with the terns, they have been well studied and efforts made to protect them from the same factors which adversely affect the Little Terns. Gibraltar Point is one of few sites in Britain where the three species of small plover have nested. In 1979 there was an extraordinary occurrence. A pair of Kentish Plovers arrived and settled down to nest in an area of saltings and shingle, slightly north of the main beach area, but nonetheless in an area where visitor access was unrestricted. A female was confirmed to be incubating two eggs on 30 June. Mindful of the significance of this event and their vulnerability to egg collectors the whole episode was kept so confidential that it is possible that only two or three people knew of the occurrence. It is known that the two eggs hatched but the resulting chicks were seen away from the nest on only one occasion before being lost. This was the first nesting of Kentish Plovers in Lincolnshire and the last time that the species nested in Britain.

Post-breeding dispersal and summer passage

Amongst the breeding waterbirds on the lagoons, immature Mediterranean and Little Gulls are frequent. Some of the earliest returning waders such as Green Sandpiper and Spotted Redshank can also appear from late June. Of all the summer rarities that have occurred, from Sardinian Warblers to Red-footed Falcons, it is perhaps the waders, terns and herons that have been the most prevalent and have included Lesser Yellowlegs, Long-billed Dowitcher, White-rumped Sandpiper, Terek Sandpiper, Whiskered Tern, Caspian Tern, Great White Egret and Purple Heron. Spoonbills are now virtually annual, including a group of four birds that spent most of the summer here in 2002.

However, for sheer numbers of birds moving during the summer, Swifts provide the most impressive annual spectacle. Commencing from late June and at a peak during July, daily counts have regularly exceeded 10,000 heading south. A count of 25,000 was made on 16 July 1997 and a movement on 28 June 1979 was counted throughout the day from a single watch point resulting in a total of 22,000. The log for that day states that some 1,700 were passing south per hour, but the movement was occurring over a large front and up to 40,000–50,000 birds could have been involved. These movements are now regularly attended by a Hobby or two and sometimes coincide with a migration of Sand Martins such as the 5,600 which accompanied 10,000 Swifts on 19 July 1995. During such vast movements Alpine Swift has passed through on occasion, but the county's second Little Swift fortunately paused over the Mere for a short while on 25 June 2002.

Irruptions of Crossbills have provided another very interesting summer feature in some years. The first such occurrence to be detailed involved 57 birds from 14 to 17 August 1959, but more recent influxes have seen more than 200 passing through during June and July. Peak day counts have included 90 on 6 July 1991 and 110 on 27 June 1997. Although most are on the move, small numbers, often involving family groups always stop in the pines in the Beach Car Park and often come down to drink in the puddles, soon becoming a popular attraction for visiting birders and photographers.

Some of the other early signs of juvenile dispersal include the appearance of Pied Wagtails around the water bodies and the build up of Starlings on the salt marsh (up to 4,000 by 11 July 2005). The progeny of early-nesting Wheatears from elsewhere are usually in evidence before the close of July, but the regularity of juvenile Wood Warblers and Redstarts at this time is almost inexplicable given that neither species has nested regularly in the county since the 1990s. The first records of the year of Treecreeper and Kingfisher occur as a result of juvenile dispersal and the occurrence of all three species of woodpecker on 10 August 1988 involved the first Lesser Spotted for the observatory.

Another feature of the post-breeding period is the build up of juvenile Kestrels that disperse to the coast. Five to ten can be seen in a day, mostly trying to test hunting skills on the voles and insects of the Old Salt Marsh. Some allow very close approach along the South Marsh Road – this is not usually a good sign and the statistics relating to juvenile survival are clearly shaped by starvation at a time when the nights are becoming colder.

Autumn

Autumn migration gets underway with the return of Arctic-breeding waders from July, a build-up of terns on the beach and increasing seabird movements into August and then the vast arrival and passage of migrants overland. The main period – late August to October – always provides bouts of intense activity (peaking in September when over 120 species can occur in a single day, e.g. 126 on 29 September 2007). Although migration slows into November, ongoing movements well into the month merit its inclusion as part of the autumn.

Autumn – sea and shore

Casual observations of the sea during July produce Gannets and Fulmars from east coast colonies, small numbers of Common Scoters and Manx Shearwaters and occasional unexpected sightings such as summer-plumaged Great Northern Diver. There is also the annual mystery of up to 40 summer-plumaged Great Crested Grebes. Southbound waders move into the Wash in flocks low over the sea, from late July and through August. Knot, Redshank, Turnstone, Golden Plover and godwit flocks contain many individuals in summer plumage.

Sandwich Terns use this corner of the Wash as a staging post on migration and are a very prominent feature of the early autumn, with nationally important numbers of birds involved. Pairs arrive and the shrill calls of their still-dependent young can be heard as they beg for food. The roost builds up during the late after-noon and the continuous calling of often over 1,000 birds creates a din that is audible from a considerable distance. Offshore as the tide ebbs, massive feeding flocks can develop, which predominantly involve the Sandwich Terns coming and going between the sea and shore with a turnover of birds obviously being drawn in from the north and leaving to the south. Gannets, large gulls, other species of terns and Kittiwakes are usually also involved. At any one time as many as 2,000–3,000 birds can be involved, although day counts of Sandwich Terns alone have reached 8,000.

Not surprisingly, the first of the autumnal skuas are attracted, many pausing to steal a meal and then continuing elsewhere, giving a considerable turnover of individuals – possibly 80–100 on peak days in August. Ed Mackrill enthused about an afternoon's tern watch in a submission to the Lincolnshire Bird Club Forum on 28 July 2007:

> *Just returned from an amazing evening watching terns and skuas at Gib. Point. From about 16:00 this afternoon to when I left at 20:00 there was a large gath-ering of terns and attendant skuas on the sand/shingle banks just across the creek from the beach opposite North Building. Birds were coming and going all the time*

and the following are just one count: Sandwich Tern – 870 roosting and bathing,
Common Tern – 142 roosting and bathing, Arctic Tern – 36 but surely many
more and coming and going all the time, Kittiwake – 62 roosting and bathing
and Arctic Skua – constantly present – 16 in the air at once, 11 actually on the
beach roosting amongst the terns. All ages.

All of this action was very close and skua events with terns were often virtually
overhead. I personally cannot remember when I have had such fabulous views of
Arctic Terns and Arctic Skuas. Perfect for photographs. This situation was the
same yesterday afternoon/evening and with the present tides is likely to be the
same for the next few evenings. I strongly recommend a visit to Gib. Point to see
this spectacle. As the birds are close please take care not to disturb them and take a
hat as the midges and sandflies were hungry when the wind dropped!

When settled, the tern and gull roosts can be scanned for other species. As
suggested above there may be hundreds of Common Terns along with smaller
numbers of Arctic Terns. With so many birds rarer species do occasionally turn
up, such as the odd Roseate Tern, and there have been single records of both
Caspian and Gull-billed Terns and two sightings of 'orange-billed terns'. The gull
roost builds up through the summer when Lesser Black-backed Gulls are at their
most prominent and a few Yellow-legged Gulls join the considerable numbers of
non-breeding Herring and Great Black-backed Gulls. Kittiwakes often roost with
the terns on the beach and have attracted the occasional Sabine's Gull as
company.

There has never been a fixed sea-watching site at Gibraltar Point: watchers
have generally been reliant upon finding the closest ridge that gives some degree
of altitude for looking down across the seascape, such that the birds themselves
are not lost to view behind the waves, and to avoid any sand-blow. Outcrops of
scrub may give shelter from a northerly, but there is not much protection from
any wind with an easterly vector.

There is no doubt that given the right conditions, seabird passage can be as
engaging as any other aspects of migration here (see Table 3). September is the
key month for Arctic Skuas and Manx and Sooty Shearwaters and the largest
counts often involve birds northbound into a northerly wind. It is not unusual for
a good day to produce all four species of skua, Sooty and Manx Shearwaters,
Sabine's Gull and Leach's Petrel, along with three-figure counts of Gannets,
Fulmars and auks and perhaps rarer species such as Balearic Shearwater, Storm
Petrel or Grey Phalarope. The latter is probably overlooked as so many waders
move up and down the near-shore environment. Numbers of Red-throated
Divers and sea duck such as Common Scoter, Eider, Red-breasted Merganser, and
maybe the odd Scaup or Long-tailed Duck become more regular into late
autumn. Whooper Swans arriving from Iceland occasionally settle on the sea.
When things are good, it is difficult to leave the watch and having just nipped out
to look at the sea for an hour, birders have often returned home starving, dehy-
drated and hypothermic at dusk!

In some years, large-scale displacement of Little Auks has been apparent
during northerly blows. Often such a 'wreck' will involve exhausted and starved

Table 3. *Peak autumn seabird numbers at Gibraltar Point (and direction of movement).*

Fulmar	796 N	09/09/97
Sooty shearwater	358 N	16/09/05
Manx shearwater	181 N	09/09/97
Storm petrel	2	29/10/89
Leach's petrel	35 N	11/09/89
Gannet	2050 N	27/09/07
Bonxie	83 S	19/09/99
Arctic Skua	270 S	18/08/63
Pomarine Skua	78 S	09/11/07
Long-tailed Skua	6 N	13/09/96 + 29/09/02
Kittiwake	7000 S	08/11/01
Little Auk	1088 S	09/11/07
Razorbill	350 S	30/10/06
Guillemot	56 N	22/10/93
Puffin	7	28/10/83

individuals as well as those that are confused enough to associate with flocks of Starlings or Sanderling. On the 23 October 1993 one was found on the roof of the Field Centre shed and successfully released. In 1995, a massive influx saw 327 moving mostly north in four hours. Several that had joined Starling flocks offshore carried on migrating inland with them so little wonder that 10 were later brought to the observatory from as far afield as Grantham and Bingham. Three were later released, the others perished and post mortems confirmed starvation.

The inbound Starlings can provide a fairly dramatic sight on their own, with flocks numbering into the thousands on some days. When Starlings are on the move, other land migrants, such as Skylarks, Redwings and Blackbirds can also be seen coming in off the sea and such ungainly migrants as Snipe, Woodcock, Jack Snipe and Water Rail. On 2 November 1995 an amazing seven Short-eared Owls arrived off the sea during the day. Tired passerines arriving during daylight, having endured substantial overnight flights, can be a target for raptors such as Merlins that habitually fly out to sea to intercept them and even opportunist skuas will take advantage. On one occasion, a Blackbird (which had probably left northern Europe the previous evening) was only 300 metres from shore when forced into the sea by two Great Skuas after a sustained attack. On another occasion, stunned sea-watchers stood transfixed as a Goldcrest struggled in low from the sea, up the beach and almost between their legs!

Autumn visible migration

Even from the first full year of recording, in 1949, there was an appreciation of the vast numbers of birds passing overhead and much effort was put into quantifying these movements. Unsurprisingly, the autumn passage involves not only significantly more birds than the spring, but also a wider range of species.

Most counts are made from Mill Hill, where birds are moving south along the dune line. Often they are moving at or a little above eye level, or it may even be possible to look down on passing migrants, particularly on mornings with low cloud. Passage can be under way from dawn and usually tails off into the latter part of the morning, but this is not always the case, with pipits, finches, larks and Starlings often still moving in good numbers later on and hirundines and Swifts passing throughout the day.

The general pattern of autumn migration over the dunes commences in August with the departing of Swifts and Sand Martins, along with a trickle of Yellow Wagtails and Tree Pipits. The participants of the 1985 ringing course, whilst noting passage Swifts on 31 August, managed to pick out an accompanying Alpine Swift. Such passing rarities are quickly away as they pass at high speed. Mindful of this, when the shout went through the Field Centre, Chris Mead, the course leader, leapt from the shower and appeared in the centre garden clad only in a towel to hide his modesty!

Raptors, too, are unpredictable and rarely linger, but many can be on the move during early autumn. On a good, clear, warm day when thermals are rising from adjacent farmland, it is worth scanning to the west for thermalling Buzzards or Marsh Harriers gaining height before migration. An exceptional 48 Kestrels passed south on 11 September 1998 with six Marsh Harriers and an Osprey. Whilst on 6 September 2004 an unprecedented raptor migration involved totals of 16 Buzzards, five buzzard sp., Honey-buzzard, an Osprey, eight Sparrowhawks, and 16 Kestrels on a day when many hirundines and passerines were also on the move.

Raptors do not always follow the presumption of arriving during good weather though. Indeed, light drizzle on 14 August 1999 did not deter eight Marsh Harriers and a duo of Buzzard and Osprey from their southward journey – almost hugging the contours of the dunes in such conditions. Strong easterly winds and rain also brought the first significant arrival of Honey-buzzards to the reserve with three on 14 September 1993. They have been annual in autumn since then and there have been some incredible influxes. In 2000, a total of 34 birds during September commenced with a dark juvenile on the 17th. It came in off the sea and over the Visitor Centre car park to the delight of birdwatchers as it almost coincided with the passage of a very elegant and vocal Crane, to be followed by a very impressive 25 Honey-buzzards on the 20th.

This event was thought unlikely to be repeated, but a similar influx occurred on 14 September 2008. With several Honey-buzzards reported on the east coast the previous day, local birders were alert to the likelihood of one or two appearing at Gibraltar Point. Several birders assembled at Mill Hill on that morning and the first Honey-buzzard drifted through at 06:30 hrs, having possibly roosted on the reserve overnight. Other individuals duly followed and were picked up arriving from the north. By mid-morning a total of 16, mostly dark morph, juvenile Honey-buzzards had given spectacular views and photo opportunities to the small crowd which included a 1980s wardens' reunion!

Increasingly more Swallows and House Martins pass through during September. They are omnipresent components of the autumn migration into October, but on some days Swallows have been the most numerous species. Some 60,000 moved through between 11 and 14 Sept 1954, an estimated 40,000 on 25 August 1964 and a further 30,000 on 9 September 1995, when the majority passed in three half-hour waves. On 9 September 1974, 25,000 Swallows flew south following 24,000 the previous day. However, what was extraordinary about passage on the 9th was the immense accompanying movement of 11,000 Meadow Pipits. This species regularly achieves four-figure day passage counts, but this was a record for the observatory. Meadow Pipit and Siskin were the only two species to feature prominently in a southerly passage on a morning of continuous light drizzle on 12 September 2008. Flocks of up to 600 Meadow Pipits and 300 Siskins culminated in totals of 7,620 and 4,140 respectively. On good days, these two species can be accompanied by other passerines, typically Chaffinches, Linnets, Goldfinches, Greenfinches, Reed Buntings and sparrows (mostly Tree Sparrows).

As autumn progresses further into October, Goldcrests can be seen bush-hopping south through the scrub blocks. More surprising was the scale of Blue Tit migration in October 1949. Over 1,440 birds headed south-west during the first half of the month, with 500 on the 12th. At this time, the predominance of Meadow Pipits gives way to the Rock Pipit and up to 500 passage birds have been counted during a day. The finch component changes slightly to include more Bramblings and a few Twite and there is a definite increase in Skylarks on the move. Occasional Woodlark and Shore Lark can be detected and Snow and Lapland Buntings become frequent. Such movements may bring near-annual Richard's Pipit or Hawfinch.

Most years will see some considerable movements of Starlings and Redwings, but more unusual are the spontaneous movements of small numbers of Bearded Tits, often flying at great height with only their 'pinging' calls giving them away – bizarre behaviour for a secretive reed-bed dweller. On some occasions they may be drawn to the small patches of reed around the lagoons or great willowherb on the dunes.

The flavour of raptor immigration changes, too, during the later autumn when, in many years, Rough-legged Buzzards have been seen. Multiple arrivals are not unusual either. Six passed through between 22 and 28 October 1973 and the following year five arrived on the 22 October alone. In 1994, three came in over the Freshwater Marsh during the course of the afternoon on 24 October. A good arrival of raptors on 4 October 1998 involved a Rough-legged Buzzard, a Buzzard, Peregrine, Hobby, Merlin, several Kestrels and up to 10 Sparrowhawks. This was a particularly good autumn for Sparrowhawks, with up to 19 counted during mid-October. One of the most impressive sights to be witnessed by migration watchers was an immature White-tailed Eagle that made its way south along the Lincolnshire coast on 27 October 1985.

Some good visible migration continues into November, with Woodpigeons, Rock Pipits, Skylarks and finches and the occasional late surprise, such as the two Red-rumped Swallows on 14 November 1988. An exciting development in the study of bird migration was under way during the late 2000s. The Central Science Laboratory came to Gibraltar Point to trial radar techniques for monitoring bird migration in offshore windfarm areas as part of environmental impact research. Information was gathered on numbers of birds, and altitude and direction of travel relative to the windfarm sites.

Autumn – falls of migrants

Overnight arrivals of grounded birds generally commence with Willow Warblers in August when up to 200–300 can be seen, often preceding more significant numbers later in the month: over 1,000 were ringed during the annual ringing course 26–31 August 1985. It is not unusual during a good fall to see Willow Warblers in groups of 20–30 feeding in sallows and moving through the dune scrub.

A ripe crop of elderberries is appreciated by the *Sylvia* warblers and scanning the elders is the best way to see species such as Blackcap and Garden Warbler. Some of the most productive elder clumps can be overseen from the old Sleeper Track or the Mill Hill viewpoint. Redstart and Pied Flycatcher are expected components of migrant arrivals at any time from mid-August onwards. Although many of these early autumn migrants may be 'British' birds, question marks remain over the origin of some of the more unusual immigrations to the site, such as the 300 Dunnocks on 27 August 1961, and the arrival of five Great Spotted Woodpeckers on 26 August 2006, including a group of four that dropped out of the sky into the Beach Car Park pines.

European migrants have featured in falls as early as 16 August 1992 when two Icterine Warblers and a Barred Warbler arrived on the East Dunes with a fall of 290 Lesser Whitethroats, 150 Whitethroats, 56 Garden Warblers and 230 Willow Warblers. Another early arrival involved six Icterines on 19 August 1958. At this time, it is likely that coverage of the reserve was concentrated at the southern sector of the East Dunes (mostly the Ringing Hollow), so there may have been even more. In addition to the two scarce warbler species mentioned, the other classic scarce drift migrants to be expected during such early autumn arrivals include Red-backed Shrike, Wryneck and Bluethroat, although as the years have passed all have become scarcer.

In 1976 up to five Wrynecks were seen daily between 24 and 26 August, with 10 individuals ringed during that period. The following year, again up to five Wrynecks arrived with four Red-backed Shrikes on 20 August. There have been up to four Bluethroats in a week (September 1956) and eight Barred Warblers in some autumns (e.g. 1981 and 1982). The 2000 annual report, in stark contrast, is devoid of autumn entries for either Wryneck or Barred Warbler. However, this poor state of affairs was rectified two years later when one of each shared a patch of scrub on Rock Ridge during a fall on 10 September, which also brought Red-breasted Flycatcher, Icterine Warbler, 83 Yellow Wagtails, 120 Redstarts, Black Redstart, 80 Pied Flycatchers, 25 Spotted Flycatchers, 35 Wheatears, and 26 Tree Pipits.

Drift migrants continue into September when some of the largest volumes of birds have been involved in falls – again 1958 gets a mention for the 200 Pied Flycatchers and 200 Redstarts that arrived with 100 Wheatears on 4 September, but an exciting period for birds brought three Bee-eaters, three Wrynecks and a Greenish Warbler in the preceding two days.

Not all birds arrive overnight. Continuous and detailed day watches over small areas of the site (such as the Ringing Hollow) have enabled a fuller under-standing of the arrival time of landbirds during fall events. No migrants were evident when the Ringing Hollow was checked at 07:15 hrs on 15 September 1968, but several birds were present at 08:10 hrs, including Garden Warbler and Redstart, when the area was checked again. An arrival was underway and later the area held 14 Garden Warblers, 13 Redstarts, four Ring Ouzels, a Wood Warbler and a Wryneck. The arrival continued the following day, bringing 200 Redstarts, 70 Garden Warblers, 40 Blackcaps and a male Bluethroat.

On 18 September 1995, after a fairly quiet morning various Redstarts, Robins, Wheatears and Pied Flycatchers were seen freshly arrived on the Field Centre garden wall and on the lawn by mid-afternoon. There was a frenzy of bird activity. Obviously something large-scale was happening. With only two birders on site there was a lot of ground to cover. Looking across to the Storm Ridge there was an incredible number of Redstarts, Wheatears and other migrants hopping out from scrub to feed on bare sand and shingle – a Wryneck was seen flying in low over salt marsh from the sea and landed in the same area. The sheer number of birds darting in and out of the scrub made counting tricky but by dusk the following counts were made: 481 Redstarts, 70 Wheatears (mostly on rocks by the Wash Viewpoint), 17 Whinchats, 30 Tree Pipits, 600 Meadow Pipits, 94 Robins, 66 Pied Flycatchers, Red-breasted Flycatcher, Richard's Pipit, 15 Chiffchaffs, 39 Willow Warblers, 64 Goldcrests, 24 Spotted Flycatchers, 15 Song Thrushes and a Goshawk over the Old Salt Marsh.

As autumn deepens, the dune scrub can be positively 'ticking' with migrant Robins and Song Thrushes freshly arrived. Willow Warblers are subtly replaced by Chiffchaffs and likewise, Stonechats replace Whinchats. Goldcrests, having been virtually absent for four months, become common. Firecrests are to be expected accompanying them from time to time. Woodcock are flushed from dune scrub when passing and, if lucky, a Long-eared Owl may be found at roost in thick elder or hawthorn.

Scarce migrants from the east include annual Yellow-browed Warblers (up to nine in a day), and near annual Red-breasted Flycatcher, Richard's Pipit, and Common Rosefinch. Rarities have come in the form of Little Buntings, Arctic and Greenish Warblers, Olive-backed Pipits, the only two Lincolnshire records of Short-toed Lark, the county's second Blyth's Reed Warbler and the only Citrine Wagtail.

Probably the most spectacular feature of the period is the arrival of thrushes. Substantial groups of Redwings, Blackbirds, Song Thrushes and Fieldfares just tumble out of the sky at high speed. The first indication of this event will be the incredible noise of the air passing through their wings as they drop – fairly unnerving if one does not realize what is happening – and after a moment, the birds come into view, flocks of anything up to 300 stalling and plummeting into cover. Having just arrived, it is remarkable how they then seem determined with the business of onward migration; vast flocks soon moving on, between south and west, and the day after an arrival, only a fraction will remain.

October 1990 will be remembered for a very significant fall of thrushes and other migrants grounded by poor weather. On the 18th a two-hour search of the West Dunes and Plantation had revealed an arrival of thrushes brought down by fog during a light northerly. Even in this short time 750 Fieldfares and 430

Redwing were counted, along with good numbers of Robins, Blackbirds, Song Thrushes and Goldcrests. Of the warblers, an interesting grey-looking Willow Warbler of the Scandinavian race *Phylloscopus trochilus acredula* was also seen with four Chiffchaffs. The wind changed to a light north-easterly overnight and there was thick mist and occasional drizzle. One of only two observers on site that day, residing in the old Coastguard Tower, was woken by the calls of thrushes flying around the buildings before dawn. Peering out of the window, he was greeted by two Goldcrests sitting on the window ledge. It was clear that something unusual was happening. The log entry for the day records:

> *A staggering day for land migrants, with huge falls of thrushes, the likes of which not seen since 1965. A minimum of 9,500 Fieldfares carpeted roadside fields and flocked in the dunes. Redwings numbered 6,200 and Robins were up to 140 with 160 Blackbirds, 95 Song Thrushes and four Ring Ouzels. Up to 2,000 Starlings were present and moving through inland as were finches. Bramblings were in greater numbers than Chaffinches. One flock numbered 70 and the day total exceeded 340. Sallows and elders were dripping with Goldcrests – well over 1,000.*

These figures would almost certainly have been substantial underestimates due to the poor visibility, low number of recorders involved and the mobility and turnover of the birds. A fall on 22 October 1988 again brought many Redwings and Blackbirds and some 1,600 Goldcrests overnight. The unusual component of this arrival of eastern birds though, was the first mainland British record of a Northern Waterthrush. Trapped in a mist-net and barely visible in the field after ringing, it is difficult to draw any conclusions about its journey. However, a bird in Dorset some years later coincided with a fall that also brought good numbers of Redwings, Firecrests and Bramblings.

A more typical associate of the thrush arrivals is the Waxwing and small parties usually arrive during October or later, again keen on hawthorn or even rose hips. Another obvious and annual visitor is the Great Grey Shrike, once regular through autumn and winter. October is now the classic month for its arrival and up to three have been seen in a day (7 October 1998), actually visible simultaneously along the Storm Ridge and West Dunes. October 1960 also produced a good crop of three grey shrike records during the month which involved two Great Grey Shrikes and Lincolnshire's first Lesser Grey Shrike.

As the leaf cover is blown from the trees during autumn gales, it becomes a tough existence for insect feeders such as crests and warblers, but the sallows and sycamores usually hang on to some foliage well into October. This is prime Pallas's Warbler habitat – almost annual by the late 2000s with some days bringing two and even three birds. The first Pallas's Warbler for the county was found here on 19 October 1968, with another at Anderby Creek less than 20 kilometres up the coast. A remarkable coincidence occurred on 23 October 2003, when a Hume's Warbler was found at Gibraltar Point – a first for the county – later that day a second was found at Anderby Creek!

That autumn had been remarkable for *Phylloscopus* warbler records at Gibraltar Point – with seven species recorded around the Plantation alone, including the

Hume's Warbler, a Radde's Warbler, two Pallas's Warblers, Wood Warbler and at least nine Yellow-browed Warblers, as well as Willow Warbler and Chiffchaff.

The extent to which autumn migration continued into November was not fully appreciated until 1960 when the Trust took over the old coastguard buildings and there was a resident warden on site to keep records. Indeed, the following year, on 5 November, after light northerly winds and overnight rain, a spectacular and unprecedented arrival of Blackbirds was witnessed. The log account details: 'a constant stream of birds from dawn until dusk – it is estimated that less than 1% came near the traps'. Over 850 were ringed that day when the total number of Blackbirds was estimated at 100,000. This remains the largest arrival of any species at the Observatory in its history. Although September and October may be regarded as the holy grail of autumn birding by some, this event alone demonstrates the potential for the most significant ornithological event of the year to occur in November. In addition, this month has produced a list of scarce and rare birds to almost rival October, including a Pied Wheatear in 2000, a Red-flanked Bluetail in 2002 (when they were still rare enough to draw a crowd of several hundred birders), two Dartford Warblers and even a Dipper of the nominate European form, Black-bellied Dipper *Cinclus cinclus cinclus* perched on a pond-dipping platform briefly in 2008.

As already mentioned, the one single bird that Gibraltar Point will always be remembered for is the American Redstart in November 1982. The bird was only the fourth for Britain and Ireland and followed one on Islay the previous week. During the period of its stay there was very good coverage of the reserve by visiting birders and many other 'good' birds were recorded. Up to six Firecrests could be seen around the Plantation, often close to the redstart. A Serin was found on 13 November, but another remarkable event happened on 15 November. The log reads:

> *Yet another new species put in an appearance this morning when Ron Overton discovered an adult male Isabelline Shrike (believed to be* Lanius isabellinus phoenicuroides*) in the West Dunes. Good views were obtained by all observers between 12:00 hrs and 14:00 hrs, though it was reported later, showing in a bush with the American Redstart! Is this a novel example of detente or simply a close shave for the latter!*

It was no coincidence that one of the authors and many other visiting birders first became acquainted with this magnificent east coast site that month.

Autumn – waterbirds

Wader interest on the freshwater and brackish lagoons (Tennyson's Sands, Jackson's Marsh, Fenland Lagoon and the Mere), is at its peak as water levels drop through July and into August. The turnover of birds is such that these features often hold a different selection of birds at dusk to those there at dawn.

Whatever the weather has to offer, the series of spacious hides provides good shelter and good views. Little Stint, Curlew Sandpiper, Ruff, Spotted Redshank and Little Ringed Plover can all be seen in small numbers alongside roosts of Black-tailed Godwit, Greenshank and the 'local' Redshank and Avocet. Numbers of the latter are augmented during the autumn by birds that have presumably bred around the Humber, while the godwit flock has grown to 300 or so in recent years. Careful scanning through the godwits on 5 July 2004 led to the discovery of a summer-plumaged Long-billed Dowitcher which became a daily companion to the godwit flock, remaining until the end of September. It was presumed to be the same bird returning in July 2006, which found itself in the company of a Nearctic neighbour in the shape of a Lesser Yellowlegs that had been present on and off since June.

Greenshanks are always loyal to the Fenland Lagoon, with a daily roost of up to 70, often with good gatherings of Redshanks on the high tide. A count of roosting Redshanks here totalled 1,017 birds on 4 August 1997 – an amazing number for such a small area. Detailed counting of this tightly packed roost also led to the finding of a Broad-billed Sandpiper lurking between the legs of the roosting 'shanks. This lagoon has also hosted the only Buff-breasted Sandpiper, but otherwise provides visitors with good close up views of Grey Plover, Oystercatcher and Curlew.

The Mere has consistently been a magnet for waders when its water levels are low. Being the only significant freshwater body on the site for over two decades, it has hosted some 34 species of wader, including Wilson's Phalaropes in spring and autumn, Broad-billed Sandpiper, Temminck's Stints and Pectoral Sandpipers. 'Pecs' have been regular but in no way annual or to be expected. However, working on the adjacent hay meadow on 18 August 1990, Mark Grantham had a premonition, or just a lucky hunch as he took a break, heading toward the hide he exclaimed, 'I'm just going to the Mere to find a Pec.' Sure enough there was one – a juvenile!

The same hide saw a queue of birders forming outside in September 1983 to get a look at a Citrine Wagtail that was feeding on mud in front of the hide, the first Lincolnshire record and still a mainland novelty at the time. Less of an identification problem, and also right below the hide occasionally during its stay was the first Great White Egret for the reserve on 11 July 1993. It made the Mere look like a mere puddle!

The fringes of Sea Club-rush and reed along the muddy margins of the Mere have proved an ideal attraction for several Spotted Crakes over the years. Water Rails have not been proven as a breeding species but are usually present by mid-autumn, occupying the lagoon margins and ditches, the dune slacks and the salt marsh creeks. As the new lagoons have developed fringing vegetation, they too have started to attract Water Rails, a Spotted Crake and even the rarer herons, such as an immature Night-heron roosting with Little Egrets in the Jackson's Marsh hedge during autumn 2007, following an adult in the same area that spring.

Out on the estuary at low tide, vast swathes of feeding waders traverse the mud even by early autumn. Large numbers of Redshank flock in to feed on the high estuary and as the tide ebbs away Ringed Plovers approach their peak numbers for the year. The immigration of adult waders precedes the arrival of the year's juveniles and there is much evidence of summer breeding colours from

Sanderling, Dunlin, Knot, Bar-tailed Godwit, Grey Plover and the immaculate Turnstone. Although this last species does not winter here in any numbers, the early autumn throughput has seen up to 250 migrants on the estuary.

Little Stint and Curlew Sandpiper can be located consorting with the Dunlin, when time and tide permit. In practice, observations are made too infrequently always to detect peak arrivals of these scarcer species out on the estuary. However, some estuary counts have coincided with good arrivals, as on 10 August 2004 for example, when 73 summer-plumaged Curlew Sandpiper were out on the mud (with another four on the lagoons). The sheer numbers of birds out on the flats makes rarity-finding a hard task and waders such as White-rumped Sandpiper are doubtless overlooked. The only confirmed record occurred in June 2007 and the county's first Terek Sandpiper was found on 18 July 2005.

With the arrival of passage and wintering populations of waders and the juveniles of the year, the numbers of waders in the Wash swells to a peak during September and October. The autumnal high tide roosts on the highest tides provide an ornithological wonder that is difficult to rival and has involved the largest single species day count for any species, a record 150,000 Knot were estimated on 25 August 1953. Another spectacular roost occurred on the high tide of 10 October 2006. Counting started at first light in order to record the whole fly-past over one and three-quarter hours to the peak of the tide at 08:44 hrs. The single observer was left almost stunned by the numbers involved in the roost arrival. His final tally for Knot alone was 122,000! The largest single flock to arrive contained almost 30,000 Knot, a vast stratum, stretching for about two kilometres. The whole roost of nearly 157,000 waders of six species comprised: 122,000 Knot, 9,500 Grey Plover, 9,000 Dunlin, 8,850 Oystercatcher, 6,600 Bar-tailed Godwit and 1,000 Sanderling. On this occasion, the main roost area was full to capacity and sub-roosts formed on the open beach in various spots up to Seacroft.

The large tides during the autumn usually cause extensive flooding of the series of strip saltings all the way up the reserve, leaving a series of large, shallow, temporary pools. These are a great attraction for gulls, waders and some dabbling ducks. The floods are usually the best areas to check for flocks of juvenile Little Stint and Curlew Sandpiper where there are occasionally over 20 of each and both Grey and Red-necked Phalaropes have been found here.

Incoming migrant ducks will pause on these floods before heading further inland to the lagoons. During September, there can be over 1,000 dabbling ducks on the lagoons, predominantly Teal, a couple of hundred each of Wigeon and Mallard, various Gadwall and Shoveler and occasional Pintail or Garganey. It is hoped that as the grazing marsh beyond becomes well established, Wigeon will be attracted in greater numbers. Lapwings and Golden Plovers are already becoming accustomed to this new grassland habitat.

Hopefully the above gives a flavour of what can be expected through the seasons at Gibraltar Point. The reserve contains a wide variety of habitats, which result in a wide range of species whatever the time of year and almost whatever the weather.

BIRD RINGING

The observatory building is the centre of activity for the trapping of migrants during spring and autumn. A series of displays that complement the information available to visitors at the Visitor Centre have recently been produced, detailing the history of the observatory and its ringing activities. Since the observatory opened in 1949 and up to the end of 2008, a total of 182,889 birds have been caught and ringed, the most numerous of which are detailed in Table 4.

In the first few years the vast majority of the birds were caught in the Heligoland trap, at the time the most effective means of catching large numbers of fledged birds prior to the widespread introduction of mist-nets. Among the more interesting species caught were Bluethroat, Yellow-browed Warbler, Red-breasted Flycatcher and Black Redstart. A further trap was built in August 1951, at the limit of the vegetation on the ridge to the south-west of the original trap (the success of which is praised in the 1951 Report) and a third, even larger one, followed in the 1960s. By 1959 the number of birds ringed had exceeded 11,000. Among the new species added to the list in this time were Nightjar, Rose-coloured Starling, Greenish Warbler and Barred Warbler.

The great advantage of Heligoland traps is that they are not affected by adverse (and particularly windy) weather conditions as much as mist-nets, and can continue to be used in the strong easterlies which are often the best conditions for large numbers of migrants at the observatory. Unfortunately the two later traps were removed when significant repairs became necessary. The original one was retained as an educational tool for visiting school groups, but has now been dismantled because a new Heligoland trap has been built on the Storm Ridge, thanks to a generous donation from George Gregory. Anticipation of what treasures it may produce is high, as a single 60-foot net used on the same site a few years ago was responsible for as much as 85% of the annual catch at the observatory.

The introduction of mist-nets reduced the reliance on the Heligoland traps and meant that a wider area of the reserve could be used for trapping. One of the first places mist-nets were used was in an area of Elder scrub eastwards of the original Heligoland trap behind the observatory building in the East Dunes, which

Table 4. *The 10 species most frequently ringed at Gibraltar Point to 2008.*

1949	2008	1949–2008
1 Blue Tit	1 Goldcrest	1 Blackbird
2 Blackbird	2 Greenfinch	2 Willow Warbler
3 Willow Warbler	3 Blackbird	3 Dunnock
4 Whitethroat	4 Swallow	4 Goldcrest
5 Great Tit	5 Chaffinch	5 Whitethroat
6 Chaffinch	6 Siskin	6 House Sparrow
7 Dunnock	7 Willow Warbler	7 Swallow
8 Pied Flycatcher	8 Goldfinch	8 Blue Tit
9 Redstart	9 Dunnock	9 Greenfinch
10 Song Thrush	10 Robin	10 Robin

became known as the Ring, because it was cut out in two long lines running north to south, joined at the ends of the rides so forming a giant ring, measuring several hundred feet in length. A multitude of birds have been caught in this area, the rarest of which is probably the Northern Waterthrush. On another ringing session a few years ago, also in October, the ringers were amazed to see about 1,500 Blackbirds drop out of low cloud straight into the middle of the Ring. A busy morning ensued until the birds dispersed, by which time several hundred had been ringed, showing that anything can happen at an east coast observatory.

Other areas used include a wet dune slack known as Buckthorn, although it now has less Sea-buckthorn in it than some other areas, as sallows have spread through much of the lower dune slack. The water it holds means it has a high insect population and it yields a significant proportion of the breeding birds ringed, including large numbers of Dunnock, Wren and Whitethroat, together with a steady flow of migrants. It was in Buckthorn that Lincolnshire's first Pallas's Warbler was caught on the 19 October 1968, as already mentioned. Still a very rare vagrant in Britain and Ireland at that time, it was duly ringed after detailed biometrics had been taken. A phone request to a senior ringer to come and confirm identification received the reply that he was just leaving home to drive up the coast to confirm another Pallas's. Confirmation of both was duly made, but to this day, no one knows whether the Gibraltar Point or the Anderby Creek bird was the first for the county. Within ten years these two county records had increased to twenty-three. However, only three more have been ringed at the observatory, one in 1994 and the other two in 2008. It was also in Buckthorn

The Heligoland trap constructed on the Storm Ridge at Gibraltar Point in 2008 can be operated in conditions that are unsuitable for mist-netting (Mark Grantham).

that the observatory's first Thrush Nightingale was ringed on the 23 May 2003, thereafter having a net ride in Buckthorn named after it known as Sprosser Corner.

The large amounts of Sea-buckthorn on the reserve lead to a huge berry crop on the female bushes in the autumn, which is a welcome food source for migrants, especially members of the thrush family. Up to 10,000 Fieldfare, 7,800 Redwing and 1,000 Song Thrush have been recorded feasting on this berry crop. These large numbers never stay long though, usually departing westwards as soon as the food supply is exhausted. Fieldfares in particular have been very difficult to catch and ring; one solution has been to place two-shelf wader nets next to Roadside Pond in the West Dunes. The wader nets move less in the wind and the birds always go for a drink and a bath just before roosting. This technique has been very successful on occasion.

There have been several key strands to the work of the observatory over the years. An important one was the analysis of ringing recoveries to shed light on bird movements. There was sufficient evidence as early as 1955 for Ted Smith and Dick Cornwallis (1955) to give authoritative comments on bird movements both in Lincolnshire and beyond. Even so, they expressed the hope that the establishment of a chain of observatories along the east coast might fill in the many gaps remaining in our knowledge. They also made an important contribution to bird identification, ageing and sexing at the time (Cornwallis & Smith 1960). For ringers trained in the early years this guide, together with Ken Williamson's warbler identification guides, formed the backbone of their training. Gibraltar Point has also played an important part in the training of ringers – through the BTO ringing courses which started at the observatory in 1962. Courses were first led by Ken Williamson, followed by Bob Spencer and then the charismatic Chris Mead.

In more recent years the focus of the ringing scheme has been on monitoring bird populations and to this end a Constant Effort Site (CES) was established in a scrub block north of Aylmer Avenue in 1990. To maximise the value of the data there are strict rules for CES visits that require ringers to operate at the same time each day once in every ten-day period between May and August. The CES project operates nationwide and yields detailed information on annual variations in bird populations and breeding success. In 1992 a second site was added in the East Dunes, but by 1994 it was proving far too labour intensive to operate both sites and the East Dunes site was abandoned.

A fairly recent development in the efforts to increase the number of birds ringed is the use of tape lures. Tapes of bird song are played at suitably sheltered nets and the effects can, on occasion, be dramatic. On 1 October 2002, although the first Corn Bunting for ten years had been caught, there appeared to be little else around. In an effort to boost the catch a tape-lure playing Goldcrest song was deployed by a net in the Buckthorn. Ten minutes later the net had caught two Firecrests and a Cetti's Warbler (only the second for the observatory and only about 50 metres from where the first was trapped). This was pretty good, but there were also 112 Goldcrests in the net!

In 2008 more than 9,000 birds were ringed, over 2,000 more than the previous highest total, in 1980. Numerous species have been ringed in record numbers, notably Greenfinch, which has become the sixth species to have over 1000 individuals ringed in a calendar year. Amongst the highlights of the year have been the third, fourth and fifth Black-tailed Godwits, the fourth Curlew, the tenth Bluethroat, the third and fourth Pallas's Warblers and the fourth Waxwing. With an upsurge in the number of young ringers involved with the observatory, the future is looking bright. Who knows what is waiting to be caught?

OTHER FAUNA AND FLORA

The National Nature Reserve covers around 430 hectares and stretches along nearly five miles of the Lincolnshire coastline. The recording area is split into compartments to take account of habitats created and land additional to the original area established in 1948, the most significant being Croftmarsh, 40 hectares lying to the west of the main reserve, where a system of lagoons, scrapes and reedbeds has been created with grazing marsh beyond. The whole of this area is now designated a Local Nature Reserve.

The most important habitats are contained within the main NNR and are afforded SSSI status. Here, intertidal beach, sand and mudflats develop into sand dunes and salt marsh, and all stages of development are represented from the intertidal zone to pioneer colonization of mud and sand through to mature habitats.

Offshore, Harbour Porpoises are often seen, particularly in the autumn, with evidence of local breeding. Records of other cetaceans are mostly of unfortunate strandings, involving Common and Atlantic White-sided Dolphins, two Sperm Whales, two Northern Bottlenose Whales together, and a Minke Whale. However, two live Minkes toured this part of the North Sea in July 2004. During the summer months, small numbers of Common Seals give birth to their pups on the beach, the main colony being on the sandbanks further out into the Wash. Their numbers fell greatly during two phocine distemper virus episodes in 1988 and in 2002. A few Grey Seal pups may be seen on the beach in November.

On the high beach, the limit of tidal reach is demarcated by a strandline, typically involving much Hornwrack, harbouring sandhoppers and other invertebrates. Pseudoscorpions may be found under the larger items of driftwood. The seeds of various oraches germinate here after being washed up alongside the unique Prickly Saltwort, which has a limited coastal distribution, being part of the strandline community, and is the host plant for a rare moth. The first salt marsh plants, Glasswort and Annual Sea-blite are important seed-bearers for winter finches, buntings and larks. As siltation occurs on repeated tides, the development of middle marsh flora involves such species as Sea Aster, English Scurvygrass and Sea-milkwort. The Common Sea-lavender grows densely to produce a carpet of mauve flowers in summer, a popular spectacle for visitors. Later, Sea Aster provides colour and then a copious seed source. Sea-purslane fringes the marsh creeks and is good cover for nesting Redshank and Reed Bunting. The mature marsh is dominated by the Sea Couch which out-competes most other plants. This tall, dense grass is favoured by an unusual cricket called the Short-winged Conehead.

Despite regular tidal inundation, a healthy population of Field Voles inhabits the salt marsh and attracts Kestrels and Short-eared Owls. A diverse range of invertebrates also has to withstand the tidal flooding and includes a variety of scarce moths such as the Crescent Striped, Star-wort, Dog's Tooth and the Scarce Pug. The latter, feeding on Sea Wormwood, is found at only a handful of UK sites. The Old Salt Marsh here represents a fairly rare example of mature marsh along the Lincolnshire Wash coast, where continuous marsh reclamations occurred until the 1980s.

The transition area from salt marsh to dune is hospitable to an unusual suite of plants more typical of a Mediterranean landscape. This includes the Rock Sea-lavender, Sea-heath and Shrubby Sea-blite, all species at the northern limit of their range. Patches of the Shrubby Sea-blite provide more structural diversity to the marsh edge. Extensive linear areas of bare sandy mud in this zone provide important refuges for colonies of solitary wasps and other aculeate Hymenoptera. This group has been well studied by Dr Michael Archer. Over 120 species occur on site (half this number makes a site worthy of SSSI status). Most impressive, the Red-tailed Sand Wasp at up to four centimetres, can provide a shock when first seen!

Following establishment of Sand Couch, Lyme-grass and Marram on young dunes, the grey dunes develop attractive carpets of lichens and mosses and a variety of dwarf dune herbs including Dove's-foot Crane's-bill, Germander Speedwell, Spring Vetch, Parsley-piert, Common Cornsalad, Early Forget-me-not, Bird's-foot, mouse–ears and a range of yellow composites including Mouse-ear-hawkweed, Cat's-ear and Autumn Hawkbit. The species richness is maintained by close grazing, which also helps to suppress a dense coverage of Sea-buckthorn. Although management by the Trust has involved a grazing regime of primitive sheep and cattle in relatively recent times, it is the rabbit grazing that has histori-cally been the most important factor affecting the dunes and saltings. Overall, it has been the most influential mammal on site. Myxomatosis in the early 1950s devastated the population, and there has followed a pattern of population build up and demise with notable periods of plague populations in the mid-1970s and again in the mid- to late 1990s before the virus again had a major impact. Heavy rabbit grazing has at times resulted in the formation of large areas of bare ground and the extensive growth of Ragwort, both factors probably benefiting a wealth of dune specialist thermophilous insects. Adversely, their activity has probably promoted the spread of Rosebay Willowherb over considerable areas of impor-tant dune vegetation. Large swathes of these purple flowers have been typical of the East Dunes landscape, but management here has concentrated on the control of this species. Success has been achieved in recent times through grazing with Hebridean sheep.

Much of the floristic spectacle on the grey dunes involves early flowering species, particularly annuals that wither by mid-summer. In some years, Pyramidal Orchids can put on a splendid show on the dunes. Dewberry is omnipresent and provides a nectar source for invertebrates as well as succulent berries for *Sylvia* warblers on autumn migration. A further abundance of berries is produced annually by the typical dune scrub consisting of Sea-buckthorn, Elder, Wild Privet and Hawthorn. The Sea-buckthorn is able to invade even the youngest stable dunes, where it shades out the dwarf dune herbs and enriches the dune system with leaf litter and nitrogen through root nodules. As a native species, it is restricted to this part of the east coast but its invasive quality renders it a management problem. This shrub has few monophagous associations but the most significant is the micromoth *Gelechia hippophaella* that was first described at Gibraltar Point. Clearance management and browsing by primitive sheep are important in restoring and maintaining dune grassland. Again, Rabbits have undoubtedly had a role in suppressing scrub historically.

Large local populations of Stoat, Weasel and Fox clearly benefit from the availability of rabbit prey, but the Fox is also the most significant factor impacting on the important shorebird populations of Little Tern and Ringed Plover. Of the other larger mammals, both Badger and Reeves' Muntjac have recently colonized the site. European Roe Deer are seen occasionally and Chinese Water Deer was first recorded in about 2005. Hedgehogs are rarely seen and seem to have trouble maintaining a presence on the reserve – maybe due to the aforementioned Badgers.

Bat sightings are mostly confined to the Plantation and Sykes Farm area or around the water bodies. Both Common Pipistrelle and Soprano Pipistrelle occur frequently, and there are regular records of Brown Long-eared Bats (mostly involving mist-net captures). In recent years Daubenton's and Natterer's Bats have been recorded. Interestingly, the only known roost concerned a nursery colony of Nathusius' Pipistrelle bats – the first confirmed breeding of this species in Britain.

Of the aquatic mammals, Water Shrew is present but very seldom recorded, whilst national recognition is achieved as a stronghold for the Water Vole, with some animals becoming habituated to human presence along Mill Pond Road. A complex arrangement of ponds, ditches and borrow pits has been created, mostly since the 1970s, and provides a range of hydrological conditions.

Plants restricted to coastal brackish environments include the Beaked Tasselweed and Brackish Water-crowfoot, discovered during extensive botanical surveys by the late Marson Peet. A fringing of Sea Club-rush is quick to develop along the margins and is an important refuge for dragonflies and other insects.

The Odonata were studied in detail during the 1980s by Eric Blood who plotted the breeding distribution of the seven resident species at the time. The following decade saw five additions to that list: Black-tailed Skimmer, Emperor Dragonfly, Broad-bodied Chaser, Four-spotted Chaser and Azure Damselfly. There were also temporary occurrences of Red-veined and Yellow-winged Darters. The most surprising was the rapid arrival of breeding Small Red-eyed Damselfly in the mid-2000s.

These wetland features are within the wider Freshwater Marsh, separated from the salt marsh and tidal inundation by the Bulldog Bank. This marsh, which is really relict salt marsh, has a variable water table but is usually seasonally flooded, encouraging the development of a dune slack community with fine sedges, rushes and Cuckooflower, Selfheal, Fairy Flax and Common Fleabane to name a few. In dry years, Yellow-rattle can dominate and Pyramidal Orchids are ubiquitous. This habitat is maintained by summer cattle grazing.

True dune slack runs through the centre of the East Dunes ridge system. However, much of the area had scrubbed over by the 1940s, save for a small open area established by the military for bomb disposal. In recent times, scrub clearance has led to the restoration of a much larger open slack system and the flora has been quick to respond. In particular, there is now a rich spread of Southern Marsh-orchids. The southern end of this slack system demonstrates succession from Wood Small-reed, through scrub and up to Goat Willow canopy. The small reed is the food plant of a moth, the Kent Black Arches, and is the favoured nesting haunt for Harvest Mice, whilst the willow trunks are peppered with the exit holes from the Lunar Hornet Moth.

One of the flagship species of the dune slack is the Natterjack Toad, reintroduced in the 1990s, many decades after its extinction here. The reeling of the males on warm spring evenings is audible from afar. In addition to the common amphibians, Great Crested Newt is seen occasionally. The only reptile is the Grass Snake. Marginal slack habitat may be the last stronghold for the Marsh Moth, now restricted to only two sites in the UK.

Much invertebrate recording was carried out by Keith Payne in the 1970s, providing a useful record of many species and their distribution over the reserve. Four species of Orthoptera were acknowledged at that time, but 20 years later two species of Groundhoppers, Common and Slender, were discovered in association with slack habitat.

Another prominent insect survey carried out on site is a butterfly transect. Amongst the 23 species of resident breeding species, the Green Hairstreak is one of the most interesting. Coming close to extinction in the mid-1980s it has made a remarkable comeback on the mature dunes with mixed scrub and short grassland. Perhaps more remarkably, the Brown Argus recolonised the site in the mid-1990s after local extinction 30 years previously. This specialist of short dune vegetation relies upon Common Stork's-bill as a food plant, and as with the above species is dependent upon an ant association to successfully sustain part of the lifecycle. The establishment of the White-letter Hairstreak from about 2003 was a welcome addition to the reserve's butterfly fauna, with a small colony now associated with the elms at Plantation/Sykes Farm. This followed the Speckled Wood which became a resident of this small woodland block in the mid-1990s, since when it has become widely seen over dune habitat too. The isolated population of Wall butterflies has continued to thrive outside the range of its alarming decline elsewhere.

The reserve sees its share of insect migration involving dragonflies as mentioned above, and butterflies including annual influxes of Painted Ladies, a scattering of Clouded Yellows, and the occurrence of Camberwell Beauty on three occasions. The diversity of migrant moths, though, has been extensive and major migrations in 1996 and 2005 have involved such species as Convolvulus and Bedstraw Hawkmoths, Delicate, White-point, Gem, Scarce Silver Y and Scarce Bordered Straw to name but a few. For all these migrant insects the trend has been one of increase, particularly for southern species.

ACCESS AND ACCOMMODATION

Gibraltar Point is situated on the north-west corner of the Wash and is only accessible via Skegness from where it is well signposted as part of a network of tourist attractions. The approach road passes Seacroft Golf Course before reaching the two car parks. The first, the Beach car park, provides access to the northern part of the reserve, the Freshwater Marsh, Freshwater Mere, North Saltings and the main beach. The second is situated immediately adjacent to the Visitor Centre and the Wash Study Centre, towards the tip of the West Dunes and overlooking the Old Salt Marsh. The broad vista over various habitats renders it popular as a watch point, particularly for raptors for those who prefer not to stray too far from the car.

Skegness is quite well served by bus and train, but there is no continuity of public transport from there to the site, hence the majority of visitors arrive by car. Taxis are, of course, readily available from Skegness. A recently established cycle route has encouraged more visitors on pedal power and there are those hardy folk who will walk either down the road or along the beach or dune edge from Skegness. It is important to appreciate that careful planning and reference to tide tables is essential for those planning to walk along the beach in either direction. Greenshank Creek provides an intertidal challenge and walkers are strongly encouraged to come inland and follow the East Dunes edge just seaward of the Golf Course, as a safe alternative.

Upon arrival at the site, there is a car parking charge to pay. All proceeds from car parking are invested back into the reserve by the Trust. The reserve is open every day of the year from dawn till dusk. Car parks are closed overnight during busy periods to avoid problems with boy-racers and their ilk. All other facilities, access to the reserve, Visitor Centre and toilets are free and there are free leaflets available at the Visitor Centre. A 'Walkabout Guide' also obtainable from here interprets the full visitor route covering 5.6 kilometres (3.5 miles) with information on history, management and wildlife of the varied habitats from a series of numbered posts. The Visitor Centre is open daily with seasonal opening times. The centre houses an exhibition featuring displays on the principal habitats: sand dunes and salt marsh and their wildlife and management. Site-specific bird information is detailed in a CD-ROM exhibition and there is a series of further interactive displays in the adjacent Nature Discovery Room. Two marine tanks house a range of locally occurring marine fauna and flora, providing great interest to the public and educational groups. The centre houses a gift shop and café with a wonderful view over the marshes and the Wash to Norfolk from 'The Lookout'.

A daily information board is maintained to highlight current events, features of wildlife interest and daily bird sightings. This is reliant to some extent upon visitors reporting their sightings to the team of volunteers who facilitate visitor reception at the centre. Bird records received from day visitors are always welcomed and can be made on field record sheets and submitted to the Visitor Centre. However, there is a dearth of recorders who are prepared to make comprehensive counts of all the common species.

A network of footpaths enables visitor access to all the main habitats. Most of the recognised paths are surfaced to a reasonable standard and the full circular route is accessible to wheelchairs and mobility scooters. Visitors are encouraged to stay on the footpaths to avoid causing disturbance in the dunes and marsh. There is a series of birdwatching hides overlooking the lagoons, which allow close views of waterbirds.

Additionally, a sanctuary area is set up annually to protect the shorebird colony on the southern foreshore during the breeding season. This also limits access to the Wash salt marsh and intertidal areas to the south where errant visitors could fall foul of the network of tidal creeks or decide that they can walk out across the seemingly endless flats to Hunstanton (this has happened on occasion!). The zoning of the beach in this way works well as the majority of summer visitors are attracted to the vast sandy beach to the north of the shorebird sanctuary.

During the autumn and winter, the shorebird sanctuary fence is removed and visitors may walk right down to the estuary. In an ideal world, however, visitors would recognise the needs of feeding and roosting waterbirds and avoid undue disturbance so that the area could realise its full potential. The northern section of the reserve provides continuous open access to dunes, saltings and foreshore and is generally a much quieter area for visitors. This vast area north of the main recording area is seldom visited by birders either.

A series of by-laws are enforced by the site wardening team; there are controls on dogs such that they must only be brought onto site on a short lead and are not permitted on the beach from April to September. Other prohibitions include cycles (with the exception of the aforementioned cycle track), horse riding, camping and fires through to 'touting, hawking or begging'!

Formal arrangements need to be made for coach parties or group bookings. Naturally, there are restrictions on day visits to prevent the overuse of the site. Site staff oversee all educational visits by schools and are available to guide general interest groups or birdwatching and natural history groups. A series of events is organised for visitors throughout the year and these run from the Visitor Centre for a small charge. Bird walks are scheduled on a monthly basis to watch migration during spring and autumn, winter waterbirds or autumn wader roosts, there are bat walks, moth nights, pond dips, plankton trawls and bug hunts for all ages.

The Wash Study Centre, the Trust's Field Station, was developed around the 1850s Coastguard Station and this now provides accommodation for the observatory. The observatory building, the old wartime shelter, remains a secure ringing base with occasional sleepovers by the more hardy, but in general, higher standards of accommodation (and fewer earwigs) are expected by visitors today. The centre is fully equipped to host up to 36 residents on a fully catered basis. The accommodation block provides twin and single rooms in a basic but comfortable setting, with dining room, laboratory, computer suite, library and common room, which provides an ideal meeting place for an evening social or log call for even large groups. The adjacent sun lounge provides a superb view over the marshes and dunes and across the Wash to Norfolk. Some exciting migrations have been witnessed from here and the garden is a magnet for chats (particularly

Black Redstart, Wheatear and Whinchat), wagtails, pipits and finches, attracted to the old compound wall or the lawn.

The venue is generally operational from March to November with occasional bookings possible outside of this period, e.g. the winter meeting of the Bird Observatories Council. Schools, colleges and universities generally patronise the centre on weekdays, with natural history and birdwatching clubs and societies taking weekend slots. Additionally, a range of residential courses are available concerning natural history topics, photography, painting and so forth. The annual ringing course is scheduled for the early autumn period and is run by the Nunnery Ringing Group.

All course details, accommodation charges and booking information can be obtained direct from the Wash Study Centre. As already mentioned, all day and residential visitors are requested to contribute natural history records to the site. General information concerning the reserve, habitats, wildlife and facilities can be found on the Lincolnshire Trust website.

Observatory opened:	11 April 1949
Total number of bird species recorded at the observatory:	321
Best bird year:	2008
Number of species recorded:	232
Total of birds ringed at the observatory:	182,889
Number of species:	171
Best ringing year:	2008
Number ringed:	9,034
Number of species:	77

Hilbre

by Chris and Steve Williams

THE ISLAND

Hilbre is the largest of a chain of three tidal islands at the mouth of the Dee Estuary on the west coast of England. The estuary divides North Wales from England with the Wirral Peninsula lying on the English (northern) side. Hilbre is situated approximately two and a half kilometres from the town of West Kirby on the Wirral. It can only be reached from the town on foot and then only at certain states of the tide. The nearest point to the mainland is actually Red Rocks, Hoylake, but it is not safe to cross to the islands from there.

The Dee Estuary ranks as one of the most important estuarine sites in Britain, described as '... one of the most important winter-bird haunts in Britain ...'

Chris and Steve Williams are brothers who have almost been brought up on Hilbre, being the sons of Peter Williams, the chairman of Hilbre Bird Observatory from 1982 to 2009. They have both been active members of the observatory since the early 1980s, and together have amassed more than 3,000 day-visits to the island. Chris has lived within walking distance of Hilbre all his life and has combined his love of birds and the duties of ringing secretary and ringer-in-charge at Hilbre with being Coastguard Station officer for Hilbre and subsequently working for the RNLI at Hoylake—all in his spare time. Steve, despite periods living in Norfolk (whilst at University) and Hong Kong (working and birding), has always been drawn back to the Wirral Peninsula and Hilbre in particular and now combines the roles of secretary, records secretary and report editor, whilst living within sight of Hilbre.

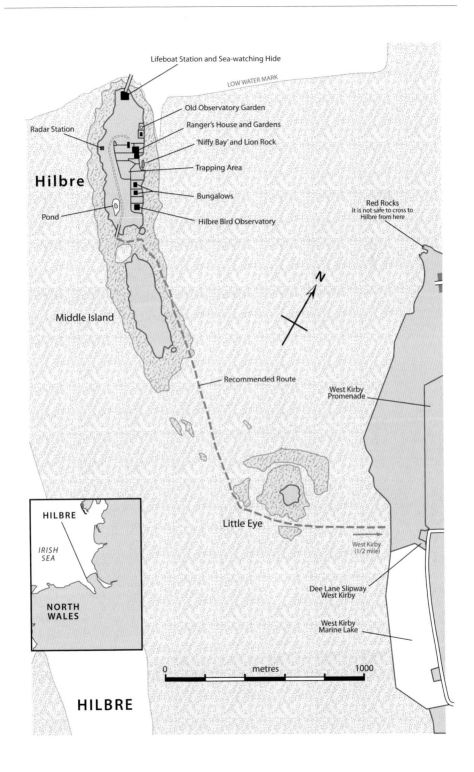

Lifeboat Station and Sea-watching Hide

LOW WATER MARK

Old Observatory Garden

Ranger's House and Gardens

Radar Station

'Niffy Bay' and Lion Rock

Trapping Area

Hilbre

Bungalows

Red Rocks
It is not safe to cross to
Hilbre from here

Pond

Hilbre Bird Observatory

N

Middle Island

Recommended Route

West Kirby
Promenade

HILBRE

IRISH
SEA

Little Eye

West Kirby
(1/2 mile)

NORTH
WALES

Dee Lane Slipway
West Kirby

West Kirby
Marine Lake

0   metres   1000

HILBRE

(Ratcliffe 1977). It was first notified as an Site of Special Scientific Interest (SSSI) in 1954, declared a Special Protection Area (SPA) and Ramsar site in 1985 and designated a Special Area of Conservation (SAC) in 2001. The Hilbre islands are a small but significant part of the estuary's ornithological life and geography. They were declared a Local Nature Reserve on 26 July 1983 and have been designated as a Regionally Important Geological and Geomorphological Site. They have regional significance as the only islands, albeit tidal, on the north-west coast of Britain between North Wales (Anglesey) and Cumbria (Chapel Island and Walney). They also provide one of the only examples of rocky shoreline between Great and Little Ormes Head in Conwy and St Bees Head in Cumbria, making them the only significant habitat in the region for many species of marine and littoral flora and fauna.

The islands are made up of red Bunter Sandstone with a covering of short grassland. The principal habitats are maritime grassland and heathland, cliff and ledge vegetation and tidal rocky foreshore. The few trees and bushes on Hilbre are in the private gardens and paddocks that are associated with the cluster of buildings of various ages (including the bird observatory) occupying the lower, east side of the island.

Hilbre itself is the largest of the group, covering just 4.65 hectares and rising to 18 metres at its highest point. The island plateau supports one of the best examples of sub-maritime heath in the region due to the influence of the sea on the island's microclimate and the associated exposure to sea spray and gale-force winds. The heath and grassland communities contain a number of regionally rare species of plants and invertebrates.

The islands suffer from the continual problems of coastal erosion and considerable human interference. Many people visit the three islands – Hilbre, Middle Island (but also known as Little Hilbre Island) and Little Eye – particularly in summer, for educational, ornithological and general recreational purposes. This puts added pressure on the vegetation and causes disturbance to birds and animals. The islands are also vulnerable to environmental effects from any developments occurring in the Dee Estuary or along the coast.

In ornithological terms, the islands' location in the rich feeding-grounds of the estuary makes them important as a roost-site for wintering waders and Hilbre's position at the extreme north-west point of Wirral, jutting out into the Irish Sea, makes it one of the prime sea-watching locations in north-west Britain. This location also makes it a focal point for passerines migrating along the North Wales and Wirral coastlines in spring and autumn.

The exposed position means that Hilbre suffers from winter and autumn gales, which can result in good sea-watching conditions. However, the North Wales mountain ranges to the south-west protect Hilbre from rainfall and, being tidal, Hilbre seldom suffers heavy frosts. During the summer months Hilbre is often warmer than the nearby mainland, although the sea breeze can be deceptive and many day-trippers to the islands fall victim to sunburn.

HISTORY

Hilbre has long attracted the attention of naturalists, with records of society visits going back to the nineteenth century. In fact Brownbill (1928) quotes the visit of John Leyland in the sixteenth century to check it for a shipping centre and mentions that Rabbits were resident there. In the late 1840s, the Liverpool Zoologists & Botanists Society made annual field trips to Hilbre and the Dee Estuary to record the natural history they encountered and supplied the William Brown Museum with their records. *The feathered folk of an estuary* (Farrar 1938) was illustrated with what were perhaps the first photographs of the wading birds of the Dee and Hilbre.

Lewis Jones, the island keeper between 1888 and 1923, published his records from Hilbre in the Dock Board magazine, *The Mersey*, under the pseudonym 'Islander'. He recorded all forms of natural history, although he concentrated mainly on birds that he shot and collected, as was the fashion of the day. His book *Atgofion Ynyswr*, published in 1939, contained chapters on the wildlife of Hilbre, whilst *The Vertebrate Fauna of Cheshire & Liverpool Bay* (Coward 1910) had appeared earlier. Eric Hardy (Merseyside Naturalists' Association) followed with visits from the 1920s onwards, with many of his notes, including those from Hilbre visits, appearing in his book *The birds of the Liverpool area* (1941). Coward's apprentice and follower, A. W. Boyd, a local Cheshire naturalist, followed up with *The Country Diary of a Cheshire Man* (1946), which was mainly a compilation of notes taken from his observations around Cheshire, but included Hilbre, which he visited from time to time.

Two local West Kirby naturalists – William (Billy) Wilson and Walter Griffiths, both Hilbre devotees of the time – encouraged more local men such as Norman Ellison ('Nomad' of BBC Radio fame) and thereafter John Gittins, Professor John Craggs and George Richards to become interested in the ornithological aspects of Hilbre in the 1930s and 1940s. A small booklet *The Birds of North Wirral* (Griffiths and Wilson 1945) contained many references to Hilbre. This was followed by *Birds of the Hilbre Islands, Cheshire* (Craggs & Ellison 1955), reprinted from *The North Western Naturalist* 1944, a wonderful yearly list of natural history events from the north-west of England and Wales. Eric Hosking, the pioneering bird photographer, used the islands to photograph waders on a fairly regular basis and Roger Tory Peterson, P. A. D. Hollom and Guy Mountfort visited in the late 1940s. The illustration on Plate 32 of *A Field Guide to the Birds of Britain and Europe* (1954) was painted by Peterson on Hilbre from 'Niffy Bay'.

Despite this historical attention from naturalists, a group of local birders who were visiting the islands regularly felt that much more could be learned through systematic observation and the ringing of birds. The foundations were laid for the creation of a bird observatory on the island, which came into being in spring 1957. Its founding members were Bob Anderson, Tony Bell, John Craggs, John Emmett, John Gittins, Tony Land, Peter Lowry, Geoff Pass and George Richards, and the primary role was, and still is, to promote the study and ringing of birds on and around the Hilbre island group.

The main movers in the creation of the observatory were John Gittins, a

The official opening of the observatory building in 1962.

dynamic West Kirby man with a long association with the island and Professor John Craggs, who was already ringing House Sparrows on Hilbre as part of his long-term study of the small colony then resident there. Fuller appreciations of the work and character of these two memorable and much-loved personalities can be found in obituary notices in the Hilbre Bird Observatory Reports (Gittins *et al.* 1999, Anderson 2001). These two founders would become long-standing members and created the foundations of what Hilbre Bird Observatory has become today.

Over the intervening 50 years, the bird observatory has not only built up a vast amount of information on the birds of Hilbre, but also on the mammals, invertebrates, flora and geology of these beautiful islands. This general interest is reflected in the comprehensive volume on Hilbre edited by Craggs in 1982 *Hilbre – the Cheshire island: its history and natural history* as well as in the observatory annual reports.

In those early years birding was very different from today, and more localised. The leisure market had yet to take off, equipment was more basic, information more limited and travel was far more restricted and expensive. The beginnings of the Hilbre Bird Observatory should be read in this context. Although the primary motivation of the founder members was to learn more about the birds passing through the island and the waders feeding around its shores, there was also the attraction of contributing to wider knowledge.

The network of major observatories was, by then, established and a case was recognised – notably by Ken Williamson of the British Trust for Ornithology (BTO) who offered early encouragement to Hilbre – for smaller 'mini-observatories' to supplement information by filling the geographical gaps in the network.

There were two key developments that enabled the observatory to take off in 1957. The first was the use of a building to act as a base for ringing activities, which also provided the members with shelter from the harsh weather and, importantly, a place to boil water on a Primus stove for tea. The 'building' was actually a tiny garden shed known affectionately as 'the Wendy Hut'. Members of the Whiteley family, who leased a holiday bungalow on the island and who are still present today, kindly loaned the Wendy Hut to the observatory during this time (1957–1962).

The other key development was the permission to construct a small Heligoland trap in one of the gardens. The original Heligoland site is still in use, though the trap has been re-built several times. In more recent years two further Heligolands have been constructed in the east-side paddocks.

The importance of the work of the bird observatory on Hilbre was soon recognised by the local Council, who own the island, and in 1962 they provided the bird observatory with a new home. A purpose-built 30-foot cabin with a six-berth bunkroom was transported to the island and became the most northerly building on the island. The bushes and trees have grown up around it from 1962 to the present day, providing a first stop for migrants arriving on the island at the northern end. In addition, a small sea-watching hide, for observing passing seabirds, was erected, which enabled members to shelter from severe gales whilst watching such majestic birds as Leach's Petrels.

In 1982, Peter Williams took over as chairman of Hilbre Bird Observatory and under his passionate and ebullient stewardship over the next 25 years the observatory went from strength to strength. Sadly Peter passed away in March 2009, but fortunately he saw Hilbre obtain accredited bird observatory status in 2008 and read this chapter in draft before he died aged just 65. In 1989, the observatory was fortunate to obtain, thanks to the previous occupants (the Dixon family), the tenancy of the southernmost bungalow on the island, which continues to provide reasonably comfortable accommodation with a separate ringing and recording laboratory – far removed from the original tiny garden shed.

The same year saw the demolition of the original timber cabin to make way for a pond and the reconstruction of the sea-watching hide. The opportunity was taken to enlarge the hide and clad it in sandstone so that it blended in with the old Lifeboat Station at the north end of the island. This was done so that more of the members (and if room is available, members of the public) can enjoy sea-watching at Hilbre even in very poor weather.

Members maintain the observatory building and three Heligoland traps in fine order (despite the annual effects of winter gales), and the observation and ringing work of the observatory continues with as much relish, except we now have a little more comfort, as in those early pioneering days of the late 1950s. Possession of a permanent base and more recently the use of off-road vehicles (the observatory has permission to use one vehicle) have led to improved coverage. Observatory members will normally be present on most weekends, with added effort (early morning visits and full-time residence on the island) at peak migration periods. Typically, members will now visit the island for ringing or recording purposes on 225 or more days in the year.

Over the years we have had many people to thank for allowing us to work on the islands – particularly Dr Mcafée and Mr Lowe who kindly allowed us to construct Heligoland traps on their leased land and to carry out our activities unhindered. Most of all we wish to thank Wirral Borough Council, particularly the Education Department (formerly Leisure Services and Tourism), who continue to provide us with space to carry out the important work of monitoring Hilbre's wildlife – especially its birds. Many of the islands' Keepers and, subsequently, Rangers have been helpful and patient with us over the years and we thank them all.

Aspects of observatory life on Hilbre

When we asked members of Hilbre Bird Observatory to provide us with accounts of their best bird days on the island, we had many to choose from and these will form part of a new publication in the not-too-distant future. However, one stood out as almost perfectly describing a first visit to Hilbre and of observatory life in general. The following is written by a youthful observatory member, Brian Tollitt:

> *It was new-moon dark when we left West Kirby behind to spend the night at the Obs on Hilbre Island. "What's an Obs?" I remember thinking. Our guide, the trustable Mr Williams, said, "Trust me, head for the flashing light and follow my footsteps carefully".*
>
> *My size-seven feet in size-nine wellies and little legs tried to keep pace as we plodded forever through the gloop and the black. The flashing light didn't seem to get any nearer and even though I was hiding behind my Dad the horizontal sand on the wet westerly wind blasted my cheeks.*
>
> *We reached the danger of Redshank Bend where the outgoing tide went straight over the size nines causing a slow-motion five-yard bladderwrack-induced slither into the slop. Strange cries from neurotic wading birds filled the air, sensory overload – a different world.*
>
> *We got to the obs which was immediately recognisable as a den with bunks. Perfect. The candles, Tilleys and the Calor fire went on and more importantly the kettle. Trouble was the gale had brought the waves right over the island and filled the water tank with salt water. I think I had my first beer that night.*
>
> *In the morning I was shaken awake and parted the condensation on the window to see that the tide was in and we were marooned on the island. Field mushrooms and breakfast, new people or were they characters to meet, goats and horses, Heligoland traps and mist-nets, Redstarts, Whitethroats, Wheatears and Willow Warblers and even Quail and Corncrake, log books and roll calls and on that very first day eighteen species of birds I hadn't seen before.*
>
> *Some days are more memorable than others but even though I was young this first day on Hilbre was life-changing. Since then every day on Hilbre has been a best day.*

Observatory gatherings

Hilbre meetings have been held regularly each year since the inception of the observatory in 1957. Initially, meetings of the elected committee were held in the back room of a small terraced house on the mainland in West Kirby. These quite formal affairs were used, as now, to discuss items relevant to the running of the observatory and on many an occasion to thrash out views and policies.

Whilst the general running of the observatory is delegated to the various committee members, an AGM is also held. These meetings were held in the larger and more practical surroundings of a function room in or above a local hostelry (which clearly has additional benefits). Although these benefits were a welcome distraction, they also fuelled some of the more colourful debates, particularly in the politically volatile times of the late 1970s and early 1980s.

Over many years the gatherings became amalgamated into the now-annual barbeque, which first took place in 1993 after our second move to the present observatory building. These events are a great opportunity for regular and nationwide members to get together for a great social event and provide the opportunity for all kinds of interesting, informative and also amusing discussions. Generally the 'Barbie' is held in August with the objective of combining good migration weather with fine outdoor socialising.

August can be a fantastic time on the islands and if you get lucky you can have a great morning's ringing followed by a, hopefully, not too serious meeting and then on to the eating (freshly caught mackerel and shrimps perhaps?) and maybe even the odd tipple. Good numbers of calling Little Terns will be diving and feeding around the islands at this time, with big flocks of Common and Sandwich Terns attracting the odd skua and almost anything can happen bird-wise at this time of year.

Indeed, these 'Barbie' days have produced some great birding, making for memorable weekends. As well as good numbers of Willow Warblers, caught and ringed, including the odd controlled bird, highlights over recent 'Barbie' weekends have included Long-eared Owl, Hobby and a fine Woodchat Shrike caught on the 'morning-after' in 1998 (no doubt that blew the cobwebs away!). It is also the peak Grey Seal time, good for moth trapping and excellent for some of Hilbre's plant and marine life – the island is often at its sparkling best at this time of year with the tide in and the sun beating down, more Mediterranean than Irish Sea!

Wader nights

For many at the observatory it is the waders and wader ringing on Hilbre that hold an extra special place in their ornithological lives. Winter wader ringing on the islands is a particularly arduous and often unrewarding endeavour; however, when things go well it can also be extremely satisfying. What an accomplishment it must have been for the early observatory pioneers to hear that a Hilbre-ringed Purple Sandpiper had been found in Greenland, a first record for the BTO ringing scheme. Even today Purple Sandpipers would be a close contender for many as a 'special' bird, as colour-ringed individuals are carefully studied and their return is eagerly awaited every autumn.

Waders were on the agenda from the 1950s when early efforts were made with assistance from Lockley's ringing book, in the form of clover-leaf traps and double clap nets. Dazzle-netting was carried out at night (there was no light pollution at all in those days) with the aid of converted ex-RAF Aldis lamps and extremely heavy battery packs. The observatory assisted a great deal in the early 1960s with the development of the then-experimental cannon nets (particularly by catching large numbers of Oystercatchers) and had great success up to 1970 with the use of clap netting.

However, it was decided that although the rewards of clap netting and so forth were high, it could not continue on the islands whilst there was a large amount of disturbance (from other sources) at roosts around the Dee Estuary. The islands were one of the only safe havens in the estuary for roosting waders and the observatory was keen to assist in the prevention of general disturbance in the estuary. With daytime wader ringing not being possible, the alternative was night-time mist-netting, which was thought to cause minimal disturbance to roosting birds, and this activity continues to this day. As mentioned, this is not an easy exercise and conditions are rarely right for a good catch: many a long night has been spent preparing colour-rings by the light and hiss of a Tilley lamp to no avail. However, we are still keen to pursue the activity and, with the log-burning stove and a good pan of 'scouse' (lamb stew) on the go, it is not that much of a chore!

Purple Sandpiper, Redshank and Turnstone now form part of our ongoing colour-ringing studies and continue to throw up interesting results. Hilbre appears to obtain its reward for all the hard work and often small catches in the form of above-average recoveries and controls.

Spring mornings

Setting out from West Kirby shore with a slight south-easterly breeze behind you and Hilbre just visible ahead in the early morning mist, one wonders with eager anticipation what lies ahead – and one's pace quickens to the calls of a wagtail or unseen pipits passing overhead. Your arrival at the south end of Middle Island is greeted by a Wheatear or, better still, you flush a Ring Ouzel from the grassy slopes of the west side – it flies off south down the 'Ridge' and your pulse is now racing and not solely due to the long walk or heavy rucksack on your back.

Arriving on Hilbre, you see more Wheatears on 'Wheatear Hill' and Tree Pipits can be heard buzzing overhead. When the sun bursts through the mist later in the morning the odd Yellow Wagtail can be heard and occasionally one drops down and adds some bright yellow to the pink and green blanket of Thrift and grass that cloaks the west side of Hilbre at this time of year. The sound of calling terns comes from the sea, just out of sight behind the mist. Approaching the first area of bushes and trees at the northern tip of the island (where most migrants first arrive) your anticipation is heightened by the soft disyllabic call of a Willow Warbler – the rest of the morning is yours alone as the tide surrounds the island, cutting you off from the mainland. Almost everything you see, find or catch is newly arrived – and has probably spent the winter in Africa.

For some, late April is the best time for birding on Hilbre, combining good numbers of common migrants with the chance of a rare bird, as well as good sea-watching; winter waders are still present, but not for long, and the occasional large raptor flies over. Recent Aprils have produced Dartford and Subalpine Warblers, Woodlark, Wryneck and most recently Red-breasted Flycatcher, in 2007.

BIRDS

Hilbre is famous for the wintering waders that roost on the islands as well as along West Kirby and Hoylake beaches. It is also well known for its sea-watching and in particular for Leach's Petrels. Indeed, the two species regarded as Hilbre special-ities are the Leach's Petrel and the Purple Sandpiper. However, more recently it has also become known regionally for its wintering Brent Geese and the spring passage of Little Gulls.

Birding around the islands provides visitors with the chance of seeing a diverse range of species in a relatively short period of time. Visiting birdwatchers should look out for waders on the way over to the islands and along the rocky shoreline and gutters around the islands. Keep eyes, and ears, alert for the overhead passage of diurnal migrants such as hirundines, pipits and finches during the walk over from the mainland. It is worth paying particular attention whilst walking over the uninhabited Middle Island (the second largest of the group). Early mornings are best for passerine migration; grounded migrants such as wheatears, wagtails and pipits can be looked for on the west side of Hilbre and thrushes, warblers and crests can be searched for in the few bushes and trees in the east side trapping area, which is best viewed from the mound affectionately known as the old 'Air Raid' shelter (although it was in fact a generator store during the Second World War).

Later in the day, a walk to the 'North End' of the island for a sea-watch can be rewarding. This is so at any time of year, although typically during or after autumn gales is best. The area is also very productive for waders that prefer rocky shorelines, like Purple Sandpipers and Turnstone.

The seasonal round-up

Hilbre is worth a visit at any time of year. In winter the estuary provides the stun-ning, swirling flocks of waders, while the islands themselves provide great views of Purple Sandpipers, Rock Pipits and the occasional Snow Bunting amongst the commoner species. The sea is ever productive, and grebes, divers, auks and some sea-duck can always be found.

Spring is a beautiful time on Hilbre with change apparent on an almost daily basis. Migration is very weather dependent, but the best conditions can produce a variety of migrants grounded or passing over on a spring morning. The massive movements of Meadow Pipits in early spring (and autumn) are a feature of west coast observatory recording. Large flocks battling in off the sea against a stiff south-westerly breeze or a 'carpet of pipits' encountered whilst walking along the west side of the island are remarkable sights. Four-figure tallies are not uncommon, particularly in March or September. Seabirds are supplemented at this time by the arrival of terns and Gannets as well as the annual arrival and build-up of Little Gulls.

As spring turns to summer the small number of breeding species, including singing male Linnets and displaying Shelduck, add further colour amongst the island's flora. Strong winds in midsummer have produced good numbers of Manx Shearwaters over the years, with the occasional Balearic or Sooty Shearwater thrown in, and in recent years increasing numbers of Storm Petrels occur between June and August. Tern numbers build up throughout the summer, with huge roosts of Sandwich and Common Terns interspersed with smaller numbers of Little and Arctic as well as the occasional Roseate. These attract the attentions of skuas, mainly Arctic, but as summer turns to autumn Pomarine, Great and Long-tailed are all recorded on an almost annual basis these days. Later summer and early autumn can also produce falls of returning Willow Warblers, but sadly not as frequently as in the past. Wheatears are on the move and then, as autumn progresses, finches, thrushes and crests appear, and there is again the chance of a rarity.

Autumn sea-watching is very exciting. Imagine setting out from West Kirby slipway, battling against a strong north-westerly, a rucksack heavy with scope, butties and perhaps a tin of soup, your head down and eyes often closed to avoid the spray or blasting sand – the journey to Hilbre seems to take for ever – at least twice as long as usual. You arrive wet with sweat but soon cool down in the sea-watching hide where you shelter from the increasingly persistent sea spray. The squall showers become more frequent as the tide rises and the wind buffets the hide's flaps. The first Leach's Petrel sighting of the year, flitting over the now massive waves, is an incredible, heart-stopping moment; ever fresh, every year. Also possible are all four skuas, as are Sabine's Gull, Grey Phalarope, Little Auk and other rarer species.

These days, a lift over in the Land Rover makes sea-watching a less arduous event, but is it also less rewarding in some ways?

Scarce and rarer birds

A crude but significant measure of the observatory's contribution to the knowledge of Cheshire and Wirral's birds is that, despite the attention of naturalists prior to 1957, the total number of species recorded on Hilbre then stood at 157; by the end of 2008 it had risen to 256. The current figure includes an impressive list of county and regional rarities and, indeed, birds new to the county, some of which might not have been discovered had it not been for the ringing effort on the islands.

Some of the more interesting examples include the first Cheshire and Wirral record of Yellow-browed Warbler, on 13 October 1973. Hilbre has since had seven more records of this delightful, once much sought-after, west coast rarity. Two fine male Subalpine Warblers have been trapped and ringed on Hilbre, only the second and fourth records for Cheshire and Wirral. Two each of Melodious and Icterine Warblers, the latter species occurring twice on Hilbre in spring (in 1970 and 1973), were rare events on the west coast and the first and second records for Cheshire and Wirral. Other 'good' passerines have included two Woodchat Shrikes (of five county records), Pallas's Warbler, Dartford Warbler and Red-rumped Swallow (all third records for the county).

Possibly the rarest bird to occur on Hilbre was the Yellow-breasted Bunting found by Gavin Broad on 7 September 1994. Very much a Shetland speciality, this was one of the first records on the west coast of the mainland; fortunately it stayed for most of the day, becoming Hilbre's first properly twitched rarity.

Obviously seabirds are also emphasised, with the first county records of Great Shearwater (October 1971) and Cory's Shearwater (August 1980). Other species include Laughing Gull, two White-winged Black Terns, Gull-billed Terns and Collared Pratincole (the latter another county first record). Whilst in national terms Hilbre is not renowned for rarities, it is well known for rare and scarce seabirds and passerines at the county and regional level.

Changes in status

The rarities apart, the regular observations since the observatory was established have led to an improved knowledge of the occurrence and changes in status of all the species that occur on or around the Hilbre islands. There are many examples where there has been a positive change – in Storm Petrel, Brent Goose, Sparrowhawk, Osprey, Marsh Harrier, Little Egret, Long-tailed Skua and Little Gull to name a few. Some of these are simply as a result of the species increasing in numbers or expanding their range. However, for birds such as Long-tailed Skua the reason is improved awareness of identification features and for Storm Petrel and Little Gull, observer awareness of when and where to look (time of year and weather conditions) may also have played a part.

The dramatic increase in Storm Petrel records at Hilbre in the past 50 years and the significant increase since the late 1980s (Figure 1) is possibly due to a combination of factors including a change in the status of Storm Petrel in the region generally.

Similarly, the dramatic increase in Sparrowhawk records at Hilbre in the last 50 years, and particularly since the early 1980s (Figure 2), mirrors the general recovery of the species on the mainland.

Those species showing a downward trend in recent times sadly include two of our favourite species, namely Willow Warbler and Purple Sandpiper. The former has seen a decline nationally and the latter has seen numbers dwindle in the past few winters. Evidence from our colour-ringing studies suggests that the Purple Sandpiper decline may be partly due to more movement between wintering sites in North Wirral and the availability of improved feeding habitat at Wallasey and New Brighton. However, there is also a feeling that wintering birds are staying further north in the UK generally, although this latter suggestion has yet to be proved.

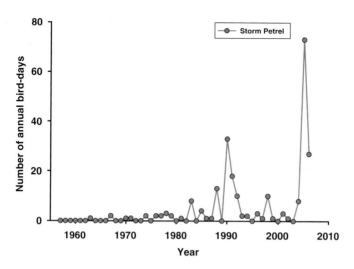

Figure 1. *Annual number of bird-days of Storm Petrels at Hilbre between 1957 and 2006.*

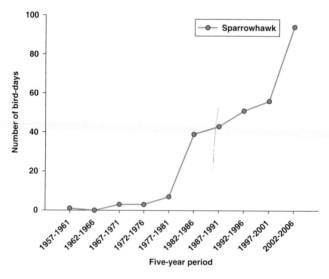

Figure 2. *Numbers of Sparrowhawk bird-days at Hilbre in five-year periods between 1957 and 2006.*

Hilbre specialities

Brent Goose

Two races of Brent Goose both occur fairly regularly at Hilbre. One is the Dark-bellied Brent Goose *Branta bernicla bernicla*, which breeds in Western Siberia and winters in very large numbers around the North Sea, particularly along the east coast of Britain but also, importantly, in the English south-coast harbours. The other is the Pale-bellied Brent Goose *B. b. hrota*, which breeds in Greenland,

Arctic Canada and Svalbard and winters in very large numbers in Ireland, especially the north-east, and in smaller numbers in western Britain.

Historically, the Dark-bellied Brent Goose was the much more frequent winter visitor to Hilbre, occurring in small numbers each year. Indeed, only *c.*30 Pale-bellied Brent Geese were recorded at Hilbre between 1957 and 1977. However, small numbers of Pale-bellied birds were seen wintering with the Dark-bellied birds between 1988 and 1990. Since 1993, Pale-bellied birds have become annual and have increased dramatically around Hilbre (and the mouth of the Dee Estuary) to over 100 birds in the last two winters (Figure 3).

Dark- and Pale-bellied Brents flock together on Hilbre, although family parties of each tend to stick fairly close together within the larger flock. We are always on the lookout for birds of any species with colour rings (as we colour-ring so many waders, Wheatears and Linnets ourselves). On 10 November 2005 a Pale-bellied Brent Goose with yellow colour rings and lettering was seen with the Hilbre flock. A couple of quick e-mails later and we learned that the bird had been colour-ringed by the Irish Brent Goose Research Group – in Iceland on passage in May 2005. There then followed a series of sightings of this bird at Hilbre and elsewhere, which enlightened us as to the likely origins and movements of Pale-bellied Brents that occur on Hilbre. Here follows the brief history of 'XXYY', as she is affectionately known (ringers were able to tell her sex when she was ringed).

XXYY was ringed on 10 May 2005 at Álftanes/Skógtjörn, Hafnarfjördhur, in Iceland and she remained there until 28 May 2005. Her next sighting was in Northern Ireland at Greyabbey, Strangford Lough, on 14 October 2005, where she stayed until at least 22 October. She was next seen at Hilbre on 10 November

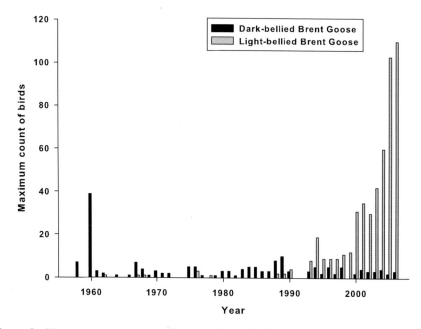

Figure 3. *Maximum winter counts of Dark and Pale-bellied Brent Geese at Hilbre 1957 to 2006.*

2005, remaining only until 22 November. This was interesting in itself, as we had long believed that birds arriving at Hilbre during the autumn simply arrived and stayed to winter, being joined by others throughout the winter. However, XXYY showed that at least some birds use Hilbre as a staging post before moving further south.

After leaving Hilbre she was at Langstone Harbour in Hampshire on 8 December 2005 and stayed in the area for the rest of the winter. She was last seen there on 14 April 2006 and was back in Iceland at Hafnarfjördhur, Álftanes/ Skógtjörn on 28 April, where she remained until 24 May. After this she presumably headed further north-west to Greenland or Arctic Canada for the summer but there were no reports. The next sighting was back at Strangford Lough on 30 October 2006, where she remained until 17 November. Subsequently seen at Hilbre on 29 November and remaining until at least 16 January 2007, she then relocated briefly to Beddmanarch Bay, Anglesey, on 4 February 2007, presumably heading westwards in preparation for her annual trip north-west.

On 20 April 2007 she was back in Iceland where she was seen, for the first time, with an 'associate'. After a last sighting there on 25 May, XXYY was next recorded during July on breeding grounds at Bathurst Island, part of the Canadian Arctic Archipelago. She arrived back at Strangford Lough on 17 October 2007 and was last seen there on 29 October before being found again at Hilbre on 15 November, remaining at least into December. An amazing insight into one bird's life – it is incredible to think that these birds fly more than 4,000 kilometres in about six weeks from their Arctic breeding grounds to winter in Britain and Ireland and then make a similar journey, only stopping off in Iceland en route, during their northward spring migration.

Subsequently, further colour-ringed birds have arrived with the Hilbre flock, including one bird originally ringed in Canada.

Leach's Petrel
Sea-watching has always attracted birders to Hilbre, and no seabird more than Leach's Petrel – now adopted as the logo for Hilbre Bird Observatory. Long associated with a north-westerly gale in the autumn, there is perhaps no better place to watch this enigmatic petrel on the mainland of Britain, in terms of location, ambience and views of the birds themselves (but of course we are biased!).

They occur almost annually at Hilbre, sometimes in quite large numbers (for example 663 on 17 September 1978). Autumn storms push birds into the Irish Sea and when winds veer to the north-west birds are pushed into Liverpool Bay. As they continue south they follow the coast around the bottom of Liverpool Bay and head westward past the north end of Hilbre. Some analysis was carried out on the massive movements observed during autumn 1978. However, there is plenty of scope for further analysis of weather patterns and our records for this fascinating species.

The annual bird-day totals of Leach's Petrels recorded at Hilbre clearly fluctuate depending on the severity and direction of gales in September and October, the peak months for occurrence at Hilbre (Figure 4). Prolonged strong north-westerly winds (for two or three days) are required to produce good numbers.

During strong north-west winds, large numbers of Leach's Petrels can be forced into Liverpool Bay and afford excellent views as they pass the northern end of Hilbre (Paul Bowerman).

Purple Sandpiper

The winter flock of Purple Sandpipers is a particular feature of ornithological interest at Hilbre. Away from their breeding grounds, these small attractive waders are found almost exclusively on seaweed-covered rocky shores. Their favourite area on Hilbre is at the bottom of the lifeboat slipway at low tide and on the ledges at the North End during high tide.

Hilbre Purple Sandpipers usually start to arrive in mid-October and peak at around 50 birds in December/January, although numbers fluctuate from year to year. The last birds leave Hilbre in early May and head for their breeding grounds. Rather than flying to Scandinavia, which is where birds seen on the east coast of Britain generally breed, they probably make for Greenland. Early evidence of this was provided by a bird ringed at Hilbre on 7 February 1959 and found in southern Greenland on 27 October 1964 – the first foreign recovery of a BTO-ringed Purple Sandpiper.

Purple Sandpiper numbers have been declining in Britain for the past two decades and this is reflected in the maximum flock counts at Hilbre. It appears that this may be part of northwards redistribution, as opposed to a decline in the population as a whole, but it is not a well-surveyed species nationally.

Little Gull

Little Gulls spend much of their time in winter offshore around parts of the British Isles, the west coast of Europe and the Mediterranean (Cramp & Simmons 1983, Olsen & Larsson 2003). It is now well documented that there is a wintering population in the Irish Sea which roosts on sand banks to the south of Dublin Bay

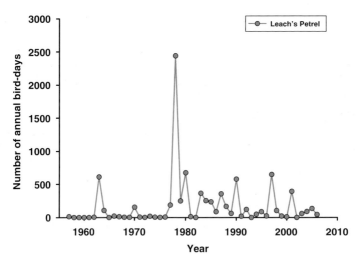

Figure 4. *Annual bird-day numbers of Leach's Petrels at Hilbre 1957–2006.*

off the coast of County Wicklow. There used to be a wintering population some-where off Liverpool Bay, which accounted for the good numbers occurring off Seaforth and Hilbre during winter gales in the past and generally for the records in the 1970s and 1980s at Hilbre (Figure 5). However, there have been very few winter records of good numbers in the past decade from either Hilbre or Seaforth.

The Little Gull passage in Liverpool Bay during spring has long been a feature of birding in the north-west region, particularly at the prime site at Seaforth Nature Reserve, Lancashire, which is probably their most important spring passage stopover site in Britain. However, since the early 1990s, spring passage

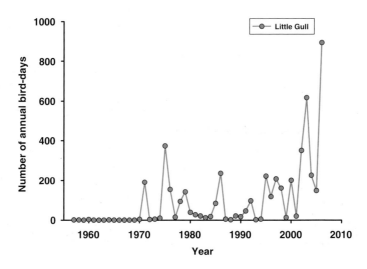

Figure 5. *Annual bird-day numbers of Little Gulls at Hilbre 1957–2006.*

has been observed at Hilbre with increasing regularity and in increasing numbers.

In recent years the typical arrival time in Liverpool Bay is from mid- to late March. At this time they are generally feeding up in the Liverpool Bay area and are visible from Hilbre but not from the mainland. The largest count occurred on 20 March 2006 when a remarkable 628 were seen moving eastwards in the space of about three hours. In a regional context this is the highest ever March day-count anywhere in Liverpool Bay. The previous highest Hilbre count was 257 on 26 March 2002. Other previous highs in March, all at Seaforth Nature Reserve, were: 262 in 1985, 258 in 1990 and 222 in 2004. The highest day-counts in the region occur in April and all have been from Seaforth Nature Reserve/Crosby Marine Park with peak counts of *c.*750 in 2001, 683 in 1989 and 650 in 1987. It is probable that these are the largest spring counts in Britain up to and including 2007. From early April numbers start to build up on the sand banks around West Hoyle (west of Hilbre) and later at Seaforth, reaching a peak in late April when many set off eastwards overland, presumably towards the North Sea and beyond. This perhaps surprising behaviour has been corroborated by regular spring records of Little Gulls at 15 inland locations to the east of Seaforth (Messenger 1993). Furthermore, ringing recoveries have linked the Irish Sea wintering population with breeding birds in the Baltic and more particularly Finland.

The spring passage observed from Hilbre is typically more condensed and less prominent than at Seaforth. However, for the first time, in spring 2004, Little Gulls were watched from Hilbre, roosting on the sand bank during low tide, and

Little Gulls, a feature off Hilbre in early spring, are increasing in number and regularity, with more than 600 birds seen on occasion (Ben Porter).

subsequent observations suggest that this is perhaps becoming a more regular event. It is also interesting to compare numbers at Hilbre and Seaforth with the wind direction. Whilst it has long been considered that easterly winds bring Little Gulls to Hilbre in spring, this is not apparent from observations in recent years.

There is still much study to be done on Little Gulls, but certainly they are extremely attractive, charismatic and dainty gulls and their arrival during the spring in Liverpool Bay is something to look forward to each year at Hilbre.

Breeding birds

The limited land area of the islands makes it relatively easy to study and ring the limited populations of resident birds. The House Sparrow colony described by Craggs (1967, 1976) was largely dependent on livestock foodstuff and disappeared many years ago. However, a number of passerine species still breed on the islands, and are studied through five-year cycles using territory-mapping methods.

Of particular interest are the flourishing Linnet colony (the subject of an ongoing study) and Wrens (the habitat having once been regarded as unsuitable). Additionally, about 15 pairs of Shelduck now breed – a significant increase from the two or three pairs to be found when the observatory opened. Skylarks bred for many years, but have recently ceased to do so, although birds have been recorded during the breeding season and we continue to monitor the situation.

Ringing

Despite the time and expense involved in their maintenance, the Heligoland traps remain a mainstay of ringing at Hilbre and are sited in the limited cover available on the island. They are effective on an exposed site even when weather conditions prevent mist-net use and are supplemented, for passerine trapping, by the mist-nets and some small wire Potter traps.

It was always accepted that large numbers of birds would not be ringed on Hilbre (waders, briefly, apart). Nevertheless, the observatory has ringed over 34,000 birds of almost 100 species since 1957 (excluding the early rocket-netting of Oystercatchers which involved several thousand birds). This relatively modest total has, however, produced some useful results. A very high proportion, almost 88%, of Hilbre's ringing is of passerines and obviously a large proportion of these birds are migrants.

Willow Warbler is clearly the dominant passerine species and over 10,000 have now been ringed, representing nearly 1% of those ringed by the BTO. Interestingly, in the early years, ringing expanded our knowledge of the numbers of birds present at an assumed 'well-watched' site. In 1957 it was known that a few could be seen frequenting the gardens, but nobody then guessed that 50, 60 or 100 individuals could be present, and ringed, in a single day.

Unsurprisingly, observatory members have taken a particular interest in patterns of Willow Warbler movements. It is encouraging that we have had Willow Warbler recoveries and controls from many other British and Irish observatories including Bardsey, Calf of Man, Copeland, Dungeness, Heysham, Holme, Portland and Walney (and sometimes several from each). Obviously west and south-west coast observatories dominate our recoveries and controls, but records from the east and south-east coast include a bird ringed at Holme Bird Observatory on 12 May 1969 and controlled at Hilbre on 8 May 1970 and another ringed at Hilbre on 10 August 2004 and controlled at Dungeness on 17 April 2006.

The pattern of recoveries and controls on and from Hilbre is also interesting in that we have had a number of both from Scotland and Northern Ireland. This leads us to believe that the majority of Willow Warblers passing through Hilbre (particularly in August) are from these breeding areas, and to a lesser extent Northern England, which is emphasised by the fact that birds ringed in these areas during the breeding season are caught on Hilbre during August or in some instances the following spring.

There are also several foreign recoveries and controls of Willow Warblers and these have helped add to the 'bigger picture'. For example, a bird ringed in Switzerland on 9 April 1980 was caught on Hilbre six days later; another ringed in Belgium on 23 April 1987 was caught at Hilbre on its return south on 17 August 1989 and one ringed at Hilbre on 12 September 2002 was captured in southern Spain on 6 October 2002. This latter bird was at a traditional fattening area and was probably at its last stop before crossing the Sahara.

Weather patterns have also been closely studied at Hilbre by the bird observatory, particularly in respect of the arrival of significant numbers of Willow Warblers and other migrants. Classic spring conditions include a situation where an area of high pressure centred over North Africa and the Iberian Peninsula moves north-eastwards, producing south-easterly winds from the continent in conjunction with the arrival at Hilbre of a south-moving front at or near dawn, giving rise to cloud cover and/or rain. The overall effect is that lots of nocturnal migrants are grounded (which typically includes Willow Warblers). Numbers of migrating passerines at Hilbre do not compare with those recorded by the observatories on Bardsey, Walney or the Calf of Man in the Irish Sea, but Hilbre is only a very small island of 4.7 hectares (11.5 acres), compared to, say, Bardsey with 180 hectares (444 acres).

The largest fall of Willow Warblers ever to occur on Hilbre was on 5 August 2004 when high pressure to the north over Scotland produced clear skies, light winds and a north-easterly airstream, which were ideal conditions for birds to leave their breeding grounds. However, a front moving eastwards across the Irish Sea arrived at Hilbre at dawn, and hundreds of Willow Warblers were grounded. The count of grounded migrants that day included a record of over 400 Willow Warblers and three Sedge Warblers, five Whitethroats, two Spotted Flycatchers, a Garden Warbler, four Greenland Wheatears *Oenanthe oenanthe leucorhoa* and a Redstart.

Enquiries at other north-west coastal stations on the same day were revealing and the comments received included 45 Willow Warblers at Bardsey, 10 at most on Walney and very few migrants at all on the Calf of Man. It is apparent that this exceptional fall was not part of a broad front, as no similar falls were reported between Walney in Cumbria and Bardsey on that morning. What is perhaps even more remarkable is the fact that there were hardly any migrants at Red Rocks Marsh Nature Reserve, on the Wirral, which is less than one mile east of Hilbre. Although different patterns of migration have been observed simultaneously on Hilbre and at Red Rocks (Craggs 1982), seldom has it been more pronounced than on this day.

Obviously, the general weather pattern across the country needs to be right for falls of migrants on our coasts, but the events of 5 August 2004 indicate that local weather conditions can be a very significant factor in migration, not just at Hilbre, but at all coastal migration stations, and despite over 50 years of research we still find it difficult to predict the large falls.

Other species, though ringed in smaller numbers, have added to local knowledge and produced interesting recoveries. Grasshopper Warbler is a good example and was not recorded at Hilbre prior to the establishment of the bird observatory in 1957. A remarkable 225 birds have been ringed in the 50 years since, representing just over 1% of Grasshopper Warblers ringed in the UK during that time. The recovery in Scotland of a Hilbre-ringed bird in 1963 was an early reward for our work. The number of Grasshopper Warbler bird-days at Hilbre were significantly higher in the early days of the 1960s and early 1970s than during the following 20 years or so, although a slight increase has been noted again in more recent years (Figure 6).

Prior to the introduction of Potter traps in the early 1990s we only caught very small numbers of Wheatear on Hilbre, mainly in the Heligoland traps and occasionally in mist-nets. However, the advent of 'Potters', used along the west side path, affectionately known as 'Wheatear Way', means that we have now ringed over 400.

We have been colour-ringing Wheatears at Hilbre for about a decade, but

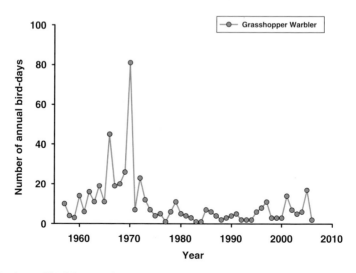

Figure 6. *Annual bird-day numbers of Grasshopper Warblers at Hilbre 1957–2006.*

despite our efforts we are still waiting for our first sighting away from Hilbre. Whilst in one respect this is very disappointing, in another sense it is interesting that our birds have not been recorded at other local coastal sites such as Red Rocks, North Wirral, and along the Dee Estuary coastline or even in North Wales, all of which are very close by. Similarly, returning colour-ringed birds have not been sighted at Hilbre in subsequent seasons.

Useful data are also provided by the measurements of captured Wheatears and an example of this is in Figure 7, which plots wing length of spring males against the capture date. One conclusion that can be drawn from these data is that if a male is captured on Hilbre before 15 April it is likely to be a nominate race bird, *O. o. oenanthe*, whereas if it is captured after 15 April it is likely to be of the Greenland race, *O. o. leucorhoa*. The corresponding date for females is 1 May as females arrive later in spring than males. Obviously, there is an overlap zone in terms of timing and wing lengths.

However, it is also apparent that Greenland Wheatears occur more frequently in spring than the nominate race. This is supported by recording work, but the figures may be slightly skewed by the fact that observations have revealed that, at Hilbre at least, Greenland birds appear more attracted to our Potter traps than are the nominate race.

We assume that the nominate birds are those that breed in Britain and Ireland, whereas our 'Greenland' birds could breed anywhere from Iceland through to Canada and we look forward to a colour-ring sighting that will perhaps go some way to answering this question.

We have always been interested in Purple Sandpipers, which have sadly reduced in numbers in recent years, i.e. from a peak of over 70 in the 1960s to a

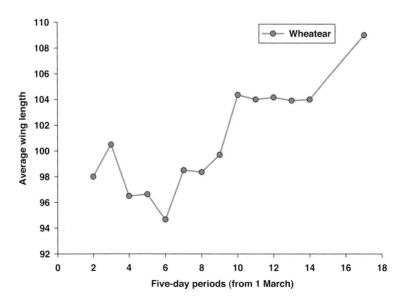

Figure 7. *Comparison of wing lengths of male Wheatears caught at Hilbre with arrival dates.*

maximum of only 29 birds during 2006 (although numbers rose to 39 during winter 2007/08). Colour-ringing demonstrated the return of individuals year after year and, as mentioned earlier, one bird was found in Greenland. Other recoveries and sightings include birds as far north as the Outer Hebrides (the latter on spring passage). Similarly, with our colour-ringing of Turnstones we have had a number of birds seen or captured on passage in Iceland, as well as numerous sightings around the west coast of Britain. These colour-ringing projects continue to provide interesting insights into site fidelity and the movement and age of returning birds and many other examples of interesting recoveries and controls from our ringing efforts are to be seen in our annual reports.

Other activities at the observatory

The work of Hilbre Bird Observatory is not restricted to the daily censusing of birds and ringing. It also involves the submission of data for surveys such as the Wintering and Breeding Atlas organised by the Cheshire and Wirral Ornithological Society (CAWOS) and national surveys such as the Winter Gull Roost Survey, the Wetland Bird Survey, the Breeding Bird Survey, the Brent Goose Survey and the BTO Bird Atlas 2007–11.

The observatory regularly gives ringing demonstrations to schools, children's groups, birdwatching groups and many other interested parties that visit the island. Despite the relatively low numbers of birds ringed at Hilbre compared with some of the larger observatories, Hilbre has helped to train approximately 50 ringers over the years and currently has two trainees and a helper.

The observatory attends the Hilbre Management Committee meetings and has brought various conservation aspects to the attention of the Wirral Borough Council. It also attends the Dee Estuary Conservation Group meetings and presentations, and it has assisted Natural England in respect of cockling activities on the Dee Estuary. It has gathered and digitised more than 50 years' data on the Grey Seal haul-out for the benefit of various authorities, including for Wirral's Biodiversity Action Plan for Grey Seals, Clwyd's Biodiversity Action Plan and to the Countryside Council for Wales.

The observatory assisted the Wildfowl and Wetlands Trust in coordination with the BTO with their questionnaire 'Changes within the Dee Estuary Special Protection Area (SPA)'. The observatory also assisted with the final editing of the Management Plan for Hilbre.

Each year the observatory contributes its data electronically to CAWOS for storage in its database of records for the county and for production of the CAWOS annual report. Hilbre's contribution is significant in terms of the number of records and its range of species and is particularly important for wader and sea-bird records. Between 5–10% of the county's records for the year are usually supplied by Hilbre Bird Observatory alone. Furthermore, the observatory has sponsored various species for the publication '*Birds in Cheshire and Wirral – A breeding and wintering atlas*' (Norman 2008). Hilbre first implemented the 'electronic log-book' concept in the late 1980s and we have a database of bird records going back almost 20 years. The ringing data from 1957 to present day have now been computerised and we will concentrate next on inputting the rest of our daily census data and other records.

The data we have stored are constantly being put to good use, not just for analysis by the observatory but by interested conservation bodies and groups, which often ask for information. Of course, it is now much easier and quicker to respond to such requests and to allow access by others to our records.

OTHER FAUNA AND FLORA

Grey Seals

The observatory and its members have monitored the haul-out of Grey Seals on the West Hoyle sand bank just west of Hilbre for more than 50 years and the dramatic rise in maximum counts recorded there since 1951 is shown in Figure 8.

Other mammals

The observatory records all other aspects of mammal life on and around Hilbre, including monitoring the island's population of Field Vole as well as the less frequent visitors such as the occasional Fox, Weasel or Stoat. The appearances of Harbour Porpoise, whales and other cetaceans, as well as other forms of sea-life, are also recorded by the observatory in the annual reports.

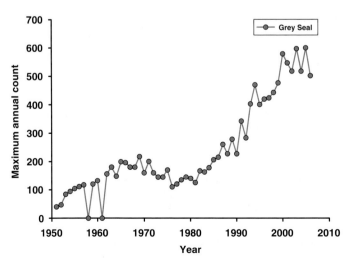

Figure 8. *Annual maximum Grey Seal counts at Hilbre 1951 to 2006.*

Invertebrates

Observatory members have recorded butterflies consistently for decades, building up a valuable record of change over the years. Professor Roger Dennis has used these data in papers and a book addressing the mechanisms of colonisation and extinction for butterflies on British islands, the Hilbre data comprising the most complete data set available to him (Dennis & Shreeve 1996).

Interest in other invertebrate groups has always been marked, and moth trapping and the recording of dragonflies and damselflies (Odonata) has become more popular since the early 1990s. For a small island, the variety of species recorded is impressive and in the last decade the lists of moths and Odonata known from Hilbre have increased substantially, in line with increased recording effort. There are presently 276 moths and 17 species of Odonata on the lists, the latter being particularly impressive as there is very little standing water on the islands (although there is a current conservation project to remedy this).

Specialists within the observatory membership engage in the concerted recording of spiders, molluscs, ants, bees, wasps and parasitic wasps, and other groups, all of which are recorded in the annual reports.

Flora

The Hilbre habitat, unique in the north-west of Britain, boasts several regionally special plants. The predominant flora associations are heath plant communities comprising Common and Bell Heather, and the cliff-top plant communities comprising mainly Thrift, Buck's-horn Plantain, Danish Scurvygrass and Rock Sea-spurrey. The most important plant species include Rock Sea-lavender, Sea Spleenwort, Field Mouse-ear, Slender Trefoil and Pellitory-of-the-wall.

The future

Writing this chapter and providing a brief account of the observatory and its work has confirmed that the aims of the founder members have been achieved and that our efforts have made a contribution, however modest, to the wider knowledge of the birds that use the islands and the estuary.

Hilbre may be small geographically, as are the ringing totals, but it neatly fills the gap in the 'island' west coast bird observatories between Bardsey and Walney. Those of us who are fortunate to have spent 25 years or more enjoying the islands and their birdlife learn something new each year. Fortunately, the observatory is now better housed, better equipped and perhaps, most significantly, better manned and covered than it has ever been – we are always looking forward, with eager anticipation, to what the next season might produce, never mind the next half-century!

ACCESS AND ACCOMMODATION

Hilbre, Middle Island and Little Eye are very exposed tidal islands and the dangers of attempting to cross to them at the wrong time or by taking the wrong route cannot be stressed enough. Over the years many avoidable rescues have proved necessary and, tragically, there have also been fatalities because visitors have not taken basic precautions.

Access to Hilbre is usually on foot from the mainland at West Kirby, taking around 45 minutes for the average walker. The route is generally from Dee Lane slipway, around the back of Little Eye, on along the east side of Middle Island and around the rocks to Hilbre. This route should always be checked before leaving and there is a notice board at Dee Lane. Checking the tide times is absolutely crucial, making sure allowances for British Summer Time are taken into consideration. A minimum of three and a half to four hours must be left before high water if crossing. Tides at Hilbre vary hugely and no two crossings will ever quite be the same.

One must be prepared for a long day if staying over high tide. Wellies and foul weather gear are essential; even if the weather looks fine it can suddenly change at Hilbre. It can be very easy to experience sunburn on the islands, even on overcast days. On sunny days, cool sea breezes mask the strength of the sun – so sun cream is essential. If you stay over the tide, you must allow for being on the island for a minimum of six to seven hours before you can begin your return journey, and you will need food and drinks to cover that period. You can start your return journey two to three hours after high tide. Groups of six or more visiting the islands require a permit from Wirral Ranger Service.

Hilbre Bird Observatory now occupies the most southerly building on the main island, which has a laboratory annex where most of the scientific work is carried out, a lounge, a small kitchen and some sleeping accommodation. The observatory welcomes daytime visitors, but is not permanently manned, so it is always better to make an arrangement beforehand. There are many good bed-and-breakfasts available locally on the mainland for those who wish to get over to the islands for early morning migration and again, contact with the observatory will provide all the necessary information.

Annual reports have been produced from 1957 to the present day and are available for purchase from the observatory or via our website and visitors are encouraged to send their sightings to the observatory by e-mail or in the case of a rarity to ring or text 07976 205574 immediately.

Acknowledgements

Thanks to all the members and friends of Hilbre Bird Observatory past and present for recording and ringing birds, and all aspects of natural history on the islands, without whom this chapter would not have been possible. Thanks to Graham McElwaine of the Irish Brent Goose Research Group for all of the information on movements and sightings of colour-ringed Brent Geese and to Steve White of Seaforth Nature Reserve for information and comments on spring Little

Gull passage in Liverpool Bay. Finally, special thanks are reserved for the late Pete Williams, father of the authors and Chairman of Hilbre Bird Observatory (1982–2009), for reviewing and commenting on an early draft of this chapter and without whom there would simply be no bird observatory on Hilbre. This chapter is dedicated to his memory and the legacy he has left on Hilbre.

Established 1957 and accredited to the Bird Observatories Council in 2008	
Total number of bird species recorded at the observatory:	256
Best bird year:	1976
Number of species recorded:	166
Total of birds ringed at the observatory:	34,004
Number of species:	98
Best ringing year:	1968
Number ringed:	1,734
Number of species:	43

Holme

by Sophie Barker and Jed Andrews

INTRODUCTION

Holme is one of the brightest avian jewels in North Norfolk's coastal crown. It stands like a sentinel at the western end of the North Norfolk coast and the eastern mouth of the Wash. Migrants following the coastline from the east pass the finest example of coastal marshes in Britain, extending from Weybourne to Hunstanton, and over such well-known sites as Salthouse, Cley and Blakeney Point, Holkham Pines, Wells Woods, Scolt Head and Titchwell, before reaching Holme. To the north-west, across the Wash, stands the nearest neighbouring bird observatory at Gibraltar Point, whilst Landguard lies down the Suffolk coast and close to Felixstowe and Harwich.

The observatory has its being in a simple carstone structure, formerly a humble garage, with an access ramp leading down beside the building from the Norfolk coast path. The building doubles as the visitors' centre. It is the hub from which the warden and his staff perform their daily duties and around which members, visitors and volunteers gather. It is also here that folk may take the weight off their

Jed Andrews became the assistant warden of the observatory in June 1994 and has been warden since 1995. Sophie Barker started as a volunteer in spring 2001 and has been assistant warden ever since.

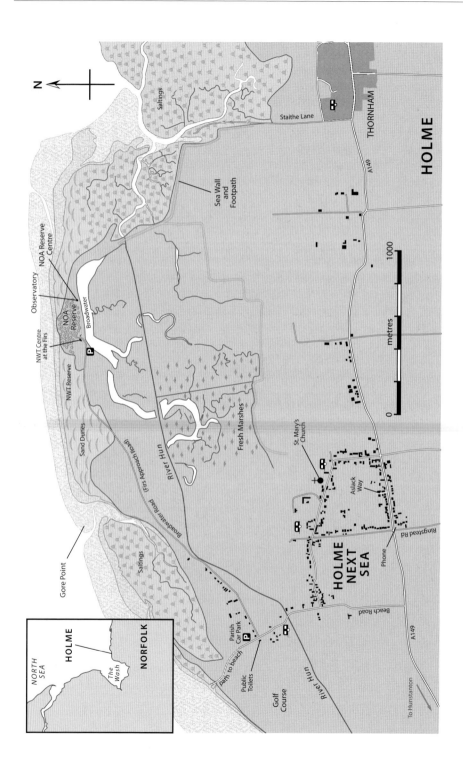

feet and perhaps a welcome mug of tea into their hands. This hub, the observatory/visitors' centre which, for the sake of simplicity, we shall call the observatory, stands in four hectares of ground, being the reserve, which comprises two disconnected areas. The first is squarish in shape and incorporates the car park and a hide. The other, larger, area is of a shape as yet undefined by geometricians, being long, narrowish and tapering and turning to a point at its south-easterly end.

The Norfolk Ornithologists Association (NOA) car park lies south of the approach road, and to the west of The Firs, where the Norfolk Wildlife Trust (NWT), formerly Norfolk Naturalists Trust (NNT), visitors' centre is situated. Visitors going to the observatory then proceed along a wide grassy bank to where the observatory sits amid an open landscape characterised by big skies and a broad panorama offering superb views. It is in close proximity to various habitats: the sea, beach, dunes, pine woods, scrub, and salt and freshwater marsh all contributing to an incredibly varied wilderness. The reserve is bounded on the north and east by the North Norfolk Coast Path with views to the North Sea and Thornham Marshes respectively. The southern boundary is at the water's edge on the north side of Broadwater, a brackish lagoon that supports a variety of wildfowl and waders, with a sluice at the east end to control the water levels. There are views here over Holme Marsh to the south, whilst the western boundary adjoins the NWT reserve.

The ringing hut is placed close to the observatory. Mist-nets are set on either side of the grassy bank both in the buckthorn and amongst the vegetation bordering the edge of Broadwater. There are three viewing hides along the bank giving close secluded views into the scrub that grows in the shelter of the pines. These hides really come into their own during substantial falls of migrants and also provide a welcome shelter from showers. Two other hides look out over Broadwater and across Holme Marsh, and one, at the southern end of the car park, is adapted for wheelchair access. Finally, a purpose-built sea-watching hide stands high in the pine trees giving extensive views over the dunes to the sea and the north-west. With so many outward-facing hides, it is no surprise that the recording area extends well beyond the reserve and as far as Thornham harbour channel to the east, to the horizon in the south, to the west end of the golf course in the west and as far as can be seen with a modern telescope to the open horizon of the North Sea. It also includes the area of the NWT reserve.

The land on which the reserve stands was part of a Second World War firing range, as at Gibraltar Point, and the grassy bank and the bunkers in the dunes are witness to the previous military presence, as is the ordnance uncovered on the beach by the sea and made safe by the Navy Bomb Disposal Team. To the east of the observatory is the east bank, formed by the Thornham sea wall. This grass bank is covered with Marram Grass and Bramble, with small pockets of Wild Privet, and with taller vegetation at the northern edge of the Broadwater. There is a dense area of Elder and Willow scrub at the east end of the reserve.

The dunes and beach are very popular with visitors, but tidal erosion has seen the dunes eroded to a high cliff in recent years, especially at the west end. More recently, this has brought the sea perilously close to the pines, and some trees have already fallen onto the beach. At the eastern end, towards Thornham channel, however, new dune is forming at a dramatic rate and the contours of the beach are changing constantly. The dunes themselves, which are subject to restricted access from April to September, are extensive and contain numerous patches of cover for migrants. Gore Point is accessible from the coast path about a kilometre west of the observatory, offering good views of the sea and the lavender marsh. The dunes to the west are attractive to migrants. The Paddocks, further still to the west, consist of mixed rough grass and scrub and provide shelter for a variety of birds. On the western edge of the recording area lies the golf course, where man-made areas of short grass and dense scrub are a favoured site for early-arriving migrants in both spring and autumn. To digress for a moment, it was also from this golf course that rumours circulated in 1974 of three albatrosses in a single week, which proved to be correct but were of the 'hole in one' golfing variety achieved by Robert Taylor of Leicestershire and were a feat unique in golf (Bob Carrick, pers. comm.).

HISTORY

The history of the observatory is so closely linked with that of the NOA that the narrative must now necessarily stray a little from the immediate area of the reserve. The NOA receives subscriptions, permit fees, donations and gifts which in part serve to pay the warden and his assistant. As at 2008, the NOA owns or manages six reserves, sites or areas of land away from Holme observatory. Whilst these do not form part of the Holme reserve, they are used to a greater or lesser extent as out-sites for observatory ringing activities and other studies.

The site of Holme Bird Observatory and the reserve first attracted the attention of the Cambridge Bird Club in the mid-1950s, and they began ringing there. It was around this time that Peter Clarke, the founder-warden of the observatory, saw the site and realised its potential as a place at which to study migration. He wrote (in Durman 1976) that:

> *Having seen the magnetic attraction that clumps of cover on the shore have for small migrants ... my enthusiastic reaction on sighting, for the first time, the magnificently isolated clump of pine trees on the shore at Holme can be well imagined. Here, it was obvious, was a unique site, unrivalled anywhere else along the Norfolk coast; not as small as the famous plantation on Blakeney Point, but not as extensive as the pine woods at Wells and Holkham ...*

Holme Bird Observatory came into being on 6 September 1962 with Peter Clarke and G. H. Byford as co-directors. The outset was far from easy and the winter of 1963 at The Firs saw some of the most severe winter weather of the century. Peter Clarke wrote that 'great icebergs littered the Holme shore and Broadwater was frozen solid for weeks. Flocks of Brent Geese and Wigeon found meagre sustenance on the frozen freshwater marshes beyond Broadwater. Water Rails attacked and killed Chaffinches too weak to escape'. In 1963, the observatory struggled financially, but this same year Richard Richardson, the honorary warden at Cley Bird Observatory, retired from his post and that observatory sadly had to be disbanded. The balance of its funds was donated to Holme Bird Observatory and, by the end of 1964, the membership had doubled. However, this progress was offset when the owner sold The Firs, leaving Peter Clarke to find alternative accommodation.

The observatory's financial difficulties continued until 1968, when so many rare migrants were found at Holme that the reserve received no fewer than 2,000 visitors, providing a welcome boost to funds. At the end of that year, Miss V. M. Leather very generously provided a permanent house for the use of the warden. Following this change of fortune, the observatory building was improved to become a ringing laboratory. In 1970, with membership continuing to increase, the NOA was formed to act as the parent body of the observatory, to further the study of ornithology in Norfolk and, as it turned out, to act as a holding vehicle for the reserves that have been acquired subsequently. The Association and the observatory are organised and managed by the same team of individuals. The early 1970s saw continuing progress, with the purchase of the site of the former Cley Bird Observatory at Walsey Hills. Kelling Quags was bought in 1984, quickly followed by the purchase of Redwell Marsh in 1985, and 1988 saw Whiddington Wood, a one-acre fruit orchard in Holme village, gifted to the care of the Association.

By this time, birdwatching was changing rapidly under the influence of the developing Birdline information service, initiated in 1986, but membership remained steady. In May 1987, a pair of Black-winged Stilts arrived on the adjoining NNT reserve. They remained there to breed successfully and departed on 31 August. This attracted great numbers of paying visitors to both sites throughout the summer and observatory staff were involved in the wardening and monitoring activities. The NOA's Annual Report for 1987 contained pictures, almost exclusively, of the stilts and their success remains a memorable event in the history of Holme.

Malcolm Cox became a volunteer deputy warden in 1992, and after two years it was formally agreed by the trustees that he would become the full-time warden at the end of January 1994, when Peter Clarke retired. In June 1995, Jed Andrews began working two days a week at the observatory as assistant warden and took up the post of full-time warden at the end of the year. Jed Andrews soon obtained his ringing permit, and ringing at the site was given a further boost when a new Heligoland trap was built in 1997, south of the main reserve path, following a donation of £1,500. Habitat management was also undertaken to restore diversity to parts of the reserve that had become overgrown and dominated by Sea-buckthorn. 1998 saw developments to Redwell Marsh in Holme, with English Nature funding ditch work and the installation of a new sluice. Meanwhile, Hempton Marsh, near Fakenham, was purchased in 1999 with a Heritage Lottery Grant, and was the Association's first inland and seventh site overall.

The North West Norfolk Ringing Group continued to ring at the observatory reserve until 1999, when the Holme Bird Observatory ringing group was re-established. An NOA-staffed constant ringing effort programme then became possible, giving the potential for consistent year-round monitoring through ringing. This brought significant renewed interest in the activities of both the observatory and the NOA and was reflected in the ringing totals, with the Holme Bird Observatory Ringing Group ringing 2,200 birds in 1999. In 2000 Rhys Dandy, who had been involved at the observatory since the age of 13, worked a full season as assistant warden. The sea-watching hide was overhauled by Peter Tilley, a very active member, who both encouraged and supported the work of the observatory. Peter also constructed the hide at Redwell Marsh in 2001. The new hide gave the site the formal visitor access it richly deserved and was dedicated to the memory of Sydney Riddell, a long-standing supporter of the NOA, whose family generously contributed to the cost of its construction. Sophie Barker became voluntary assistant warden at the observatory in 2001 and took on a variety of administrative tasks in addition to training for a ringing permit, that she quickly gained. With two full-time staff, the observatory continues to flourish, with the ringing of over 4,000 birds in 2004.

Charitable and similar organisations depend heavily on the hard work of volunteers and the generosity of benefactors. Holme Bird Observatory and the NOA are no exception! In the past, coffee mornings, jumble sales and raffles have been organised by volunteers, and the Association now runs an annual Grand Summer Draw and Sponsored Birdwatch each year. In addition, grants have been sought and applied for to fund habitat management and construction projects. A substantial Gift Aid repayment claim in 2004 funded the Association's first vehicle. Significant donations have been received from many benefactors over the years, including other charities who have made donations; the NOA office was built with a grant from the Vincent Wildlife Trust and Redwell Marsh was bought with a significant grant from the then World Wildlife Fund. Sheer hard unpaid work and practical skills have been applied to great effect. As an example, trustee Mick Townsend rebuilt the car park hide over the winter of 2006/07, free of charge. In 2006 the Association secured a Heritage Lottery Fund grant of £49,900 for the development of Hempton Marsh and was able to build visitor access adapted for wheelchairs. This increased interest in the Association locally and added to the membership base inland.

In 2008–2009 the observatory benefited directly through grants for wheelchair access facilities at the observatory and for equipment for ringing and moth trapping. These were secured from the Awards for All grants scheme and the Norfolk Coast Partnership. This has allowed the NOA to invest in the infrastructure of the observatory reserve and the site is now one of the most accessible bird observatories in the UK.

THE BIRD YEAR

In January, the observatory witnesses an abundance of wildfowl, with flocks of up to 10,000 Pink-footed Geese and over 2,000 Wigeon on the marsh. Several hundred Brent Geese are regularly seen. The Brent flocks sometimes contain a

Black Brant *Branta bernicla nigricans* or Pale-bellied Brent *B. b. hrota* and may be seen regularly until the flocks depart. At the start of the year, sea-watching can be very productive and good numbers of divers, including a few Black-throated and Great Northern, are recorded each year. Some years also see big movements of auks, particularly Guillemots. Long-tailed Duck winter offshore and up to 40 birds are regularly recorded north of the observatory, with even bigger counts off Gore Point and into the Wash. Other sea-ducks recorded include Eider, Red-breasted Merganser, the much less common Goosander, Scaup and Goldeneye. Wild swans can still be arriving in January; Whoopers are the more numerous, but Bewick's are also recorded in most years. Formerly a summer visitor, Marsh Harriers now put in a regular appearance in the winter, Barn Owls can be seen readily in daytime and Short-eared Owls will sometimes hunt the marshes too. Winter passerines vary from year to year. Snow Buntings usually exceed 100 in number, but the flocks are transient and mobile. Twite also winter around the marshes. Shore Lark can occasionally be found sheltering among the debris on the beach, but their numbers have been much reduced in recent years. Cold weather in January can bring big flocks of winter thrushes, with Fieldfares and Redwings often gathering to eat the crop of Sea-buckthorn berries, regarded as a poor but essential food for these nomadic winterers. Waxwings are sometimes attracted by the rose hips and rowan berries on the reserve, but rarely stay for long.

February can be very variable, being in some years by far the coldest month of the year with snow and ice, while other years see mild, windy weather bringing in early migrants such as Black Redstart and Avocet. Overwintering warblers such as Blackcap and Chiffchaff can be very visible as the level of natural cover is at its lowest. As the winter draws to a close, flocks of several thousand Pink-footed Geese gather on the marshes, feeding for a few weeks before setting off north to their breeding grounds. Merlin and Peregrine are very active during February and can sometimes be seen at rest as well as hunting. In some years Hen Harriers are also regularly seen, and Short-eared Owls are a possibility. Seabird activity can start to decrease during this month; however, Slavonian and Red-necked Grebes are often present, sometimes in surprising numbers.

If mild, March often sees the departure of geese and Wigeon for their breeding grounds, and spring migration begins, usually around mid-March, with the passage of Pied Wagtails and Meadow Pipits. Early Chiffchaffs and Wheatears are generally recorded in the third week, and the first Swallows and Sand Martins arrive by the end of the month. Cranes are often seen moving along the coast at this time. In many years they are seen flying along the line of the ridge, and sometimes their calls are audible as they pass overhead. In some years, significant numbers of Blackbirds and Goldcrests, generally seen as autumn migrants, make return movements through Holme in March and can be the most common species in terms of ringing. Black Redstarts and Stonechats are often to be found on the east bank, and Ring Ouzels can likewise be found towards the end of the month, sometimes in significant numbers. Tree Sparrows are unusual migrants, which are also recorded here in March.

By April, most of the geese have gone. Chiffchaffs and Willow Warblers begin to sing as they pass on their way north, although a few will stay on site to breed. Other warblers, such as Blackcaps, Whitethroats, Lesser Whitethroats and Sedge Warblers are also to be found now, and Grasshopper Warblers and Nightingales can accompany them, sometimes singing in dense vegetation. Less usual species such as Sardinian Warbler have been recorded in April, and Wrynecks, Hoopoes and Bluethroats have also been recorded in this month. In some years Redstarts are the only notable migrant to pass through in any numbers. Larger migrants include Hobby and Montagu's Harrier, and in some years White Storks have been tracked flying along the coast. When southerly winds prevail, rarities such as Black Kites have been recorded, and Alpine Swift and Red-rumped Swallow are also a possibility. Waders begin to migrate at this time, with Greenshank, and Common, Green and Wood Sandpipers pausing on the surrounding marshes, or simply calling as they fly through. Less common waders to have been seen here include Temminck's Stint and Curlew Sandpiper. The Meadow Pipit passage, which begins in March, continues into April and increasingly includes Tree Pipits, Yellow and White Wagtails *Motacilla alba alba*. House Martins and Swifts also begin to arrive and Garganey can sometimes be seen feeding on undisturbed pools. Cuckoos and Turtle Doves hail the arrival of spring in earnest.

May usually brings with it a significant emergence of insects and vegetation is often in full leaf by the start of the month. Spotted and Pied Flycatchers can be seen here, the weather becoming an increasingly dominant factor in their appearance. This is a key month for Reed Warblers; often very late to arrive and set up territory, and initially outnumbered by Sedge Warblers, they become dominant during the course of May. Wheatears arriving this late in the spring tend to be of the larger Greenland race *Oenanthe oenanthe leucorhoa*. Many migrants are still arriving, and include less common species as the month wears on; Tawny Pipit, Dotterel, Black Tern and Osprey can be among them. Bee-eaters are tracked along the coast almost annually in May, sometimes to be picked up by birders as they fly past or over the observatory. The passage of hirundines and Swifts generally peaks in May, with Swallows being the most numerous in most years. Tawny Owl nestlings are generally ringed during this month, and have bred in the pines on the reserve for decades. Common resident species are busy brooding or feeding young. The end of May also sees the first fledgling birds on the reserve, often Chaffinches or Blackbirds.

June is marked by the cessation of migration and an intensification of breeding activity, and young Dunnocks, Robins and Chaffinches are among the first juveniles to appear. Rarities are few and far between in this month, but can include species such as Surf Scoter, Honey-buzzard, Red-backed Shrike and Common Rosefinch.

In July, sea-watching becomes increasingly productive with good numbers of terns, including occasional Arctic Terns, Gannets and Kittiwakes, not to mention Manx and Sooty Shearwaters and Arctic Skuas when the winds are right. Early returning Wigeon are often noted during this month. Return passage of waders is also apparent, with Greenshank and Green, Common and Wood Sandpipers recorded. Little Stints and Curlew Sandpipers are also possible. Common Crossbills often drop in at Holme during July, sometimes in flocks of over 15

A young local birder, Connor Rand, is seen here admiring three Tawny Owl chicks at Holme after they had been ringed (Jed Andrews).

birds. A rare bird for the reserve, Treecreeper is most-regularly ringed in July, and Kingfishers are unusually visible too, with young birds sometimes found in unexpected habitats such as the scrub. Juvenile warblers are also numerous in July, including Reed and Sedge Warbler, Whitethroat and Lesser Whitethroat, Blackcap, Chiffchaff and Willow Warbler. Towards the end of the month, favourable north-easterlies can bring early Spotted and Pied Flycatchers back to the reserve and juvenile Tawny Owls can sometimes be seen in broad daylight, before they learn their nocturnal etiquette.

August is the first month of true return migration at Holme. Some very big movements of hirundines and Swifts can be recorded, with numbers sometimes running into thousands. When conditions favour migration, this can produce good numbers of Pied Flycatchers, and on occasion these have been ringed on the Continent just a few days before. Wheatears, Whinchats, Stonechats, Redstarts, Garden Warblers and a variety of other migrants can be brought here in August on migration, including the elusive Barred and Icterine Warblers. Movements of Willow Warblers can be accompanied by a Wood Warbler. Red-backed Shrikes also occur on an almost annual basis. The last week of August and first week of September are the perfect time for Greenish Warblers, which have been recorded at Holme on at least seven occasions, five of them being trapped and ringed. Early winter returns, such as Fieldfares and Redwings, are generally first recorded here. On the sea, the variety of skuas increases, with Great and

Pomarine Skuas becoming more frequent, and Arctic Skuas becoming more numerous than in July.

September is the first of the two biggest months at Holme in terms of migration. North-westerlies during September can produce a continuous visible passage across the spectrum of seabirds and the more unusual can include Leach's Petrel, Cory's Shearwater, Sabine's Gull and Long-tailed Skua. Strong winds can sometimes bring seabirds very close inshore and they can even be seen flying over land. The first geese return in September, with Pink-feet on the marshes. Falls in September include less obvious species such as Great Spotted Woodpecker and Song Thrush. Robins are famed for moving in big numbers during September, and these are believed to be Continental birds, as born out by the occasional ringed individuals from Scandinavia. Many of the autumn species which arrive first in August, continue to do so in September, Redstart, Garden Warbler and Pied Flycatcher being among the most notable. Easterlies towards the end of the month have sometimes produced Red-breasted Flycatchers, and Yellow-browed Warblers also appear at this time given similar conditions. Ortolan Bunting and Bluethroat have also been recorded here in September.

October is the most consistently productive month in terms of ringing and visible migration, with the second and third weeks producing the biggest numbers. During this period Goldcrests and Blackbirds are usually the most commonly ringed species, but winter thrushes also move at this time, and Ring Ouzel has also occasionally been caught in October. Another very commonly ringed species in October is Greenfinch, which is attracted to the feeding station in very high numbers. Ringing shows that these passage birds are almost exclusively juveniles, and many show eccentric moult (the unusual replacement of several of the juvenile primary feathers), more than at any other time of year at the observatory. Firecrests can also pass through, often in the latter part of the month, and Yellow-browed and Pallas's Warblers are recorded in most years. Other *Phylloscopus* warblers, such as Radde's and Dusky, are also occasionally recorded during this month. Tern numbers decrease at this time, but a great deal of skua activity is often stimulated by strong north or westerly winds. Duck passage is considerable, with Wigeon and Teal moving consistently throughout the month, often with less abundant species such as Pintail. Auk activity also becomes more visible: Little Auks and even Puffins can be seen with the right weather conditions. High tides produce breathtaking numbers of Bar-tailed Godwits, Knot and other waders, the water level transforming the chain of dunes into an isolated island north of Thornham Marsh.

November often sees a big passage of Starlings, which are accompanied by winter thrushes and occasionally by a disorientated Little Auk. Finch movements also continue during November, with Chaffinches, Greenfinches and Bramblings often still on the move. Lapland Buntings can sometimes be found, most commonly with Skylarks feeding on the fields at the back of Thornham Marsh, an area also favoured by Twite. Hen Harriers have arrived by this time, and can be seen hunting at dusk over the marshes, whilst Long-eared Owls have been recorded both at Holme and at Redwell at this time, sometimes feeding in broad daylight, and usually in the afternoon.

December brings things full circle. Pink-feet in their thousands, Wigeon and Brent Geese are on the marshes across which Peregrine and Merlin hunt, whilst auks, sea-ducks and divers are the main attraction offshore, and Snow Buntings move along the beach to feed. Whooper and Bewick's Swans can be seen, and occasionally a glimpse of a Bittern can be caught across the marsh. An early cold snap can bring winter thrushes and a variety of other species onto the Sea-buckthorn to feed. Water Rails become surprisingly tame, and, if the ground freezes, Snipe and Woodcock become more visible as they are forced into the open to find food.

Amongst the many ringing recoveries, of particular interest are the first British-ringed Blackcap to be controlled in Syria and the first British control of a Blackcap ringed in the Czech Republic.

The Sea-watch programme at Holme Bird Observatory
by Professor Fred Cooke

In 2005, the NOA began a cooperative programme of systematic seabird counting at Holme Bird Observatory. The primary objective of this programme was to learn more about the patterns of use of the near offshore region by seabirds and to monitor possible changes over time. This was thought to be particularly important at a time when major new structures, such as wind farms, were being developed. A secondary objective was to provide NOA members and visitors with an exciting way of having an enjoyable time birding, but at the same time participating in the scientific programme of NOA.

Seabirds were defined for this programme as any species primarily using the open seas and visible from a coastal watch point. Included were gulls, terns, tubenoses, skuas, auks, sea and migratory ducks, divers, grebes, cormorants and gannets. However, observers were encouraged to record any other birds that were moving along the shore, or were seen to arrive from the sea. A typical observation period would last at least 30 minutes, and observers watching out to sea with telescopes would record their start and finish time, numbers of each species seen, direction of flight (if flying), weather conditions, state of tide and number and names of observers. Where possible, the sex and age of the birds, and possibly the state of moult were also noted. Interesting behaviours were sometimes recorded. Most of the sightings were made from the top of the sand dunes which gave an elevation of about two metres above the beach. However, in really foul weather conditions, a sea-watching hide is used. Over the years many members have enjoyed contributing to the data collection and some have become regulars. When we first started the programme, some sceptics thought that nothing new would be discovered. After all, birders have recorded seabirds from the shore in Britain and Ireland for many years. But the results have shown that there was still a lot to be discovered, and that it was very important to develop a standardized method of recording the information. All our results were reported in terms of the number of birds seen per fixed time interval and we used the number per hour. This allowed comparisons under varying conditions and between different places. Collecting data in this way also recorded when NO birds of a particular species were seen, and in this way peak migration times could be deduced.

We divided the year into ten-day periods (called deciles), and aimed to collect at least five hours of observation in each decile. The effect of this was to divide each month into approximately three equal parts, an early, mid and late. In fact during peak migration we often watched for more than 30 hours per decile, or roughly three hours per day. We tried to make observations in all weathers, all stages of the tide and all times of day. We could then explore which conditions, on average, were optimal for observing seabirds and deduce when seabird migration was at its peak.

We have been collecting data since 2005, and have made contact with other groups who were using the same methods as ourselves. This has allowed us to look at some regional variation in both distribution and timing of the sightings. Two observation sites in Suffolk, Kessingland in the north and Thorpeness in the south, where similar data have been collected for several years, provided interesting comparisons and showed important regional variations in the migration patterns. Many more Gannets and skuas were seen during the spring at these sites in comparison with Holme, showing that most migrating Gannets in the spring move directly north rather than taking the more leisurely route along the west Norfolk, Wash and Lincolnshire coasts.

Several interesting patterns are beginning to emerge. Most species, as expected, show similar patterns of distribution and numbers in each of the four years, but

Many projects at observatories rely heavily on assistance from their members and volunteers, as with the NOA members seen here at Holme, participating in the sea-watch programme headed by Professor Fred Cooke (Jed Andrews).

there are some notable exceptions. The period from 30 December 2006 to the end of January 2007 produced a massive increase in the number of auks (up to 80 per hour), Cormorants (40 per hour), Red-throated Divers (52 per hour), Kittiwakes (35 per hour) and Little Gulls (25 per hour), but not of other wintering seabirds. Presumably this event coincided with a massive increase in some marine organisms on which these species fed. These species all arrived in the area within a day or two and stayed, with numbers gradually decreasing until numbers were back to normal at the end of January. Usually these species are seen in much smaller numbers at this time of year, so it would be interesting to know if this increase coincided with any known oceanographic event. The increase in numbers of Red-throated Divers coincided with a drop in the number seen at Thorpeness, which may indicate that wintering divers were influenced by changes in food distribution.

Overall numbers of seabirds have averaged around 30 per hour throughout the first half of the year, but increased to more than 100 per hour with notable peaks in September and again in November. The first peak coincided with the autumn movement of Gannets and the second with the arrival of wintering ducks from the east. There is little detected spring migration of these species at our site. We have plotted the distribution patterns of all the birds that we monitor throughout the year and Figures 1 and 2 show two species, Gannet and Fulmar.

These graphs help us to plot the distribution of seabirds throughout the year and inform our members about what they can expect at different times of the year. In the example of the Fulmars, the species is usually present because of the proximity of a breeding colony at nearby Hunstanton, but the graph shows that the birds leave the area completely for a short period in October and November after breeding is completed, but return to establish territories as early as December.

Most birders imagine that sea-watching is best done in the early morning, but we found that, apart from the very late afternoon, a similar number of birds,

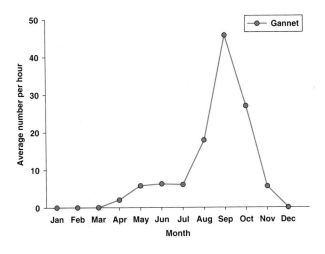

Figure 1. *Numbers of Gannets per hour passing Holme Bird Observatory, monthly average over four years (2004–2008).*

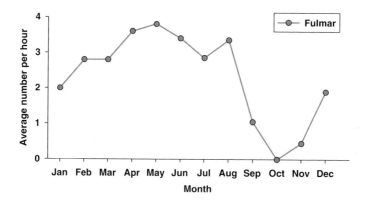

Figure 2. *Numbers of Fulmars per hour passing Holme Bird Observatory, monthly average over four years (2004–2008).*

averaging around 30–40 per hour, could be seen throughout the day. As expected, strong winds with a northerly element produced not only more unusual species such as shearwaters, storm-petrels and skuas, but also more individual birds. More surprisingly, however, under all other wind conditions and directions (including light or no winds) similar numbers of birds were detected.

We detected an interesting pattern of sightings of Eider Ducks, which had two peaks of observation (Figure 3). In the November–December period there was a movement of birds flying west and in March a slightly higher peak of birds flying east. This supports ringing data which suggest that Eiders wintering in the Wash are Continental birds, rather than birds moving down the coast from further

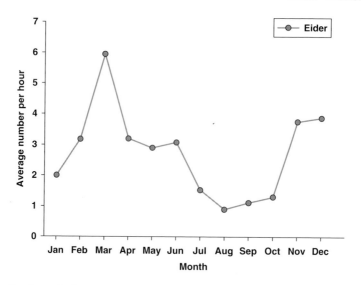

Figure 3. *Numbers of Eiders per hour passing Holme Bird Observatory, monthly average over four years (2004–2008).*

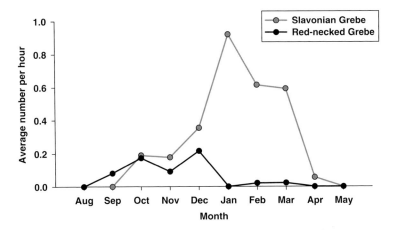

Figure 4. *Comparison of numbers of Slavonian and Red-necked Grebes per hour at Holme Bird Observatory, monthly average over four years (2005–2009).*

north in the British Isles. Small numbers of non-breeding Eiders can be seen throughout the summer months too, occasionally showing signs of moult.

Another interesting finding has been the observations of wintering Slavonian and Red-necked Grebes. Although both species are well known as winter visitors, our observations suggest that the Slavonian Grebes generally appear after 1 January, whereas the less common Red-necked Grebes are more likely to be seen before the end of the year (see Figure 4).

This is just a sample of the findings from our systematic long-term monitoring of seabirds at Holme Bird Observatory. With time we may be able to detect long term declines or increases, but this will require more years of data collection. Seabirds are often not monitored very effectively by the various census methods employed by the British Trust for Ornithology (BTO) and our approach has the potential for being expanded to other locations for a more complete national coverage. Figure 5 shows that the number of Long-tailed Ducks has declined in each of the four years of our study, but this may be a local phenomenon and more data are required.

As this programme continues and as more data accumulate, we will be able to discover more about the distribution and timing of appearance of some of our more intriguing species of birds. More sophisticated analytical statistical approaches will be needed and more comparisons with other sites need to be made. Happily, this is now a serious prospect, as the BTO is planning to carry out analyses of the dataset gathered at Holme and is considering how best to use it to create a national sea-watching monitoring scheme. The potential of our observations, which have given members of the NOA and others hours of enjoyable birding, is already bearing fruit.

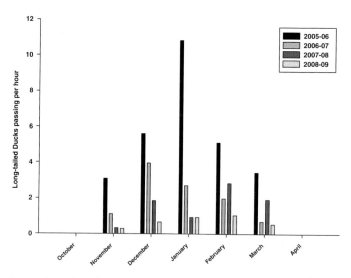

Figure 5. *Comparison of numbers of Long-tailed Ducks passing per hour at Holme Bird Observatory 2005–2009.*

Conservation in action

The bird data gathered at the various NOA sites is available for use in evidence in respect of planning and development matters. The relevant sea-bird data were made available regarding proposed off-shore wind farms and a development at Wells-next-the-sea. Our data was also relevant to a couple of applications affecting land near to Redwell Marsh.

SPECIAL DAYS

The Isabelline Shrike
related by Jed Andrews

Monday 14 October 1996 was a real red-letter day for the NOA when a new species was added to the list of rarities, thanks to honorary life member Maurice Eccleshall's sharp eyes. A first-winter Isabelline Shrike was identified and could have been the bird reported from the eastern side of the county the day before. I had travelled the two hours to Horsey with friends, leaving before daylight on the Sunday, to see the shrike only at a distance. One of my friends had map-read us to the site. Unfortunately, however, the map reference would have placed us eight kilometres offshore in the North Sea, as we discovered when we arrived at the beach with the map telling us there was some distance still left to go!

The bird, which had been at Horsey Gap, had not been seen since late Sunday afternoon, whilst our bird had been located at 14:45 hrs on Monday afternoon. Karen Ellis, on being told of the bird, contacted me – as usual, a rarity on my day off! And the headless chicken routine began. Left boot on right foot, start motorbike, go back indoors for crash helmet and binoculars, proceed to the observatory at warp speed. On arrival the bird was perched just a few metres away on a Bramble patch. First impressions were that it was not the same bird. The tail looked duller – or was this just a trick of the light? Does a view from a few metres compare directly with a bird scoped from 100 metres? With the news released to Birdline East Anglia, birders started turning up in good numbers which help increase the funds.

By early evening a sizeable crowd had gathered and watched as a Long-tailed Tit became the shrike's first victim. The tit was promptly skewered on a broken willow twig where it was plucked and partly eaten, before the shrike moved to a nearby Elder, and once again spiked the remains onto a broken twig. During its stay, prey items included dragonflies, beetles and wasps, all of which were scattered around the reserve in various larders. I watched the bird until it went to roost just before dark, hoping and praying that it would stay until the weekend when the masses would converge on the reserve and bring much-needed revenue.

Tuesday 15 October saw an early start to relocate the bird. First light revealed the shrike exactly where it had gone to roost. A check on the tit remains failed to find the ring it had carried on its left leg. By the end of this, the second day, over one hundred birders had paid to see this Asian traveller. Wednesday 16th and the shrike was still present. Its movements were now getting predictable and, although its range had extended slightly, the bird was looking settled. Its appetite was quite amazing, feeding ferociously on almost anything that moved. Again, over a hundred birders had 'ticked' it during the day.

Thursday 17th and the shrike was present for its fourth day, which started wet, and was relocated early, 'showing' at times down to as close as a metre and posing for some exceptionally fine photographs. It was present again on the 18th, although its range had now extended across the Broadwater, and to the western end of the reserve. For the first time in the week, over 400 birders had seen it and provided other site records as well. On the 19th the shrike had extended its stay and the weekend birders were arriving in vast numbers.

On the 20th it was still present for a seventh day, but was showing signs of moving on. It was now venturing as far west as the Firs. A Bittern flying west along the Broadwater was an added bonus for the assembled masses. Rain set in during the afternoon and it seemed that this was the signal for the shrike to leave, although it lingered for the first half of the day on the 21st. During its week-long stay we had received much praise, a lot of revenue and many new members. The longest distance twitch prize must surely go to Trevor Donaldson, an NOA member, and his mates from Aberdeen, well done Trevor.

The Great Skua
related by Jed Andrews

17 September 2001 was a bright, quiet day. The autumn had so far been uneventful, and with all the observatory's mist-nets open all day, just four birds had been caught; two Reed Warblers, one Reed Bunting and a Red-breasted Flycatcher. The

latter was a promise of things to come, and with north winds forecast for the 18th, a very early start was agreed and the nets were open before dawn.

The first bird caught was a retrap Tawny Owl, first ringed as an adult by me five years before, and a species not often mist-netted at Holme. After processing the owl and renewing our acquaintance, I was walking along the bottom of the east bank, head down, hands in pockets, contemplating the day's ringing. When I looked up in the half light, a large, dark bird was flying towards me very low. At first I thought it was a Long-eared Owl, but on seeing me approaching the bird banked to reveal white flashes in its primaries – a Great Skua. The bird was tired and struggling to gain height. Seeing that it was in difficulty, I followed and it swerved to try and cross the Broadwater, but dropped too quickly and crashed into a Bramble bush. With no thought for my own safety, I leapt and caught it, Peter Bonetti style. The skua immediately seized me, but I determined that it would not get away as it bit into my hand. In the meantime a good sea-watch was underway, with several members in the sea hide enjoying the proceeds of the north wind.

Hurrying back along the east bank with the skua under my arm, I fell to my knees outside the ringing shed, almost panting my last. I showed the bird to Sophie Barker, who had been sleepily arranging the ringing shed for the day's catching. She immediately ran to the sea-watch hide to tell the intrepid sea-watchers: 'Jed's got a Great Skua!' 'We've got loads out here' came the reply, but it was quickly explained that this was not in the warden's binoculars, but in his grubby mitts. As the sea-watchers charged down from the hide, the ringing shed was brought to order and the bird was calmly ringed and processed. It inflicted further minor injuries to me, but as a first-year bird, it was tired and thin, and it was decided to take it into care and let it rest. It was placed in a quiet place in a sturdy box – not sturdy enough, however, and with one flick of its wings, the unfortunate container was flattened. A stronger box was then found, and the skua was left to recover until the early afternoon.

After some discussion, it was decided that Redwell would be a better release site than at the observatory, because it could readily be picked up again if it had difficulty taking off. An admiring crowd gathered on the marsh with cameras and video recorders and the bird was transported the short distance to the marsh. Then came the moment of truth – the box was opened and the skua burst out. Its first attempt at take off ground to a halt and it stood still, surveying its surroundings. The watching birders held their breath. Afraid that the release attempt had failed, I began to walk after the bird. My approach was enough motivation for the skua, which again ran and took off, this time struggling into the air. It steadily gained height and was soon circling many metres up, getting its bearings before it sailed off east towards the coast. The observers watched as it became a faint speck on the horizon – the observatory's first, and so far only, Great Skua ringing record.

The Rose-breasted Grosbeak on 4 and 5 May 2006
related by Jed Andrews

Observatory wardens know that almost any bird can turn up at coastal sites, but credibility was stretched to breaking point early on 4 May when I was about to set off for the observatory and the phone rang. It was Les Watson, a friend in the village. 'You may think I'm daft, Jed, but I think I've got a Rose-breasted Grosbeak in my garden'. Making no judgements, I made haste for the garden and got a detailed description, but there was no sign of the offending bird. After an hour without success, the NOA staff left to get on with the day's work, but asked for immediate news of the bird's return.

After a long day, I was cooking my tea of sausages and mash when the phone rang again. It was Les. 'You know that bird' 'Is it back?' I asked. 'It's in my hand', said Les, 'it's just hit the window!' 'I'll be round in a nanosecond'. I fled leaving my tea to go cold. When I arrived Les showed me the bird, which had stunned itself but was already showing signs of recovery. It was clear that Les was right, and there was little doubt that this was indeed a female Rose-breasted Grosbeak. It was decided to keep the bird overnight and make sure it had recovered. I returned home around 22:00 hrs for a very cold supper!

The following day the bird appeared to be fully recovered and, after consultation with the BTO, the bird was ringed and released. Les was less than keen on the idea of having hundreds of people around his garden and permission to move the bird elsewhere was refused, so the exact location had to be kept secret. This did not go down particularly well with the local birding community, but there was no choice in the matter and, as with many rare birds, decisions need to be taken which may not always please everyone.

This Rose-breasted Grosbeak was the first for Norfolk, and the first British and Irish spring record. The only other east coast records for Britain were a bird at Leigh-on-Sea in Essex from 20 December 1975 to 4 January 1976 and a bird at Bridlington, North Yorks on 5 and 6 November 1991. It remains one of our most exciting birds for many years.

OTHER FAUNA AND FLORA

Mammals

Mammals at the observatory have included Rabbit, Brown Hare, Fox, Stoat, Weasel, Grey Squirrel, Water Shrew, Pygmy Shrew, Common Pipistrelle, Reeves' Muntjac and European Roe Deer, while the sea has produced Sperm Whale, Common and Grey Seal, and Harbour Porpoise.

Reptiles and amphibians

The pond is home to good numbers of Common Newts, and Common Toads are abundant in the early spring when they come out of hibernation. Natterjack Toads can occasionally be found on the reserve; one was heard in the wall just outside the visitors' centre in 2002, and two were found in the same year, feeding around the moth trap in the small hours. In general, however, they are confined to the marshes. Common Lizard can be found when sunny conditions favour their basking behaviour. Again, the area around the observatory is the best place to see them.

Invertebrates

The short grass grazed by rabbits is particularly good habitat for Small Copper and Brown Argus butterflies, which can be seen between May and October. Green Hairstreaks are common in April and May, and Speckled Wood frequents the shady areas of the reserve. Grayling are common here in the summer, often alighting on the concrete hard standing, on the building itself, and on any pale clothing. Ringlets can be found in the areas of longer grass and tall flowers. Visible butterfly migration occurs, with Painted Lady a very abundant species in some years. However, common species such as Small White and Red Admiral also migrate, especially during periods of easterly winds, and can be seen flying in the dunes, along the beach and even over the sea itself. Immigrant species such as the Clouded Yellow and the rare Camberwell Beauty have been recorded here.

Moth trapping has taken place at the observatory over most of its history and a daily census of moths and butterflies on the reserve is also kept, largely between March and October, when multiple moth traps are run. Dragonflies and damselflies are recorded, but not currently on a daily basis. The census can show when insect migrations occur and the conditions that often produce them. It also shows how the weather and habitat management influence the numbers of many of these species. For example, the cutting of the east bank in 2002 produced a significant increase in the growth of Lady's Bedstraw, which in turn produced high numbers of Small Elephant Hawkmoths, which feed on bedstraw, in 2003. The increase took a further year to become apparent because the life cycle of the moth takes a year to complete.

Common resident moth species include Cinnabar (a Ragwort feeder), Pine Beauty, Drinker, Emperor Moth and Oak Eggar. Lunar Hornet Moths take two years to mature in the trunks and roots of mature willows, and are found on the reserve when conditions favour their hatching. Hawkmoths breeding on the reserve include Pine, Eyed, Poplar, Elephant, Small Elephant, Privet, and in recent years Hummingbird Hawkmoth. Other migratory hawkmoth species are caught in most years, including Convolvulus, Bedstraw and Striped. Major moth migrations occur in some years (most notably the Silver Y), while in 2003 an invasion of Hummingbird Hawkmoths gave rise to a small breeding population at the site. Also recorded in recent years were Marbled Clover, Pale Pinion, Red Sword-grass, Red-necked Footman, Orange Footman and Scarce Merveille du Jour. The moth species count stands at 449, in part due to an increasing interest in micromoths, which are being identified by macrophotography undertaken by the warden.

Other insects of note include dragonflies and damselflies. Swarms of Southern and Migrant Hawkers occur here in late summer, and both egg-laying and hatching can be seen on the pond. Banded Demoiselle has been recorded on the reserve, most recently in 2003. In 2004, a three-day swarm of migrant hoverflies was witnessed and the remains of hundreds and hundreds were swept up in the visitors' centre, whilst many more thousands were visible on the tide line. Ladybirds can also invade, as they did in 1976 and 1995. These mass migrations are thought to result from an abundance of aphids on the Continent, allowing the population to multiply very rapidly.

The plants

The characteristic habitat of the reserve is formed by the dominant plant species of the site, of which the Corsican Pines, Sea-buckthorn, various Willows, Sycamore, Elder and Bramble are the most abundant. When the observatory was first established, scrub vegetation was sparse, but Sea-buckthorn, which grows very quickly, was dominant until recent years, when rigorous management restored a balance with other species. There is a surprising variety of species on the reserve. Most readily noticed in spring is the Tamarisk, which in May is covered in tiny pink flowers that attract Green Hairstreak and Small Copper in particular, while in the autumn the yellow Buddleja in front of the visitors' centre attracts dozens or even hundreds of Painted Ladies, and Hummingbird Hawkmoths often feed there. Small areas of Wild Privet occur on the reserve, together with Dog-rose, Alder and Hawthorn. A patch of Wild Gooseberry is located just opposite the observatory, and Wild Asparagus grows in many places among the scrub. East of the observatory a small patch of Gorse grows. A single Rowan tree grows among them, quickly found by hungry Waxwings when bearing berries in winter. A single Silver Birch is situated at the back of the scrub on the north-west side of the reserve, and is a good place to look for *Phylloscopus* warblers in autumn. A single small Oak tree grows south of the Heligoland trap on the west side of the reserve.

In winter and early spring the floor of the wood is carpeted with Springbeauty, a colonising plant introduced to Britain from America. Its tiny white flowers embedded in their single leaves are very distinctive. A species that is increasingly abundant on the reserve is Traveller's-joy, which has led to an increase in the catch of Fern moths and Small Waved Umber in recent years. Along the east bank a colourful variety of flowers thrive in the short grass, including Stonecrop spp., Common Centaury, Scarlet Pimpernel and Common Bird's-foot-trefoil. Towards the eastern end of the east bank, Sea Bindweed grows among the Marram. Areas of scrub on the reserve are interspersed with impressive stands of Rosebay Willowherb, and Bittersweet can be found everywhere. Hound's-tongue and Viper's-bugloss can be found in areas of shorter grass, and Evening-primrose plants benefit from the relative warmth and shelter near the observatory. Early Marsh-orchids, of the subspecies *coccinea*, grow up every year around the pond and Pyramidal Orchids can be found in the lee of the pines.

Other flora to be found at Holme includes a selection of fungi, including Jelly Ear, which thrives on Elder, puffballs which grow in the short grass following rain, and Wood Blewit and Barometer Earthstar which can be found in the pines.

ACCESS AND ACCOMMODATION

The observatory is generally manned seven days a week throughout the year, but is sometimes closed on Mondays outside peak times. For more information telephone 01485 525406 or visit the observatory website. The reserve is open to members from dawn to dusk and from 09:00 hrs to 17:00 hrs to permit holders. Daily permits should be purchased at the observatory (current price £3). The

NWT reserve next door opens at 10:00 hrs and closes at 17:00 hrs, but visitors need not purchase an NWT permit unless they wish to visit that reserve.

Holme Bird Observatory reserve can be approached by car from the A149 which runs round the coast from Kings Lynn to Cromer. At the western end of Holme-next-the-Sea, take the first turn to the left coming from Hunstanton following signs for NNT reserve (noting that the signs have not been changed as yet, as of April 2010, even though NNT is now known as NWT) and NOA Watch Point. Carry straight on for a kilometre, ignoring the temptation to explore the chalk, flint and mellow brick of the village, and cross the hump-back bridge over the River Hun. Turn right just before the public car park at more of the aforesaid signs (if you reach the Golf Course, you have gone a little too far). Then follow the rough gravel track for about one and half kilometres. There is a five-barred gate halfway along the track on the NWT reserve. NOA visitors can proceed through the gate and continue to the NOA car park, which is clearly signposted on the right. To reach the observatory, visitors should look for the signs whilst going eastwards, keeping the large square Victorian house (The Firs) on their left. Then proceed along the grassy bank through the pines.

The reserve can also be approached on foot along the North Norfolk Coast Path, which runs from Hunstanton to Cromer and connects with the ancient Peddars Way a little to the west of the reserve. To approach from the west, it is best to park in the Council car park near the Golf Course, just beyond the right turn to the approach track. From Thornham, turn off the A149 at Staithe Lane, Thornham. If you intend to park near the Coal Barns, it is advisable to check the tide times as high tides can affect the parking area. Then walk west along the footpath on the top of the Sea Wall. Depending on the direction of your approach, turn left or right off the Coast Path at the Holme Bird Observatory sign. Rail travellers will make their way to Kings Lynn and then to Holme on the local bus service (presently the Coast Hopper), both services running frequently.

Although there is no accommodation on site, a full list of local accommodation can be obtained from the Holme-next-the-Sea website or from the observatory. The observatory has a telephone and internet connection, heat and light and offers comfort and shelter. There is an excellent bore hole, which provides enough clean water for making tea and washing up! However, the observatory is still without toilet facilities and fresh running water.

Visitors are encouraged to leave their sea-watching and other bird records for the recording area at the observatory or to send them in by e-mail. Copies of the annual report are available from the observatory or by post.

Observatory opened:	1962
Total number of bird species recorded at the observatory:	319
Total of birds ringed at the observatory:	75,920
Number of species:	159
Best ringing year:	2004
Number ringed:	4,462
Number of species ringed:	72

The Isle of May

by Niall Campbell, Mike Martin, Mark Oksien, Stuart Rivers, David Thorne and Margaret Thorne

THE ISLAND

A traveller on the East Coast railway line near Dunbar, idly looking out across the mouth of the Firth of Forth, might be forgiven for taking the long grey shape with impressive sides and tall superstructure to be that of a battleship sailing south. To the knowledgeable traveller, these features would quickly resolve themselves into the west cliffs of the Isle of May, crowned by the great grey stone tower of its lighthouse.

The Isle of May lies in the mouth of the Firth of Forth, eight kilometres south-east of Anstruther in Fife and 16 kilometres north-east of North Berwick on the Lothian shore. Although a small island of about 57 hectares, it is the largest island off the east coast of mainland Britain. The length of the north-west–south-east axis is about 1.6 kilometres and the maximum width a little over 500 metres. The volcanic olivine-dolerite sill, of which it is formed, dips from the top of the 45-metre cliffs on the sheer west side to low rock upstands and skerries on the east. In

The authors are all members of the committee of the Isle of May Bird Observatory and Field Station Trust.

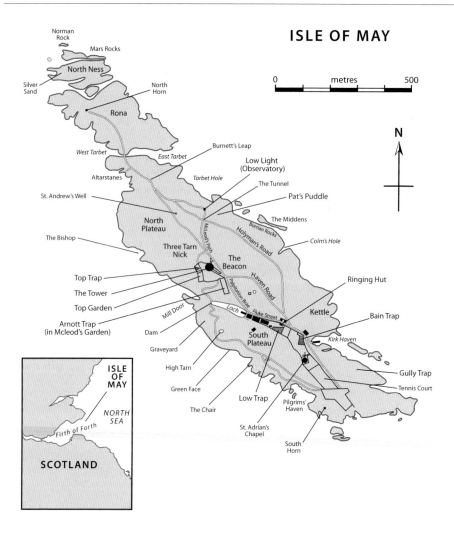

this plane, there are faults, the smaller of which have allowed the formation of geos, caves, natural arches and stacks, while larger ones have developed to separate off the North Ness and Rona. The largest fault forms a pronounced cleft. It is the site of various buildings related to the main lighthouse – engine rooms and stores and also the former keepers' houses, known as Fluke Street. Soil is thin and vegetation poor, except where developed by past lighthouse keepers for gardens or by the observatory for cover. For the most part, the island is covered in rough grass kept short by Rabbits and undermined by their burrows and the burrows of Puffins. The tidal range is 4.3 metres and there are two very small sandy beaches.

Rainfall, at 56 centimetres a year, is amongst the lowest in Scotland and, though there may be running water after winter rains, the small pools which develop at this season dry out in summer, being replenished infrequently by thunderstorms. The only permanent water is 'the Loch', a murky body of water artificially dammed to provide water for the lighthouse machinery. Strong winds are a common feature of the weather on the May. Those from the east tend to be more powerful, having a longer fetch, right across the North Sea, whereas westerlies are modified by the proximity of the mainland. Haar – dense sea fog – is a feature of warm high pressure periods at any time throughout the summer.

THE ISLAND'S HISTORY

The Isle of May would have been seen by early settlers in Fife over 8,000 years ago, and a potsherd found on the island by archaeologists, possibly made around 2,000BC, shows that visits were made at this time at least. In common with many far more remote islands, it was attractive as a place of Christian life, for burial, religious settlement and pilgrimage. In the May's case this extended over more than eight centuries prior to the Reformation.

At the start of this period, an Irish or Pictish monk called Ethernan, who probably lived in the seventh century, settled on the May. Later there were violent Viking raids on the religious settlements and the monks were put to the sword. The island's association with martyrdom made it a place of pilgrimage. Places of worship and devotion were built. St Ethernan was Latinized to St Adrian and the May was much visited by pilgrims touring the other holy sites of Fife. King James IV visited a number of times, both as pilgrim and sportsman (to shoot seabirds). The religious buildings have been fully excavated and now have interesting explanatory material for visitors. In the mid-sixteenth century, the monastic buildings left the hands of the church and part of the priory buildings became a fortified manor. The May was used in 1580 as a quarantine station for immigrants, 'infectit with the pest'. It also gained a reputation as a haunt of smugglers.

The archaeological excavations not only revealed the religious buildings, but also information about the birds. The remains of 26 bird species have been identified, although these were not necessarily island birds as they may have been imported for food. However, it would be surprising if the human population did not make use of locally available produce. That birds were consumed by people is evident from butchery marks on the bones of a number of species found and remains have been identified dating from the fifth to the nineteenth centuries.

Not surprisingly, seabirds are prominent among the remains found. These include adult and young Gannets, and also Cormorants and Shags. Although Gannet and Cormorant no longer breed, both are known to have done so during the nineteenth century. Herring Gull, Lesser Black-backed Gull, Great Black-backed Gull, Black-headed Gull and Kittiwake have also been identified. Auk species feature strongly, with Guillemot predominating as it does at present. Single Puffins have been identified, their sparsity reflecting the bird's status on the island in the later nineteenth and first half of the twentieth centuries. There is a single Black Guillemot record. This species is not even recorded annually now, though it is known to have bred in small numbers in the early nineteenth century. Of all the archaeological remains, perhaps the most intriguing are those of the Great Auk *Pinguinus impennis*, a species only present in the Status Logs of one other British bird observatory. Bones from a minimum of five individuals, covering the whole period from the fifth to the nineteenth century, have been recovered. We can only guess whether this species bred or even occurred naturally on the island, as there is plenty of evidence that the Great Auk was salted and transported from various points around the British coast. The remains of geese, duck and waders have also been found, as well as a few passerines.

The May lies on the sea route to Scotland's capital and it was necessary to make it safer for shipping. In 1636 the first lighthouse in Scotland, a beacon tower with an open coal-fired grate at its top, was built on the May. It required 400 tons of coal to keep it going for a year and the ground surrounding the beacon is still thick with cinders. With three keepers to maintain the Beacon and their families, a small village developed. The Beacon functioned for 180 years until the opening of the current lighthouse, fuelled by oil, on 1 February 1816. The original beacon still stands (though in a truncated form) thanks to Sir Walter Scott, the novelist, who saved it from total destruction when visiting the island with Robert Stevenson of the famous lighthouse-building family.

It was Stevenson who designed and built the grand new lighthouse that replaced the Beacon. This lighthouse is a magnificent structure, with battlements, and looks more like a church or a castle. Its interior, with its huge spiral staircase and Commissioners' Room, is equally grand. The fixed light lantern was replaced by a revolving one in 1844 and converted to electricity in 1886, the first in Scotland to be so powered. During this period, up to 1924, large numbers of birds were attracted and killed there. But the electric light was costly to run and it then reverted to paraffin, with a significant reduction in bird casualties. The lantern, following automation, is again powered by electricity, but the problem of birds being killed there is a thing of the past, due to the much reduced candle-power of the light.

The Low Light, the bird observatory's current home, built in 1843 and 1844, is much more modest. It has a short white tower, which had in it a fixed light to assist shipping entering the Tay. Attached to the tower are single storey buildings that now provide the observatory's living quarters. They are not spacious but they are snug. Perched above the sea on the rocky east coast of the island, the Low Light is protected from prevailing south-westerlies and the view from the small terrace in front is surely one of the best from any bird observatory in Britain and is an excellent place for sea-watching. On a clear day can be seen the thin white pencil of the Bell Rock lighthouse, 35 kilometres to the north.

In 1814 the island was bought by the Commissioners of Northern Light Houses who were responsible for all the lighthouses around the coasts of Scotland. The lighthouse on the May was initially an island station, which meant that the keepers and their families lived there. With its re-designation as a rock station in 1972, the families left to live on the mainland. Then in 1989 the lighthouse became automatic and for the first time in 353 years there was no resident keeper on the island. This ended a long and happy association between the keepers, some of whom took a close interest in birds, and the residents of the observatory.

Despite its powerful light and the existence of foghorns at the north and south ends of the island (now silent), ships were occasionally wrecked on the May. One wreck in particular, that of the Danish steamer *Island,* which grounded in fog just below the Low Light on 13 April 1937, was of particular benefit to the observatory in the provision of crockery and also – for a period – exotic food and drink.

In 1956 the Northern Lighthouse Board entered into a 99-year agreement with the Nature Conservancy under which the island became a National Nature Reserve. In 1989 the island was transferred to the ownership of the Nature Conservancy Council. It is currently in the ownership of Scottish Natural Heritage (SNH), its successor body and its continuing status as a National Nature Reserve has recently been reviewed and confirmed.

The island's status as a major nature reserve and the attraction of its seabird colonies, particularly the Puffins, has meant a steady growth of day visitors to the island in the summer months. SNH employ two resident wardens on the island in the summer to receive visitors and tell them about the island's wildlife. In 2008 over 7,000 day visitors landed on the island. A visitor centre providing a display about the island is situated close to Kirk Haven. Whether one is interested in birds or not, a visit to the May in high summer, with thousands of Puffins whirring through the air like insects and cliffs packed with noisy auks while terns scream over their colonies, is an impressive experience.

Since the island first came into the hands of the Nature Conservancy, and later SNH, there has been a steady growth in ornithological research work, which is concentrated on the seabirds. The lead in this has been taken by Professor Sarah Wanless and Professor Mike Harris. Up to 15 research students may be present during the summer, resident in Fluke Street. When the seabirds (and their researchers) leave at the end of the summer, a new group of researchers takes up residence – the Sea Mammal Research Unit from St Andrews University. They study the significant Grey Seal population that comes to the island to breed and produce pups in October and November.

In 1710, Sir Robert Sibbald drew up a list of seabirds of the May. However, one of the first naturalists known to have visited the May was Charles Darwin in 1826. Darwin was a medical student at Edinburgh University at the time and his wide interests in natural history took him to the shores and the islands of the Forth. Other visitors followed. At the end of the nineteenth century, Dr Eagle Clarke, amongst others, was studying migration, particularly on islands. He visited the Flannans, Sule Skerry and Fair Isle, resulting in papers on migration at lightships and lighthouses. The Misses Baxter and Rintoul, two keen ornithologists based in Fife, knew him and his writings and were inspired to further the study of migration using the Isle of May as their base. From 1907 until 1933, apart from the years of the First World War, they made spring and autumn visits, and from their observations put forward their concept of migrational drift published in *Ibis* in 1918. This was an important contribution to explaining the relationship between weather and migration. During that period they spent a total of 684 days on the island, keeping careful records. At the time an accepted mode of identification was by 'securing' specimens, and the 'Good Ladies' must have cut interesting figures, dressed in tweeds and carrying their guns. Their beautifully kept records periodically contain the phrase, 'We procured it', followed by a set of measurements. However, many of their records are based on good field identification or

The observatory on the Isle of May helps with the ringing of adult and young Guillemots and other seabirds essential to CEH studies (Steve Stansfield – www.wildlifeimages.eu).

on long hours spent during the night, recording the birds attracted to the lantern of the lighthouse.

In 1929, a group of young men who were at, or had just left, the Edinburgh Academy formed the Inverleith Field Club. This was expanded into the Midlothian Ornithological Club (MOC) whose members played a major role, along with the Misses Baxter and Rintoul, in establishing the Scottish Ornithologists' Club (SOC) in 1936. Aware of Baxter and Rintoul's work on the Isle of May, two MOC members visited the island in September 1932. In autumn 1933, a larger MOC party went out, but their studies obviously had to take their place alongside other interests. As the Log records, '... many of us observed a migrational rush for the first time. A game of football was in progress against the lighthouse keepers when the goalie noticed a Red-spotted Bluethroat. By the time the game was finished a total of six had been seen, along with numerous other species.'

Two articles inspired the MOC: W. B. Alexander's writing in *British Birds* (1934) about the Heligoland Bird Observatory and Ronald Lockley's article in *The Countryman* (1931) about the bird observatory he established on Skokholm. W. B. Alexander, then of the British Trust for Ornithology, provided much valuable help and encouragement and visited the May. With his involvement and that of Lockley, the Isle of May Bird Observatory was started on 28 September 1934 and now has the status of the longest continuously functioning observatory in Britain.

The first Heligoland trap, the Low Trap, was erected and put into use from the beginning, facilitating the future of the 'new' method of trapping, ringing, description and release, a fundamental change of approach from that of their predecessors with their shotguns. A second Heligoland, the Top Trap, was built in the spring of 1938 prior to the requisitioning of the island by the Navy. Before the Second World War, the observatory was housed in 'The Lookout', a coastguard building high on the middle of the island, but, when it reopened in 1946, the move was made to the Low Light and for 60 years this has been the visitors' accommodation. Three further traps have been built over the years, the Bain Trap in 1948–49, the Gully Trap in 1952 and the Arnott Trap in 1975 to bring the complement to five, though the Gully Trap is not currently in use. From the establishment of the observatory to the end of 2008, some 267,388 birds of 182 species have been ringed.

When the island was requisitioned by the Navy in 1938 in preparation for war, the observers were ejected at short notice and the island became HMS May Island, under naval command. The observatory was taken over and huts were built to accommodate over 70 service personnel, manning the radar defences of the Forth.

The members of the MOC, who had started the observatory only five years earlier, joined the Forces and were scattered over the world. Almost miraculously, all survived and throughout the war they continued bird watching. George Waterston, captured in the fall of Crete, planned his next bird observatory – Fair Isle – in his prisoner of war camp. Frank Elder, the first secretary of the observatory, and Ian Munro met up during an artillery battle in northern Europe and compared notes on Firecrests observed following the Normandy landings. Donald Watson in Burma noted Yellow-browed Warblers and Red-breasted Flycatchers – familiar to him from the May – during the Battle of Arakan. Donald was to become a distinguished bird artist after the War. Maxwell Hamilton, who had joined the Navy, was sunk twice, once within sight of the May.

In 1946 the observatory reopened. On 23 January 1947 the MOC transferred control to 'The Isle of May Bird Observatory and Field Station Committee' which in turn became a Charitable Trust in 1985. Valuable financial assistance was provided by the four older Scottish Universities in the post-war period.

From the start, it was run as a cooperative venture. It has remained so ever since, reliant upon a steady succession of volunteers, onshore, responsible for administration by serving on the committee, and offshore, to undertake the maintenance and development of facilities. There is no resident warden and each party is required to complete the logs daily in the usual format. The 'Chatty Log', the record of the daily doings of the observatory, has been kept from the very start and, with a current lifespan of 76 years, is a document of some historical importance. Its 18 handwritten volumes cover the whole gamut of subjects, many mundane, such as food and the weather, but references can be found to political, legal and social changes and all the major world events which occurred when the Low Light was occupied. The logs give a wonderful insight into the companionable life of a small observatory; the observers, never more than half a dozen, gathered round a driftwood fire, writing up the day's observations by a paraffin or, latterly, gas lamp. Above all, it is a wonderful illustration of the fun and excitement of birdwatching.

The logs record the excitement of new species for the island, for Scotland or for Britain and Ireland, the busy October days ringing huge numbers of Blackbirds and thrushes, and the problems faced by those who were stranded by bad weather, with their stores dwindling. One of the most interesting birds first described in the Chatty Log is the Hoodwink (*Dissimulatrix spuria*). However, it will be a familiar species to many at bird observatories round Britain and Ireland. Its field characteristics were recorded as "elusive, usually only a glimpse of part of the back obtained. Only perches beyond the range of strong binoculars". The song was described as "teww-twee-swee-swee-brr" and also as resembling the words, "See you outside the Odeon, Saturday". Its plumage was described as "buffish-tan shading to tannish-buff", with "the soft parts (i.e. the hard parts) pinkish horn shading to hornish pink". The description, of which this is only an extract, was written by Professor M. F. M. Meiklejohn who regularly visited the May after the war. 'Maury' Meiklejohn was Professor of Italian at Glasgow University and a distinguished ornithologist, but it is for his delightful contributions to the log that he is specially remembered on the May.

The importance of wind direction for migration was realised early on. It was well known that westerly winds were likely to mean that nothing of interest would be seen. Maury Meiklejohn's *Ode to the West Wind* is a famous expression of the frustration felt during periods of prolonged westerly wind. It starts:

> *Far on the wide Hungarian plain*
> *The Hoopoe waves his tawny crest –*
> *But not at us. The wind remains*
> *Perpetually West.*

It was with feeling he wrote in the log:

> *There was an old man of the May*
> *Who knelt on the North Ness to pray*
> *'O Lord, I have sinned –*
> *But why need the wind*
> *Blow westerly day after day?*

The log records delays and enforced stays created by stormy weather. Dr Joe Eggeling, author of the excellent standard work on the Isle of May (1960, 1985) and a major figure in running the observatory after the War, was marooned for 11 days in April 1958. In the days before mobile phones there were many anxious watches in rough weather to see whether a fishing boat had set out from Fife or not. Observers remember with gratitude their journeys with Willie Hughes in the *Fair Morn*, Jimmy Smith in *Breadwinner* and the Gatherums in *Aspire*, before the swift passages in RIBs with Niall White and Colin Murray.

The log also contains illustrations. It charts the artistic development of Keith Brockie, from his first visit to the May to his present position as one of Scotland's leading wildlife artists. *One Man's Island*, his illustrated account of a year on the May, is a beautiful book which captures brilliantly every aspect of the wildlife of the May. The bird artist Derek Robertson has also been a regular visitor to the island and his drawings also illustrate the log.

THE BIRDS

The ornithological spectrum of the Isle of May is rich and diverse. This account opens with discussions of two equally important aspects of the island's ornithology, first migration and then the seabirds. These are followed by two other interesting families, the waders and the raptors. Next come some paragraphs on the breeding birds not previously discussed and then a few comments on the island's contribution to the Scottish ornithological scene. Finally, there is a summary, partly in tabular form, of the status of migrants, be they common, scarce or rare.

The position of the Isle of May provides an excellent focal point for the study of migration and movement of birds. With the exception of seabirds, breeding in their tens of thousands, the annual totals of birds that breed do not exceed a few tens of a handful of species, including Oystercatcher and passerines such as Rock Pipit and Pied Wagtail. Non-breeding passerines occurring on the island can

Exceptional falls of migrants can occur on the Isle of May when the weather conditions are right, and as many as 15,000 Goldcrests have been recorded on a single day (Steve Stansfield – www.wildlifeimages.eu).

reasonably be classed as 'on migration', from presumably locally bred Willow Warblers, with wing lengths so short as to suggest the flight from Fife would be a challenge, and other trans-Saharan passage warblers touching down for a brief respite, to the Scandinavian thrushes which arrive on passage in many thousands in the autumn. The island can support good numbers of waders, many as passage birds, but others wintering on the island. There is evidence of rocky-shore species, such as Purple Sandpiper and Turnstone, flying to the island for the hours of darkness to feed and roost, perhaps avoiding rats and other nocturnal predators on the mainland.

Various forms of visible migration are associated with the Isle of May. These include typical diurnal passerine movements of coasting birds, such as Skylarks, hirundines, Tree and Meadow Pipits and Linnets. On clear days these species can be observed passing over the island, often at a considerable height and only rarely making landfall, whilst in more overcast conditions, or if there is rainfall or mist, they may touch down for a while. Numbers are seldom large, although there have been exceptional movements of up to 4,500 Swallows, 7,000 Meadow Pipits, 30,000 Blackbirds, 10,300 Fieldfares, 8,000 Song Thrushes, 10,000 Redwings, 1,000 Willow Warblers, 15,000 Goldcrests and 4,000 Bramblings.

A second form of passage involves drift migration, as explored by Baxter and Rintoul. Drift migration is responsible for the appearance of birds, coming from or heading to Continental destinations, which have been deflected from their intended route by adverse weather conditions, whether in spring or autumn. The conditions that tend to bring these birds down in greatest numbers involve locally east or south-east winds, with drizzle or rain and generally poor visibility, linked to appropriate pressure systems, and wind direction and strength on the Continent, which encourage the birds to set off in the first place. It is assumed that in fairer weather with better visibility the birds will make their landfall on the more hospitable looking mainland.

When conditions are right for landfall on the island, spectacular numbers of many species, both common and more unusual in Britain, can appear. A good illustration is the week of 18 to 26 August 2001, which started with light easterlies and a haar on the first afternoon, with only a Robin and a handful of Willow Warblers present to suggest that any migration was happening. Overnight conditions worsened with drizzle and strengthening easterlies continuing through the next day, by the end of which some 120 birds had been ringed, including: two Wrynecks, three Tree Pipits, two Robins, three Whinchats, a Wheatear, a Grasshopper, an Aquatic, five Icterine, 19 Garden, three Barred, and 28 Willow Warblers, two Whitethroats, 47 Pied Flycatchers and a Red-backed Shrike. Other birds seen included: 19 Green and a Wood Sandpiper, six Reed Warblers, three Lesser Whitethroats, and a Wood Warbler. By the next day, 20 August, many had already moved on.

Autumn migration from late September into November typically involves Scandinavian night migrants making landfall on the island between dawn and the early afternoon. As with drift migrants, the weather conditions associated with the largest falls involve winds from an easterly quarter, with drizzle or rain. Even on fairly clear days a slight shower can result in a deluge of birds, such as thrushes tumbling out of the sky from a height of several hundred metres, and carpeting what minutes before had been a relatively passerine-free island. The North Sea haar can be something of a mixed blessing for those hoping for a spectacular fall, as it seems at times that birds pass over in the clear skies above, presumably migrating at a height where they can see the mainland clearly.

Whilst most of the autumn migrants move through fairly quickly, as evidenced by the lack of significant numbers of re-trapped birds, at other times some individuals or groups of birds, such as Brambling, can take up residence for a period of days or even weeks. Small numbers of, for example, Short-eared Owls even overwinter.

The observatory's logs all bear witness to some thrilling autumn falls. Perhaps one of the most memorable series of days was in October 1989, when following several days of westerlies, and a very quiet island, the wind turned east on the 27th, and stayed there until the 29th, when it backed to the north-west. On the 27th, with continuous rain from the morning onwards, birds arriving included: three Merlins, a single Corncrake, Jack Snipe and Snipe, four Woodcocks, two Ring Ouzels, 50 Blackbirds, 70 Fieldfares, 50 Song Thrushes, 1,000 Redwings, four Blackcaps, and single Chiffchaff, Brambling and Snow Bunting. In addition, 'flyover' birds included a further 400 Fieldfares, 150 Song Thrushes, 4,000 Redwings and a Lapland Bunting. On the 28th, arrivals included: a Sparrowhawk, six Woodcocks, four Long-eared and two Short-eared Owls, 12 Black Redstarts, three Ring Ouzels, 150 Blackbirds, 150 Fieldfares, 5,000 Redwings, two Blackcaps, 10 Chiffchaffs, 30 Goldcrests, 400 Starlings, 15 Chaffinches, 30 Brambling, a Twite, six Yellowhammers and six Reed Buntings. Although the wind had backed to the north-west on the 29th, birds continued to arrive, including: a Kestrel, 30 Long-eared Owls, three Blackcaps, a Pallas's Warbler, 10 Goldcrests, four Greenfinches and 10 Twite. However, very few of the passerines remained two days later.

There have been several instances of passage of irruptive migrants. Waxwings have occurred in a number of years, but are probably under-recorded as the observatory has often closed by early November; and Common Crossbills, occasionally from June to September, usually in numbers of fewer than 10, although exceptionally 85. Pallas's Sandgrouse have been recorded twice, with up to 40 in May 1888, as part of the biggest-ever irruption into the British Isles, followed by two on 11 May 1975.

Raptors

The only raptor to breed recently on the Isle of May is the Peregrine which bred prior to 1930 and has occasionally done so since. However, it is notable that the range of species recorded has increased in recent times, with several first records occurring in the past 25 years.

One of the juvenile White-tailed Eagles released in Fife in 2008, as part of the programme to reintroduce the species to Scotland, spent a fair part of August and September of that year on the island.

Honey-buzzard has been recorded six times, with an even spread of spring and autumn occurrences, all since 1983; and there has been a single record of Red

Kite, in August 2003. Three species of harrier have occurred. Marsh Harrier, with all nine records since 1974, is seen more often in spring than in autumn, whilst Hen Harrier is most frequently recorded in October. There is a single record of Montagu's Harrier.

Goshawk is represented by a single bird in September 2000, whilst Sparrowhawk is recorded most years between March and May, and again between July and November, with some birds staying for several days. Buzzard has been increasing in frequency in recent years, and with just over 30 records in total has been almost annual since 1994. There is a single record of Rough-legged Buzzard, in October 1982. Osprey has been recorded on 37 occasions, with almost two-thirds since 1963; most records are of single birds, but two were seen in May, June and September of 1977.

Kestrel is the most frequently recorded bird of prey, with significantly more autumn than spring occurrences. Counts of two or three birds are not uncommon, with an exceptional count of 31 in September 1969. There are two records of Red-footed Falcon, both in the month of May, in 1969 and 1973. Merlin occurs occasionally in spring, between March and May, and more regularly between July and November, with a maximum count of three. Hobby has been recorded four times, in June 1993, September 2000, May 2006 and May 2008, and a white-morph Gyr Falcon was seen in April 1979. Peregrine has been recorded in most months, most regularly between February and May, and August and October.

There are records of four species of owls for the Isle of May. Barn Owl has been recorded at least 12 times, with two birds ascribed to *Tyto alba guttata*, the dark-breasted race. The first record was in 1934, followed by three in 1961, singles in 1977, 1985 and 1996 and the remainder since 2000. A bird seen in January 2006 was thought to have been present since the previous year. There is a single record of a Tawny Owl from September 2008. Long-eared Owls have been recorded in every month, less frequently in spring, and most regularly from September to November. There have been several multiple records, including a spectacular total of 50 in October 1989 and birds can stay for several days. Short-eared Owl is occasional in spring between February and May and more regular in autumn between July and November. Single records are the norm, though multiples are not unusual and the maximum count is nine in October 1978.

Waders

The Isle of May, with its rocky and pebble shores and limited areas of fresh water, some of which dry out for the greater part of the year, is not renowned as a site for wading birds. In spite of this, the observatory's status log bears records for 29 wader species, four of which have bred. Oystercatcher breeds annually with up to 39 nests recorded, though with typically fewer than 10 young fledging, whilst Ringed Plover attempted breeding only once, unsuccessfully, in 1977. There is an early record for Lapwing from 1897 and records for most years between 1976 and 1986, with an indication that only one chick fledged. Redshank bred once in 1912, there being no record of the outcome.

Only Oystercatcher, Curlew, Purple Sandpiper, Redshank and Turnstone are recorded throughout the year. There is evidence of passage migration for all five, in both spring and autumn, with larger numbers in the latter half of the year. Purple Sandpiper is recorded in every month. Maximum counts for these species are: Oystercatcher 147 (September 1948), Purple Sandpiper *c.*400 (September 1979), Curlew autumn counts of 167 (October 2002) but typically up to 120, Redshank 200 (August 1972) and Turnstone 516 (September 1990).

Few individual species, other than seabirds, have attracted study resulting in published papers from the Isle of May. An exception is the Purple Sandpiper, which has been studied by various ringing groups from the east of Scotland. Many of these studies in Scotland have their genesis on the Isle of May, both in terms of devising methods for counting and trapping for ringing and biometric and moult studies. One biometrics study led to the description of different populations based on bill lengths: one short-billed population and the other long-billed (Atkinson *et al.* 1981). Further work established that the short-billed population originated in Norway, whereas the long-billed population is believed to originate from Canada. Several birds which were colour-ringed in Norway were sighted on the Isle of May, including one that returned for 14 years (Rae *et al.* 1986). It was from these studies that the southern Norwegian breeding origin of the birds wintering in the east of Scotland was established. The proportion of short-billed birds proved to be higher on the Isle of May than in any other part of Britain. Studies here and elsewhere also established that the two populations differed in their migration phenology (Nicoll *et al.* 1988). Short-billed birds start arriving back on the Isle of May in July and immediately commence their moult. With an average start date of 16 July for females and 24 July for males, the complete moult takes 61 days (Summers *et al.* 2004). Colour ringing of Purple Sandpipers also showed that the Isle of May birds exhibited strong site fidelity to the island, both within and between years (Atkinson *et al.* 1981), whilst a radio-tracking study showed that the island was used as a night-time refuge by some birds which foraged on the mainland by day (Summers 1995).

A number of wader species are recorded on passage on a reasonably regular basis. Ringed Plover are typically seen in April and May in spring and August and September in autumn, usually as single birds, but there is a maximum count of 32. Golden Plover can be seen in all months between March and November, with a few winter records and a maximum count of 50 in October 1985. Lapwing can be seen from mid-February to May and again from August to November with occasional winter records, the peak count being 159 in October 1978.

Knot are a rare spring migrant, but more frequent in autumn between July and October and single bids are the norm, although a flock of 120 has been recorded. Dunlin can be seen irregularly in small numbers during May, but in larger numbers in autumn between August and November, with a highest count of 80 in October 1982. Jack Snipe is an irregular passage migrant between March and May and again from August to November with a peak count of six birds, and there are occasional winter records. Snipe follow a similar pattern, except they are slightly more numerous with a peak count of 16. Woodcock occur in small numbers in spring, but are generally much more numerous in the autumn with counts occasionally reaching 40 birds in October and November. There were exceptional counts of 100 in November 1962 and 60 in November 1982, whilst in some years they are absent.

Small numbers of Whimbrel can be seen on spring passage from March to May, with larger numbers in autumn between August and November, and a peak count of 70 in August 1980. Greenshank are rare in spring, with only four records in May and June, although they are more frequent in autumn from July to November, mostly as single birds but with a maximum count of four. Common Sandpiper are irregular in spring, typically from mid-April to June, but are more regular in autumn between July and October, with a maximum count of 50 in August 2001.

Wader species, rare for the Isle of May, are also recorded. There have been two spring records of Stone-curlew, and for Dotterel there are three spring and 10 autumn records, including an attraction to the lantern of the lighthouse of several hundred birds, with a few reported killed on 30 August 1914. Grey Plover are slightly more numerous, with 30 records between 1951 and 1999, and a maximum of four individuals.

Sanderling have been recorded on 14 occasions with all but one in autumn, between July and October, and a maximum of three birds. Little Stint was first recorded in 1946, since when there have been 28 autumn records, with a maximum of 11 birds in 1996. Curlew Sandpiper was first recorded in 1902, with five subsequent autumn records, mostly singles but with a maximum of 13 in 1991. For Ruff there is a single spring and seven autumn records.

Black-tailed Godwit was first recorded in 1902, with 11 records, in both spring and autumn months; whilst Bar-tailed Godwit is more regular in autumn than spring, with a maximum of 30 birds in September. All Spotted Redshank have been in autumn, from July to October, with about 25 records of single birds, and one record of two birds. Green Sandpiper has produced 16 records between April and May, with rather more in autumn from July to October, and a maximum of 19 in August 2001, and there have been two records of Grey Phalarope.

Seabirds

For a visitor to the May in early summer, the overwhelming impression is of seabirds. The Firth of Forth holds seabird colonies of international importance, the Bass Rock with its huge Gannet colony is clearly visible much of the time and the May itself is a major seabird station.

The island has one of the most intensively studied seabird communities in the world and the study of seabirds has formed part of the work of the observatory since its inception. Observations of their activities were recorded beforehand by lighthouse keepers and visitors, though this was not done systematically until censuses were made by Baxter and Rintoul in 1921 and 1924. During the 1960s and early 1970s, Dr John Coulson and his students undertook research on gulls and Shag, but subsequently most projects have been organised by Professors Mike Harris and Sarah Wanless of the Centre for Ecology and Hydrology (CEH). Current research is based on long-term studies (over 30 years) of ringed auks,

Shags and Kittiwakes to understand the population dynamics of these birds. This has involved the use of the latest technological advances, such as geolocation loggers, time-depth recorders and miniature cameras, to follow the activities of birds away from the colony during both the breeding and non-breeding seasons.

Results from this work are making a major contribution to improving our understanding of the threats to North Sea seabirds from climate change and industrial fishing for Sand Eels. Scottish Natural Heritage undertakes annual censuses of most of the seabirds and the observatory supports CEH's research by supplying rings and manpower to help ring the large numbers of adult and young seabirds essential for the studies. The history and present status of the individual seabird species on the May is as follows.

Fulmar was first recorded in 1914 and confirmed breeding in 1930, the number of occupied nests reaching 108 in 1979. This more than trebled to a maximum of 382 Apparently Occupied Sites (AOS) in 1997, following which there was a period of decline from 2001 to 2004, to below 250 AOS and a recent revival to between 280 and 300.

Manx Shearwaters are observed from the island throughout the summer in varying numbers, but in recent years, particularly from 1996, more activity by prospecting birds has been noted over and on the island. There has been one confirmed record of successful breeding in 2008.

From a few pairs of breeding Shags in the 1820s, and only six pairs in 1934, numbers grew steadily to 1,100 in 1973, reaching a peak of 1,919 occupied nests in 1987. Fortunes have fluctuated considerably since then with a crash to 403 in 1994, and another to 281 in 2005, both following massive mortality in the seabird 'wrecks' of the preceding winters, but with signs of a small recovery to 2008.

Before 1930 the Lesser Black-backed Gull was known as a passage migrant, but from an initial pair in that year there was sustained expansion to 2,100 pairs in 1972. Herring Gull was first recorded breeding in 1907 and around 3,000 pairs were present by the late 1950s, even at a time when eggs were collected and despatched to the mainland for human consumption. Herring Gull breeding numbers reached 15,000 pairs in 1972. At the instigation of the observatory, a population management programme was implemented for both species in order to reduce numbers significantly. This was repeated in 1985, and Lesser Black-backed Gull numbers have been fairly stable since 1995 in the range 1,450–1,800 pairs per year, with a peak of 1,944 in 2008. Herring Gull numbers only exceeded 3,000 pairs in 1999 and 2000 and were about 2,850 in 2005.

From 1962, small numbers of Great Black-backed Gulls attempted to breed, with up to four pairs in the early 1970s, while, from a single pair in 1985, double figures were reached in 1998, with 14 pairs, and a maximum count of 33 pairs in 2005. Peak numbers occur in the autumn when the seals have their pups, with up to 2,000 birds recorded.

With a known presence spanning nearly four centuries, the breeding population of Kittiwakes will have experienced many fluctuations. The recorded peak of more than 8,100 AOS came in 1990, but numbers then gradually declined to between 3,000 and 4,000 nests in 2006–2008.

Breeding of Sandwich Terns was annual from 1926 to 1956, with a peak of about 1,400 pairs in 1946. Breeding resumed in 1998 when two pairs bred, though unsuccessfully. In 1999, there were 110 birds incubating. On 11 August 1999 a mobile crèche of 87 large young made its way down to the rocky tideline at Burrian, but by 14 August none remained, either washed away or predated by gulls. Subsequently, breeding has been erratic, with 500 pairs in 2001 and none in 2005.

A few pairs of Roseate Terns bred between 1935 and 1956, with a peak of up to 20 pairs in 1946, but it was 1995 before breeding was attempted again, though unsuccessfully, a situation repeated in 1996 and 2000. Two young were ringed in 2001, but disappeared before fledging, since when only occasional prospecting birds have been seen.

Common Terns have had a long but far from continuous history as a breeding bird, with notable absences from the mid-eighteenth century until the First World War, and again from 1957 until success was proved in 1980, perhaps a positive outcome of the reduction in gull numbers. In between times the colony peaked at 5,000 to 6,000 pairs in the period immediately after the Second World War. In recent years, the figures have fluctuated between 415 pairs in 1999 and two pairs in 2002.

With 800 pairs of Arctic Terns in 1936, the recorded maximum, the species was always less numerous than the Common Tern up to the abandonment of the mixed colony in 1957. Since its return in 1980 this situation has been reversed. Arctic Terns have increased to over 900 pairs in 2000 and 2001. In the succeeding four years, it has settled within the 500–650 range, with two new sub-colonies developing from 2004.

The Isle of May was home to the largest single Puffin colony in Britain in 2003, with 69,300 breeding pairs (Richard Brown).

Guillemot is a long-established breeder whose numbers grew steadily to about 6,000 pairs in 1969 and to a peak of 19,000–20,000 pairs in the period 2002–2004, since when there has been a decline. Similarly, Razorbill is long established as a breeder, but even in 1883 they were not as numerous as Guillemot. The population grew to a fairly stable level, mainly in the 2,500–3,500 range, between 1995 and 2005.

The small numbers of Puffin which bred up to the 1950s did so in rock fissures on the cliffs and stacks, but between 1957 and 1961 a colony was established in the Rabbit warren on the Burrian involving up to 100 pairs. The peaty turf was increasingly exploited such that the population was estimated at 3,000 to 4,000 in 1972. By 1981, there were estimated to be 8,500 occupied burrows, 20,106 in 1992, 42,000 in 1998 and 69,300 in 2003, at which time the Isle of May had the largest single colony of Puffins in Britain and Ireland. Wanless, Harris and colleagues (Wanless *et al.* 2003) considered that 'the island could in theory have room for a quarter of a million burrows and an associated population of three-quarters of a million adults and immatures'. In 2008, the population was thought to have declined to 42,000 pairs.

From 286 nests in 1979 the Eider population exceeded 1,000 for the first time in 1995 and has remained roughly in the range 800–1,200 since then. Shelduck also attempt to breed annually in small numbers.

Of other species recorded, but not breeding, the Gannet is the most noticeable with the stream of birds passing between the Bass Rock and the feeding grounds a constant backdrop. Great Skuas regularly predate auks and Kittiwakes and later in the season Arctic Skuas harry food-carrying terns and Puffins. Pomarine Skua is almost annual. Mediterranean, Little, Sabine's, Black-headed, Common, Iceland and Glaucous Gulls have all been recorded.

Autumn sea-watching brings records of Sooty Shearwater, with a maximum day-count of 669 in September 2002, and six records of Balearic Shearwater since 2000. Black Terns are occasional at this time. Later in the year, Little Auk can be numerous, but the passage of over 100,000 in a single day in October 2006 was unprecedented in Britain.

As at many other locations around the coast, using recorded calls of Storm Petrels as a lure at night has demonstrated that there is a considerable summer movement of birds past the island. Since 1979 over 1,000 birds, and five Leach's Petrels, have been ringed, although sight records of both species are rare. There is a winter Cormorant roost but none remain to breed. Black Guillemots are recorded in about one year in two, usually between September and May, but there are occasional summer sightings, while the Sooty Tern in July 1989 was an unexpected visitor.

Passerines

It is the scarce and rare passerines which earned the Isle of May its early reputation as a migrant and vagrant hotspot. A total of 128 passerine species (all Category A on the official British List) have been recorded on the Isle of May, plus several Category D and likely escapes, including Chestnut Bunting *Emberiza rutilla*, Red-headed Bunting *Emberiza bruniceps* (seven birds), Lazuli Bunting *Passerina amoena*, Daurian Redstart *Phoenicurus auroreus* and Pallas's Rosefinch *Carpodacus roseus*. The 128 passerine species can be loosely grouped as follows by their current status (bearing in mind that most of the species which have bred are commonest as migrants).

Breeding passerines

Since 2000 only a couple of passerine species have bred on the May. One is Rock Pipit, which has undergone a dramatic decline from up to 60 pairs in the 1950s, and a minimum of 49 territories in 1994, to only six territories but good breeding success in 2001 and just one pair in 2005 – though up to nine pairs bred in 2007. The other, Pied Wagtail, retains a toehold as a breeder with three pairs in 2005, six in 2006 and eight in 2007, but has never bred in large numbers.

Former or irregular breeders

Species which have bred on the Isle of May include:

Swallow	first noted in 1959, then regular 1971–2000
Meadow Pipit	last bred in 1986
Wren	occasionally up to 1997
Wheatear	in small numbers up until 2000
Blackbird and Song Thrush	neither known to have bred in over 20 years
Willow Warbler	once in 1992
Carrion Crow	irregularly up to 2000
Starling	last in 1999
House Sparrow	between 1925 and 1947
Tree Sparrow	between 1907 and 1922
Linnet	most recently in 1998
Black Redstart	have been observed in several summers and almost certainly bred in 1994 and 2006.

Common passage migrants

Around 35 species come under this broad heading, with birds which breed locally and throughout east Scotland often greatly supplemented by birds from northern Europe. They include the following species: Skylark, Sand Martin, House Martin, Meadow Pipit, Tree Pipit, Wren, Dunnock, Robin, Redstart, Wheatear, Whinchat, Ring Ouzel, Blackbird, Song Thrush, Fieldfare, Redwing, Sedge Warbler, Willow Warbler, Whitethroat, Garden Warbler, Blackcap, Chiffchaff, Goldcrest, Pied Flycatcher, Chaffinch, Brambling, Greenfinch, Goldfinch, Siskin, Linnet, Twite, Lesser Redpoll and Reed Bunting.

Uncommon or scarce passage migrants

About 30 species occur in small numbers that average up to 10 individuals annually. Members of this group are: Yellow Wagtail, Grey Wagtail, Waxwing, Bluethroat, Stonechat, Mistle Thrush, Grasshopper Warbler, Reed, Icterine and Barred Warblers, Lesser Whitethroat, Yellow-browed Warbler, Wood Warbler, Spotted and Red-breasted Flycatchers, Red-backed and Great Grey Shrikes, Jackdaw, Rook, Tree Sparrow, Common Redpoll, Common Crossbill, Common Rosefinch, Bullfinch, Lapland and Snow Buntings, Yellowhammer and Ortolan Bunting.

Scarce vagrants

Five species have been noted on an irregular basis, but have records exceeding 30 birds. Shore Lark has been recorded 10 times in spring and about 22 times in autumn with a maximum count of four (3 October 1976). Long-tailed Tit is occasional in autumn between 26 September and 5 November with a maximum count of 20 (11 October 1992). Treecreeper can be seen in both spring and autumn with seven records from March and April, one in June and over 45 from mid-July to mid-October. Hooded Crow is seen mainly in the autumn and House Sparrow formerly bred, but declined rapidly once the lighthouses were no longer manned.

Rare vagrants

This group includes 56 species, just under half (44%) of the passerine total recorded on the island, which range widely in their potential origins. The figures give the total number of individual birds recorded and the last year in which they were recorded:

Birds breeding on the adjacent mainland

Dipper	10, last in 2004
Coal Tit	15, 1996
Blue Tit	16, 2005
Great Tit	28+, 2005
Magpie	one in 1986
Corn Bunting	13, 2006

Birds breeding elsewhere in Britain and Europe

Woodlark	19, 1997
Nightingale	20, 1996
Marsh Warbler	26+, 2007
Firecrest	20, 2004
Bearded Tit	one record of four birds in 1999
Golden Oriole	four, 1997
Raven	eight, 2004
Parrot Crossbill	one, 1953
Hawfinch	five, 1991
Cirl Bunting	six, 1976

Birds breeding in Europe (but not Britain and Ireland)

Calandra Lark	one, 2006
Short-toed Lark	five, 1998
Red-rumped Swallow	two, 2001
Red-throated Pipit	two, 1988
Citrine Wagtail	one, 1968
Thrush Nightingale	17+, 2008
Red-flanked Bluetail	one, 1975
Pied Wheatear	one, 1909
Black-eared Wheatear	two, 1980
Lanceolated Warbler	one, 1987
Aquatic Warbler	seven, 2001
Blyth's Reed Warbler	three, 2007
Eastern Olivaceous Warbler	one, 1967
Booted Warbler	two, 1992
Melodious Warbler	six, 1998
Subalpine Warbler	10, 2007
Sardinian Warbler	one, 1981
Greenish Warbler	12, 2004
Arctic Warbler	four, 1996
Lesser Grey Shrike	one, 1997
Woodchat Shrike	four, 2003
Rose-coloured Starling	two, 1991
Arctic Redpoll	one, 1982
Two-barred Crossbill	two, 2001
Pine Grosbeak	one, 1954
Ortolan Bunting	no precise figure available, 2001
Rustic Bunting	19, 1999
Little Bunting	30, 2000
Yellow-breasted Bunting	12, 1989
Black-headed Bunting	one, 1949

Birds breeding further afield

Olive-backed Pipit	four, 2005
Siberian Thrush	one, 1954
Paddyfield Warbler	one, 1988
Pallas's Warbler	eight, 2001
Hume's Warbler	one, 1994
Radde's Warbler	six, 2005
Dusky Warbler	one, 1985
Isabelline Shrike	one, 1950

It is this group which has provided 11 species that the Isle of May has added to the Scottish List, and it includes four which were new to Britain and Ireland (Table 1).

The Isle of May also provided the first British record of the Siberian race of

Table 1. *First records for the British and Scottish lists contributed by the Isle of May*

British firsts	
Pied Wheatear	19 October 1909
Siberian Thrush	1–4 October 1954
Eastern Olivaceous Warbler	24–26 September 1967
Isabelline Shrike	26 September 1950
Scottish firsts	
Nightingale	9 May 1911
Melodious Warbler	27 September 1913
Radde's Warbler	8 October 1962
Firecrest	30 September–3 October 1959
Woodchat Shrike	19 October 1911
Pine Grosbeak	8–9 November 1954
Ortolan Bunting	2 May 1885

Stonechat, *Saxicola torquata maura*, an immature male, despatched to the museum specimen drawer by the 'Good Ladies' on 10 October 1913.

As mentioned earlier, many historical records and observations confirm that the lighthouses on the island were a major attraction to birds migrating at night, while the foghorns also provided cues for landfall in foggy or misty conditions. It may be speculated that the subsequent decommissioning of the foghorns made the island less of a focus for birds, along with the increased illumination on the mainland shores. While there are fewer migrants compared to the earlier half of the last century, this almost certainly reflects general reductions in population levels across Europe and beyond rather than a reduced attraction of birds to the Isle of May itself. This can be well illustrated by examining the occurrence of various scarcer migrants in recent years.

These scarcer migrants can be grouped into three broad categories according to their relative frequency compared with records in the neighbouring recording areas of Fife and Lothian. In particular, the comparison is with the easternmost portion of Fife, from the East Neuk to Fife Ness, which has recorded the bulk of scarcer passage migrant records immediately to the north of the May, and the equivalent stretch of the Lothian coast: from Musselburgh to Thorntonloch. In none of the species considered below (17 passerines and Wryneck) was the total of birds recorded in recent years (1990–2008) similar in all three recording areas. This presumably reflects the differences in the complex combination of factors operating on the migrants flying over the outer part of the Forth Estuary, such as wind speed and direction and the vector on which the birds are travelling, the factors causing them to make landfall – local visibility and rainfall – and perhaps not least the ease with which observers are able to locate migrants on the ground in the three areas.

In many instances, the occurrence of scarce migrants on the May is greater than in both of the other areas (and often the entire east coast of Scotland). In a few instances, numbers on the May, though still frequent, closely match those of one of its adjacent recording areas, while in the third group are species which are more regular in either Lothian or Fife. The position for some of the individual species is as follows.

Thirty-three Wrynecks have been noted on the May from 1990–2008, compared to 22 in Fife and 12 in Lothian. Yellow Wagtail still maintains a small breeding population in Lothian (breeding in Scotland being restricted now to Lothian and the Scottish Borders) and bred in Fife up to 1983 (and again in 2001–2003). The 95 birds recorded on the May from 1990–2008 compared to about 70 in Fife, while since 2000 there have been five years with just a single bird reported, which undoubtedly reflects the decline of this bird as breeding species in northern Britain and Europe. In the case of Bluethroats (93 or more for Isle of May; 23 for Fife and four for Lothian in 1990–2008), there has been a notable decline over the last 25 years in birds found in spring along the entire east coast of mainland Scotland, and the only records south of Aberdeenshire in many years are from the May.

The May has recorded around 112 Reed Warblers from 1990 to 2008, while mainland Fife shares a similar total and could potentially have had nearer 190 birds but for the difficulty of estimating the passage at Fife Ness in 1998. The annual totals for Fife and the Isle of May show a good correlation, which is perhaps indicative of birds following the coast on autumn migration. Lothian had just over 30 birds in the period. There have been 48 Icterine Warblers on the May since 1990, over twice as many as in Fife in the same period and about six times more than in Lothian. A total of seven Greenish Warbler records came from the May in 1990–2008, with five from Fife but none in Lothian. The total of 76 Yellow-browed Warblers from the May since 1990 exceeds the 64 in Fife, and is about twice the total in Lothian in this period. The total from the May might well have been higher given better coverage in the late autumn. Barred Warbler was recorded nearly three times more frequently than in Lothian and almost twice as often as in Fife during the same period (51; 18; 26). Wood Warbler is scarce in the east of Scotland but has had a small Lothian breeding population (last bred in 2003). The total of 37 records from the May over the period is similar to the 40 from Fife, but there is very limited correlation between the annual totals.

A total of 10 Firecrests from the May from 1990 to 2008 is matched by birds seen in Lothian, whereas Fife managed 16 in the same period, though only in three of the 16 years (1990, 2001, 2004) did all three recording areas have birds in the same year. The May has recorded 24 Red-breasted Flycatchers since 1990 compared to at least seven in Lothian and 15 in Fife. At least 65 Red-backed Shrikes were noted from 1990 to 2008, compared to 47 in Fife and 37 in Lothian, while the general absence of observers on the island from November to April almost certainly means that Great Grey Shrike is under-recorded with just five records from the May since 1990, but at least eight from Lothian and 14 from Fife during this time.

Perhaps most marked of all is Common Rosefinch, where the Isle of May has recorded at least 71 birds from 1990 to 2008, but Fife has had just four, while Lothian and Dundee and Angus have managed only two each, with eight in the Scottish Borders and 25 in North-east Scotland (Aberdeenshire) in the same time period. Interestingly, a female/immature ringed on the island on 10 October 1987 was trapped the following day at Pefferside on the Lothian coast just north of Dunbar – a nice piece of evidence for movements of birds between adjacent areas. Lapland Bunting is another species where the lack of observations on the island from November to April probably under-represents its true status. The 51 birds noted on the May from 1990–2008 is close to the total of about 60 in Fife, but both are well below the 200 or so noted in Lothian.

The ability of the Isle of May to attract bunting species, which are notably rare on the Scottish mainland, is also evident from the records of several species. The May has been host to six Cirl Buntings, but only one has ever been found else-where on the Scottish east coast (in Angus 1928), while the total of 19 Rustic Buntings recorded on the island compares to five in north-east Scotland, four in the Scottish Borders, two in Lothian, one in Dundee and Angus, and none in Fife. Thirty Little Buntings far exceed the five ever found in Fife and two in Lothian and there have been 13 Yellow-breasted Buntings, yet only three from Fife and only two elsewhere on the Scottish mainland (Highland 1982, Moray and Nairn 2004). In the period from 1990 to 2008, 13 Ortolans have been recorded on the May compared with just two each from Fife and Lothian. The May serves to indi-cate that these birds do pass through or over East Scotland, but are seldom found on the mainland coast.

The Isle of May has often presented the first evidence that many species typi-cally associated (in Scotland at least) with the Northern Isles, or St Kilda and the Western Isles, do also occur (albeit in much smaller numbers) along the east coast of Scotland. A long list of monopoly-breaking records from the May includes: Calandra Lark, Red-rumped Swallow, Olive-backed Pipit, Red-throated Pipit, Citrine Wagtail, Thrush Nightingale, Black-eared Wheatear, Red-flanked Bluetail, Lanceolated Warbler, Aquatic Warbler, Paddyfield Warbler, Blyth's Reed Warbler, Booted Warbler, Subalpine Warbler, Sardinian Warbler, Greenish Warbler, Little Bunting and Yellow-breasted Bunting.

The incidence of 'falls' on the island remains a regular, if unpredictable, occur-rence and continues to provide hope and inspiration for the occupants of the Low Light. It is clear that the Isle of May continues to be a focus for migrant and vagrant passerines and expects to remain a source of significant records well into the future.

OTHER FAUNA AND FLORA

Mammals and invertebrates

With the island occupying its gatekeeper's position at the entrance to the Forth, and having a long history of occupation, it is unsurprising that an interesting list of sea mammals has been recorded.

Those which are regularly seen are Minke Whale, Harbour Porpoise, and Bottlenose and Common Dolphins. For all these species, most sightings fall between July and September, but Minke Whale has occurred in early June and both it and Harbour Porpoise have been noted in the last week of October. Numbers of Minke Whale at any one time generally range from one to five, and occasionally 10, but there have been occasions when there has been mixed feeding activity involving other species such as Harbour Porpoise. In September 2002 there was the exceptional sight of up to 25 Minke Whales in feeding groups to the east of the island accompanied by Gannets, Kittiwakes and Sooty Shearwaters.

Harbour Porpoises sometimes occur in double figures, with a maximum recent count of *c*.40 in August 1997, but the most remarkable record is from April 1969 when a glut of Sprats in the Forth attracted an estimated 800 individuals. Between 1963 and 1965 one animal regularly escorted the observatory boat on its crossings to and from the mainland. Bottlenose Dolphins have been a regular feature of July and August sailings, providing entertainment and excitement, particularly to those on the tourist boat, but they tend to remain nearer to the mainland shore rather than frequenting the environs of the island.

Of the larger cetaceans, a Humpback Whale was off the west cliffs in June 2003 and a Fin Whale was noted in July 1981. The sighting of Sperm Whale in June 1992 was the more impressive in that it involved a group of four large and two small animals. Killer Whales have been recorded thrice, once in March and once in May with three animals on each occasion, plus a single in June, and Long-finned Pilot Whale once, at the end of July.

Grey Seals are considered to have bred historically, but in the twentieth century there was no evidence until a pup was seen in 1956. For 20 years up to 60 animals used the island as a haul-out with only occasional breeding, but by 1980 there were 310 pups and in 2006 there were over 1,800. Common Seals are scarce visitors, the paucity of sandy strand meaning that the island has little attraction for them.

There are two relatively recent records of Basking Shark, one in early October 1997 and the other in late September 2002.

On land, the evidence of man's long association with his surroundings is provided by the Rabbits, whose presence was recorded as early as 1329 and which were a major source of income to the monks. The letting of the right of pasturage in 1803 included the use of the warren, but they were almost exterminated by myxomatosis in 1955. Another bout of disease in 2008 again almost wiped out the Rabbit population. The fortunes of the island's House Mouse have similarly waxed and waned, but estimates of a possible population up to 6,000 at the end of summer may explain why migrant owls are in no rush to move on in late autumn. Eels are still present in the freshwater loch, judging from reports of infrequent sightings.

No domesticated animals remain, though when lighthouse keepers were resident they had, at various times, sheep, cows, goats, ducks and hens to supplement their diet, horses for transporting coal and stores, dogs and cats, and ferrets to exploit the Rabbits. During the Second World War a pig was kept.

Since the turn of the millennium, bats have been seen, with Common Pipistrelle noted on one or two days each year between May and October, whereas formerly they were occasional. Historically, a bat 'with ears like a ram's horns', caught at the Tower of the Low Light in September 1938, could only have been a Brown Long-eared.

The finding of a Stoat's skull is also recorded, presumably brought in by a gull. The island, it is hoped, is too far offshore for that other mustelid, the American

Mink, to make a crossing under its own power, but with animals regularly seen in the East Neuk harbours, vigilance is necessary to ensure that no 'hitch-hiker' arrives by boat.

The island's Lepidoptera have received more attention of late, with regular moth trapping taking the species list beyond 180. Clouded Yellow butterflies are scarce visitors. Occasionally there are exciting movements, such as that in 1996 when more than 500 Painted Ladies and 300 Small Tortoiseshells were amongst tens of thousands of Silver Y moths streaming across the island from the south-east and heading on into Fife.

Flora

The island's diverse natural and man-made habitats support an interesting range of plants that have been well studied and mapped. Species distribution and abundance have been influenced by past fluctuations in population levels of seabirds, Rabbits and Grey seals, and probably by relatively recent changes in climatic conditions. The predominantly rocky terrain provides opportunities for typical crevice plants, such as Buck's-horn Plantain, English Stonecrop, Danish Scurvygrass and Procumbent Pearlwort, with Common Saltmarsh-grass and Lesser Sea-spurrey associated with areas of high gull, Shag or seal density. However, the plant which dominates this habitat, and much of the island, with spectacular large white flowers in spring, is Sea Campion. Often accompanied by equally attractive Thrift, which blooms only where pressure from grazing Rabbits permits, the Sea Campion thrives in a variety of habitats, sometimes in vast swathes.

Closely grazed areas of Red Fescue-dominated acid grassland, as by McLeod's Path and south of Three Tarn Nick, are studded with Tormentil and Heath Bedstraw. Yorkshire-fog thrives in neutral grassland, accompanied in damper areas such as the Tennis Court and McLeod's Path by Silverweed or, as along Holyman's Road, by Lesser Celandine and Creeping Buttercup. Weed species including Common Sorrel, Orache, Common Chickweed and mouse-ears, *Cerastium* spp. are common in disturbed ground around Puffin and Rabbit burrows and in areas of high gull density. Creeping Thistle, Nettle, Common Sorrel, and Hogweed thrive in the previously cultivated gardens and disturbed areas along roads. They also grow with Lesser Burdock and Ragwort on the cinder areas between the Tower and Beacon. Another human influence on the flora has been tree and shrub-planting in the gardens and by the Tunnel beside the Low Light to provide shelter for migrating birds. Of the species recently used, Elder, Willow, *Salix* sp and Birch have proved successful. Sycamore and Hop have survived from earlier plantings.

Because there are no streams on the May and the Loch is polluted, aquatic plants are confined to small brackish pools, spring-fed and poorly drained depressions, and peaty runnels. Common Water-starwort, Shoreweed, Curled Dock, Floating Club-rush and Small Sweet-grass occur in pools on the North and South Plateaux, from which Least Water-parsnip and Marsh Pennywort have also been recorded. Round-leaved and Ivy-leaved Crowfoot, Lesser Spearwort and Blinks may be found in seasonally wet areas such as Pat's Puddle. All these damper parts of the island appear to be gradually drying out, so the future of these species is uncertain. A recent study of bryophytes by Dr David Chamberlain (2006) indicates a continued decline in species numbers attributed to loss of wetland and aquatic habitats and eutrophication associated with an increase in the Puffin population.

Sea Spleenwort and Scots Lovage can be seen on cliffs near the South Horn, Sea Milkwort is abundant in cracks in the path above Altarstanes, Sea Fern-grass (the Darnell's Fescue [Darnel] referred to in the observatory's special notes) grows on the walls of McLeod's and Top Gardens and Henbane is well established near the Low Light and Beacon. Common Spotted-orchid is recorded regularly, but Northern Marsh-orchid has not been seen in recent years. This and other rarities may yet be rediscovered.

ACCESS AND ACCOMMODATION

Access to the Isle of May for those staying at the observatory is from Anstruther in Fife, by means of a RIB, of the type used as inshore lifeboats. The observatory arranges a trip out to the island every Saturday during the period when it is manned (from the beginning of April to the end of October) to take out visitors who are staying at the observatory. Visitors have to make their own way to Anstruther. While there are buses to Anstruther from Edinburgh (change at Leven), and elsewhere, the RIB often leaves quite early in the day so that most observatory visitors come to Anstruther by car.

In addition, during the summer months (May till September) a trip boat (the *May Princess*) sails daily from Anstruther to the Isle of May (subject to weather and demand). This makes day visits possible, with about 2–3 hours on the island. It also makes it possible for visitors to the observatory to come and go from the island other than on a Saturday, if necessary. Neither form of transport is guaranteed since landing depends on the weather and visitors should plan accordingly.

The capacity on the RIB is limited. There is no shop on the island and visitors must bring all their food with them. There will be no opportunity to re-provision, so it is necessary to take enough food for the whole stay and for a day or two more – in case it is not possible to get off on the expected day. If visitors are planning to do more than bring on the equivalent of a rucksack and a large box of groceries per person (particularly if it is a full group of six people), they need to contact the boatman in advance to discuss whether a second journey may be necessary. If this should prove to be the case they will need to pay for the second run. With this in mind, visitors should note that there are a number of items that are normally available as a result of previous parties leaving spares, but this cannot be relied upon, and it is sensible to bring your own toilet-paper, kitchen roll, dish towels, washing-up liquid, scourer, matches and fly-papers (July/August in particular).

Please remember that the journey by RIB is eight kilometres, takes about 20 minutes and can be wet. It is therefore strongly advised that all kit and food is covered to make it fully waterproof.

The observatory accommodates a maximum of six in the Low Light which is an old lighthouse. There are bunk beds with mattresses, and a plentiful supply of blankets and pillows. Most people take a sleeping bag, but sheets and a pillow-case are all that are needed. Two of the bunks are in the living room; the other four are in the bedroom. There is a chemical lavatory but there is no bath or shower. There is an emergency food shelf and two small fridges but no deep freeze. Cooking and lighting is by calor gas. There is no electricity. Pots, pans, cutlery and crockery are all provided.

The observatory is an entirely voluntary enterprise and, unlike some larger observatories, does not employ a warden. Visitors, therefore, are required to manage for themselves, both in terms of their domestic needs and in maintaining the field-work recording. The observatory has a regularly updated manual with advice on running everything, from the gas and water supplies to completing the daily census and migration logs. The observatory's principal function is to keep ornithological records and all visitors to the observatory should regard this as an essential task. During migration periods it is important that there should be expe-rienced ornithologists in the party to ensure that accurate records are kept. Outside these periods, all those with an interest in natural history are welcome.

There are four Heligoland traps. The observatory supplies all rings and is well equipped with pliers, balances, rulers and identification guides. The observatory has a supply of bird bags, but welcomes the fact that many ringers bring their own. Mist-net poles are available, but visitors need to bring their own nets, spring-traps, tape-luring gear and torches. There is a ringing hut in which all this equipment is kept and to which birds, other than seabirds, are taken for ringing.

Those whose principal interest in visiting the island is photography should make arrangements in advance to get the required permit from the SNH Office at Cupar, Fife (01334 654038), but this is not needed for taking more casual photos or photographing birds in the hand whilst ringing.

Visitors are normally expected to book for a week. Full details of how to book and who to get in touch with are on the observatory's website. Whilst school and university parties are welcome it should be remembered that the observatory can only accommodate a total of six persons.

The observatory is run by the Isle of May Bird Observatory and Field Station Trust. The subscription is currently £15 a year; members receive the observatory's Annual Report and benefit from a priority period for booking accommodation.

Observatory opened:	1934
Total number of bird species recorded at the observatory:	279
Best bird year:	1998
Number of species recorded:	159
Total of birds ringed at the observatory:	267,388
Number of species:	182
Best ringing year:	1982
Number ringed:	9,998
Number of species:	77

Landguard

by Nigel Odin

THE LANDGUARD SITE

L andguard Bird Observatory is situated on the peninsula at the southern point of the Suffolk coast, immediately adjoining the seaside town of Felixstowe. The observatory operates from Landguard Right Battery, which consists of a man-made military structure and associated earthworks built up over the last hundred years. The recording area itself comprises a mere 26 hectares, making the daily census of birds extremely manageable. Unfortunately, the observatory buildings are not readily accessible to the casual visitor as the area is enclosed by rifle fencing to protect the ancient monument (and visitors) from potential harm. Several of the rooms have been adapted to accommodate an excellent observation point, ringing room, offices, welfare facilities and dormitory accommodation.

Landguard is an unusual site in that residential housing and a caravan park abut its north-eastern boundary and the UK's largest and busiest container port

Nigel Odin is indebted to his uncle who introduced him to the wonders of wild birds from a young age and to members of the Cardiff Naturalists' Society, who developed this interest. He was assistant warden at Sandwich Bay Bird Observatory from December 1985 to July 1987 and until November 1988 at Dungeness Bird Observatory. He spent the spring of 1989 at North Ronaldsay Bird Observatory before becoming warden at Landguard Bird Observatory from July 1989 to July 1995, after which he remained in Felixstowe.

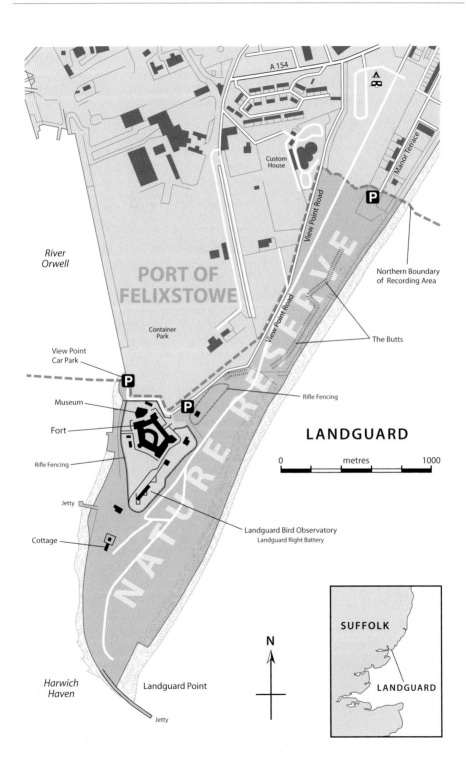

A 154

Custom House

View Point Road

River Orwell

PORT OF FELIXSTOWE

Container Park

Northern Boundary of Recording Area

Manor Terrace

The Butts

View Point Car Park

Rifle Fencing

Museum

Fort

LANDGUARD

0   metres   1000

Rifle Fencing

Jetty

Landguard Bird Observatory
Landguard Right Battery

Cottage

NATURE RESERVE

N

Harwich Haven

Landguard Point

Jetty

SUFFOLK

LANDGUARD

occupies the inland area on the banks of the River Orwell. Consequently, the skyline is dominated by vast cranes, radar towers and line upon line of stacked containers, with the sight of shipping continuously moving in and out of Harwich Haven towards the ports of Felixstowe, Harwich and Ipswich. These gargantuan ships, whose sheer size beggars belief, are up to 350 metres in length and carry in excess of 9,000 containers. The whole area is lit up by powerful lights 24 hours a day, 365 days a year and, although dimmed in recent years, it is still possible to read a newspaper by them at midnight. Evidence of man's influence on the area is all around you due to a long military presence and the needs of shipping and sea defences. It is difficult to imagine a less likely site for a bird observatory.

With easy access from Felixstowe and a diverse range of attractions, the Landguard Peninsula attracts between 600,000 and 700,000 visitors a year. The chief attraction is undoubtedly ship-watching and general recreational activities, such as walking and exercising dogs, are also common pastimes. Other popular attractions include Landguard Fort, Felixstowe Museum and the Landguard Nature Reserve. All this human pressure has not prevented a large part of Landguard being designated as a Site of Special Scientific Interest (SSSI) for its shingle plant communities and migrant landbirds. Additionally, recent research by the observatory has revealed the importance of the site for other taxa that would qualify it for SSSI status. Various parts of the site are also designated as a Scheduled Ancient Monument, a Local Nature Reserve and a County Wildlife Site, reinforcing the importance of the peninsula. With the interesting and busy seaside town of Felixstowe nearby, a varied range of potential activities is available along this very small stretch of the Suffolk coast. To accommodate and promote these diverse interests at Landguard, the various landowners and other interested parties came together to form the Landguard Forum (recently renamed the Landguard Partnership) and help manage the peninsula for the benefit of the entire community.

Geomorphologically speaking, the site consists of mixed sand and shingle of varying depths overlying muddy estuarine deposits. The northern end of the recording area has only a shallow covering of sand and shingle, with none at all in places, but further south towards the point the shingle is up to 16 metres deep. Despite the best efforts of longshore drift, the point is prevented from extending south-westwards by continuous dredging of the estuary to keep the channels open for shipping at all stages of the tide. A walk along the bare shingle reveals pebbles of diverse origin, with sharp eyes spying amber or fossilised sharks' teeth. Coal and old leather shoes from shipping sunk during the World Wars are regularly washed up, particularly after onshore gales, and the observatory organises monthly litter picks on the beaches, in conjunction with Suffolk Coastal District Council.

With all this sand and shingle, water retention is limited, except where the old estuarine deposits are not overlain with shingle. Apart from a few scattered Brambles and Elders on the open areas, cover for migrants is confined to areas near the old buildings. Ten Holm Oaks survive on the seaward side of the observatory ridge and a number of hybrid poplars and Sycamores grow on the landward side, where they are partially sheltered from the salt spray and easterly winds. Tamarisk and Privet prosper on the well-drained slopes and a few Hawthorns struggle to survive where the soil pH is higher. This vegetation was originally planted by the military as camouflage for the defences and the soil at the base of some of the earthworks is now at a slightly higher pH level as a result of creep. In general, vegetation at Landguard is extremely slow growing due to the poor quality soils, combined with a lack of water and the presence of a large and hungry population of rabbits capable of munching on anything and everything. In mid-winter rabbits can even be seen several feet off the ground on top of Bramble bushes, tree climbing or stealing food put out for the birds and the sight of a rabbit eating a discarded sausage roll or ham sandwich has to be seen to be believed.

Landguard is very exposed to the elements, in particular the wind and salt spray, and has one of the lowest rainfalls in Britain with an annual average, from 1969 to 2008, of just 536.9 millimetres (with a range of 390 to 756 millimetres; John Rowlands pers. comm.). Consequently the site can look extremely parched, uninviting and desolate.

HISTORY AND DEVELOPMENT OF THE OBSERVATORY

Due to its location overlooking the mouth of the strategically important Harwich Haven, military fortifications at Landguard were first built on the orders of Henry VIII and date back to at least 1543. The Dutch, under the command of Admiral de Ruyters, attacked the fort on 2 July 1667, but they were sent packing, thanks to the fort's defenders, under the command of Captain Nathaniel Darell. The imposing fort that now occupies the site was largely built in the 1740s, but was significantly altered during the reign of Queen Victoria. Landguard Right Battery, within which the observatory now resides, was constructed in the late 1890s and early 1900s, with various alterations and additions up to the Second World War. Abandoned in 1956, the area was largely neglected for the next 25 years, pillaged for anything of value and vandalised. But this was also the period when local naturalists started to visit the site. Ornithologically, little was known about Landguard, apart from references to a couple of Storm Petrels at the lighthouse in 1883 and a Snowy Owl, shot in 1885. Fire destroyed the lighthouse in 1925 and it was not rebuilt.

A hundred years ago the town of Felixstowe consisted of just a few houses, but expanded with the coming of the railway, which made trips to the seaside accessible to the mass of the people. The continuous growth of the port has also helped the town's population increase to 24,000 and another 6,000 live in nearby villages. By the 1970s the docks were acquiring land at an alarming rate, despite the fact that a large chunk had been designated as an SSSI to protect it. Local naturalists were alarmed at the loss of such valuable habitat, which was increasingly tarmacked over in the name of development, and were fighting a valiant rearguard action to protect what was left along the coastal fringe. Fortunately Suffolk County Council and Suffolk Coastal District Council took up ownership of the coastal strip, with the county council designating their holding as a Local Nature Reserve in 1975. These measures effectively prevented the docks from spreading to the North Sea.

Landguard became better known amongst the wider birding community with the occurrence of a Woodchat Shrike for five days in August 1977 and Suffolk's third Pallas's Warbler in October of the same year. Both species were national rarities at the time and, although the locals were starting to record many of the migrants passing through, it often takes a few rarities to spark a wider interest. Then in 1981, if anyone hadn't yet heard of Landguard, the appearance of a Lark Sparrow for nine days made national headlines and put the site on the map. This bird is the site's only addition to both the British and Western Palearctic lists (Charlton 1995), and local observers began to mull over the possibility of what other rarities might be discovered if regular coverage could be achieved.

The abandoned military buildings remained in government hands, as despite being offered the opportunity to take on the entire site, the local authorities were properly concerned about future expense. In 1982 the Landguard Right Battery was enclosed behind an imposing chain link and barbed wire fence to prevent public access. Although the local birders had thought that Landguard would be a good site for a bird observatory, it is amazing to think the construction of a security fence would be the major catalyst. The inaugural committee meeting to set up an observatory was attended by Bill Last, Steve Piotrowski, Derek Moore and Mick Wright. An agreement with the owners allowed the Suffolk Wildlife Trust to lease the site from November 1982 so that an independent observatory could be developed. I doubt that the owners had any idea back then what they were letting themselves in for! Net lanes were cleared, a Heligoland trap was built and some of the buildings were made more useable. Links were quickly developed with the neighbours, Halls Aggregates, to allow observatory members access to the welfare facilities alongside the new observatory at all hours.

Although there was some ringing in the late 1970s and early 1980s, it was the formation of Landguard Ringing Group in February 1983, following the official opening of the observatory in the previous November, which really got things going. The pioneers at that time had very little observatory experience between them, but they more than made up for this with enthusiasm and hard work. A large boost undoubtedly came in the guise of the government's Manpower Services Commission scheme, allowing renovation work to be undertaken. A second Heligoland trap was built (sadly now defunct) and a ringer-warden was employed. Like most government schemes designed to get people off the dole, this one ultimately came to an end (in 1988), leaving something of a void and only a small band of volunteers to run the site. By now though, the quality of the record keeping was beginning to reach bird observatory standards.

I was employed from July 1989, initially on a short-term contract, to look after the adjoining Nature Reserve in addition to the observatory. A report written following this stint was just the stimulus needed for the employment of a Ranger to manage the entire peninsula from the following spring. Derek Moore, then director of the Suffolk Wildlife Trust, was a great driving force in raising funds for this position as he realised that if the fledgling observatory and adjoining Nature Reserve were to survive and prosper then something needed to be done. Fortunately at this time, John Davies at Suffolk Coastal District Council appreciated the importance of Landguard as a resource for the entire community and, along with Derek, badgered the other members of the Landguard Forum to support the initiative, and the Landguard Ranger's position was created from April 1990, to be filled by me. This was only possible through funding from all of the partners, including Suffolk County Council, Suffolk Coastal District Council, Felixstowe Town Council, English Heritage, Natural England, Landguard Bird Observatory, Felixstowe History and Museum Society, Harwich Haven Authority, Port of Felixstowe and the Suffolk Wildlife Trust. This provided a much-needed boost for all the Landguard regulars and a period of stability for the observatory.

The following five years not only saw regular recording to observatory standards, but also allowed a vast improvement in the protection of the nature reserve and the ground nesting birds using it. As the remit of Suffolk Wildlife Trust evolved, resources were diverted to other areas, and by July 1995 I had left the Ranger's position. Paul Holmes took over the post and a separate Ringer/Warden was employed at migration times for the next few years. During Paul's time as Ranger, the emphasis of the Ranger's post gradually evolved from biological recording and reserve wardening towards other priorities and he ultimately left in 2001 to pursue a career in teaching. The Suffolk Wildlife Trust then relinquished the lease of the Right Battery from which the observatory operated, effectively abandoning it to its own fate. Despite these unforeseen developments, the now high standard of recording was maintained throughout this period.

However, these events provided just the impetus the observatory needed and, in 2002, the Landguard Conservation Trust was formed. One of its main tasks was to take on the lease so that the observatory could continue to function, flourish and develop. Beforehand, in 1997 and 1998, English Heritage had spent a considerable sum of money on renovation work at Landguard in an attempt to help preserve the entire monument and they were happy to lease Landguard Right Battery to Landguard Conservation Trust for the benefit of the observatory. The newly acquired charitable status allowed the fledgling Landguard Conservation Trust to apply for funding to further upgrade the facilities in the Right Battery. This allowed the important educational work of the observatory to continue and further funding followed from the Suffolk Environmental Trust, Suffolk Coastal District Council and other generous individuals. Members of Landguard Conservation Trust now raise funds to employ a seasonal warden, which complements the volunteer effort. Naturally, an observatory does not run itself and a lot of hard work has had to be done behind the scenes over many years to enable it to grow and develop. Whilst Landguard Bird Observatory first opened in 1982, it was only when the BOC modified its rules as to the provision of accommodation that, in 1997, it became an accredited observatory.

Meanwhile, further developments are in hand nearby as part of the Felixstowe South Reconfiguration: namely an expansion of the docks out into the River Orwell. This will not only result in even larger ships coming into port, but also in enhancements to the existing dock viewing facilities, including a visitors' centre, café and a permanent landing stage for the Felixstowe/Harwich/Shotley foot-ferry.

THE BIRDS

Ornithologically, the early part of the year can be extremely tedious. Mediterranean Gulls and Turnstones are easily seen scavenging in the View Point car park or scrounging bait from fishermen and small numbers of Snow Buntings favour the bleak shingle areas in most winters. Snow Buntings are easily attracted to millet and 250 were trapped in the Felixstowe area during a three-year study in 1997–1999. This revealed that 90% were first-winter birds, of which two-thirds were females and fewer than 1% were adult males. In terms of racial composition, 85% were of the Icelandic race *Plectrophenax nivalis insulae* and the remaining 15% were of the nominate race *P. n. nivalis* (Odin 2003a). It is fascinating and instructive to listen to birders picking out adult males in the wintering flocks when wiser heads know that they are often looking at young males of the nominate race that stand out from the rest of the flock. Most adult males, it seems, stay near the breeding-grounds with very few venturing this far south in the winter.

We are now building up a valuable database on our Mediterranean Gulls, both of birds ringed here and re-sightings of colour-ringed birds from the Low Countries. Our wintering Turnstones are fairly site-faithful. One regular individual, ringed here, was recorded present in the field in the Netherlands from its ring number by a sharp-eyed birder with a powerful telescope and it appears that the bird has a regular staging point in the Netherlands as it goes to and from its breeding-grounds, but visits us in the mid-winter period.

Apart from these enigmatic winter species, the only birds present are a few common species in very small numbers. Nevertheless, it is well worth a walk around in the winter to help one appreciate the rest of the year. This paucity of common species is partly the result of a recent run of mild winters, as a freezing cold spell from the east can reward those well wrapped up against the elements with some excellent birding. Waterfowl are then pushed out of the Baltic and the Low Countries, with cold and patient sea-watchers witnessing such winter gems as Smew, in addition to the mass of Wigeon.

A truly memorable sight was a flock of 71 Scaup moving south close in to the beach on 11 February 1991. Also passing are flocks of hungry Lapwing and Skylark heading south-west in search of unfrozen feeding grounds. As no mist-netting is carried out in the winter, ringing totals are normally rather dire then, unless a cold spell attracts birds to the food in the mouth of the Heligoland trap. A few apples are all that is needed to draw in winter thrushes and the only two Corn Buntings trapped at Landguard were enticed to grain in the cold spell of February 1991. Gulls are also easier to trap in cold weather, not just because of the cold, but because fewer folk are out with bags of bread in harsh conditions. People in this part of the world feed bread to gulls in the car parks due to an acute shortage of ducks in duck ponds!

Spring migration

Following mild winters, spring gets going in middle to late February with the evocative calls of Curlews abandoning local estuaries and flying north. Linnets begin to return from wintering grounds as far south as the Iberian Peninsula and a trickle of Stonechats passes through, the origin of which is a bit of a mystery as some show characteristics of the Continental race *Saxicola torquatus rubicola*. However, a small fall of five birds on 27 February 2008 included a ringed female, when none had been present the previous day. This bird was spring-trapped and found to have been ringed in the nest in Cumbria in April 2006, perhaps giving an indication as to the origin of at least some of the birds on spring passage. The first Blackbirds and Song Thrushes are moving by the month's end, but the first signs of spring don't start until early March if it's been a hard winter.

According to most accounts, British-breeding Great Tits are very sedentary, but nobody explained this to the Great Tits that visit us, with March being the peak month for spring movements. The March of 1994 was particularly busy when over 400 passed through, mostly from the 6th to the 11th, with a maximum of 100 on the 10th. These numbers are a ringer's nightmare as Great Tits are prone to finding mist-nets with little or no encouragement. However, the hard work is rewarded by the recoveries which suggest that our passing Great Tits buck the national trend and that movements of over 100 kilometres are not unexpected. Whilst ringers like to dream that all these spring migrants are moving back to the Continent, having spent the winter in Britain, the reality is different as all the proven movements so far have been within East Anglia.

Migration throughout the remainder of March and into April is dominated by birds moving back to the Continent after the winter or migrants coming into the country for the summer. A light south or south-easterly wind at this time of year, with a bit of murk and drizzle thrown in for good measure, can produce a fall of chats and Firecrests. Just the sort of weather in which you might opt to stay indoors is just the sort of weather to get the Landguard regulars out hoping for a Bluethroat of the white-spotted southern and central European race *Luscinia svecica cyanecula* amongst the Black Redstarts and Wheatears that Landguard is famous for. Wing measurements of spring Wheatears show that 44% are of the Greenland race *Oenanthe oenanthe leucorhoa*, with 15% of the nominate race *O. o. oenanthe*. Those indeterminable on wing length, though, do show plumage characteristics indicative of Greenland race birds. Wheatear numbers in March can be very poor if conditions for migration are good, when British breeding birds fly directly on to their breeding areas without needing to pause, at Landguard at any rate. Greenland race birds have appeared as early as 8 April, though peak numbers occur at the end of April and into early May. Landguard is an excellent site for them to fatten up on their long way to the north and west, where their nesting grounds will still be frozen over when British Wheatears are already incubating their first clutches. Weight gain of migrants is such that some birds are positively obese by the time they leave.

Warblers trickle through in spring, with the occasional impressive fall such as on 2 May 2004 when at least 100 Whitethroats passed through. National rarities start to put in an appearance from the end of April, with one major unexpected rarity in 1997 being a Spectacled Warbler. This bird, the second record for Britain, was found by Mike Marsh and stayed for a week.

Regular monitoring of bird numbers over the years allows us to produce trends that indicate the fortunes of a species. Sadly, several appear to be in terminal decline, with the status of once-common species such as Cuckoo, Turtle Dove and Spotted Flycatcher being indicative of a sorry state of affairs. Whether numbers will recover has yet to be seen, but it should be remembered that whilst Whitethroats were ubiquitous (prior to a massive population crash in 1968 and 1969), Landguard's largest spring fall was, nevertheless, in 2004. What is important here is that monitoring has to continue.

Late May and June sees spring migration grinding to a halt, except for a few 'laggards' and traditional late spring migrants such as Reed Warbler and Spotted Flycatcher. Yet, this time of year can still produce a good run of scarcities and rarities when few other migrants are present, especially in easterly-influenced weather conditions. One memorable morning was 30 May 1992, following a week of east and south-easterly winds that had already brought us a singing Greenish Warbler. Jim Askins was covering the early netting session and my lie-in was interrupted at 04:15 hrs, to be awoken to the sight of a superb male Red-breasted Flycatcher. After this, the heavens opened up with some phenomenal thunderstorms, temporarily bringing catching to a stop. When the deluge had passed we were treated to an excellent selection of unexpected birds, including a young male Red-footed Falcon, four Grey-headed Wagtails *Motacilla flava thunbergi*, a Marsh Warbler, a Wood Warbler and a 'White Wagtail' of one of the eastern races that we never did put a name to. Other migrants, though, were conspicuous by their absence. This is often the case at this time of year – Britain and Ireland's eighth Trumpeter Finch turned up at the end of May 2005 on a morning that was almost completely devoid of any other migrants.

Throughout both spring and autumn migration periods, observers spend the first few hours each morning recording the 'vis. mig.' (visual migration). These counts involve standing on top of the observatory ridge counting the little dots flying over. Most birds are identified by call or by the observer's familiarity with the jizz of a species. This somewhat specialised form of birding can be very frustrating for birdwatchers who, by definition, like to watch birds, as it is essentially bird-recording and not birdwatching. Strangely, regardless of the season, most birds follow the coast in a south-westerly direction. Migration can often be confusing and birds flying south in the spring will definitely have you scratching your head. Sorry folks, but some birds migrate south in the spring!

Diurnal or daytime migrants, such as the Goldfinches, Linnets and Yellowhammers that have spent the winter in Britain, migrate for the first few hours in the morning and then settle somewhere suitable to feed for the remainder of the day. It is thought they roughly follow the East Anglian coastline and become concentrated at Landguard Point before crossing the mouth of the River Orwell into Essex. Many then probably turn east over Kent, gaining height so that they can see the 'other side', and move across to the Continent. Interestingly, it is not quite that simple, as further north up the Suffolk coast at Orford Ness, 'vis. mig.' is almost non-existent, with birds presumably cutting inland at this point, and further south, at Walton-on-the-Naze in Essex, migration is also poorly recorded as birds presumably cut inland of this prominent headland.

Not only do (some) birds that have wintered in Britain and Ireland move south in spring, but returning summer migrants can do the same. If I haven't totally confused you by now, then the concept of Swallows and Yellow Wagtails flying south in spring certainly will. What is thought to be happening here is that some summer migrants overshoot their intended destination in warm southerly-influenced weather conditions and basically turn around and reorientate, following the coast back south until they reach their intended arrival location.

If conditions over the river mouth are murky or foggy, some of these diurnal migrants will come to ground at Landguard until the weather improves, rather than risking flying out over water. Conditions may be good enough to follow the East Anglian coast, but they hesitate if fog is encountered. This then gets really confusing for observers, as birds that have just headed past in a southerly direction often turn round and head back northwards over the docks, following the river bank. Hopefully these complexities haven't put you off birding at Landguard, but don't worry if you get frustrated at being unable to put a name to everything that flies over. And remember that not all birds with distinctive calls are identified, even by the experts. It is indeed concerning to think how many rarities we may have missed. With a bewildering range of escaped cage birds also on the move the situation can become very confusing as not all escapees are as easily identifiable in flight as a Scarlet Macaw *Ara macao.* 'Vis. mig.' in spring runs mostly from March to early June and in autumn from mid-July to November and is at its most spectacular from the end of September to mid-November.

The breeding season

During summer, Landguard Nature Reserve supports a small population of Ringed Plovers that peaked at 14 pairs in 1997. Numbers then declined to just four or five pairs, with only six chicks surviving to fledge in the past 10 years. Site fidelity is high, but the adult population is getting aged and only persists due to recruitment from elsewhere. Oystercatchers and Little Terns often attempt to rear young, but with very poor success recently. However, Linnets are still present in good numbers and in some years the observatory rings as many as 10% of the total ringed throughout Britain and Ireland. Wheatear and Black Redstart have both nested, but not in recent years, although a few pairs of Black Redstarts still manage to rear young on the adjoining dock complex.

Autumn migration

'Autumn' passage is a difficult concept to explain in June when summer has often hardly arrived. Ornithologically speaking, autumn is the period after the breeding (or attempted breeding) season, so the time of autumn passage varies from species to species and from bird to bird. June is an odd month as not only do oddities turn up, but juvenile dispersal brings us species that we don't record here at other times of the year. Coal Tits (of the British race *Periparus ater britannicus*) only tend to appear here at the end of June and our two records of Marsh Tit were also of dispersing juveniles at this time of the year. Some very rare birds have also been noted in mid-summer, when a male Black-headed Wagtail *Motacilla flava feldegg* on 30 June 1985 was only the fifth British record. Crossbills start moving in eruption years and autumn is already under way for Lapwings and Curlews. The latter trickle south all day and night as failed and non-breeders head down from the hills to moult on the estuaries.

Early autumn migration is thus a fairly relaxed, unrushed affair with as much juvenile dispersal as long-distance migration. Records of Great Spotted Woodpeckers have increased in recent years; indeed, there were no records at all in the 10 years prior to the formation of the observatory, but a spectacular increase has occurred since (Figure 1).

This mirrors increases elsewhere in Suffolk and also nationally across its range. Great Spotted Woodpeckers of the British race *Dendrocopos major anglicus* are supposedly highly sedentary, though the Landguard records show a light spring passage from mid-March to early June, with juvenile dispersal from the end of June until as late as early December – and with just a couple of mid-winter sightings. Interestingly, none of the 82 birds trapped have been adults. Two were thought to be of the more migratory nominate race *D. m. major*, due to their longer wing-lengths, but the rest are presumed to be of British origin. Speculation that the continental race *D. m. pinetorum* (from west and central Europe) might also occur has yet to be confirmed by ringing recoveries (Coulson & Odin 2007).

Three recoveries of Great Spotted Woodpecker have resulted from ringing activities at Landguard. One, ringed on 29 June 2002 was, unusually, killed by a dog, 26 kilometres away, on 24 November the same year; another ringed 77 kilometres away at Burgh Castle, Norfolk, on 16 November 2002 was controlled at

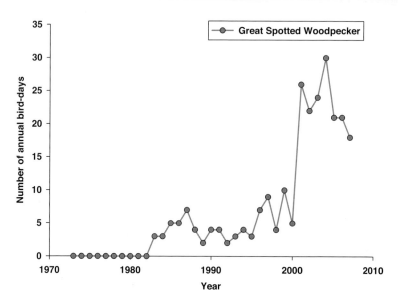

Figure 1. *Annual bird-day numbers of Great Spotted Woodpeckers at Landguard 1973–2008.*

Landguard on 5 April 2003; and a third, ringed on 23 August 2003 was re-caught 112 kilometres to the north at Sheringham on 18 September 2003. These are more distant than might be expected for a sedentary species, but perhaps population pressure is forcing juvenile birds to wander more in search of a territory.

One of the earliest autumn migrants to leave our shores for Africa is the Wood Warbler, with peak passage in the last week of July and early August. Wood Warbler is now almost extinct as a breeding species in Suffolk and it is almost exclusively juveniles which stop at Landguard on what is presumably the first leg of a long-haul journey to wintering areas in equatorial Africa. Pied Flycatchers also start to appear at the end of July and early August, with numbers at Landguard greatly influenced by the prevalence of easterly-influenced weather. Local birders in August and September know that westerlies bring us migrants of British origin on their way south, with Willow Warblers always the dominant species.

Easterlies bring us fewer birds in total, but as soon as Pied Flycatchers start to appear the chance of a Wryneck, Red-backed Shrike or Ortolan Bunting is greatly increased and the ringers have been known to ring almost as many Pied Flycatchers as Willow Warblers in an August dominated by easterlies. Interestingly, with westerlies, migration is done and dusted by mid-day but with easterlies it continues all day and in some cases doesn't even start until mid-afternoon with the arrival of birds which have crossed the North Sea. Unsettled weather with showers and murk thrown in for good measure is always more exciting for observers, although a lot less pleasant for the birds attempting to migrate, and the periods immediately following thunderstorms can result in a large number of grounded birds. Clear sunny conditions produce some visual migration early on, but sometimes the peninsula can appear almost bird-less apart from flocks of feeding Linnets and a few Wheatears lingering here to fatten up on their way south.

September was formerly the peak month for east coast migration hot spots, but this has become hard work on most days, with very few grounded migrants present in recent years. This may be due to changing weather patterns, but many believe there have been huge declines in migratory bird populations across Europe over the past 50 years. However, there are still some impressive falls, with, for example, three Wrynecks, 25 Whinchats, 60 Redstarts and an Icterine Warbler on 19 September 1995.

Clear skies with north-westerly winds are the curse of Landguard in the autumn when the bushes can seem completely devoid of life, but the Barred Warblers seen here are just as likely to be found on such apparently bird-less days as in falls during easterlies. As in the spring, some superb birds can turn up on days when little else is around, with Saturday 4 September 1993 bringing us not only Suffolk's first Yellow-breasted Bunting and the first Rose-coloured Starling in the county since 1960, but also a Barred Warbler for good measure. The next Saturday brought only the second British record of a 'Caspian' Stonechat of the race *Saxicola torquatus variegata* and an excellent, accurate description and sketches taken in the field resulted in its correct identification, as it wasn't realised at the time exactly what had been encountered (Ling 1996). Not to be

As well as impressive falls, winds from the east can bring good numbers of migrants to the east-coast observatories with Wrynecks featuring on a regular basis (Steve Stansfield – www.wildlifeimages.eu).

outdone, the ringers trapped a magnificent first for the county at this time of the year in the shape of a Lanceolated Warbler which, undoubtedly, would have been overlooked but for the perseverance of those manning the nets.

Although Landguard is known for unusual birds, this is only because we are persistent enough to spend the necessary man-hours counting, scrutinising and correctly identifying common species. For example, in the large flocks of Starlings we have encountered five juvenile Rose-coloured Starlings in recent autumns, the only other Suffolk record being a juvenile found at Benacre Broad in 2007 by, unsurprisingly, a Landguard stalwart. It is only by becoming familiar with common species that we tend to notice the unusual ones, which are really little more than an occupational hazard of spending many hours in the field.

The migratory activity of some common species, say Wrens and Dunnocks, is best understood by looking at the ringing data. The number of Wrens present at Landguard is largely dependent on the severity of the winter weather. Following runs of mild winters, up to three pairs attempt to breed but may not survive after a cold snap and it can take several years before they start nesting again. Several individuals winter on site but, once again, they can be killed off by freezing conditions. Annual ringing totals have varied from 22 in 1986 to 158 in 1993. Generally, no new Wrens are ringed from the end of November to early March, with new birds being trapped in early March and peaking in early April. Although numbers are small, some individuals do appear to have different plumage characteristics, leading to speculation that they may actually be of Continental origin.

Post-juvenile dispersal from nearby and the progeny of our own local pairs account for a handful of new birds ringed in the summer months, but none at all have been trapped from mid-May to August following hard winters when the local population perishes.

The autumn passage of Wrens gets underway in mid-September and continues into November, with a marked peak of activity from the third week of September and through October. The best day-total was 17 ringed on 17 October 1993 contributing to a monthly total of 96. The bulk of these autumn Wrens could well be of a fairly local origin when juveniles wander in search of suitable sites or move down to the coast to spend the winter. However, as in the spring, some individuals show structural and plumage features which differ from those of the local birds (Odin 1996). Are we perhaps getting some foreign birds?

The Dunnock is also a ubiquitous species in Britain and up to 15 pairs nest at Landguard, producing large numbers of young in some years. The species' occurrence at Landguard involves more than just the local breeding population and is best considered by an analysis of the ringing data. Small numbers are ringed on spring passage from the end of February to early May. The prolific local breeding population and juvenile dispersal from nearby sites account for new birds ringed in the summer months, but the trapping of new adults from early May until autumn passage is almost unknown.

Autumn passage gets underway in September and peters out in the first week of November. Quite large numbers pass through in some years, with a day-maximum of 36 new birds ringed on 1 October 1984, out of an estimated 100 present on site. However, a good autumn passage of Dunnocks does not always follow years in which good numbers of juveniles have been ringed here in the summer months, suggesting that some of the autumn birds are not of local origin. Interestingly, Dunnocks are often seen flying south in the autumn, with a 'vis. mig.' daily-maximum of 36 on 19 September 1992, which is a bizarre sight for those more used to seeing their Dunnocks grovelling around at ground level in the bushes. We await our first foreign recovery for this species which is surely more migratory than many people believe.

By the end of September the last of our summer visitors are departing and the first winter visitors arrive. Song Thrush passage starts at this time and greyer northern Continental nominate race *Turdus philomelos philomelos* birds are far commoner on passage than their browner local cousins. Trapping shows that many of the Song Thrushes move through quickly and are subsequently re-caught in western France and the Iberian Peninsula (with one to Morocco), where many sadly end up in the cooking pot. Why birds from the Low Countries should migrate through our area to Iberia, which includes a couple of sea cross-ings en route, remains a mystery.

Overhead movements of hirundines, pipits and finches can be spectacular at the end of September and into October and on some days over 10,000 birds have been counted moving overhead in the first few hours of a morning. Most 'vis. mig.' is done and dusted by 10:00 hrs, save on exceptional mornings when it can carry on a bit longer. The species most frequently involved are Swallow, House Martin, Meadow Pipit, Greenfinch, Goldfinch and Linnet, with good numbers of

Siskin and redpolls in irruption years. Observers here hope that the good people of southern England will keep their bird feeders well stocked in winter to feed the hordes of Greenfinches that pass through here in some autumns, as that's probably as far as they go. By way of contrast, many of our Linnets are known to be heading for Spain.

A light spring overhead passage of Grey Wagtails peaks in mid-March to mid-April, with a handful of dispersing juveniles turning up throughout the summer in most years. Autumn passage runs from the end of August to mid-November, with a distinct peak from mid-September to early October, whilst none has been recorded from December to February. In the early years of the observatory the annual bird-day totals were in single figures, but increased to 119 bird-days in 2005, though the reasons for this are unknown. This species has been declining nationally, which suggests that more attention needs to be paid to the vast banks of data held by bird observatories, in addition to traditional methods of population monitoring, to present a more balanced view of such bird populations. There is no reason why the species should stop here on migration so, to find out where they are going, a CD of Grey Wagtail song and calls is piped through to speakers at the small pond in the mouth of the Heligoland trap, luring inquisitive juveniles down to investigate. Morning use of these calls from the end of August to the end of October has so far led to three recoveries: a bird trapped the following spring, 125 kilometres away in Greater London; another taken by a cat the following spring 66 kilometres away in Lowestoft; and an individual trapped on 9 September 2008 which was re-caught 225 kilometres across the North Sea in Holland exactly one month later. But it's a start, considering almost nothing is known of the destination or origins of the Grey Wagtails that fly over east coast migration sites.

Another species engaging the minds of ringers and birdwatchers over recent years is the 'redpoll complex', which was recently 'split' by the elevation of two of the races or sub-species to full species status. Thus, Lesser Redpoll *Carduelis cabaret* and Common Redpoll *Carduelis flammea* are the redpoll species to be found regularly at Landguard. In autumn, redpolls start to pass through at the end of September, with passage continuing into November. Archival ringing information on Common Redpolls is limited due to its former status, but fortunately extra data was noted on the ringing schedules for many birds trapped here in the past, which has allowed old records to be assigned retrospectively to one species or the other. Very few records of Common Redpoll had been noted before November, until 2005, when several adults were trapped in mid-October in easterly winds. Interestingly, these early adults were trapped on days when no Lesser Redpolls were present and were often caught in the late morning, suggesting they were fresh in after crossing the North Sea. The normal peak of redpoll catching here is in the first few hours, with birds starting to appear early in the morning, often before the sun is up. Lesser Redpolls only rarely occur on easterlies and the best trapping conditions are on clear sunny mornings with light west or north-westerly winds. Into November, the Common Redpolls occur more frequently mixed in with the Lesser Redpoll flocks. These are presumably birds that have arrived on the easterlies and then joined up with their near-cousins before wandering down to Landguard.

The Common Redpolls in November are mainly birds in their first-winter, which is where the fun starts. Adults of both species are easily separated as are the majority of the juveniles. However, youngsters are occasionally trapped with plumage characteristics that really have us scratching our heads. Is the difference between these two species as clear cut as the birding establishment would have us believe? Or do they grade into each other or even interbreed? Much has still to be learned about Common Redpolls and their movements, and the timing of their spring passage in southern Britain has been overlooked in the past. Currently, catching in the spring is revealing that they move through Landguard in May following influx years (Odin & Cope 2005). No doubt we will unravel the complexities in forthcoming years, but we might end up with more questions than answers.

At the same time as the work on redpolls is proceeding, observers are treated to one of the great Landguard migration spectacles. Woodpigeons move south in late October and the first half of November in vast numbers. Our 'best' autumn to date was 1994 when a staggering 86,109 were counted. In 2005, a total of 81,098 moved south on 13 days from 22 October to 14 November, including 30,700 on 4 November and a truly awesome record count of 45,550 the next day. A few feral Rock Doves usually get caught up in all this excitement and at least 669 Stock Doves were noted amongst the 2005 movements. There has been much speculation in relation to the origin of these birds, with some suggesting that they are of Fennoscandian origin. There are a number of reasons, though, why this may not be the case. Movements only occur on bright sunny mornings with wind speeds of less than force 6 to 7 and stop almost immediately if the weather changes, becoming overcast or rainy. Easterly winds are unproductive, but cool crisp north-westerly winds produce the biggest counts. Movements start about an hour after first light and are normally petering out by 10:00 hrs.

The Woodpigeons are not seen coming in from the sea, but move in a south-westerly direction roughly parallel with the coastline and in a wide band from a kilometre offshore to about five kilometres inland. The migrating birds can be concentrated into quite a narrow corridor on some mornings and it is only over the sea that strong north-westerly winds drift them further out. Birds departing from Suffolk towards Essex occasionally change bearing to a more west-south-westerly direction, gaining height as they go out over the water at the tip of Landguard Point. If flocks were of a Continental origin they wouldn't be seen here so soon after dawn, unless they had migrated into East Anglia unseen on previous days or overnight. We suspect the flocks are leaving Suffolk woodlands not long before they come en masse over our heads at Landguard. Other diurnal migrants from the Continent, such as Starling and Chaffinch, presumably set off from the Low Countries at first light at the same time of year as these pigeon movements occur and do not start arriving from the sea until much before 11:00 hrs. If Woodpigeons were Continental drift-migrants, then presumably they wouldn't be passing over here so early in the day. None of the birds involved in these mass migrations are caught by the observatory for ringing as they do not pause to feed and the bulk of any we do ring are juveniles caught soon after fledging. British Woodpigeons seem to be rather sedentary and the bulk of the birds trapped here get shot, in the winter months, within 20 kilometres. This has not prevented two of our young Woodpigeons venturing to France and getting shot there, so maybe some local birds do get caught up with the migrants. In summary, the current ringing data do not enable us to interpret the observed large-scale movements (Wernham *et al.* 2002).

Sea-watching is carried out in autumn from the top of the bird observatory ridge, which has an excellent sheltered spot from where to watch in poor weather conditions. Waders and waterfowl regularly move south, with many autumns producing counts of Brent Geese in excess of 10,000. The evocative calls of Brents, chattering amongst themselves, can be a moving experience and one can imagine the sheer relief of these tired flocks as they get their first sight of the vast estuary in front of them, providing a welcome site for feeding and resting. The adults must be extremely pleased to bring their youngsters to a safe haven after their first major flight over the open ocean.

The most interesting sea-watching conditions at Landguard are often when the weather is at its worst. A good onshore wind with heavy, squally showers can bring a range of seabirds within sight of the patient watchers in the observatory, who can be rewarded with Sooty Shearwaters, Leach's Petrels, skuas and perhaps even a Sabine's Gull. As the autumn progresses, it is interesting to watch the passage of different species. Early autumn brings a steady passage of Oystercatchers, Curlews and terns. The first Wigeon and Pintail start to go by in September and from mid-October onwards Goldeneye and saw-billed duck appear, along with Shelduck returning to our shores from moulting grounds in the Waddenzee.

In autumn, as in the spring, it is often the rarities that really get the pulse going and 26 October 1995 was one of those days with very few birds around, starting just after first light with the discovery of a superb adult male Red-flanked Bluetail. Whilst this bird was being processed, a Rough-legged Buzzard headed past and later that morning a Red-rumped Swallow flew through with a couple of Swallows. All this on a day when the ringers managed to ring only 14 birds, albeit including the 'bluetail' and two Long-eared Owls! Nearby, a Pied Wheatear was in the docks and a total of three Pallas's Warblers and a Yellow-browed Warbler were at other sites on the Felixstowe peninsula.

Ten days later was another day of few birds, the only real interest being a Desert Finch *Rhodospiza obsoleta* that dropped in briefly during the morning. Much discussion followed as to its origin, until a large pipit was found at lunchtime. This was duly identified as a Blyth's (Marsh & Odin 1994) and was, at the time of its discovery, the second British record. Interestingly, the first British record was a specimen collected in October 1862 and correctly identified at the Natural History Museum (then based in London) by Ken Williamson in 1963. The Landguard bird gave excellent views over the next week to over 2,000 observers and was one of the biggest twitches ever recorded at the time. However, this figure has been exceeded several times since, following the increasing interest in rare birds and the use of pagers, and at least 6,000 visitors saw Trumpeter Finch here in 2005.

October and November falls can keep ringers incredibly busy, with the biggest total to date being on 16 October 1988 when 506 birds were ringed, including 268 of the estimated 500 Robins present that day. Autumn falls can often bring a single dominant species but little else, and 239 Blackbirds were ringed on 17 November 2005 out of the 247 birds trapped.

Autumn slowly peters out at the end of November and winter sets in. This doesn't prevent observers going out, though, as autumn often has a sting in its tail as on 6 December 1985 when the third British record of a Southern Grey Shrike (of the central Asian race *Lanius meridionalis pallidirostris*) was discovered (Marsh 1987). At this time, any cold spell on the near Continent can bring an influx of waterfowl moving offshore, with Fieldfares and a small number of Woodcock. Fewer Blackbirds now reach Britain at the traditional time of mid- to late October, possibly due to milder winters and the increased prevalence of bird-feeders in urban gardens on the Continent, and their peak passage period is slipping later and later into November. December sees the 'laggards' arriving, but this might be the peak time in future years if current trends continue.

When the observatory's pioneers first visited the peninsula, they surely dreamed of the rarities to be found with more regular coverage. Apart from those already mentioned, other county firsts have included Crested Lark, Thrush Nightingale, Desert Wheatear, Paddyfield Warbler, Subalpine Warbler, Sardinian Warbler and Dusky Warbler. Other memorable events were the obliging Great Shearwater seen following a trawler close inshore for over half an hour, the observers' shock on finding a Yellow-billed Cuckoo, and the discovery of a dead Red-billed Tropicbird on the tideline (Knox *et al.* 1994), together with the exceptional ring recoveries, particularly a Robin recovered in Russia and the recapture of a Goldcrest ringed in the Czech Republic. I think we can say that we, and the pioneers, can be well pleased.

OTHER FAUNA AND FLORA

Mammals and reptiles

Offshore, seals are regular enough, but cetaceans are thought to avoid the peninsula due to the underwater noise generated by the high density of shipping using the area. This has not prevented stray whales from visiting and there has been a pleasing rise in the number of sightings of Harbour Porpoise in recent years. Bats are infrequent visitors and a large 'fruit bat' flying around over the estuary one morning was definitely rather surprising and presumably ship-assisted. Other mammals recorded include Yellow-necked Mouse, right at the northern edge of its British range, and a House Mouse, trapped in 2004, was the first to be recorded at the observatory, although it was probably a pest species in the days of military occupation. Grass Snakes were recorded for the first time in 2004, which seems to tie in with an increase in this species' range throughout east Suffolk. Unfortunately, in almost 500 years of military occupation, the human occupants of the site were more interested in soldiering than biological recording.

Invertebrates

Moth traps have been run nightly from March to November since 1991 and the number of species recorded is fast approaching 900. At least 20 Red Data Book species have been recorded and the micromoth *Agonopterix curvipunctosa* is regular here but only rarely recorded elsewhere in the UK (Odin 2003b, 2004). Other notable micromoths recorded include *Ethmia bipunctella*, *Melissoblaptes zelleri* and *Pima boisduvaliella*. Worryingly, many of the scarcer grass moths have been getting rarer over the years or have even disappeared for reasons unknown. Four of the first five British records of Pale-shouldered Cloud were found here (Odin 2003c), as well as an impressive list of rarities which easily rivals the list of rare birds. We have even recorded four species here which are classed as extinct in Britain (Many-lined, Small Ranunculus, Orache Moth and Gypsy Moth). Very little moth recording was carried out prior to 1991, so when a couple of Spurge Hawkmoths were trapped in 2003 it was interesting to discover that the species had formerly been noted here when a caterpillar was found by the Rev. E. N. Bloomfield around 1865. Common butterfly species enjoy the natural grassland areas and attractive migrants, such as Camberwell Beauty and Swallowtail, are on the site list. Landguard is of national importance for recording migrant insect species, and it is interesting to count the Red Admirals and Hornets migrating south alongside the birds in the autumn.

With such a highly specialised habitat it would be a surprise if a number of other rare and specialised insects were not present. Although other taxa are less well studied, Red Data Book species recorded at Landguard include a spider, a parasitic fly and a sand wasp. Nationally scarce species include a hairy-legged bee, a nomad bee, a flea-beetle, a weevil, a hoverfly, a yellow-faced bee, a mining bee, a leaf-cutter bee and Roesel's Bush Cricket.

Flowering plants

Landguard is of international importance for its vegetated shingle. Botanically, the site has been well studied and nearly 500 species of flowering plants have been recorded, including over a third of all British grasses. Regional and national rarities, including the aptly named Stinking Goosefoot, grow here and Landguard is currently the only British site for Woody Fleabane. Just above the bare wave-washed shingle the density of Sea-kale is one of the highest in the world. This then gives way to rabbit-cropped acid grassland dominated by lichens. Man-made earthworks around the military structures and sea defences support accidentally and deliberately introduced scrub. County rarities include Small-flowered Buttercup, Upright Chickweed and Ray's Knotgrass, along with a large number of nationally rare plants including Sea Pea, Suffocated Clover and many grasses. Dittander was formerly dominant but has been cut back in recent years due to its invasive nature, despite the fact that it is a nationally rare plant. Interestingly, the Tamarisk on the ridges was first introduced into Britain at Landguard, and the Hoary Cress on site is another military import, said to have arrived with soldiers returning from the conflicts in the Crimea.

ACCESS AND ACCOMMODATION

Landguard is easily accessed along the A14, and following it east past the entrance to the Port of Felixstowe leads the visitor over a level crossing. Taking a right turn at the traffic lights, the open access areas of Landguard Nature Reserve are accessible from the three car parks which are signposted with brown 'leisure and tourism' signs. Landguard Bird Observatory is managed by Landguard Conservation Trust under licence from English Heritage on land owned by the Department of Culture, Media and Sport. Membership of the observatory is available to anyone interested in its aims and 'Friends of Landguard Bird Observatory' support the observatory and receive regular newsletter updates.

Visits to the observatory depend on the availability of volunteers to show you around and must be arranged in advance by contacting Landguard Bird Observatory, at View Point Road, Felixstowe, Suffolk IP11 3TW; on telephone 01394 673782. Please see the observatory website for current arrangements, recent annual reports and latest bird news. All members and visitors must also undergo a Health and Safety induction before being allowed onto the site. Basic dormitory accommodation and welfare facilities are available for members and visitors, and Felixstowe has plenty of hotels and bed-and-breakfast establishments. For more local information, contact the Tourist Information Centre on 01394 276770.

Observatory opened:	November 1982
(accredited to the Bird Observatories Council: 1997)	
Total number of bird species recorded at the observatory:	294
(plus 45 escapes and one tide-line corpse)	
Best bird year:	2004
Number of species recorded:	205
Total of birds ringed at the observatory:	147,215
Number of species:	157
Best ringing year:	1998
Number ringed:	9,622
Number of species:	81
Best years for number of species ringed:	1988 and 1997
Number of species ringed:	84

North Ronaldsay

by Kevin Woodbridge

DESCRIPTION

The Orkney Islands lie off the northern coast of mainland Scotland. North Ronaldsay is isolated in the far north-eastern corner of the archipelago, with Shetland a further 80 kilometres beyond, to the north-east. On reasonably clear days, both Fair Isle (40 kilometres to the north-east) and Foula (80 kilometres to the north-north-east), with their height and cliffs, are easily visible from the island, but the opposite cannot be said; even on the clearest days it is difficult to pick out the lighthouse on low-lying North Ronaldsay from these islands, and the land is only discernible in the calmest of conditions.

The larger island of Sanday is the nearest neighbour to the south, separated by

Kevin Woodbridge came to North Ronaldsay in 1977 as the island's general practitioner and has been associated with the North Ronaldsay Bird Observatory since its foundation. He took a break from his medical career in 1976 to work at Gibraltar Point Bird Observatory as shorebird warden and volunteer, during which time he undertook his ringing training. He has chaired the BOC from 1994 to the present time, and has served on the Ringing Committee of the British Trust for Ornithology.

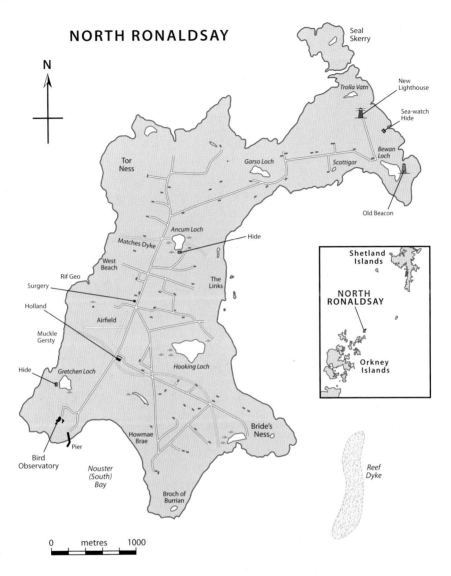

NORTH RONALDSAY

N

Seal
Skerry

Trolia Vatn

New
Lighthouse

Sea-watch
Hide

Tor
Ness

Garso Loch

Scottigar

Bewan
Loch

Old Beacon

Ancum Loch

Hide

Matches Dyke

West
Beach

Rif Geo

Surgery

Holland

Airfield

Muckle
Gersty

Hide

Gretchen Loch

The
Links

Hooking Loch

Shetland
Islands

NORTH
RONALDSAY

Orkney
Islands

Bird
Observatory

Pier

Howmae
Brae

Nouster
(South)
Bay

Bride's
Ness

Broch of
Burrian

Reef
Dyke

0   metres   1000

the shallow but treacherous North Ronaldsay Firth. The Firth, nearly five kilometres at its narrowest, and never swum, is open to the Atlantic at its western end with the North Sea to the east – a recipe for spectacular seas with massive swells from both directions meeting high winds, all stirred up by an 11-knot tide. To describe waves as being as big as cathedrals is hardly an exaggeration; it is definitely not the place for the inexperienced to be messing around in small boats. Further south, stretching some 64 kilometres along the east coast of the Orkney archipelago, lie Stronsay, Deerness (on the east Orkney mainland) and the southern isles of Burray and South Ronaldsay (linked by the Churchill Causeways, also known as the Churchill Barriers) together with a number of smaller holms and islets. This entire coastline is known to be good for migrant birds, but they are rarely found in the concentrations that occur regularly on North Ronaldsay.

About 24 kilometres to the west lie Westray and Papa Westray, most notable for their breeding seabirds. Eday is a similar distance away, but more central among the north isles, lying off the west side of Sanday and south of Westray. The Red Head of Eday is clearly visible from North Ronaldsay and the regular visiting Peregrines presumably originate from this area. In fact, all the outer northern Orkney isles and the inner island of Rousay can be seen from the south end of North Ronaldsay, though Stronsay can only be located by its wind generators, peeping above Sanday in the foreground. Wideford Hill, beside Kirkwall, and the hills of Evie on mainland Orkney, can also be seen in good visibility, some 48 kilometres distant, but the mainland of Scotland is well below the horizon.

The geological substrate of North Ronaldsay is sandstone formed from sedimentation onto an ancient lakebed. This has created an excellent source of flagstones, reflected in the vernacular building style. Vertebrate fossils are rare, despite the famous fossil fish sites in the region, but petrified sand ripples and mud cracks are common. This sandstone is overlain with a varying depth of glacial clay, with substantial additional accumulations of shell sand on the south and east side of the island, forming extensive sandy bays between rocky outcrops, with some remnant inland dunes. The exposed Atlantic coasts on the west and north sides of the island are entirely rocky and display a succession of low cliffs, boulder-beaches and small bays with varying grades of shingle. The low cliff stretches are punctuated by deep inlets known as geos (the 'g' is soft in the local dialect), sometimes terminating in a shallow cave; one of them, Rif Geo, retains

Whilst rough seas can be an issue for the ferry-crossing to the island, large numbers of seabirds can be counted on sea-watches during autumnal gales (Kevin Woodbridge).

an arched roof.

Similar, but less dramatic, rocky shorelines also occur on the coasts most open to the south-east and exposed to the North Sea. Off the north end of the island, Seal Skerry marks the northern extremity of Orkney. It is reputed to be accessible on foot during extreme spring ebb tides, though still requiring a waist-deep wade, but it would be foolhardy to take on the challenge. About a mile to the east of the southern arm of the island lies the Reef Dyke, a submerged rock and the site of many wrecks. Again, it is claimed that a man has stood dry-footed (in waders) on the dyke at extreme spring-ebb, but with the strong tide-rips in the area it is hardly to be recommended for sport.

Agriculture has affected the whole of the island, right down to the littoral zone, where the unique seaweed-eating sheep graze on fronds of washed-up kelp. A drystone wall – the Sheep Dyke – encircles the island to exclude the sheep from the farmed land, and this defines a distinct foreshore area. For much of its length, the dyke is built immediately above the beach, where it can be vulnerable to exceptionally high tides and storm-surges, leaving a relatively narrow corridor of beach at high tide. A dyke in Scotland, it should be said, is a wall, not a drainage ditch. On the east side of the island, it cuts several hundred metres inland to leave an extensive area of closely grazed sward (known as The Links), the flora here reflecting the underlying shell-sand. On the north end around the lighthouse, at the north-west corner at Tor Ness and along much of the west coast (the west beach), the dyke again runs well inland, leaving extensive areas of well-cropped coastal heath where vestigial heather and Glaucous Sedge can be found on a clay/rock substrate. One area on the west side, just north of the airfield, is closed off from the foreshore grazing area and croft land extends to the rocky shore for about half a mile. Here, the grazing pressure is much less and abundant areas of flowering thrift can be found along with less disturbed areas for nesting birds. Within the Sheep Dyke lie the 50 or so habitations and the agricultural land.

The island is generally low-lying. Its highest point is just 30 metres above sea level at Holland, close to a covered water-reservoir, but there is a subtle relief (particularly noticeable when cycling!), and Holland House, the School and Community Centre and the old coastguard watch point towards the north end are all sited on prominent ground. There is no true central village, but more of a scatter of croft houses distributed fairly evenly throughout the island. However, the airfield, shop, doctor's surgery, kirks, post office, the memorial hall, and the school and community centre are all loosely concentrated in the southern centre of the island. Crofts are generally no more than five to 10 hectares in size, and few of the original fields are larger than a hectare, except on the three larger farms of Holland, Howar and Kirbist in the south end, where fields have been amalgamated. Many field boundaries are marked by drystone dykes in various states of repair, which, along with the associated overgrown field headlands, provide a substantial habitat for migrants throughout the island.

Holland House sits prominently on high ground and is the seat of the island's laird, though the estate is now fragmented and most of the crofts are in private ownership. Its large garden is the main ringing site for the observatory. Another prominent building is the new lighthouse, 'new' being its status when first lit in

1854, as opposed to the nearby Old Beacon which was first illuminated in 1789. This was also an important site for ringing, until access was lost following automation in the late 1990s.

Until recently and including the first few years of the observatory's existence, agricultural practice was highly traditional with a rotation of crops and grass. A crop of bere (a primitive and hardy strain of barley) or oats would be followed by a year of neeps (swedes) with an undersown crop of grass in the third year. The grass would be used for hay or grazing for several years until its quality declined, when the cycle would be started again.

All this was achieved with the use of light tractors, which had replaced the horses. Crops were gathered as sheaves using binders and then 'stooked'; hay was turned in the sun and 'square baled'. Both were then built manually into stacks for the winter feeding of cattle. The result was a rich patchwork of varied habitats from bare ground to deep grassland, providing a wonderful resource for breeding birds and migrants in spring and autumn, not to mention the birding opportunities both there and in the numerous 'tattie' (potato) patches. Currently, however, grass has become the main fodder crop, managed through 'round-bale' silage making. Cereals are no longer grown except when used as a nurse crop for under-sown grass seed, which is now silaged in summer before ripening, so no loose grain becomes available for birds to glean. Regrettably, only a handful of tattie patches are now cultivated as these previously provided a sheltered haven on every croft for autumn migrants. Much heavier machinery is used and far fewer people work the land. The exceptions to this are the 14 hectares managed by the observatory and some sacrificial crops which have been planted on the island recently through agri-environmental incentive schemes.

Some of the poorer land has fallen into disuse or is used only for rough grazing, particularly the area to the west of Garso Loch where much rank grassland can be found on very sandy soil. Otherwise, the only substantial areas not used agriculturally are the wetlands. The three largest of these are at Ancum, Bridesness and Hooking, where extensive Yellow Iris beds surround open water and provide a haven for breeding water birds. As there is little or no shooting, they are also favoured by passage birds. An abundant flora is also associated with the wet margins that are pink with Ragged-Robin in season, whilst the more open areas are richly studded with Northern Marsh-orchids. Wild mint there assaults the nostrils when ringing gull and tern chicks. The considerably smaller Loch of Garso is similarly endowed, as is the diminutive area by Scottigar, but the lochs of Gretchen, Bewan and Trolla Vatn (Water of the Trolls) are completely different, being oligotrophic with no associated wetland margins.

ISLAND HISTORY

The island has been continuously inhabited from prehistoric times (Tulloch 1974). As elsewhere in Orkney, there are numerous archaeological sites scattered across it. Two massive earthen banks crossing from east to west, the Muckle Gersty and Matches Dyke, reputedly once defined three roughly equal areas of the island as territories for three brothers.

There is no documentary record of this, but the dykes are still evident despite agricultural erosion and, where undisturbed, leave one contemplating how such massive engineering was achieved without mechanical aids. Similarly lost in the mists of time is the story of the standing stone, known locally as 'The Stan Stane', just to the north of the observatory, a lone sentinel with an enigmatic hole perforating it above head height. It has been suggested that it may be an outlier to a putative stone circle on the Tor Ness hill at the north-western corner of the island, though definitive evidence of this is lacking. The ancient tradition of dancing around the stone on New Year's Day has been revived in recent years. Growing numbers encircle the stone whilst holding hands and dance around it to music. A splash of sacrificial whisky is offered to the stone prior to its imbibing by the assembled crowd!

Howmae (pronounced 'Hoomy') Brae, above Nouster (or South) Bay, lies to the east of the observatory and was excavated by Dr William Traill, then owner of the island, in the late nineteenth century, revealing two Iron Age wheel houses with associated artefacts. Half a mile further along the coast, by the Point of Burrian, is the Broch of Burrian dating from a later era, probably the late first century BC or early first century AD (MacGregor 1972). The broch is known locally as 'the Castle', which well describes its original fortified structure. It also was excavated by Dr Traill who found Pictish artefacts, including the well-known Burrian Cross, a Christian symbol on stone, suggesting that the broch remained in occupation probably at least to the ninth century and the coming of the Vikings.

The Norse invasion period was documented in the 'Orkneyinga Saga' and includes some of the island's earliest recorded history. At this time it was referred to as 'Rinansay', believed to be derived from St Ninian, a favoured saint of the Picts. The first event would be around the end of the ninth century when Halfdan High-leg was hunted down and executed on the island by Turf Einar. Maybe with prescience of the ornithological future of the island he 'carved an eagle on his back in this way: he stuck his sword into the body by the backbone, cut all the ribs away, and there drew out the lungs. That was Halfdan's death'.

Mention is made of a chain of beacons to warn of hostile fleets approaching from the North and the island beacon at Rinansay was lit as soon as Fair Isle's was seen. The beacons were in use again recently, for example on the Golden Jubilee of Queen Elizabeth II's accession and the fiftieth anniversary of VE day. Moving to the twelfth century, the colourful character of Ragnathe, the wise woman, appears. She owned a large farm on the island and gave good counsel to the Earls of Orkney. She was also instrumental in promoting poetry in the court of Earl Rognvald, but might have been best noted for her attention-grabbing head-dress of red horsehair.

From the fourteenth century, the Orkney Islands came increasingly under Scottish domination; in 1468 they were pledged, along with Shetland, for dowry security for the marriage of the Danish princess Margaret to James III of Scotland. Many a wistful remark has been passed since, suggesting that the pledge be redeemed and Danish rule restored, usually following some particularly inappropriate dictum from Westminster or Holyrood. Orkney retains a strong Norse tradition and is proud of its connections. Following the surrender to Scotland, the islands suffered a dark period of plunder, exploitation, oppression and feudalism at the hands of the Stuart Earls, but it may be that 'North Ronaldshay', as it had come to be known, escaped the worst excesses because of its remoteness. Though many thousands of people reportedly died in a famine in Orkney in 1634, there is documentation of a thriving farming and fishing culture on North Ronaldsay. In 1662 the Reverend Alexander Smith was banished to the island (for holding anti-establishment views), as he would have trouble in gaining any influence in Edinburgh from this remote ministry.

The history of the island is much more thoroughly documented from the eighteenth century onwards, a major early landmark being the purchase of the island by James Traill from Archibald Nisbet in 1727 for the sum of 2,000 guineas. Through the 1745 rebellion the Traills had a tough time, being considered sympathetic to the rebel cause. The family, originally from Fife, have been very influential estate owners in Orkney, and the descendants of James continue as successive lairds of the island. They are still active in island affairs, although the extent of the estate holding has been considerably reduced since the Crofting Reform (Scotland) Act 1976, which gave tenants the right to buy their croft land and housing. The ornithological record of North Ronaldsay owes a great deal to this family, both historically and in recent times, through its association with the observatory. By 1773 the island was described as having crops of a quality that 'excels most of Orkney', and by 1791 the population had risen to 420.

Shipwrecks were a feature during this period (16 between 1773 and 1788), so the original 'Beacon' was conceived, and completed in 1789. This icon of North Ronaldsay, which was featured in the TV programme 'Restoration' in 2006, proved to be of little practical use as it was not visible from every direction and created a false sense of security for mariners. Wrecks continued regularly, with 11 between 1796 and 1799. The lantern was extinguished in 1806 and the striking interlocking stone ball, which now crowns it, was transferred from the more recently built tower at Start Point on Sanday. The 'new' North Ronaldsay lighthouse was commissioned in 1854 and continues to shine – it too has a special place in the ornithological record.

Seaweed, as a resource, has been of great importance to the island, both as a fertiliser for the land or fields and for burning (as kelp) to create soda ash. For near on 200 years, running into the early part of the twentieth century, this was the main industry on the island. In the eighteenth century and up to about 1840 it was primarily produced to supply the soap and glass industries, but demand then fell, to recover around 1880 when it became a major source of iodine until early in the twentieth century. This was a profitable business for the estate, but also supported a considerable resident population, which peaked at 546 in 1881 and drove the establishment of a true cash economy within the island. Later in the twentieth century, from the 1950s to the early 1990s, seaweed was gathered and air-dried to supply the alginate industry, but alternative supplies again proved cheaper and the 'tangle' gathering business was abandoned. Remnants of the kelp-burning pits are still visible on many of the shorelines on the island.

More famously, seaweed was exploited through confining the native sheep to the foreshore where, over the course of 200 years or so, they have become physiologically adapted to a seaweed diet. This variant of the primitive northern short-tailed group are known as North Ronaldsay Sheep, a breed endemic to the island. The Sheep Dyke that keeps them on the beach is now a Schedule A listed monument, having the same status as St Magnus Cathedral in Kirkwall. The dyke was completed, to the extent that it finally confined the sheep to the foreshore, in 1832, and the initial grazing regulations, with the 'Sheep Court' managing them, were formulated by 1839. The Sheep Court remains the regulatory body for the flock and the foreshore grazing, an arrangement as unique as the sheep, and is increasingly active following new gourmet interest in the meat and the historic designation of the Dyke.

Throughout the twentieth century, the island reflected developments as the effect of two World Wars and the mechanisation of agriculture impacted on both the population and farming practice. Following the decline of the kelp industry, egg production became very important. In the second half of the twentieth century, beef production became central to the economy, supplemented by work on road maintenance and the water supply, and local appointments such as postman and school janitor.

Transport links developed with the building of the pier at Nouster early in the twentieth century and its extension in 1964. The air service was established in 1968 and is the lifeline-link to the island. There are now daily passenger flights, and a weekly air freight service. There are also several ferries a week, depending on the time of year. Tourism is a recent development, mainly following the establishment of the bird observatory, and boosted by higher subsidies for the air service, which brings the fares closer to those of the ferries to neighbouring islands.

There has been a school on the island since around 1835 but, after the Second World War, selective secondary education was offered for talented pupils at Kirkwall Grammar School, with the children being lodged in digs. Following the building of the school hostel in Kirkwall, the school became a modern comprehensive; this was possibly to the advantage of the children, but probably to the detriment of the community, as few former pupils have returned to the island since its inception.

A government scheme for supplying medical services to the Highlands and Islands brought a resident doctor to the island in 1915. This post has been held by me since 1977, though the decline in population to its current level of well below 100 and the change in roles among allied health professionals, such as the development of family-nurse practitioners, has called into question the continuation of the practice. As my arrival on the island and the development of the observatory are inextricably linked, the following section will be written in the first person and to an extent autobiographically.

ORNITHOLOGICAL HISTORY

Buckley & Harvie-Brown (1891) laid out the first comprehensive overview of the archipelago's birds, but with little detail regarding North Ronaldsay. Alan Briggs (1893, 1894), however, provided a magnificent snapshot of the birds of the island from the 1890s whilst staying for extended periods at Holland House, presumably as a guest of the Traills.

In his somewhat bloodthirsty accounts Briggs (1894) pursued the Victorian philosophy of 'what's hit is history, what's missed is mystery' – birdwatching robustly backed up by double-barrelled shotgun! His writings effectively gave a bird report for the island for 1892 and 1893, albeit rather thin and not comprehensive, but with a number of interesting records which contrast with more recent times. A typical passage gives a flavour of his writings:

> SHORT-EARED OWL (Asio accipitrinus) [flammeus] – Saw one, a male, on 2 December 1892, which rose out of some reeds by the edge of a small loch, where I was after Snipe. I killed it and a Snipe, left and right. I came across another on the night of 3 December when I was waiting for duck. It circled round me several times but I refrained from shooting it. I hear from the natives at times that they have seen a Cat-face among their turnips, and I fancy in most cases they mean this bird.

As well as the changes in nomenclature since Briggs, the comparative changes in occurrence are of great interest, for instance he records in 1893 'Land Rail *Crex pratensis* [Corncrake] Abundant […] I saw six nests in one rushy field' and 'Common Bunting *Emberiza miliaria* [Corn Bunting] with 15 or 16 breeding pairs'. A single calling Corncrake is now celebrated and attracts special protection measures; Corn Bunting has been extinct as a breeding bird since the late 1960s, and is now rarer on passage than Rustic Bunting.

Some less usual birds of this period still remain on the island as stuffed specimens at Holland House, such as Pallas's Sandgrouse, Squacco Heron and Snowy Owl. At least these testify to the accuracy of the finder's identification skills, though the camera and the rarity record form have thankfully supplanted the shotgun.

Though occasionally visited by ornithological luminaries such as Ronald Lockley and David Lack during the twentieth century, it wasn't until the arrival of Ken Walker, as a lighthouse keeper, that the continuous recording of the island's birds began again. It should not be overlooked that many of the islanders had and still have a strong interest and expertise in birds. However, due to a combination of their retiring natures, the isolation of the island and the mere handful of authoritative naturalists in Orkney until the latter half of the twentieth century, many interesting ornithological events must have remained formally unrecorded. Whilst there is a local anecdote about Johnny Ancum being ribbed – 'I see you are lifting your tatties by crane this year' after a Crane took up residence in his tattie patch one autumn, there is no reference to this bird in the official Orkney record.

Ken Walker arrived on the island in 1964 with a strong interest in birdwatching and both summarised the island's records to date and gave another invaluable snapshot of the island's birds from 1964 to 1966. These are published as an appendix in an account of the island by Mary Scott (1967). By this time Corncrake had become *Crex crex* and Corn Bunting *Emberiza calandra*, but sadly, however, there were as few as ten calling crakes and six pairs of buntings. He also noted the last breeding Red-necked Phalaropes in 1952.

One of Ken's early moves was to advertise via the British Trust for Ornithology (BTO) for someone to come to the island to train him to ring birds, as it had become clear to him that regular lighthouse attractions gave the opportunity for many to be marked. In return, he offered free board and accommodation. Michael King responded to the call and subsequently became a long-term stalwart of North Ronaldsay, continuing to visit in most years following Ken's departure right through to my early years on the island and beyond. Along with Ken, he pioneered the use of mist-nets at Holland House gardens. In many ways they laid the foundations for the development of the observatory, partly through their records and not least by seeding the idea locally as a potential development, pointing across the water towards Fair Isle where the observatory had brought much benefit to the community.

When Ken left the lighthouse service to join the seaweed processing industry, he continued his birdwatching as a hobby and still had a crucial part to play in the development of the observatory. Michael King last visited North Ronaldsay in the early 1990s, after which he concentrated on developing a ringing operation in West Africa, satisfied that coverage of the island no longer needed his regular visits, though Alison Duncan and I reciprocated with a number of long-distance winter trips to help in West Africa, studying wintering British trans-Saharan migrants. Michael died in 2002 and Ken in 2008.

Also around the mid-1960s, the island was beginning to attract a wider interest and, though no resident birder remained after Ken's departure, some coverage was achieved in most autumns and in some springs until I took up the resident mantle in 1977. Michael King was of course a regular, but notable were a group of birders from Hampshire including Bob Gomes, Jim Williams, Eddie Wiseman and Dave Wooldridge who, between them, made repeated visits into the early seventies. Jim continued visiting, having acquired an Orcadian wife, Ruth, and moved to the county. He is now the county recorder for Orkney and, incidentally, Eddie later became recorder for Hampshire and Dave for the Isle of Wight!

Other regular visitors during this period included Eddie Balfour, who came out with Jim, and David Lea (one time warden of Lundy Bird Observatory) who always managed to time his very popular annual Royal Society for the Protection of Birds (RSPB) film show at the hall for late September. Andrew Ramsay also made an annual autumn ringing visit in the later 1970s, often overlapping with Michael King, generally in the October school break, as at the time he was teaching at Kirkwall Grammar School. Andrew became my ringing trainer when I arrived in Orkney and carried me through to acquiring my 'A' permit.

My journey to North Ronaldsay started at the end of a two-year hospital appointment, when I chose to seek a working environment with more natural diversity than central Manchester, abandoning a career in hospital medicine. Having gained an appointment as a trainee general practitioner in the Outer Hebrides starting in October 1976, I took up the position of Little Tern warden at Gibraltar Point Bird Observatory in the April for the princely sum of £5 per week plus board, funded by the WWF. George Evans was the field centre warden and it was he who had persuaded me to take on the job, having known me from previous excursions to Bardsey when he was the observatory warden there. After the tern job had finished, I stayed on as a volunteer until I was due in the Hebrides and I gained my 'C' permit recommendation at the autumn ringing course led by Chris Mead. Dick Lambert had arrived as reserve warden that year and I was his trainee.

Then followed the move to north-west Scotland, albeit a brief one. My interest in birds soon became known and, not long after my arrival, the practice receptionist, Iris Walker, invited me to meet her husband – Ken Walker. They knew that the Orkney Health Board was looking for a doctor for the North Ronaldsay practice and thought it was just the place for me, and I'll never forget the now familiar but then alien-sounding house names – Purtabreck, North Gravity and Gerbo, tripping off their tongues with stories of the people there. I discussed this with my trainer, Dr McIntosh, who encouraged me to apply even though it would leave him without support in his practice for many months. The interview took place very close to Christmas, but we stayed over on the island for a night beforehand and it was everything and more than I imagined. The moonlit walk back from the surgery to Garso with the Wigeon whistling from Ancum Loch and the unexpected Brent Goose at Bewan stick in my mind; I was offered the job the next day and moved to the island in early February 1977.

During the last years of the 1970s and early 1980s, I worked towards my 'A' permit, particularly with Andrew Ramsay, both on and off the island. Jim Williams and Michael King came over at least annually, Eric Meek had also appeared on the scene as Orkney RSPB Officer, and a young and enthusiastic Martin Gray had become a regular visitor and trainee ringer. Holland House Gardens became established as a permanent ringing site, with many thanks to the laird, Captain D. J. T. Robertson, who has always been most supportive of the study of birds through ringing. The arrangement is now embodied in a long-term agreement between the observatory and the estate. These were heady times with a tight band of enthusiasts, Andrew phoning euphorically with a Common Nighthawk in his hand, Eric discussing over the phone what turned out to be a Tennessee Warbler, Iain Robertson calling from Fair Isle to 'grip' me with a Yellow-browed Bunting ('Got you back there!') – all good pioneering stuff. By this time I had naturally become involved with the island community and was well aware of its problems, including a lack of employment opportunities and depopulation. Gundry had ceased making mist-nets and Knox Nets took over, but later went out of business. On one of my annual pilgrimages to the BTO Ringers' Conference at Swanwick, I discussed the possibility of developing a mist-nest-making industry on the island with Chris Mead. Being a small-volume, high-value product which could be posted, coupled with the security of an off-shore island and a ringer fundamentally involved with the operation, it proved to be 'a goer' and the North Ronaldsay

Netting Group (a partnership cooperative) is still operating, making its 20,000th mist-net in 2008.

THE DEVELOPMENT OF THE OBSERVATORY

To train a band of islanders in mist-net-making techniques, Chris Mead came to the island with Adrian Cawthorne, a scientific officer with the BTO, in June 1981. Between training sessions, we spent many happy hours in brilliant weather ringing Arctic Tern chicks in the large colonies that were thriving on the island at the time. Adrian loved the place and we arranged for him to come back that autumn for the migration. His wife, Wendy, was a doctor and for the following autumns she worked for two weeks as my locum while Adrian and I 'hit the birds' becoming close friends in the process. By 1984 we were seriously discussing the possibility of establishing a bird observatory, having recognised the quality of the migration through the island and another, if more ambitious, opportunity to boost its economy. He left that autumn with the intention of seeing what he could do to promote the idea from the BTO and scientific angles and I undertook to investigate the strategic possibilities locally.

Adrian was not at the January 1985 Ringers' Conference; it was announced that he was ill and couldn't attend. I really couldn't understand why Chris (Mead) seemed so stand-offish until I returned to the island to find a message to ring him. Adrian had died suddenly and unexpectedly after a short illness just before the conference and it had been decided to suppress the news, even from the BTO staff, to avoid casting a deep cloud over the proceedings. He was 29 years old. Chris had intended to catch me at the end of the conference to tell me, but I had left early for transport reasons. It had taken me two days to get back to the island and was long before the era of mobile phones. I immediately left again to attend Adrian's memorial ceremony, and it was at this point that it became inevitable that one way or another North Ronaldsay Bird Observatory would happen.

The Adrian Cawthorne Memorial Fund was established with the principal objective of developing a bird observatory on North Ronaldsay. Its trustees included Chris Mead, John Marchant (Adrian's close friend from schooldays in Portsmouth, ringing trainer, work colleague and neighbour), Stephen Baillie, Eric Meek, Colin Mackenzie-Grieve, Wendy, who took the chair, and me. It was never the intention to raise funds for the whole project, but a substantial sum was raised to act as seedcorn finance to encourage grant aid from public agencies, at that time the most likely being the Highlands and Islands Development Board (HIDB) and Orkney Islands Council (OIC). With the approval of North Ronaldsay Community Council and after a presentation by Eric and myself, a local steering group was formed to progress the project. The vogue for funding projects in the region at the time was to encourage the formation of community cooperatives and it was generally agreed that this would realise the highest percentage of public funding from both the OIC and the HIDB, so the various interested groups held a series of meetings to establish a cooperative to take this forward.

As it turned out, irreconcilable differences emerged within the local steering group, leading to a deadlock in progress towards a cooperative. The observatory was already operating from Twingness, the low-energy house I had built, and it was generally considered that developing there was more practical than trying to start from scratch. Eventually, after many reports, projections and meetings, where various methods of forming a management structure were discussed and dismissed, Ralph Palmer from the HIDB wrote to me, frankly stating that the community route was clearly not going to work, but they would do everything they could to back me if I was willing to take the project forward on a private basis. The Memorial Fund and OIC were also willing to support this way forward. I recall discussing all this with Duncan Robertson (the laird) and his comment was 'The best committee is a committee of one.' Though counter to my natural philosophy, I couldn't help but think at the time that he had a point!

A meeting of the Memorial Fund held in Tring (the BTO was then based at Beech Grove before its move to Thetford) in the early summer of 1986 will be forever etched into our memories. Wendy Cawthorne, very much the driving force of the fund, had travelled up from Hampshire where she had taken a General Practice post. The substance of the meeting concentrated on fund raising; it was very strongly Wendy's view that Twingness should be developed as the observatory's long-term base and efforts should be directed towards acquiring it for running by the proposed cooperative venture. After the meeting I returned to my parents' house in nearby Beaconsfield where I normally stayed when down for meetings of the fund. I was called the next morning by my mother to take a 'phone call from a distraught Jane Marchant, John's wife. Wendy, with Charlotte (her toddler daughter with Adrian) had stayed overnight with them after the meeting and they had found Wendy dead, from natural causes, in her bed in the morning. Wendy was 30 when she died.

This second tragedy in the genesis of the observatory hardly bears dwelling on. It reinforced the determination of everyone, culminating with Chris Mead formally opening the observatory in June 1995. Suffice it to say that when Chris, John Marchant and I fixed the memorial plaque for the Cawthornes to the hearthstone of the original croft house, at the heart of the completed buildings, there was a tangible yet unspoken sense of relief, joy, poignancy and closure between us. Not to mention a tot of whisky.

From the mid-1980s onward, it becomes impossible to mention all the many people who have contributed to the establishment and continued operation of the observatory. A list of those who wardened the ornithological side is appended, but this is only the tip of the iceberg when it comes to acknowledging all the ancillary staff, volunteers, locals and students on projects, who have helped with tasks from mixing concrete to cooking dinners (and often both!).

1986 was the year of the Hedgehog deportation when Jane Watson coined the term 'NADM' (never a dull moment), which pretty well sums up what it has been like ever since. Following an exponential rise in the Hedgehog population on the island, which began with two introduced animals in 1972, the 'Hedgehog saga' became an international news story when Loganair agreed to fly them out to pastures new, away from the eggs and hatchlings of the ground-nesting birds of the island on which they had a devastating effect. Spike Milligan wrote to the

Guardian expressing his concern about the reports of exploding Hedgehogs in Orkney, demanding that we be told publicly of this new secret weapon. We in turn wrote to him to ask if he would become a figurehead for the observatory to which he readily agreed. Regrettably perhaps, this was never really followed up, but the memorial fund benefited substantially from all the publicity.

At the annual general meeting of the Bird Observatories Council in January 1987, North Ronaldsay Bird Observatory became officially accredited, having met the required criteria. Mike Pennington became the first official warden and a wave of willing helpers and volunteers began to appear, not least a contingent of the Royal Scots Dragoon Guards led by Major Tony Crease who put enormous energy into converting the old croft-house into a serviceable bunkhouse. They even donated a set of army bunks and mattresses for the purpose. They also set telegraph poles for Heligoland traps with Martin Gray, but my abiding memory is of 18 of us manhandling the huge flagstone that still forms the doorstep to the central entrance of the observatory. I had to re-site it in 2004 following extension work but, not having an army to hand, we used a JCB.

In September 1987, Alison Duncan came for a visit with her friends Raymond Duncan and Judy Cooper (now Judy Duncan), following a talk I gave about the observatory to the Scottish Ringers' conference at Carrbridge the previous year. She still hasn't gone home! The observatory has become central to her life and she central to the life of the observatory, since she became Warden in 1988, and her contribution to the development and running of the complex has been immense. Arriving well-qualified with a first-class honours degree in Zoology from Aberdeen, and rapidly upgrading her long standing 'C' permit from Grampian Ringing Group to an 'A' permit, her scientific credentials were impeccable, but in her quiet and unassuming way she has also become a highly effective administrator and domestic manager. Her companionship and support through all the trials and tribulations of the observatory's development have been invaluable; what more can I say – we married in 2001.

In 1988 the first wind generator was moved from Myres Hill near Glasgow, where it was being evaluated by the Energy Studies Unit of the University of Strathclyde, to its permanent site at the observatory. Wind-generated power had been an ongoing aspect of the low-energy building project for some years, in association with Professor John Twidell and a series of students. Principal among these was Andrew Stepek who stayed with us for many months. He had the place totally wired with temperature sensors (silver-foil-coated toilet-roll centres with a thermocouple in the middle hanging from the ceilings of every room at a fixed height), ammeters, kWh meters, an anemometer and most memorably the data logger which loudly spewed out a print from all the data points on the hour every hour of every day. This was located in the old house dormitory and moved with the bunks into the temporary dormitory in the main lounge when renovations were started. Visitors took a few nights to attune themselves before obtaining a full night's sleep, only to wake up mystified when there was a power cut and the data logger fell silent. I am convinced that Andrew, always the scientist, used a thermocouple even when preparing his signature dish of chilli con carne.

The period from 1988 to 1994 was one of consolidation for the ornithological establishment, with the standardising of recording protocols, the further development of a computerised recording system (new ground in those days) and an expansion of the ringing effort as more ringers became available. In parallel with this, plans for developing the building were pursued, including the addition of a second aero-generator, again with help from Professor Twidell but this time through De Montfort University, Leicester, where he had moved to head the AMSET Centre. Tree-planting and excavations for pools proceeded to improve the attractiveness of the immediate surroundings for migrants, and the fields were fenced to allow a traditional rotation of crops to complement the growing flock of North Ronaldsay Sheep (currently 100 ewes). All this was done on a shoestring budget. Legal wrangles over the title offered as security were delaying access to potential grant funding and when these were finally settled, it did little more than cover the cost of materials. This is not to say that the funding bodies were other than extremely generous, just that our plans were ambitious; however, a substantial percentage of the costs could not be grant-aided from public funds and the memorial fund fell some way short of the difference.

The salvation in this situation was that the grant funding bodies were willing to accept 'work in kind' in the form of documented hours of contributed labour in lieu of cash to match-fund the project. We could not afford a contractor but, with some skilled advice and employees, Alison and I became project managers, ordering all the materials, organising the works and, along with many unsung heroes (it would be invidious to pick out individuals without listing everyone), contributed many thousands of hours of hard labour to put it all together. These were intense times, happy and sometimes hilarious, but not without stress – deliveries via an unreliable once-weekly ferry made for hair-tearing frustrations, such as when the blocks arrived and the merchant forgot to put in the cement, which arrived two weeks later. By 1995, when Chris Mead performed the formal opening ceremony, we had completed the spanking-new observatory, with four guest rooms, one of them downstairs, en-suite and adapted for disabled use, five four-bedded dormitories with a shower block below, an Assistant Warden's room and a four-roomed Warden's flat, with the energy for all the heating and much of the hot water being derived from wind and sun.

Of course, the bird work continued during and after the first building period and the island developed an increasingly high profile in the birding world, attracting more and more visitors, who found more and more birds (particularly the more glamorous ones), which in turn attracted yet more visitors. Not only was the reputation of the observatory spreading among birdwatchers, it was also attracting both general and specialist visitors who wished to use the accommodation. These varied from general tourists to sheep aficionados and lighthouse 'collectors' (yes, they do exist!). By the late 1990s it was becoming clear that the establishment was neither adequate nor properly configured to meet the new demand. A three-phase plan for development was hatched, all continuing the low energy specifications, and after an initial rejection for phase one, grant funding was obtained from Orkney Islands Council and Orkney Enterprise (the local enterprise company that succeeded the old HIDB) for each phase in turn as the development progressed. There was another substantial input of own labour, in all three phases, and the observatory was by this time generating a modest income, which enabled the retention of a building contractor for each, all of whom were happy to accept our input to defray costs.

Phase one saw the building of the large vaulted octagonal lounge to the south of the main building, incorporating a bar and digital projection facilities. A full hotel licence was granted for the premises. This space gave enormous new flexibility by allowing the dining area in the conservatory to be cleared after meals and reset for breakfast. It also provided room for a café service at lunchtime, à la carte evening meals and functions, and a place to call the log in the evening by projecting the database onto the big screen. Football on the big screen is also ever popular! Also, as part of this phase, the three guest rooms upstairs were upgraded to include en-suite facilities. Delays to the building schedule, not least as a result of having to air-ambulance the senior building partner off the island with a heart attack, saw us up all night, nailing down the floor, before the grand opening ceremony in July 2001, and Jim Wallace, deputy First Minister for Scotland at the time, helping us carry through the furnishings just before the crowds arrived to see him perform the official opening. All was alright on the night indeed, just!

Phase two involved converting the original barn and byre into a self-contained hostel with one two-bedded and two four-bedded (one en-suite) dormitories plus a self-catering kitchen, all of which became operational in 2003. This reduced the need for dormitories in the main building. Phase three involved building in the gap between the main blocks of the original buildings and cannibalising three of the original dormitories to form three new enlarged en-suite rooms, thus completing the current complement of four doubles, two twins and one single. The remaining two dormitories are now used for staff accommodation, which remains in short supply. Phase three also saw an extension and complete upgrading of the kitchen facilities, a new laundry room, and renovation of some outbuildings to form an equipment store and the ringing hut.

Though phase three was effectively completed in 2005, a power circuit was not installed in the ringing hut until 2008 when it became fully operational, and other outstanding minor works still need to be done.

It is safe to say now that the observatory has reached maturity both ornithologically and structurally. However, there is little doubt that we will need the enthusiasm and goodwill of the many friends and supporters of the observatory in years to come, to enable its central purpose, the monitoring of bird migration through North Ronaldsay, to be maintained.

BIRDS

An overview of migration

North Ronaldsay lies latitudinally north of the southern tip of Norway and only just shy of the southern tip of Greenland, the coordinates at Holland House ringing site being 59°22′N, 2°26′W. From a migrant's point of view, it sits at the tip of a broken peninsula formed by the chain of the Orkney Islands stretching north from the Caithness coast, with open sea beyond for some 80 kilometres to

Shetland, punctuated only by the island of Fair Isle. The effect of this geography is to concentrate migrants heading north and east and to offer a landfall for those heading the other way. Its rich variety of habitats provides shelter and feeding opportunities for most styles of avian diet, enabling it to sustain migrants for extended periods.

Not surprisingly, land bird migration through the area is dominated by birds heading into or leaving Scandinavia, comprising species typical of British east coast migration in general. Additionally, the Northern Isles are open to the west and north and form a conduit for migration through to the Faeroes, Iceland, and Greenland and on to northern Canada. The longer distances on this flyway mainly involve shorebirds and wildfowl, but a few passerines regularly venture beyond the Western Palearctic region as far as Greenland.

Added to this is the potential for British birds to reach the islands, both as spring overshoots and dispersing autumn juveniles. The same applies to continental breeding species in increasing levels of rarity as distance increases and, of course, to southern, eastern and transatlantic vagrants well beyond their normal migratory pathways, which mix in with the migrants of the region. All this can add up to some spectacular migratory events and on its day can provide some of the most exciting birding in the country.

A further dimension to the interest is the seabird passage past North Ronaldsay. The island effectively marks the northern end point of the British east coast and seabirds leaving the North Sea are funnelled past the north of the island to enter the Atlantic Ocean. There is regularly something of interest at sea, even if only large summer feeding movements of auks, but after a north-westerly storm has passed through and the wind backs to the south-east, especially in autumn, a spectacular passage of seabirds emptying out of the North Sea can be observed at close quarters. That is, if you can drag yourself away from the fall of passerines that has also arrived with the south-easterly ...

Winter is not without interest. A number of species from the far north, although less common further south, overwinter here. Good numbers of wildfowl are also present, and influxes of these can reflect harsh continental conditions. Storms can bring large flocks of gulls ashore, which, when picked over, often produce unusual species or forms. Summer visitors include a variety of breeding passerines, waterfowl, seabirds and waders, often with some non-breeding individuals, probably derived from overshoots or late-moving failed breeders, with occasional unexpected extralimital breeding.

In general, migration through the island in spring is lighter than in the autumn as a result of several factors. To start with, there are significantly fewer birds, following heavy first-winter mortality in many species, and birds tend to move north as conditions improve with less risk of becoming storm-stayed, though this can still occur. There is also an advantage in being first onto the breeding grounds to claim the best territories, which encourages a more direct and faster migration. Additionally, a number of species (for example Redwing) follow a circular winter migration pattern, taking a more easterly return track in the spring and thereby missing the Northern Isles at this season, whilst being 'main-line' through them in autumn. Conversely, in autumn, there are many inexperienced juvenile birds on the move with poorly tuned navigational skills. When coupled with the predominant weather, often a series of depressions moving into the British Isles and creating offshore continental winds, these birds may cross the North Sea and end up staging in the Northern Isles.

For North Ronaldsay, the ideal winds for arrivals of migrant birds from the continent are between south-east and north-east; anything south of south-east leads to the 'shadow' effect of other land upwind of the island (i.e. Sanday, Stronsay, Mainland Orkney and Caithness) and anything north of north-east is 'shadowed' by Shetland and Fair Isle. This is not to say that large movements don't occur on winds outside these parameters, but there is a filtering and moderating effect with less of a sense of 'rawness' about the birds when many have not made their first landfall here and are island-hopping to continue their journey.

The passage of successive weather-fronts leads to the grounding of migrants. The perfect conditions for this in both spring and autumn are east to south-east winds with a Scandinavian-based 'blocking' anticyclone and a depression heading into central Scotland with an associated rain-front arriving over the island in the evening, and with clear conditions over the continental coast at dusk. Hopefully the rain will be clearing with calm conditions for mist-netting at first light the next morning and the island just heaving with migrants! Of course arrivals can and often do continue through the day, in fair and foul weather, but waking up to an overnight arrival of spectacular proportions takes some beating.

Staying with birds arriving with winds from the eastern half of the compass, these predominantly originate from continental Europe, with a wide spectrum of migrant species. Leaving aside sea and shore birds for the moment, their frequency of occurrence on North Ronaldsay will depend on the proximity of their normal range, the size of the population, and their migratory habits. This is well illustrated by the regular occurrence of species scarce elsewhere in Britain such as Common Rosefinch, Icterine Warbler, Red-backed Shrike, Wryneck, Red-breasted Flycatcher and Bluethroat, all of which appear annually in varying numbers and all of which breed on the nearer continent. However, these birds cannot represent the bulk of their moving population, suggesting that North Ronaldsay lies on the margins of the main migratory pathway of these species.

That North Ronaldsay lies on the main migration route for some species is best exemplified by the thrushes, with breathtaking numbers of Redwing, Fieldfare and Blackbirds, and lesser numbers of Song Thrush and Ring Ouzel sometimes pouring out of Scandinavia and making landfall on the island in the early hours, often with large flocks sweeping down the island later on and heading south across the North Ronaldsay Firth in broad daylight. This is very much an autumn phenomenon, and especially so for Redwing, which take an anticlockwise migration route over the winter, with the continental nominate race *Turdus iliacus iliacus* being as scarce in spring as it is common in autumn. Thrushes that winter predominantly in the British Isles, such as Blackbird and Song Thrush, can however turn up in large numbers in 'fall' conditions in spring, though rarely in autumnal numbers. Another feature of these 'main route' species is that adults are well represented among the juveniles, in contrast to species of more variable occurrence, which are represented predominantly by juveniles. This is presumably a consequence of their immature navigational skills, the more experienced adults managing a more direct route. With finches such as Chaffinch and Brambling, the adults similarly move with the juveniles, and can also arrive in significant numbers.

Willow Warbler and Blackcap are the commonest migrant warblers and both occur in greater numbers in autumn than spring. However, Willow Warbler is commoner than Blackcap in spring, whereas there are more Blackcaps than Willow Warblers in autumn. These differences probably reflect the differing migration strategies, with the Willow Warbler following a longitudinal north/south migration, whereas Blackcaps have a strong westward vector in their autumnal movement, with a much more northerly wintering range.

A similar explanation might account for the unusual predominance of Whitethroat in spring, with Lesser Whitethroat showing a fairly equally weighted pattern but with slightly more in autumn. Here, the Whitethroat has the longitudinal migration, with that of the Lesser Whitethroat vectored to the south-east, but there are also significant differences in breeding range, with the Lesser Whitethroat not extending so far west as the Whitethroat, and being absent from Iberia, Ireland and most of Scotland. Interestingly, Lesser Whitethroat was one of the surprise extralimital breeders on the island, a pair having nested at Holland House gardens in 1988, a most unusual record.

All three flycatchers (Pied, Spotted and Red-breasted) mainly conform to the pattern of 'almost exclusively birds of the year' arriving in the autumn, with fewer records in spring. The data for Spotted Flycatcher are, however, still completely skewed by a remarkable arrival in May 1992 which started around lunchtime, and by late afternoon it seemed that every fence post on the island had a Spotted Flycatcher feeding from it. To put it in context, a double-figure day count in spring would usually be exceptional, but on this day a conservative count of 382 was logged, and this was far from a complete census, representing only birds casually seen and counted. A total of 136 birds was ringed from this movement (not even double-figures are ringed for this species in some years) and one bird bearing a Norwegian ring was controlled, neatly suggesting the origin of this population or, perhaps more accurately, its target destination.

Before moving on from the 0–180° sector, it is worth mentioning two more species – Red-backed Shrike and Wryneck – sharing the migratory characteristics associated with trans-Saharan migrant passerines. Unlike the Great Grey Shrike, which shows the more typical pattern of being commoner in autumn, the Red-backed Shrike is very much a spring bird, which from a birding point of view is great, with males turning up in spanking breeding plumage and the fewer autumn birds mainly being less strikingly plumaged youngsters. Wrynecks have, however, shifted from being a predominantly spring bird to being most frequently seen as an autumn migrant, possibly reflecting the south-eastward retraction of the breeding range away from the near continent.

For many migratory non-passerines, it becomes a little complicated to assign the origins of a species to one sector, as many regular migrants can approach the island from the continent or from the north-west and the subspecies involved can often only be separated with certainty through biometrics. This is especially true for waders and wildfowl, for which the island is well placed with its varied shore-line habitats and wetlands. In fact most of the species that regularly track through the area from breeding grounds to the north-west, in Canada, Greenland and Iceland, have a sub-arctic or boreal distribution which extends across northern Europe into Asia, with many being circumpolar.

Dunlin is a good example of this extended distribution: the subspecies *Calidris alpina arctica* from north-east Greenland, *C. a. schinzii* from south-east Greenland, Iceland, Britain and southern Norway and *C. a. alpina* from northern Fennoscandia and across western Siberia are all represented on migration. Ongoing colour-ringing studies of Sanderling and Purple Sandpiper are being undertaken to elucidate the migratory strategies of geographical subpopulations, and North Ronaldsay is a key site for annual cannon-netting activity, particularly in the spring.

One of the reasons for targeting Purple Sandpipers and Sanderling on the island in spring is that, along with Ringed Plover, numbers crescendo in May to a stunning peak of hundreds of birds until there is a sudden departure, presumably direct to their breeding grounds. How much this is a gathering prior to departure and how much turnover of birds occurs is difficult to assess, but hopefully the ringing studies will tease this out in time. Whilst on the subject of waders and colour rings, an interesting record was the spring sighting of a southward-moving colour-ringed female Dotterel on North Ronaldsay on 19 June 1990. The timing of this lends support to the understanding that the Scottish and Norwegian breeding populations are linked, with movement between the populations (Whitfield 2002). It is possible that some females may lay a clutch in Scotland before moving north with the spring amelioration to start a second nest with a different male in Norway, leaving the Scottish male to rear the first brood (Rik Smith – pers. comm.).

Of course some wader species have clearer origins, such as the Icelandic race of Black-tailed Godwit *Limosa limosa islandica,* which is the usual form passing through the island, and the almost regular Buff-breasted Sandpipers and other scarcer Nearctic waders that come from across the Atlantic. However, the regular Pectoral Sandpipers could be coming from either direction and their frequent appearance in easterly conditions suggests, perhaps, that these are not mainly transatlantic in origin.

Similarly wildfowl, which occur in great variety on migration, do not always have easily defined origins. This is complicated by the number of species breeding on the island, and whereas the summer visiting (and breeding) Shelduck can reasonably be assumed to follow the rest of the British and Irish population in a 'moult-migration' across the North Sea, the wintering Long-tailed Ducks could come from almost anywhere in the Arctic. Although it is speculated that they are Icelandic, the one national piece of hard evidence is of a Scottish-ringed individual, which was shot in Finland. There is plenty of evidence to suggest that the majority of passage geese come from Greenland and Iceland. However, it is probable that the smaller Svalbard populations of Pink-footed and Barnacle Geese make occasional landfall in easterly conditions, though heavy autumn goose passage is always associated with strong westerly weather – a spectacular sight in September which can, to a degree, soften the loss of continental passerine arrival with these winds. Whooper Swan passage is also associated with westerlies at this time of year, and is sometimes quite light with little more than our regular wintering party arriving. Nevertheless, Ancum Loch has been seen to be white-over with birds, leaving new arrivals to crash down, and force others to take flight!

Many other duck species appear in good numbers in autumn to augment the local breeding populations, and it is obvious that Wigeon, Teal, Pintail and Mallard numbers far exceed anything that could represent local productivity. Weather patterns associated with their arrival suggest a continental origin. This is also probably true for the smaller numbers of Pochard, Tufted Duck and Scaup. But the Shoveler and Gadwall present both in autumn and through the winter would appear to comprise mainly resident birds.

Raptors are well represented, though rarely numerous, and none breed on the island. Almost anything can turn up (and has!), though the more local breeding birds from the island group, such as Merlin, Peregrine and Hen Harrier, are the most regular and also appear both on passage and in winter. Kestrel is a common migrant and can be quite numerous in autumn, though rarely reaching double figures in a day. Sparrowhawk is similarly common but more frequent in the spring. Ospreys moving in and out of Scandinavia are a regular sight, but can pass very high and probably are frequently missed unless the local Ravens point them out. Many other species on the British list have been recorded but, perhaps surprisingly, the island is still waiting for its first authenticated sighting of Golden Eagle.

Seabird passage

Seabird passage is a notable feature of the island. Although there is some movement through the Pentland Firth and threading between the Orkney Islands, it seems that the bulk of the birds moving between the Atlantic and the North Sea use the 'Fair Isle passage' between Fair Isle and North Ronaldsay. These birds often cut close in to the north-east corner where there is a sea-watching hide for sheltered viewing and consistent monitoring. Bill Bourne commented in the early days of the observatory that North Ronaldsay could become the 'Cape Clear' of Scotland, but though it would be generous to make this comparison with the illustrious 'Cape', there can be few places to rival it for quality sea-watching in Scotland.

The visible passage is predominantly east to west and the most rewarding period for watching is in the autumn months, from August to October, though it is always worth a look at any time of year. Staggering numbers of seabirds can be seen on the move, particularly Gannets, Fulmars, Kittiwakes and auks, with good numbers of skuas and shearwaters regularly among them. It is a prime site for Sooty Shearwaters, with numbers per hour reaching three figures on a good day. Other scarcer species such as Sabine's Gull, Long-tailed Skua and Cory's Shearwater are usually seen annually. Phenomenal events occur occasionally, such as the unprecedented passages of Great Shearwaters in August 2006 and

2007 which on some days exceeded the total number previously recorded in the whole of Orkney up until that time. However, sadly, there has been a noticeable decline in passage numbers of many seabirds in recent years in parallel to their breeding crash, though this has led to a new interest in analysing the copious sea-watching data held by the observatory.

Breeding birds

The breeding birds of the island do not escape the attentions of the observatory and their changing fortunes have been monitored and recorded over the years. Numbers are included in the census log, there is regular ringing of the young and other ongoing studies are undertaken.

The dynamism of populations is as visible here as it is in changing migration patterns. By way of contrast, compare first the loss of the Corncrake and Corn Bunting with the rise of the Curlew, and also the extinction of breeding Twite with the massive colonisation of Linnet. There has been a huge fall in House Sparrow numbers and, of course, a severe decline in the breeding status of both Black-headed Gull and Arctic Tern from common to scarce breeder. Black Guillemots seem to be 'holding their own', with a substantial breeding population. However, there is concern that predation from skuas, which have lost their traditional quarry species, the aforesaid terns, may adversely affect their breeding success.

It is also feared that breeding wader species lose many if not all of their young to the skuas. On Seal Skerry, the Cormorant colony has now shrunk to a handful of nests, where previously in excess of 100 young could be ringed on a single annual visit.

Vagrants and scarce birds

It naturally follows that a site with large numbers of migrants will tend to concentrate the scarce and vagrant species among them. North Ronaldsay is no exception. Perhaps because it is geographically nearer than much of the rest of Britain to the main breeding grounds and migration routes of a number of continental species, some scarce British species are considered regular on the island and other, rare, species are merely scarce on North Ronaldsay.

Hence it is usual to get multiple annual records of species such as Marsh Warbler and Common Rosefinch and it would be an exceptional year when one or more of the regular Northern Isles rarities did not turn up. Both Lanceolated and Pallas's Grasshopper Warblers have occurred on the island, but their rarity compared with their virtually annual appearance just 40 kilometres away is probably explained by the large areas of heavily vegetated wetland on North Ronaldsay, giving such skulking species plenty of opportunity to hide. Rarities have been described for close on 200 years now, dating back for example to a Snowy Owl in 1812, through Pallas's Sandgrouse in 1882, Scops Owl in 1892, Squacco Heron in 1896, Sociable Plover in 1926, to Roller in 1966, with many others on the way. Perhaps unsurprisingly, the number of recorded rarities has really taken off since the 1980s and the establishment of the observatory.

The location's quality might be best illustrated by a list of some of the vagrants that have turned up during the first 20 years of the observatory's existence. These include Little Bustard, Black-throated Thrush, Yellow Warbler, Yellow-browed Bunting, Siberian Thrush, Spanish Sparrow, Southern Grey Shrike, Yellow-rumped Warbler, River Warbler, White-throated Sparrow, Pallid Swift, Collared Flycatcher, Brünnich's Guillemot, Siberian Blue Robin, Calandra Lark, Sykes's Warbler, Veery and Cretzschmar's Bunting to name some of the rarest, with a large supporting cast of 'lesser' rarities far too long to list here. Twitching (of the mass variety) has developed over the same sort of time scale as the observatory and such birds listed above inevitably attract the attentions of twitchers, with their high-octane emotions, and present particularly challenging transport logistics for these intrepid souls.

The observatory has always been pleased to share news of rarities with the rest of the birding world, though facilitating a major twitch can become highly disruptive to the routine work. The invasion of twitchers, by both air and sea, is on the whole an enjoyable phenomenon. Old acquaintances are renewed, gossip is caught up on and above all there is the pleasure of sensing the tangible relief of the crowd when the bird 'shows'. Islanders, too, can share the fun. One of the earlier twitches was before the days of a bar on the island and the old *Orcadia*, complete with liquor licence, was regularly chartered out to the island. This resulted in a two-way flow, of twitchers up the island to the bird and islanders down to the floating pub. Of course, there have been 'hairier' moments, such as when one small charter plane clipped the perimeter fence of the airfield,

Visiting 'twitchers' at the Holland House ringing hut on North Ronaldsay awaiting the release of a Citrine Wagtail after ringing and processing (Kevin Woodbridge).

bounced up off the runway and then retired to Kirkwall, where it circled the airfield while air traffic control inspected it from below for damage. True to the spirit of twitching, the passengers, after making a safe landing in Kirkwall, immediately commandeered another plane out to the island and saw their bird!

Not all twitches are successful (probably an essential element of the twitching ethos) and one well-kent editor of a birdwatching magazine, having just arrived in Scilly, could not get up to the island before darkness on the day the bird was found. His devastation later the next morning, when it had to be conceded that the bird had moved on, really brought home how profoundly he and his colleagues feel about seeing these birds and it still rankles with him many years after the event. The names of the aforementioned vagrants and twitchers are withheld to protect the innocent (but mainly the author).

Returning to the main focus of the observatory, the daily census (as with many observatories) is conducted to a protocol based on the work of Hussell & Ralph (2005). The island is divided into six areas designed to contain as far as possible a roughly similar spectrum of habitats (part of the coast, a wetland, some agricultural land, sheltered gardens and so forth) and these are visited on a daily rotating basis, with the seventh day being a day of rest, spent sitting in the sea-watch hide for at least twenty minutes, which is defined as the minimum sampling time to calculate a rate of passage, specifically for sea-watches. This provides a pragmatic basis for reasonable consistency of recording to enable statistically valid year-on-year comparisons to be made.

Ringing

Trapping and ringing the birds is also central to the monitoring activity, with the main focus for this being the garden at Holland House with its dense Fuchsia cover, Sycamore stands, Elder and Whitebeam, blackcurrant 'scrub' and open rides. A recent planting of Japanese Rose has been very successful in drawing birds out from the denser areas and the stands of New Zealand Flax can often harbour the unexpected (e.g. roosting Long-eared Owl). The exposure of the island to wind has resulted in these hundred-year-old Sycamores barely attaining four metres at their highest, so mist-nets placed before them catch everything from skulkers to canopy-loving species. The variety caught there is astounding, from Bee-eater to Water Rail, through Honey-buzzard, Spanish Sparrow and Red-footed Falcon to Veery; in fact so much so that a freshly dead Storm Petrel slipped into a net was not considered the slightest bit spurious by the ringer-in-charge until the smirks gave away the ruse!

Much other ringing activity takes place away from the gardens; nets are set up below the observatory during the summer for tape-luring petrels, and subsidiary mist-netting sub-sites are operated at the doctor's surgery garden and anywhere else that offers an opportunity, such as a Starling roost in a derelict building. Nets are also set up around the observatory to supplement the mini-Heligoland there and used, along with spring-traps, for more targeted ringing as opportunity arises, perhaps for Common Crossbills on thistles or to confirm identification.

Dazzling in the darker months of the year is a regular activity, mainly for waders but the occasional duck, swan or goose also comes through the door and even Grey Herons have been caught this way. A crow-trap near the observatory has been very successful for catching gulls, but a substantial by-catch of Starlings has also resulted and a Great Skua was eventually tempted in by a mixture of rotting bait, the details of which need not be described.

Cannon-netting for waders depends on outside help, not least from Colin Corse of the Orkney Ringing Group, who holds a cannon-netting licence. The studies are very much guided by Ron Summers, who often attends the event, along with any Highland Ringing Group members who care to come along, and with reinforcements from Orkney Ringing Group. Inevitably there is a strong social aspect to these occasions, and members of the observatory staff reciprocate by helping with cannon-netting activity elsewhere in Orkney when feasible, along with other Orkney mainland mass activities such as the summer swan round-up. Whilst catching wildfowl has never been successful in terms of numbers caught, considering the numbers on the island (and whilst duck traps have come and gone), it remains an ambition of the observatory to mark substantially more of these species. Only a few centres nationally generate most of the recovery data, and little information is available from outlying sites.

The other major activity is, of course, pullus (chick) ringing in the summer, which over time gives a fair index of breeding numbers and success, particularly for the seabirds and especially for Fulmars, Black Guillemot (Tysties) and terns, for which special censuses are made each year. Greylag Geese have recently

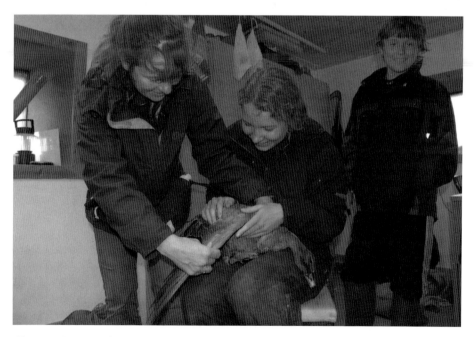

Observatories are excellent places for ringers to extend their knowledge of less-commonly trapped species. Alison Duncan, seen here on the left, is explaining how to age a Pink-footed Goose (Kevin Woodbridge).

colonised the island, wader species targeted include Oystercatcher, Ringed Plover, Lapwing, Snipe, Curlew and Redshank and a variety of passerines including Skylark, Rock Pipit, Swallow, Blackbird, and Linnet are regularly ringed before fledging. The success of Blackbird, House Sparrow and Linnet is also monitored through the BTO's RAS (Retrapping Adults for Survival) scheme, though it may now be that House Sparrows have become so scarce that insufficient birds are retrapped each year to provide a significant sample.

Because of the island's exposed position and the generally fierce and variable weather, it is not possible to operate a controlled sampling of migration through a timed net-opening protocol, as is done for example at Ottenby Bird Observatory in Sweden. Migration monitoring is therefore primarily through the daily census supported by 'maximum effort' ringing, i.e. at least a morning and evening session at Holland House, whenever weather allows during the migration periods.

The data generated from the daily census and ringing activity from the inception of the observatory in 1985 are available in their entirety in electronic form. Originally, the census log was loaded on to a database programme using a 'BBC-B micro-computer'. Each species' record (species/date/number/notes) was loaded from and then saved to a '5¼ inch' floppy disc during call over. Some observers at the time thought this to be an annoyingly tedious process. Thank goodness it was done though, as it saved the effort that would have been required to digitise it all retrospectively had the traditional paper log been adopted. In the late 1980s an Olivetti PC was bought (with a massive 20-megabyte hard drive) that could cope with Microsoft Works, which was configured to meet the required specification for the census log, and the data from the BBC-B system were transferred to it. This provided a slick, convenient and robust system for 'logging' and, despite the massive advances in computing and many generations of the 'Works' suite since, the same database format is still being used daily, both here and at other observatories, pending the development of a better successor, which so far has proved elusive.

Similarly B-RING, the original software produced with the BTO for managing ringing data, was adopted early in its development in 1987 and, thanks to sterling work by Mike Pennington, the ringing data back to 1985 were entered onto it. B-RING has now been superseded by IPMR (Integrated Population Monitoring Recorder), which is considerably more sophisticated and can also handle the nest record data.

This electronic resource has already proved its value through many studies, either using the local data on its own or in conjunction with wider studies. It has been demonstrated that observatory data can be used for population monitoring (Woodbridge 1996), and this has underpinned projects such as the investigation of Ring Ouzel population changes where other census techniques have proved inadequate. Local studies have been performed on Rock Pipit, and a number of students have used the ongoing monitoring of breeding Fulmar as the centrepiece of their final-year project or attachment report. Not all students have necessarily been studying zoology or environmental science; a geography student recently related the North Atlantic Oscillation to the annual variation of the number of migrants (Law 2008), and engineering students have undertaken a number of studies into the performance of the wind generators. Some of these studies remain to be published and there are ample opportunities for others.

As all ringers are aware, ringing data are submitted electronically to the BTO and contribute to the national data set. Recoveries and controls relating to the island are always of interest, often informing us about which populations are visiting the island and their migration routes, or simply impressing by the awesome journeys they undertake. For instance, the Arctic Tern caught by a Captain Cook (sic) on a ship off Ghana was extremely interesting. Another outstanding recovery relates to an American Golden Plover ringed on the island and shot in Italy. However, this record has yet to be officially accepted by the Italian Records Panel and will be the first record of this species for Italy if accepted – it was presumably eaten in ignorance of this!

Interestingly, a study in the somewhat contentious area of ringing rarities (Woodbridge & Duncan 1998, 1999) examined the fat score of birds defined as rarities by the BBRC (British Birds Rarities Committee) and compared this to that of their commoner fellow travellers. It was found that the rarities were in a similar body condition to their co-migrants and we argued that there was no requirement to treat these birds in any way differently from the standard criteria for trapping and handling, though of course there might be other considerations unrelated to these processes.

Climate change has opened up a new and important use for observatory data as an indicator of phenological change, and Scottish Natural Heritage recently made a request for all the North Ronaldsay census data for use in a report commissioned on phenological indicators of climate change (Sparks *et al.* 2006). The analysis showed an average trend towards an earlier arrival date for migrant birds of 0.26 days per year over a period of 20–30 years. Similar trends were apparent from a comparison of dates for first egg-laying, the emergence of insects and the flowering of plants. Significantly, the author of this publication comments on the North Ronaldsay data – 'Shortage of time has meant that the huge potential from this data set has not been realised.'

This emphasises both the importance and the under-utilisation of the data, even though it is all available electronically and has enabled more to be done than could possibly be thought of otherwise. It is a fact of life, especially for those at the 'coal face', that the sheer effort of collecting the data, alongside the basic running of the observatory (with all that involves, from ensuring a good meal is on the table for staff and visitors to unblocking the drains), leaves little time for more analytical work. Each year's data, however, is more valuable than the one before in the context of extending the data run, just as 'the best bird to catch' is one with a ring on as it already has a history. So the overriding principle is that the basic function of the observatory has been discharged as long as the data are gathered consistently and are secure.

OTHER FAUNA AND FLORA

Typical of an island fauna, many mammalian species are not represented and in fact only six wild terrestrial mammals occur. There are two species of mouse – the House Mouse and the Wood Mouse (possibly better named here as the Long-tailed Field Mouse). The latter is rather scarce and is particularly interesting as it shows the classic isolation phenomenon of being larger than its mainland congeners, its measurements falling well outside the typically described range. Though the mice were no doubt unintentional introductions by man, both Rabbit and Hedgehog were planned introductions; the Rabbits, as elsewhere, for food, and the Hedgehogs by the local postman with the intention of keeping his greenhouse clear of slugs!

The Rabbits are abundant and are now entirely a pest species, as the local population has been discouraged from eating them by the recurrent outbreaks of myxomatosis. They do provide carrion for gulls and corvids, mainly as frequent road kills and sometimes after a shooting assault on them, but sadly their main predator is the feral Cat, which they sustain in unwelcome numbers. The population of Rabbits on the observatory's land is well suppressed by the humane operation of sunken drop-traps, and the feral Cat problem is being addressed by a programme of sterilization. It is of interest that tom-cats are better given a vasectomy rather than a castration; thus they remain hormonally intact and still defend and retain their territory and queens, but only 'fire blanks'. This programme is not being run by the observatory, which would be more in favour of humane destruction once caught, but nonetheless welcomes the initiative, which is part-funded by Cats Protection (formerly the Cat's Protection League) with local Cat lovers, as it should at least reduce the feral Cat population.

The two Hedgehogs escaped from their greenhouse and were either a pair (in a veritable Garden of Eden with no other terrestrial insectivores or ground predators to compete with) or one at least arrived pregnant. Whichever it was, by the mid- to late 1980s this unchecked population had exploded and they were regularly found raiding the tern colonies and munching their way through wader eggs and chicks. In deference to the general public sentiment surrounding this species and with the ulterior motive of drawing wider attention to the folly of introducing a ground predator to an island of ground-nesting birds, it was elected to embark on a mass deportation that attracted press interest of unimagined intensity. This was done under licence from the (then) Nature Conservancy Council, and even attracted a film crew from Japan with the unforgettable line of 'flee, too, wun, acsun!' The deportation certainly reduced the population to the current level so that they no longer pose a threat and it is hoped that a fatal gene will emerge consequent upon the inevitable in-breeding and they will eventually die out. Two interesting aspects of this population are that they are flea-free, having been dusted on arrival, and show a sex-linked penetrance of around 30% for pale pelage in females, again reflecting their narrow genetic ancestry.

The sixth terrestrial species and only true colonist is the Otter. These are rarely seen and sometimes their presence is only detected by their spraints. It is likely that they are absent from the island for extended periods, though they have been known to breed on several occasions. The nearest population is on Sanday, and it is remarkable to realise that these animals must cross the North Ronaldsay Firth, with its massive tide-race, to reach the island.

Bats regularly occur in Orkney in small numbers. In the last 20 years most records on North Ronaldsay have been of Pipistrelles, not usually formally identified to species, due to brief views in poor light. Furthermore, continental species are probably as likely to occur as British ones, though some may derive from the small colony of Common Pipistrelles found on Hoy, the most northerly in Britain. The earliest record for bats is in late April and the latest is for early November. They are most often recorded in autumn with easterly or south-easterly winds. Pipistrelle-type bats were seen on several days in August 1990, but a record of three on 13 August 1996 was exceptional. A Noctule caught at the Lighthouse in June 1976 was only the third record of this species in Scotland; there was another on 2 September 1992 and a Brown Long-eared Bat on 26 September 2006 was the fourth record for Orkney.

Domestic animals are mainly farming-related, with beef cattle being central to the agricultural output from the island. The endemic seaweed-eating North Ronaldsay sheep are widely described and need no more detail here other than to mention that the observatory manages a flock of about 100 ewes, which supplies the kitchen with plenty of the uniquely flavoured mutton. A few horses are kept and the occasional goat, pet dog and cat, but the school guinea pig is sadly no more – after its 'terrible murder' by a dog on school open-day.

There is a substantial, though diminishing, Common Seal colony at the south end of the island. Grey Seals are common all round the island and in particular haul out in numbers on Seal Skerry. Grey Seals do occasionally pup, but only in small numbers, the majority presumably attending the mass rookeries elsewhere in Orkney. Among the Cetacea, Killer Whales are probably the most spectacular and are regularly seen offshore, especially in the summer months. Harbour Porpoises are regular, but mainly noted in calm conditions, and Risso's Dolphin is the next most commonly sighted species. A number of other species are occasionally seen or have been washed up, including Sperm Whale, Long-finned Pilot Whale, Minke Whale, and White-sided and White-beaked Dolphins. One other notable marine animal to be recorded more regularly in recent years is the Basking Shark.

Among the invertebrates the Lepidoptera are the most studied. The commonest butterflies are immigrant Red Admiral and Painted Lady, with scarcer records of Peacock and an occasional Common Blue and Large White. Green-veined White used to breed but is now extinct, and the Small Tortoiseshell, which was quite regular and often appeared after winter hibernation, has not been recorded for some years. A moth trap has been run over many years and substantial numbers of records are available, although activity is somewhat dependent on the interest of the staff. No exceptionally rare moths have been recorded, but of general interest are the recent colonisation by the Magpie (moth), sporadic invasions of Silver Ys in spectacular numbers and the occasional Hummingbird and Convolvulus Hawkmoths, which are always pleasing to see.

The littoral and inshore waters have been studied by visiting marine biologists who report generally that they are in pristine condition, although they do not contain any exceptional colonies or species requiring special protection.

A comprehensive plant list is kept by the observatory and made available to visiting botanists who are always welcome to update it. As the island is predominantly farmed and most of the coastal heathland is degraded by the attentions of the North Ronaldsay sheep, there are few areas where plants can flourish undisturbed. The wetlands are the main such places. Here, dense stands of Yellow Iris are interspersed with more open areas, becoming a riot of Ragged-Robin among the horsetails and Marsh-marigolds midst the blue forget-me-nots and purple marsh-orchids The observatory manages areas of coastal heath and species-rich grassland (under its control through an agri-environmental scheme) on which Violets, Glaucous Sedge, Wild Pansy, Grass-of-Parnassus, Adder's-tongue, Northern Marsh-orchid, Wild Thyme, Kidney Vetch, Spring Squill and Tormentil thrive, with controlled grazing. There are no particularly rare species on the island, apart from some rather obscure stoneworts to be found in some of the lochs. The Orkney speciality – Scottish Primrose – does not occur and the sheep ensure the Oysterplant can't get a toehold on the beaches.

Acknowledgements

The observatory would be nothing without the succession of staff, volunteers and visitors. Some are long-term, others come for a very short visit and many return year after year – all contributing to the development and continuation of the work of the observatory, directly or indirectly. Originally, we were all multi-tasking omnicompetent volunteers – who could forget Ian Fisher's sausage casseroles or Bob Simpson's 'porrk in coiderr', the mass concreting teams and 'West! West!' shouted at Kevin Scott (also famous for being kicked in the 'lower abdomen' by a freshly slaughtered sheep) when moving the trusses off the old croft house. Then there was the tender kiss given to the first British-ringed Bee-eater on its release by Phil Bloor, or Alison suddenly disappearing vertically downwards in the reed bed at Hooking when the floating mat of iris collapsed under her.

There are so many anecdotes – from a young Heather Woodbridge famously saying to Steve Stansfield 'Let's get out of here!' when a roosting Black Kite leapt out of the bushes at Holland beside her, to the visitor discovered trying to dry his boots in the microwave and the inevitable cracks about beef Wellington and choux pastry, and finally the American visitor's first question after slipping and breaking his arm on the rocks – 'Who can I sue?'. We're still not sure if he was joking. And numerous romances have blossomed – there has even been a wedding ceremony, with an imported minister, in the observatory's main lounge followed by in-house catering. Suffice it to say that there have always been many happy and hilarious occasions at North Ronaldsay Bird Observatory and long may they continue.

ACCESS AND ACCOMMODATION

Getting to North Ronaldsay

Subsidised Loganair flights from Kirkwall operate daily and are the usual method of reaching the island from mainland Orkney, being charged at ferry-equivalent rates. The scheduled ferry from Kirkwall operates on Tuesdays and Fridays in summer and on Fridays only in winter. Always check with Orkney Ferries on the afternoon before sailing for re-scheduling due to weather and tides. A number of Sunday excursion sailings also operate in the summer but not every week. Small boats may be chartered and can be a reasonably economic alternative for larger parties, though the landing at North Ronaldsay pier may be difficult as it is very exposed.

There are many alternative ways of travelling to Orkney, depending on preferred methods and budget. Air connections are available from anywhere in Britain via Aberdeen, Edinburgh or Glasgow, arriving in Kirkwall to connect with same-day flights out to the island. Loganair operate flights between Kirkwall and Wick or Inverness. There are roll-on roll-off vehicle ferries from Aberdeen, Thurso (Scrabster) and Gills Bay in Caithness and a summer passenger-only ferry operates from John o' Groat's which connects in high season with the through coach service between Inverness and Kirkwall, sometimes known as the 'Orkney Bus'.

Wick and Thurso have railway stations, Wick, Thurso and John o' Groat's have coach connections and cars can be left at the ferry terminals or airport if desired.

Accommodation

The observatory is open to visitors all year though, very occasionally, serviced accommodation may not be available when the members of staff take winter holidays. Additional discounts are available by negotiation to groups of ten people or more and special rates and arrangements can be made for students wishing to undertake a project or attachment. Part-time domestic positions are sometimes available for those wishing to help for an extended period with the ornithological work.

The climate on North Ronaldsay tends to be mild in winter (rarely below freezing) and cool in summer (rarely reaching 20°C), so visitors are advised to bring some warm clothing and be prepared for wet weather. A stout pair of boots is also recommended.

At the Guest House, there are four double rooms, two twins and one single. All are en-suite with tea/coffee making facilities and telephone extensions are available. One of the twin rooms is on the ground floor and is adapted for use by disabled visitors. Families are welcome and cots or additional floor couch-beds for children can be set up in rooms. It is regretted that pets cannot be taken into the house, excepting guide/assistance dogs. The hostel annexe is self contained with ten bunk spaces and a self-catering kitchen. One four-bedded dormitory is en-suite with the other four and two-bedded dormitories sharing washroom facilities. Dormitories may be single-sex or mixed, and meals can be included. Campers may be given permission to pitch on observatory land and use the bathroom facilities for a modest daily fee. Please note that Loganair will not carry fuel for camping stoves, but meals can always be taken in the observatory.

Meals and the licensed lounge

A full cooked breakfast and evening meals (including a choice of North Ronaldsay mutton) are available daily on an individual or half-board basis. Non-residents are welcome and vegetarian and special diets are catered for. Lunches are available in the observatory café or packed to order. Evening à-la-carte meals are also available. A wide selection of quality wines, beers and spirits is stocked and the lounge is open to non-residents. Digital projection and video conferencing equipment is available and its use for private functions, lectures and meetings is welcomed. Wi-Fi internet access and office facilities are also available.

Staffing now is of course far more formal and differentiated than hitherto. The Warden is supported by a domestic supervisor and a cook with a variable team of domestic helpers. There are two full-time assistant bird wardens, several volunteers (who are often working as domestics part-time to earn their keep) and, of course, our visitors, who are welcome to contribute to the recording effort.

Useful contacts for travellers

Wardens, Bookings and Residents	01857 633200
Fax	01857 633207
Postal address	North Ronaldsay Bird Observatory
	Twingness
	North Ronaldsay
	Orkney, KW17 2BE
Loganair (Kirkwall Airport)	01856 872494 / 873457
Orkney Ferries (N.R. Ferry)	01856 872044
British Airways	0844 493 0787
Flybe	0871 700 2000
NorthLink Ferries	(Scrabster–Stromness and
	Aberdeen–Kirkwall)
Stromness Terminal	01856 851144
Reservations	0845 6000 449
Thomas & Bews (John o' Groats Ferry)	01955 611353
Pentland Ferries (Gills Bay – S. Ronaldsay)	01856 831226
Ridgway Travel (local travel agent)	01856 873359

(Note: above contacts correct in December 2008)

The North Ronaldsay Bird Observatory Report is to be found within the Orkney Bird Report for the year, copies of which can be requested from Jim Williams on 01856 761317, by post from him at Fairholm, Finstown, Orkney KW17 2EQ or by e-mail. Interesting aspects of the observatory's ringing records are to be found in the Ringing Report which is also within the Orkney Bird Report.

Records of birds and other sightings are always welcome from visitors to the island who are not able to attend the call over (daily log), and should be sent to the Warden at the observatory.

The observatory opened in the spring of 1985 and was accredited in January 1987	
Total number of bird species recorded at the observatory:	330
Best bird year:	2003
Number of species recorded:	215
Total of birds ringed at the observatory:	73,329
Number of species:	211
Best ringing year:	1992
Number ringed:	3,943
Number of species:	117

Portland

by Peter Mowday†

INTRODUCTION

Often shrouded in mists or swept by Atlantic gales, the Isle of Portland can prove itself a magical place for naturalists. All too often the first-time visitor will travel straight down the major roads to Portland Bill and fail to explore the cliff paths and byways. Portland's secrets need to be carefully sought out, for the rewards can be surprising. Situated almost midway along the English Channel coast, the Isle of Portland seems to hang like a pendant southwards from the neck of what has become known as the Jurassic Coast World Heritage Site, being the 150 kilometres of coast between Exmouth and Swanage.

In geomorphological terms, Portland is not an island because it is linked to the Dorset coast by the spectacular, 29 kilometres long, Chesil Beach. This is thought to have resulted from the redistribution of collapsed cliff debris some 10,000

Peter Mowday was the honorary secretary of the observatory from 1988 until his death on 15 November 2007 and was instrumental in setting up the very successful observatory bookshop.

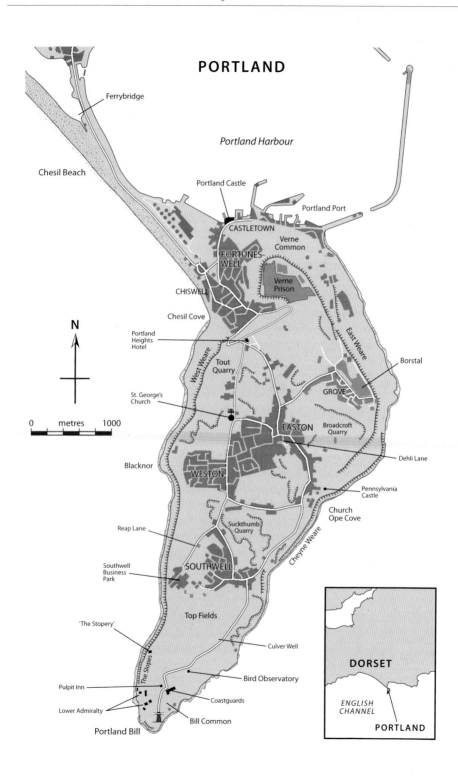

PORTLAND

Portland Harbour

Ferrybridge

Chesil Beach

Portland Castle

Portland Port

CASTLETOWN

Verne Common

FORTUNES-WELL

Verne Prison

CHISWELL

Chesil Cove

Portland Heights Hotel

West Weare

Tout Quarry

East Weare

Borstal

St. George's Church

GROVE

N

Blacknor

WESTON

EASTON

Broadcroft Quarry

Dehli Lane

0　　metres　　1000

Pennsylvania Castle

Church Ope Cove

Reap Lane

Suckthumb Quarry

Cheyne Weare

Southwell Business Park

SOUTHWELL

Top Fields

'The Stopery'

Culver Well

The Slopes

Pulpit Inn

Bird Observatory

Lower Admiralty

Coastguards

Bill Common

Portland Bill

DORSET

ENGLISH CHANNEL

PORTLAND

years ago. Landslips similar to those now known and visible today as the Undercliff, near Lyme Regis, stretched all along the coast from Portland to Bridport in the west until rising sea levels carried the huge quantities of flint and chert in longshore drift to create today's beach. The larger pebbles are more readily moved than the smaller ones and the continuous drift has resulted in the larger potato-sized pebbles being at the leeward Portland end of the beach in the east grading down to the smaller pea-sized ones at the north-western end of the beach at Bridport. It is claimed that local fishermen can quite accurately locate their position along the Beach merely by examining the size of the pebbles.

Portland is a lozenge-shaped slab of limestone lying almost north-north-east to south-south-west and is 6 kilometres long and 2.5 kilometres at its widest. Highest in the north, where the cliffs reach 150 metres not far from the Verne Citadel, the land drops sharply to Chesil Beach. In the other direction, the land slopes down to a mere six metres above sea level near to the Trinity House obelisk at the 'Bill'. Most of the underlying rocks are of the late Jurassic period, some 135 million years old, and belong to the Kimmeridge, Portland and Purbeck groups. The bedrock is covered by one or two metres of Quaternary drift and various features make Portland a geological and geomorphological site of international importance. Here are some of the largest landslips in Britain (on the north-east coast), two raised beaches (at Portland Bill), some of the best examples of the Purbeck fossil forest and two ammonite zones.

The modern road and the line of the disused railway run out from the mainland along the eastern edge of the barrier beach and cross the sea at Ferry Bridge. Although it had been possible to walk to and from the Island along the beach, doubtless a long and tiring exercise, boat crossings were made at Ferry Bridge. The actual (treacherous) ferry crossing at nearby Small Mouth, in a small boat positioned between two ropes slung across the water, was the means of access for centuries and, despite petitions to George III, it was not until the 'Great Gale' of 1824, in which 136 houses were destroyed and the ferryman drowned, that a decision was taken to build the first bridge, which ultimately opened in 1838. In 1865, the Weymouth to Portland railway line was opened, affording Portland easier access to the mainland so that its resources could be better exploited. Whereas the first road bridge of 1838 linked an isolated population of 2,670 to mainland Dorset, it had reached 13,000 by 2006 and the resulting pressure on land use has reached critical levels.

Farming, fishing and quarrying, where once over 500 people were employed, were the dominant occupations and the available farmland occupied the thin Quaternary layer of calcareous soil enclosed in small fields edged with dry stone walls. Sheep, cattle and horses predominated and some cereal crops were grown on relatively poor soils. In general, the landscape was treeless, bereft of hedges and windswept. Today, few of the small fields survive, save for a relict group in the north-east corner and those on the slopes down to the Bill. There are only tiny, isolated patches of unaltered calcareous soils. By 2000, all the arable fields had disappeared as farming declined and only one or two part-time farmers remained in 2006. Nowhere was it possible to earn a full-time living from the land. Cattle and sheep are now seen infrequently and fields are increasingly grazed by horses or left fallow. The available land is poorly managed and the dry stone walls are often in disrepair. However, the Portland Ranger has begun to rebuild the walls with a small conservation group, visiting experts and volunteers from the Young Offender Institution. The Portland Bird Observatory now farms some 14 hectares for wildlife and at long last the remaining farmland is beginning to improve.

Weymouth and Portland Borough Council advertises the allure of the island's flora and fauna and its unique environment, but could do more to protect such an investment. The 'Court Leet', a loose group of local landowners, oversees a grass-cutting policy which often seems to destroy the very flora the visitors are being encouraged to explore! Despite local neglect and seemingly continual development, Portland still has a superb natural history, with over 550 plant species and 352 birds recorded.

Portland is rightly famous for its building stone, which is renowned the world over for its durability and fine cutting properties. Many buildings made use of Portland Stone, which was much favoured by Sir Christopher Wren when he planned the rebuilding of London, following the Great Fire of 1666. In more modern times, Portland Stone was used to face the United Nations Building in New York and it is still much in demand. However, the increased quarrying has begun to threaten the geological interest and many geological outcrops have all but disappeared.

Portland's landscape is scarred by quarrying. Disused quarries are soon taken over by scrub where the dominant species are often Bramble, Elder, Sycamore, Buddleja and Cotoneaster. Where quarries have been filled in after extraction the resulting topsoil is a mixture of quarry waste and the original thin calcareous soils. Even so, plants typical of chalk and limestone still dominate. Some quarries, such as Broadcroft, have been used as landfill sites, whilst others such as King Barrow and Tout have become nature reserves or are used for cultural purposes. The quarrying and weathering have resulted in an almost continuous exposure of rock around the coast, which accentuates the feeling that Portland is a very dry place, particularly when viewed from the air. There were originally five or six wells, but there was never much surface water. Thus, garden ponds and the observatory ponds in particular, remain ecologically very important.

There are five major settlements on the island: both Castletown, which developed to service the harbour, and Fortuneswell lie to the north of the high cliffs, whilst Easton, Weston and Southwell occupy sites on the sloping limestone 'lozenge'. Portland Harbour and the necessary breakwaters were created using convict labour in the mid-nineteenth century. Until then, the largest buildings on Portland had been the Norman Rufus Castle and Henry VIII's Portland Castle. The nineteenth century saw the construction of the prison at the Verne Citadel and the Borstal, an austere building, which still dominates the landscape of the East Weares. Improvements to the harbour led to the development of the dockyard, which became of increased importance to the Royal Navy.

The Second World War saw further development and the destruction of an area known as 'the Mere', lost to wildlife for use as an oil storage area and a Fleet Air Arm base. Early in this century the oil storage units were removed and the base closed. Further developments to the sailing facilities helped lead to the selection of Weymouth as the sailing venue for the 2012 Olympic Games, a welcome consequence of which was the temporary postponement of a proposal for windfarm turbines to be sited along the breakwaters. The Royal Society for the Protection of Birds (RSPB) and others opposed the proposals, which may well be reconsidered after 2012.

There are few trees. In the north, a thin belt of trees known as North Woods grows alongside the footpath down from the Portland Heights Hotel to Underhill. It was from this footpath that Thomas Hardy, in his novel *The Well-Beloved* had Jocelyn Pierston observe Avice as she performed in a concert. Nowadays it often repays a visit, especially during a period of migration, and there is another small piece of woodland in the cleft between Pennsylvania Castle and the town museum. Disused quarries hold clumps of Sycamore, Ash and Elder, but hedges are rare and are temporarily formed in the spring by the prevalent umbel-lifer Alexanders, although all too frequently this wayside plant is destroyed through thoughtless cutting policies.

HISTORY

The Portland Bird Observatory (PBO) was established as a result of early pioneering work by Dr. K. B. Rooke who made the first autumn migration survey in 1951. He was joined by other enthusiasts such as Dr. J. Nash, A. J. Bull, Miss D. Crosby and Miss T. F. Almack. A management committee was formed in 1955 and Heligoland traps were constructed at the disused Admiralty Radio Station. 1959 found the observatory temporarily homeless, but later that year Eric Brotherton and his daughter Helen were able to purchase the Old Lower Lighthouse in which the observatory is now housed. Following the move the observatory gained accredited status in 1962.

Lighthouses have stood at or near the site since 1716. The first light was coal-powered but proved inefficient, so the elegant 19-metre tower was built to work in conjunction with the Old Higher Light and provide day and night bearings for all shipping passing the Bill and the Shambles. By 1789 the Lower Light had become the first lighthouse in the world to utilise an Argand lens of glass. It was powered by oil and visible well over 29 kilometres away on the far seaward horizon. Cannon were based at the Lower Light in 1804 in anticipation of a Napoleonic attack but were never fired in anger. They had been removed well before 1869 when the lighthouse was replaced by the present building, which operated until 1906 when both it and the Higher lights were replaced by a new single, 36-metre, automatic lighthouse, which is still in use today.

The Old Lower Lighthouse became a private dwelling and was once used as a tea room (where it was fashionable for nannies to take tea) and as a restaurant. It reverted to domestic use and was in a partly dilapidated state by the time it was purchased by Eric Brotherton. He and his daughter Helen then lovingly restored the tower and one of the light keeper's cottages. Unfortunately the second cottage had to be destroyed and around the repaired tower the Brothertons built

Portland is one of the first observatories to record Afro-Palearctic migrants, such as Grasshopper Warblers, in spring (Steve Stansfield – www.wildlifeimages.eu).

the present accommodation block. At a slightly later date an annexe, laboratory and garage were constructed. Throughout its existence the Portland Bird Observatory has owed a huge debt of gratitude to Miss Helen Brotherton; she was a very active chair of the General Management Committee, but sadly died on 6 August 2009.

The ethos and aims of the observatory still largely reflect those originally envisaged when she established the complex. A raised patio was built overlooking what has become the famous observatory garden. Planting took place to provide resting migrants with some cover and a large pond was constructed. The present warden, Martin Cade, claims with some pride that he can't think of a single spot in Britain from where more bird species have been recorded.

On 18 March 1961 the observatory was officially opened by Sir Peter Scott, who was elected as the first president. Systematic recording of migration began in 1961 with the appointment of a full-time warden and there has been one in post ever since. Migration is monitored through observing visual passage, counting and recording a daily census and trapping. Although a log is no longer called at an appointed time each day the daily census nevertheless continues and visitors are welcome to read the sightings pad in the lounge overlooking the sea. Visiting naturalists are encouraged to add their sightings.

The observatory began renting farmland in 2002 and now holds 14 hectares. The closure of the Borstal farm unit in the mid-1990s led to the loss of arable land

and many of the arable weeds disappeared, with the consequent demise of the Corn Bunting as a breeding bird. Gradually, the fields became occupied by horses. The observatory recognized the need for a mix of horse paddocks and arable land, so the move was made to acquire as much land as possible. A tractor and farm machinery were purchased in 2006, repair work started on walls, fences and gates and a wide mix of seeds were planted to farm the land for wildlife. Planting is being interspersed with grassland strips to provide nesting sites for Skylarks and Meadow Pipits and leave habitat suitable for wintering owls. Plans are advanced to create a small spinney of trees and shrubs such as Birch, Hawthorn, Tamarisk, Gorse and Sycamore. The project is supported by the PBO General Committee, Natural England, RSPB, the Dorset Wildlife Trust, and Weymouth and Portland Borough Council.

PORTLAND'S BIRDING YEAR

Any description of the birding year on Portland can be thrown into disarray by freak weather systems. Portland is the driest part of Dorset, with an average precipitation of 636 millimetres compared with 1070 millimetres, after the air has risen over the chalk hills, at Winterborne Abbas to the north. Dorset's average precipitation is 883 millimetres. Portland is wettest during autumn and winter, but any moisture soon evaporates or soaks away into the porous limestone. It is also part of the coastal fringe and is therefore much affected by the sea temperature. The winter temperature range is between 5–7°C (compared with the wider temperature ranges of central Dorset) and as much as 17–18°C in the summer. Strong winds, predominantly from the west, are common and snow and ice are rare.

Britain has few birdwatching sites to rival Portland. Its position on the south coast is ideal as one of the first landfall sites for migrants and it is perfectly placed for sea-watching. Portland has an impressive species list and has five times produced first records for Britain and Ireland: Calandra Lark in 1961, Orphean Warbler 1955, Asian Desert Warbler 1970, Savannah Sparrow 1982 and Lesser Short-toed Lark 1992.

Spring migration usually commences in early March with Wheatears and Chiffchaffs, although the earliest Wheatear was recorded on 18 February and Chiffchaffs occasionally overwinter. The up-channel movements of seabirds begin, mainly with divers, Fulmars, Gannet, Common Scoter, Kittiwakes and auks. Migrant numbers gradually build up and these can now include Black Redstart, Ring Ouzel and Firecrest. Look for the first two species in the quarries or along the cliff, whilst Firecrest might well linger in the observatory garden or in Penn Woods. Common migrants arrive during April and May when significant falls are possible, especially of Willow Warblers and Chiffchaffs.

This period also witnesses the return of Turtle Dove, Tree Pipit, Yellow Wagtail, Redstart, Whinchat, Garden Warblers, Blackcaps and Grasshopper Warblers. Reed and Sedge Warblers appear, along with both Pied and Spotted Flycatchers. Most years see a few Wood Warblers and the occasional Nightingale. Sub-rarities such as Hoopoe and Serin can occur anytime now and most years someone records a Stone-curlew. Both Bee-eater and Woodchat Shrike are annual and there are often reports of Wryneck, Short-toed Lark, Richard's and Tawny Pipits, Bluethroat, Icterine and Melodious Warblers at this time. Red-breasted Flycatcher, Red-backed Shrike and Ortolan Bunting have also occurred at this season. Hirundine movements increase, and are followed by Swifts from late on in April.

Merlins appear in March and April, with most Hobbies passing inland in May. Other raptors pass through at this time; there are often a few Short-eared Owls and of the larger raptors it is possible to see all three of our harriers. Ospreys are annual and Honey-buzzards, Red and Black Kites also occur. Rare birds occasionally overshoot from southern and eastern Europe and in recent decades Portland has hosted Red-footed Falcons, Scops Owl, Alpine Swift, Red-rumped Swallow, Black-eared Wheatear, Rock Thrush, Fan-tailed Warbler, Subalpine and Sardinian Warblers, Iberian Chiffchaff, Woodchat Shrike, Rose-coloured Starling and Black-headed Bunting. Presumably *en route* to wetter locations, Little Bitterns, Night-heron, Cattle and Little Egrets and Spoonbill have all made brief visits.

By early April, Manx Shearwater, waders, skuas and terns have all joined the up-channel movements of seabirds which peak early in May. Birdwatchers are attracted by the prospect of Pomarine Skua and the distinct chance of seeing Long-tailed; Arctic and Great Skuas occur and the terns begin to feature. Sandwich, Common and Little Terns are most likely, but Arctic, Roseate and Black are recorded in most years. At this time gulls could include both Glaucous and Iceland and there can often be a passing Mediterranean or even a Ring-billed Gull.

The commonest sea-duck is undoubtedly the Common Scoter, but there might also be Velvet Scoter, and Eider and Long-tailed Ducks are possible. Unsettled weather can produce quite large numbers of Storm Petrels. A small overwintering flock of Purple Sandpipers may still be located on the rocks near the Trinity House Obelisk and just occasionally the season might produce rarities such as a White-billed Diver, which flew over in March 1997.

Now that the observatory is engaged in farming we can hope for more occurrences of Dotterel and perhaps other rare waders which like to linger on ploughed fields. The vertical West Cliffs support small colonies of Guillemots and Razorbills and one or two pairs of Puffins return every year to nest on the top of the cliffs well hidden within the compound. Four or five pairs of Peregrine now nest and there are usually two pairs of Ravens, whilst Fulmars, Rock Pipits, Jackdaws and Stock Doves nest on the cliffs and several pairs of Little Owls use the scattered quarries. As summer draws near there are greater movements of Manx Shearwater and a few Balearic Shearwaters pass the Bill.

Mid-summers are not bird-less just because the bulk of inward migration is over. June and July have recorded Greenish Warbler, Eastern Olivaceous Warbler, Common Rosefinch, Red-rumped Swallow and Sykes's and Blyth's Reed Warblers, as well as an Egyptian Nightjar which occurred in June 1984. By July, the autumn passage can be under way, often led by Swifts. Of the returning birds that pass through Portland, Pied Flycatchers appear in August and September but Black Redstarts, Ring Ouzels and Firecrests are usually later in the year. August is also the best time to catch up with two of Portland's 'reliable' scarce migrants, the Melodious Warbler and the Wryneck, which attract many bird-watchers. Aquatic Warbler has been recorded in recent years. Ortolan Buntings regularly turn up from late August and the return of stubble fields will, hopefully, see these birds stay longer.

By September, movements of Skylarks, Meadow Pipits, thrushes, finches and buntings have begun. These can last well into October. The best month for Tawny Pipits is September, whilst Richard's Pipits occur a little later. Three Blyth's Pipits have been recorded in the Top Fields in recent years. The growing number of horse paddocks could see a rise in the records of rare pipits. September and October also bring the possibility of Barred and Yellow-browed Warblers and Red-breasted Flycatchers, whilst late October is a better time to expect Pallas's Warbler. The visual passage of thousands of finches can be quite impressive at this time of the year and may include Brambling, Siskin, Common Redpoll and Goldfinch.

At this time many of the rarities originate from Siberia and Scandinavia, with Blyth's, Olive-backed, Pechora and Red-throated Pipits all occurring. The warblers have included Pallas's Grasshopper, Booted, Greenish, Arctic, Hume's, Radde's and Dusky Warblers and buntings have been represented by Rustic, Little and Yellow-breasted Buntings.

From further south, Portland has hosted Red-footed Falcons, Pallid and Alpine Swifts, Short-toed Lark, Pied and Desert Wheatears, Subalpine, Sardinian, Orphean and Western Bonelli's Warblers. American landbirds have included Yellow-billed Cuckoo, Cliff Swallow, Red-eyed Vireo, Northern Parula, Bobolink and Northern Waterthrush. Short-eared and Long-eared Owls can often appear in October or November, with some staying on to overwinter, and there have been autumn reports of Baird's, Pectoral, Buff-breasted and Upland Sandpipers.

Given the right conditions, sea-watching can be rewarding. The main species to be seen include Fulmar, Manx Shearwater, Gannet, Common Scoter, Arctic and Great Skuas, Kittiwake, Sandwich, Common and Arctic Terns and auks. July and August have recorded both Cory's and Great Shearwaters, but such sightings are rare indeed. Sooty Shearwaters are usual and there are both Pomarine Skua and Little Gull at this time. Sometimes storm-driven birds will include Leach's Petrel, Grey Phalarope, Long-tailed Skua, Sabine's Gull and Little Auks. Throughout the late autumn, Brent Geese numbers build up on the Fleet and numbers can reach 2,000. In recent years there have usually been a few Pale-bellied Brents *Branta bernicla hrota* at Ferry Bridge and the chance of a Black Brant *B.b.nigricans*. Portland Harbour will contain over 300 Red-breasted Mergansers, five species of grebe and usually both Great Northern and Black-throated Divers.

By the New Year, the Brent Geese numbers will have reduced to fewer than 400 but on land, cold weather movements can result in sudden increases in thrushes or even in the arrival of a Waxwing. Woodcock sometimes stay a while in the Hut Fields round the observatory and on one occasion an overwintering Dark-eyed Junco was discovered! Recent winters have seen the build up of Mediterranean

Gull numbers at and around Ferry Bridge, with 61 being counted in February 2007, and Water Rail can be found in most winters in either Culverwell or the observatory gardens.

FINDING THE BIRDS AT PORTLAND

The visitor's first impression of Portland might well be of a dour, grey landscape, somewhat blighted by industry. If the visitor travels straight to the Bill tip and returns by the same route then that first impression remains dominant. To fully appreciate Portland one has to walk and explore all the byways and footpaths. Portland surrenders its secrets only to the visitor prepared to explore. There is a nearly complete round-the-island footpath, which is largely within the SSSI of the coastal strip. Even local birdwatchers can be guilty of neglecting some of these best areas and many make immediately for the observatory and the area of the Bill, especially during spring and autumn migrations. Fear of missing something exceptional means that other parts of Portland get overlooked.

In the first edition of this book (1976), Frank Clafton wrote 'To the naturalist, only the Verne Common, a scrub-covered plateau above the dockyard and below the Verne Citadel, and the East Weares, an overgrown lunar landscape stretching from the picturesque Church Ope Cove to the dockyard, remain as areas worthy of exploration.' This is misleading. The entire island needs attention. Ferry Bridge and Chesil Beach can be highly productive and the West Weares below the West Cliffs remain significantly under-watched and under-recorded. In Frank Clafton's day, the observatory recording area more or less covered the land south and south-west of Southwell village, but a decision was made in the 1990s to extend it all the way from the Bill to the bridge at Ferry Bridge. Virtually everywhere is worth investigation, but those listed represent the sites most often visited by the local birdwatchers. All the map references refer to Ordnance Survey Landranger Map 194.

Portland Bill (SY676682)

This area includes the low cliffs to the east and west of the Trinity House Obelisk, the extensive Bill Common, the Bill Slopes and the higher cliffs mostly contained within the perimeter fence of the research base. The area also contains the Bill Quarry to the west of the main lighthouse. Birdwatchers tend to congregate at the Obelisk or along the rocks above the Pulpit Rock where good views can be had of Guillemots, Razorbills and the occasional Puffin. Kittiwakes and Shags share the cliffs.

In the right weather conditions, seabirds pass very close to these sites which can also be very good for Bottlenose Dolphins and, occasionally, other, rarer cetaceans. The Bill Common can be good for gulls and passerines, including Wheatears and pipits. Waders such as Whimbrel and Curlew often make temporary stops here. The large public car park at the Bill should be used when accessing these sites.

Portland Bird Observatory (SY682689)

This area includes the gardens around the Old Lower Light. Access to the gardens is restricted, but any unusual species which has been trapped in the observatory's mist-nets is brought up and shown to visitors on the patio over-looking the sea. The walls and bushes around the garden can easily be viewed from outside the observatory. The observatory ponds often attract migrants, which might stay for a while, but generally speaking the birds move on quickly and progress through the island and on to mainland Dorset.

Hut Fields (SY682687)

These fields adjoin the observatory. They are well worth investigating and contain Bramble and Elderberry scrub which often conceals visiting migrants. The hut fields are privately owned and care should be taken to remain on paths and not to intrude on the hut owners. The nearby Observatory Quarry in the adjoining field is also privately owned. Little Owls sometimes nest here and the quarry can be excellent for migrants, particularly for Wrynecks in early autumn.

Observatory arable land (SY683693 & SY685695)

The PBO arable project is discussed elsewhere in this chapter, but suffice to say that all the arable land can be viewed from the tracks and footpaths. Helen's Fields contain some arable strips. Visitors, everywhere, are requested to keep off walls and crops.

Top Fields and Helen's Fields (SY684697)

From the observatory these sites can be accessed via the track which runs north almost opposite the entrance. Pass through the arable land farmed by the obser-vatory and at the obvious 'T' junction turn right to arrive at Helen's Fields. Access here is via the kissing gate. The path crosses the site and emerges onto a public footpath at SY685695. If the visitor continues along the main track he or she will pass through horse paddocks and arrive at Southwell Farm barns. This area can be very good for migrants and at the right times can yield Golden Orioles or birds such as Woodchat Shrike. Look out for Yellow Wagtails and pipits in the horse paddocks.

Weston Fields (SY685709)

The fields are privately owned but can be viewed well from Barleycrates Lane which lies off the main road from Weston to Southwell and is accessed alongside the isolated Community Centre. From this entrance, it is possible to walk through to the West Cliffs where visible migration can sometimes be impressive.

Cheyne Weares and Duncecroft Quarry (SY693704)

These can be accessed either via a footpath south out of the cliff top car park, which takes the walker down into what remains of Duncecroft Quarry (the site of a thriving colony of Wall Lizards), or by walking left down the path eventually to join up in Church Ope Cove. This is an area of collapsed undercliff and is rich in flora and insect life. Before reaching the Cheyne Weares car park there is a small pull-in at 691703. From here walk slightly south before viewing the cliffs for Peregrine.

The 'Hump' (SY687707)

This is an obvious mound covered in Sycamores, Elders and Bramble, immediately south of the last of a line of cottages. Respect the gardens and progress around the base of the hump to view both the trees on the mound and the sunken ditch on the left at the rear of the cottage gardens. This area is excellent for warblers, especially occasional Hume's, Pallas's and Yellow-browed Warblers.

The Craft Centre (SY687708)

There is a track-way leading south from the left of the Craft Centre on Weston Street. This takes the walker into a mass of scrub and pathways developed on old

Firecrests are seen regularly during spring and autumn at Portland (Steve Stansfield – www.wildlifeimages.eu).

quarry spoil. The area is sometimes excellent for migrants and has often held shrikes, Hoopoe, Lesser Whitethroats and other warblers. It is a rich butterfly area; it is good botanically and is one of the better areas for Adders and Slow-worms. Look for these under waste boards or corrugated iron sheets.

Pennsylvania Castle, Woods and Church Ope Cove (SY697713)

It is possible to park on the road close to Pennsylvania Castle or in the small car park almost opposite the Portland Museum. A footpath is signposted to the left of the privately owned castle. This path descends through what is known as Penn Woods and passes through the cliff top remains of St Andrews Church, joining the steps down to Church Ope Cove. An alternative approach can be made by going down the lane past the museum to reach the top of the Cove steps to return in reverse order. These woods can be very productive and are often, at the right time of the year, good for Pallas's and Yellow-browed Warblers and for Red-breasted Flycatchers. Occasionally, this is the site for Treecreeper and Tawny Owl, both rare birds for Portland.

The Grove and Nicodemus's Knob (SY698726)

This area is reached from the A354 on the northern outskirts of Easton by turning east along Grove Road. St Peter's Church sometimes holds migrants and it is possible to walk from the Young Offender Institution southwards viewing gardens and fields along the cliff top. There is access down a signposted path onto East Weares below the institution. A blind left turn just west of the church will take the visitor into a scrubby area of waste land leading north towards the Verne Prison. Over in the north-east corner stands Nicodemus's Knob and a series of small walled fields. This area is botanically rich and often holds migrants. Watch the cliffs for Peregrine and Ravens.

Tout Quarry and Priory Corner (SY685725)

Tout Quarry currently holds a collection of rock sculptures and is soon to be designated as a nature reserve in the care of Dorset Wildlife Trust. There will be a link under the road into King Barrow Quarries Nature Reserve. Grayling and Wall butterflies are found here. The area is often good for Ring Ouzel and the scrubby clefts often hold migrants. There are Little Owls and the area once held a Black-eared Wheatear. From Priory Corner it is possible to view the scree slopes which drop away towards the West Weares. In 2006 the site proved just how exciting Portland can be when a new shieldbug for Britain, *Eurydema ornatum,* was discovered just days after the publication of a new field guide (Evans & Edmondson 2005).

King Barrow, viewing grounds and North Woods (SY692732)

King Barrow Quarries have been taken over by Dorset Wildlife Trust as a nature reserve, which can be accessed by parking on the viewing grounds behind the Portland Heights Hotel. These grounds overlook the Chesil Beach, Underhill and the Harbour, with mainland Dorset and Weymouth to the north. The area is often a superb vantage point during migration and often proves interesting when watching raptor movements. Migrating Ospreys, Hobbies, kites and buzzards can sometimes be observed from these vantage points. North Woods lie immediately to the north of the hotel. A footpath runs down to Underhill. Visitors should respect the privacy of the householders whilst searching for migrants here.

East Weares (SY704716)

The East Weares stretch from just north of Church Ope Cove all the way along the line of the disused railway until it enters the old naval base at Castletown. This area lies at the foot of the cliffs on which the Young Offender Institution sits. Much of it is impenetrable boulder scree, but it is the area, world renowned, for its lichen flora. Watch here for Peregrines and Ravens and search for visiting swifts and hirundines hawking along the cliffs. It was at this site that the British Primitive Goats were released in mid-2008 with the so-far beneficial effect of forging paths through the scrub.

Verne Common and Naval Cemetery (SY693740)

To access this extensive site take the Verne Common Road out of Fortuneswell, signposted to HM Prison and to the Royal Navy Cemetery. After leaving the housing estate, park on the left and walk down the metalled path to the cemetery. The area is extensive and in places impenetrable. Around the cemetery look for migrants. Wood Warblers sometimes stay a while in the trees around the grave-yard, Nightingales have nested and several rarities such as Iberian Chiffchaff, Cliff Swallow, Great Grey and Woodchat Shrikes have been found here and in some winters the dense tree cover holds a roost for Long-eared Owls.

Chesil Beach and West Weares (SY684732)

Chesil Beach can be a very good sea-watching site. Birdwatchers often shelter in the lee of huts at the southern end of the bay. If the winds are blowing into the bay this can be a very productive site and will often hold Sabine's Gulls, terns, skuas and Grey Phalaropes. The West Weares lie south of the huts and are often under-watched. This is the site of the endemic Portland Hawkweed and should be investigated for Ravens, Peregrines and Wheatears.

Portland Castle, Harbour and New Bunds (SY683742)

This area has changed greatly over the last few years. Park in the castle car park and walk through to view the harbour. This area can hold Little Egrets and the occasional Black Redstart or Kingfisher. Start looking for harbour specialities here or progress further around using the recently constructed footpath. The newly created grassland areas sometimes hold gulls and these areas and the bunds along the roadside are worth investigation when looking for pipits or when looking through the Starling flock for possible Rose-coloured Starling. With the development of the boating facilities there are now car parks from which to scan the harbour for divers, ducks and grebes.

Ferry Bridge, Small Mouth and the disused railway line (SY668754)

Portland Harbour and the Fleet are important wintering areas for Brent Geese, divers, grebes, mergansers, other ducks and waders. Ferry Bridge is the site of the Fleet Nature Reserve. There is a large car park and visitor centre. This is the best site from which to view waders, gulls and wintering Brent Geese. Little Egrets feed here and Kentish Plovers are annual. The goose flock regularly holds Pale-bellied Brent Geese and most winters produce a Black Brant. In recent years, large numbers of Mediterranean Gulls have been recorded. Dunlin, Ringed Plover, Oystercatchers, godwits and Turnstones are commoner along the Harbour shores accessed across the road where visitors often scan the Harbour from the disused railway line. Visiting Small Mouth can sometimes reward the viewer with very close views of divers and sea-duck. The winter of 2006/07 produced not one but two Red-breasted Geese.

Remarkable days

Portland does witness spectacular ornithological events and amongst the memorable was 9 September 1956 when the day list included a Quail, 250 Turtle Doves, two Wrynecks, over 100 Whinchats, three Bluethroats, seven Corncrakes, a Barred Warbler, 40 Pied Flycatchers, three Tawny Pipits and five Ortolan Buntings.

In 2000, there was a remarkable raptor passage between 23 September and 2 October. During this period there were 72 records of Honey-buzzard, with 16 on 29 September and a minimum of 35 on 30th. During those days small groups of birdwatchers could be seen on every vantage point across the island. The same period produced multiple sightings of Osprey and 25 Buzzards on 30 September including a party of 12. One or two days earlier raptors migrating south from Scandinavia and Eastern Europe had met with unfavourable easterly winds, which forced them to cross the North Sea. The weather then settled and the birds trickled south to leave the country over the various well-watched sites along the south coast. Few watchers who made the effort will forget the excitement of those days.

Individual species can and do cause as much excitement. It seemed that 10 February 2002 was just a routine day, well ahead of any spring passage. Martin Cade, the warden, took a phone call from Ashleigh Snaith who said that she had been walking her dog close to the West Cliffs at Weston when her attention had been drawn to what appeared to be the corpse of a bird that the animal had discovered in rough grass ahead of her. As she approached, the 'corpse' moved its neck and she realized that the bird was still alive, but obviously unwell as it made no attempt to stand up, let alone to fly. Being concerned for the bird's welfare and curious to learn its identity, she picked it up and took it to her home before contacting the observatory. By the time the warden arrived the bird had been placed into an empty shoe box. Imagine Martin's surprise when the lid was duly lifted to reveal an Allen's Gallinule. Attempts to save the bird failed and it died after an hour or two, at which time it weighed 82 grams as opposed to the expected 140–170 grams.

There had been only one previous British record of this tropical African species and most of the 38 previous Palearctic records were during the winter months. Any vagrancy is likely to occur at the height of the African dry season between December and March. The low body weight would suggest that the bird had made a prolonged over-water passage before being discovered. Ironically, the bird had made landfall only a very short distance from the Weymouth birth-place of William Allen, after whom the species was named following the collection of an individual from the River Niger in September 1841.

Ringing

There have been spectacular ringing days as well, but perhaps the most amazing events were in the spring of 2007. To place the two days within the context of the history of ringing on Portland one needs to appreciate that there are usually several days each year when over a hundred birds are caught and ringed and one or two 200-bird days. Bird-days of over 300 are not annual events and there had only been two previous days when 400 or more birds had been caught. On 17 April, heavy cloud cover rolled in from the north and by dawn there was a brisk northerly headwind providing ideal conditions for a fall of migrants. It turned out to be the best day in the 46-year history of Portland Bird Observatory, with the day's garden ringing total of 502 birds easily exceeding that of 410 achieved on 19 April 1997. A further 138 birds were trapped in Culverwell, a copse some 150 metres to the east. On that day estimates of common migrants in and around the observatory included 1,000 Willow Warblers, 300 Wheatears, 300 Blackcaps, 250 Chiffchaffs, 80 Redstarts, 25 Tree Pipits, 15 Yellow Wagtails, 15 Grasshopper Warblers, six Ring Ouzels, six Pied Flycatchers and four Short-eared Owls!

With a combined total of 640 birds mist-netted, few expected that record to stand for only a few days, but on 4 May the garden total of ringed birds reached a staggering 531! The days prior to the 4th had all been clear, but the morning opened with heavy cloud at dawn and another huge fall of birds in and around the garden. Again, estimates included 1,000 Willow Warblers with 250 Garden Warblers, 250 Blackcaps, 250 Whitethroats, 100 Wheatears, 60 Sedge Warblers, 30 Redstarts, 15 Reed Warblers, 12 Pied Flycatchers and six Lesser Whitethroats.

The history of trapping on Portland makes fascinating reading. No birds were mist-netted in 1955 and only 4,296 birds of the 14,444 ringed between 1956 and 1962 were trapped using mist-nets. The records for those years clearly illustrate the wide variety of trapping methods and also indicate just how labour intensive trapping was (Table 1). Volunteers were far more numerous 40 years ago. Far more joy seems to be found nowadays in the pursuit of rarities than in recording the movements of common bird species within a localized area.

Table 1. *Bird-numbers caught by various methods at Portland 1955–1962*

Trap type	1955	1959	1962
Heligoland traps	782	1,038	701
Mist-nets	Nil	729	1,391
Dyke traps 1 & 2	Nil	10	12
Funnel traps 1, 2, 3 & 4	Nil	65	5
Spring nets	24	1	1
By hand	Nil	4	8
Swedish wader traps	84	Nil	Nil
Ringed as nestlings	50	Nil	40
Hand net	Nil	1	Nil
Government sparrow trap	13	8	3
Hat!	Nil	1	Nil

By 1962, mist-nets were responsible for more than 60% of the 2,247 birds trapped during the year. 2005 saw the dismantling of the remaining Heligoland trap and, although other trapping methods are occasionally used, 100% of the birds trapped in 2006 were caught using mist-nets. By the end of 2008, 192,280 birds of 193 species had been trapped and ringed, of which those most frequently ringed are set out in Table 2.

Table 2. *Bird species most frequently ringed at Portland 1955–2008*

Willow Warbler	40,471
Linnet	14,427
Chiffchaff	13,941
Greenfinch	11,434
Swallow	10,522

The present warden, Martin Cade, has never ringed a Corn Bunting on Portland and 2004, 2005 and 2006, yielded the three lowest recorded Linnet totals. Both these species have declined due to changes in agricultural practice and are amongst the target species now that the observatory is farming the land around the lighthouse.

OTHER FAUNA AND FLORA

Mammal fauna

Mammals are relatively poorly represented and some records are of non-residents which enter Portland by travelling over Chesil Beach. When Frank Clafton was writing in 1976, he recorded regular sightings of Pygmy Shrew, but records have been few and far between in recent years. Common Shrew, Wood Mouse, Bank Vole and Field Vole are probably the commonest small mammals, whilst the most often recorded is the Rabbit, which periodically suffers greatly from myxomatosis. The Fox numbers fluctuate wildly, with a high of about 400 individuals estimated from the numbers recorded at two feeding stations in central Portland. House Mice and Common Rat are common and there are the two mustelids, Weasel and Stoat, although Weasel is much more widespread. Badgers, Brown Hares and Grey Squirrels have been recorded as have European Roe Deer and Reeves' Muntjac.

The sea mammals include regular sightings of Bottlenose Dolphin as well as Humpback, Killer and Minke Whales. Grey Seals are common visitors and there are infrequent sightings of Common Seals. There has been a single record of Harp Seal. Harbour Porpoise, White-beaked Dolphin and Common Dolphin have been recorded but are not frequent visitors.

Bats are almost certainly under-recorded, but the list does include Greater Horseshoe, Whiskered, Natterer's, Serotine, Noctule, Common Pipistrelle, Barbastelle, Brown Long-eared and Grey Long-eared. As previously mentioned, eight British Primitive Goats from the Valley of the Rocks, Exmoor, were released onto East and Penn's Weares in mid-2008. These goats were specially chosen for a grazing trial to help control scrub that threatens to encroach wildlife-rich open habitats and the project is funded by Natural England.

Reptiles and amphibians

Portland's dryness militates against this group, but the island holds Adders and Slow-worms in suitable habitats and, alongside Common Lizard, there is a spectacular and thriving colony of Common Wall Lizards in Duncecroft Quarry.

Insect fauna

With over 550 plant species and the island's geographical position, it is not surprising that Portland sometimes teems with a rich and varied insect life. There are 40 species of butterfly on the list and some are very special to the Isle. The island form of Silver-studded Blue is to be found on patches of Common Bird's-foot-trefoil, whilst Adonis Blues favour Horseshoe Vetch along with the Chalkhill Blue. Small, Holly and Common Blue are also present. Graylings and Walls are to be found in the quarries and along the pathways and tracks and there are two small colonies of Lulworth Skippers, though their sites have been damaged by vandalism in recent years.

Portland remains one of the best sites in Britain to find that spectacular North American insect, the Monarch, during late autumn if the weather conditions are right. As if to underline that almost anything can turn up on Portland, the spring of 2007 saw not one but two examples of overwintering Large Tortoiseshell, followed by a similar but even more spectacular emergence of a Camberwell Beauty in early April.

Moths can be equally exciting and 1,191 species of macro and micro moths have been recorded. Spectacular falls can be achieved on nights when the weather is muggy and the breeze southerly. Thundery weather from the continent can result in moths being drawn into Britain from deep within Europe and occasionally from North Africa. Add to those, the occasional opportunistic wanderers from elsewhere in Britain and it is little wonder that Portland is something of a Mecca for visiting lepidopterists. Whenever possible the Centre uses multiple moth traps which visitors can often view in the early mornings. Local specialities such as the Portland Ribbon Wave and the Four-spotted can be joined by such species as Striped Hawkmoth, Scarlet Tiger, Privet Hawkmoth or even the enigmatic Death's Head Hawkmoth.

Wherever there is water, and the observatory is blessed with several ponds, there can be large numbers of dragonflies and damselflies. The rare Red-veined Darter bred on the Island in the late 1990s until the breeding site was destroyed by landfill. Hoverflies are monitored and recorded on a regular basis, but some other groups, such as beetles, have received scant attention to date.

Other well-documented groups include grasshoppers and allied insects amongst which Portland is host to Scaly Cricket which lives just above the tideline in the Chesil pebbles at Ferry Bridge. Studies of spiders began a few years ago and amongst the interesting Portland fauna is the spectacular Wasp Spider. Woodlice, land snails and slugs are studied annually and details are available at the observatory.

Flora

The Isle of Portland has long been known for its flora. There are two endemic species, Portland Hawkweed and the Sea-lavender (*Limonium recurvum* subsp. *recurvum*) which attract botanists from far afield. The variety of Portland's vascular plants, with a total exceeding 550 species, is quite amazing for such a small area where the soils are generally thin, and taking into account developmental pressure and scant protection from the authorities. Whilst the whole island is botanically important, visitors should be certain to explore the shores at Ferry Bridge and Small Mouth as well as the line of the disused railway which used to connect Portland and Weymouth along the western edge of Portland Harbour. Here plants such as Sea-holly, Wild Asparagus, Sea Beet, Little-robin, Yellow Horned-poppy and Hare's-foot Clover can be found alongside Oraches, Goosefoots, Seablites and Glassworts and other plants of both sandy and pebble-strewn shorelines.

The cliffs contain botanical excitements such as Wild Cabbage, Rock Samphire, Golden-samphire and the Sea-lavenders. The endemic Portland Hawkweed can be found along the West Weares. The quarries and thin replacement soils still contain large numbers of flowers common to calcareous soils and at four or five locations Early Gentian and Autumn Gentian can be found. There are small pockets of arable land, mainly in the area south of Southwell village, and although such species as Corncockle and Pheasant's Eye have now disappeared, Shepherd's-needle and both Round-leaved and Sharp-leaved Fluellen occasionally recur. The list goes on. There are 39 species of vetch or clover, seven species of willowherb, eight of spurge and nine of cranesbill, together with 11 goosefoots and oraches and seven poppies.

Other botanical treasures can be found in and around Church Ope Cove, for it is here that the tiny Hairy-fruited Cornsalad and Rue-leaved Saxifrage can be found. Eight different orchids have been recorded and Portland remains a good place to find Autumn Lady's-tresses and Bee Orchids (*Oprhys apifera* var. *trollii*). In recent years the sub-species *Ophrys apifera-tollis*, known as Wasp Orchid, has been discovered at three sites. The area of small fields around Nicodemus's Knob is botanically rich and the Verne Common area holds flowers of relict woodland.

Macro fungi are generally poorly represented on Portland, although the range of species increases with the numbers and variety of farmed animals. The Bill Common and the area known as the Hut Fields can be productive if searched for Waxcaps and mushrooms. Parrot Waxcap, Blackening Waxcap and Scarlet Waxcap have all been found on the Common in recent years.

Portland is world famous as a site especially rich in lichen and bryophyte flora and particularly for species associated with a Mediterranean–Atlantic distribution. Recent discoveries by both Bryan Edwards and Vince Giavarini have added three lichens new to Britain. The richest area for exploration appears to be the boulder-strewn debris of the East Weares where baseline monitoring has identified 50 of the richest boulders. Durdle Pier and Penn's Weare also seem exciting locations for lichenologists and account for many of the lichens which figure prominently on the citation sheet for the Isle of Portland Site of Special Scientific Interest.

ACCOMMODATION AND MEMBERSHIP

Once described as 'The Hilton' of bird observatories, Portland offers basic accommodation at reasonable rates. The observatory is housed in the Old Lower Light or Lighthouse a few hundred metres from the very tip of Portland Bill. The observatory has space for up to 28 overnight visitors accommodated in two or four bunk dormitories. There are shower rooms and toilets and a large kitchen for those who are self-catering. There is also a self-contained flat housed in the old light keeper's cottage. This facility can sleep up to six and has a lounge, kitchen and shower room. The observatory is ideal for small parties of school and college students, but it is not as suitable for young children as there are no play facilities. Visitors are asked to provide their own sleeping bags, sheets, pillow cases and towelling. Pillows and blankets are provided and there are heaters in all the rooms. The observatory is a no smoking area and visitors are asked not to bring dogs. There are wheelchair ramps at ground floor level within the observatory building and in the grounds and there is limited parking space. The observatory is open all year and bookings can be made via the warden on 01305 820 553 or via the observatory's website.

Weekends can be very busy and the observatory is often booked months in advance. Full membership is available to interested parties and application can be made via the observatory or via the membership secretary, Nicholas Wright,

15, The Knap, Wyke Regis, Weymouth 01305 777991. There are in excess of 800 members whose memberships entitle them to a copy of the annual report, regular newsletters, reduced overnight fees and discounts in the observatory bookshop. The bookshop is housed in the old laboratory and carries a comprehensive stock of new natural history titles as well as a good selection of second-hand books. There are particularly good selections of Poyser and New Naturalist titles. The shop is open every Wednesday, Thursday, Saturday and Sunday from 10 to 4 throughout the year. Further details are available on 01305 826625 or 01225 700728 or on the (very popular) observatory website where most of the second-hand books valued over £10 are listed. This page is updated monthly, but the natural history news is revised and updated daily.

A bus service operates from Weymouth to Portland and the buses will stop on request at the observatory gates.

Observatory opened:	18 March 1961
Total number of bird species recorded at the observatory:	352
Best bird year:	2005
Number of species recorded:	218
Total of birds ringed at the observatory:	192,280
Number of species:	193

Sandwich Bay

by Pete Findley

FIRST STEPS

Inevitably it begins with a small band of enthusiasts and the Sandwich Bay Bird Observatory story is no exception. After visits to Fair Isle Bird Observatory, the Isle of May and Gibraltar Point, the acorns of ambition were sown. Sandwich Bay was not the first choice, but sites on the Isle of Thanet at Foreness Point and others, such as Kingsdown and St Margaret's at Cliffe near Dover, lacked a precise site for ringing and an agreeable landowner. The matter was settled by a fortunate and timely fall of Robins.

Although not on a headland or an island, Sandwich Bay was clearly a place where migration happened and the chance to find, catch and ring migrants provided the catalyst for the decision. It was fortunate indeed that this site was selected. With the benefit of hindsight, it was every aspect of the study and conservation of our flora and fauna that benefited and an internationally important area for wildlife, geology and history has been preserved. None of the founders

---

Pete Findley is a trustee of Sandwich Bay Bird Observatory Trust and the senior ringer at the observatory.

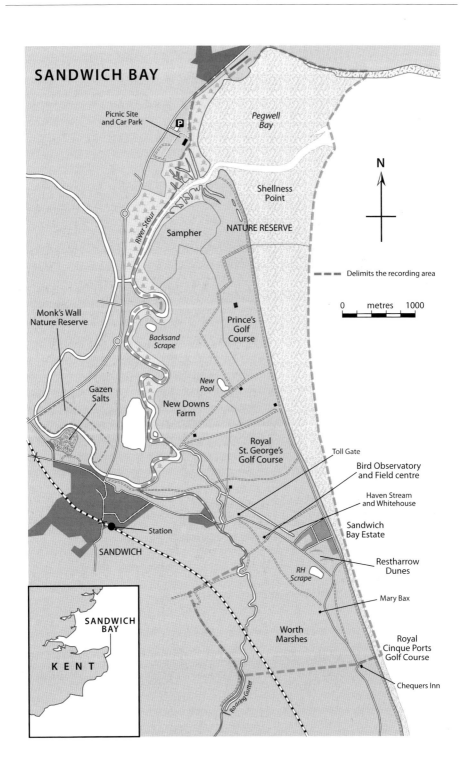

would have dreamt, over 50 years ago, of the European protection now afforded to the area, nor that the observatory would have its own well-equipped and spacious Field Centre, albeit after years of tireless effort, with over 850 members and accommodation that can only be described as plush.

THE BAY

Sandwich Bay is the most easterly of the British and Irish observatories and lies only 40 kilometres from Calais and the north-western coast of Continental Europe. The observatory's greater recording area is bounded by the River Stour from the Cinque Port of Sandwich to the east. The northern border follows the shoreline and southernmost chalk cliffs of Thanet, towards Ramsgate, whilst to the east are the dunes of the shore running south to the Royal Cinque Ports Golf Club. The caravan park forms the southern boundary, whilst the railway from Sandwich to Deal forms the western one.

The principal recording area is around the Sandwich Bay Estate, surrounded as it is by a world-famous golf course, farmland and the sea, and the permanent ringing sites are here. Almost the whole area is of special scientific interest for one reason or another and in the original conservation appraisal it was described thus:

> The estuary of the River Stour together with the intertidal dune and salt marsh complex of Sandwich Bay makes up a habitat of ecological value unique in the county. Indeed, due to its proximity to Europe, a strong element of continental flora and fauna make it an area of national and international importance.

The beach down to Deal is shingle which, due to a northerly drift, is now creeping towards the estuary, threatening the natural sand dunes. The shingle beaches slope steeply, but the sandy area to the north has a shallower profile. At low tide, little sand is exposed near the Estate, but towards the estuary the sandy area broadens extensively. Marram grass is the initial fixer of the dunes and golf courses predominate on the inland side. The three championship courses in fact preserve many hectares of dune grassland and are consequently rich in flora.

The saltings and mudflats to the north are forever changing shape as the sand dunes inevitably grow relatively rapidly northwards. At the time when the Roman garrison at Richborough Castle was at its height, the area around the Estate and observatory would have been under the sea and the shoreline would have been at the site now known as Mary Bax. A recent dig there found evidence of Roman pottery, coins and copious shells.

The farmland is crossed by reed-fringed ditches and many of these are valuable in their own right, being rich in unusual flora and insect life. They are also the haunt of Water Voles and Harvest Mice.

SANDWICH BAY BIRD OBSERVATORY FIELD CENTRE

The premises

Sandwich Bay has not always been a wardened bird observatory and in those early years the core activities were the responsibility of various ringing and records secretaries. The observatory has always had a governing body, elected at an Annual General Meeting. This, since the formation of the charitable trust, is a council of trustees of which Bill Oddie has been President since 1977. The main work of running the Field Centre and its attendant activities is undertaken by a growing team of volunteers coordinated by a number of committees.

Perhaps the most dramatic change in the fortunes of the observatory came about with the purchase of the buildings and their immediate environment. The planning began in 1996, but it was not until 1999 that the funding began to come together. The Heritage Lottery Fund formed the basis of our bid for a new home and this was matched by an Interreg grant from Brussels. The latter was perhaps the more difficult to obtain and finalise. It was part of the European Transmanche Fund which, as its name suggests, involved us being 'twinned' with the wetland reserve of Oye-Plage near Calais. Regular exchange visits take place and it is interesting to note how much power local mayors have within the devolved political structures of France. This contrasts starkly with the centralised control in our country. Oye-Plage has many similarities to the Sandwich Bay area, with coastal dune systems, a large scrape and colonies of breeding terns. Some notable differences include the regular and substantial passage of Spoonbills to and from the Dutch colonies and carpets of Natterjack Toads in spring.

One of the most immediate benefits of owning our own plot of land is having a car park. Instead of parking on the side of the track we can now accommodate 45 cars, provided a willing and firm volunteer car park attendant is present to organise proceedings. The original buildings were formerly First World War officers' quarters, comprised of three sturdily built bungalows. The central one was used as the observatory and those on either side as the farmer's stores. There are many affectionate accounts of the old building, including having to scrape the ice from the inside of the window to discover what the weather was like outside. The best seat in the house was said to be on the stove. There was a constant stream of second-hand sofas and an annual winter battle with the rodent population and the birds in the roof – Starlings, and especially Little Owls, scuttling and squawking at night. And the local fire brigade well remember the smouldering roof above the stove one night in 1986, for each fireman splashed into the pond with impressive-looking equipment on the way in.

1998, however, saw the 'beginning of the end' with the long-awaited connection to the mains drainage system and by the summer of 2000 the change was complete and, of the old buildings, only the concrete pillars remained. A wet winter during construction had delayed completion, but included such unusual delights as newts in the kitchen and sticklebacks in the car park. The new building is named the Sandwich Bay Bird Observatory Field Centre and heralded the expansion of the Trust's activities and interests to become a 'bird observatory plus' whose joint interests and activities are inextricably linked. It is four times larger than the previous headquarters.

The activities

The first bungalow now houses our lecture theatre, nearly 18 metres long. Up to 80 people can be comfortably seated and weekly events include a beginners' bird-watching club every Wednesday and an 'improvers' club (some have been beginners for 20 years!) every Tuesday evening from September to April. Between May and early September a series of outdoor visits to local birding local-ities takes place. As this happens every week with a planned programme, members can attend regularly or not as they choose. A friendly environment and a chat over tea and biscuits in the interval encourage a relaxed atmosphere. The 'Tuesday Club', in one form or another, has been fronted by Mike Briggs for over 20 years now and is a major source of willing volunteers.

On Thursday evenings, speakers deliver a slide show to an average of 55 people, mainly on bird-related topics from around the world, but also on subjects ranging from dragonflies, butterflies, and moths, to interesting locations and single-species studies. The programme follows a similar pattern to Tuesdays with a different series of outdoor summer walks. Visiting speakers have come from as far afield as the north of England and Poland. We finish in time to include a trip to the local hostelry.

There are also weekly walks and talks on Friday afternoons specifically designed to include those who would not wish to travel at night. Each Sunday morning is now devoted to our new Natural History Photographic Club which includes a monthly workshop where members can display their photographs on the walls of the lecture theatre. Members of this increasingly popular club range from the professional and experienced to those who have just purchased their first digital camera and want to know how to get the best from it.

The lecture theatre increasingly hosts meetings of local organisations, such as a Poetry Group called 'Split the Lark' and the Sandwich Bay Estate Residents' Association. It has a large projection screen and displays of local flora and fauna around the walls. At one end is the main office, the hub of the observatory's activ-ities. Between the first bungalow and the middle is the main entrance to the Field Centre, and the shop which sells a range of ecologically related goods and in particular a wide range of books and bird food. There is also a large kitchen.

The middle bungalow hosts a large classroom and dining room and a very extensive library. School parties, younger visitors and groups such as Brownies are inspired by the facilities and equipment including a range of microscopes. Exhibitions include an extensive set of macro-moths and butterflies, a gruesome collection of skulls and a virtual beach. Beachcombing is a popular activity and children can bring back their often malodorous treasures and identify them from our extensive reference collections.

Education is a central theme to our work here and we are very conscious of the need to encourage the next generation to take an interest in the environment to lead to its continued protection. In cooperation with the Royal Society for the

The new field centre at Sandwich Bay, with its purpose-built classroom, is central to many educational activities for school children and others. Pond-dipping is shown here with the RSPB Wildlife Explorers Group (Margaret Douet).

Protection of Birds (RSPB) we have started a Wildlife Explorers club for children eight to twelve years old. Many local schools visit us during the summer term. The most popular activities are beachcombing, pond dipping, searching for reptiles under habitat boards and watching birds being ringed and processed. Regular repeat visits are booked and the Field Centre is becoming well known as an educational resource. Pfizer, the well-known pharmaceutical firm, generously sponsors the travel costs for these classes.

The third bungalow and the connecting section are devoted to warm, spacious and comfortable accommodation which is now of a superior standard and bookings are increasing rapidly. This is locally relevant in the context of a recent assessment for the promotion of Natural East Kent, in which the need for high quality rooms at a reasonable cost was stressed.

The separate Ringing Room has an office and space in the main room for up to 20 visitors to watch the processing of birds. Sunday mornings are particularly busy, and the ringers give demonstrations of the ringing and talk about the birds if time allows. This is proving very popular with members of the public and facilitates instruction about ringing and migration in general and the British Trust for Ornithology (BTO) Ringing Scheme in particular. Most folk are fascinated by explanations of identification features, ageing and sexing, fat scoring, feather tracts, moult and accounts of the life histories of various species. The state-of-the-art Ringing Room allows the ringers to deal efficiently with the birds in an atmosphere of caring for the birds. The opportunity to demonstrate the scientific aspects of observatory work is particularly valuable.

An observation tower in the centre of the main building gives extensive views towards both Deal and Sandwich. This enables us to check the marshes and nearby golf courses for ornithological interest. A workshop, greenhouse, reed-fringed pond and a sheltered bird-feeding area complete the headquarters amenities.

In the Sandwich Bay chapter of the first edition of this book (Durman 1976), Dennis Harle noted that membership had fluctuated but then stood at 40, approximately half of whom were described as 'committed to practical management'. The number of individual members currently stands at over 850 and is beginning to rise rapidly. At no time has there been a concerted membership drive, so it is interesting to consider why this might be happening. The buildings themselves create a good impression and the activities already described are major contributors. There is much more.

People are the greatest resource and the atmosphere is welcoming and encouraging. The entire centre is run by a team of committed volunteers who have regular meetings at which their views can be heard. The many activities and events previously described are organised to support a variety of interests.

Monthly boat trips, leaving from Sandwich Quay, travel downstream to the estuary at Pegwell Bay. As many as 25 birdwatchers can be floated to a part of our recording area, which is otherwise difficult to get to at best. This provides an opportunity to make detailed monthly counts, of waders in particular. Around 60 species of bird are usually found on the three-hour trips. As many as 10,000 Lapwings and 8,000 Golden Plovers have been recorded in winter and up to 1,000 Sandwich Terns, 60 Little Egrets and 130 Common Sandpipers in the summer. These excursions have given us a new insight into the numbers of birds migrating through our area. Those who regularly make the trip gain an insight into the seasonal changes on the River Stour and a close look at Common Seals, which loaf on the sandbanks and cannot be seen from Pegwell Bay.

Courses and workshops are put on throughout the year as single or two-day events and have included a wide range of topics including raptors, moths, fungi, photography, bird identification (waders and gulls), orchids and spring flowering plants. Close by are a number of excellent birdwatching locations and trips are organised to Stodmarsh, the Isle of Sheppey, Dungeness and Rye Harbour.

We have hosted many ringing courses and Sandwich Bay is not only able to provide large numbers of birds to ring and process, but also a wider range of species than most ringers are used to. We also have the advantage of Swallow, Yellow Wagtail and wader roosts; we use many forms of trap, and tape lures; and there is always the chance of a fall of migrants.

Birdwatching courses have taken advantage of our proximity to France and a ferry journey at the right time of the year can be very rewarding. But do remember not to be eating breakfast when a White-billed Diver flies by! Open days and wine and wisdom evenings, where more of the former leads to less of the latter, encourage participation at all levels. Sponsored birdwatches, quizzes, question and answer sessions and Conservation Team events all help to foster a spirit of cooperative endeavour.

THE EMPLOYMENT STORY

A more unusual facet of observatory life since 1983 has been the utilisation of various Government schemes to encourage people into work. The first of these was the extremely successful Manpower Services Commission's Community Programme, which enabled us to offer employment to a wide range of helpful people. We took on skilled craftsmen and those wanting to learn a trade but lacking the opportunity. The fabric of the old observatory building received much-needed attention from floor to ceiling. The plumbing, electrics and heating were all transformed, their new-found reliability being both a novelty and a luxury. After a regime of trial and error, the fireplace constructed in the Common Room provided welcome warmth. However, three experiments were necessary before the chimney was able adequately to conduct smoke from the building.

The committee of the time gleefully drew up a long list of targets and matched it to a monthly timetable. The first 11 months were filled with exciting projects and we were pleased with our planning, until we realised the only job left for a team of four in December was to demolish a rickety old notice board. The scheme itself was well funded and a new Ringing Room and single bedroom, a spacious work shed and a well-organised store for all the new tools of the trade gradually appeared to meet our growing needs. As many as 19 people were so employed in 1986.

Conservation and our primary activity of recording flora and fauna received welcome attention and we were able to employ wardens and assistants whose efforts began to reveal the true potential of the area. At one point we had a warden, deputy warden, senior assistant warden and several assistants. With all this manpower, the ringing and bird-recording increased dramatically and records began to be set.

The care of our nature reserves reached a new height as we were able to attract a range of skilled conservationists who had often been trained to a high standard by the British Trust for Conservation Volunteers. The flora and wider fauna received greater attention as marine biologists, botanists and various entomologists extended the database. An additional benefit of this influx of wide ranging knowledge and skills was our ability to represent environmental concerns at planning application meetings and public enquiries. Successes followed one another and, with the River Stour Society, we supported the overthrow of the Broad Oak reservoir proposals. We were also able to present data and trends at two enquiries concerning Pegwell Bay, one in respect of a proposed hotel complex, with its attendant activities, and the other a proposed road to the Port of Ramsgate. Neither application succeeded.

The second work opportunity scheme, in 1988, was taken over by the East Kent Training Agency. It provided us with a team to work on our reserves led by a Conservation Officer. This scheme differed from the Community Programme in that it was skills rather than project-based. It metamorphosed into schemes run by South Kent College of Technology and Kent TEC in 1991 and eventually the New Deal programme in 1998. The latter involved much training both in health and safety and for qualifications in the use of chainsaws, forklift and dumper trucks, 360° diggers, road rollers and, most fun of all, telescopic handlers. Of course, participants (up to a maximum of 42) had to practise these skills on habitat management, laying car parks, digging ponds and other tasks of benefit to the Trust and the local community. Supervisors who were ringers, birders or conservationists brought additional benefits, helping the observatory to its highest ringing total and with three more Ringing Courses. It was particularly rewarding to be able to provide numerous work opportunities in a field well known for its paucity of jobs. Many participants went on to work with the Nature Conservancy Council, for county conservation trusts and for other bird observatories.

THE NATURE RESERVES

The Sandwich Bay Bird Observatory Trust (SBBOT) currently owns or manages seven sites as nature reserves, ranging from less than half a hectare to over 10 hectares in size, and hopes to expand this number shortly.

Our initial dabblings in habitat management stemmed from our need to establish a regular ringing site. In the early 1970s the Whitehouse Paddock was secured under a gentlemen's agreement with the Royal St George's Golf Club. It quickly became established as our primary ringing area because of its proximity to the observatory. As a Site of Special Scientific Interest, we were restricted to maintaining a small patch of willow carr. The rest of the paddock hosted some rare plants, such as Yellow Bartsia, as well as some large patches of Green-winged and Southern Marsh-orchids. This paddock was regularly grazed either by horses or a notorious donkey. Many ringers remember this creature with less than affection. If you lost the game of 'dodge the donkey', it invariably nipped the final part of you to cross over the stile.

The second area established primarily for ringing, in 1978, was the Haven Stream. This abandoned canal, originally dug from Sandwich to the sea, has been mostly filled in towards the port itself. Silting of the River Stour began to restrict access to the ancient Cinque Port of Sandwich in the middle of the sixteenth century and this three-kilometre cut was a failed attempt to save it. Eventually, dredging the Stour proved more effective, but not before the influence of the town as a port was reduced. The recent Haven Stream project involved considerable fund-raising, hundreds of metres of stock-proof fencing and a great deal of tree planting. The latter activity proved only too successful and considerable cutting and pollarding are now necessary to preserve any of the original character of the open reed-filled cut.

During the 1960s, 1970s and 1980s, considerable effort was put into extending the amount of cover and food for migrants. Several techniques were employed ranging from extensive planting schemes to the efforts of Dennis Batchelor, for nearly 50 years 'Mr Sandwich Bay', who walked around the recording area with pocketfuls of willow twigs and stuck them in the ground wherever he thought they would grow. The theory was that if you planted a hundred, at least a few would survive. The results were considerably better than these theoretical odds and 20 years later we hear the cry 'there's too much cover!' Our keen Conservation Team is gradually addressing this issue with chainsaws and a box of matches. A balance between being able to see, count and catch the migrants and their need for cover and food will be soon reached.

Our first success with a specific nature reserve was the negotiation of an agreement to manage 1.2 hectares of neglected farmland on the edge of our recording area. Downsbridge Nature Reserve was created in 1984 with the management of derelict hedges and planting a wildflower meadow, digging a small pond and converting a First World War concrete bunker into a 'bat cave'. Downsbridge survived for ten years as a reserve until new landowners decided to return it to agricultural use. During that time it was appreciated by various bees, frogs, dragonflies, bats and visitors alike and was a useful trial-run for expanding our skills and knowledge of a broader view of conservation.

Charitable Trust status was finally granted to the observatory in 1984 with the objects of '… the advancement of the education of the public by:

a) The study of birds, their distribution and migration
b) The study and conservation of flora and fauna in the area of Sandwich Bay, Kent and in such other areas adjacent thereto as may from time to time be considered reasonable and appropriate …'

The Trust Deed, though interestingly devoid of useful punctuation, has served us well to this day. It has helped our fundraising activities and allowed us to own land and employ people. The first benefit of Trust status, in 1987, was a successful appeal for funds to purchase Restharrow Dunes Nature Reserve. The establishment of this SSSI has meant the protection of such well-known areas as the Little Gully, Big Gully, Waldershare Gully (all part of the old Haven Cut) and the Elms. The area has considerable botanical, entomological, geological and ornithological interest. Indeed, one of the main arguments in favour of the grant-aid application was the occurrence of a tiny moth, a leaf-miner prospering under the name of *Stigmella repentiella*, new to Britain and discovered in 1957 on the rare Creeping Willow in the trapping area.

It is primarily a botanical reserve of grazed dune grassland with three gullies, an elm plantation and a triangle of land planted with migrant birds in mind. The gullies are damp, with some willow, and are the sites for the various Heligoland traps and net-rides. The acquisition of this land finally secured ringing sites, which can be used as manpower allows.

In the same year we were leased a 2.6 hectare field in the centre of the Sandwich Bay Estate by David and Julia Hunter. Imaginatively named the Middle Field Nature Reserve, the reserve committee decided to create a mosaic of habitats which include a pond, marshland, a reed bed, some small mixed copses and much grassland. Trial and error have been the watchwords here, but the Conservation Team now has the area under control. It is one of the best sites for hatches of Marbled White butterflies, the newly arrived Wasp Spider and Black-tailed Skimmer dragonflies, whilst Southern Marsh-orchid has recently colonised the reserve.

At the time of the demise of Downsbridge, a new nature reserve was created following a substantial bequest from the estate of Miss Shirlaw. This involved the creation of a two and a half hectare site to be known as Backsand Scrape, leased on land owned by Mr Hulme. A bold and exciting project was designed to replace some of the wetland damp pasture habitat, so characteristic of the area during the early to mid-twentieth century, but lost to subsequent years of drainage. The water level is controlled by natural means and during construction it was estimated by means of three sticks and line-of-sight. This was arrived at by the use of a small shooters' pond, already present, and incorporated into the design. The precise design was discussed on site by a committee of three; whilst one wanted it dug deeper and one shallower, the third was ambivalent. The end-product, with three islands, has been extremely successful; Oystercatcher, Redshank, Little Ringed Plover, Gadwall, Tufted Duck, Little Grebe and recently, Ruddy Duck, have all nested. Pegwell Bay and the River Stour are close by and the scrape supports good numbers of roosting waders, particularly Redshank, Greenshank and Common and Green Sandpipers. Rarities such as Baird's Sandpiper, Marsh Sandpiper, Red-necked Phalarope and several Pectoral Sandpipers have occurred here. Many species come to bathe and drink and the scrape is host to many species of dragonflies and damselflies. The ringing of freshwater waders is possible, particularly during August, and up to 75 Common Sandpipers have been ringed in a year. Two 'members-only' hides give excellent close views of many tricky-to-identify species.

Regular ringing at Backsand Scrape has given us some interesting insights into the life histories of several hard-to-catch species. Green Sandpiper, for example, is a species which shows some remarkable site-fidelity, with one adult individual caught in late July over a period of five years. This bird presumably completes its breeding, and arrives early at Backsand at around 23 July. It usually spends around three to four weeks here, until late August, during which time it completes at least two-thirds of the moult of its primary feathers. It has not been caught later than 22 August and doubtless moves on further south, completing its moult either on its way to, or at, its ultimate wintering grounds.

Although Backsand Scrape is an excellent place to watch birds, it is difficult to get to at times, particularly after rain. In spite of its success, we were continually on the search for an alternative closer to the observatory, preferably with easy access. After many exploratory discussions, plans and negotiations, our local farmer, Richard Daw, agreed to lease us about five hectares of arable land that had repeatedly failed to produce much of a crop. Composed almost purely of sand and exposed to strong winds, the upper surface regularly blew away whilst prolonged water-logging did little to improve its utility.

There were two particular advantages to this field. First, it was adjacent to land the observatory already owned, named Restharrow Dunes Nature Reserve, and secondly, the Ancient Highway ran alongside between the two plots, affording easy access. Work began on Restharrow Scrape in 2001, the observatory having obtained a 10-year lease. Advice from a hydrologist who knew the area particularly well was that pumping, holding and draining schemes would be largely ineffective. Sand, he pointed out, drains very effectively and we would need to adjust the level of the scrape to the natural water table.

A few trial bore holes established the water table level, and we began to make plans. Digging such a large hole would require considerable mechanical help and the Royal School of Military Engineering at Chatham kindly reconnoitred the site and returned with a squad of sappers and two 20-ton diggers to create phase one. With military precision, the site was transformed into a scrape with an island and two deep water channels. The excavated material formed a bank around the perimeter which helped to reduce disturbance. It also provided the base for a route to the new hide by way of a short concrete path with a bay for wheelchair access. A single car-parking space, connected to a gate accessible by wheelchair, completed the picture. The site is very easily accessed from both Deal and Sandwich and has proved increasingly popular with members of the public and the Trust alike.

The recent Open Golf Championships provided us with considerable income when we rented out the observatory building and accommodation, together with the Restharrow Dunes field, to a hospitality company. This was put to good use in extending the scrape. Fortunately, the digger driver was a local duck-shooter who intuitively scraped out bird-friendly muddy edges. However, the water evaporated quickly in dry summers to a point where animals were able to roam in. A further week's digging in autumn 2005 deepened the external channel to prevent this and resulted in three distinct islands. One of these was topped with 10-millimetre shingle, proving an instant success with Oystercatcher, Lapwing, Greylag Goose and Little Ringed Plover. All raised broods the following spring and further patches of shingle are planned for the other islands. Additional food is supplied on the scrape for wildfowl during the winter months, thus giving an alternative feeding area for ducks from the nearby shooting pools.

Inevitably, the hide has proved too popular at times, particularly when we have larger groups of visitors at our regular events. A project such as this can be a victim of its own success and yet further improvements will be required. In the meantime it is an ideal place to watch several pairs of Lapwings raise their broods, Hares box in the adjacent grassland and the Yellow Wagtails and Linnets and other smaller birds that come to drink and bathe.

The overall effect of managing our reserves has led to a change in the birdlife within our recording area. The increase in coppice, scrub and woodland has added Sparrowhawk, Jay, Blackcap, Nightingale and both Great Spotted and Green Woodpecker to the list of breeding species. Additional wetland breeders include Gadwall, Tufted Duck, Ruddy Duck, Coot, Greylag Goose, Canada Goose and Little Ringed Plover. There has also been an increase in the diversity of butterflies, moths and dragonflies. The flora has been maintained and, with careful management, the field surrounding the Restharrow Scrape may well be transformed from thistle forest to a more valuable meadow.

Our involvement with nature reserves does not end with those that we own or manage ourselves. The negotiations for the Sandwich Town nature reserve at Gazen Salts (formerly Gallows Fields) were conducted by one of our founder members, Dennis Harle, who went on to design and manage it. Our involvement centred on its development, supporting the management and, probably most importantly, establishing long-term funding for the project through various councils and grant-making trusts. Our participation continues to this day with considerable representation on the management body. The original plan was to turn Gallows Fields into a mosaic of habitats with a central pond and hide and a collection of pinioned ducks and geese. A warden was employed to oversee the daily running of the site, the principal purpose of which was to enable the towns-people of Sandwich to have somewhere to walk for a little relaxation.

Long-standing members of the observatory were also instrumental in setting up an adjacent, much larger, site called Monk's Wall Nature Reserve. Again, this was an area of pasture that now has a mosaic of grassland and wetland features. While Gazen Salts Nature Reserve has largely developed into woodland, Monk's Wall has a much more open aspect with larger areas of wet meadow and open water. Problems with the mains water supply, which was leaking into the Reserve throughout the year, have meant that many summers have been rather wet; often coinciding with hosepipe bans! The land is owned and funded by Pfizer who operate adjacent to the reserve and it is particularly pleasing to be able to work with the business community on such an environmentally friendly venture in a mutually beneficial way. Members of SBBOT are well represented on the management committee in an advisory, planning and reserves management capacity. The area can attract large numbers of Lapwings in winter and has hosted a number of rarities including Slender-billed Gull, Terek Sandpiper and a North American duck, the Canvasback.

Over the years, the National Nature Reserve at Pegwell and Sandwich Bays, owned mainly by Thanet and Dover District Councils and the National Trust, has been well supported by the observatory. In the early days we fought side by side with other conservation organisations and often provided the bulk of the data for the case for protection. The site is now managed by the Kent Wildlife Trust and a succession of observatory members have been honorary wardens and have sat on the management committee. Our more recent involvement has been of a prac-tical nature. We have provided manpower at work-parties and accommodation for seasonal wardens at reasonable cost. We also supply water for the project to reintroduce Natterjack Toads.

The nearby Ham Fen Nature Reserve, a site for the reintroduction of the European Beaver, also benefited from the training programme under the New Deal Scheme. The use of diggers and dumper trucks to construct a pond provided ample training opportunities in yet another authentic situation.

BIRDS

Caring for birds

Being known as a place where birds are studied suggests to members of the public that we are also a bird rescue centre. The summer is often typified by a succession of 'orphaned' chicks and, in particular, partly fledged Herring Gulls. One year we had a crèche of 17 young birds, necessitating the construction of a large aviary over a concrete floor with running water and an endless supply of dog food.

Winters are usually less busy unless there is an oil spill in the English Channel, when many auks are brought in by concerned members of the public.

One such year was 1983 when we were inundated with Guillemots. An urgent call went out for Fairy Liquid detergent, a kiddie's paddling pool, old towels and newspapers. Old socks with the toes cut off were also in demand. These were slipped over the birds to prevent preening. Negotiations followed with the local vets for Kao-biotic tablets and with the local fishing fleet at Deal for kilo after kilo of sprats.

After seeking expert help from local rescue centres, likewise swamped with seabirds, the clean-up began. Every feather had to be cleaned with detergent and a constant stream of warm water. It was not simply a matter of removing the oil with detergent but all the impurities, including the detergent itself. It was amazing to watch the plumage change from black to chocolate brown in colour under the jets of water as the feather's own fine structure reassumed its water repellent qualities. Then there was Gurnard the Gannet who occupied pride of place at the top of a stepladder, but developed a manic hatred of one particular male visitor and refused to let him into the building.

Migration

The study of birds has been the main object of the observatory since the early 1950s. Having over 50 years of daily census counts puts us in a unique position, along with the other observatories, to show changes both in population and distribution. We are, however, aware that birds are part of and depend on the environment in which they live. It is this changing relationship that we also hope to record. Conservation, ringing, surveys using transect methodology and various projects and studies all help us to fit the pieces into the jigsaw.

'Falls' or arrivals of migrants, grounded by conditions or circumstance, are the icing on a birder's cake and a just reward for the days spent recording commoner species. One fall, which remains as a highlight, occurred on 15 September 1968. A front lay across Kent and the rain forced northern and eastern migrants to land on the East Kent coast. Night migrants, such as warblers, thrushes and flycatchers, leave their breeding grounds if they have accumulated enough fat reserves and the night is clear overhead. If they can see the stars by which to navigate, they set off and with good fortune they complete part of their longer migration over a single night. If they encounter bad weather, they make landfall wherever they can. Should dawn find them over water, such as the North Sea, they have no option but to keep flying, usually into the wind.

By mid-morning on this particular day, birds began to drop onto the coast through the low cloud. Ninety-one species were recorded on the Estate alone and seven rarities were present. A brief search in the damp conditions at 10:30 hrs produced little, but the rain stopped an hour later and birds began to arrive. Before long, a gathering of 350 Redstarts, 400 Robins, 250 Garden Warblers, 175 Willow Warblers, 100 Whitethroats, 40 each of Sedge Warblers, Ring Ouzels, Blackcaps and Pied Flycatchers and 20 Lesser Whitethroats provided a colourful addition to the bushes. Rarities were everywhere including five Wrynecks, eight

Bluethroats, at least two Icterine Warblers, two Red-throated Pipits, a single Red-backed Shrike and a Corncrake. Further excitement was provided by a large but unidentified raptor, probably a spotted *Aquila* eagle. The species mix suggested a Fenno-Scandinavian origin where conditions the night before had been clear with light winds – ideal for departure.

The movement of diurnal migrants, or visible migration in the daytime at Sandwich, generally involves finches, pipits, hirundines and thrushes coasting along the beach. Numbers can be huge if conditions are right and 5 November 1961 saw some 50,000 Blackbirds, 5,000 Fieldfares, 3,500 Redwings and many flocks of larks, finches and Starlings move southward towards the shortest Channel crossing at Dover.

Waders and gulls

Many observatories, particularly on islands, are operated from spring through to autumn. Not so Sandwich Bay, which is both operable and operated all year round. Interesting numbers, of waders in particular, are present in winter. Nationally important numbers of Golden Plover traditionally spend the winter on the pasture and have recently taken to roosting at Pegwell Bay. Counts of between 5,000 and 10,000 are frequent, as are those of Lapwings.

Pegwell and Sandwich Bays have subtle differences in sediment composition. The River Stour deposits fine particles as mud in Pegwell Bay, whereas the purer sand of Sandwich Bay provides a contrasting habitat. Waders such as Curlew, Redshank and Dunlin, with sensitive, probing beaks, detect their prey by touch and prefer the softer mud of Pegwell. The harder packed sand on the Sandwich Bay side is better suited to those waders with larger eyes and shorter beaks, such as Grey Plover, Sanderling and Ringed Plover that can pick their prey visually from close to the surface. The pattern of occurrence for these species in 1985 is shown in Table 1.

Table 1. *Monthly bird-day numbers for selected waders at Sandwich Bay in 1985.*

	Jan	Feb	Mar	Apr	May	Jun	Jul	Aug	Sep	Oct	Nov	Dec
Dunlin	3,210	1,206	644	290	300	31	220	322	300	340	1,100	1,200
Redshank	208	402	309	259	73	36	300	265	260	302	245	252
Curlew	298	453	564	205	72	77	350	407	354	411	357	270
Sanderling	62	100	183	86	68	52	16	73	80	60	60	80
Ringed Plover	83	88	65	121	131	47	70	387	430	280	120	107
Grey Plover	271	271	211	75	23	16	6	10	52	140	200	194

Ringed Plovers have received much attention from both counters and ringers. With average wing lengths of 136.9 millimetres for males and 137.5 millimetres for females, our local breeding birds of the nominate race *Charadrius hiaticula hiaticula* are the largest of the various breeding populations. This would confirm the statement in *Shorebirds* (Hayman *et al.* 1986), for instance, that '...the largest, palest individuals are in S Britain and France and are much more distinct from *Charadrius hiaticula tundrae* than are the nominate birds from Greenland'. These local birds are largely sedentary, or at best, short-distance migrants. They raise up to three broods per year, though they are heavily predated, and they can utilise man-made (e.g. car parks) as well as natural sites for nesting. The adults have a post-breeding moult, often beginning in late July, and usually completed by the end of September or the beginning of October. The local birds contrast starkly with the smaller, darker race *C. h. tundrae* from Fenno-Scandinavia and Siberian Russia. These attractive and often visually distinct birds migrate through Sandwich Bay during September, sometimes in their hundreds and it is this highly migratory population from the north that swells the numbers of Ringed Plovers at this time of year.

In addition to the winter waders, large numbers of gulls roost in Pegwell Bay. During storms in the Channel, the larger gulls shelter in the estuary and, during the eighties in particular, many loafed about on the sand, doubtless replete with scavenged refuse from a large and nearby tip. These loafers would harass other birds and especially the local breeding Little Terns and no doubt this was a factor contributing to the eventual demise of the once strong tern colony. The gulls have always had one or two devotees but hardly what one could call a fan club. At least six recorders would be required to make a coordinated count of the Pegwell Bay roost as the birds fly into it from various directions. Preferably, each would have a scribe to write down the numbers called out, particularly just before dusk, when large influxes can occur quickly in poor light.

Almost annual coordinated counts were held from 1979 to 1989 during January or February and the peak counts were Black-headed Gull 22,000 (1981), Herring Gull 15,000 (1986), Common Gull 4,200 (1986), Lesser Black-backed Gull 31 (1989), Great Black-backed Gull 8,450 (1986), Glaucous Gull four (1984) and Kittiwake 56 (1984). Other species of gull were recorded but not regularly. Nowadays, the numbers of Mediterranean, Yellow-legged and particularly Lesser Black-backed Gulls would be very much higher. Incidentally, it was calculated that the weight of gulls roosting in Pegwell Bay on 1 February 1986 was about 32 tonnes.

We hope to gain as much information as possible about our birds and occasionally we can build up an interesting life history. One such individual was a Black-headed Gull caught and ringed on the first day of the 1980s at our first ever cannon-netting session and it was already in adult plumage. The ring number was next read through a telescope by a Danish birder in Copenhagen, on 4 July 1984, 888 kilometres away. It was later caught in Copenhagen on 31 March 1987 and the ring was read in the spring of both 1988 and 1990. The Danes re-caught it in 1992 and fitted a large white Darvic ring bearing the inscription UK1. It was last seen in Denmark that year on 29 June. With the large, easy-to-read, Darvic ring, it was recorded at Walmer (a few miles south of Sandwich) between 10 November and 2 December of the same year and it was subsequently to be found nearly every day in Deal between 11 November 1993 and 6 March 1994. On 2 April 1994 it was back again in Denmark and was seen on four occasions up to 11 July. It was next found, again at Deal, on 17 November where it stayed until 20 February 1995. This was 5,506 days (more than 15 years) after it was first caught by us and approaching at least 17 years. After publicity in the local papers it became quite the celebrity on Deal promenade as an increasing number of admirers sought it out with their spare cake and bread.

Ringing a gull with a large and obvious coloured ring and a simple code to read increases dramatically the chances of it being reported again later. Sandwich Bay Bird Observatory started catching Mediterranean Gulls in 1991 and has ringed nearly 70, many with individually coloured Darvic rings. The observatory is responsible for the coordination of the British colour-ringing effort for this species and 'our' birds carry a yellow ring. Likewise, a white colour-ring on a Mediterranean Gull would indicate that it was ringed in Holland, green in France, light blue in Germany and so on for some 10 countries. The life histories of the birds marked by us at Folkestone are in many cases spectacular. Our first 50 colour-ringed birds had a 100% recovery rate, mainly due to the enthusiasm and dedication of local and continental birders. The Mediterranean Gull, as a species, has a surprisingly large number of followers, particularly on the continent.

The very first colour-ringed bird from Folkestone, number 01P, accumulated 166 sightings, 54 of which were foreign. All this effort involved 12 observers at 11 locations in three countries. It has since been re-ringed with a new green Belgian Darvic. Number 02P has performed even better with 236 sightings, 69 of which are foreign, from nine sites, and the bird is now 10 years old. Most of the Folkestone birds are associated with French, Belgian or Dutch sites, but two are regularly found in Hampshire and singles have been recorded in Essex, Italy and Germany and as far away as the Ukraine. There were over 1,000 at Folkestone in December 2005, a staggering increase on early numbers.

Winter

Wintering Great Crested Grebes can be present in surprising numbers and can drift offshore with the tide around the whole of East Kent. A typically good year was 1997, with peak winter monthly figures between 668 and 692. During that year, by comparison, there were none from April to October.

Significant winter numbers of Stock Doves are recorded. Apart from the local breeding population, figures rise from mid-October onwards and over a thousand can be found on the farmland at New Downs. There was a peak of 3,500 birds on 1 December 1992, when most were roosting in Prince's Plantation. However, a decline has been noted recently.

Two passerines, Corn and Snow Buntings, can also be present at this time of year in significant numbers. Corn Buntings have had a stronghold at Sandwich Bay for some time and the fact that birds were known to be present here in every month was quoted as evidence of their resident status in the county (Harrison 1953). In 1994, 43 singing males were present at an average density of 3.6 males per square kilometre, whereas the national average for farmland is 2.4 pairs per square kilometre. A single kilometre square just south of the observatory held 16 singing males. However, the number of pairs in any population is not easily determined as some males are known to be polygamous, a position further complicated by the likely presence of a few unmated males. Numbers at Sandwich Bay for 1986 are indicated in Table 2.

Table 2. *Monthly bird-day numbers of Corn Bunting, Sandwich Tern, Common Sandpiper, Long-eared Owl and Starling at Sandwich Bay in selected years.*

Species	Year	Jan	Feb	Mar	Apr	May	Jun	Jul	Aug	Sept	Oct	Nov	Dec
Corn Bunting	1986	266	580	120	81	43	27	44	31	49	79	195	209
Sandwich Tern	1997	–		58	25	116	22	121	1,076	412	3	–	–
Common Sandpiper	1984	3	2	3	7	12	1	142	162	46	1	1	1
Long-eared Owl	2000	–	–	3	6	2	1	2	1	13	17	10	7
Starling	2000	2,350	1,600	3,816	970	385	898	1,967	3,300	6,450	30,000	7,000	3,500

It is felt, however, that numbers at Sandwich Bay have been declining since about the turn of the new century.

Snow Buntings are an attractive species. During the mid-eighties, several Scottish ringers turned their attention to the large numbers present in their areas. This triggered several parallel studies as far south as Sandwich Bay. Although the numbers here are small by comparison with the four-figure flocks often encountered in Scotland, this study yielded much valuable information in a local context. During January 1960, Snow Buntings came to feed on wheat during hard weather and over 200 were ringed. The information from these early catches was limited, to the extent that ageing and sexing at that time was based on *The Handbook of British Birds* (Witherby *et al.* 1938), which made no reference to racial differences.

In the more recent study it was found that baiting with wheat only worked well in hard weather. Their natural food comprises the much smaller seeds of coastal plants, particularly Sea Sandwort, so a foreign finch mix based on Panicum Millet was used in the grain dump. This proved so successful that we were able to catch them even in very mild weather.

The study showed that our Snow Buntings in mild winters are young, Icelandic and female. Young males and adults of either sex are more likely to appear in cold weather. Males averaged slightly larger than females and lipid fat scores increased towards winter/early spring. It was also noted that this species occupies a highly specialised ecological niche rarely shared by other passerines except, at times, Skylark and Shore Lark. Consequently, their susceptibility to a variety of man-made influences such as coastal defence work, oil pollution and habitat erosion (by large numbers of summer holidaymakers) is a factor to keep in mind.

Spring

Spring arrives with subtlety at Sandwich Bay. Many plant species are flowering earlier, and Chiffchaffs and Common Sandpipers have begun to overwinter in gradually increasing numbers; many common species nest earlier. Mid-February sees the start of a more noticeable migration with an increase in male Chaffinch numbers. These birds are thought to be wintering in France or further west in England and begin moving through in March in good numbers, by which time we are looking for 'the usual suspects', the early arrivals, such as Wheatear, Sand Martin, Garganey, Swallow, Firecrest and Black Redstart.

South coast observatories to the west invariably record the first arrivals of summer migrants before Sandwich Bay and it is a red-letter day if the situation is reversed. However, the element of competition is always there and it is with a species such as Lesser Whitethroat, arriving from an easterly direction, that we stand our best chance of success.

The continental race of Great Tits *Parus major major*, so dull and grey in comparison with our bright yellow and green local birds, have started to appear in fair numbers in early spring and three-figure counts have occurred. Linnets, Goldfinches, Siskins and Greenfinches all move back through the area in substantial numbers in spring and it is at this time of year that we hope for a flush of Golden Orioles, Kentish Plovers, Montagu's Harriers and Icterine Warblers.

Yellow Wagtails have always added a welcome splash of colour to our springs. They nest in good numbers around the pastures and the autumn roosts have built up to 2,000 during August. Most of the Yellow Wagtail subspecies have turned up here. Birds of the continental nominate race, Blue-headed Wagtail *Motacilla flava flava*, are regular, particularly in early May, and often stay to breed. Worth Marshes is a 'wagtail-lovers' paradise (or nightmare, depending on your point of view). Among the nesting British race of Yellow Wagtails *M. f. flavissima*, there are often pairs of pure Blue-headed which breed true-to-form youngsters.

Unfortunately, there are also mixed race pairings producing hybrid young-sters. Add to this the return of the hybrids in any following year, which in turn pair up with Yellows or Blue-headed or, heaven forbid, other hybrids and the melting pot is boiling. Imagination is further stretched if youngsters from these combinations return to breed. Unsurprisingly, identification to race often causes considerable discussion.

With spring ending in June and autumn beginning in July, it would be easy to miss the delights of summer if you were to concentrate on migration alone. The show of sand dune and coastal plants, such as Lizard Orchid, Sea-holly and its associated Common Broomrape, and Sea Aster, brings botanists from far afield and engenders much interest among the locals. Butterflies and dragonflies have gained an increasing following, but the real 'growth industry' is moths.

Its similarity to birdwatching is worth noting and there is much to study. Up to 350 regular larger (macro) moths are recorded at Sandwich Bay, though another 500 or so smaller (micro) moths are there to be found by the true enthusiast. There are handfuls of tricky species, all appearing virtually the same, there are migrants and there are specialists as to both habitat and locality. A number of the larger species look simply spectacular. It is no wonder that emptying the trap each day is an increasingly popular activity at this time of the year.

Breeding birds

Surveying the breeding birds, constructing nest boxes and ringing the subse-quent chicks are also beginning to gain momentum as the changes in our avian fauna become more newsworthy. House Sparrows are a prime example, with many parts of the country reporting declines. Here at Sandwich Bay, the numbers have also contracted. The formerly frequent flocks of 50 or so are now absent from the Bramble patches in the agricultural areas. Tidiness may be restricting breeding numbers as well-groomed farms and farmland, and efficient farming methods, tend to reduce both feeding and nesting opportunities. Our regular recording area, the Estate, is now the stronghold. An abundance of bird tables and nest boxes by the dozen seem to keep the population healthy here. Annual ringing totals of over 500 are still possible.

Breeding terns at the accreting dunes and sandbar system in the mouth of the estuary have long held our interest. From as early as 1792, when William Boys, the Sandwich historian, left a record of 164 bird species for the area, the varying fortunes of terns and plovers have been monitored. It was he who collected the type specimens of Sandwich Tern and Kentish Plover and sent them to the ornithologist Dr John Latham who named them. Little Terns and their (mis)fortunes are well documented. In 1930 there were seven pairs. Numbers fluctuated between 60 and 80 pairs in their heyday in the mid-thirties, but very few were present over the next seven decades. Productivity is extremely variable as a number of factors seem to work against them. Attempted predation by Foxes, Hedgehogs, loafing gulls and the ever-prospering crows, tests the ability of the adults to keep marauders at bay. Other factors favour loss. Heavy downpours, exceptionally high tides, increasing human disturbance and once, a hovercraft, limping along with a damaged skirt and ploughing through the colony, have all taken their toll. The last breeding attempt by these diminutive and vulnerable seabirds was in 1994, and although we, and the Kent Wildlife Trust, continue to expend resources on their behalf, only memories of the past and hopes for the future remain.

Sandwich Terns can be with us all year round, but individuals are not present every winter. Migrants begin to arrive in March. Pairs are observed displaying each year, the males offering tempting presents of fish fry and Sand Eels as part of their courtship. Unfortunately, they have not stayed to nest in recent years, though the habitat seems suitable. However, spectacular numbers pass through in August as the colonies empty in Belgium, Holland and north-eastern Britain. Bird-day counts in a typical year are detailed in Table 2.

The early autumn

July sees Lapwings gathering together in flocks. Hundreds, sometimes thousands, of Sand Martins arrive on the marshes. Adult waders, particularly Common and Green Sandpipers, put in an appearance and we eagerly await the first flush of south-bound Willow Warblers amongst which we search for elusive migrant Wood Warblers.

The build-up of Common Sandpipers on the river is often spectacular. By early August many birds of the year, perhaps only ten weeks old, swell the numbers of moulting adults already present. Birds caught at Backsand Scrape reveal a pattern of autumn site fidelity as an increasing number of these twitchy, rear-bobbing birds have been ringed in previous years. A typical pattern of bird-day counts is shown in Table 2. With a highest ever count of 300 in August 1962 and 165 birds considered notable in the 1983/84 'Birds of Estuaries Enquiry' (Salmon & Moser 1984), the continuing substantial counts along our estuary must be very important.

The numbers of any species migrating over Sandwich Bay during darkness must be considerably more than are grounded. In recent years, birds have been tape-lured into a maize field adjacent to the observatory during August. Sedge, Reed and Grasshopper Warbler tapes work particularly well and 300–400 birds can be caught on a good morning. This exercise gives us considerable food for thought when we realise that the numbers naturally recorded in our area must be just 'the tip of the iceberg'. The majority of nocturnally migrating birds will simply fly over and not be observed.

The peak counts for migrant birds during August include typical species such as Willow Warbler, Swift, Sand Martin, Wood and Green Sandpipers, Pied Flycatchers, Whimbrel, Greenshank and Yellow Wagtails. September brings to mind Chiffchaffs, Whinchats, Whitethroats, Lesser Whitethroats, Garden Warblers, Blackcaps, House Martins and Swallows, and we especially recall the roost of approximately half a million of the latter in the maize field on 15 September 1996. The last main month of migration, October, suggests Meadow Pipits, Lesser Redpolls, Siskins, Black Redstarts, Goldfinches, Linnets, Starlings, Blackbirds, Song Thrushes, Jays and especially Goldcrests.

Many species have been studied in depth at various times and House Martins were subjected to a considerable amount of attention in the 1980s. Many were tape-lured and several hundred could be caught in a day at times of peak move-

Sightings of Hobby have increased quite dramatically in recent years at Sandwich Bay, where they can be seen chasing migrant House Martins and Swallows (Rob McEwen).

ment. Some large movements have been recorded, with at least 100,000 in 1986 and possibly even nearer a million moving south on 21 September.

Very little is known about the wintering grounds of this species. House Martins have feathered tarsi and feet and it was felt, for instance, that the BTO metal rings might be overlooked on birds found dead. Rings tinted pink or blue were trialled and in 1986 alone, 7,488 were fitted here. Recoveries or controls from within Britain increased dramatically, with several from as far north as Scotland and west to Gloucester. These recoveries indicated the importance of Sandwich Bay as an exit point for House Martins from all over Britain. There were also many local controls, emphasising the diverse origins of the huge flocks which pass through in autumn. Whilst there were single recoveries from France and Algeria, nothing was learned about the wintering areas in Africa, despite the colourful rings. Unlike Swallow and Sand Martin, no terrestrial winter roosts of House Martins have been identified in Africa. We have now ringed over 22,000 of the birds, 6,000 more than for Swallow, for which species we have three South African recoveries by comparison.

Amongst the owls are some highly migratory species and there are several Long-eared Owl roosts nearby in winter. Although the species probably nests regularly, the paucity of summer records here shows just how difficult it is to prove breeding. In the hand, this owl is a defiant and fierce bundle of feathers and many a ringer has learned the hard way to avoid the feet rather than the beak. However, most are recorded on the Estate as migrants in October and the pattern shown in Table 2 is typical of many years.

Raptors are having mixed fortunes. Numbers of Rough-legged Buzzard, Hen Harrier and Kestrel have shown a slight general decline since the 1950s and 1960s. Merlin, Montagu's Harrier and Honey-buzzard would appear to be holding their own, but the rest demonstrate an increase. Hobby sightings have increased considerably since the seventies, as have Marsh Harrier, Osprey and Peregrine. In more recent years Buzzard and Red Kite have also shown a sudden increase.

Perhaps the most dramatic change in fortunes is for the Sparrowhawk, as detailed in Table 3.

Table 3. *Monthly bird-day numbers of Sparrowhawks at Sandwich Bay in selected years from 1968 to 2003.*

Year	Jan	Feb	Mar	Apr	May	Jun	Jul	Aug	Sept	Oct	Nov	Dec
1968	–	–	–	2	–	–	–	–	1	–	–	–
1977	1	–	–	1	–	–	–	–	4	4	–	1
1987	1	1	4	10	4	–	–	–	–	3	–	–
1995	16	9	13	22	13	2	–	3	21	27	22	25
2003	35	18	73	82	52	39	4	69	90	70	36	15

While the Sparrowhawk populations in many parts of the country recovered in the 1970s and 1980s, following the earlier well-documented collapse, it was only in the late 1990s that the species penetrated all the way into the south-eastern corner of Kent. This gradual return to its former breeding range culminated on the Estate with a pair successfully raising two chicks in 2006.

Late autumn

October is an exciting and long-awaited month. An extract from the monthly summaries of 1988 epitomises the expectations and possibilities.

> *There were two periods of south-easterlies, the first during the first few days of the month and then again from 13th to 23rd. October started with a fall of Chiffchaffs on the 1st, accompanied by Barred Warbler, two Icterine Warblers, two Ring Ouzels, Tree Pipit and a Red-backed Shrike. There were also two Lesser Spotted Woodpeckers on the Estate and eight Lapland Buntings flew over. The following day, Ring Ouzels had increased to five, seven Bearded Tits were also present and the first Yellow-browed Warbler of the autumn arrived. The next few days were quieter but records included another Yellow-browed on the 4th, which stayed to the 11th, accompanied by another one on the 8th, Hobby on the 5th, Wryneck on Prince's Beach from 5th to 7th and Quail on the 7th and 12th. Late summer migrants included Turtle Dove to the 10th, two Swifts on the 5th, Sand Martin to the 9th, Whitethroat to the 10th and four Arctic Terns on the 7th. The really exciting period started on the 13th, as the wind became south-easterly and high pressure established over the continent. On that day Goldcrest and thrush numbers, including Ring Ouzel, rose. The 14th produced two Firecrests, a Chiffchaff of the Siberian race* Phylloscopus collybita tristis *and a Treecreeper on the Estate and the first Hen Harrier of the autumn. The 15th saw a Leach's Petrel flying through the dunes, eight Ring Ouzels and a Jack Snipe. At about midday a 'red-tailed' Shrike was found in the Mary Bax area which turned out to be an Isabelline Shrike – the first for the observatory and for Kent. This bird was later trapped and then released on the Estate giving excellent views the following day as it moved off across Worth Marshes. The most spectacular day was the 16th when a large fall took place. This initially involved Robins, with up to 500 on the Estate, but thrushes were also much in evidence and were seen to arrive continuously during the day, with 500 Redwings, 150 Song Thrushes and over 100 Blackbirds recorded. Other movements included 10 Grey Wagtails, 10 White Wagtails* Motacilla alba alba, *56 Chaffinches, 200 Goldfinches, 160 Siskins, 190 Lesser Redpolls, 30 Bramblings, two Merlins in off the sea and two Bean Geese were seen at Mary Bax's Stone. Also present on the Estate were seven Black Redstarts, 180 Goldcrests, a Garden Warbler, a Yellow-browed Warbler and another* P. c. tristis *Chiffchaff. The best confirmed record for the day was an Olive-backed Pipit which was trapped in the Elms, yet another 'first' for the observatory. The day was rounded off by a Barn Owl of the continental dark-breasted form* Tyto alba guttata *that was seen near the Tollgate in the evening. Over the next few days Robin and Goldcrest numbers remained high and Black Redstarts peaked at 13 on the 19th. Other records included 142 White-fronted Geese on the 17th and up to seven Bean Geese on 18th, when a Common Redpoll was also present. The 19th produced yet another rarity, a Short-toed Treecreeper, which was trapped in the Whitehouse bushes and was present intermittently in the Elms, where it was released, until the 24th. This, the observatory's third record, proved to be a very big attraction.*

A very late Swift was present on the Estate on 24th and a Sparrowhawk was seen on the 25th. Sea-watching on 26th produced 500 Brent Geese, five Velvet Scoters, two Pomarine Skuas and a Little Auk. A Little Stint was at the Point from 26th to 30th and Hen Harriers were recorded daily from 26th. The next day a Great Northern Diver flew south and a Shore Lark appeared on Prince's Beach and remained until the following day. A very late Red-backed Shrike was seen on 28th when a Red Kite flew over Pegwell Bay. Strong north-easterly winds on 9th gave better sea-watching with Sooty Shearwaters, Slavonian Grebe and Little Auks, as well as 43 Bewick's Swans coming in off the sea. On the Estate there was a Yellow-legged Gull, a Rough-legged Buzzard flew over and three Little Auks circled the observatory building. Another Little Auk was on the sea on 30th and yet another was seen swimming in front of the hide at Pegwell. A Whimbrel and nine Bewick's Swans were also seen and there were four Whooper Swans on Worth the following day.

In many years Starlings feature in October and November. It may be that numbers simply appear to increase day by day, whilst on others, flocks can be seen flying in off the sea over the coastline. They still breed here in good numbers, but the summer flocks of juveniles tend to number hundreds nowadays, rather than thousands. In addition, the numbers immigrating are less frequently in five figures and the winter flocks tend to be more fragmented. We are still talking of large numbers, however, and the pattern of high autumn and winter numbers is illustrated for 2000 in Table 2.

Local Starlings tend to move only short distances, with most recovered within eight kilometres, but an occasional first-winter bird will venture as far as Essex, Sussex or London. The immigrants, arriving in large numbers from the continent, journey here from as far eastwards as Russia. Many move further into Britain but only rarely beyond.

Blackbirds prosper at Sandwich Bay. The residents in summer comprise the adult breeding population, their young and, no doubt, a few unmated non-breeders. There appears to be very little movement of the birds during this season though numbers can be high. Up to 70 young birds may be seen in the area by the end of June (e.g. as in 1962). Before the hard winter of 1962/63 the average number of breeding pairs on the Estate was 20. Numbers recovered fairly rapidly over two years or so, from only six pairs in 1963, to 10–15 pairs in 1964 and back to its former level a year later. The local breeding population tends to remain in the area. Of 339 recoveries of ringed local birds, only three were further away than 6 kilometres, of which one was in France.

Autumnal Blackbird passage is usually noticeable at Sandwich Bay from late September to mid-November. The largest numbers appear in the third and fourth weeks of October and the first week of November and vary considerably from year to year. They do not normally involve more than 300 birds on any one day and numbers more often range from 70 to 150 for counts on the Estate. On a good day, a further 200 may be found on the marshes, particularly in the area of Hawthorns known as the Sampher. The first of three exceptional years was 1961 when, on 4 and 5 November, over 12,000 Blackbirds were associated with a westerly movement of an estimated 50,000 birds over the Bay. In subsequent summers, one recovery from those ringed was from just across the Channel. There were also two recoveries from Norway and one from Sweden, which go some way to suggest the origins of these birds. In 1966, 1,400 Blackbirds passed north-west in the afternoon of 26 October.

The third departure from the norm was in 1977, when a large movement occurred on 17 and 18 November. Observations were limited on both days to the Estate area, where energies were concentrated on ringing. The major proportion of the birds involved were young males, compared with 1966, when birds of all ages and sexes were caught. There were probably at least 5,000 birds arriving on a broad front between Ramsgate and Deal on 17 November. The three large movements referred to had several elements in common. The Blackbirds involved were always moving in a westerly or north-westerly direction. They were accompanied by several other species common to all three movements, namely Fieldfare, Redwing and Song Thrush. Thirdly, the movement was centred on Sandwich Bay, while the movement nationally was in a very narrow band, especially across the English Channel.

Analysis of the accumulated ringing recoveries and dates of capture reveal an interesting pattern. The Continental birds arrive from late September to mid-November but mainly in October, to be followed by the Scandinavian birds arriving from late October, but mainly in November. The Continental birds pass through to winter in France, with none, or very few, apparently wintering here, but often return from their wintering grounds via our area in March and early April. The Scandinavian birds, however, remain here, mainly in the orchards, and have usually left by the end of February or early March. As stated earlier, the British Blackbirds at Sandwich Bay are almost entirely sedentary, with only an occasional individual moving more than six kilometres.

Sea-watching and visible migration

Sea-watching in a bay is hard work and requires many long hours and a telescope. Several species spend time offshore in winter, including Common Scoters, Guillemots, Razorbills, Red-throated Divers and the aforesaid Great Crested Grebes. However, it is October and November that are best for variety, when strong winds are necessary, specifically from the north-west. On a good day, several hundred Gannets will fly past with a handful of the other birds mentioned above. Skuas, shearwaters and Little Auks all add a little spice as do Dark-bellied Brent Geese *Branta bernicla bernicla*, which can pour by in their thousands. Once, in 1974, a passage of 44 Little Auks was recorded.

Visible migration, watching day-flying migrants move north or south along the coastline, known colloquially as 'viz migging', is a productive activity that can be combined with sea-watching in any September and October. There is also probably no better way of improving one's knowledge of bird calls. A particularly interesting movement occurred from 1–10 October 1974 and its details are recorded in Table 4.

The table illustrates not only the numbers, but also the variety, of birds.

Table 4. *Bird-day numbers for selected visible passage migrants at Sandwich Bay 1–10 October 1974.*

	1st	2nd	3rd	4th	5th	6th	7th	8th	9th	10th
Skylark	40	4	35		110	30	20	150	306	123
Swallow		340		30	10		10			11
House Martin		5,300		1,500	80	110	80	25	26	30
Fieldfare									3	1,667
Song Thrush		6							28	19
Redwing									3	5,820
Blackbird		50						8	20	17
Great Tit										1
Blue Tit	5	15			8	100				22
Dunnock						6	2	2		1
Meadow Pipit	40	50			15		15	10	31	19
Rock Pipit									5	4
Grey Wagtail		4			1	3	1		1	2
Starling							20		1,186	886
Greenfinch									2	6
Goldfinch		80		200	90				115	32
Siskin		10					7		18	7
Linnet		180			180		8		12	204
Twite									1	
Redpoll sp		20			5	120	3	1	12	92
Chaffinch							2	1	21	6
Brambling							1		4	23
Reed Bunting							3	5	4	17
Tree Sparrow		300			150	150	10	25	11	98

The rarities

A number of rarities have been mentioned already and there is no doubt that more arrive in October than at any other time. The first notable rarity at Sandwich Bay in modern times was the Red-flanked Bluetail of 28 October 1956. Other first records for the county are Pallas's Warbler, Thrush Nightingale, Black-headed Bunting, Sociable Plover, Terek Sandpiper, Blue-winged Teal, Ring-billed Gull, Arctic Warbler and Isabelline Shrike.

Perhaps the rarest bird of all, though, was the Swainson's Thrush, known then as Olive-backed Thrush and caught on the Estate on 27 October 1976. This is still our only American passerine record and one of very few recorded anywhere on the east coast of Britain. Not only was it a 'first' for Sandwich Bay and the county, but also for England. It was only the fourth for Britain and Ireland following one at Skokholm and two in Ireland. A skulking bird, it was extremely hard to see subsequently, even though we knew which bush it was hiding under.

The thrill of finding a rarity, confirming it and managing the folk who want to see it, is not quickly forgotten. One such occurrence was the Sharp-tailed Sandpiper found by Bill Fletcher on 4 September 1987. The day had already started well with two Red-backed Shrikes, an Icterine Warbler and a Wryneck. The scene is set and the following account is in Bill's own words.

'The 4th of September was possibly the most exciting day of the year here at the Bay and certainly one of the most hectic. This was fortunate for me, because it meant that nobody had time to cover much of the greater recording area, which included the excellent little flooded meadow near Roaring Gutter, which had come to be known affectionately as Worth Scrape.

I arrived at Worth Scrape early evening with reasonably high hopes of finding something good. In past weeks it had been producing good numbers of Ruff, Wood, Green and Common Sands [Sandpipers], Greenshank, Spot-shank [Spotted Redshank] and L.R.P.s [Little Ringed Plovers], so on a day like the 4th the idea of finding something like a Pec [Pectoral] or Broad-billed [Sandpiper] seemed quite possible; the idea of finding something really good like a Solitary, Sharp-tailed or Stilt Sand seemed somewhat unlikely, after all the Wood Sand seemed a really good bird for the Scrape when they first started turning up just a few weeks earlier.

This time however a helicopter scared most of the waders off just before I got there, leaving just two Ruff, two Wood Sands and two L.R.P.s. I was just about to move on to Roaring Gutter, which was the direction in which some of the waders flew, when I changed my mind. It was a calm, warm evening, the light although fading was bright and crisp, so I decided to relax on the bank of the North Stream and wait to see if any of the waders came back, which turned out to be one of my better decisions, not because anything did come back, surprisingly enough it didn't. What changed this decision from being a bad one to a good one was a bird sleeping by a small pool, just out of sight in the right hand corner of Worth Scrape meadow.

As I jumped the bottom gate, I disturbed a wader about 15 yards in front of me and as I came to a halt and raised my bins, we were about 12 yards apart, a little too close for comfort, the bird crouched and stared at me in a snipe-like fashion and like a snipe it looked as if it would explode into flight at any moment, so I backed off, the bird got up, looked around and decided to join the two Wood Sands on the large pool, allowing me brief flight views.

Well, at this point I thought it might be a good idea to stop and have a good think about the situation I'd just found myself in. I'd just flushed and as yet had only brief views of a sandpiper that looked more like a Sharp-tailed than anything I could think of (I've seen a few in Australia). It was getting late in the day and it was a long run back to the Obs. I stood staring at this bird feeding contentedly with the two Wood Sands for a moment, thinking and looking really hard, and the bird continued obstinately to not look like anything other than Sharp-tailed. I think it was probably at this point that my heart rate really began to increase and also at this point I realised that I would have to get a lot closer without flushing the bird, and this would have to be done as quickly as possible, it wasn't going to be easy. I didn't have a scope with me and the bird was with two fairly flighty Wood Sands. This objective however was made distinctly easier with the help of a herd of sheep, which obligingly stayed between me and the bird, allowing me close enough views through their legs to see the main distinguishing features, which were the presence of spotting and barring on the sides and flanks and streaking on the under-tail coverts. After seeing all I needed to, I tore off back to the Obs and the telephone. *A quick reference to Shore Birds while I got my breath back, then a quick phone call to Dave Howe, I was driven back to the spot passing Aron [Sapsford] the Warden with his passengers Colin Davison, Richard Newton and Bill Bufford, who were on their way back from Dungeness. We screamed to a halt and I yelled "Sharp-tailed on Worth Scrape" at them, the expression on all of their faces was quite priceless, and after a moment of apparent panic and rapid repetitions of "What?" they did a quick U-turn and followed. Picking up John Hollyer en route, who apparently when confronted with the sound of an unfamiliar Irish voice screaming "Sharp-tailed Sand on Worth Scrape" down his corridor, responded in a way that could only be explained by many years of hard and regular training for just such an event. Meanwhile back at the Scrape the bird had moved back to its original corner and it took only a moment to relocate it, the bird was quite close and the sun was behind us producing excellent light conditions. Aron and company arrived a few moments later followed by John van der Dol with Pete Findley and Dennis Batchelor; Keith Ellis was next and good old Dave Howe was the last to arrive whilst poor old Roger Lawrence was looking in the wrong place and had to wait till the next morning to see the bird.*

After getting our fill of the bird the situation was discussed and it was decided that it was logistically possible to organise public viewing as long as it could be coordinated from the observatory. Richard Newton was the main man in arranging things for what was expected and turned out to be a very busy weekend, Dick Daw [the farmer] kindly allowed us the use of one of his fields close to the Obs for parking and special arrangements were quickly made with the Toll Gate and later with the Estate Management who were extremely cooperative. Signs were put up from the Obs to the bird, C.B's were used and the car park manned right through. The whole event went like clockwork, and by and large the bird performed well too, though it could have been a little closer and it did disappear from time to time onto a small pool on the other side of the railway line, this alternative spot was located late on the evening of the 5th by Pete Findley with some effort involved. In the end the bird stayed for two weekends receiving well over 1,000 visitors and went down in history as one of the most well-run twitches to date.

The bird was an adult in worn summer plumage, which had the effect of generally darkening the bird, most of the rufous and buff had gone from its upperparts and most of the chevrons had been replaced by smudgy spotting, though the undertail coverts still had distinct fine streaking. The cap was dark red and the supercilium was white and very distinct. The jizz was most similar to that of a Pec though noticeably heavier in bill, with shorter neck and legs. The stance was generally more vertical and the movements generally more laboured enhancing the effect of an altogether stockier bird. In flight the bird looked dark and uniform with an indistinct wing-bar and indistinct off-white sides to a black rump. The jizz was a little like a small short-winged Ruff. Calls were similar to Pec's but softer renditions of 'tchurt-tchip-tchip', 'trit-treep' and 'breet-brit-bret' were heard.'

Some rarities yield more information than others and catching a bird that has already been ringed in its place of origin is perhaps the most useful of all. Such an event occurred on 15 August 2006. After considerable planning and preparation, the morning dawned cloudy, warm, still and dry. These ideal conditions allowed an experienced ringing team to set 11 nets in the maize field next to the observatory. Catching in the maize has been carried out for the last seven years and the number of migrants supported by each crop appears to relate directly to the aphid numbers present. There were many migrant birds in the maize at this time, mainly Reed Warblers and Sedge Warblers. Considerable physiological and phenological data have been collected about this temporary habitat and how we consider various species are supported by it. That particular morning we ringed 209 birds including 126 Sedge Warblers, 35 Reed Warblers and 15 Grasshopper Warblers.

At about 07:30 hrs, Amanda Parker extracted and identified an Aquatic Warbler during the mid-morning rush. It was carrying both a numbered Belarus ring and an orange colour ring. Catching a rarity prompts certain general considerations and an assessment of the condition of all the birds was made. They were clearly fit and healthy (many of the Sedge Warblers were carrying considerable amounts of lipid fat) and the weather and feeding opportunities were good. Eventually a small amount of time was allotted for telephoning local birders while the team processed the other birds carefully, efficiently and rapidly.

Information was released to the internet via KOSNET, the county ornithological website and Mark Grantham of the BTO responded within hours with the news of its origins. The importance of the record in conservation terms became apparent very quickly as the Belarus Ringing Scheme was able to provide almost instant information concerning its origins. This clearly demonstrated the value of ringing chicks in the nest and then speedily digitising the data. A brief but adequate description and wing formula were taken before full processing, photographing and release at the Field Centre pond. The bird's primaries, tertials and tail feathers were glossy and fresh indicating that it was a young bird, probably about two months old. Adult plumage would have been worn, as an adult bird would not have moulted since the previous late autumn or winter. With a muscle score of two (on a range of 0–3), it was clearly fit and healthy.

The previous history of this young Aquatic Warbler was intriguing. The parent female had two clutches and this bird, which came from the first clutch of five chicks in a nest found by Yurko Valera, was ringed on 12 June 2006 at the Kosnuki monitoring plot, Sporovski Ramsar site, Beresa, Belarus by Dimitry Zhuravlev. It was also fitted with an orange colour ring to make it more visible and easily identifiable in the field. The distance covered by the bird on this, the first stage of its migration, was about 1,650 kilometres. Due to its low visibility and a small worldwide population (thought to number between 12,000–32,000 pairs), its wintering grounds are largely unclear. There are records from the West African wetlands (in Senegal, Ghana, Mali and Mauritania) though the important wintering sites have yet to be identified. The species is classed as vulnerable in Europe, which holds more than 95% of the known world breeding population and Belarus is the centre of that population. It is therefore satisfying to be able to place a piece in the jigsaw puzzle. In terms of conservation, this is perhaps the most important bird ever caught at Sandwich Bay.

Ringing

Ringing at Sandwich Bay began in 1952. The unofficial fledgling bird observatory first saw the light in 1959 and achieved official accredited status in 1962. At this time, officers' quarters of First World War vintage, in splendid dereliction, were acquired at the present site and they were ready for improvement!

The catching and ringing of our migrant bird population and the taking of biometric data has always been at the centre of our activities. The first trapping device, a Heligoland, was to be built in what was known as Slazenger's Garden, which was then cluttered with accoutrements for the defence of the realm during two World Wars, including blocks of concrete and bundles of wire. The passage of time had added bushes and shrubs and over this cheerful neglect was formed the first Heligoland Trap, constructed of several rolls of second-hand chicken wire supported by many handy pieces of driftwood. It was very late autumn and it was nearly a week before a confused bird was out-manoeuvred and triumphantly caught. This first Great Tit laid the foundation for the thousands of birds that followed.

Seven more Heligolands of various designs have followed and the latest, made of scaffolding poles and galvanised rectangular mesh netting, is a far more durable, sturdy, and sophisticated structure than the first. Some were more successful than others and the one with the mist-net across its mouth told its own story. Driving the birds gently from bush to bush with various 'pishings', 'shooshings' and twig-waving always evokes anticipation and brings out the best of man's cooperative hunting instinct. Inevitably, it is the intriguing little brown skulker, nipping out when halfway into the trap, which causes most discussion at the evening log-call.

Many other catching devices have been constructed, ranging from the quite ridiculous to the down-right fiendish. Box traps, chardonnerets and various walk-in constructions have abounded, including mini portable Heligoland traps, such portability depending, of course, on the availability of lusty trainee ringers. One particular idea, namely a tent-like clap-net mounted on a floating platform and pushed out to sea for passing terns to rest on, worked well on dry land. At sea, however, tide drag on the line and other dynamics ensured that the tern was fully 50 metres away by the time the net 'snapped up', even to a half-closed position. The smallest chardonneret imaginable, about the size of a cigarette packet, was amazingly successful and provided endless entertainment as Blue Tits struggled heroically to reach peanuts.

We are frequently asked if the birds 'mind' being caught. We then tell the story of the year we concentrated on catching Greenfinches in a box trap outside the kitchen. Following release, some immediately flew straight back to the food in the box trap and were trapped five or more times a day. The lengths some birds will go to for a peanut!

Our best species' totals years were 1988 with 117 and 1985 with 116, when a large team of dedicated ringers were present. The highest annual ringing totals occurred in 1986 with 18,329 birds ringed, eclipsed in 2000 by a British Bird Observatories record of 21,088. High totals and a very wide range of species make Sandwich Bay an ideal venue for training. To this end, many ringers have advanced to 'C' or 'A' permit level while being here. We have run 12 ringing courses, all of which have been thoroughly enjoyable and rewarding, not only for the participants but also for the organisers. A ringing course is an ideal forum for the exchange of ideas and gaining new experiences. Popular activities here at Sandwich Bay have included Yellow Wagtail roosts, ringing at Stodmarsh, taking part in a cannon-netting session and experiencing a fall of migrants. Inevitably, unusual birds are caught and these have included Ruff, Little Ringed Plovers, Mediterranean Gulls, Spotted Crake, Cetti's Warblers, Bearded Tits, Hobby and even Aquatic Warbler.

Cannon-netting has been a feature at Sandwich Bay since 1980, with the ringing of over 1,000 Starlings, and 2,000 waders and 3,500 gulls, represented by more than 25 species. Apart from the novelty and excitement of waiting for a catching opportunity, ringers are given ample experience in handling unusual birds, fitting tough rings and taking a range of unusual measurements. A catch of 30 Great Black-backed Gulls can only be described as a bruising encounter, and you soon learn to stand well clear of a ringer with one of these tucked under his arm.

Many of the ultimate rewards of ringing at a bird observatory are the recoveries and controls. Of the more exceptional birds ringed at Sandwich Bay have been two Turnstones found nesting in Arctic Canada, with Knot and Swallow recovered in South Africa. A Common Gull from Russia, the Aquatic Warbler from Belarus and a Goldcrest from Lithuania have been controlled here, the latter a bird weighing 5.6 grams and caught just 13 days after it was ringed.

Our ringing of Turnstones on the Thanet coast has shown this species to be incredibly long lived and site faithful. The recoveries from Arctic Canada, of two birds while nesting, clearly identifies their origins and their return to the same patch of rocks and beach for the winter, year after year, is reassuringly predictable in contrast with the sporadic occurrences of our beloved vagrants. It is, however, notable that such dependable birds impose a weighty conservation responsibility. Misuse or adverse change to any part of this coast could affect part of a species' population and thus risk reducing biodiversity.

It is said that there are more planning applications in the south-east of England and in Kent in particular, than elsewhere in the country. Having a large database of useful information has enabled the observatory to advise on or oppose many planning applications. Much time and effort has been put into providing data for the government conservation body of the time (now called Natural England), various local councils, the RSPB, the Kent Trust for Nature Conservation (now the Kent Wildlife Trust) and also into representing the observatory at various public enquiries. Our data and resources have been used to resist proposals for hoverports, ferry terminals, hotel complexes, reservoirs and extensive road systems through nature reserves, and also in relation to proposed habitat destruction within a Site of Special Scientific Interest (SSSI). These lengthy and exhausting exercises occurred mainly during the 1970s and 1980s. It is pleasing to record that the Thanet and Sandwich Bay coasts were designated as a Special Protection Area (SPA) and Ramsar sites in 1992, in part due to our efforts and data, and relieving us of much of the pressure of fighting rearguard actions so that we have since been able to make more progress on the conservation front.

OTHER FAUNA AND FLORA

Mammals and other vertebrates

Over 30 species of mammal have been recorded, including six species of cetacean and eight bats. Hares are an increasingly common sight and are never more noticeable than when boxing in the spring. All the common species of mouse, shrew and vole occur and there are regular records of Water Vole along the dykes on the marshes, Pygmy and Water Shrew around the Haven Stream, Yellow-necked Mouse in the older grassland and Harvest Mouse in the reed-filled ditches amongst the fields. There is also a record of an itinerant European Roe Deer. European Beaver are being introduced nearby, but none has escaped this way, so far.

Amphibians and reptiles are well represented and Grass Snakes, Common Lizard, frogs and toads are present in good numbers. The recent addition of Natterjack Toad and Sand Lizard to the Kent Wildlife Trust Reserve follows long and determined efforts at reintroduction.

Invertebrates

Since pre-Roman times, changes in the coastline at Sandwich Bay have created a diverse range of habitats, as dunes have steadily displaced the sea, which now laps against the shore more than a mile from the ancient port of Sandwich. Although much of the land that lies between the town and the sea is now given over to agriculture, many habitats exist that are rare in the UK, particularly closer to the shore, and these hold an outstanding variety of nationally rare plants and invertebrates.

It is not only birds that feature prominently as migrants at Sandwich Bay. Of the Odonata, 23 species of dragonfly and damselfly have been recorded, including some that are currently expanding their ranges northwards. Among these, Southern Emerald Damselfly and Small Red-eyed Damselfly have both recently colonized the area and Red-veined and Yellow-winged Darters have been seen in recent years. Notable species, rare or local in Kent, have occurred at Sandwich Bay including Variable Damselfly, Four-spotted Chaser and Black Darter, while it is one of only two sites in the county known for the nationally rare Scarce Chaser.

Although the nearby chalk downs hold a greater range of resident species, a wide variety of butterflies has been recorded at Sandwich Bay, together with a wide range of uncommon to rare migrants, including Swallowtail, Camberwell Beauty, Pale Clouded Yellow and Bath White.

Migrant moths also feature prominently in the observatory's records and while Death's Head and Convolvulus Hawkmoths are among the more spectacular of these, Hummingbird Hawkmoths are an annual feature. Recent warm summers have increased the frequency with which some previously rare or infrequent species are occurring, a trend that is likely to accelerate as climate change takes hold. Most notable, though, was the discovery of the afore-mentioned species, new to Britain in 1957, the tiny leaf-miner *Stigmella repentiella*.

Fungi and plants

Naturalists have spent a great deal of time compiling data on the many and varied species of fungi at Sandwich Bay, some of which are rare. Although only a brief glimpse can be given here of the area's variety, species include Velvet Shank, the almost unworldly Barometer Earthstar, Verdigris Agaric, the imposing Wood Blewit, delicate Fairy Inkcap and Sulphur Tufts.

Spring brings a carpet of Early Forget-me-not, Rue-leaved Saxifrage and other tiny-flowered species that exist with speedwells and chickweeds on the more permanent dunes, where Wild Onion, a very pretty allium, is found commonly during summer. An amazing array of orchids also grace the Bay and include 13 of Kent's 30 species.

Along the footpaths and in rough grass in summer tall Lizard Orchids wave gently in the breeze in concert with the bright blue spikes of Viper's-bugloss whilst the rare Bedstraw Broomrape clings to its parasitic existence on the roots of bedstraw plants. Wetter areas of the dune slacks hold abundant Southern Marsh-orchids and, in the height of summer, Marsh Helleborines, while beyond the dunes, the seashore is dominated by clumps of prickly Sea-holly, interspersed with patches of pink-flowered Common Restharrow. The Yellow Horned-poppy is one of the most distinctive summer plants of the shingle beaches, while at the other extreme the pretty Yellow Bartsia is known from only two sites in Kent and is rare and in danger of extinction. It flowers in late summer and the observatory has a special management programme to assist with its protection.

We now operate both as a bird observatory and a field centre. Thus, we are beginning to attract a greater number of visitors with a wider range of interests and this will undoubtedly lead to a strengthening of interest in the non-avian aspects of the area and add substantially to our knowledge.

ACCESS AND ACCOMMODATION

Access to Sandwich from London is by train from Charing Cross or Waterloo and by coach from Victoria. When visiting by road, take the M2 and then proceed via Canterbury, or the M20 and then by way of Dover. Within Sandwich follow signs to the Golf Courses. About 300 metres past the diurnally manned Toll Gate at the entrance to the Sandwich Bay Estate, you will find the Field Centre building on the right, a short distance along the well signposted track. The roads through the Sandwich Bay Estate are private and the current arrangement is that visitors to the observatory pay a much reduced entrance fee of £1, for access to the observatory car park only. Members enter free.

The accommodation, by general observatory standards, is excellent. There is a large kitchen, a common room, several showers, an eight-bed dormitory/family room and four modern double bedrooms, some with washbasins. In addition there is an attractive self-contained flat with its own access and a modern kitchen, double bedroom, sitting room and bathroom. The entire observatory, with the exception of the observation tower, is wheelchair-friendly, as are many of our reserves.

Annual reports have been scanned on to the observatory website. Our telephone number is 01304 617341 and the postal address is Guilford Road, Sandwich Bay, Kent, CT13 9PF.

The observatory was opened as a Ringing Station in 1952 and accredited as an observatory in 1962.	
Total number of bird species recorded at the observatory:	330
Best bird year:	2008
Number of species recorded:	241
Total of birds ringed at the observatory:	347,865
Number of species:	217
Best ringing year:	2000
Number ringed:	21,088
Number of species:	113

Spurn

by Geoff Neal

THE SPURN PENINSULA

Located on the south-eastern tip of the Holderness plain, which forms the northern banks of the Humber Estuary, Spurn Point (as it is known, but otherwise Spurn Head) is a narrow sandy promontory, approximately five kilometres long, forming a sweeping curve which continues the line of the coast. The sand which forms the spit has been transported along the Holderness coast by longshore drift, but the energy in the waves transporting the material is reduced where the North Sea meets the outflow from the Humber Estuary and the material is deposited as a result.

Historical accounts have enabled us to deduce that there have been five 'Spurn points' over the last 1,000 years. Each spit grows until it becomes unstable and is destroyed, to be rebuilt slightly to the west of the former one. These natural cycles

Geoff Neal first visited Spurn in 1973 and fell in love with the place, returning every year since. He was coopted onto the committee in 1986 and has twice served as honorary treasurer. He has recently resigned from the committee after 20-years' service and is the author of the recently updated *The Birds of Spurn* (1996) entitled *Birds of the Spurn Peninsula* (2007).

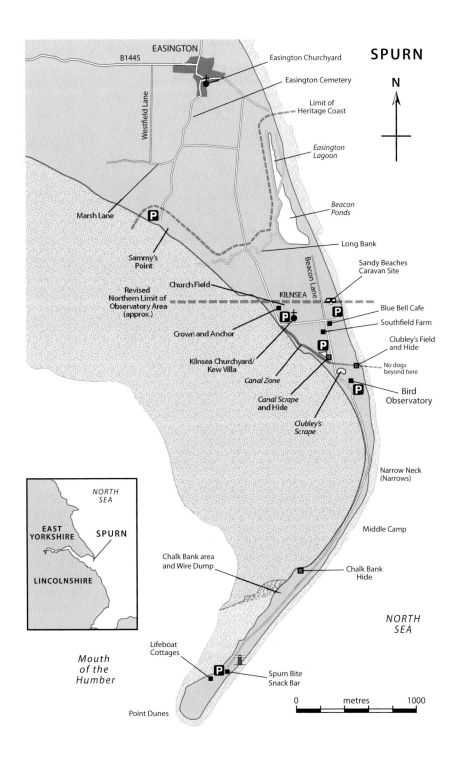

EASINGTON

B1445

Westfield Lane

Easington Churchyard

Easington Cemetery

Limit of
Heritage Coast

*Easington
Lagoon*

SPURN

N

*Beacon
Ponds*

Marsh Lane

Long Bank

Sammy's
Point

Sandy Beaches
Caravan Site

Revised
Northern Limit of
Observatory Area
(approx.)

Church Field

Beacon Lane

KILNSEA

Blue Bell Cafe

Southfield Farm

Crown and Anchor

Clubley's Field
and Hide

Kilnsea Churchyard/
Kew Villa

Canal Zone

No dogs
beyond here

Canal Scrape
and Hide

Bird
Observatory

*Clubley's
Scrape*

NORTH
SEA

EAST
YORKSHIRE

SPURN

Narrow Neck
(Narrows)

LINCOLNSHIRE

Middle Camp

Chalk Bank area
and Wire Dump

Chalk Bank
Hide

NORTH
SEA

*Mouth
of the
Humber*

Lifeboat
Cottages

Spurn Bite
Snack Bar

0   metres   1000

Point Dunes

last approximately 250 years, but the current spit is past the end of its cycle and has been artificially maintained by man-made sea defences. These began to break down in the late 1970s and little remains of them today, with the result that the peninsula is now in constant danger of breaching. In fact the road to the Point has been destroyed and washed away between the 'Warren' and the 'Narrow Neck' on several occasions in recent years, necessitating its reconstruction, each time a little further to the west. The present road has probably reached its limit, being now practically on the Humber tideline, with nowhere else to go. It has already been flooded on the highest tides with considerable deposition of sand, forcing temporary closure. Clearly, this road link is of particular importance as the RNLI lifeboat and full-time crew are based at the Point, along with the jetty and the control tower for the Humber Pilots and Vessel Traffic Services.

The Point area is heavily vegetated, particularly with Sea-buckthorn, which forms dense stands in some areas. This makes the area very important for migrant birds, providing both shelter and food, and in autumn often holds large numbers of birds, particularly thrushes. Seeing and counting these birds has its own difficulties due to the impenetrable nature of the vegetation, but a number of paths and net rides have been cut and maintained in recent years by volunteers from the observatory and the Yorkshire Wildlife Trust (YWT), thus improving access. A considerable amount of ringing activity is carried out in this area, particularly during the annual British Trust for Ornithology (BTO) ringing course in October and there is a permanent Heligoland trap here at the edge of the old parade ground.

Moving north from the Point, the peninsula begins to narrow around the area of the lighthouse (now disused) and the sandy beach on the Humber estuary side

Strong winds coupled with high tides, eroding the coastline, continue to threaten access to the Point at Spurn (Spurn Bird Observatory Trust).

becomes more muddy as the extensive mudflats of the estuary take over, providing feeding areas for large numbers of wading birds. Moving further north past the old 'tank ditch' you come to the area known as the 'Wire Dump' which gets its name from the fact that after the war it was used by the military as a dumping area for large quantities of surplus wire. When I first started visiting Spurn in the early 1970s there was still some evidence of this in the form of heaps of rusting wire scattered about, but you would be hard-pressed to find much sign of it now. The area is now mostly rough grassland with the remains of a small area of salt marsh, which is flooded only on the very highest tides. At the southern end there is another Heligoland trap where the grass is kept shorter for trapping Meadow Pipits, using tape lures, during migration in September. The area to the north is known as 'Chalk Bank', due to the infilling of a former breach with large quantities of chalk, much of which can still be seen on the shore. An area here was cleared of buckthorn and fenced off some years ago and is now grazed by sheep for at least part of the year; perhaps unsurprisingly, this area is now known as the sheep field. There are two small hides just to the north, overlooking a wader roost on the Humber shore, although on very high tides many waders fly off to Lincolnshire, or north to the Beacon Lagoons Nature Reserve.

The peninsula now narrows again through the area known as 'Middle Camp'. Many people drive straight through here, but a walk along the road can be productive, as with the finding of a Lesser Grey Shrike in September 2005. The next point of interest is the Narrow Neck or 'the Narrows' as it is known. This is the site of the observation point where visible migration counts are carried out, the infamous 'Narrows Watches'. For many years a famous Spurn landmark, the Narrows Hut, a wooden migration watch shelter, was situated here to provide (minimal) protection from the weather. This was burned down by vandals in 1984 and subsequently replaced with a breeze-block structure which, unfortunately, resembled a toilet, and was often used as such by day visitors when unmanned. It finally succumbed to coastal erosion in 2004 and we now have a wooden structure once again, a little to the south of the original watch point.

Continuing north again along the latest 'new road' you pass places with names such as 'Black Hut', and 'Iron Gates', both structures having long since disappeared, and arrive at the Warren, site of the observatory buildings, and also the YWT information centre and the point at which a car admission fee to the peninsula is collected. Many people are under the erroneous impression that this money goes to the observatory, but in fact it goes into the coffers of the YWT. The peninsula once more begins to broaden at the Warren as the Humber bank turns to the north-west and then subsequently west. Much of the area north of the Warren consists of farmland and is known generally as 'the Triangle' as it is bordered on two sides by the road from the Warren to the Blue Bell (a former inn and shop, now housing the Spurn Head Heritage Coast centre and a small café) and from the Blue Bell to the Crown & Anchor Inn, with the Humber bank making up the third side. The hedges and bushes in this area can be very productive for migrants, although restricted access to much of the area can prove frustrating.

Running parallel with the Humber bank is an area of brackish water known as 'the Canal'. This was formed by excavations for flood defences along the Humber shore, following the disastrous flooding of the early 1950s. More recently a scrape has been excavated in the south-eastern corner of the Triangle and a hide built to overlook this. Unfortunately it has not proved very productive for waders, but is good for dragonflies and has been instrumental in adding several new species to the Spurn breeding-bird list, namely Little Grebe, Mute Swan and Coot. The northern limit of the Triangle is the Kilnsea road, running from the Blue Bell, westwards to the Crown and Anchor, which plays a pivotal role in the non-birding activities of observatory residents and visitors. Along this road are several private dwellings, the former church, now being converted into living accommodation, and Kew Villa, recently purchased by the observatory and used as housing for the observatory warden. The garden has become a useful additional ringing site, as well as being very productive for the moth trap. A small private caravan site is maintained here, licensed by the Caravan Club, and this provides an additional source of income for the observatory. An area to the north of Kew and the church has also been purchased and is known as the Church Field. A management programme is being implemented to improve the area for wildlife and to install viewing facilities. This includes activities such as tree and hedge planting, the excavation of a pond and the planting of a sacrificial crop to provide for autumn feeding. The purchase of this land has necessitated the northward extension of the observatory recording area's boundary, which at one time ended at the Kilnsea road (allowing a slight diversion for the churchyard, as good birds were found to turn up there on a regular basis). This additional area goes some way towards compensating for the land which has been lost to coastal erosion over recent years.

FOUNDING THE OBSERVATORY

Following visits to Spurn by several members of the Yorkshire Naturalists' Union (YNU) in the late 1930s, a communal log for ornithological observations was instituted in 1938. This included a roll-call of species, the beginnings of a recording system, which later became standard in bird observatories. Realising the potential of the Spurn peninsula for the regular observation of bird migration a group of enthusiasts, notably Ralph Chislett, George Ainsworth, John Lord and R. M. Garnett, had the idea of setting up a bird observatory, with Warren Cottage at the northern end of the peninsula as an ideal headquarters. Unfortunately, the outbreak of war forced them to put their plans on hold, but a lease for Warren Cottage was obtained from the War Department when hostilities ceased and Spurn Bird Observatory was established shortly afterwards under the auspices of the YNU with the afore-mentioned enthusiasts forming the first committee. A preliminary meeting was held in September 1945 to decide on the site for a Heligoland trap, work on which was begun almost immediately, and the first bird (a Blackbird) was ringed on 17 November. The first minuted committee meeting was held on 9 March 1946 and the observatory was opened to visitors at Whitsuntide that year.

Initially coverage was limited to the main migration seasons, and extended to

Ralph Chislett, seen here outside Warren Cottage, was one of a group of far-sighted enthusiasts who foresaw the birding potential of the Spurn peninsula and set about establishing the bird observatory that eventually opened in 1946 (Spurn Bird Observatory Trust).

winter weekends in the early 1950s to trap and ring some of the large numbers of Snow Buntings which used to occur at that time of year and gradually coverage was increased (whenever possible) to include the late spring and summer. In 1959 there was an important development when the Yorkshire Naturalists' Trust (now the Yorkshire Wildlife Trust) became the owners of the peninsula and thus the observatory's landlord. A full-time warden was appointed by the Trust in 1960, and although he had no official connection with the observatory, the presence of an observer on the peninsula all-year-round inevitably helped to improve the ornithological coverage. This was especially the case from 1963 when Barry Spence was appointed, in conjunction with a growing interest in birds and their migrations, and more birdwatchers were using the observatory.

There was accommodation for seven visitors in Warren Cottage when the observatory opened and facilities included two chemical toilets, the Warren Heligoland trap and for ringing, an ex-army hut. Over the next ten years a further five Heligoland traps were constructed along the peninsula, although only three remain today. In 1959 the observatory gained the use of the Annexe, one of two ex-War Department bungalows built at the Warren during the early 1950s, thus increasing the accommodation capacity to 17 and providing much improved toilet facilities. Over the years the accommodation and facilities have been gradually improved to try to make the visitor's stay at Spurn as comfortable as possible. Other improvements have also taken place; in 1968 part of one of the derelict buildings at the Point was converted into a ringing laboratory ready for the first BTO Ringing Course, held in autumn of that year and, in 1971, part of one of the derelict buildings at the Warren was converted into a ringing laboratory. The other part of this building became a laboratory for use by Leeds University students, but it became available to the observatory in the mid-1980s when the university no longer needed it. Subsequently, it was converted into self-contained accommodation for two, complete with kitchen facilities, and although officially known by the somewhat unimaginative name of Room F (the rooms in the Annexe being known as Rooms A, C, D and E – whatever happened to Room B?), it was somewhat irreverently christened 'Dunbirdin' by regular visitors to Spurn.

In 1965, a sea-watching hut was erected east of the Warren beyond the line of the former railway track. Due to coastal erosion it became necessary to move this in late 1974, when it was hoped that it would last at least as long as it had in its first position. Alas this was not to be, as the rate of erosion increased dramatically in the mid-1970s, necessitating a further move in early December 1977. In that year a clay bank had been built across the field behind Warren Cottage (Clubley's Field) to prevent the flooding of arable land by wind-blown sea water, but on 11 January 1978 Spurn suffered its worst flooding ever when a strong to gale-force north-westerly wind combined with a spring tide. In late 1981, a large quantity of boulder clay became available due to extensive construction works at Easington and this was used to build up and extend the bank across Clubley's Field, south towards Black Hut and north beyond Big Hedge, to join up with an existing bank (built in 1974) behind the scrape. In 1982 the sea-watching hut was repositioned on top of this bank, where it remained until the bank itself was washed away in the early 1990s. The original observatory hide was eventually dismantled, following the erection of a larger (and more comfortable) public hide by the YWT in conjunction with the Heritage Coast project.

A number of other changes to the observatory recording area began to take place from the early 1970s, including extensive building operations at the Point, commencing in 1974, with the construction of a new jetty for the Humber Pilot boats, new housing for the Spurn lifeboat crew, and the conversion and renovation of various existing buildings for use by the coastguard and the pilots. In 1981, the lines of wartime concrete anti-tank blocks running from the seashore to the 'Canal Zone' were removed to fill in a breach at the Narrow Neck. This resulted in the southward extension of the Scrape field by the farmer up to Big Hedge and the start of a gradual decline in the condition of this hedge and its attractiveness to birds. In 1982, a local resident excavated a pond for shooting purposes in the wet area adjoining the Canal Zone. This never really proved successful and the land was later purchased by the YWT and the pond enlarged to become what is now known as 'Canal Scrape'.

A period of considerable change began in 1988 when the Spurn peninsula was designated as part of the Spurn Head Heritage Coast. Projects undertaken included the enlargement of the Canal Scrape with a hide overlooking it, a hide to overlook the Humber wader roost at Chalk Bank and the restoration of the short-turf habitat there, the provision of additional car-parking space and footpaths. A major project was the renovation of the Blue Bell in Kilnsea for use as offices, an information centre and a small café, which became fully operational in 1995. Another project has been the recent creation of a scrape and pond on Clubley's Field.

In 1996 the observatory celebrated its fiftieth anniversary and employed a full time seasonal warden for the first time in its history. This position has since been expanded and the observatory now enjoys the services of a year-round warden. In 1998, with a view to the future, Kew Villa was purchased with money bequeathed by the late John Weston, a long time committee member, who sadly died in 1996. This was followed in 1999 by the purchase of a strip of land adjacent to the property which will provide a base for the continuation of the observatory when the current premises are (inevitably) lost to the sea. The 'Friends of Spurn Bird Observatory' finally became a reality in 2003, after many years of discussion. Membership of this organisation holds numerous advantages, not least of which is a reduction on overnight accommodation charges, but also includes a free copy of the observatory's annual report, regular newsletters, and preferential admission to viewing areas on land owned by the observatory. I am pleased to relate that this has proved very popular and the membership has already reached a healthy total.

Wardening

For many years Spurn Bird Observatory did not have an official warden. From his arrival in 1963, as the reserve warden, Barry Spence took on the day to day running of the observatory, taking bookings, looking after the finances and keeping order on a voluntary basis. Barry was afforded some relief from his duties in 1996 when a seasonal warden was appointed to cover the period from spring to autumn. The first incumbent was Dave Boyle, a southern lad, who proved very popular with everyone. The following year his place was taken by Mike Pilsworth, who now works full-time for the Royal Society for the Protection of Birds at their Blacktoft reserve and is a Spurn committee member. The appointment was extended to a permanent year-round one in 1998 and Dave Boyle returned to take his place as Spurn's first full-time warden. However Dave's itchy feet got the better of him in early 2001 and he left for foreign parts, having since worked in such exotic places as Ascension Island, Hawaii and the Hebrides. His place was taken in spring 2001 by Paul Massey, who stayed for just a year, to be followed on a temporary basis by local birder Martin Stoyle. Paul Collins took on the position in spring 2003 and remains there to this day, another highly popular and well-liked southerner.

THE BIRDS

During the 30-odd years that I have been visiting Spurn I have often been asked by first-time visitors 'Where is the best place to go to see birds?' On a serious note, the answer can be 'anywhere'. Birds can and do turn up just about anywhere along the peninsula, sometimes in the strangest of places. Who would expect to see a Nuthatch on a steel boat jetty, or a Dipper on the beach? It's happened at Spurn. Of course occurrences of birds are very much dependent on weather conditions, particularly wind direction and strength. Most people will tell you that the 'best' wind for Spurn is from the east or south-east as this is the most likely to produce falls of Continental migrants and rarities, particularly in September and October. Under these conditions it is worth checking everywhere to see what has arrived, although it sometimes seems that easterlies attract more birdwatchers than birds and it is difficult to find anywhere that has not already been checked thoroughly several times. Personally I prefer south-westerly conditions which can produce spectacular visible migration movements and being of limited mobility, especially in recent years, it means that I can stand in one place at the Narrows and let the birds fly past me, rather than having to walk round looking for them.

For those interested in sea-watching, the best winds are from the northern quarter, i.e. between north-west and north-east and preferably at least force 6, and although the numbers of birds seen cannot match those at some of the more famous headlands, the right conditions can still produce some spectacular movements. Depending on the time of year these can include divers, Fulmars, Sooty and Manx Shearwaters, Gannets, all four skuas, terns and auks (including good numbers of Little Auks in some years). Seawatching can also prove to be of interest in southerly winds, but in this case wildfowl are more likely to be on the move (and sometimes waders).

The least productive winds at Spurn are from the west, particularly light north-westerlies, but visitors should not despair as even then anything can turn up at any time under any conditions. The birds do not always follow the rules anyway as on numerous occasions the conditions have appeared ideal for visible migration, but the birds just don't appear. On the other hand, one of the best migration days I have experienced was in late October when a force 7 to 8 north-westerly wind made it difficult to stand up. Flocks of finches and buntings were literally pouring south past the Narrows. Obviously there are other factors involved at which we can only guess.

A year in the life of Spurn

The year starts quietly at Spurn, especially on New Year's Day, when any observers who are present are likely to be somewhat below peak condition. Apart from the resident species there may be small numbers of Fieldfares and Redwings present, along with a few Snow Buntings and possibly a Stonechat or two. In some years Waxwings may be seen occasionally, but normally only in single figures. There is still plenty to look at on the Humber, where there is a regular wintering flock of up to 500 Dark-bellied Brent Geese *Branta bernicla bernicla*, sometimes joined by small numbers of Pink-footed Geese or occasionally even Barnacle or Bean Geese. Waders are also still present in good numbers and attract the attention of Merlin and the occasional Peregrine. Good numbers of Red-throated Divers occur offshore in some years, together with occasional Great Northerns, and winter storms can also produce numbers of other seabirds, particularly Kittiwakes and sometimes Little Auks. Other visitors of note can include Water Rail, Short-eared Owl, Blackcap, Twite and Lapland Bunting. Unusual and out of season records do occur, such as the Short-toed Lark on 12 January 1992 and the two records of Bittern in early January.

February normally continues in a similar vein to January, but in early March come the first signs of migration as Lapwings start to fly south, although they have recently become much less numerous. As the month progresses they are joined by such species as Skylarks, Meadow Pipits and Pied Wagtails, along with small numbers of finches and buntings. It should be mentioned here that the vast majority of visible migration at Spurn is in a southerly direction, even in spring. The reasons for this are not clearly understood, but presumably the shape of the peninsula is partly responsible. One of the few species that is regularly seen flying north or north-west in spring is Meadow Pipit, but even then numbers flying south are normally greater.

The first spring migrants to arrive are normally Wheatear, Chiffchaff and Black Redstart, usually around the 20 March, give or take a few days. Records over the last 40 years indicate that average first arrival dates for some species have been getting slightly earlier, though conversely other species do not seem to have been affected (Table 1). Other March arrivals frequently include Sand Martin, Ring Ouzel and Blackcap and in some years Sandwich Tern and Swallow. In 1988 the first 'spring' migrant of the year was an Alpine Swift on 20 March.

Migration really gets under way from the middle of April, with most species putting in a first appearance during the second half of the month. Visible migration, though not as spectacular as in autumn, can still include good numbers of hirundines and finches, particularly Goldfinches and Linnets, while most days will produce small flocks of Jackdaws and Rooks attempting to push south, with many turning back when they see the width of the Humber and realise that they have to cross this expanse of water. The last species to arrive are usually Reed

Table 1. *Changes in average first arrival-dates for selected spring migrants over ten-year periods from 1966 to 2005.*

	1966–1975	1976–1985	1986–1995	1996–2005	Change over 1966–2005	Average 1966–2005
Sandwich Tern	9/4	5/4	3/4	31/3	9 days	5/4
Sand Martin	11/4	8/4	1/4	26/3	16 days	5/4
Swallow	9/4	11/4	6/4	1/4	8 days	7/4
House Martin	22/4	19/4	19/4	14/4	10 days	18/4
Reed Warbler	22/5	17/5	12/5	5/5	17 days	14/5
Chiffchaff	28/3	28/3	21/3	15/3	13 days	23/3
Willow Warbler	12/4	10/4	8/4	3/4	9 days	8/4

Warbler and Spotted Flycatcher, and often not until early May. This is the month when the more unusual species sometimes turn up, such as Bee-eater, Wryneck and Red-backed Shrike. Over the years a number of rarities have occurred in May, among them Red-throated Pipit, Thrush Nightingale, Rock Thrush, Blyth's Reed Warbler, Great Reed Warbler, Western Bonelli's Warbler, Woodchat Shrike, Song Sparrow and White-throated Sparrow, to name but a few.

June is normally somewhat quieter although there is still plenty of interest. Most records of Quail and Marsh Warbler have occurred in this month and other species which have occurred include Great White Egret, Red-footed Falcon, Lesser Crested Tern, Pied Wheatear, Booted Warbler, Marmora's Warbler, Sardinian Warbler and Rose-coloured Starling. Late June, along with early July, is normally the peak time for Swift movement, and several thousand frequently fly south in a day, with as many as 20,000 on two occasions.

July sees the start of the return wader passage as numbers begin to build up on the Humber, with small parties flying south offshore. Spurn is not well-known as a site for rare waders, due to the lack of fresh water and the huge area of mudflats where they can 'get lost' among the flocks of Knot and Dunlin. However, some 'goodies' have occurred in July, for example Greater Sand Plover and Pacific Golden Plover. Visible migration really gets under way in August as hirundines start to move with the Sand Martins coming first, followed by Swallows. House Martins are often the last to appear, although the biggest numbers of the latter two species are normally seen in early September when Meadow Pipits add to the spectacle. Other species taking part include *flava* wagtails and small numbers of raptors such as Marsh Harriers, Sparrowhawks and Kestrels. From mid-September these are joined by Rock Pipits, Linnets, Siskins (sometimes) and other finches.

September is also the time when easterly winds are eagerly awaited, in the hope that there will be falls of Continental drift migrants, with a few scarce migrants or rarities amongst them. Some of the more regular scarce species are Barred Warbler, Icterine Warbler, Wryneck, Red-backed Shrike and Yellow-browed Warbler.

As the days shorten and the weather starts to turn colder, winter thrushes start to arrive with Redwings usually the first, followed towards the end of October by Fieldfares. To see flocks of these birds coming in off the North Sea is one of the most satisfying birding experiences at Spurn. Many of these continue in a westerly direction or turn south and head down the peninsula, but if it has been a hard crossing they will land in the fields and the buckthorn, particularly at the Point, to rest and feed up before continuing their journeys inland.

October is normally the month for the real rarities, which have included Yellow-billed Cuckoo, Pallid Swift, Calandra Lark, Olive-backed Pipit, Pied Wheatear, Asian Desert Warbler, Hume's Warbler, Radde's Warbler (seven were present on 1 October 2000), Penduline Tit, Isabelline Shrike, Nutcracker and Parrot Crossbill. At one time Pallas's Warbler would have been classed with these, but over 90 have now been recorded since the first record on 22 October 1960, with up to four in a day on some occasions. Other species to be looked for in October are Long-eared Owl, Richard's Pipit, Firecrest, Great Grey Shrike and

Lapland Bunting, while visible passage tends to be mostly made up of Skylarks, Meadow and Rock Pipits, Starlings and finches, particularly Greenfinches and Goldfinches. Early November usually sees the migration winding down, although this is often the best time for Blackbird arrivals and rarities have included Rufous Turtle Dove, Chimney Swift and Dipper. Things really quieten down from mid-November and Spurn settles down to endure another long, dark winter.

Migration monitoring and ringing

In the early days of the observatory emphasis was very much on ringing, using a variety of traps, particularly the Heligoland traps, but also including smaller portable traps such as 'sparrow' traps and 'Potter' traps. In those days it appeared to be very difficult to get any record accepted, apart from the commoner birds, unless the bird had been trapped. From the early 1950s more attention began to be paid to birds on the move. Sea-watching (originally termed 'ocean gazing') was occasionally mentioned in the log and some observers began to take an interest in visible passage, as appears from an entry in the log for 10 September 1954: John Cudworth stood at the narrowest point counting migrants for four hours from 04:15 hrs. He identified Grey Wagtails, Tree Pipits and Yellow Wagtails passing as well as Swallows and Meadow Pipits. His figures are recorded as a monument to his keenness as well as a record of migration.'

This appears to be one of the first records of what has now come to be known as a 'Narrows Watch'. Prior to that most mentions were of half-hour sample watches,

The relative comfort of the modern-day sea-watching hides was probably not anticipated by the hardy pioneers of the observatory's early years, here sea-watching from the Narrows (Spurn Bird Observatory Trust).

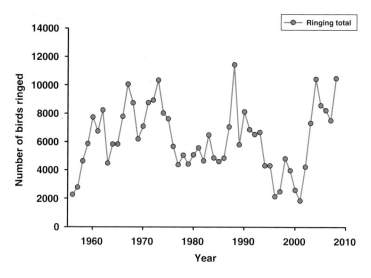

Figure 1. *Numbers of birds ringed annually at Spurn 1956–2008.*

and counts of birds moving were very rarely noted. Nowadays, along with the daily census of grounded migrants, the Narrows Watch has become one of the main activities of Spurn birders, dependent of course on suitable weather conditions. Ringing remains another major observatory activity, but its popularity has fluctuated somewhat over the years (Figure 1) with fewer ringing groups coming to stay at the observatory, particularly during the late 1990s and reaching an all-time low in 2001. Fortunately at present a keen warden means that ringing is once again flourishing. An annual ringing course is held, usually in the second or third week of October, and is popular with both trainee and experienced ringers alike.

The non-passerines

No two years' migration seasons are ever the same at Spurn, and it seems that there will be unusually high numbers of one or two species in every year, while others may be scarce or even absent. It is noticeable, however, that certain species seem to be on an upward trend. A good example is Pink-footed Goose, a regular autumn passage migrant and mostly seen flying south or south-east offshore, presumably heading for wintering areas on the Wash or the Continent. Up to 1995, the maximum recorded in a day had been 330 (in 1958), to be followed later by 370 on 26 October 1996, 1,100 in 1998, 1,844 in 1999, 2,900 on 31 October 2000, 4,610 on 31 October 2004 and 6,510 on 5 November 2005. Spring numbers are boosted by return passage skeins moving to the north or north-west in February and March, to a maximum count of 1,672 on 13 March 2005. Another member of the wildfowl family which is on the increase is the Whooper Swan, again mostly as a late autumn passage migrant. In 1995 the daily maximum was 28, but this has increased gradually over recent years and now stands at 117 (all flying south) on 22 October 2006. Conversely, the Bewick's Swan has become considerably scarcer. Up until the early 1980s it was considered to be the commoner of the two 'wild' swans, but numbers have decreased until there are only one or two records in most years.

Nowadays, as has already been mentioned, a regular wintering flock of Brent Geese is present and small numbers are also seen passing south offshore in most years, but the other geese are somewhat irregular at Spurn with, for example, between one and four records per year on average of White-fronted. The Canada Goose is recorded in most years with the majority of records in June, while Barnacle Geese are most regular in October. There have been 29 records of Bean Goose, four of Snow Goose and two of Red-breasted. Shelduck is present throughout the year and is an occasional breeder, whilst Wigeon and Teal are common autumn migrants. Most of the other species of dabbling ducks are seen in only small numbers, and the same can be said of most of the diving ducks, but sea ducks are sometimes seen in good numbers, particularly Common Scoter and Eider. There is a single record of Ferruginous Duck (from 1962), four of Surf Scoter, 13 of Smew and five of Ruddy Duck.

The Little Grebe bred first in 1995 and annually since 2000. The Red-necked Grebe is a scarce visitor with a total of 86 records, but has been recorded in all months, while there are 34 records of Slavonian Grebe and only ten of Black-necked. Black-browed Albatross has been seen on two occasions, there are 29 records of Cory's Shearwater, ten of Great Shearwater and 54 of Balearic. Much more frequent are Manx and Sooty Shearwaters, which are regularly seen offshore, particularly in autumn, whilst Storm Petrel and Leach's Petrel are seen only irregularly.

Another example of a species on the increase is the Little Egret, in line with the situation nationally. The first record was in 1993, followed by three in 1996, a singleton in 1999 and four in 2000. Sightings then increased annually to a total of 516 bird-days in 2008 with a daily maximum of 17 and it has been recorded in every month except February. Grey Herons have also become more noticeable as passage migrants in recent years, with singles or small groups regularly observed passing south or coming in off the sea and continuing to the west. Other members of the heron family are only occasionally seen at Spurn. There are six records of Bittern, four of Great White Egret and three of Night-heron, plus a single record of Purple Heron. White Storks have occurred seven times, there are two records of Black Stork, three records of Glossy Ibis and 49 of Spoonbill.

The raptors have seen considerable increases in numbers over recent years. A prime example is the Marsh Harrier which has gone from being a fairly scarce bird in the 1960s to a fairly common passage migrant, seen mainly in spring, but increasingly so in the autumn (Table 2).

Similarly, Hen Harriers have become more regular since the mid-1970s, although the increase has been somewhat less dramatic than that of the Marsh Harrier. Conversely, the Montagu's Harrier, which was once recorded almost annually, began to decrease from the mid-1970s, although it has become annual again since 1992. Just to complete the set, a Pallid Harrier was seen in April 2003.

The increase in Sparrowhawk numbers also began during the early 1980s and continues to the present day (Table 2). The fact that at least some of these birds are Continental and Scandinavian migrants has been demonstrated by recoveries of Spurn-ringed birds in Norway, Denmark, Sweden and Germany, and the recovery of a German-ringed bird at Spurn. The Goshawk, however, remains a very rare bird at Spurn, with a total of only 10 records. The Red Kite has also become a more regular visitor, though it still remains scarce. There were 12 records in the observatory's first 40 years (to 1995), and a further 21 since. Ospreys have also been seen more regularly in recent years, with 33 records in the first 40 years and over 150 since. Numbers of Merlin, Hobby and Peregrine have also increased since the mid-1980s, particularly so in the case of the Peregrine (Figure 2) and Merlin (Table 2).

Buzzard records have increased slightly in recent years, but the Rough-legged Buzzard remains very scarce, with only 47 records. The Honey-buzzard is also a scarce migrant, with a total of 79 individuals recorded, 15 of which flew south on one memorable day in September 2000. Small numbers of Kestrels can be seen moving south at Spurn on suitable days during autumn and are most probably British birds, although there is a single recovery of a Finnish-ringed bird and the species is occasionally seen coming in off the sea. Numbers on any one day seldom get into double figures, but 98 were recorded on 22 September 1969, with the maximum in recent years being 94 on 28 September 2000. There are two

Table 2. *Increases of selected raptors: average number of bird-days per year for Marsh Harrier, Sparrowhawk and Merlin at Spurn at five-year intervals from 1966 to 2005.*

	1966–1970	1971–1975	1976–1980	1981–1985	1986–1990	1991–1995	1996–2000	2001–2005
Marsh Harrier	2.8	3.2	5.8	9.6	23.2	32.8	52.8	76.4
Sparrowhawk	16.8	14.4	23.8	61.2	176.4	222.6	358.0	406.2
Merlin	6.6	7.2	24.6	69.2	99.4	113.2	135.6	132.8

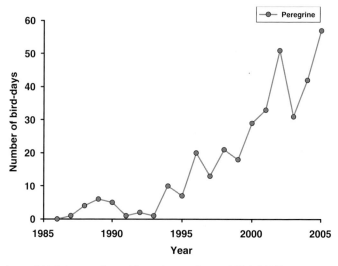

Figure 2. *Annual bird-day numbers of Peregrines at Spurn 1986–2005.*

records of Black Kite, four of White-tailed Eagle (all between 1982 and 1990), and Red-footed Falcons have occurred on 15 occasions.

Moorhen and Coot both breed at Spurn, whilst Water Rails are regular in very small numbers as passage migrants and also in winter. The Corncrake (with 51 records) has always been an uncommon visitor, and particularly so in recent years. Spotted Crakes have occurred seven times and there is a single record of Little Crake. Cranes have become of more regular occurrence of late, and from eight records up to 1995, the total now stands at 31, with a maximum count of seven birds flying south together in March 2002.

As mentioned previously Spurn is not particularly known as a site for the occurrence of rare or scarce waders, but numbers of the commoner species on the Humber Estuary can be spectacular and most species (apart from the Turnstone) seem to be on the increase in recent years. The commonest species is most certainly the Knot. Pashby (1988) wrote: 'The general impression is of a considerable fall in numbers over the past 10–15 years' and there was a maximum count of 9,000 up to 1985, but subsequently numbers began to increase and by 1995 the maximum stood at 15,000. Since 1998 numbers have regularly reached 25,000 or more, with an autumn maximum of 100,000 on 21 August 2008, and 35,000 in winter on 26 February 2000. Although a total of 104 Knot has been ringed at Spurn there are no foreign recoveries; but this is not the case with the Dunlin, another species that has increased in numbers in recent years. Well over 9,500 have been ringed at Spurn and there are recoveries from a number of overseas locations, the majority being from Sweden, Finland and Denmark, but also several from Poland, Germany, the Netherlands and France, and singles from Canada, Russia, Latvia and Norway. There are also good numbers of recoveries of foreign-ringed Dunlins at Spurn, with the majority being from Sweden (31) and Norway (30).

Other wader species which have shown considerable increases are Ringed Plover (from a maximum of 238 up to 1995 to regular counts of over 500 and a maximum of 955); Golden Plover (from a maximum of 500 up to 1985 to 10,000 in 2004 and 2008); Grey Plover; Black-tailed Godwit (from a maximum of four up to 1985 to 730 on 4 November 2008); Bar-tailed Godwit and Redshank. One species which seems to have become increasingly scarce in recent years is the Little Stint, a species considered to be a regular passage migrant up to the late 1980s. A Finnish-ringed Little Stint was found dead under wires at nearby Easington in 2001, but there have generally been very few sight records in recent years. Other interesting wader recoveries include a Russian-ringed Grey Plover, a Finnish-ringed Curlew, a German-ringed Kentish Plover and a Spurn-ringed Woodcock in Spain.

Considering that the Avocet is now breeding in good numbers along the Humber, there are relatively few occurrences of this species at Spurn, with a total of only 95 records since it was first recorded in 1958, although it has become more regular in recent years. The lack of suitable freshwater also means that many of the species which prefer this habitat are seen less frequently. Ruff and Common Sandpiper are reasonably regular, with smaller numbers of Green Sandpipers, whilst a few Wood Sandpipers occur nearly annually, mostly in May and August. Greenshanks can sometimes be present in reasonable numbers, but the Spotted Redshank remains a relatively scarce bird at Spurn, and there is a single record of Marsh Sandpiper. All three phalaropes are rarities here; Grey, the most regular, has a total of 31 records, and there are seven for Red-necked and two for Wilson's.

The commoner species of gulls are usually present in varying numbers at Spurn and there can sometimes be fairly substantial movements offshore, particularly of Herring Gulls. Little Gulls are often seen in small numbers throughout most of the year and can be spectacular in autumn, as witnessed in 2003, when birds appeared to be feeding well offshore from early August and using the Humber for roosting, going out north-east in the morning and returning in the evening. A count of 2,000 was recorded on 4 August, and then an incredible 10,000 came in close to Kilnsea cliff in the evening on 12 September, an amazing sight! Numbers reduced after this, although there were several more counts of over 1,000 and 4,500 on 22nd. One or two Sabine's Gulls occur in most autumns, with a total of 106 recorded since the first sighting in 1953, but of course it is not unknown for immature Kittiwakes to be mis-identified as this species, especially at long distances. Mediterranean Gulls have shown an increase in recent years with a maximum of eight on 19 August 2007. A few Glaucous and Iceland Gulls occur in most years, with most being just fly-pasts, but there are no accepted records of any of the rarer species of gulls, as yet, save for a Caspian Gull seen in July 2001.

Tern numbers can be spectacular at Spurn. In early autumn, large numbers pass south close inshore on their way to roost in the evening. Many of these can be seen returning north in the early mornings, but they are then much further out to sea and often only discernible as silhouettes against the rising sun to the east. The Common Tern is the commonest species, although in the past many of these were recorded as 'Commic' (unidentified Common or Arctic Tern). With increased observer awareness and better optics, the vast majority can now be assigned to specific species. Counts of 4,000–5,000 Common Terns are fairly regular, with more on occasions and, exceptionally, 22,500 on 19 August 2006, followed by an incredible 30,000 the following evening. Arctic Terns occur in considerably smaller numbers and the autumn maximum up to the end of the twentieth century was 140, but this now stands at 1,430 as from 11 September 2003. Conversely Arctic Terns are often the commoner of the two species in spring, especially after east or south-easterly winds, when they can be seen flying east or north-east out of the Humber. Black Terns are often involved in these easterly movements, particularly in May, and a maximum count of 222 was recorded on 3 May 1997. They are also often seen in the evening roost movements in autumn as are Sandwich Terns with up to 6,000 birds present, but numbers have been considerably lower in recent years. Counts of Roseate Terns in these movements have increased steadily over recent years, apart from a 'blip' in 2001 and 2002 (Figure 3).

Little Terns breed nearby and the observatory has been involved in organising wardening facilities for the colony for a number of years now, with the help of generous donations from local business. Small numbers still attempt to nest on the peninsula in some years, and two pairs reared three young in 2006, the first

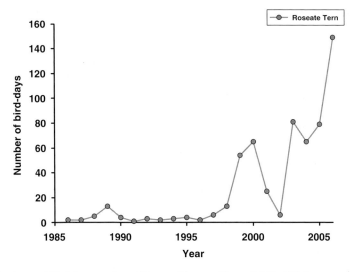

Figure 3. *Annual bird-day numbers of Roseate Terns at Spurn 1986–2006.*

successful breeding since 1993. Other terns to have occurred are Gull-billed (with two records), Caspian (eight records), Lesser Crested (two records, almost certainly relating to the same bird) and White-winged Black (four records).

Large numbers of auks can often be seen passing offshore, mostly Guillemots or Razorbills, but with many being too far out for specific identification. Puffins occur in small numbers (day maximum of 158) and there are nine records of Black Guillemot. Little Auks are very irregular in their occurrence, but can sometimes be seen in good numbers in late autumn or early winter, particularly after northerly winds, with a highest count of 1,767 on 29 October 1983.

There are a number of old records of Pallas's Sandgrouse (between 1888 and 1890), but it is unlikely that this species will occur again. Large movements of up to 10,000 Woodpigeons formerly occurred, particularly in November and December, but numbers have been considerably lower since the late 1960s. They do seem to be making a bit of a comeback recently, however, as 2,450 were recorded flying south on 4 November 2005. A similar situation exists with the Stock Dove, the maximum count of 261 occurring in January 1958. They were much scarcer in the 1970s through to the 1990s, but a new autumn maximum of 193 was recorded on 4 November 2003, and a new spring maximum of 151 on 26 March 2006. The species also bred for the first time in 2006, in an owl box, where a pair raised six young from three broods. Turtle Doves bred at Spurn for the first time in 1999 and have continued to breed every year since with up to four pairs (possibly five) in 2005. Numbers of migrant birds, however, have been much reduced in recent years. There is a single record of the Rufous Turtle Dove, on 8 November 1975. Numbers of Cuckoos have also decreased, but there does seem to have been a slight upturn over the last few years (Figure 4).

The Great Spotted Cuckoo has occurred twice, in 1982 and 2003, and there is a single record of Yellow-billed Cuckoo from October 1978. The most frequently

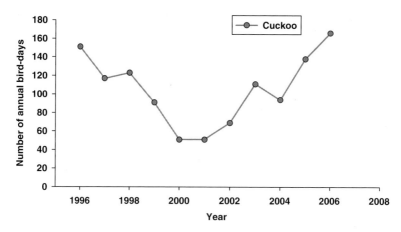

Figure 4. *Numbers of bird-days per year for Cuckoo at Spurn from 1996 to 2006.*

occurring owls at Spurn are the Barn and the Short-eared. Barn Owls are regularly seen throughout the year, normally singles but up to four have occurred in a day. Most are believed to be local breeding birds from the Kilnsea and Easington areas. A pair attempted to breed within the observatory recording area in 2001, but without success. There is very little evidence of migration, apart from two records of the dark-breasted race of Barn Owl, *Tyto alba guttata*, in 1990 and 2005, both in late October. Short-eared Owls can occur throughout the year, but are commonest in autumn, particularly October, and there is also some evidence of spring migration. Long-eared Owls have also occurred in every month, although only once in February, and again the largest numbers are recorded in autumn as with Short-eared Owls, particularly following easterly winds, when up to 23 have been present (15 November 1986). There is an interesting ringing recovery of a bird ringed at Spurn in October and found dead in Lithuania in July of the following year. Tawny and Little Owls are only irregular visitors and there are single records of both Snowy and Tengmalm's Owl.

The Nightjar is but a rare visitor, with a total of 29 records, which include an interesting observation of one flying around the mercury vapour moth trap late at night in August 1999. Impressive movements of Swifts can occur, with peak numbers normally in late June and July, when several thousand frequently pass south in a day. Maximum counts of 20,000 have occurred on two occasions. Spurn has also done well for the rarer swifts, with two Pacific Swifts, a Little Swift, two Chimney Swifts, two Pallid Swifts and 15 records of Alpine Swift. Kingfishers are irregular visitors but have occurred in every month except December, always as single birds. Bee-eaters, conversely, are less frequent but have been recorded in small groups on several occasions, with a total of 41 records involving 58 birds and a maximum of seven on 23 May 1999. The 22 records of Hoopoes have all been of single birds.

The Wryneck is a regular but uncommon passage migrant, commonest in late August and September, but with reasonable numbers sometimes occurring in

Table 3. *Average number of bird-days per year for Wryneck, Yellow Wagtail, Firecrest and Red-backed Shrike at Spurn at five-year intervals from 1966 to 2005.*

Species	1966–1970	1971–1975	1976–1980	1981–1985	1986–1990	1991–1995	1996–2000	2001–2005
Wryneck	43.4	41.0	38.6	29.4	30.6	17.8	18.8	20.2
Yellow Wagtail	445	269	678	700	1,116	688	1,332	1,093
Firecrest	1.6	14.8	17.8	19.2	12.6	19.0	36.6	72.6
Red-backed Shrike	7.4	16.6	47.0	27.4	20.2	19.2	14.4	10.2

spring, mostly in May. Its occurrences have been less frequent in recent years (Table 3).

The Green Woodpecker is a rare visitor, with a total of only 11 records, but the Great Spotted Woodpecker, although of only irregular occurrence, appears to be increasing in frequency. Most are seen in autumn, but the presence of the recent overwintering bird in 2001/02 means that it has now been recorded in every month. Some autumn birds are attributable to the northern nominate race, *Dendrocopus major major.*

The passerines

Skylarks are breeding residents, although in considerably lower numbers than formerly. They are also a regular constituent species of autumn visible passage, although again in much reduced numbers, very rarely reaching 1,000 in a day compared with the 10,000 recorded on 28 October 1971. The Woodlark is a fairly regular but uncommon migrant, with a total of 85 records for the periods between March and May, and September and December. Shore Lark is a fairly regular but uncommon migrant, again recorded in lower numbers than in past years, and with occasional records in winter. There are 20 records of Short-toed Lark, including sightings in both December and January. Other species of larks recorded are a Black Lark (the first British record), on 27 April 1984 and Calandra Lark, on 3 October 2004.

The hirundines are among the most obvious visible migrants at Spurn, when several thousand frequently pass south in a day, given the right weather conditions. Swallows are the commonest, with a maximum of 45,000 recorded, along with 15,000 House Martins on a single day. Sand Martins are usually seen in smaller numbers, although there can be up to 2,000 on occasions and an exceptional 12,000 were recorded on one late August day in 1996. Swallows breed in some of the old buildings along the peninsula and Sand Martins occasionally in the sea cliff. House Martins have attempted to breed on the Lifeboat Cottages at the Point, but all the nests collapsed and there is just a single breeding record from a farm in the northern part of the area. Red-rumped Swallows are seen occasionally, particularly in spring, and there have been 37 records in all, including the first for Yorkshire in May 1964. Totally unexpected was a Cliff Swallow, which was seen on three days in October 1995.

Another of the most numerous visible passage birds is the Meadow Pipit. Peak numbers occur around the second half of September, up to 20,000 having been recorded on a couple of occasions. Considerable efforts have been made over the years to catch and ring them during their diurnal migrations, using tape lures in the Heligoland trap at the 'Wire Dump', and over 27,000 had been ringed up to the end of 2008, producing an excellent series of recoveries, including 34 from Spain, 11 from Morocco, three from Algeria and two from Italy. Small numbers of Tree Pipits are sometimes recorded, with a maximum count of 70 birds, but numbers in some recent years have been very low. Rock Pipits are also recorded flying south, and they are most numerous in October, but Water Pipit remains a rare bird at Spurn, with a total of only 15 records. Richard's Pipits are uncommon autumn migrants, with around 170 records, only three of which have been in spring. Of the rarer pipits there is a single record of Pechora, seven of Olive-backed, 12 for Red-throated and 13 for Tawny.

The Yellow Wagtail is a regular migrant in both spring and autumn, with peak numbers from mid-August to early September. It seems to be getting more regular in recent years (Table 3) and has bred occasionally. The Blue-headed race, *Motacilla flava flava*, is fairly regular, particularly in spring. The Grey-headed race, *M. f. thunbergi*, has been recorded more often than not in the years since it was first identified at Spurn on 26 May 1965 and there is a single record of Ashy-headed, *M. f. cinereocapilla*. The birds that are seen (flying south) overhead are usually recorded as '*flava*' wagtails, as it is only when they are grounded that they can be assigned to a subspecies.

The Grey Wagtail is principally an autumn migrant, with the vast majority of records in September and October, but recorded in all months except December. Numbers of this species have also been increasing in recent years. The status of the Pied Wagtail was formerly the same as the Grey, but it has been a regular breeder since 1990, with four or five pairs breeding annually since the turn of the century. The Waxwing is an irregular and uncommon visitor, with most records from late October to December, but there was an exceptionally late record on 13 May 2007. There are two records of the Dipper, from October 1962 and November 1999. Both the Wren and the Dunnock are resident and breed in good numbers in most years. There is some evidence of migration for the Dunnock, with a few birds being seen flying high to the south in autumn, and ringing has provided evidence of Continental movements with three controls from Norway and a Spurn-ringed bird recovered in France, near Paris. There was also an obvious arrival of Continental birds in March 2005, with 61 on the 27th, rising to 145 on the 28th. Unusually most of these birds were to be seen feeding on the tide wrack along the Humber shore.

The Robin also breeds in small numbers but is principally an autumn migrant, with peak numbers in September and October and a daily maximum of 2,000. Good numbers of Robins have been ringed at Spurn and there are foreign recoveries from 12 countries, including Switzerland, Italy, Spain and Poland, along with several controls at Spurn of foreign-ringed birds, from Finland and Sweden, and elsewhere. The Nightingale is an uncommon migrant, with a total of 56 records, mostly in spring, with just seven in autumn. There have also been 12 records of Thrush Nightingale, including three different birds in May 1984, two of which were present at the same time, in good voice. The Bluethroat is recorded in most years and at least 174 birds have now been seen, 105 in spring with 104 in May (from the 3rd), and one on 11 June 2003. In addition there are just two records of the southern European White-spotted race, *Luscinia svecica cyanecula*, in April 1958 and 1966.

Black Redstarts have been recorded in all months, but peak numbers occur from late March to mid-May, and in October. Redstarts, Whinchats and Wheatears are all common migrants, Redstarts and Whinchats being much more numerous in autumn than spring, but Wheatear numbers are more or less equally balanced between the two seasons. There have been three occurrences of Pied Wheatear, the first being a first-summer male trapped and ringed on 20 June 1991 and rediscovered further north at Scarborough two days later. There is also a nineteenth century record of Black-eared Wheatear for the area. Stonechats have been recorded in every month, but are most numerous from late September to November. 'Siberian' Stonechats of the race *Saxicola torquatus maura/stejnegeri* have been identified on 13 occasions, mostly in autumn, but there is only a single spring record. A somewhat surprising record was of a male Rock Thrush in May 1984.

The thrushes make a significant contribution to ringing numbers at Spurn, with the totals for Blackbird, Fieldfare, Song Thrush and Redwing between them constituting over 23% of the total numbers ringed. This is reflected in the number of recoveries, particularly of Blackbirds, with many from the Scandinavian countries and such diverse places as Estonia, Latvia, Italy and Albania. Unusual recoveries of Fieldfares have been reported from Austria, Greece and Yugoslavia, amongst others, and for Redwings from Russia, Italy and Sardinia. Most foreign recoveries of Song Thrushes are from Portugal, Spain and France and Spurn-ringed Ring Ouzels have been recovered in Morocco, Italy, Spain and France. Perhaps not surprisingly, there are no foreign recoveries of the Mistle Thrush.

Of the warblers, several species breed at Spurn, the Whitethroat being the most numerous, but other regular breeding species include Sedge Warbler, Reed Warbler, Lesser Whitethroat and Blackcap, and occasional pairs of Grasshopper Warblers and Willow Warblers. Most of the other commoner species occur in varying numbers as both spring and autumn passage migrants. There are over 200 records of Icterine Warbler and the Barred Warbler is fairly regular in autumn, averaging between 10 and 20 bird-days in most years. The Pallas's Warbler was at one time considered to be a rare visitor, but it has become more frequent in recent years and a total of 98 birds have now been recorded, with up to four present in a single day, while the similar Yellow-browed Warbler has amassed a total of at least 400 records. There have been 49 records of Marsh Warbler (a pair bred successfully in 2008), and Spurn has an impressive list of rare warblers, including Cetti's, Lanceolated, River, Savi's, Aquatic (eight records), Blyth's Reed (three), Great Reed (three), Booted (seven), Melodious (three), Marmora's, Subalpine (20), Sardinian, Asian Desert, Greenish (18), Arctic (seven), Hume's (three), Radde's (19), Dusky (eight) and Western Bonelli's (five).

Unusual ringing recoveries include Blackcaps from Lebanon and Greece, and

Willow Warbler from Algeria, but the highest recovery rate among the warblers is for the Booted, with a total of six ringed for one recovery (in Belgium). Another interesting record is of a Blackcap ringed in Switzerland and controlled at Spurn. Goldcrests are often very numerous in autumn, with up to 2,000 sometimes present, and an exceptional 4,000 on 10 October 1959, while the Firecrest occurs in much smaller numbers but has been increasing in recent years (Table 3).

There are a number of overseas recoveries of Goldcrest, mostly from the Low Countries but also from Ireland and Switzerland, whilst birds ringed in Norway, Sweden, Denmark and Finland have been controlled or recovered at Spurn. Spotted Flycatchers are regular migrants with peak numbers occurring in late May and again in September, whilst the Pied Flycatcher is much more numerous in autumn than in spring. The Red-breasted Flycatcher is a fairly regular autumn migrant, with a total of 220 records, of which 18 were in spring and a maximum of five on 24 September 2008.

Most members of the tit family are normally regarded as fairly sedentary, but there is evidence of migration at Spurn, with small numbers of both Blue and Great Tits making their way slowly south down the peninsula in autumn, and there is a recovery of a Spurn-ringed Blue Tit from France. Coal and Willow Tits are irregular visitors and there are only 13 records of Marsh Tit. Long-tailed Tits are irregular wanderers, but bred for the first time in 2007. Two birds of the northern Scandinavian white-headed race *Aegithalos caudatus caudatus* were seen on 18 October 2005. They were relocated about three miles away the following day, where they spent most of the winter, one of them paying three brief visits to Spurn again in April 2006. There is a single record of Penduline Tit, the first for Britain, on 22 October 1966. The Treecreeper is an irregular visitor with a total of 69 records, and the Nuthatch is a fairly recent addition to the Spurn list, with only six records, the first being in July 1998.

The Golden Oriole is a scarce migrant with a total of 82 records; the vast majority (77) were in May and June, but there has also been one in April, one in July, two in September and one in October. Of the shrikes, the Red-backed is the commonest, although it has been less regular in recent years, after numbers peaked in the late 1970s (Table 3).

Great Grey Shrike numbers were highest in the early 1970s and this is another species which has become less frequent, although there has been a slight recovery in recent years. It is scarce in spring with just 20 records, but more frequent in autumn, with over 200 records from September to November, and a late one on 3 December 1978. Of the rarer shrikes there have been two records of Isabelline and six of Lesser Grey, four of which were between 1959 and 1970, followed by a long gap until 2005, when, surprisingly, two different birds occurred. The Woodchat Shrike has occurred on 11 occasions, mostly in May and early June.

Rooks, Carrion Crows and Jackdaws are regularly to be seen in small parties flying south in both spring and autumn, although many 'lose their nerve' and return north before crossing the Humber. Hooded Crows were formerly much more numerous than in recent years, and were regular migrants recorded in most months, peaking in late October and early November, with a maximum of 330 on 5 November 1960. Nowadays there are on average, only a couple of records of single birds each year, and occasional absences. The Raven is a very rare bird at Spurn, with only five records, and there are also three records of Nutcracker, all of single birds flying south during the 1968 invasion, one each in August, September and October. The Jay is normally a scarce visitor but is occasionally recorded in good numbers, such as in the autumn of 1983, when there were 94 bird-days in October, including a maximum of 39 on 19th. This was followed by a good spring in 1984 when there were records almost daily from 20 April to 19 June with a maximum of 29 on 30 May and 1 June. The Starling can be a very numerous bird at Spurn, up to 20,000 have occurred on several occasions, mostly flying south or coming in from the east. There have been 10 records of Rose-coloured Starling since the first in 1984, including four different birds in 2005. Numbers of House and Tree Sparrows are much reduced in recent years, although both species are holding their own and there have been signs of a slight recovery in the past few years, with Tree Sparrows particularly becoming more evident during visible passage in autumn.

Perhaps surprisingly, there are three species of American passerine on the Spurn list. The one with the best claim to being a genuine vagrant is a Red-eyed Vireo, trapped and ringed on 30 September 1990. The other two were both seen in May and could possibly have been ship-assisted. The first of these, a Song Sparrow, trapped in May 1964, was the second record for Britain and Ireland and also for Europe, while a White-throated Sparrow trapped in May 1983, was the first Yorkshire record.

Some members of the finch family are amongst the most common diurnal migrants and good numbers are seen passing south in suitable conditions. The most numerous are Greenfinches, Goldfinches and Linnets. Chaffinches were formerly a common diurnal migrant, with up to 3,500 recorded in a day in 1960, but numbers in recent years have dropped off considerably, and seldom exceed 300. However, there were unusually high numbers recorded in early spring 2006, including a maximum of 1,357 on 1 April. There are a number of foreign recoveries of Spurn-ringed Chaffinches, mostly from Norway, Germany, the Netherlands and Belgium, although there is also a recovery at Spurn of a bird ringed in Finland. Brambling and Siskin are both regular migrants, although numbers vary considerably from year to year. Siskin generally occurs more regularly now than hitherto.

Foreign recoveries of Spurn-ringed Bramblings include birds from Finland and Spain, while there is an unusual recovery of a Siskin from Italy. Redpolls also occur on passage, particularly in autumn, but in smaller numbers, and Twite too, but irregularly. Even more irregular in their appearance are Common Crossbills and Bullfinches, although they cannot really be classed as rarities, like the Parrot Crossbill (with three records), the Arctic Redpoll (15 records) and the Serin (41 records). The Hawfinch was also considered a rarity until the 1980s, but has become more regular in recent years and a total of 88 birds have now been recorded, with up to five present in a day. The Common Rosefinch has also become more frequent in the last couple of decades, with over a hundred records to its credit, and two pairs attempting to breed in 2000, unfortunately with no apparent success.

The commonest of the buntings at Spurn is the Reed Bunting, which still breeds in small numbers and can occur in good numbers on autumn passage. Unfortunately this can no longer be said for the Yellowhammer and the Corn Bunting, both of which have declined dramatically at Spurn, as elsewhere. Snow Buntings still occur in small numbers, but are much less numerous than they were in the 1950s and 1960s, and small numbers of Lapland Buntings occur in most autumns, and occasionally in winter. There are 27 records of Little Bunting, mostly in autumn but there is one spring record. Of the rarer buntings there are single records of both Cirl (1964) and Rock Bunting (1965), four records of Yellow-breasted Bunting and 10 records of Rustic Bunting. There are interesting recoveries of Snow Bunting from Belgium, Norway and Iceland, and of Reed Bunting from Norway and Sweden.

SOCIAL ACTIVITIES

A nightly roll-call is held in the common room, giving an opportunity for residents and visitors to report their sightings and to find out what has been seen during the day; however, most sightings of interest are already common knowledge thanks to a short-wave radio system used by regular visitors. The system is licensed for use by the observatory and the YWT and most locals and regular visitors have their own handsets, while there are a limited number of sets available for use by observatory visitors. Most social activities are centred on the local pub, the Crown and Anchor, and people tend to gravitate there after (or sometimes instead of!) attending roll-call. Quizzes or live music sessions are occasionally arranged as fund-raising activities for the observatory and a sweepstake is held on most Saturday nights, based on the first rare or scarce bird to be identified the following day. The 'proceeds' are used to purchase books for the observatory library. A major social event is the annual Friends of Spurn Bird Observatory barbeque held at Kew Villa, normally on the first Saturday in August. Copious quantities of food and beer are consumed before folk retire to the pub (which is fortunately just next door) to carry on the festivities.

OTHER FAUNA AND FLORA

Mammals, reptiles and amphibians

Mammals are relatively inconspicuous at Spurn, but of the larger species, Fox and European Roe Deer are regularly seen. Both Grey and Common Seals are generally present offshore in very small numbers and Harbour Porpoises are seen regularly. Sadly, most records of other cetaceans are of stranded individuals, one of the most recent being the well-publicised Sperm Whale on the Humber mudflats. Water Voles used to be relatively common in the 'canal' but are rarely seen nowadays. There are occasional records of Harvest Mouse and a single Grey Squirrel has put in a few appearances in recent years. Hedgehogs are occasionally seen, usually dead on the road and there is some evidence of visits by Badgers from their nearby sett, but no definite sightings as yet. As its name suggests, Rabbits were once common in the Warren area, but their numbers are much reduced in recent years, due mainly to myxomatosis, but in part also to habitat loss and drowning following inundation by the sea. Other mammals present include Hare, Stoat and Weasel, and Common, Pygmy and Water Shrews.

Of the reptiles and amphibians, Common Lizards are regularly encountered, particularly around the observatory buildings and there are very occasional sightings of Grass Snake. For a couple of years there were regular sightings of two Ocellated Lizards in the Chalk Bank area, doubtless released animals, but these seem to have succumbed to the weather. Common Newts still breed in several of the freshwater habitats and there is a colony of Marsh Frogs in the garden pond at Kew Villa in Kilnsea, whilst there are also occasional sightings of Common Frog and Common Toad.

Invertebrates

Apart from the birds, the groups receiving most attention at Spurn are the invertebrates, particularly the butterflies, moths and dragonflies. Up to the end of 2006, a total of 29 species of butterfly had been recorded, including a number of migrant species. Southerly passage of Red Admirals is regular in autumn, and up to 200 in a day are sometimes recorded flying south, to be joined in some years by Small Tortoiseshells. Another regular immigrant is the Painted Lady, although no genuine southerly passage has been recorded, and Clouded Yellows are sometimes seen, whilst there have been four records of Camberwell Beauty. Of the resident species, there have been a number of recent colonists, which are now established as breeding species, notably Green Hairstreak (1983), Comma (1984), Holly Blue (annual since 1989), Speckled Wood (1992), Brown Argus (1997) and Essex Skipper, first recorded in 2003. Wanderers with only a single record include Swallowtail, Large Tortoiseshell and White Admiral.

A considerable amount of effort has been put into moth trapping over the years and the list now boasts 817 species (to the end of 2006), consisting of 431 macromoths and 386 micromoths, while new species continue to be recorded. New macromoth records in 2007 included Toadflax Brocade and Clouded Magpie. Many of these species are common and widespread, but quite a number are of restricted distribution in Britain, examples being Scarce Pug, Sand Dart, Shore Wainscot, Star-wort, Crescent Striped and Lyme Grass. As with birds, Spurn is particularly suited to receiving migrants and apart from the regular species such as Dark Sword-grass, Silver Y, Rush Veneer and Rusty-dot Pearl, other regular migrants include Pearly Underwing, Hummingbird Hawkmoth and Convolvulus Hawkmoth. Less frequent immigrants include such species as Bordered Straw, Scarce Bordered Straw, and Great Brocade. One particularly unwelcome colonist is the Brown-tail, a very rarely recorded insect until about four years ago, but now a serious pest southwards from the Narrow Neck.

A total of 23 species of dragonflies and damselflies have been recorded at Spurn and numbers of many have been increasing in recent years due to the creation of additional freshwater habitat. Recent colonists include Emperor Dragonfly, Broad-bodied Chaser, Black-tailed Skimmer and Red-veined Darter. A number of species have been recorded only as vagrants, including Banded Demoiselle (four records), and Large Red Damselfly (two), and there are single records of Southern Hawker, Lesser Emperor, Brown Hawker, Norfolk Hawker, Downy Emerald and Vagrant Darter. The Coleoptera (beetles) are another well-studied group.

Plants

Spurn is important botanically and despite loss of much habitat it still harbours a number of locally important species. One of the characteristic plants is Sea-holly, and Spurn is the only known Yorkshire site for Suffocated Clover, although this is very difficult to find nowadays as much of its short-turf habitat has been lost with the reduction in the Rabbit population. The dominant plant along most of the peninsula is the Sea-buckthorn with a few scattered Elders and a ground cover of Claytonia. Pyramidal Orchids are still fairly common in some areas.

ACCESS AND ACCOMMODATION

Spurn Bird Observatory is situated at the northern end of the Spurn peninsula, half a mile from Kilnsea. Access by public transport is not particularly good. There is a bus service to Easington, three miles to the north, from Hull from Monday to Saturday, but there is presently only one direct service each day. Otherwise it is necessary to take a bus to Withernsea, 10 miles to the north, and then another bus to Easington. Fortunately, on bank holidays and Sundays (from Good Friday until the last Sunday in October) there is a direct service from Withernsea all the way to Spurn Point, four times daily. For timetables check the website of the East Yorkshire Motor Services Ltd or telephone their enquiry line on 01482 222222.

Naturalists wishing to stay at the observatory should apply to the warden, Kew Villa, Kilnsea, via Patrington, Hull, East Yorkshire, HU12 0UG, stating the dates of the nights that they wish to stay, with possible alternatives, and enclosing a s.a.e. Alternatively, they can telephone and leave a message on the answer phone (01964 650479) or e-mail the warden. Visitors stay at their own risk. The observatory also maintains a small touring caravan site (available to Caravan Club members only) and bookings and enquiries may be made in the same way.

Unfortunately, some of the rooms used for accommodation at the observatory have been deemed unsuitable for habitation from the end of 2009. It is expected that some accommodation will be available for visitors after this time, but the capacity will be reduced. It is therefore even more important to book well in advance and intending visitors should contact the warden for up to date information.

At the time of writing the charge for staying at the observatory is £8.00 a night, or only £5.00 to members of Friends of Spurn Bird Observatory. These charges are subject to change. Payment should be made to 'Spurn Bird Observatory Trust', via the warden. Visitors under 16 years of age can only be accepted if accompanied by a responsible adult.

Cooking facilities are available at the observatory, with crockery, cutlery and kitchen utensils provided. Food may be bought in Easington (half-day closing Tuesday) or in Withernsea, where a full range of shops and services (including banks) is available. Please note that the nearest available petrol to Spurn is at Patrington or Withernsea, both approximately 10 miles away. There are two cafés at Spurn which both serve excellent fare. The Blue Bell near Sandy Beaches Caravan Site is open most weekends, and all bank holidays from either 10:00 hrs or 11:00 hrs until 16:00 hrs or 17:00 hrs. It is occasionally open during the week. The Spurn Bite Snack Bar is situated at the point near the Lifeboat Cottages and sells the highly acclaimed 'Spurn Biter' (best served with beans) or excellent full breakfasts with a wide range of other snacks. It is open most weekends throughout the year from 10:00 hrs until approximately 16:30 hrs. The Crown and Anchor Inn in Kilnsea also sells meals at lunchtimes and in the evening.

Blankets and pillows are provided on the beds, but sheets and pillow slips (or sleeping bags and pillow slips) must be brought, as must soap and towels. A bath and a shower are available for residents and guests. Rooms must be kept clean and tidy and all breakages made good. Please respect other observatory residents and keep noise to a minimum at night time. Smoking is not allowed in any of the observatory buildings. Camping, caravans and sleeping in cars are not allowed and under no circumstances may dogs be brought onto the reserve.

Visitors wishing to take part in ringing should first get permission from the warden and should hold a current BTO permit ('A' or 'C') or be supervised by a permit holder with whom the responsibility for accuracy rests. Traps must not be driven unless there is a registered ringer present. Only rings provided by the observatory are to be used. Visitors are not entitled to publish records or photographs made whilst using the facilities of the observatory without first obtaining permission from the committee.

Rights of ownership of the peninsula are vested in Yorkshire Wildlife Trust Ltd. Visitors to the observatory are expected to observe the regulations issued for the guidance of the public. These include the avoidance of certain marked areas in the breeding season and bans against fires, tents, uprooting of plants, shooting and so forth. Membership of the Yorkshire Naturalists' Union and/or the Yorkshire Wildlife Trust Ltd. carries no right of entry to observatory premises or traps, except by arrangement with officials of the observatory or the warden. Other properties on the peninsula are also let and cannot be visited except by arrangement with the tenants.

To join 'Friends of Spurn Bird Observatory', you can obtain a membership form from the visitor centre or from the warden, or by writing to the Membership Secretary, 114 Everill Gate Lane, Broomhill, Barnsley, S73 0YJ. Alternatively you can download a membership form from the observatory's website. To see a very comprehensive bibliography for the Spurn area, follow the link to 'wilgilsland' on the observatory website.

Observatory opened:	1946
Total number of bird species recorded at the observatory:	351
Best bird year:	2006
Number of species recorded:	248
Total of birds ringed at the observatory:	346,507
Number of species:	229
Best ringing year:	1988
Number ringed:	11,435
Number of species ringed:	85

Walney

by Colin Raven and Keith Parkes

WALNEY ISLAND

Think of island bird observatories and thoughts immediately turn to intrepid voyages over rough seas in tiny boats or turbulent air crossings and rough landings in small planes on airstrips teetering atop isolated, remote and windswept isles. However, the landscape of Walney Island is far less austere and the journey far tamer, requiring nothing more strenuous than a short car journey across Walney Channel via the small bridge that links the island to Barrow-in-Furness on the mainland.

Walney is the largest of a small group of islands that occupy the relatively shallow waters of Morecambe Bay off the south-western tip of Cumbria in north-west England and was formed during the last glaciations when large quantities of rock, sand and clay were deposited and later uncovered as the ice sheet retreated. Forming a natural breakwater for the mainland, Walney Island is a good example of a barrier island, a relatively rare geomorphological feature in the British Isles. Fairly flat, low-lying and windswept, the only 'hills' are the sand dunes at the north and south ends and the mounds of red boulder clay overlaid with sand and turf in the centre of the island.

Much of Walney Island is composed of this red boulder clay and large expo-

Colin Raven is the current Cumbria County Recorder, has been Walney recorder since 1992 and has been actively involved in the work of Walney Bird Observatory for over 20 years.
Keith Parkes is a founder member of Walney Bird Observatory and has been secretary since 1965.

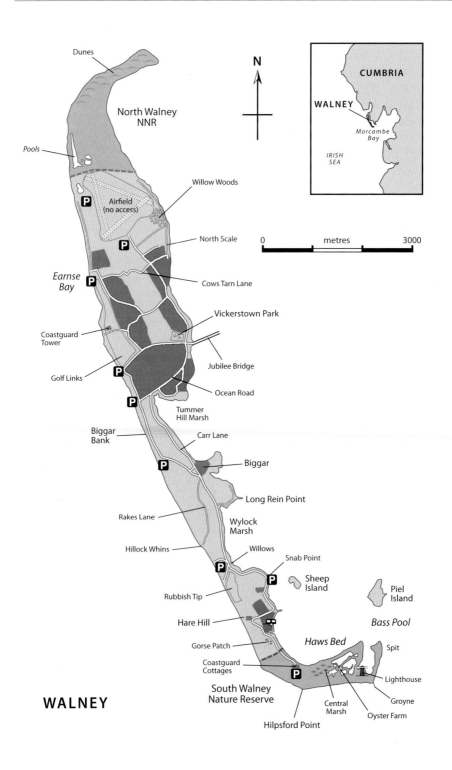

Dunes

North Walney
NNR

Pools

Willow Woods

Airfield
(no access)

North Scale

Earnse
Bay

Cows Tarn Lane

Vickerstown Park

Coastguard
Tower

Jubilee Bridge

Golf Links

Ocean Road

Tummer
Hill Marsh

Biggar
Bank

Carr Lane

Biggar

Long Rein Point

Rakes Lane

Wylock
Marsh

Hillock Whins

Willows

Snab Point

Sheep
Island

Piel
Island

Rubbish Tip

Bass Pool

Hare Hill

Gorse Patch

Haws Bed

Spit

Coastguard
Cottages

Lighthouse

WALNEY

South Walney
Nature Reserve

Central
Marsh

Groyne

Oyster Farm

Hilpsford Point

N

CUMBRIA

WALNEY

Morcambe
Bay

IRISH
SEA

0   metres   3000

sures are especially prominent along the western shore at Hillock Whins and Hare Hill. Beneath this boulder clay, the island is composed almost entirely of three Mercian mudstones, Hambleton, Singleton and Kirkham. Hare Hill, at 16 metres above sea level, towards the southern end of the island and the area further north around the now abandoned coastguard tower at 23 metres above sea level, are the highest points on the island.

The western shore faces the full force of the Irish Sea and is exposed to the ravages of the prevailing westerly winds which, coupled with the action of the tide, have, over the centuries eroded away what was once a far wider island. Although normally a gradual process, this erosion can be strikingly dynamic at times and when gale force winds coincide with high tides the island may be breached – as most recently in February 2002. At such times, the low-lying areas can be severely flooded for lengthy periods and large amounts of sand, shingle and clay are swept out to sea. Indeed, much of the south end has been formed by the action of the tides that have washed gravel and sand down the island past Hilpsford Point and onto the beaches near the groyne, where a steady expansion of the spit continues to this day.

Despite numerous attempts to stem erosion by the construction of sea defences, in the past 250 years the island has narrowed by over 300 metres in places. Erosion on the eastern shore is a far less dynamic event; small bays and channels have formed slowly over many years through the combined action of water seepage from the land and the ebb and flow of the tide across the large area of mudflats. In addition to sea erosion, the wind continuously winnows away exposed sand, both from the shoreline and the surface. This is then covered by Marram that has helped form the extensive dune systems that exist at both ends of the island (Dean 1990).

Extensive nature reserves are to be found at each end and the island still supports a semblance of agriculture in the vicinity of Biggar. The island also protects large expanses of inter-tidal mudflat and salt marsh from destruction by the Irish Sea; these salt marsh habitats are steadily expanding as Common Cordgrass creeps relentlessly outwards across the mudflats. Now around 16 kilometres long and between 350 metres and 1,500 metres wide, Walney Island covers a total of 1,362 hectares – one of the largest recording areas of any of our observatories. It can be divided into four main areas.

North Walney National Nature Reserve, at the northern end of the island, is relatively sparsely vegetated. The 144 hectares of sand dunes and rough grassland that extend northwards from Earnse Bay encompass a variety of habitats. Salt marsh, reed-bed and Gorse scrub along the eastern shore give way to dune heath in the centre and an assortment of shallow man-made pools along the western edge. Created as a National Nature Reserve as recently as 1985, it is currently administered by Natural England.

Urban Walney, at the centre of the island, is essentially a residential suburb of Barrow-in-Furness. The bulk of the island's human population of around 12,000 is concentrated in the area between the airfield to the north and Biggar to the south. It holds a mixture of council estates, terraced houses and sumptuous residences that house a mainly itinerant workforce. The strong winds and salt-laden air mean that the shrubbery is generally sparser and smaller than that found further inland. However, the private gardens and allotments and the area around Vickerstown Park, which holds the largest trees on the island, are green oases within this concrete jungle.

On the east side of the island between North Scale and the airfield is Willow Woods. This is a small, relatively sheltered wooded area dominated by stunted Ash, Willow and Oak that has developed and matured since the Second World War. The coastal strip of Biggar Bank and a golf course provide a green corridor along the western seaboard linking the north and south ends of the island.

Rural Walney, the area between Ocean Road and South Walney Nature Reserve, holds the major part of what remains of agricultural Walney, historically the mainstay of arable farming in the area and considered 'the granary of Furness'. Nowadays agriculture is chiefly pastoral, with the fields mainly used for animal grazing and silage pasture. Some of the fields are still surrounded by their original thick Hawthorn hedges and offer welcome protection to a variety of migrant passerines and a small number of breeding species. Along Rakes Lane, which runs south-west from Biggar, the hedgerows, reed-filled ditches, wet meadows and areas of rough grazing give a glimpse of early Walney. The ridge and furrow lines still visible in some of the fields are a legacy of medieval times. However, some mechanisation is already in evidence and it is perhaps only a matter of time before modern farming practices are introduced to the island with the consequential grubbing out of hedgerows and drainage of wet meadows.

South Walney Nature Reserve is an area of shingle ridges and degraded sand dunes concealing freshwater pools and brackish lagoons – the result of recently ceased gravel extraction. Removal of sand and gravel started in the late nineteenth century and continued until 2002, although activity was on a much reduced scale during the final years and limited to the winter months. The excavations quickly became flooded and have led to a network of 11 relatively sheltered brackish lagoons. A condition of the extraction licences saw the area landscaped when operations ceased and mitigation has seen the creation of isolated islands and several areas of shallows within the pools complex.

In the 1970s an oyster farm was established to utilise the lagoons and a circulation system was created inter-connecting the pools with the tidal flow via a sluice. This provides a regular food supply for the seedling Portuguese Oysters and has increased the salinity of the water, ensuring that the pools remain ice free in harsh weather. Freshwater habitats are still to be found in the central marsh. One of the earliest excavations and significantly shallower than the others, this area remains isolated from the rest of the pools complex, while the marsh and pool near the entrance gate are sited on a long-flooded meadow. Vegetation is sparse on the 130 hectares of the reserve and much of the early work by observatory members involved planting a number of sheltered sites. A mixture of trees and shrubs, mainly Willow, Elder and Bramble, is enhanced by a small reedbed in the central marsh and now forms the main area of attraction for migrant passerines.

THE OBSERVATORY'S HISTORY

Walney Island has been known for centuries as a haven for large colonies of gulls and terns and its importance was first recognised by an Act of Parliament passed in 1553 prohibiting the taking or destruction of eggs of the Black-headed Gulls and terns which bred in profusion at that time. In 1896 an amendment to the Wild Birds Protection Act 1894 gave protection to a wider range of the island's breeding birds following representations to Sir Matthew Ridley, the Home Secretary, from concerned local naturalists. More recently, much of the island's wildlife protection arises under the Wildlife and Countryside Act 1981 and the European Union's Habitats Directive and Birds Directive. The northern end of the island falls within the boundaries of the Duddon Estuary Site of Special Scientific Interest (SSSI), Special Protection Areas (SPA), European Marine Site (EMS) and Ramsar site, while the south end is part of the Morecambe Bay SSSI, SPA, Special Area of Conservation (SAC), EMS and Ramsar site designations and the South Walney and Piel Channel Flats SSSI.

Although some spasmodic recording of the birds on the island has occurred since at least the middle of the 19th century, regular observations and ringing only commenced at the south end of the island in the early 1960s. South Walney Nature Reserve was established in 1963 and shortly afterwards a Cattle Egret was found stalking the field immediately to the north of the reserve. Walney Island, under the careful guidance of Eric Pithers and Howard Tickle, achieved full accredited bird observatory status in 1965.

Unlike the majority of observatories, Walney Bird Observatory has always been operated with the generous help of volunteers. It has been un-wardened, in the sense of having had no permanent or seasonal paid warden. Fortunately, several of the South Walney Nature Reserve wardens have worked tirelessly to support the work of the observatory over the years. In the first full year of operations almost 6,000 records, involving 141 species, were logged. Two Heligoland traps were built on the South Walney Nature Reserve, one within the garden of the Coastguard Cottages, and the other along the northern boundary wall. Limited mist-netting was also carried out on the few days when weather conditions allowed. Each of these early years saw up to 1,000 birds ringed, including Cumbria's first Melodious Warbler in 1964 and Britain's third White-throated Sparrow in 1965. Two additional Heligoland traps were built in the central marsh in 1967 and 1972, but despite this, the ringing figures deteriorated dramatically with disillusioned observatory stalwarts linking the failure of some of the finest but emptiest Heligoland traps ever built to the burgeoning gull colony.

While it is true that ground-nesting species such as Meadow Pipit, Skylark and Reed Bunting ceased to breed in the spreading colony, there is little evidence to support the view that migrating passerines were reluctant to rest and feed there. The reason for the observatory's nadir in the early 1970s was perhaps more due to an ebbing of enthusiasm amongst the small band of observers upon whom the observatory relied, coupled with a lack of finance to support the employment of a full-time warden (Dean 1990).

Upon the formation of South Walney Nature Reserve, the Lancashire

Naturalists' Trust appointed Walter Shepherd as a non-birding, non-resident, 'caretaker warden' in 1963. County boundary changes saw control transferred to the Lake District Naturalists' Trust (now the Cumbria Wildlife Trust) in 1974 and the observatory's fortunes were boosted with the timely appointment of Mike Thom as the first full-time resident bird warden in 1975. As a result, for the first time, the area had daily coverage throughout the year with the consequential increase in the collection and collation of records. 1975 also saw Cumbria's first and only King Eider. There was a welcome stabilisation in the ringing totals.

Tim Dean took over in 1979 and his seemingly boundless energy and enthusiasm saw the observatory go from strength to strength. Although warden to the South Walney Nature Reserve, Tim was a staunch supporter of the ideals of the observatory and as a result membership reached unparalleled heights and the collation of records became more organised. The increase in observers allowed recording activities, hitherto concentrated on the South Walney daily recording area, to be extended to include casual observations from sites across the remainder of the island.

The increased emphasis on recording also produced a series of BBRC rarities. There was a Nutcracker on the tideline in 1979, Hume's Warbler in 1982, Gyr Falcon in 1983 and a Western Bonelli's Warbler singing from sycamores in the centre of the island in 1984. The following year there was a Black Stork at Snab Point, a Desert Wheatear near the lighthouse in 1986 and a Wilson's Phalarope in 1989. In 1992 there was a Roller in the dunes at North Walney and a Booted Warbler at South Walney, while who can forget the mass twitches that took place for Britain's eighth Paddyfield Warbler in 1982 or the 11th Greater Sand Plover in 1988?

In 1983, a fifth Heligoland trap was built to complement the existing garden trap and mist-netting activities were initiated at Willow Woods at the north end of the island, resulting in annual ringing totals of well in excess of 1,000 birds.

The early 1990s saw a steady fall in membership and the unexpected departure of Tim Dean, after almost 14 years of mentoring, to take on new challenges with the Royal Society for the Protection of Birds (RSPB) on Orkney. However, the observatory was again fortunate when Bill Makin was appointed as the new South Walney Nature Reserve warden and his dedication to recording amply filled the huge void left by Tim Dean. A sixth Heligoland trap was constructed on the north-east corner of South Walney Nature Reserve in 1993, a year that also saw the beginning of more concerted mist-netting activities at the south end. However, daily observations and recording were not neglected and were rewarded in autumn 1984 with a Baird's Sandpiper and Britain's 11th Southern Grey Shrike.

Although financial restraints continued to limit ringing, mainly to migrating passerines, the extra effort put in at this time saw excellent numbers of birds ringed and culminated in a record total of 2,496 birds of 60 species ringed for 1995. Computerisation of bird capture data was implemented in 1996 and tradition was maintained when Bill Makin was persuaded to help with the reconstruction of the main Heligoland trap in the central marsh, which had finally succumbed to severe winter gales.

Unfortunately, Bill left in 1998 and since then there have been numerous short-term appointments to the post of South Walney Nature Reserve warden. This, sadly, has provided for less continuity and empathy with the recording work of the observatory. Despite this, exciting birds have continued to be found. Records have included Spotted Sandpiper in 1998, Britain's second American Coot in 1999, Blue-winged Teal in 2000, Fea's/Zino's Petrel in 2001 and, more recently in 2002, the first Squacco Heron in Cumbria for over 100 years. This well-watched individual spent several days feeding along the water-filled ditches bordering the south end caravan site and occasionally posed on the adjacent fence posts to the delight of its well-travelled audience.

At the modest end of the observatory buildings pecking order, Walney Bird Observatory spent many years based in a series of cold, damp and draughty second-hand caravans. However, 2002 saw Cumbria Wildlife Trust generously supply a modern Portakabin for observatory use. Situated inside the walled garden of the Coastguard Cottages within South Walney Nature Reserve, it provides a ringing facility of comparative luxury with the associated benefits of running water and an electric heater!

At the present time, the observatory has turned full circle and is once again heavily reliant on the hard work of a handful of local observers and ringers to provide the bulk of the records and undertake ringing activities and surveys. In addition to the ongoing long-term studies into migration, core activities include censuses of the Lesser Black-backed Gull, Herring Gull and Eider populations and coordination of the island's monthly WeBS count.

Other shorter-term projects have also been undertaken, including studies of the migration routes, feeding patterns and associated flight heights of birds using the Eastern Irish Sea Flyway, to assess the impact of offshore windfarms, while the first comprehensive breeding bird census for the whole island has just been completed. This hard work and dedication has produced fitting rewards, with 190 species recorded in 2003 – the highest annual total to date; 12,500 records involving 189 species were recorded in 2005, with the autumn arguably one of the best on record for local rarities. Barred Warbler, Yellow-browed Warbler, Golden Oriole, Ortolan Bunting, Little Bunting, and Cumbria's first Cetti's Warbler were all recorded. Most recently, 2007 saw Cumbria's second Serin and Britain's fourth Hudsonian Whimbrel *Numenius phaeopus hudsonicus* – a long-staying summering individual that attracted some of the largest crowds of birders ever seen on the island. Cumbria's first Rustic Bunting was found in 2008, along with a supporting cast of Bluethroat, Barred Warbler, Yellow-browed Warbler and Ortolan Bunting amongst over 12,300 records involving almost one million birds. In excess of 1,000 birds are still ringed annually.

THE BIRDS

Winter and spring migration

As New Year dawns, Walney Island plays host to a number of local winter specialities. The area is the only reliable regular wintering site for Greenshank and Black
Guillemot in the north-west of England. A flock of Twite is seen regularly, fleeing
from the talons of one of several wintering Merlin, and a small gathering of
Purple Sandpipers clings to the rocks in the vicinity of Biggar Bank. Light-bellied
Brent Geese *Branta bernicla hrota*, from the Canadian High Arctic, mingle with
birds of the Dark-bellied race *B. b. bernicla* from the Russian tundra on the salt
marsh at high tide. In addition, the presence of a small group of Little Egrets on
the island brightens any winter's day. Numbers are currently increasing, with
birds regularly seen stalking the tidal pools along the sheltered eastern shore.

The beginning of the year sees wildfowl numbers reach a peak. Shelduck,
Wigeon and Teal abound on the sheltered salt marsh habitats and smaller
numbers of Pintail are also present. The island also holds waders in numbers of
international and national importance with large high tide roosts of up to 10,000
Knot and 2,500 Redshank, along with 13,500 Oystercatcher, 800 Grey Plover and
10,000 Dunlin. In addition, there are spectacular flocks of Lapwing, Golden
Plover and Curlew which wheel overhead, suggesting the presence of a hunting
Peregrine. Furthermore, the location of Walney Island means that the sights and
sounds of migration are never far away and early morning soon produces thousands of Pink-footed Geese.

These take advantage of the favourable settled conditions associated with
periods of high pressure to begin the journey north to Scottish staging posts,
before heading off towards the Icelandic breeding grounds. Severe weather at
this time can produce spectacular cold weather movements, with birds fleeing for
more hospitable climes in Ireland. Skylark, Fieldfare and Redwing are the most
likely birds to appear, while Woodcock can be found skulking in the Marram and
sub-rarities have included Bittern, Shore Lark and Chough.

Red-throated Diver and Red-breasted Merganser become more prominent
offshore in late February when calm conditions reveal both species in numbers of
national importance as they begin to move north. Westerly gales can produce a
strong passage of Kittiwakes, while this is potentially the best time to search for
Glaucous Gull and Iceland Gull. Lesser Black-backed Gulls, returning north
from their wintering grounds, are perhaps the first harbingers of spring on the
island as they begin competing for territories with the non-migratory Herring
Gulls that have remained close by throughout the winter.

Wildfowl numbers begin to decline, bugling flocks of Whooper Swans move
north towards Iceland and mid-March sees the first Sandwich Terns returning to
feed offshore. The bushes soon hold Stonechat and Goldcrest, generally accompanied by the first Chiffchaff and Wheatear, and the occasional Black Redstart
takes up temporary residence.

Early April sees increasing numbers of courting Eiders coming ashore at the
south end in search of favoured nest sites and feeding flocks of up to 170 Little

Colour-ringing studies of Brent Geese have shown that one particular pair has spent several winters on Walney, returning each spring to their Canadian breeding grounds after staging at Strangford Lough in Northern Ireland (Steve Stansfield – www.wildlifeimages.eu).

Gulls can occur offshore amongst increasing numbers of Sandwich Terns. Up to 1,000 Turnstone make the western beaches internationally important for this species as they jostle with dog walkers and beachcombers before heading for northern breeding grounds, possibly as far afield as the Canadian High Arctic.

Summer migrants continue to move through the area but are generally less numerous than during the autumn. Calm weather in early April produces the first Swallows and Willow Warblers that are generally outnumbered by a strong Meadow Pipit passage. Towards the end of the month, migration activity usually occurs in a rush; White Wagtails *Motacilla alba alba* flit ghostlike along the tide-line, a few Blackcaps appear and Redstarts provide a welcome splash of colour. Sightings of Merlin and Peregrine begin to decline, but Osprey and Marsh Harrier are occasionally seen overhead, though they are quickly encouraged north by the gulls, while Hooded Crow is a traditional spring migrant. The large numbers of Common Scoter moving north are usually accompanied by a few Velvet Scoters.

May produces an influx of the Greenland race of Wheatear *Oenanthe oenanthe leucorhoa*, while Whitethroat, Sedge Warbler and Grasshopper Warbler quickly become well distributed at traditional breeding sites across the island. Whinchat, Garden Warbler, Spotted Flycatcher and Swift then bring the bulk of spring passage to a conclusion. However, the possibility of something unusual means that hopes remain high and notable records at this time have included White

The western beaches of Walney island are an internationally important site for up to 1,000 Turnstones in spring (Ben Porter).

Stork, Crane, Bee-eater, Hoopoe, Bluethroat, Golden Oriole, Red-backed Shrike and Cumbria's first Serin. The first significant gatherings of Gannet, Fulmar and Manx Shearwater reappear offshore, Arctic Skua can usually be relied upon at this time and Guillemot numbers reach a peak during onshore winds.

A noticeable passage of Arctic Terns occurs and early morning movements of up to 1,000 birds have been recorded in recent years as they move into the mouth of Morecambe Bay. Anecdotal evidence from sightings at inland waters suggests that these birds then spiral up and head overland, across the Pennines, to the North Sea. Common and Little Terns also appear to feed offshore at this time. The western beaches now hold Arctic-bound flocks of up to 600 Ringed Plover, 1,000 Sanderling and 2,500 Dunlin, with numbers achieving national or even international importance. Loose flocks of over 100 Whimbrel can be found feeding in the fields to the south of Biggar over the high tide.

Breeding birds

Although a few tardy summer migrants are still moving through in early June, the island is in the throes of a breeding frenzy. However, local rarities at this time have included Nightingale, Greenish Warbler, Red-breasted Flycatcher, Woodchat Shrike and the first Dartford and Subalpine Warblers for Cumbria.

South Walney Nature Reserve then becomes the breeding ground for an internationally important mixed colony of Lesser Black-backed and Herring Gulls, with the gullery long-recognised as the largest ground-nesting colony in Europe, holding around 41,000 pairs at its zenith. However, regular census work shows that the size of the colony has been in almost perpetual decline since the late 1970s, with numbers decreasing dramatically in recent years.

The Herring Gulls first nested sporadically from 1904, but it was not until 1928 that a regular colony became established. Numbers rose slowly at first, with 35 pairs present in 1934 and 120 pairs shortly after the Second World War. A steady increase saw 9,500 pairs in 1965 before the population peaked with 25,000 pairs in 1977. Following a crash in the 1980s and a period of relative stability in the 1990s, 9,560 pairs were counted in 2000. The census of 3,080 pairs in 2006 established a fall of 87.7% since 1977, 67.8% of which had occurred since 2000 (Chadwick & Raven 2006).

Lesser Black-backed Gulls were first recorded breeding in 1926 and numbers increased from 200 pairs in 1934 to 21,000 pairs in 1974. Although some fluctuation was noted in population levels throughout the 1980s and 1990s, in contrast to the Herring Gull, the trend for Lesser Black-backed Gull was one of increase. The 2002 census figure was 19,000 pairs, but the species' fortunes have changed dramatically since then, down to 10,354 pairs at the last census, giving a decline of 52.9% since 1996.

Nationally, Herring Gulls and Lesser Black-backed Gulls appear in the Birds of Conservation Concern Red and Amber Lists produced by the British Trust for Ornithology (BTO) respectively (Eaton *et al.* 2009) as species of conservation concern. At South Walney, it would appear that a combination of pressures conspires to impact on local population levels and productivity.

While avian botulism has been noted for many years, outbreaks have become an increasingly regular sight within the colony. A number of especially virulent outbreaks have occurred in recent years, with high mortality rates noted amongst both adults and chicks. Although little data is available on these mortality rates, around 5–10% of breeding adults were considered to have succumbed in an outbreak in 2000. The current trend for periods of warm weather during the breeding season, perhaps the result of climate change, is likely to accentuate the problem. The bacterium *Clostridium botulinum* is widely dispersed in soils and wetland sediments, but ingestion of the organism itself is not harmful. It becomes dangerous when the toxin is produced as a by-product of the bacterium's growth. The organism multiplies rapidly in conditions of high temperature and humidity and it is unsurprising that stagnant pools and decomposing carcasses are well known to support toxin production. Water sources easily become contaminated since the toxin is water-soluble.

Although Lesser Black-backed Gulls are generally considered to favour South Walney's flatter areas, holding thicker vegetation, and Herring Gulls prefer sand dunes with clumps of Marram, it appears that birds tend to shun areas where the vegetation becomes dense and invasive. Unlike areas of Marram, which are visible at the pre-incubation stage, these areas are flat and relatively featureless at the beginning of the breeding season and it would appear from casual observations that birds desert nests that become engulfed by dense vegetation as the season progresses. This feature has been more pronounced latterly, probably because of the added nutrients deposited, until recently, by winter grazing cattle and also by the gulls themselves.

Recent Herring Gull studies at South Walney show that tall clumps of vegetation moderate the microclimate of the nest site and provide protection to incubating birds from both diurnal heat gain and nocturnal heat loss and could also provide chicks with shelter from sun, wind and rain (Kim & Monaghan 2005). However, chicks raised in areas where the vegetation is particularly invasive could be prone to a greater risk of hypothermia if they become wet and bedraggled when hiding amongst dense damp nettle beds or lush grass.

Mammalian predation is an additional factor, although the impact on productivity is thought to vary with the predator. Since the first animals were noted in the 1980s, Foxes have become an increasingly common sight on the island and they are now considered to be the main external source of predation in the colony, with losses amongst eggs and chicks considered commonplace. In 2004, 50% of the monitored clutches on a study plot were destroyed in a single night. Stoats and Weasels also occur in the colony during the breeding season, but it is thought that the extent of their predation is negligible. The decline of the Rabbit population, which was devastated by myxomatosis in the late 1990s, has significantly reduced alternative food sources for predators, as has the dramatic reduction in the size of the Eider colony.

A number of other factors are likely to have contributed to the decline. Previously available habitat in the colony has been lost to sand and gravel extraction, with recent surveys showing that around 25,000 square metres of prime nesting habitat has disappeared since 1995. Changes in practice at refuse tips will have significantly reduced scavenging opportunities as the waste is now covered as soon as it is dumped. The closure of the local tip in 2001 and 2002, at one time a rich feeding ground for these omnivorous gulls, has also exacerbated the situation. Moreover, feeding opportunities will have been affected by the reduction in size of the commercial fishing fleet in the Irish Sea – because less offal is discarded – and also by the reduction in the release of untreated sewage into Morecambe Bay.

Finally, the possibility that birds are deserting South Walney for other nearby colonies cannot be overlooked. However, since the late 1990s, a colour-ringing scheme has been in operation to establish if there is any inter-colony movement between South Walney and the nearest large Lesser Black-backed Gull colonies at Tarnbrook Fell, Lancashire and on the nearby Ribble Estuary. To date, this study has produced little supportive evidence – indeed these colonies are also in decline. Although the Seabird 2000 Census (Mitchell *et al.* 2004) concluded that South Walney remains the largest mixed gull colony in Britain and Ireland, the latest population estimates of 10,354 pairs of Lesser Black-backed Gull and 3,225 pairs of Herring Gull (in 2008) means that status would appear to be under threat.

Through the course of history, Walney Island has boasted a total of around 90 breeding species and although the huge Lesser Black-backed and Herring Gull colony currently continues to dominate breeding figures, the diversity of habitat across the island supports a wide range of additional species and latest estimates suggest 2,715–3,070 breeding pairs of a further 67 species. These include nine species which appear in the Birds of Conservation Concern Red List (Eaton *et al.*

2009). Comparatively healthy populations of House Sparrow (200–220 pairs), Starling (190–210 pairs), Skylark (150–170 pairs), Linnet (100–110 pairs) and Lapwing (55–60 pairs) still exist on the island, with smaller numbers of Song Thrush (15–20 pairs), Grey Partridge (8–10 pairs), and Grasshopper Warbler (5–6 pairs) also present. In addition, a further 10 species on the Birds of Conservation Concern Amber List can be found breeding on the island, including Meadow Pipit (195–205 pairs), Dunnock (75–85 pairs), Reed Bunting (75–85 pairs), Willow Warbler (20–25 pairs), Redshank (12–15 pairs), House Martin (10–15 pairs), Bullfinch (5–6 pairs), Barn Owl (2–3 pairs) and Kestrel (2–3 pairs) (Raven 2005).

Nevertheless, there have unfortunately been some losses during the life of the observatory. The dynamics of seabird populations have seen the demise of a number of species, with Sandwich Tern, Common Tern, Arctic Tern and Little Tern, all lost as breeding birds. Nationally declining species such as Corncrake, Snipe, Stock Dove, Rook and Yellowhammer have also gone, while Red-breasted Merganser, Cuckoo and Mistle Thrush are no longer breeding annually. However, a combination of the maturation of suitable habitat on the island and national population increases has seen these losses tempered by the addition, as breeding species, of Greylag Goose, Canada Goose, Shoveler, Red-legged Partridge, Pheasant, Coot, Collared Dove, Little Owl, Lesser Whitethroat, Blackcap, Long-tailed Tit, Coal Tit, Magpie, Raven, Bullfinch and, most recently, Reed Warbler.

Walney Island is also renowned for holding the southernmost Eider colony in Britain and, although a decline has occurred recently, nationally important numbers are still present offshore throughout the year. From a single nest found at the south end in 1949, numbers rose slowly at first with just 20 nests located in 1962. However, from this meagre beginning a rapid increase occurred with 125 nests in 1966, 375 in 1976, 650 in 1983 and 1,000 in 1986 ultimately peaking with 1,500 nests in 1991 and 1992. A reversal in fortunes was first noted in 1992 when viral duck enteritis affected the South Walney population and an estimated 16% of breeding females died.

Further pressure has come from Foxes, which find incubating females easy prey, and the lifting of restrictions on the commercial harvesting of mussels. The escalation in these commercial activities within Morecambe Bay has increased competition for the birds' main food source. As a direct consequence, the number of nests fell steadily to 1,000 in 1994, 700 in 1998 and 400 in 2001. However, there is some evidence to suggest numbers have stabilised in recent years, with the current count steady at around 300 nests.

In addition, South Walney holds a colony of Great Black-backed Gulls. A single pair reportedly bred in 1946 and a slow increase in the size of the colony followed. Numbers peaked at 120 nests in 1998, making Walney one of the largest colonies in England at the time; thereafter, numbers began to decline. Eighty nests were counted in 2000; however, in 2008 the breeding population was estimated at 65–70 pairs suggesting something of a stabilisation. The birds have long nested on the isolated islands and spits created during sand and gravel extraction. Unfortunately, continued extraction reduced the size of many of the islands and narrow spit areas, forcing some of the pairs to move to less favoured, land-locked sites where the eggs and young were prone to Fox predation. However, the cessation of extraction and subsequent creation of new islands and spits appear to be having an impact. In 2005 there was a marked improvement in productivity, mainly from birds nesting on the islands and narrow spits. A total of 42 nests were monitored producing 70 young at a productivity rate of 1.67 young per nest (Raven 2005).

Autumn migration

As the breeding season comes to an end the Eiders are 'noticeable' by their absence, Shelduck disappear overnight and the first Teal reappear. The large numbers of gulls and terns attract marauding Great Skua and Arctic Skua. Other feeding movements include Gannet, Fulmar and Manx Shearwater, with flocks of up to 1,000 of the latter congregating offshore, while good numbers of Common Scoter are again on the move. A relatively recently discovered phenomenon is the late summer presence of Storm Petrels feeding close inshore after moderate westerly winds. Balearic Shearwater has also been recorded annually in recent years. Garganey move through in early autumn and return wader passage includes Green Sandpiper, Wood Sandpiper, Common Sandpiper, Ruff, Greenshank, Spotted Redshank and Black-tailed Godwit. Nationally important flocks of up to 2,500 Curlew assemble on the island, with many favouring the salt marsh habitats around Biggar.

August heralds the onset of return passerine migration. Calm days see southbound passerines flying overhead, with Pied Wagtails *Motacilla alba yarrellii* and Swallows most prominent and, although much reduced in recent years, a few Yellow Wagtail and Tree Pipit. The bushes hold migrant Willow Warbler, Redstart, Whinchat, Whitethroat, Sedge Warbler, Garden Warbler and Spotted Flycatcher, and the area is always worth searching for something more unusual. There have been early autumn records of Tawny Pipit, Icterine Warbler, Barred Warbler and Melodious Warbler (although the observatory has recorded 17 individuals over the years, this latter species has yet to turn up elsewhere in Cumbria). Further wader passage consists of large flocks of Ringed Plover, Sanderling and Turnstone along the western beaches. Cormorants are most noticeable at this time, with up to 280 birds – a nationally important number – roosting on the island and offshore navigation towers over the high tide.

The gulls have dispersed from the south end by September and relative tranquillity descends over the area. However, migration continues apace; the first skeins of Pink-footed Geese wing their way south to winter on the Lancashire Mosses or in Norfolk and, although at no time as regular, a few flocks of northbound Barnacle Geese head back to the Solway Firth after overshooting their intended destination. The sky is now alive with Meadow Pipits, Skylarks, Swallows, and Pied and White Wagtails *M. a. alba*. Rock Pipits also occur in this movement, Grey Wagtails replace Yellow Wagtails and the bushes now predominately hold Robin, Stonechat, Blackcap, Chiffchaff and Goldcrest, while Wheatear are on the move through the area.

Local rarities at this time have included Honey-buzzard, Corncrake, Greenish Warbler, Red-breasted Flycatcher, Golden Oriole, and the first Marsh Warbler and Ortolan Bunting for Cumbria. Wildfowl and wader numbers steadily increase and a few Little Stint and Curlew Sandpiper can usually be found amongst the internationally important numbers of Redshank that frequent the sheltered eastern salt marshes and gravel pools. Sandwich Terns remain offshore, with Great Skua and Arctic Skua still in attendance when the winds are onshore. Stronger westerly gales usually produce Leach's Petrel and occasionally Pomarine Skua. Cory's Shearwater, Sooty Shearwater, Sabine's Gull and Wilson's Petrel – one of only a few land-based sightings in Britain – have also been recorded at this time.

The flow of migrant passerines continues through October. Diurnal movement now involves Linnet, Chaffinch and Greenfinch, mixed with Siskin, Lesser Redpoll and a few Bramblings, while the forerunners of the overwintering Twite flock return. Calm early morning conditions produce spectacular movements of high-flying Jackdaws heading south out into Morecambe Bay. Whilst not overrun by traditional east coast specialities, Walney Island is the Cumbrian location most likely to turn up an unusual passerine at this time and recent surprises include Richard's Pipit, Firecrest, Yellow-browed Warbler, Pallas's Warbler, Bearded Tit, Lapland Bunting and Little Bunting.

The sea holds returning Red-throated Diver and Common Scoter, while a few Gannet and Kittiwake are still to be seen. Dramatic large-scale early morning movements of Razorbill can occur in calm conditions, with passage rates of as many as 2,500 birds per hour recorded in recent years. Skeins of Pink-footed Geese continue to stream south and are joined by an increasing number of Whooper Swans, mainly in small family parties. Wintering wildfowl and wader numbers begin to build, Jack Snipe appear amongst good numbers of Snipe, while both Red-necked Phalarope and Grey Phalarope have occurred on the pools at this time.

The final passerine movements of the year involve continental Redwing, Blackbird, Song Thrush and Fieldfare as October ends and November begins.

As the year draws to a close, it is still worth checking offshore as the sheltered waters of Bass Pool have held Red-necked, Black-necked and Slavonian Grebes, Great Northern Diver, Velvet Scoter and Long-tailed Duck, while Little Auk can appear off the west shore after strong westerlies. In addition, the local status of Shag, a scarce bird in north-west England, has changed radically in recent years, with small numbers now roosting regularly throughout the winter on the newly constructed navigation towers marking the entrance channel to Barrow Docks and feeding off Hilpsford Point.

Passerines are less evident at this time, but include mobile flocks of Twite, Goldfinch and, occasionally, Snow Bunting that frequent the dunes and salt marsh and are harried daily by Merlin and Sparrowhawk. Short-eared Owl and Barn Owl regularly hunt the island towards dusk and Peregrines are attracted to feast on the vast flocks of wintering waders that are again in residence.

The meticulous daily recording of the migrants moving through Walney Island during the spring and autumn passage periods over the last 25 years means that a wealth of data has now been collected by the observatory. Figures 1 and 2 show annual totals for a selected number of long-distance migrant species, mainly with a breeding distribution biased to the north and west of Britain. Although short-term fluctuations could be a result of local weather patterns or observer effort, data analysis can establish long-term trends in population levels.

The records emphasise the downward spiral shown by the majority of trans-Saharan migrants that arrive every spring to breed in Britain and Ireland, as they struggle to cope with a combination of climate change and habitat loss.

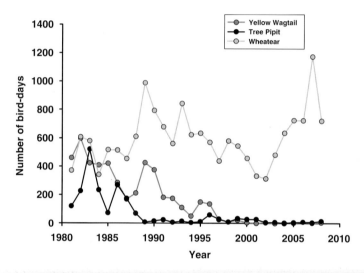

Figure 1. *Annual bird-day totals of Tree Pipit, Yellow Wagtail and Wheatear at South Walney 1981–2008.*

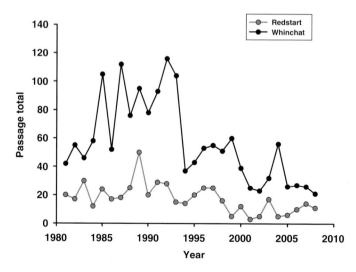

Figure 2. *Annual bird-day totals of Whinchat and Redstart at South Walney 1981–2008.*

Spectacularly serious declines in Tree Pipit and Yellow Wagtail populations since the late 1980s are well illustrated (Figure 1), while a long-term steady decline in the numbers of Redstart and Whinchat is also evident (Figure 2). However, there is some cause for optimism; the Wheatear would appear to be bucking the trend for decline, with the data indicating relatively stable population levels (Figure 1). In general, these observations reflect national trends and are complementary to other long-term population studies such as the BTO's Breeding Bird Survey.

Ringing

Since the formation of the observatory, the major and continuously operated ringing site has been located at South Walney, with additional, less intensive, activities undertaken in the north and centre of the island. A total of 52,563 birds, of 135 species, have been ringed between 1964 and the end of 2008, including 3,654 pulli, at an average of 1,168 birds per annum. Although day catches exceeding 100 birds are rare, the best ringing total for a single day was on 13 August 1997 when an exceptional 251 birds of nine species were trapped during a large fall of Willow Warblers. While the vast majority of passerines trapped at the south end are passage migrants, the North Walney ringing site holds a good breeding population of both resident and migratory species. Accordingly, adults on their breeding grounds and juveniles at their natal sites were, until recently, monitored for longevity and site fidelity.

Unfortunately, the area is currently out of bounds due to restrictions put in place following an upgrade to the airfield, allowing it to be used by the Eurofighter. Interestingly, very few of the birds ringed elsewhere on the island are re-trapped at South Walney as they start their migration south or complete their northward return the following spring. Similarly, not many individuals ringed on the Cumbrian mainland are re-trapped on the island. For example, large numbers of Pied Flycatcher chicks are ringed annually in Cumbrian woodlands, but only two bearing Cumbrian rings have been caught on Walney Island, where the species is a relatively uncommon passage migrant.

The seemingly low average annual ringing figure embraces 55 non-passerine and 80 passerine species, with non-passerines making up only 7.6% of the total. This may seem strange when it is considered that Walney Island sits on the mouth of Morecambe Bay and is a stronghold for wildfowl and waders, as well as holding a large gull colony. However, a number of factors contribute to the apparent discrepancy.

Initial efforts to catch wildfowl with cannon nets and a floating tunnel trap at South Walney achieved little success and were discontinued. However, over the years, Wigeon, Teal, Mallard and Eider have been caught in the Heligoland traps and a proposal to build a trap specifically for wildfowl is currently under consideration. In addition, when the observatory was first accredited, there was already a very active Wader Ringing Group based on Morecambe Bay. At the time, it was accepted that this group would continue to undertake the ringing of waders within the observatory recording area and some large catches were made on the island during the late 1960s and 1970s, including single cannon net catches of over 2,000 Oystercatcher and 3,000 Knot. Annual, though usually much smaller, catches are still made by the group and consequently the ringers working at the observatory have not attempted to catch waders, taking only those which occasionally appear in Heligoland traps or well-placed mist-nets. These include Little Stint, Black-tailed Godwit, Wood Sandpiper and Grey Phalarope. Additionally, a small number of wader chicks, such as Oystercatcher, Ringed Plover and Lapwing, are ringed each year.

Similarly, the ringing of young gulls, particularly Lesser Black-backed Gull, was already under way in the early 1960s, under the auspices of the Animal Behaviour Research Group from Oxford University. Involving local ringers, the project was subsequently led by Professor Niko Tinbergen, who later became a Nobel laureate and whose involvement with Walney Island is described in a recent and interesting biography (Kruuk 2003). This activity continued after the observatory was set up and a succession of universities and ringing groups have usually ringed over 1,000 young gulls each year. By comparison, the observatory has ringed only a token number. However, the catching of adult gulls has been attempted on a number of occasions, using the dazzling technique, with reasonable success. This has resulted in the ringing of a total of 204 Lesser Black-backed Gulls and 295 Herring Gulls and on one memorable night, 65 birds were caught in less than three hours, demonstrating the potential available with suitable conditions and willing volunteers.

One gull species has, however, received far more attention. As the number of breeding Great Black-backed Gulls steadily rose, increasing numbers of young birds were ringed. A total of 1,728 have been marked since 1968 of which 221 birds (12.7%) have been recovered, virtually all being found dead. Interestingly, the recoveries show that these gulls do not venture far from their natal colony, with over 66.0% of those recovered away from the colony moving less than 40 kilometres. With the exception of three birds found on the east coast of Eire and one moving 409 kilometres north to the Grampian Region of Scotland, the majority have dispersed no further than the Solway Firth, the Isle of Man or North Wales. This limited dispersal emphasises the mainly sedentary nature of the species. The age breakdown shows that 25.0% fail to survive their first winter, but the mortality rate drops thereafter. Most recoveries involve birds that were active in the colony, where it is more likely that they will be found. Although the oldest ringed bird to date achieved an age of 20 years and 355 days, the average age of birds that survive the first year is only 6 years 171 days.

Influenced by these limiting factors, 92.4% of the birds ringed by the observatory have been passerines. Initially, most were caught in the newly constructed Heligoland traps with a few taken in mist-nets. The prevailing westerly wind, combined with lack of vegetation, meant that there was little cover to enable mist-nets to be used to great effect. As the trees and shrubs planted in the early years took hold, additional cover was created for migrants and better sheltered mist-netting sites were produced, resulting in a change in the proportion of birds caught by this method. Consequently, in the past 10 years almost 50% of captures have been made with mist-nets. Of the 80 passerine species trapped and ringed, 15 are represented by singletons and include rarities such as Paddyfield Warbler,

Booted Warbler, Subalpine Warbler, Woodchat Shrike, and White-throated Sparrow. Conversely, the most frequently ringed species have been Willow Warbler (with 9,707 birds representing 18.5% of the total), Goldcrest (4,341 and 8.3%) and Robin (4,041 and 7.7% respectively).

Walney Island is situated along the Eastern Irish Sea Flyway, with a geographical position that is almost central to the whole of Britain and Ireland. Consequently the large falls of continental migrants, which are regularly experienced along the east coast of England and Scotland, rarely occur on the island. Indeed, recoveries of ringed birds suggest that many of the birds passing through Walney Island are of Scottish origin, following the coastline south during autumn and returning north to their breeding areas in the spring.

Of 4,041 Robins ringed, 39 (1.0%) have been recovered in Britain and, more unusually, one moved 1,667 kilometres to Spain. Most are young birds captured in autumn and, although a few individuals ringed at migration points in Britain have occasionally reached Spain, these are thought to be of Fennoscandian origin (Wernham *et al.* 2002). The majority move less than 100 kilometres further south to winter in suburban sites around Lancashire, Merseyside and Yorkshire. The six recoveries (15.0%) in the breeding season have been from north and eastern Scotland, with the exception of an early spring record in north Cumbria of a bird that, it is assumed, was moving further north. Three recoveries in the Isle of Man were of adult birds in the autumn of later years that were again, presumably, moving south on a slightly more westerly route.

A similar pattern of migration strategy has started to appear in recoveries of Greenfinch, Goldfinch and Chaffinch. These three species have recently been caught in increasing numbers, again mainly as young birds in autumn. There are now winter recoveries for all three further to the south in England, demonstrating movements predominantly less than 100 kilometres, but with one Greenfinch moving 248 kilometres to Gloucestershire. In direct contrast, all spring recoveries are to the north, extending from the Cumbrian coast into western Scotland. A series of retraps on the island in subsequent years suggests that these species regularly follow the same basic route when moving north or south between breeding and wintering grounds.

However, some continental birds that make landfall on the east coast do continue westwards across Britain and pass through Walney Island on their journey to Ireland in the autumn, making the return journey eastward in the spring. For example, 2,616 Blackbirds have been ringed, of which 26 (1.0%) have been recovered, including three in Eire and eight in countries around the North Sea. The most distant of these recoveries was 2,000 kilometres to the east in Finland. A single Redwing recovery, 2,690 kilometres away in Russia, also gives an indication of the likely origins of some of the other thrushes that move through the island.

Foreign recoveries of less frequently caught species are always exciting, so those for a Whinchat, 2,330 kilometres distant in Morocco, and a Spotted Flycatcher 5,200 kilometres away in Nigeria (at the time the first of this species recovered south of the Sahara), are worthy of mention. Additionally, a Meadow Pipit recently moved 2,150 kilometres to Morocco, one of only 20 Black Redstarts ringed flew on to an oil rig 540 kilometres away in the North Sea and an Icterine Warbler was on Bardsey Island six days after being ringed on Walney. Of the very frequently trapped Willow Warbler, there have been but a few recoveries. Although 9,707 of these small, long-distance, trans-Saharan migrants have been ringed, only 23 (0.2%) have been recorded elsewhere as at the end of 2008, usually as controls by other ringers. Interestingly, two were in the Channel Islands, with singletons in Portugal and Gibraltar, giving some insight into the migration route taken by this species. There have also been several instances of very rapid movements of Willow Warblers, including one moving 330 kilometres overnight from Somerset to Walney Island. A number of foreign ringed birds have also been controlled on the island, notably two Sedge Warblers from the Loire region of France, a journey of 760 kilometres; a Blackcap which moved 545 kilometres from the Netherlands and an autumn Garden Warbler that travelled 750 kilometres northwest from Belgium.

Recoveries involving non-passerines are slightly more frequent and there have been some interesting returns. A Jack Snipe, one of only three ringed, was found in Spain, as was one of two Short-eared Owls, while one of just four Long-eared Owls ringed was reported 3,200 kilometres to the east at Ronga, Mariskaya, Russia. Between 1984 and 1988, Common Terns bred at South Walney and 67 chicks were ringed. One of these, fledging in 1986, was recorded annually at Seaforth, Merseyside from 1992 until 2000 and was last seen 14 years 31 days after ringing.

A number of colour-ringed birds of foreign origin have been seen on Walney in recent years and amongst the more interesting are two Light-bellied Brent Geese *Branta bernicla hrota* that were ringed in Canada and Iceland respectively and have returned each winter since 2002. Travelling as a pair, these birds have also been recorded annually at Strangford Lough in Northern Ireland and on the spring staging grounds in Iceland as they head back to their Canadian breeding grounds. A Spoonbill, ringed in the Netherlands in 1999, was seen in Spain and Mauritania before reaching Walney where it spent several days in 2002. A Black-tailed Godwit ringed in Iceland in the spring of 2003 appeared at Walney three months later.

Ringing data are also used to monitor population trends. In the early 1960s ringers frequently commented that the numbers of Whitethroat moving through the recording area mirrored those of Willow Warbler. The trend for each species, as a percentage of the annual ringing total, shows that both species did indeed follow a similar pattern at first, though there were always more Willow Warblers (Figure 3). The Whitethroat then suffered a well-documented population crash, before both species displayed dramatic declines in the early 1970s. Whilst the Willow Warbler had recovered by 1980, the Whitethroat has never regained original levels. Recent dramatic falls in the number of Willow Warblers are also clearly shown, with current totals at an all time low.

Population trends can also be generated for less migratory species such as Dunnock, Wren and Robin. The trends for all three species follow a remarkably similar pattern, rising in the early 1970s before crashing and then climbing again through the 1980s and 1990s.

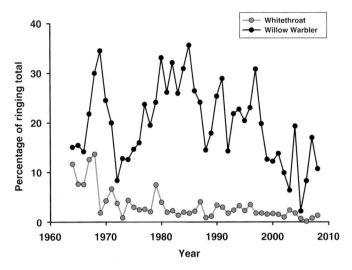

Figure 3. *Totals of Whitethroats and Willow Warblers ringed as a percentage of annual ringing totals at South Walney 1964–2008.*

Although the numbers of Goldcrest moving through Walney Island have fallen in recent years, changes in trapping methods have seen a gradual increase in the numbers ringed due to the species being more easily caught in mist-nets than in Heligoland traps. Despite this, these data illustrate the large and striking natural fluctuations in population levels shown by this species year on year.

A comparison of the species most frequently ringed in 1965, the first full ringing year for Walney, with 2008, shows considerable change (Table 1). In 1965, the 'top' species was Willow Warbler and the restricted vegetation resulted in the trapping of good numbers of Linnet, Reed Bunting and Meadow Pipit. The intervening years have seen the population levels of many species fall and nine out of the top 10 in 1965 have shown significant national population declines as at 2008, the exception being Robin, which has resisted the trend and shown a notable rise. Currently the 10 species most frequently ringed on Walney include Greenfinch, Goldfinch, Chaffinch and Wren – all species showing long-term population increases. The spectacular emergence of the finches is doubtless partially due to the popularity of feeding stations to which they are particularly attracted. In contrast, the decline in Willow Warbler numbers, long considered staple fare for ringers at the observatory, is equally dramatic.

All the Walney ringing data from 1991 have already been computerised and we are now concentrating on inputting the earlier records. Although we have only relatively recently begun to use electronic data capture for bird records, it is already proving to be an invaluable tool. The inputting of records does take more time in the short term but this extra effort is already bringing benefits. Gone are the days when many hours were needed to trawl through the daily logs to extract the data held within.

The information currently stored electronically is already being put to good use in a number of ways. The increasing pressures placed on the island's birds

Table 1. *Ten species most frequently ringed by Walney Bird Observatory in 1965 and 2008.*

1965				2008			
Rank	Species	No. ringed	%	Rank	Species	No. ringed	%
1	Willow Warbler	146	15.5	1	Greenfinch	198	15.9
2	Linnet	106	11.3	2	Goldfinch	197	15.8
3	Whitethroat	72	7.7	3	Willow Warbler	133	10.6
4	Blackbird	68	7.3	4	Goldcrest	120	9.6
5	Herring Gull	68	7.3	5	Long-tailed Tit	83	6.6
6	Robin	40	4.3	6	Blackbird	76	6.1
7	Starling	38	4.1	7	Robin	50	4.0
8	Reed Bunting	34	3.6	8	Chaffinch	42	3.4
9	Meadow Pipit	31	3.3	9	Wren	36	2.9
10	Song Thrush	31	3.3	10	Chiffchaff	32	2.6
	Total ringed	936			Total ringed	1,243	

and their environment has seen a noticeable increase in the number of requests received by the observatory for up to date and accurate data, usually requiring a fast response. Digitisation allows for a quick initial interrogation of the records to check for any relevant available data, both by site and species, and usually enables a rapid response. The data requested, in conjunction with specific surveys carried out by the observatory, have recently been used as the basis for several Environmental Impact Assessments to help judge the influence of offshore wind-farms on seabird and wildfowl migration.

Furthermore, the data have also been used to advise on lessening the impact of development on some of the island's Red and Amber listed breeding birds. The laying of gas pipelines across the island was timed to take place outside the breeding season and mitigation work to limit habitat loss was required before planning consent was given to a number of caravan site extensions. Observatory records, again backed up with additional survey work, have also assisted in blocking a recent proposal for a land-based windfarm on the island.

Once all the historical records have been added, the data set will provide an unparalleled insight into the island's birds and prove to be important in moni-toring population changes in specific species at both local and national levels. Additionally, the submission of bird records for inclusion in the County Bird Report is greatly simplified. Previously, at the end of each year the observatory had to summarise all the sightings held in the daily log and then annotate these records onto record cards prior to submission, but a complete data set can now be presented at the push of a button.

OTHER FAUNA AND FLORA

Vertebrates

Despite being of an often secretive and at times nocturnal nature, around 30 species of mammal have been recorded, though records for many are sparse.

Typically, an unmonitored Hedgehog population exists on the island with the majority of records unfortunately resulting from road casualties. The Pygmy Shrew and Field Vole, whilst only seen infrequently, are considered widespread and a mammal trapping study has found the Wood Mouse to be fairly common at South Walney. However, the once thriving Rabbit colony in the dunes at the south end was virtually wiped out by a series of myxomatosis outbreaks at the end of the twentieth century and has surprisingly failed to recover in subsequent years, although Brown Hares are still encountered regularly.

Both Stoat and Weasel represent mustelids on the island, although the former is much the commoner. The Fox is a relatively recent unwelcome arrival, while Otter, Badger and Grey Squirrel are the latest additions to the mammal list. Recent years have also seen increasing numbers of Grey Seals around the island and up to 100 congregate at a haul out through the summer months. However, there is no evidence of breeding and these haul outs are generally deserted by October, although small numbers remain offshore during the winter. In contrast, there are only very occasional sightings of Common Seal. Cetacean records are sparse despite regular sea-watching activities. Although Harbour Porpoise are now seen annually in calm conditions, other recent sightings are limited to several pods of Bottlenose Dolphin and Common Dolphin and the very occasional Minke Whale or Basking Shark.

Whilst Common Frog, Common Toad and Palmate Newt are all resident, the Natterjack Toad is the most important amphibian on the island. Known from about 40 sites in the British Isles, the dune slacks at North Walney remain a haven for small numbers, with the nocturnal calls of courting males an enthralling sound on a still spring evening. Occasional sightings of Common Lizard also occur – the only reptile to be found on the island.

Invertebrates

The pools attract a variety of damselflies and dragonflies, with Blue-tailed Damselfly and Emerald Damselfly particularly common at the north end, while Four-spotted Chaser, Brown Hawker, Common Hawker and Common Darter are also regularly recorded. A steady northwards range expansion in Britain has seen the Migrant Hawker recently colonise the island. First recorded in 2002, numbers continue to increase and the species is now by far the commonest dragonfly on the southern half of the island. Also at the northern edge of their ranges are the impressive Emperor Dragonfly and the Broad-bodied Chaser, the latter – one of only a handful of Cumbrian records – being the latest addition to the island's Odonata list.

Butterflies can be numerous when optimum weather conditions prevail, with Meadow Brown, Small Tortoiseshell, Green-veined White and Small White the most prominent residents. In total, 23 species have been recorded, including migrants such as Painted Lady – an exceptional 5,000 or more were estimated to be present at South Walney on 12 August 1996 – Red Admiral and Clouded Yellow, while a Monarch appeared in 1995. The Orange-tip and Comma are relatively new additions to the island list, but the most recent colonist is Speckled

Wood, with individuals first noted in 1999 and numbers continuing to increase annually.

An impressive moth list contains almost 500 species and is the result of regular trapping activities carried out, mainly at South Walney, since the early 1980s. A number of Cumbrian first sightings have been recorded, the most recent being Thistle Ermine, and Walney is the only site in the county for the Mallow. Local sand dune specialists include Coast Dart, Sand Dart, Portland Moth, White Colon and Shore Wainscot, while the heath holds the spectacular Oak Eggar, Fox Moth and Emperor Moth.

A number of notable continental immigrants have also been recorded and recent records include: the Vestal, the Gem, Convolvulus Hawkmoth, Death's Head Hawkmoth, Hummingbird Hawkmoth, Bedstraw Hawkmoth, Pearly Underwing, Great Brocade, the Delicate, White-speck, Small Mottled Willow, Scarce Bordered Straw, Bordered Straw and Ni Moth. However, the commonest migrant is usually the Silver Y, which at times can reach 'plague' proportions, with an estimated 50,000 at South Walney alone on 15 August 1996.

Flora

Although Walney Island is especially rich in flora, with over 470 species recorded, many botanists associate the island with one particular plant – the Walney Geranium *Geranium sanguineum var. lancastriense*. Originally discovered on the island in 1732, this subspecies of Bloody Crane's-bill *Geranium sanguineum* typically has a pale pink flower with a darker vein.

The island is also recognised for its diverse vegetated shingle communities, a rare habitat both in Britain and Ireland and also in Europe. Specialised species to be found include Ray's Knotgrass, Portland Spurge, Isle of Man Cabbage, Sea Sandwort, Spear-leaved Orache, Sea Rocket and Sea-kale. At North Walney, the mobile dunes support further coastal specialities such as Sea-holly, Sea Spurge and Sea Bindweed, with Dune Fescue, Dune Helleborine, Green-flowered Helleborine, Seaside Centaury and Variegated Horsetail in the fixed dune grassland.

Walney is at the southern limit of the Coralroot Orchid's limited British distribution and, in contrast, a few Bee Orchids still survive at the northern edge of their range. Displays of Northern Marsh-orchid, Early Marsh-orchid and Common Spotted-orchid can be spectacular. At the south end, impressive swathes of Viper's-bugloss can be found on the disturbed gravel areas along with Henbane, Yellow Horned-poppy, Hound's-tongue and Great Mullein, while close scrutiny can reveal increasing numbers of Pyramidal Orchid and Tassel Hyacinth.

ACCESS AND ACCOMMODATION

Walney Island is located at the end of the Furness Peninsula. Leave the M6 at junction 36 and follow the A590 to Barrow-in-Furness. After passing through the outskirts of the town, take the second exit, signposted 'Walney and Docks', from the large Craven Park roundabout and at the next roundabout turn right onto Jubilee Bridge, which leads directly to the island.

For those wishing to visit by public transport, the nearest railway station is in Barrow-in-Furness, on the Cumbria Coastline. This connects to the West Coast Main Line network via Carlisle and Lancaster where there are links, in turn, with regular Trans-Pennine train services. There is a daily National Express Coach service to Barrow-in-Furness from where several local buses serve Walney Island. Routes 1 and 1A cover the Biggar Bank area while Routes 6 and 6A, which terminate at Earnse Bay, are suitable for exploring the north end of the island. No suitable local bus route is currently available for the southern end of the island.

Walney Island receives surprisingly little interest from visiting birdwatchers, despite a reputation as perhaps the finest birding site in Cumbria. Those who do visit usually head for the famous reserve at the southern end of the island, and in doing so, miss out on some excellent areas on the way. Whilst receiving relatively little attention, numerous sites across the island have produced exciting birds over the years. A few suggestions are given below which can add variety to a full day's birding on the island, perhaps based around a visit to South Walney Nature Reserve. Although there are only a few public footpaths and several areas are out of bounds, notably the golf course and airfield, the narrow width of the island allows even these locations to be viewed from the road or shore. When visiting the island, please avoid disturbing high tide wader roosts and walking along the tide line during the breeding season.

On crossing the bridge, visitors are greeted by the sight of the tallest trees on the island. Turn right at the traffic lights and park on the roadside by The Ferry public house. This area around Vickerstown Park has produced a selection of woodland species that are rarities on the island, early morning probably being the optimum time to visit. For Willow Woods and the airfield, continue along the road to North Scale and head straight on through the village to the end of the road where limited parking is available. A public footpath runs east through Willow Woods to the channel side from near the airfield entrance gates. The airfield can be best scanned from the discretionary footpath running west, owls hunt the area at dusk and waders roost over the high tide. The area supports typical garden species and an assortment of warblers during the breeding season.

North Walney National Nature Reserve can be accessed from North Scale by heading west along Cow Tarns Lane and then right into West Shore Road. Ample car parking is available at Earnse Bay or you can drive along the rough track that runs north from here and park at the end. A myriad of paths give open access and many profitable hours can be spent here throughout the year as this is a large area with a variety of habitats.

To explore the southern end of the island, turn left at the traffic lights and follow Ocean Road before turning into Carr Lane. Tummer Hill Marsh, immediately on your left, can be viewed from the roadside or from atop the embankment. The autumn and winter period sees it come into its own as impressive numbers of wildfowl and waders are pushed up onto the salt marsh over the highest tides and eventually fly over Carr Lane to roost in the adjacent fields. Alternatively, continue along Ocean Road to Biggar Bank where there are several car parks at the roadside. Although popular with families and dog walkers, the foreshore holds good numbers of waders outside the summer months, despite the disturbance, with Purple Sandpiper a speciality. A sea-watch can be undertaken from any of the car parks along Biggar Bank, but the southernmost at Thorney Nook is usually favoured.

The hedgerows and gorse around Biggar hold migrants and breeding passerines, while waders can be found in the fields, this area being the best site on the island for Whimbrel during spring passage. Continue through Biggar along Carr Lane for 0.75 kilometres and park in the lay-by on the right. Wylock Marsh can be checked from here for wildfowl and waders.

Cross the road and follow the path that runs north-east out to Long Rein Point. An under-worked area, the sheltered hedgerows should be checked for migrants, and this is also a good spot to view the upper reaches of Walney Channel. After another 0.75 kilometres, look for the large sandstone boulders on the right that mark the entrance to a car park overlooking the western shore. The Willows by the entrance are one of the few areas of cover on the southern part of the island and regularly attract the commoner migrant passerines.

Sea-watching can also be good from the elevated car park, which gives better views in rough seas than other sites on the island. A further 0.5 kilometres along the road is Snab Point; park in the lay-by on the left and check the surrounding scrub for passerines. This small area has produced a fine selection of rarities amongst the commoner migrant species. The flooded fields attract waders and the high tide wader roost on Sheep Island can also be viewed from here. After a further 0.5 kilometres, at the entrance to the south end caravan site, take the private metalled road which leads to the South Walney Nature Reserve car park, a distance of about 1.5 kilometres. Do not neglect this approach – driving slowly can produce a number of migrant species in both spring and autumn at the gorse patch and along the fence posts (Makin 1996).

The reserve is open throughout the year from 10.00 hrs to 17.00 hrs (16.00 hrs in the winter). There is a small charge for admittance and day permits and trail leaflets can be obtained from the kiosk in the car park. Access is limited to a number of permitted waymarked trails to limit disturbance. These range between one and four kilometres in length and lead to the eight hides that provide good views over the most productive areas. Wheelchair access to Bank Hide, adjacent to Coastguard Cottages, is possible from the car park where there are related toilet facilities.

Accommodation is available at South Walney Nature Reserve in one of the three Victorian cottages, which were occupied by coastguards and their families until the mid-1950s. The other two cottages are now permanent homes for the warden and assistant warden. Fully furnished, the cottage can accommodate up to 10 people throughout the year on a self-catering basis. Bookings for individuals or parties can be made through the warden at: Coastguard Cottages, South Walney, Walney Island, Barrow-in-Furness, Cumbria, LA14 3YQ or by contacting the reserve office on 01229 471066. In addition, there are a number of establishments offering bed and breakfast facilities in the urban area of the island or nearby on the mainland.

Membership of Walney Bird Observatory is available in three grades (family, individual or junior) to anyone interested in birds or natural history. Subscriptions cover daily permit charges to South Walney Nature Reserve and a copy of the Annual Report. A fourth grade (friend) is available to people who may not visit the area frequently but wish to receive a copy of the Annual Report and show their support for the observatory and its aims. For further information contact Walney Bird Observatory at: Coastguard Cottages, South Walney, Walney Island, Barrow-in-Furness, Cumbria, LA14 3YQ.

Visitors are encouraged to submit bird sightings and, indeed, records for all branches of natural history, particularly the unusual and the unexpected. This may be done by referring to the observatory website, which details the point of contact. It is hoped that this website will be developed comprehensively in the medium term to provide additional information on where to watch birds on the island, lists of species seen and so forth.

Observatory opened:	1964 (BTO accredited in 1965)
Total number of bird species recorded at the observatory:	292
Best bird year:	2003
Number of species recorded:	190
Total of birds ringed at the observatory:	52,563
Number of species:	135
Best ringing year:	1995
Number ringed:	2,496
Number of species:	60

Appendices

APPENDIX 1: CHECKLISTS OF BIRDS AND RINGED BIRDS

These checklists give the total numbers of species recorded at each observatory up to 31 December 2008, along with the number of each species ringed up to the same date. The species list only features those in Categories A, B and C of the British Ornithologists' Union checklist of British Birds. Records of national rarities only appear if they have been accepted by the British Birds Rarities Committee or Irish Rare Birds Committee and those of local rarities if they have been accepted by local records committees and appear in the official observatory list. Records which were not accepted have not been included.

Each observatory is represented in a single column in each of the two tables. The British (English) vernacular and scientific names follow the BOU checklist of birds, and are used throughout the text.

The status codes in the checklists (A to H) are used to depict the relative abundance of the birds recorded for each site.

Status Code	Description
A	Very abundant – in excess of 5000 birds recorded on average per annum
B	Abundant – 1001 to 5000 birds recorded on average per annum
C	Common – 251 to 1000 birds recorded on average per annum
D	Fairly common – 51 to 250 birds recorded on average per annum
E	Uncommon – six to 50 birds recorded on average per annum
F	Scarce – one to five birds or records on average per annum
G	Rare – 21 to 50 records
H	Vagrant – Fewer than 20 records

The far right column in the species checklist gives the number of observatories at which a species has been recorded. For example, the figure for Goldcrest is 18 as it has been recorded at every observatory, whereas Summer Tanager scores just one, having been recorded at only one observatory.

It is interesting to note that of the 588 species recorded in Britain and Ireland to the end of 2008, 498 – or 85% – have been recorded at the 18 observatories. Of course, many of these species have been recorded away from observatories, for example House Sparrow and Robin, but some of the rarer species have only been seen within the recording areas of observatories. The observatories are seen to be well positioned to record many migrant species.

The ringing table depicts the number of birds of each species ringed at each observatory, as well as the number of birds of each species ringed collectively at all the observatories (totalled in the far right hand column). The total of species ringed at each observatory appears at the foot of each observatory column. Over three million birds of 370 species have been ringed by the observatories over the past 60 years representing a contribution of over 8% to the total of 36,165,157 ringed in the British Isles up to the end of 2008 (Coiffait *et al.* 2009). The 370 species ringed at the observatories represent 85% of the 431 species ringed in Britain and Ireland, giving some indication of the species diversity passing through the observatories.

All the information contained in this appendix has been supplied and checked by the observatories and every effort has been made to ensure its accuracy.

Footnote. Citril Finch. The record of Citril Finch from Fair Isle in 2008 is still awaiting official acceptance on to the British List by the BOURC.

APPENDIX 1a: CHECKLIST OF SPECIES RECORDED

Common Name	Scientific Name	Bardsey	Calf of Man	Cape Clear	Copeland	Dungeness	Fair Isle	Filey	Flamborough
Mute Swan	Cygnus olor	H	H	F	G	E	H	E	F
Bewick's Swan	Cygnus columbianus	H	H		H	G	H	F	G
Whooper Swan	Cygnus cygnus	G	F	G	E	H	D	D	E
Bean Goose	Anser fabalis				H	H	G	H	H
Pink-footed Goose	Anser brachyrhynchus	H	H		G	H	D	A	C
White-fronted Goose	Anser albifrons	F	H		F	F	F	G	F
Lesser White-fronted Goose	Anser erythropus			H					
Greylag Goose	Anser anser	G	G	G	E	D	C	D	D
Snow Goose	Anser caerulescens	H				H		H	H
Canada Goose	Branta canadensis	H	H	H	G	E	G	C	D
Barnacle Goose	Branta leucopsis	H	H	G	H	G	D	E	F
Brent Goose	Branta bernicla	G	H	G	E	A	G	D	D
Red-breasted Goose	Branta ruficollis								
Egyptian Goose	Alopochen aegyptiaca					H		H	H
Ruddy Shelduck	Tadorna ferruginea					H		H	H
Shelduck	Tadorna tadorna	E	E	F	C	C	F	D	D
Mandarin Duck	Aix galericulata							H	H
Wigeon	Anas penelope	E	F	F	F	B	D	B	B
American Wigeon	Anas americana						H	H	H
Gadwall	Anas strepera		H	F	H	E	G	E	E
Teal	Anas crecca	E	E	D	D	C	D	A	B
Green-winged Teal	Anas carolinensis						H	H	H
Mallard	Anas platyrhynchos	D	E	C	C	C	E	C	C
Black Duck	Anas rubripes						H		
Pintail	Anas acuta	G	H	H	H	D	F	E	D
Garganey	Anas querquedula	H	H	H		F	H	F	F
Blue-winged Teal	Anas discors			H				H	
Shoveler	Anas clypeata	H	H	H	H	D	F	E	E
Red-crested Pochard	Netta rufina					H		H	H
Pochard	Aythya ferina	G	H	H	H	E	F	E	E
Redhead	Aythya americana			H					
Ring-necked Duck	Aythya collaris			H		H	H		
Ferruginous Duck	Aythya nyroca		H			H			
Tufted Duck	Aythya fuligula	G	H	G	F	D	E	D	D
Scaup	Aythya marila	H	H	H	H	E	F	F	E
Eider	Somateria mollissima	G	B	H	C	C	C	D	C
King Eider	Somateria spectabilis						H		H
Steller's Eider	Polysticta stelleri						H	H	
Harlequin Duck	Histrionicus histrionicus						H	H	
Long-tailed Duck	Clangula hyemalis	H	H	G	H	F	E	E	E
Common Scoter	Melanitta nigra	D	E	C	E	A	F	B	B
Surf Scoter	Melanitta perspicillata	H		H		H	H	H	H
Velvet Scoter	Melanitta fusca	H	H	H	H	D	F	E	D
Goldeneye	Bucephala clangula	G	G	H	F	E	E	D	E
Smew	Mergellus albellus	H	H			G	H	H	H
Red-breasted Merganser	Mergus serrator	F	G	H	E	C	E	E	E
Goosander	Mergus merganser	H	H	H		F	F	E	E
Ruddy Duck	Oxyura jamaicensis					G		E	H
Red Grouse	Lagopus lagopus scotica	H	H						
Red-legged Partridge	Alectoris rufa					D		E	D
Grey Partridge	Perdix perdix	H	G			E		E	E
Quail	Coturnix coturnix	G	H	G	H	H	F	H	F
Pheasant	Phasianus colchicus	H	H	D	F	G		D	D
Red-throated Diver	Gavia stellata	E	E	E	D	A	E	C	B

Gibraltar Point	Hilbre	Holme	The Isle of May	Landguard	North Ronaldsay	Portland	Sandwich Bay	Spurn	Walney	Number of obs' recorded at
D	F	E	H	E	D	F	C	D	E	18
E	F	F	H	E		H	F	F	G	16
D	F	F	E	H	C	H	F	D	D	18
G		H		H	F	H	G	G	H	13
A	E	A	C	F	C	G	G	B	A	17
F	H	F	H	F	E	G	E	F	G	17
		H								2
D	F	D	D	E	A	G	C	E	D	18
H		H	H	H	H	H		H	H	12
C	E	D	E	E	G	F	C	E	D	18
F	H	F	D	D	C	G	G	E	F	18
B	C	B	E	A	F	B	B	C	E	18
H		H		H		H		H		5
G		D		H		H	H	H	H	10
H	H	H		H		H		H	H	10
C	A	E	E	B	C	E	B	B	B	18
H		H			H		H	H		7
C	D	B	E	B	A	E	A	B	B	18
	H	H			H		H			7
D	H	D	H	E	C	F	D	E	G	17
B	D	C	D	B	B	E	A	B	C	18
H		H			H		H	H		7
C	C	C	E	E	B	E	A	C	C	18
										1
E	D	D	G	C	C	F	D	D	D	18
F	H	F	H	H	F	F	E	F	G	17
					H		H		H	5
E	G	D	H	E	C	F	D	D	E	18
H				H			H			6
E	H	E	H	E	D	F	D	E	F	18
										1
H									H	5
							H	H		4
D	G	D	G	E	C	F	C	D	E	18
F	F	D	H	F	D	F	G	E	E	18
D	E	C	B	C	A	E	E	C	B	18
			H		H	H			H	6
					H					3
										2
F	F	D	G	F	D	F	G	E	F	18
B	B	B	E	B	E	B	D	B	B	18
		H			H	H		H		10
E	G	E	G	F	F	E	F	E	F	18
E	E	D	F	E	D	E	E	D	E	18
H	H	H	H	H	H	H	G	H	H	16
E	B	E	G	C	D	D	E	D	D	18
F	G	E	H	F	G	G	F	E	G	17
E	H	E			H		G	H	H	10
									H	3
E	H	E		F		G	E	E	F	11
E	H	E		G		G	D	D	E	13
G	H	F	G	H	G	F	F	G	H	18
D	H	E		H	E	E	C	D	E	16
C	C	D	E	C	D	C	C	B	C	18

Common Name	Scientific Name	Bardsey	Calf of Man	Cape Clear	Copeland	Dungeness	Fair Isle	Filey	Flamborough
Black-throated Diver	*Gavia arctica*	G	G	H		D	H	F	E
Great Northern Diver	*Gavia immer*	F	F	E	D	E	E	E	E
White-billed Diver	*Gavia adamsii*			H		H	H	H	H
Little Grebe	*Tachybaptus ruficollis*	H	H	E	H	E	G	E	F
Great Crested Grebe	*Podiceps cristatus*	H	H	H	G	A	H	D	E
Red-necked Grebe	*Podiceps grisegena*	H	H			E	G	E	E
Slavonian Grebe	*Podiceps auritus*	H	H			E	F	F	F
Black-necked Grebe	*Podiceps nigricollis*					E		H	H
Black-browed Albatross	*Thalassarche melanophris*	H		H		H	H	H	H
Fulmar	*Fulmarus glacialis*	B	B	A	B	B	A	B	A
Fea's/Zino's Petrel	*Pterodroma feae/madeira*	H		H		H		H	H
Bulwer's Petrel	*Bulweria bulwerii*			H					
Cory's Shearwater	*Calonectris diomedea*	H	H	C	H	G	H	H	F
Great Shearwater	*Puffinus gravis*	H	H	C		H	H	H	F
Sooty Shearwater	*Puffinus griseus*	E	F	B	F	E	E	D	B
Manx Shearwater	*Puffinus puffinus*	A	A	A	A	E	E	C	B
Balearic Shearwater	*Puffinus mauretanicus*	E	G	E	H	E		F	E
Macaronesian Shearwater	*Puffinus baroli*	H	H			H			H
Wilson's Petrel	*Oceanites oceanicus*			H					
Storm Petrel	*Hydrobates pelagicus*	D	D	A	D	H	C	E	E
Leach's Petrel	*Oceanodroma leucorhoa*	E	F	H	H	F	E	F	F
Gannet	*Morus bassanus*	B	A	A	A	A	A	E	A
Cormorant	*Phalacrocorax carbo*	D	C	C	C	A	E	F	B
Shag	*Phalacrocorax aristotelis*	C	A	C	C	E	B	D	B
Bittern	*Botaurus stellaris*	H	H			H		H	H
American Bittern	*Botaurus lentiginosus*	H							
Little Bittern	*Ixobrychus minutus*			H		H	H		
Night-heron	*Nycticorax nycticorax*	H		H		H	H	H	H
Squacco Heron	*Ardeola ralloides*					H			
Cattle Egret	*Bubulcus ibis*			H		H			
Little Egret	*Egretta garzetta*	H	H	H	H	F		H	G
Great White Egret	*Ardea alba*	H	H	H		H			H
Grey Heron	*Ardea cinerea*	D	D	C	E	D	D	E	D
Purple Heron	*Ardea purpurea*	H	H	H		H	H	H	H
Black Stork	*Ciconia nigra*					H		H	
White Stork	*Ciconia ciconia*	H				H	H	H	H
Glossy Ibis	*Plegadis falcinellus*							H	H
Spoonbill	*Platalea leucorodia*	H				H		G	G
Honey-buzzard	*Pernis apivorus*	H	H			F	G	G	G
Black Kite	*Milvus migrans*		H	H		H	H	H	H
Red Kite	*Milvus milvus*	H	H	H	H	H	H	H	H
White-tailed Eagle	*Haliaeetus albicilla*						H	H	H
Marsh Harrier	*Circus aeruginosus*	G	G	G	H	E	G	E	E
Hen Harrier	*Circus cyaneus*	F	C	E	E	E	F	F	F
Pallid Harrier	*Circus macrourus*						H		
Montagu's Harrier	*Circus pygargus*	H		H		G	H	H	F
Goshawk	*Accipiter gentilis*	G	H	H	H	H	H	H	G
Sparrowhawk	*Accipiter nisus*	D	E	C	D	D	E	E	D
Buzzard	*Buteo buteo*	D	H	H	E	F	F	F	E
Rough-legged Buzzard	*Buteo lagopus*	H	H	H	H	H	G	H	H
Golden Eagle	*Aquila chrysaetos*						H		
Osprey	*Pandion haliaetus*	G	G	H	H	F	F	F	F
Lesser Kestrel	*Falco naumanni*						H		
Kestrel	*Falco tinnunculus*	E	C	C	E	C	E	E	D
American Kestrel	*Falco sparverius*						H		
Red-footed Falcon	*Falco vespertinus*		H	H	H	H	H	H	H
Merlin	*Falco columbarius*	E	D	E	F	D	E	E	D

Gibraltar Point	Hilbre	Holme	The Isle of May	Landguard	North Ronaldsay	Portland	Sandwich Bay	Spurn	Walney	Number of obs' recorded at
F	F	E	H	E	G	E	E	F	F	17
F	F	E	H	F	D	E	F	E	F	18
					H	H				7
E	H	E	H	H	E	E	D	D	E	18
E	C	D	H	E	H	D	B	D	D	18
G	G	E	H	F	H	F	G	F	G	16
F	F	E	H	H	G	E	H	G	F	16
H	G	H	H	H	H	E	H	H	H	13
			H					H		8
D	D	D	B	C	A	C	E	B	D	18
					H	H			H	8
										1
H	H	H	H	H	H	G	H	G	H	18
H	H	H	H	H	H	H	H	H	H	17
E	H	E	D	E	C	D	H	C	G	18
E	C	D	D	F	D	A	H	C	B	18
H	H	H	H	H	H	D	H	G	H	17
										4
									H	2
H	E	H	D	H	C	D	H	F	D	18
F	D	F	H	G	E	F	H	E	E	18
C	B	B	A	B	A	A	C	A	B	18
D	A	D	D	B	B	C	B	C	C	18
F	E	F	C	E	A	C	F	D	F	18
H	H	F		H	H	H	H	H	H	14
										1
		H			H	H	H			7
H			H	H		H	H	H		12
					H				H	3
						H	H	H	H	6
E	E	D		E		D	C	D	E	15
H		H		H	H	H		H	H	12
E	D	E	E	E	D	D	C	C	E	18
H		H				H	H	H		12
		H			H		H	H	H	7
H	H	H			H	H	H	H	H	13
H		H			H	H	H	H		8
F	H	F	H	H		G	H	G	H	13
G	H	F	H	H	H	F	F	F	H	17
H		H			H	H	H	H		12
G	H	H	H	H		G	G	G	H	17
H		H	H		H			H		8
E	F	E	H	E	F	E	E	D	F	18
E	F	F	H	F	E	F	E	E	F	18
								H		2
F	H	F	H	H	H	F	H	F	H	16
H		H	H		H	H	H	H		15
E	E	E	E	D	E	E	C	C	E	18
E	G	E	G	G	G	E	D	E	H	18
G	H	F	H	H	H	H	H	G		17
										1
F	F	F	G	F	G	E	H	E	F	18
										1
D	D	E	E	D	D	D	C	C	E	18
										1
H		H	H	H	H	H	H			15
E	F	E	E	E	D	D	E	D	E	18

Common Name	Scientific Name	Bardsey	Calf of Man	Cape Clear	Copeland	Dungeness	Fair Isle	Filey	Flamborough
Hobby	*Falco subbuteo*	F	H	H		D	G	E	E
Gyr Falcon	*Falco rusticolus*			H			H		
Peregrine	*Falco peregrinus*	E	D	C	E	D	E	E	E
Water Rail	*Rallus aquaticus*	E	F	C	C	E	E	E	F
Spotted Crake	*Porzana porzana*	H		A		H	G	H	H
Sora	*Porzana carolina*	H							
Little Crake	*Porzana parva*						H		
Baillon's Crake	*Porzana pusilla*	H					H		
Corncrake	*Crex crex*	G	H	H	H	H	F	H	G
Moorhen	*Gallinula chloropus*	D	F	D	B	C	F	E	D
Allen's Gallinule	*Porphyrio alleni*								
Coot	*Fulica atra*	H	H	F	H	B	F	E	E
American Coot	*Fulica americana*								
Crane	*Grus grus*	H				G	G	H	H
Sandhill Crane	*Grus canadensis*						H		
Little Bustard	*Tetrax tetrax*						H		H
Macqueen's Bustard	*Chlamydotis macqueenii*								
Great Bustard	*Otis tarda*						H		H
Oystercatcher	*Haematopus ostralegus*	C	B	B	B	B	C	C	B
Black-winged Stilt	*Himantopus himantopus*	H				H		H	H
Avocet	*Recurvirostra avosetta*	H		H		F	H	H	H
Stone-curlew	*Burhinus oedicnemus*	H		H		G	H		H
Cream-coloured Courser	*Cursorius cursor*								
Collared Pratincole	*Glareola pratincola*						H		
Oriental Pratincole	*Glareola maldivarum*								
Black-winged Pratincole	*Glareola nordmanni*						H		
Little Ringed Plover	*Charadrius dubius*	H	H			F	H	E	F
Ringed Plover	*Charadrius hiaticula*	D	F	F	E	D	C	D	D
Killdeer	*Charadrius vociferus*	H		H					
Kentish Plover	*Charadrius alexandrinus*						H	H	H
Greater Sand Plover	*Charadrius leschenaultii*								
Caspian Plover	*Charadrius asiaticus*						H		
Dotterel	*Charadrius morinellus*	G		G		G	F	H	F
American Golden Plover	*Pluvialis dominica*			H			H		H
Pacific Golden Plover	*Pluvialis fulva*						H		
Golden Plover	*Pluvialis apricaria*	E	D	E	E	E	C	D	D
Grey Plover	*Pluvialis squatarola*	F	G	G	H	C	F	E	E
Sociable Plover	*Vanellus gregarius*								
Lapwing	*Vanellus vanellus*	E	E	E	D	D	C	C	C
Knot	*Calidris canutus*	E	G	F	E	C	E	C	C
Sanderling	*Calidris alba*	E	H	G	G	C	E	C	D
Semipalmated Sandpiper	*Calidris pusilla*						H		
Red-necked Stint	*Calidris ruficollis*						H		
Little Stint	*Calidris minuta*	G	H	H	H	G	F	F	F
Temminck's Stint	*Calidris temminckii*	H					H	G	G
Least Sandpiper	*Calidris minutilla*								
White-rumped Sandpiper	*Calidris fuscicollis*			H			H	H	
Baird's Sandpiper	*Calidris bairdii*	H					H	H	H
Pectoral Sandpiper	*Calidris melanotos*	H		H			G	H	H
Sharp-tailed Sandpiper	*Calidris acuminata*								
Curlew Sandpiper	*Calidris ferruginea*	F	H	H		G	F	F	G
Stilt Sandpiper	*Calidris himantopus*								H
Purple Sandpiper	*Calidris maritima*	C	D	E	D	F	C	D	D
Dunlin	*Calidris alpina*	D	E	E	E	C	D	C	C

Gibraltar Point	Hilbre	Holme	The Isle of May	Landguard	North Ronaldsay	Portland	Sandwich Bay	Spurn	Walney	Number of obs' recorded at
E	G	E	H	E	G	D	E	E	H	17
	H		H		H			H	H	7
E	D	E	F	E	E	E	E	E	E	18
E	H	E	G	F	E	E	E	D	F	18
H		H	H	H	G		H	H	H	14
H										2
								H		2
										2
H	H	H	G		E	F	H	F	H	17
D	H	D	F	F	B	F	C	C	D	18
						H				1
D	H	D	H	H	B	F	D	D	D	18
									H	1
G	H	E	H	H	G	H	H	G	H	15
										1
					H					3
								H		1
										2
B	A	C	D	B	A	D	A	A	A	18
H		H								6
D	H	E		E	H	G	F	E	H	15
H		H	H	H		F	H	H	H	13
							H			1
H	H	H					H	H		7
		H								1
		H					H			3
E	H	E		F	H	F	D	E	H	15
C	B	C	E	C	A	C	B	C	C	18
										2
H	H	H		H		F	H	H	H	11
								H	H	2
										1
H	H	H	H	H	E	F	H	G	H	16
		H			G	H	H	H		8
		H			H		H	H		5
B	E	B	E	C	A	D	A	A	B	18
B	B	B	G	C	E	D	B	C	C	18
		H					H			2
B	E	B	E	C	A	D	A	C	B	18
A	A	A	F	C	B	D	C	A	A	18
B	B	C	H	D	A	D	C	C	C	18
					H					2
										1
E	F	E	G	F	E	E	E	F	F	18
H		F		H	H	H	G	H	H	12
							H			1
H		H			G	H	H	H	H	10
					H	H	H		H	8
H		F			G	H	H	H	H	12
							H			1
E	F	E	H	F	E	E	E	D	E	17
										1
F	C	F	C	E	B	E	F	E	E	18
B	A	B	E	B	B	B	A	A	A	18

Common Name	Scientific Name	Bardsey	Calf of Man	Cape Clear	Copeland	Dungeness	Fair Isle	Filey	Flamborough
Broad-billed Sandpiper	*Limicola falcinellus*								
Buff-breasted Sandpiper	*Tryngites subruficollis*	H	H	H			H		H
Ruff	*Philomachus pugnax*	F	H	G	H	G	E	E	E
Jack Snipe	*Lymnocryptes minimus*	E	F	F	H	F	D	E	F
Snipe	*Gallinago gallinago*	D	E	C	E	E	C	D	D
Great Snipe	*Gallinago media*	H					G	H	
Long-billed Dowitcher	*Limnodromus scolopaceus*		H				H	H	
Woodcock	*Scolopax rusticola*	E	E	F	G	E	C	E	D
Black-tailed Godwit	*Limosa limosa*	F	H	G	F	E	F	E	E
Bar-tailed Godwit	*Limosa lapponica*	E	F	E	F	B	E	E	E
Whimbrel	*Numenius phaeopus*	C	E	D	D	C	D	D	D
Curlew	*Numenius arquata*	C	C	B	C	C	C	C	D
Upland Sandpiper	*Bartramia longicauda*						H		
Terek Sandpiper	*Xenus cinereus*						H		
Common Sandpiper	*Actitis hypoleucos*	D	E	D	E	E	E	E	E
Spotted Sandpiper	*Actitis macularius*	H		H			H		
Green Sandpiper	*Tringa ochropus*	F	H	F	H	E	E	E	E
Solitary Sandpiper	*Tringa solitaria*			H			H		
Spotted Redshank	*Tringa erythropus*	G	H	G	H	G	H	F	F
Greater Yellowlegs	*Tringa melanoleuca*								
Greenshank	*Tringa nebularia*	E	F	F	F	E	E	E	E
Lesser Yellowlegs	*Tringa flavipes*	H		H			H	H	H
Marsh Sandpiper	*Tringa stagnatilis*								
Wood Sandpiper	*Tringa glareola*	H	H	G	H	F	F	F	F
Redshank	*Tringa totanus*	C	E	E	C	E	C	C	C
Turnstone	*Arenaria interpres*	C	D	D	C	B	C	D	C
Wilson's Phalarope	*Phalaropus tricolor*			H					
Red-necked Phalarope	*Phalaropus lobatus*	H	H	H			G	H	H
Grey Phalarope	*Phalaropus fulicarius*	G	H	E	H	G	G	F	F
Pomarine Skua	*Stercorarius pomarinus*	F	F	D	E	D	F	E	D
Arctic Skua	*Stercorarius parasiticus*	E	F	D	E	C	C	C	C
Long-tailed Skua	*Stercorarius longicaudus*	G	H	G	H	F	F	E	E
Great Skua	*Stercorarius skua*	E	E	C	E	D	C	C	C
Ivory Gull	*Pagophila eburnea*						H	H	H
Sabine's Gull	*Xema sabini*	F	G	F	H	F	H	F	E
Kittiwake	*Rissa tridactyla*	A	A	B	A	A	A	A	A
Slender-billed Gull	*Chroicocephalus genei*					H			
Bonaparte's Gull	*Chroicocephalus philadelphia*	H				H		H	H
Black-headed Gull	*Chroicocephalus ridibundus*	A	D	D	B	A	D	A	A
Little Gull	*Hydrocoloeus minutus*	E	G	E	H	C	H	C	B
Ross's Gull	*Rhodostethia rosea*			H				H	H
Laughing Gull	*Larus atricilla*					H	H	H	H
Franklin's Gull	*Larus pipixcan*								H
Mediterranean Gull	*Larus melanocephalus*	D	H	H	F	C	H	E	E
Audouin's Gull	*Larus audouinii*					H			
Common Gull	*Larus canus*	D	E	E	B	A	C	A	A
Ring-billed Gull	*Larus delawarensis*	H		H			H	H	H
Lesser Black-backed Gull	*Larus fuscus*	C	B	B	A	A	D	C	C
Herring Gull	*Larus argentatus*	B	A	A	A	A	A	A	A
Yellow-legged Gull	*Larus michahellis*	H	H	H		D		H	E
Caspian Gull	*Larus cachinnans*					F			H
Iceland Gull	*Larus glaucoides*	H	H	G	H	G	E	F	F
Glaucous Gull	*Larus hyperboreus*	H	H	G	H	F	E	F	F

Gibraltar Point	Hilbre	Holme	The Isle of May	Landguard	North Ronaldsay	Portland	Sandwich Bay	Spurn	Walney	Number of obs' recorded at
H					H	H	H	H		5
H		H			G	H	H	H	H	12
E	G	D	F	F	D	F	F	E	E	18
E	H	F	F	F	D	H	E	E	E	18
D	F	D	E	E	A	D	C	C	C	18
					H			H		5
H					H		H	H		7
E	G	E	E	E	D	E	E	D	E	18
D	E	C	H	F	D	E	E	C	D	18
B	B	A	G	C	B	C	B	B	C	18
D	C	D	E	C	D	C	D	C	D	18
C	A	B	D	B	B	C	A	C	B	18
						H				2
H							H			3
D	F	E	E	E	E	E	C	D	E	18
					H			H		5
E	G	E	F	F	E	F	C	E	F	18
										2
E	F	E	G	G	F	G	E	E	F	18
H										1
D	F	E	F	E	E	E	D	C	E	18
H		H				H	H			10
		H		H				H		3
F	G	E	H	H	E	F	F	E	F	18
C	A	C	D	C	A	E	B	A	B	18
D	A	D	C	C	A	D	C	C	C	18
H		H						H	H	5
H		H			F	H	H	H	H	13
H	G	H	H	H	F	F	H	G	H	18
F	F	D	F	E	E	E	F	E	F	18
D	D	D	E	D	C	D	E	B	E	18
G	G	F	H	F	F	F	H	E	H	18
E	F	C	E	E	C	D	F	D	E	18
						H	H			5
H	G	F	H	H	G	F	F	F	H	18
D	C	B	A	B	A	A	E	A	C	18
										1
					H					5
A	A	A	E	A	A	B	A	A	C	18
E	C	D	E	D	E	D	E	B	E	18
					H	H				5
	H	H				H	H			8
										1
E	F	F	H	D	E	D	E	D	G	18
										1
B	A	B	E	A	A	B	A	C	D	18
	H	H			H	H	H		H	11
D	B	D	A	A	D	B	C	C	A	18
B	A	B	A	A	B	A	A	B	A	18
F	G	H		H	H	E	E	E	H	15
H				H			H			5
G	G	F	H	H	E	F	H	F	H	18
G	G	F	G	H	E	F	H	F	F	18

Common Name	Scientific Name	Bardsey	Calf of Man	Cape Clear	Copeland	Dungeness	Fair Isle	Filey	Flamborough
Great Black-backed Gull	*Larus marinus*	D	A	B	C	A	A	C	A
Sooty Tern	*Onychoprion fuscata*								
Bridled Tern	*Onychoprion anaethetus*		H						H
Little Tern	*Sternula albifrons*	F	H	D	H	D		F	F
Gull-billed Tern	*Gelochelidon nilotica*					H	H	H	H
Caspian Tern	*Hydroprogne caspia*	H				H	H		H
Whiskered Tern	*Chlidonias hybrida*					H			H
Black Tern	*Chlidonias niger*	F	H	E	H	C	H	E	E
White-winged Black Tern	*Chlidonias leucopterus*					G	H	H	H
Sandwich Tern	*Sterna sandvicensis*	D	E	D	C	A	F	B	A
Lesser Crested Tern	*Sterna bengalensis*					H		H	H
Forster's Tern	*Sterna forsteri*								
Common Tern	*Sterna hirundo*	E	G	E	C	A	E	B	A
Roseate Tern	*Sterna dougallii*	H	H	H	G	E	H	E	E
Arctic Tern	*Sterna paradisaea*	E	F	D	A	C	B	C	C
Guillemot	*Uria aalge*	B	B	B	A	A	A	A	A
Brunnich's Guillemot	*Uria lomvia*						H		
Razorbill	*Alca torda*	A	B	B	A	B	A	B	A
Great Auk	*Pinguinus impennis*						H		
Black Guillemot	*Cepphus grylle*	G	D	C	B	H	C	G	G
Little Auk	*Alle alle*	G	H	F	H	E	D	D	C
Puffin	*Fratercula arctica*	D	E	C	D	F	A	C	B
Pallas's Sandgrouse	*Syrrhaptes paradoxus*						H		H
Rock Dove	*Columba livia*	H	H	C	H	A	D	D	B
Stock Dove	*Columba oenas*	F	G	E	C	C	F	D	D
Woodpigeon	*Columba palumbus*	C	E	C	D	A	E	B	B
Collared Dove	*Streptopelia decaocto*	D	E	E	F	D	E	C	C
Turtle Dove	*Streptopelia turtur*	E	G	E	G	D	F	F	E
Rufous Turtle Dove	*Streptopelia orientalis*						H		
Mourning Dove	*Zenaida macroura*		H						
Ring-necked Parakeet	*Psittacula krameri*					H		H	H
Great Spotted Cuckoo	*Clamator glandarius*					H			
Cuckoo	*Cuculus canorus*	E	F	E	F	D	E	E	E
Yellow-billed Cuckoo	*Coccyzus americanus*			H					
Barn Owl	*Tyto alba*	G	H	H	H	G	H	E	E
Scops Owl	*Otus scops*		H	H			H		
Snowy Owl	*Bubo scandiacus*	H					G		
Little Owl	*Athene noctua*	E	H			F		F	E
Tawny Owl	*Strix aluco*	H	H			H		E	E
Long-eared Owl	*Asio otus*	E	F	F	G	F	E	F	F
Short-eared Owl	*Asio flammeus*	F	F	G	G	E	E	E	E
Tengmalm's Owl	*Aegolius funereus*								H
Nightjar	*Caprimulgus europaeus*	G	H	H		G	G	H	H
Egyptian Nightjar	*Caprimulgus aegyptius*								
Chimney Swift	*Chaetura pelagica*			H					
Needle-tailed Swift	*Hirundapus caudacutus*			H					
Swift	*Apus apus*	C	D	C	D	B	E	C	B
Pallid Swift	*Apus pallidus*					H	H	H	H
Pacific Swift	*Apus pacificus*								
Alpine Swift	*Apus melba*	H		H		H	H	H	H
Little Swift	*Apus affinis*			H			H		H
Kingfisher	*Alcedo atthis*	H	H	G		D	H	F	H
Bee-eater	*Merops apiaster*	H	H	H		G	H	H	G
Roller	*Coracias garrulus*						H		
Hoopoe	*Upupa epops*	G	H	F	H	F	G	H	H
Wryneck	*Jynx torquilla*	F	G	F	H	E	E	F	E

Gibraltar Point	Hilbre	Holme	The Isle of May	Landguard	North Ronaldsay	Portland	Sandwich Bay	Spurn	Walney	Number of obs' recorded at
C	A	B	C	B	A	B	A	C	C	18
			H			H				2
										2
D	C	D	G	C	F	D	E	C	E	17
H	H			H	H	H	H	H		11
H	H					H	H	H		9
H				H						4
E	F	E	G	E	H	D	F	D	G	18
H	H	H			H	H	H	H		11
B	A	B	C	C	D	C	A	B	C	18
		H					H	H		6
						H				1
C	A	C	C	B	E	B	B	A	E	18
H	G	F	F	H	H	F	F	E	G	18
E	D	E	B	E	A	C	E	C	D	18
D	C	C	A	E	B	A	D	B	B	18
					H					2
E	D	C	A	F	D	A	E	C	B	18
			H							2
H	G	F	F		B	G	H	H	F	17
E	H	E	E	E	E	F	F	D	G	18
G	G	F	A	H	B	E	H	D	F	18
		H	H		H			H		6
	F		B	B	A		C	C	D	15
D	F	D	G	C	F	B	B	D	F	18
A	E	A	E	A	D	B	A	B	D	18
E	D	G	F	C	D	D	A	C	D	18
D	H	G	F	E	E	D	D	D	G	18
						H		H		3
										1
H	H	H		H		H	E	G		10
							H	H		3
E	G	E	F	F	E	E	E	D	E	18
				H	H	H		H		5
E	H	E	H	G	H	F	E	D	E	18
						H				4
H				H	H			H		6
F	H	F		E		E	C	F	E	13
E	H	E	H	H		G	F	E	H	14
F	G	F	E	E	E	F	F	E	G	18
E	E	E	E	E	E	E	D	D	E	18
								H		2
H	H	H	H	H	H	F	H	G	H	17
						H				1
								H		2
										1
A	C	B	D	B	E	A	A	A	D	18
					H	H		H		7
								H		1
H		H		H	H	G	H	H		13
H								H		5
E	H	E	H	F		F	E	E	H	16
H	H	F		H	H	G	H	G	H	16
									H	2
H	H	G	H	H	G	F	H	G	H	18
F	H	E	F	F	E	F	F	E	H	18

Common Name	Scientific Name	Bardsey	Calf of Man	Cape Clear	Copeland	Dungeness	Fair Isle	Filey	Flamborough
Green Woodpecker	*Picus viridis*	H	H			C		H	H
Yellow-bellied Sapsucker	*Sphyrapicus varius*			H					
Great Spotted Woodpecker	*Dendrocopos major*	H	H	H	H	D	F	E	E
Lesser Spotted Woodpecker	*Dendrocopos minor*							H	
Calandra Lark	*Melanocorypha calandra*						H		
Bimaculated Lark	*Melanocorypha bimaculata*						H		
Black Lark	*Melanocorypha yeltoniensis*								
Lesser Short-toed Lark	*Calandrella rufescens*								
Short-toed Lark	*Calandrella brachydactyla*	H		H		H	F	H	H
Crested Lark	*Galerida cristata*	H				H	H		
Woodlark	*Lullula arborea*	H	H	H		E	G	H	G
Skylark	*Alauda arvensis*	C	C	C	C	B	B	C	B
Shore Lark	*Eremophila alpestris*	H	H	H		H	F	F	E
Sand Martin	*Riparia riparia*	C	D	D	D	A	E	D	C
Swallow	*Hirundo rustica*	A	B	A	A	A	D	C	B
House Martin	*Delichon urbicum*	B	C	B	B	A	E	C	B
Red-rumped Swallow	*Cecropis daurica*	H		H		H	H	H	G
Cliff Swallow	*Petrochelidon pyrrhonota*								
Richard's Pipit	*Anthus richardi*	F	H	H		H	E	G	F
Blyth's Pipit	*Anthus godlewskii*	H					H		
Tawny Pipit	*Anthus campestris*	H	H	H		G	H	H	H
Olive-backed Pipit	*Anthus hodgsoni*	H	H	H			F	H	H
Tree Pipit	*Anthus trivialis*	D	E	F	F	D	E	F	E
Pechora Pipit	*Anthus gustavi*						G	H	
Meadow Pipit	*Anthus pratensis*	B	A	A	B	A	A	C	B
Red-throated Pipit	*Anthus cervinus*	H		H	H	H	F	H	H
Rock Pipit	*Anthus petrosus*	D	B	C	E	E	B	E	C
Water Pipit	*Anthus spinoletta*	H	H	H		H		H	H
Buff-bellied Pipit	*Anthus rubescens*						H		
Yellow Wagtail	*Motacilla flava*	F	F	E	G	B	E	D	D
Citrine Wagtail	*Motacilla citreola*						F	H	H
Grey Wagtail	*Motacilla cinerea*	D	D	D	E	D	E	E	E
Pied Wagtail	*Motacilla alba*	C	B	B	D	B	C	D	C
Waxwing	*Bombycilla garrulus*	H	H			H	E	F	F
Dipper	*Cinclus cinclus*		H	H			G	H	H
Wren	*Troglodytes troglodytes*	C	B	A	C	B	D	C	C
Grey Catbird	*Dumetella carolinensis*			H					
Dunnock	*Prunella modularis*	D	D	A	D	B	D	C	C
Alpine Accentor	*Prunella collaris*						H	H	
Rufous Bush Chat	*Cercotrichas galactotes*			H					H
Robin	*Erithacus rubecula*	D	B	A	C	B	C	C	B
Rufous-tailed Robin	*Luscinia sibilans*						H		
Thrush Nightingale	*Luscinia luscinia*	H	H	H		H	G		H
Nightingale	*Luscinia megarhynchos*	G	H	H	H	F	G	H	G
Siberian Rubythroat	*Luscinia calliope*						H		
Bluethroat	*Luscinia svecica*	H	H	H	H	H	E	F	F
Siberian Blue Robin	*Luscinia cyane*								
Red-flanked Bluetail	*Tarsiger cyanurus*	H					H		H
White-throated Robin	*Irania gutturalis*		H						
Black Redstart	*Phoenicurus ochruros*	E	F	E	G	B	E	E	E
Redstart	*Phoenicurus phoenicurus*	E	E	F	F	D	D	E	D
Whinchat	*Saxicola rubetra*	E	E	D	F	D	E	D	D
Stonechat	*Saxicola torquatus*	D	B	B	F	C	F	E	E
Isabelline Wheatear	*Oenanthe isabellina*	H					H	H	
Wheatear	*Oenanthe oenanthe*	C	B	C	C	B	B	D	C

Gibraltar Point	Hilbre	Holme	The Isle of May	Landguard	North Ronaldsay	Portland	Sandwich Bay	Spurn	Walney	Number of obs' recorded at
F		F		E		F	D	H	H	12
										1
E	G	E	G	E	F	F	C	E	F	18
H		H		H		H	G			6
			H		H	H		H		5
								H		1
						H				1
H		H	H	H	F	H	H	H		14
				H						4
F	H	H	H	E	H	F	G	F		16
C	D	C	C	C	B	C	C	B	B	18
F	H	E	G	G	F	H	G	E	H	17
C	C	B	E	B	E	A	A	B	D	18
A	B	A	C	A	B	A	A	A	A	18
B	C	B	D	A	D	A	A	A	D	18
H	H	H	H	H	H	G	H	G		15
						H		H		2
H	H	E	H	H	F	F	H	F	H	17
				H		H				4
H	H	H	H	H		F	H	H	H	16
H		H			H	H	H	H		12
E	E	D	E	D	E	C	E	D	E	18
					H	H		H		5
B	A	B	B	A	A	A	B	A	A	18
H		H	H		H	H	H	H		14
D	D	D	E	D	B	D	D	C	E	18
G	H	E	H	H	H	H	F	H	H	16
					H					2
D	E	C	F	D	E	B	B	B	F	18
H		H	H	H	H		H	H		9
E	D	E	E	D	E	C	E	D	D	18
C	C	D	D	C	B	A	C	C	B	18
F	H	D	H	G	E	H	H	F	H	16
H	H		H		H	H	H	H	H	13
D	C	D	C	C	B	B	C	C	C	18
										1
C	E	D	E	C	D	B	C	B	C	18
						H				3
										2
C	C	B	C	B	C	B	B	B	C	18
										1
H		H	H	H	H	H	H			14
G	H	E	H	E	H	F	F	F	H	18
										1
G	H	G	F	F	E	F	H	F	H	18
					H					1
H			H	H	H		H			8
										1
F	G	E	E	D	E	D	E	D	F	18
E	E	C	E	D	D	C	E	C	E	18
E	E	E	E	D	D	C	D	C	E	18
E	E	E	F	E	E	C	C	C	D	18
				H	H					5
D	C	C	D	C	B	A	C	C	C	18

Common Name	Scientific Name	Bardsey	Calf of Man	Cape Clear	Copeland	Dungeness	Fair Isle	Filey	Flamborough
Pied Wheatear	*Oenanthe pleschanka*						H	H	H
Black-eared Wheatear	*Oenanthe hispanica*	H	H	H			H		
Desert Wheatear	*Oenanthe deserti*						H		H
Rock Thrush	*Monticola saxatilis*						H		
White's Thrush	*Zoothera dauma*				H		H		
Siberian Thrush	*Zoothera sibirica*			H			H		
Hermit Thrush	*Catharus guttatus*			H			H		
Swainson's Thrush	*Catharus ustulatus*			H			H		
Grey-cheeked Thrush	*Catharus minimus*	H		H			H		
Veery	*Catharus fuscescens*								
Ring Ouzel	*Turdus torquatus*	E	F	E	G	D	D	E	D
Blackbird	*Turdus merula*	D	B	A	C	A	A	B	B
Eyebrowed Thrush	*Turdus obscurus*	H					H		
Dusky Thrush	*Turdus eunomus*						H		
Black-throated Thrush	*Turdus atrogularis*						H		
Fieldfare	*Turdus pilaris*	C	C	D	E	C	A	B	B
Song Thrush	*Turdus philomelos*	D	C	B	E	C	A	B	B
Redwing	*Turdus iliacus*	B	C	C	E	C	A	B	B
Mistle Thrush	*Turdus viscivorus*	E	E	E	F	E	E	D	E
American Robin	*Turdus migratorius*	H							
Cetti's Warbler	*Cettia cetti*	H				F			H
Fan-tailed Warbler	*Cisticola juncidis*			H					
Pallas's Grasshopper Warbler	*Locustella certhiola*			H			G		
Lanceolated Warbler	*Locustella lanceolata*	H					F	H	
Grasshopper Warbler	*Locustella naevia*	C	E	F	F	E	E	F	F
River Warbler	*Locustella fluviatilis*	H					H		H
Savi's Warbler	*Locustella luscinioides*						H		H
Aquatic Warbler	*Acrocephalus paludicola*	H	H	H		H	G		H
Sedge Warbler	*Acrocephalus schoenobaenus*	C	D	C	D	B	D	E	D
Paddyfield Warbler	*Acrocephalus agricola*	H				H	H		H
Blyth's Reed Warbler	*Acrocephalus dumetorum*	H		H		H	G	H	H
Marsh Warbler	*Acrocephalus palustris*	H	H			H	E	H	F
Reed Warbler	*Acrocephalus scirpaceus*	E	G	E	H	B	E	E	E
Great Reed Warbler	*Acrocephalus arundinaceus*	H	H	H		H	H		
Thick-billed Warbler	*Acrocephalus aedon*						H		
Eastern Olivaceous Warbler	*Hippolais pallida*			H			H		
Booted Warbler	*Hippolais caligata*	H				H	H	H	H
Sykes's Warbler	*Hippolais rama*			H			H		
Icterine Warbler	*Hippolais icterina*	F	G	F	H	F	E	F	F
Melodious Warbler	*Hippolais polyglotta*	F	G	F	H	F	H		H
Blackcap	*Sylvia atricapilla*	C	D	D	E	D	C	D	D
Garden Warbler	*Sylvia borin*	D	E	E	F	D	D	E	E
Barred Warbler	*Sylvia nisoria*	G	G	F	H	G	E	F	F
Lesser Whitethroat	*Sylvia curruca*	F	F	F	H	D	D	E	E
Orphean Warbler	*Sylvia hortensis*								
Asian Desert Warbler	*Sylvia nana*								H
Whitethroat	*Sylvia communis*	C	C	C	E	B	D	C	C
Spectacled Warbler	*Sylvia conspicillata*							H	
Dartford Warbler	*Sylvia undata*	H		H		E	H		
Marmora's Warbler	*Sylvia sarda*								
Ruppell's Warbler	*Sylvia rueppelli*								
Subalpine Warbler	*Sylvia cantillans*	H	H	H	H	H	F	H	H
Sardinian Warbler	*Sylvia melanocephala*	H	H	H		H	H	H	H
Greenish Warbler	*Phylloscopus trochiloides*	H	H	H		H	G	H	G

Gibraltar Point	Hilbre	Holme	The Isle of May	Landguard	North Ronaldsay	Portland	Sandwich Bay	Spurn	Walney	Number of obs' recorded at
H		H	H		H	H		H		9
		H	H			H		H		8
		H		H		H	H		H	7
		H				H		H		4
					H					3
			H		H					4
										2
							H			3
						H				4
					H					1
E	F	D	E	E	D	D	F	D	F	18
B	D	B	A	A	B	A	A	A	C	18
										2
										1
					H					2
C	E	B	B	C	B	B	C	B	D	18
D	D	C	B	B	C	B	B	B	C	18
B	E	B	B	B	A	B	C	A	D	18
D	F	E	F	E	E	E	C	D	E	18
										1
H		F		H		G	E	H	H	10
		H				H				3
					H	H				4
			H	H	H			H		7
E	E	E	F	F	F	D	E	E	E	18
H					H			H		6
		H		H		H	H	H		7
		H	H		H	G	H	H		12
E	E	C	D	E	E	C	B	D	C	18
			H	H	H				H	8
H		H			H	H		H		11
H	H	H	G	H	F	G	H	F	H	16
D	H	C	E	D	E	C	B	D	F	18
					H	H	H	H		9
										1
			H			H	H			5
			H		H	H		H	H	10
					H	H				4
G	H	G	F	G	E	F	G	E	H	18
	H		H	H	H	F	H	H	H	15
D	E	D	D	C	C	B	B	C	E	18
E	F	D	D	D	E	C	D	D	E	18
F		F	F	F	E	F	H	E	H	17
D	F	E	E	C	D	D	D	C	E	18
						H				1
						H		H		3
C	E	D	D	C	E	B	B	C	C	18
				H						2
H	H			H		E	G		H	10
								H		1
		H								1
H	H		H	H	H	G	H	H	H	17
H		H	H	H	H	H	H	H		15
H		H	H	H	H	H	H	H	H	16

Common Name	Scientific Name	Bardsey	Calf of Man	Cape Clear	Copeland	Dungeness	Fair Isle	Filey	Flamborough
Arctic Warbler	*Phylloscopus borealis*	H		H			F	H	H
Pallas's Warbler	*Phylloscopus proregulus*	H	H	H		F	G	G	E
Yellow-browed Warbler	*Phylloscopus inornatus*	F	G	E	H	F	E	E	E
Hume's Warbler	*Phylloscopus humei*						H	H	H
Radde's Warbler	*Phylloscopus schwarzi*	H		H		H	H	H	H
Dusky Warbler	*Phylloscopus fuscatus*	H	H	H		H	H	H	H
Western Bonelli's Warbler	*Phylloscopus bonelli*	H	H	H		H	H	H	H
Wood Warbler	*Phylloscopus sibilatrix*	F	F	F	H	F	E	F	F
Chiffchaff	*Phylloscopus collybita*	B	C	C	D	B	D	D	C
Iberian Chiffchaff	*Phylloscopus ibericus*					H			
Willow Warbler	*Phylloscopus trochilus*	A	B	C	C	B	C	D	C
Goldcrest	*Regulus regulus*	B	B	B	C	B	C	C	B
Firecrest	*Regulus ignicapilla*	E	F	E	H	D	H	F	E
Spotted Flycatcher	*Muscicapa striata*	C	D	E	E	D	E	E	E
Asian Brown Flycatcher	*Muscicapa dauurica*						H		H
Red-breasted Flycatcher	*Ficedula parva*	F	G	F	H	G	F	F	F
Taiga Flycatcher	*Ficedula albicilla*								H
Collared Flycatcher	*Ficedula albicollis*	H					H	H	
Pied Flycatcher	*Ficedula hypoleuca*	D		F	E	H	E	E	D
Bearded Tit	*Panurus biarmicus*		H	H		F		H	H
Long-tailed Tit	*Aegithalos caudatus*	G	E	F	H	G		D	C
Blue Tit	*Cyanistes caeruleus*	E	E	B	H	C	H	C	C
Great Tit	*Parus major*	E	D	B	G	C	G	C	C
Coal Tit	*Periparus ater*	E	E	D	F	E	H	D	E
Willow Tit	*Poecile montana*	H				H		G	F
Marsh Tit	*Poecile palustris*					H		G	H
Nuthatch	*Sitta europaea*	H				H		H	H
Treecreeper	*Certhia familiaris*	F	F	G	H	G	H	E	E
Short-toed Treecreeper	*Certhia brachydactyla*					H			
Penduline Tit	*Remiz pendulinus*	H				H			
Golden Oriole	*Oriolus oriolus*	G	H	F		G	G	H	G
Brown Shrike	*Lanius cristatus*						H		H
Isabelline Shrike	*Lanius isabellinus*	H				H	H		H
Red-backed Shrike	*Lanius collurio*	G	H	G	H	F	E	F	F
Lesser Grey Shrike	*Lanius minor*			H			G		H
Great Grey Shrike	*Lanius excubitor*	H	H			H	F	G	F
Southern Grey Shrike	*Lanius meridionalis*						H		
Woodchat Shrike	*Lanius senator*	G	H	H	H	G	G	H	H
Jay	*Garrulus glandarius*	H				E		F	G
Magpie	*Pica pica*	D	E	A	D	B	H	D	D
Nutcracker	*Nucifraga caryocatactes*						H		H
Chough	*Pyrrhocorax pyrrhocorax*	D	B	B					
Jackdaw	*Corvus monedula*	C	D	B	C	D	F	C	C
Rook	*Corvus frugilegus*	E	D	E	E	E	E	C	C
Carrion Crow	*Corvus corone*	D	D	H	E	C	E	C	C
Hooded Crow	*Corvus cornix*	G	B	B	D	H	E	G	F
Raven	*Corvus corax*	D	C	C	E	H	D	H	H
Starling	*Sturnus vulgaris*	A	A	A	B	B	A	A	A
Rose-coloured Starling	*Pastor roseus*	H	H	H		H	G	H	H
House Sparrow	*Passer domesticus*	F	F	B	G	B	D	C	C
Spanish Sparrow	*Passer hispaniolensis*								
Tree Sparrow	*Passer montanus*	F	F	G	G	D	F	C	C
Red-eyed Vireo	*Vireo olivaceus*	H		H		H			
Chaffinch	*Fringilla coelebs*	A	B	B	D	B	C	C	C
Brambling	*Fringilla montifringilla*	E	E	E	G	D	C	D	C
Serin	*Serinus serinus*	H	H	H		F	H	H	H
Citril Finch	*Serinus citrinella*						H		

Gibraltar Point	Hilbre	Holme	The Isle of May	Landguard	North Ronaldsay	Portland	Sandwich Bay	Spurn	Walney	Number of obs' recorded at
H		H	H		H	H	H	H		12
H	H	F	H	F	H	F	G	F	H	17
F	H	F	F	F	E	F	F	E	H	18
H			H		H	H	H	H	H	10
H		H	H	H	H	H	H	H		14
		H	H	H	H	H	H	H		14
		H		H	H	H	H	H	H	14
F	H	F	F	F	E	F	F	E	G	18
D	D	D	D	C	D	A	C	C	D	18
						H				2
C	C	D	C	C	D	A	C	B	C	18
C	C	B	C	B	C	B	B	B	C	18
E	G	E	H	D	H	C	E	E	G	18
E	F	E	E	E	E	C	E	D	E	18
										2
G	H	F	F	H	F	F	H	E	H	18
										1
		H			H					5
E	G	D	D	E	E	D	E	C	F	18
F		D	H	H		F	F	F	H	13
D	G	D	H	E	H	E	C	D	E	17
D	F	D	H	D	H	C	B	C	D	18
D	F	D	H	C	G	C	B	C	E	18
E	F	D	H	E	H	F	F	E	E	18
F	H	H		H		H	H	F	H	12
H	H	H		H		H	H	H	H	11
H	H	H		H		H	H	H	H	12
F	H	F	F	H	H	F	F	F	G	18
						H	H			3
H							H	H		5
F		H	H	H	H	F	F	F	H	16
										2
H		H	H		H	H	H	H		11
F		F	F	F	E	F	F	E	H	17
H		H	H				H	H		8
F	H	F	G	H	F	G	H	F	H	16
			H		H	H			H	5
H	H	H	H	H	H	F	H	H	H	18
F	H	E		F		F	C	E	G	12
D	F	E	H	D	H	D	B	C	D	18
H		H				H	H	H	H	8
	H			H		H			H	7
D	E	D	G	E	E	C	B	C	B	18
E	F	D	G	E	E	D	B	C	E	18
D	C	D	E	D	D	D	B	C	D	18
F	H	G	H	H	C	G	H	F	F	18
H	G		H	H	C	E	H	H	F	17
A	C	A	C	A	A	A	A	A	A	18
H		H	H	H	G	G	H	H	H	16
E	E	F	G	C	A	B	B	B	C	18
					H					1
D	F	F	G	E	F	F	E	C	D	18
						H		H		5
B	C	B	E	B	D	B	B	B	C	18
D	F	C	D	D	C	C	E	C	E	18
H	H	H		H		F	H	G	H	15
										1

Common Name	Scientific Name	Bardsey	Calf of Man	Cape Clear	Copeland	Dungeness	Fair Isle	Filey	Flamborough
Greenfinch	*Carduelis chloris*	C	B	B	D	A	E	C	C
Goldfinch	*Carduelis carduelis*	C	B	C	D	B	F	C	C
Siskin	*Carduelis spinus*	D	C	D	E	D	D	D	C
Linnet	*Carduelis cannabina*	B	B	B	C	B	E	C	B
Twite	*Carduelis flavirostris*	G	F	H	E	G	C	F	D
Common Redpoll	*Carduelis flammea*	G	H			H	D	F	F
Lesser Redpoll	*Carduelis cabaret*	D	C	E	D	D	F	E	D
Arctic Redpoll	*Carduelis hornemanni*	H	H				F	H	H
Two-barred Crossbill	*Loxia leucoptera*						G		H
Common Crossbill	*Loxia curvirostra*	F	F	G	H	G	E	F	F
Parrot Crossbill	*Loxia pytyopsittacus*						G		
Trumpeter Finch	*Bucanetes githagineus*					H			
Common Rosefinch	*Carpodacus erythrinus*	F	G	G	H	H	E	G	F
Pine Grosbeak	*Pinicola enucleator*								
Bullfinch	*Pyrrhula pyrrhula*	E	H	F	H	E	E	E	E
Hawfinch	*Coccothraustes coccothraustes*	H	H	H			H	F	H	G
Black-and-white Warbler	*Mniotilta varia*			H					
Blue-winged Warbler	*Vermivora pinus*			H					
Tennessee Warbler	*Vermivora peregrina*						H		
Northern Parula	*Parula americana*								
Yellow Warbler	*Dendroica petechia*	H		H					
Blackburnian Warbler	*Dendroica fusca*						H		
Yellow-rumped Warbler	*Dendroica coronata*		H	H			H		
Blackpoll Warbler	*Dendroica striata*	H		H			H		H
American Redstart	*Setophaga ruticilla*			H					
Northern Waterthrush	*Seiurus noveboracensis*			H					
Common Yellowthroat	*Geothlypis trichas*	H							
Summer Tanager	*Piranga rubra*	H							
Scarlet Tanager	*Piranga olivacea*				H				
Lark Sparrow	*Chondestes grammacus*								
Savannah Sparrow	*Passerculus sandwichensis*						H		
Fox Sparrow	*Passerella iliaca*				H				
Song Sparrow	*Melospiza melodia*	H	H				H		
White-crowned Sparrow	*Zonotrichia leucophrys*						H		
White-throated Sparrow	*Zonotrichia albicollis*	H		H			H		H
Dark-eyed Junco	*Junco hyemalis*	H				H			
Lapland Bunting	*Calcarius lapponicus*	F	H	F	H	E	E	E	E
Snow Bunting	*Plectrophenax nivalis*	F	F	E	G	E	C	D	D
Black-faced Bunting	*Emberiza spodocephala*						H		H
Pine Bunting	*Emberiza leucocephalos*	H					H	H	H
Yellowhammer	*Emberiza citrinella*	F	F	F	G	C	E	D	D
Cirl Bunting	*Emberiza cirlus*	H				H			
Rock Bunting	*Emberiza cia*	H							
Ortolan Bunting	*Emberiza hortulana*	G	H	G		G	E	H	H
Cretzschmar's Bunting	*Emberiza caesia*						H		
Yellow-browed Bunting	*Emberiza chrysophrys*						H		
Rustic Bunting	*Emberiza rustica*	H	H	H		H	E	H	H
Chestnut-eared Bunting	*Emberiza fucata*						H		
Little Bunting	*Emberiza pusilla*	H	H	H		H	E	H	G
Yellow-breasted Bunting	*Emberiza aureola*	H		H			F	H	H
Reed Bunting	*Emberiza schoeniclus*	E	D	C	D	C	E	D	D
Pallas's Reed Bunting	*Emberiza pallasi*						H		
Black-headed Bunting	*Emberiza melanocephala*	H	H			H	G		H

Gibraltar Point	Hilbre	Holme	The Isle of May	Landguard	North Ronaldsay	Portland	Sandwich Bay	Spurn	Walney	Number of obs' recorded at
B	C	A	E	A	E	B	B	A	B	18
B	C	C	E	B	F	B	B	A	C	18
C	D	C	E	C	E	C	C	C	D	18
C	B	C	E	B	A	B	B	A	B	18
E	G	E	E	G	D	G	E	E	D	18
G	H	E	F	F	D	H	F	E	H	16
D	D	D	E	C	F	C	B	C	D	18
H		H	H		F			H		10
			H		H					4
E	H	E	F	E	E	F	F	E	H	18
H		H	H		H		H	H		7
				H						2
H		H	F	H	E	G	H	F	H	17
			H							1
F	H	E	G	F	E	E	F	E	E	18
G		H	H	F	G	G	H	F	H	16
										1
										1
										1
						H				1
					H					3
										1
					H					4
										4
H										2
H						H				3
										1
										1
										1
				H						1
							H			2
										1
								H		4
										1
					H			H	H	7
		H			H	H				5
F	F	G	F	F	E	F	E	E	G	18
E	E	D	F	E	B	F	C	D	F	18
										2
H					H	H				7
E	G	E	F	E	E	E	E	D	G	18
			H		H	G		H		6
								H		2
H		H	G	G	F			H	F	H	15
					H					2
					H					2
H			H	H	G	H		H	H	14
										1
H		H	G	H	E	H	H	G	H	16
H	H	H	H	H	H	H		H		13
D	E	D	E	E	C	D	D	C	D	18
										1
			H		H	H	H			9

Common Name	Scientific Name	Bardsey	Calf of Man	Cape Clear	Copeland	Dungeness	Fair Isle	Filey	Flamborough
Corn Bunting	*Emberiza calandra*	H	H	H	H	D	G	E	E
Rose-breasted									
Grosbeak	*Pheucticus ludovicianus*	H		H					
Indigo Bunting	*Passerina cyanea*			H					
Bobolink	*Dolichonyx oryzivorus*			H			H		
Baltimore Oriole	*Icterus galbula*		H	H			H		
Total number of species recorded at each observatory		322	269	308	207	319	374	320	346

APPENDIX 1b: CHECKLIST OF NUMBERS OF BIRDS RINGED

Common Name	Scientific Name	Bardsey	Calf of Man	Cape Clear	Copeland	Dungeness	Fair Isle	Filey	Flamborough
Mute Swan	*Cygnus olor*					194			
Bewick's Swan	*Cygnus columbianus*								
Whooper Swan	*Cygnus cygnus*						50		
Bean Goose	*Anser fabalis*						1		
Pink-footed Goose	*Anser brachyrhynchus*		1				16		
White-fronted Goose	*Anser albifrons*						3		
Lesser White-fronted									
Goose	*Anser erythropus*								
Greylag Goose	*Anser anser*						90		
Snow Goose	*Anser caerulescens*								
Canada Goose	*Branta canadensis*					44			
Barnacle Goose	*Branta leucopsis*						4		
Brent Goose	*Branta bernicla*		1						
Red-breasted Goose	*Branta ruficollis*								
Egyptian Goose	*Alopochen aegyptiaca*								
Ruddy Shelduck	*Tadorna ferruginea*								
Shelduck	*Tadorna tadorna*	5			2	17	5		
Mandarin Duck	*Aix galericulata*								
Wigeon	*Anas penelope*						57		
American Wigeon	*Anas americana*								
Gadwall	*Anas strepera*								
Teal	*Anas crecca*	7	4		2	2	83		
Green-winged Teal	*Anas carolinensis*								
Mallard	*Anas platyrhynchos*	40	21		11	22	17		13
Black Duck	*Anas rubripes*								
Pintail	*Anas acuta*						2		
Garganey	*Anas querquedula*								
Blue-winged Teal	*Anas discors*								
Shoveler	*Anas clypeata*						1		
Red-crested Pochard	*Netta rufina*								
Pochard	*Aythya ferina*					1	3		
Redhead	*Aythya americana*								
Ring-necked Duck	*Aythya collaris*						1		
Ferruginous Duck	*Aythya nyroca*								
Tufted Duck	*Aythya fuligula*					9	23		
Scaup	*Aythya marila*						6		1
Eider	*Somateria mollissima*		7		93	1	171		
King Eider	*Somateria spectabilis*								
Steller's Eider	*Polysticta stelleri*								
Harlequin Duck	*Histrionicus histrionicus*								

Gibraltar Point	Hilbre	Holme	The Isle of May	Landguard	North Ronaldsay	Portland	Sandwich Bay	Spurn	Walney	Number of obs' recorded at
D	H	F	H	F	H	F	C	E	H	18
		H								3
										1
						H				3
										3
321	256	319	279	294	330	352	330	351	292	

Gibraltar Point	Hilbre	Holme	The Isle of May	Land-guard	North Ronaldsay	Portland	Sandwich Bay	Spurn	Walney	Total ringed	Number of obs' ringed at
		42		6	3	1	242	32	17	537	8
										0	0
		1			11			1		63	4
										1	1
			1		8			1		27	5
										3	1
										0	0
					23		12			125	3
										0	0
							9	3		56	3
			3				2			9	3
		2		1			2	1		7	5
										0	0
		1								1	1
										0	0
2	1	6	1				12	3	1	55	11
										0	0
2		12	2		9		2	2	1	87	8
										0	0
		2			1					3	2
1		141	10	1	42	1	4	14	13	325	14
										0	0
12	4	14	1		45	3	84	27	26	340	15
										0	0
										2	1
										0	0
										0	0
					6		1			8	3
							1			1	1
					2		1			7	4
										0	0
										1	1
										0	0
		1			1		7			41	5
		1						1		9	4
			242		22	1		2	71	610	9
										0	0
										0	0
										0	0

Common Name	Scientific Name	Bardsey	Calf of Man	Cape Clear	Copeland	Dungeness	Fair Isle	Filey	Flamborough
Long-tailed Duck	*Clangula hyemalis*						19		
Common Scoter	*Melanitta nigra*					1			
Surf Scoter	*Melanitta perspicillata*								
Velvet Scoter	*Melanitta fusca*						2		
Goldeneye	*Bucephala clangula*		1				22		
Smew	*Mergellus albellus*								
Red-breasted Merganser	*Mergus serrator*				3		3		
Goosander	*Mergus merganser*						3		
Ruddy Duck	*Oxyura jamaicensis*								
Red Grouse	*Lagopus lagopus scotica*								
Red-legged Partridge	*Alectoris rufa*					6			
Grey Partridge	*Perdix perdix*		14			54			1
Quail	*Coturnix coturnix*	4			1		9		1
Pheasant	*Phasianus colchicus*								
Red-throated Diver	*Gavia stellata*						1		1
Black-throated Diver	*Gavia arctica*								
Great Northern Diver	*Gavia immer*								
White-billed Diver	*Gavia adamsii*								
Little Grebe	*Tachybaptus ruficollis*	3				1	10		
Great Crested Grebe	*Podiceps cristatus*					1	1		
Red-necked Grebe	*Podiceps grisegena*					1	1		1
Slavonian Grebe	*Podiceps auritus*						3		
Black-necked Grebe	*Podiceps nigricollis*								
Black-browed Albatross	*Thalassarche melanophris*								
Fulmar	*Fulmarus glacialis*	150	125	92	129		17245		2
Fea's/Zino's Petrel	*Pterodroma feae/madeira*								
Bulwer's Petrel	*Bulweria bulwerii*								
Cory's Shearwater	*Calonectris diomedea*								
Great Shearwater	*Puffinus gravis*								
Sooty Shearwater	*Puffinus griseus*								
Manx Shearwater	*Puffinus puffinus*	36167	605	92	28353			1	4
Balearic Shearwater	*Puffinus mauretanicus*								
Macaronesian Shearwater	*Puffinus baroli*								
Wilson's Petrel	*Oceanites oceanicus*								
Storm Petrel	*Hydrobates pelagicus*	664	4967	13171	3646	1	31241	732	422
Leach's Petrel	*Oceanodroma leucorhoa*	32		2		3	99	2	2
Gannet	*Morus bassanus*	4	1	1	997	4	521		2
Cormorant	*Phalacrocorax carbo*	1254	7	21	44	1	7	1	1
Shag	*Phalacrocorax aristotelis*	4019	6855	22	344	1	23692		1
Bittern	*Botaurus stellaris*	1				1			
American Bittern	*Botaurus lentiginosus*								
Little Bittern	*Ixobrychus minutus*					1			
Night-heron	*Nycticorax nycticorax*								
Squacco Heron	*Ardeola ralloides*								
Cattle Egret	*Bubulcus ibis*								
Little Egret	*Egretta garzetta*								
Great White Egret	*Ardea alba*								
Grey Heron	*Ardea cinerea*	5		1	1	99	22		
Purple Heron	*Ardea purpurea*								
Black Stork	*Ciconia nigra*								
White Stork	*Ciconia ciconia*								
Glossy Ibis	*Plegadis falcinellus*								
Spoonbill	*Platalea leucorodia*								
Honey-buzzard	*Pernis apivorus*								
Black Kite	*Milvus migrans*								
Red Kite	*Milvus milvus*								

Gibraltar Point	Hilbre	Holme	The Isle of May	Land-guard	North Ronaldsay	Portland	Sandwich Bay	Spurn	Walney	Total ringed	Number of obs' ringed at
					7		1	4		31	4
							1	2		4	3
										0	0
								1		3	2
					1					24	3
										0	0
		2	1		1					10	5
										3	1
										0	0
										0	0
43		2		15		1	3	45		115	7
23		3					28	95	15	233	8
			3			1	3	1		23	8
34							1	8		43	3
							1	2		5	4
						1				1	1
										0	0
										0	0
9		1		1		1	16	25		67	9
		2				1	3	2	1	11	7
							2	1		6	5
		1					2	1		7	4
							2			2	1
										0	0
		1	1715		7203	7	150	3		26822	12
										0	0
										0	0
								1		1	1
										0	0
										0	0
4	3	2	4	1	1	11	1	2		65251	15
										0	0
										0	0
										0	0
			1131	1	8589	375	4	8		64952	14
2	1		5	1	74		1	2		226	13
1			30		8	4	6	7		1586	13
			2		336		151	2		1827	12
1		2	32850	2	24	7	5	6		67831	15
		1					1			4	4
										0	0
							1			2	2
										0	0
										0	0
										0	0
						1	1			2	2
										0	0
1		1	1		3	1	1			136	11
										0	0
										0	0
										0	0
										0	0
										0	0
					1					1	1
										0	0
										0	0

Common Name	Scientific Name	Bardsey	Calf of Man	Cape Clear	Copeland	Dungeness	Fair Isle	Filey	Flamborough
White-tailed Eagle	Haliaeetus albicilla								
Marsh Harrier	Circus aeruginosus						1		
Hen Harrier	Circus cyaneus	1	42				2		
Pallid Harrier	Circus macrourus								
Montagu's Harrier	Circus pygargus								
Goshawk	Accipiter gentilis						2		
Sparrowhawk	Accipiter nisus	97	168	23	143	108	396	50	27
Buzzard	Buteo buteo								
Rough-legged Buzzard	Buteo lagopus								
Golden Eagle	Aquila chrysaetos								
Osprey	Pandion haliaetus								
Lesser Kestrel	Falco naumanni								
Kestrel	Falco tinnunculus	41	131	2	6	93	53	1	14
American Kestrel	Falco sparverius								
Red-footed Falcon	Falco vespertinus						1		
Merlin	Falco columbarius	8	33	2	12	7	202		
Hobby	Falco subbuteo					2			
Gyr Falcon	Falco rusticolus								
Peregrine	Falco peregrinus	39	6	1			6		
Water Rail	Rallus aquaticus	217	35	1	220	138	335		2
Spotted Crake	Porzana porzana					2	19		
Sora	Porzana carolina	1							
Little Crake	Porzana parva						1		
Baillon's Crake	Porzana pusilla						1		
Corncrake	Crex crex	13	7		1	4	43		
Moorhen	Gallinula chloropus	409	38	2	1345	147	104		
Allen's Gallinule	Porphyrio alleni								
Coot	Fulica atra		1			17	15		
American Coot	Fulica americana								
Crane	Grus grus								
Sandhill Crane	Grus canadensis								
Little Bustard	Tetrax tetrax								
Macqueen's Bustard	Chlamydotis macqueenii								
Great Bustard	Otis tarda						1		
Oystercatcher	Haematopus ostralegus	868	266	5	277	59	1544		
Black-winged Stilt	Himantopus himantopus								
Avocet	Recurvirostra avosetta								
Stone-curlew	Burhinus oedicnemus					6			
Cream-coloured Courser	Cursorius cursor								
Collared Pratincole	Glareola pratincola								
Oriental Pratincole	Glareola maldivarum								
Black-winged Pratincole	Glareola nordmanni								
Little Ringed Plover	Charadrius dubius					8	1		
Ringed Plover	Charadrius hiaticula	117	1		37	215	761		6
Killdeer	Charadrius vociferus								
Kentish Plover	Charadrius alexandrinus								
Greater Sand Plover	Charadrius leschenaultii								
Caspian Plover	Charadrius asiaticus								
Dotterel	Charadrius morinellus	2				1	4		1
American Golden Plover	Pluvialis dominica								
Pacific Golden Plover	Pluvialis fulva								
Golden Plover	Pluvialis apricaria	4				2	24		
Grey Plover	Pluvialis squatarola	3				3	1	1	
Sociable Plover	Vanellus gregarius								
Lapwing	Vanellus vanellus	159	27		13	516	352	6	2
Knot	Calidris canutus	73				38	105	3	

Gibraltar Point	Hilbre	Holme	The Isle of May	Land-guard	North Ronaldsay	Portland	Sandwich Bay	Spurn	Walney	Total ringed	Number of obs' ringed at
										0	0
										1	1
					2		1			48	5
										0	0
2										2	1
										2	1
221	13	45	70	256	168	149	129	171	99	2333	18
						1				1	1
										0	0
										0	0
										0	0
										0	0
76	19	49	40	27	6	45	147	132	19	901	18
										0	0
			1		1					3	3
4	2		18	2	16		1	7	7	321	14
				2			7			11	3
										0	0
			4			2				58	6
21	1	75	10	8	65	34	69	75	4	1310	17
			1		2		2	2		28	6
1										2	2
										1	1
										1	1
1			13		1	3		2	1	89	11
11		735	9	4	80	7	225	96	76	3288	15
										0	0
2		4			4	1	13	7	7	71	10
										0	0
										0	0
										0	0
										0	0
										0	0
										1	1
79	1124	23	511	10	569	2	155	96	220	5808	16
										0	0
8		38								46	2
										6	1
										0	0
										0	0
										0	0
										0	0
7		2					35	5		58	6
846	40	59	2	138	400	12	548	682	71	3935	16
										0	0
							1			1	1
										0	0
										0	0
			1	1	1	4		4		19	9
					2					2	1
										0	0
1			1	2	447	1	13	13		508	10
13	4						15	41	1	82	9
										0	0
27		85	27		982	2	859	33	142	3232	15
138	401	1			62	1	69	104		995	11

Common Name	Scientific Name	Bardsey	Calf of Man	Cape Clear	Copeland	Dungeness	Fair Isle	Filey	Flamborough
Sanderling	*Calidris alba*	17				1	120		
Semipalmated Sandpiper	*Calidris pusilla*						1		
Red-necked Stint	*Calidris ruficollis*								
Little Stint	*Calidris minuta*	8			1	56	123		1
Temminck's Stint	*Calidris temminckii*						2		
Least Sandpiper	*Calidris minutilla*								
White-rumped Sandpiper	*Calidris fuscicollis*					1	1		
Baird's Sandpiper	*Calidris bairdii*	1					1		
Pectoral Sandpiper	*Calidris melanotos*	2				1	5		
Sharp-tailed Sandpiper	*Calidris acuminata*								
Curlew Sandpiper	*Calidris ferruginea*	6				40	6		
Stilt Sandpiper	*Calidris himantopus*								
Purple Sandpiper	*Calidris maritima*	54	32		6		190	123	
Dunlin	*Calidris alpina*	465	1	1	8	872	604	7	23
Broad-billed Sandpiper	*Limicola falcinellus*								
Buff-breasted Sandpiper	*Tryngites subruficollis*			1			1		
Ruff	*Philomachus pugnax*					17	41		
Jack Snipe	*Lymnocryptes minimus*	22	12		1	11	145	3	2
Snipe	*Gallinago gallinago*	45	34	17	11	81	522	1	
Great Snipe	*Gallinago media*						2		
Long-billed Dowitcher	*Limnodromus scolopaceus*								
Woodcock	*Scolopax rusticola*	44	19		3	17	490	10	20
Black-tailed Godwit	*Limosa limosa*					1	1		
Bar-tailed Godwit	*Limosa lapponica*	39				7	9		1
Whimbrel	*Numenius phaeopus*	71	1		1	108	17		
Curlew	*Numenius arquata*	117	24		5	18	197		
Upland Sandpiper	*Bartramia longicauda*								
Terek Sandpiper	*Xenus cinereus*								
Common Sandpiper	*Actitis hypoleucos*	68	4		1	77	70	1	
Spotted Sandpiper	*Actitis macularius*	1		1					
Green Sandpiper	*Tringa ochropus*		1			5	59		
Solitary Sandpiper	*Tringa solitaria*								
Spotted Redshank	*Tringa erythropus*					2	3		
Greater Yellowlegs	*Tringa melanoleuca*								
Greenshank	*Tringa nebularia*	3	1			10	14		
Lesser Yellowlegs	*Tringa flavipes*								
Marsh Sandpiper	*Tringa stagnatilis*								
Wood Sandpiper	*Tringa glareola*					12	19		1
Redshank	*Tringa totanus*	116	21		17	76	288	4	4
Turnstone	*Arenaria interpres*	277	36		30	7	96	1	15
Wilson's Phalarope	*Phalaropus tricolor*								
Red-necked Phalarope	*Phalaropus lobatus*						5		
Grey Phalarope	*Phalaropus fulicarius*	2				5	3		
Pomarine Skua	*Stercorarius pomarinus*						1		
Arctic Skua	*Stercorarius parasiticus*						3949		
Long-tailed Skua	*Stercorarius longicaudus*					1			
Great Skua	*Stercorarius skua*						3195		1
Ivory Gull	*Pagophila eburnea*								
Sabine's Gull	*Xema sabini*	1		1		1			
Kittiwake	*Rissa tridactyla*	1269	939		3	36	7083		14
Slender-billed Gull	*Chroicocephalus genei*								
Bonaparte's Gull	*Chroicocephalus philadelphia*								
Black-headed Gull	*Chroicocephalus ridibundus*	1			1635	1724	48		2
Little Gull	*Hydrocoloeus minutus*					5			1
Ross's Gull	*Rhodostethia rosea*								

Gibraltar Point	Hilbre	Holme	The Isle of May	Land-guard	North Ronaldsay	Portland	Sandwich Bay	Spurn	Walney	Total ringed	Number of obs' ringed at
127	180			3	538	1	1228	52	4	2271	11
										1	1
										0	0
25					17		10	48	2	291	10
										2	1
										0	0
								1		3	3
										2	2
					3			3		14	5
										0	0
23		3	1		8		18	51		156	9
										0	0
	158		666	11	325	9	38	10		1622	12
754	1546	55	20	2	558	21	1076	9771	22	15806	18
										0	0
						1				3	3
6		4	1		10		11	11	4	105	9
15	1	3	8		141	2	17	32	3	418	16
27		57	12	3	721	15	205	42	78	1871	16
										2	1
										0	0
82	2	31	107	61	38	22	41	134	9	1130	17
5	1		1		1			2	2	14	8
15	1				1	2	1	9		85	10
2			5	1	2		8			216	10
4	7		67		204		20	12	4	679	12
										0	0
										0	0
36		7	3	2	4	5	379	13	14	679	15
										2	2
5		8	2		2	1	68	2		153	10
										0	0
1					1		1			8	5
										0	0
5		6	1		4		24	7		75	10
										0	0
										0	0
2		3	1		1		17	9	1	66	10
135	129	20	216	2	178	1	455	502	19	2183	17
8	336		592	13	527	2	688	147		2775	15
										0	0
										5	1
					1	6			2	19	6
							2	1		4	3
				1	12					3962	3
					1		1			3	3
		1			8					3205	4
										0	0
										3	3
			13989		3	5	1411	4		24756	11
										0	0
										0	0
204	1	66	3	227	1200	7	3298	4	3	8423	15
					1					7	3
										0	0

Common Name	Scientific Name	Bardsey	Calf of Man	Cape Clear	Copeland	Dungeness	Fair Isle	Filey	Flamborough
Laughing Gull	*Larus atricilla*								
Franklin's Gull	*Larus pipixcan*								
Mediterranean Gull	*Larus melanocephalus*				2	2			
Audouin's Gull	*Larus audouinii*								
Common Gull	*Larus canus*		1		1235	182	239		1
Ring-billed Gull	*Larus delawarensis*								
Lesser Black-backed Gull	*Larus fuscus*	2737	309	819	1051	4	1460		
Herring Gull	*Larus argentatus*	8789	12860	326	4396	126	4488		9
Yellow-legged Gull	*Larus michahellis*					1			
Caspian Gull	*Larus cachinnans*								
Iceland Gull	*Larus glaucoides*						1		
Glaucous Gull	*Larus hyperboreus*						40		
Great Black-backed Gull	*Larus marinus*	861	2473	349	261	14	2854		
Sooty Tern	*Onychoprion fuscata*								
Bridled Tern	*Onychoprion anaethetus*								
Little Tern	*Sternula albifrons*	1				66			
Gull-billed Tern	*Gelochelidon nilotica*								
Caspian Tern	*Hydroprogne caspia*								
Whiskered Tern	*Chlidonias hybrida*								
Black Tern	*Chlidonias niger*					73			
White-winged Black Tern	*Chlidonias leucopterus*								
Sandwich Tern	*Sterna sandvicensis*				46	10			
Lesser Crested Tern	*Sterna bengalensis*								
Forster's Tern	*Sterna forsteri*								
Common Tern	*Sterna hirundo*				387	1837	482		
Roseate Tern	*Sterna dougallii*				78	2			
Arctic Tern	*Sterna paradisaea*				3432	8	11753		
Guillemot	*Uria aalge*	1800	618	3	4	3	37059		11
Brunnich's Guillemot	*Uria lomvia*								
Razorbill	*Alca torda*	4554	1288	3			11493		6
Great Auk	*Pinguinus impennis*								
Black Guillemot	*Cepphus grylle*	2		3	527		1667		
Little Auk	*Alle alle*				1	2	14		3
Puffin	*Fratercula arctica*	1320	7				13576		3
Pallas's Sandgrouse	*Syrrhaptes paradoxus*								
Rock Dove	*Columba livia*	2					130		
Stock Dove	*Columba oenas*	1	2		228	121		1	11
Woodpigeon	*Columba palumbus*	160	26	9	4	190	74	47	33
Collared Dove	*Streptopelia decaocto*	50	44	1	4	281	389	1	6
Turtle Dove	*Streptopelia turtur*	36	15	2	9	94	83		
Rufous Turtle Dove	*Streptopelia orientalis*								
Mourning Dove	*Zenaida macroura*		1						
Ring-necked Parakeet	*Psittacula krameri*								
Great Spotted Cuckoo	*Clamator glandarius*								
Cuckoo	*Cuculus canorus*	83	110		23	377	109		
Yellow-billed Cuckoo	*Coccyzus americanus*								
Barn Owl	*Tyto alba*	7				8		16	7
Scops Owl	*Otus scops*		1	1			2		
Snowy Owl	*Bubo scandiacus*						1		
Little Owl	*Athene noctua*	90				54			1
Tawny Owl	*Strix aluco*							2	33
Long-eared Owl	*Asio otus*	21	21	3	13	42	257	7	19
Short-eared Owl	*Asio flammeus*		57	1		2	18		
Tengmalm's Owl	*Aegolius funereus*								
Nightjar	*Caprimulgus europaeus*	3				2	5		

Gibraltar Point	Hilbre	Holme	The Isle of May	Land-guard	North Ronaldsay	Portland	Sandwich Bay	Spurn	Walney	Total ringed	Number of obs' ringed at
										0	0
										0	0
				9			69			82	4
										0	0
64		12	1	51	356	1	473	8		2624	13
							1			1	1
			9472	7	25	1	3		416	16304	12
		1	38208	14	63	42	839	25	422	70608	15
										1	1
										0	0
					2					3	2
					1					41	2
			348		120	5	46	1	1729	9061	12
										0	0
										0	0
308		31		7	9		27	646	34	1129	9
										0	0
										0	0
										0	0
										73	1
										0	0
7		428	2363		123		17	2	8	3004	9
										0	0
										0	0
10		59	1219		1	111	67	37	71	4281	11
			14			4				98	4
2			1161		3276		1	37	13	19683	9
2	5	3	16274		11	9	45	28	2	55877	16
										0	0
1			1671		1	5	5	4	1	19032	12
										0	0
					1034		1			3234	6
5		2	1	3	9	1	6	13	2	62	13
1		1	36343					2		51253	8
										0	0
			2		587					721	4
79		27		3	1	16	124	25	3	642	14
285	4	89	3	839	49	261	423	230	3	2729	18
27	42	80	32	506	119	53	1116	133	21	2905	18
114		69	19	48	38	55	215	46	1	844	15
										0	0
										1	1
							2			2	1
								1		1	1
228	12	54	76	40	8	31	190	325	16	1682	15
				1		1		1		3	3
49		107	1	3		3	38	18	9	266	12
						1				5	4
										1	1
12		8		40		51	81	10	21	368	10
14		33		1		3	7	7		100	8
27		3	139	64	112	8	71	105	4	916	17
12	1		16		2	3	4	12	2	130	12
								1		1	1
2	1	3		2		3	10	3		34	10

Common Name	Scientific Name	Bardsey	Calf of Man	Cape Clear	Copeland	Dungeness	Fair Isle	Filey	Flamborough
Egyptian Nightjar	*Caprimulgus aegyptius*								
Chimney Swift	*Chaetura pelagica*								
Needle-tailed Swift	*Hirundapus caudacutus*								
Swift	*Apus apus*	30	1		1	131	19	1	1
Pallid Swift	*Apus pallidus*								
Pacific Swift	*Apus pacificus*								
Alpine Swift	*Apus melba*								
Little Swift	*Apus affinis*								
Kingfisher	*Alcedo atthis*	1				19		1	
Bee-eater	*Merops apiaster*								
Roller	*Coracias garrulus*								
Hoopoe	*Upupa epops*	2	4	1	1		3		
Wryneck	*Jynx torquilla*	32	22	5	1	4	248	5	5
Green Woodpecker	*Picus viridis*	1				109			1
Yellow-bellied Sapsucker	*Sphyrapicus varius*			1					
Great Spotted Woodpecker	*Dendrocopos major*	14	3		1	164	29	23	20
Lesser Spotted Woodpecker	*Dendrocopos minor*					1			
Calandra Lark	*Melanocorypha calandra*								
Bimaculated Lark	*Melanocorypha bimaculata*								
Black Lark	*Melanocorypha yeltoniensis*								
Lesser Short-toed Lark	*Calandrella rufescens*								
Short-toed Lark	*Calandrella brachydactyla*						9		
Crested Lark	*Galerida cristata*								
Woodlark	*Lullula arborea*					5	3		
Skylark	*Alauda arvensis*	595	60	4	23	921	1372		4
Shore Lark	*Eremophila alpestris*					1	5		
Sand Martin	*Riparia riparia*	15	49	4	16	2571	8	51	20
Swallow	*Hirundo rustica*	1252	3238	505	4970	4116	265	22	702
House Martin	*Delichon urbicum*	29	67	19	1290	4452	142	2	190
Red-rumped Swallow	*Cecropis daurica*								
Cliff Swallow	*Petrochelidon pyrrhonota*								
Richard's Pipit	*Anthus richardi*	1					12		
Blyth's Pipit	*Anthus godlewskii*						2		
Tawny Pipit	*Anthus campestris*					3	3		
Olive-backed Pipit	*Anthus hodgsoni*						10		2
Tree Pipit	*Anthus trivialis*	126	450	3	26	182	669	8	7
Pechora Pipit	*Anthus gustavi*						9	1	
Meadow Pipit	*Anthus pratensis*	1817	12829	415	3109	4240	11350	323	45
Red-throated Pipit	*Anthus cervinus*						9		
Rock Pipit	*Anthus petrosus*	1149	219	63	574	5	9913	2	88
Water Pipit	*Anthus spinoletta*								
Buff-bellied Pipit	*Anthus rubescens*								
Yellow Wagtail	*Motacilla flava*	14	1		4	403	11	7	50
Citrine Wagtail	*Motacilla citreola*						6		
Grey Wagtail	*Motacilla cinerea*	13	372	33	4	5	50		4
Pied Wagtail	*Motacilla alba*	556	1088	286	104	252	841	11	841
Waxwing	*Bombycilla garrulus*		1			4	68	2	
Dipper	*Cinclus cinclus*						17		
Wren	*Troglodytes troglodytes*	3509	3768	770	3331	3458	970	653	1205
Grey Catbird	*Dumetella carolinensis*								
Dunnock	*Prunella modularis*	1422	2013	722	774	4371	2704	1092	1560
Alpine Accentor	*Prunella collaris*								
Rufous Bush Chat	*Cercotrichas galactotes*								
Robin	*Erithacus rubecula*	3741	8278	1345	2561	9885	9333	1180	2549
Rufous-tailed Robin	*Luscinia sibilans*						1		

Gibraltar Point	Hilbre	Holme	The Isle of May	Land-guard	North Ronaldsay	Portland	Sandwich Bay	Spurn	Walney	Total ringed	Number of obs' ringed at
										0	0
										0	0
										0	0
5		124	4	7	2	30	147	295		798	15
										0	0
										0	0
										0	0
										0	0
63		54		14		10	154	5		321	9
					1					1	1
										0	0
			1		1	3		1		17	9
62		34	177	20	35	71	31	167	2	921	17
9		60		79		7	223		1	490	9
										1	1
109		231	22	89	12	8	393	93	3	1214	16
1		1		3			25			31	5
										0	0
										0	0
										0	0
										0	0
			1					4		14	3
										0	0
								2		10	3
920	125	115	44	40	601	313	650	883	164	6834	17
33			2					23		64	5
438		804		14	1	301	30706	773	2	35773	16
7499	157	1470	348	2494	377	10653	17632	6208	599	62507	18
250	1	212	6	1593	61	5881	24324	353	1	38803	18
		1								1	1
										0	0
			1		2		1	5		22	6
				1		2				5	3
			1			2	2	3		14	6
			2		4	1	1	1		21	7
111	35	8	394	89	41	138	118	122	56	2583	18
								1		11	3
2423	1141	248	2540	1351	710	1857	2307	27936	2460	77101	18
								1		10	2
14	8	2	3134	3	113	290	35	32	2	15646	18
							5			5	1
										0	0
60	2	6	1	32		332	4095	53	32	5103	16
					1					7	2
3			6	126	4	257	19	11	25	932	15
81	93	46	824	48	218	469	354	166	176	6454	18
4		2	12	1	23		2	32		151	11
										17	1
5141	1352	1852	2028	1791	686	3316	4605	3645	2458	44538	18
										0	0
15355	135	3675	1881	3472	434	3011	4632	10003	1433	58689	18
						1				1	1
										1	1
1										1	1
5827	1097	3939	9067	6972	1566	5250	11132	13827	4041	101590	18
										1	1

Common Name	Scientific Name	Bardsey	Calf of Man	Cape Clear	Copeland	Dungeness	Fair Isle	Filey	Flamborough
Thrush Nightingale	*Luscinia luscinia*		1	1		3	35		1
Nightingale	*Luscinia megarhynchos*	28	8	2	1	306	30	1	2
Siberian Rubythroat	*Luscinia calliope*						2		
Bluethroat	*Luscinia svecica*		9		2	39	296	8	22
Siberian Blue Robin	*Luscinia cyane*								
Red-flanked Bluetail	*Tarsiger cyanurus*	1					2		1
White-throated Robin	*Irania gutturalis*								
Black Redstart	*Phoenicurus ochruros*	73	96	16	20	1009	164	5	19
Redstart	*Phoenicurus phoenicurus*	642	1283	19	182	3478	1876	172	271
Whinchat	*Saxicola rubetra*	130	720	2	103	1329	666	10	70
Stonechat	*Saxicola torquatus*	832	2274	254	21	621	61	7	15
Isabelline Wheatear	*Oenanthe isabellina*								
Wheatear	*Oenanthe oenanthe*	1880	2937	32	374	4605	17638	10	48
Pied Wheatear	*Oenanthe pleschanka*						1		1
Black-eared Wheatear	*Oenanthe hispanica*					1	3		
Desert Wheatear	*Oenanthe deserti*								
Rock Thrush	*Monticola saxatilis*						1		
White's Thrush	*Zoothera dauma*				1		1		
Siberian Thrush	*Zoothera sibirica*								
Hermit Thrush	*Catharus guttatus*						1		
Swainson's Thrush	*Catharus ustulatus*								
Grey-cheeked Thrush	*Catharus minimus*	2		3			2		
Veery	*Catharus fuscescens*								
Ring Ouzel	*Turdus torquatus*	108	294	2	22	321	511	8	15
Blackbird	*Turdus merula*	9207	15174	757	4288	14275	24253	2819	3460
Eyebrowed Thrush	*Turdus obscurus*	1					1		
Dusky Thrush	*Turdus eunomus*						1		
Black-throated Thrush	*Turdus atrogularis*						1		
Fieldfare	*Turdus pilaris*	168	236	1	40	71	655	32	8
Song Thrush	*Turdus philomelos*	3146	7158	369	1353	5076	3134	696	561
Redwing	*Turdus iliacus*	5082	1489	40	241	1656	9590	460	328
Mistle Thrush	*Turdus viscivorus*	11	227	3	15	379	99	1	7
American Robin	*Turdus migratorius*								
Cetti's Warbler	*Cettia cetti*					56			
Fan-tailed Warbler	*Cisticola juncidis*								
Pallas's Grasshopper Warbler	*Locustella certhiola*			1			13		
Lanceolated Warbler	*Locustella lanceolata*	2					39	1	
Grasshopper Warbler	*Locustella naevia*	1687	368	4	121	129	143	7	16
River Warbler	*Locustella fluviatilis*						9		1
Savi's Warbler	*Locustella luscinioides*						5		
Aquatic Warbler	*Acrocephalus paludicola*			1		3	25		
Sedge Warbler	*Acrocephalus schoenobaenus*	10110	4974	168	1209	11775	553	153	687
Paddyfield Warbler	*Acrocephalus agricola*	1				1	10		1
Blyth's Reed Warbler	*Acrocephalus dumetorum*	1					12		2
Marsh Warbler	*Acrocephalus palustris*	5	4			4	145	1	9
Reed Warbler	*Acrocephalus scirpaceus*	120	26	112	3	11044	330	62	99
Great Reed Warbler	*Acrocephalus arundinaceus*	2	1			3	7		
Thick-billed Warbler	*Acrocephalus aedon*						2		
Eastern Olivaceous Warbler	*Hippolais pallida*			1			1		
Booted Warbler	*Hippolais caligata*	2				1	8		2
Sykes's Warbler	*Hippolais rama*						2		
Icterine Warbler	*Hippolais icterina*	32	13	14	1	42	124	13	19
Melodious Warbler	*Hippolais polyglotta*	77	17	18	3	40	13		3
Blackcap	*Sylvia atricapilla*	3942	2058	421	240	4527	6019	447	802
Garden Warbler	*Sylvia borin*	1506	619	125	93	3453	3786	228	278
Barred Warbler	*Sylvia nisoria*	16	26	2	3	9	445	3	8

Gibraltar Point	Hilbre	Holme	The Isle of May	Land-guard	North Ronaldsay	Portland	Sandwich Bay	Spurn	Walney	Total ringed	Number of obs' ringed at
1		5	16	2	3	1	2	6		77	13
17	1	13	11	108	2	115	231	23	1	900	18
										2	1
10	1	2	184	8	27	21	20	56	1	706	16
										0	0
			1	1	1					7	6
										0	0
33	16	17	175	511	12	142	116	395	20	2839	18
1614	353	720	2899	776	217	2379	1267	3552	352	22052	18
467	151	56	955	123	32	298	1179	867	242	7400	18
55	36	47	80	26	2	637	210	231	278	5687	18
				2						2	1
351	436	57	1228	745	879	472	337	1310	109	33448	18
					1	1		1		5	5
			2							6	3
				1		1				2	2
								1		2	2
					1					3	3
			1		1					2	2
										1	1
							1			1	1
						1				8	4
					1					1	1
71	19	34	319	121	119	73	56	327	8	2428	18
18278	1537	7588	21696	15965	6892	6634	13518	56120	2616	225077	18
										2	2
										1	1
					1					2	2
944	6	789	624	209	349	60	383	2612	37	7224	18
5786	760	1891	6536	5500	1262	3361	5779	10290	1419	64077	18
2500	113	632	4851	1661	5641	1039	1454	11647	470	48894	18
233	9	74	17	23	9	8	1135	46	6	2218	18
										0	0
4		44		3		7	301		1	416	7
										0	0
					1	1		1		17	5
				1	1			1		45	6
23	233	22	104	18	6	395	266	39	87	3668	18
					1			1		12	4
					2		4	1		12	4
		1	4			11	6	6		57	8
1223	598	2079	1280	554	36	3645	20489	661	662	60856	18
			1	1	1			1	1	18	9
1			2		6	4		3		31	8
	1		24	10	15	10	14	23	1	266	14
2037	7	4004	117	975	80	1056	28184	366	15	48637	18
					1		5	1		20	7
										2	1
			1			3	1			7	5
			1			3		6	1	24	8
					2	1				5	3
23	2	14	89	29	52	42	41	76	4	630	18
	2		4	6	3	118	5		11	320	14
4230	242	2446	3124	4171	2097	9498	14819	5823	633	65539	18
1695	139	1066	2509	1307	964	4228	2686	2716	372	27770	18
63		30	202	10	85	19	16	157	8	1102	17

Common Name	Scientific Name	Bardsey	Calf of Man	Cape Clear	Copeland	Dungeness	Fair Isle	Filey	Flamborough
Lesser Whitethroat	*Sylvia curruca*	153	86	16	5	3963	830	97	122
Orphean Warbler	*Sylvia hortensis*								
Asian Desert Warbler	*Sylvia nana*								1
Whitethroat	*Sylvia communis*	6145	6033	203	914	16711	1045	256	237
Spectacled Warbler	*Sylvia conspicillata*								
Dartford Warbler	*Sylvia undata*					18			
Marmora's Warbler	*Sylvia sarda*								
Ruppell's Warbler	*Sylvia rueppelli*								
Subalpine Warbler	*Sylvia cantillans*	15	16	1	1	3	31		1
Sardinian Warbler	*Sylvia melanocephala*	1	1			2	1	1	1
Greenish Warbler	*Phylloscopus trochiloides*	4	7	3		4	24	1	1
Arctic Warbler	*Phylloscopus borealis*	2					33		1
Pallas's Warbler	*Phylloscopus proregulus*	11	2	1		24	4	8	15
Yellow-browed Warbler	*Phylloscopus inornatus*	61	30	92	3	38	166	23	41
Hume's Warbler	*Phylloscopus humei*						1		2
Radde's Warbler	*Phylloscopus schwarzi*	2			1	3	1	2	6
Dusky Warbler	*Phylloscopus fuscatus*	2	2			8	7	1	6
Western Bonelli's Warbler	*Phylloscopus bonelli*	7	2	3		3	2		
Wood Warbler	*Phylloscopus sibilatrix*	102	72	19	6	150	113	2	14
Chiffchaff	*Phylloscopus collybita*	14723	8066	1408	1596	17189	1472	264	699
Iberian Chiffchaff	*Phylloscopus ibericus*								
Willow Warbler	*Phylloscopus trochilus*	46652	36547	1274	8362	34991	4013	868	1428
Goldcrest	*Regulus regulus*	27257	37111	3726	5833	12173	1829	3401	4629
Firecrest	*Regulus ignicapilla*	236	57	61	4	1659	2	15	56
Spotted Flycatcher	*Muscicapa striata*	3469	4054	152	318	1121	827	36	69
Asian Brown Flycatcher	*Muscicapa dauurica*						1		
Red-breasted Flycatcher	*Ficedula parva*	44	16	17	1	24	60	5	17
Taiga Flycatcher	*Ficedula albicilla*								1
Collared Flycatcher	*Ficedula albicollis*	1					2	1	
Pied Flycatcher	*Ficedula hypoleuca*	1000	347	208	19	2250	997	156	203
Bearded Tit	*Panurus biarmicus*						90		7
Long-tailed Tit	*Aegithalos caudatus*	248	185	24	6	349		810	312
Blue Tit	*Cyanistes caeruleus*	955	1653	576	6	4273	2	1310	2481
Great Tit	*Parus major*	528	1016	240	17	1900	14	545	1286
Coal Tit	*Periparus ater*	303	334	215	51	297	1	149	77
Willow Tit	*Poecile montana*	1				1		2	10
Marsh Tit	*Poecile palustris*					12		2	1
Nuthatch	*Sitta europaea*	3							
Treecreeper	*Certhia familiaris*	44	57	5	18	22	1	14	93
Short-toed Treecreeper	*Certhia brachydactyla*					8			
Penduline Tit	*Remiz pendulinus*	1							
Golden Oriole	*Oriolus oriolus*	20	5	3		4	8		
Brown Shrike	*Lanius cristatus*						1		
Isabelline Shrike	*Lanius isabellinus*	1					2		
Red-backed Shrike	*Lanius collurio*	9	10	3	1	18	253	4	16
Lesser Grey Shrike	*Lanius minor*						7		
Great Grey Shrike	*Lanius excubitor*	1	3			10	114		3
Southern Grey Shrike	*Lanius meridionalis*						2		
Woodchat Shrike	*Lanius senator*	10	3		1	8	13	1	
Jay	*Garrulus glandarius*	4				62		6	
Magpie	*Pica pica*	373	389	27	97	273		10	6
Nutcracker	*Nucifraga caryocatactes*								
Chough	*Pyrrhocorax pyrrhocorax*	481	371						
Jackdaw	*Corvus monedula*	406	19	2	704	177	13		3
Rook	*Corvus frugilegus*		7		32	954	8		1
Carrion Crow	*Corvus corone*	296	1		1	307		4	7
Hooded Crow	*Corvus cornix*		93	20	52	2	48		

Gibraltar Point	Hilbre	Holme	The Isle of May	Land-guard	North Ronaldsay	Portland	Sandwich Bay	Spurn	Walney	Total ringed	Number of obs' ringed at
3216	29	397	726	1260	180	642	3681	804	56	16263	18
						1				1	1
						1		1		3	3
9630	638	667	3106	2214	81	7369	4596	4940	1710	66495	18
				1						1	1
	1			1		26	4			50	5
								1		1	1
										0	0
1	2		7	7	5	8	1	11	1	111	16
2				1	1			1		12	10
3		5	10	2	1	4	2	13	2	86	16
2			3	7		1		5		54	8
4	1	13	5	24	1	10	22	39	1	185	17
24	8	36	102	23	68	25	51	134	6	931	18
						2		3		8	4
		2	3	3	1	8	3	9		44	13
		1	1	2		4	6	6		46	12
			2	1		3		3		26	9
58	8	6	65	73	61	68	70	72	8	967	18
1334	1302	1128	1665	3842	720	15303	13295	1971	1274	87251	18
						2		1		3	2
16050	10790	1968	14754	8259	1304	43509	13557	7936	9707	261969	18
11668	2604	4436	6771	5416	1590	7420	10808	18350	4341	169363	18
89	17	86	12	590	3	1083	777	132	18	4897	18
576	174	149	1008	878	308	1871	542	1017	318	16887	18
										1	1
11	2	12	73	10	25	27	16	104	6	470	18
										1	1
		1								5	4
1565	30	579	2219	656	258	1326	1472	3625	81	16991	18
6		173				7	3525	30		3838	7
1347	85	2045	65	647	6	171	1777	574	148	8799	17
7117	167	4863	6	1999	4	1117	8534	3483	1336	39882	18
3046	26	2796	15	2057	4	1026	4106	1639	160	20421	18
149	19	558	9	49	1	17	199	132	73	2633	18
120		77		3		2	61	53		330	10
5		79		2			59	2	1	163	9
1		3		1		3	5	2		18	7
59	6	58	44	9	2	36	188	38	13	707	18
						1	4			13	3
							2			3	2
1				1	4	8	5	2		61	11
										1	1
		1			2	1	1	2		10	7
10		1	150	14	77	16	32	70		684	16
		1					1	2		11	4
9		5	55	3	11		6	40	1	261	13
				1						3	2
	1	1	2	1		11	2	7	1	62	14
21		22		14		3	152	7		291	9
138	2	21		43		66	177	47	87	1756	15
		1								1	1
										852	2
204		133	2	2	1	35	105	20	69	1895	16
		2	3		1	2	118	17	1	1146	12
	13		11	1	1	18	172	10	5	847	14
1					16					232	7

Common Name	Scientific Name	Bardsey	Calf of Man	Cape Clear	Copeland	Dungeness	Fair Isle	Filey	Flamborough
Raven	*Corvus corax*	69	5	1	11		29		
Starling	*Sturnus vulgaris*	5484	1615	51	3561	14776	28627	75	348
Rose-coloured Starling	*Pastor roseus*	1					3		
House Sparrow	*Passer domesticus*	476	164	568	20	10344	1766	139	474
Spanish Sparrow	*Passer hispaniolensis*								
Tree Sparrow	*Passer montanus*	11	91		24	2484	118	579	528
Red-eyed Vireo	*Vireo olivaceus*	1		5		1			
Chaffinch	*Fringilla coelebs*	12113	8251	189	847	1978	3193	668	1211
Brambling	*Fringilla montifringilla*	655	39	9	11	272	3890	118	133
Serin	*Serinus serinus*		1				1		
Citril Finch	*Serinus citrinella*						1		
Greenfinch	*Carduelis chloris*	2277	2893	643	287	17216	515	5296	2013
Goldfinch	*Carduelis carduelis*	593	1590	50	276	2446	20	328	686
Siskin	*Carduelis spinus*	218	368	442	75	126	569	26	38
Linnet	*Carduelis cannabina*	1512	2255	191	1619	6978	193	1109	3211
Twite	*Carduelis flavirostris*	1	3		70	6	6329		15
Common Redpoll	*Carduelis flammea*	13	9			1	757	16	5
Lesser Redpoll	*Carduelis cabaret*	580	564	18	2356	2826	36	90	8
Arctic Redpoll	*Carduelis hornemanni*						23	2	
Two-barred Crossbill	*Loxia leucoptera*						7		
Common Crossbill	*Loxia curvirostra*	2	10	3	2	4	538	6	7
Parrot Crossbill	*Loxia pytyopsittacus*						37		
Trumpeter Finch	*Bucanetes githagineus*								
Common Rosefinch	*Carpodacus erythrinus*	23	11	5	2	3	235	1	4
Pine Grosbeak	*Pinicola enucleator*								
Bullfinch	*Pyrrhula pyrrhula*	39	4	17	2	368	300	66	181
Hawfinch	*Coccothraustes coccothraustes*	3	4	2		5	26		1
Black-and-white Warbler	*Mniotilta varia*								
Blue-winged Warbler	*Vermivora pinus*								
Tennessee Warbler	*Vermivora peregrina*						2		
Northern Parula	*Parula americana*								
Yellow Warbler	*Dendroica petechia*								
Blackburnian Warbler	*Dendroica fusca*								
Yellow-rumped Warbler	*Dendroica coronata*		1	2					
Blackpoll Warbler	*Dendroica striata*	2		2					
American Redstart	*Setophaga ruticilla*								
Northern Waterthrush	*Seiurus noveboracensis*								
Common Yellowthroat	*Geothlypis trichas*								
Summer Tanager	*Piranga rubra*	1							
Scarlet Tanager	*Piranga olivacea*				1				
Lark Sparrow	*Chondestes grammacus*								
Savannah Sparrow	*Passerculus sandwichensis*						2		
Fox Sparrow	*Passerella iliaca*				1				
Song Sparrow	*Melospiza melodia*	1	1				3		
White-crowned Sparrow	*Zonotrichia leucophrys*						1		
White-throated Sparrow	*Zonotrichia albicollis*	1					2		
Dark-eyed Junco	*Junco hyemalis*	1				1			
Lapland Bunting	*Calcarius lapponicus*	7		1		3	49		
Snow Bunting	*Plectrophenax nivalis*	1		1	3	3	675		
Black-faced Bunting	*Emberiza spodocephala*								
Pine Bunting	*Emberiza leucocephalos*						3		
Yellowhammer	*Emberiza citrinella*	78	12	96	7	584	72	75	272
Cirl Bunting	*Emberiza cirlus*								
Rock Bunting	*Emberiza cia*								
Ortolan Bunting	*Emberiza hortulana*	3	1	1		6	20		

Gibraltar Point	Hilbre	Holme	The Isle of May	Land-guard	North Ronaldsay	Portland	Sandwich Bay	Spurn	Walney	Total ringed	Number of obs' ringed at
					8					123	6
3942	498	1633	2581	16973	4078	3427	18107	24064	1936	131776	18
1			1							6	4
7872	477	339	136	6892	1742	7128	7761	25105	382	71785	18
				1						1	1
4242	70	210	61	89	10	89	1854	12821	50	23331	17
								1		8	4
3208	626	2696	1739	3358	891	1341	5354	10402	1030	59095	18
866	26	485	2078	468	2193	152	479	4839	9	16722	18
						7	6			15	4
										1	1
6834	705	9149	341	21585	107	11828	14387	21289	2821	120186	18
3431	203	1107	53	3293	6	3182	3880	1860	1888	24892	18
708	7	266	751	152	265	93	213	939	8	5264	18
3383	2253	721	528	11453	4502	14965	7081	13635	1558	77147	18
173			10		206	1	46	45	10	6915	13
1	3	6	16	40	301	2	18	428		1616	15
3428	259	212	301	858	11	136	3597	2171	32	17483	18
			1		13			10		49	5
			2		1					10	3
21		46	62	10	162	1	1	78		953	16
							1	3		41	3
										0	0
3		1	63	4	91	5		22		473	15
			1							1	1
795	3	416	14	115	124	225	1391	41	87	4188	18
1		1	4	9	11	5	3	18		93	14
										0	0
										0	0
										2	1
						1				1	1
						1				1	1
										0	0
										3	2
										4	2
1										1	1
1						1				2	2
										0	0
										1	1
										1	1
										0	0
						1				3	2
										1	1
									1	6	4
										1	1
								1	1	5	4
										2	2
			8		5	3	57	13		146	9
257	13		4	55	113		401	2214	5	3745	13
										0	0
					3					6	2
791	7	186	53	161	16	66	699	588	7	3770	18
			2		1	6		1		10	4
										0	0
			8	4	2	7	1	5		58	11

Common Name	Scientific Name	Bardsey	Calf of Man	Cape Clear	Copeland	Dungeness	Fair Isle	Filey	Flamborough
Cretzschmar's Bunting	*Emberiza caesia*						1		
Yellow-browed Bunting	*Emberiza chrysophrys*						1		
Rustic Bunting	*Emberiza rustica*		1	1		1	17	1	1
Chestnut-eared Bunting	*Emberiza fucata*						1		
Little Bunting	*Emberiza pusilla*	6	2	1		1	35	1	5
Yellow-breasted Bunting	*Emberiza aureola*	1					6		
Reed Bunting	*Emberiza schoeniclus*	257	759	45	263	2596	498	93	778
Pallas's Reed Bunting	*Emberiza pallasi*						2		
Black-headed Bunting	*Emberiza melanocephala*	3					4		
Corn Bunting	*Emberiza calandra*				1	80	4		70
Rose-breasted Grosbeak	*Pheucticus ludovicianus*	1		1					
Indigo Bunting	*Passerina cyanea*			1					
Bobolink	*Dolichonyx oryzivorus*			1					
Baltimore Oriole	*Icterus galbula*		1						
Number of Birds ringed		248686	220047	32169	101717	270286	350190	26232	36554
Number of species ringed		190	154	124	138	208	271	110	147

Gibraltar Point	Hilbre	Holme	The Isle of May	Land-guard	North Ronaldsay	Portland	Sandwich Bay	Spurn	Walney	Total ringed	Number of obs' ringed at
										1	1
										1	1
1			7	2	4			1		37	11
										1	1
			7	2	7	3	1	6		77	13
			6	1	1					15	5
4010	81	974	333	29	324	106	3989	3631	768	19534	18
										2	1
			1		2	1				11	5
61			2	2		307	341	541		1409	10
		1								3	3
										1	1
										1	1
										1	1
182889	34004	75920	267388	147215	73329	192280	347865	346507	52563	3005841	
171	98	159	182	157	211	193	217	229	135	370	

APPENDIX 2: BIRDS NEW TO BRITAIN AND IRELAND WHICH WERE RECORDED AT BIRD OBSERVATORIES

by Steve Stansfield, Deryk Shaw and Richard Brown

Between them the observatories – and those ornithologists working the areas long before the observatories were formed – have been responsible for adding a total of 56 species to the avifauna list of Britain and Ireland.

Bardsey

Summer Tanager – On 11 September 1957, a first-winter male was found by R. Moss and later trapped by J. D. Gray in the Lane trap. The bird was present until the 25th.

Yellow Warbler – On 29 August 1964, a first-year male was trapped in the observatory garden by George Evans and Roger Durman, having been seen earlier in the day by Hugh Miles.

Calf of Man

White-throated Robin – A male on 22 June 1983 was found by Adrian del Nevo, J. R. Calladine and M. W. Watson. It was seen on a wall for about five minutes but then disappeared and could not be relocated.

Mourning Dove – On 31 October 1989, Aron Sapsford found a small dove in the observatory's Heligoland trap, but could not identify the bird. It was trapped and later identified by Ian Fisher. The bird was underweight, exhausted and died the following day.

Cape Clear

Fan-tailed Warbler – Found and seen only by J. T. R. Sharrock near the East Bog on Ballyieragh on 23 April 1962.

Rose-breasted Grosbeak – A first-winter male was discovered on 7 October 1962 at Trawkieran by M. P. L. Fogden and J. T. R. Sharrock. The bird was still present in an overgrown field the following day.

Little Swift – One was observed hawking insects between the North and South Harbours on the evening of 12 June 1967 by J. T. R. Sharrock.

Bulwer's Petrel – On 3 August 1975, during an evening's sea-watch in light mist from Blananarragaun, M. R. Alibone and several others watched as it headed west some 200 metres from the island.

Indigo Bunting – One found on 9 October 1985 was trapped and ringed on the 11th. The bird was present to the 19th.

Grey Catbird – Found by K. Preston near the South Harbour on 4 November 1986. The bird was seen very briefly before disappearing.

Blue-winged Warbler – A first-year male was found by Dennis Weir in Cotter's Garden on 4 October 2000, the day after Hurricane Isaac hit south-western Ireland.

Copeland

Fox Sparrow – Found by John Wilde and trapped on 3 and 4 June 1961, it was identified subsequently from the in-hand descriptions and confirmed by comparison with skins at the British Museum.

Scarlet Tanager – One trapped on 12 October 1963 was originally identified as a tanager sp. It was not until 1986 that the bird was accepted as the first record of Scarlet Tanager for Britain and Ireland.

Dungeness

Short-toed Treecreeper – One was trapped by R. E. Scott at dusk on 27 September 1969 and retrapped on the 30th. The bird was identified using biometric measurements.

Audouin's Gull – Found by David Walker on 5 May 2003 as it flew along the beach from the east.

Fair Isle

Red-rumped Swallow – First seen by George Stout on 2 June 1905 and found dead some 10 days later.

Lanceolated Warbler – Shot by William Eagle Clarke on 9 September 1908. Initially believed to be a young Grasshopper Warbler, it was re-examined following Clarke's receipt of a specimen from Orkney in 1910.

Blyth's Reed Warbler – Found by Mary, Duchess of Bedford on 29 September 1910, and shot the following day by George Stout of Busta and his brother, Stewart Stout.

Thrush Nightingale – Shot by Jerome Wilson at the South Light on 15 May 1911. Mary, Duchess of Bedford, noted in her diary 'Wilson shot what Mr Eagle Clarke says is a Nightingale. It does not seem to me nearly russet enough for our common one'. Clarke later correctly identified it.

Pine Bunting – Shot by Jerome Wilson on 30 October 1911 and sent to William Eagle Clarke at the National Museum of Scotland for identification.

. **Pechora Pipit** – First seen at Gaila by James A. Stout on 23 September 1925 and shot on the 24th by John Stenhouse. James Stout was first drawn to the bird by its unfamiliar call when flushed. Pechora Pipit was an addition to the British List for which Stenhouse had been hoping, based on knowledge of the species' breeding distribution. On retrieving the corpse, Stenhouse said 'James, I think this could be Pechora'.

Paddyfield Warbler – This bird was seen by John Stenhouse, George 'Fieldy' Stout and Jerome Wilson on 26 September 1925 and was shot by G. Stout on 1 October.

Pallid Harrier – A second-summer male identified by George Stout on 24 April 1931 was shot by J. A. Stout on 8 May. It was sent to the National Museum of Scotland but the keeper of natural history questioned the identity. George Stout wrote an indignant reply, so it was sent to the British Museum in London, where Norman Kinnear confirmed what George already knew!

Booted Warbler – One was shot by George Stout on 3 September 1936.

Grey-cheeked Thrush – Found by Willie Eunson, who saw it feeding in front of the Observatory trap on 5 October 1953. After trapping and some research, the bird was identified by Ken Williamson, and aged as a first-winter. It was roosted over-night, but was not seen again after its release in the morning.

Citrine Wagtail – One was trapped in the Gully late in the evening of 20 September 1954 and examined in failing light by Horace Alexander, Miss M. Haydock, Henry Mayer-Gross, Mrs A. W. Thom, Valerie Thom and Ken Williamson. It was first thought to be a young Yellow Wagtail with an atypical blue-grey mantle. It was roosted overnight and tentatively identified as a Citrine Wagtail the next day. It remained for four days and was followed by the second for Britain only one week later. Identification was confirmed when skins were checked in the Bird Room of the Natural History Museum in November of that year.

Thick-billed Warbler – Trapped on 6 October 1955, at Leogh, using a Yeoman net and a small portable catching-box, and examined by observers including Herbert Axell, James Ferguson-Lees, Valerie Thom and Ken Williamson. It arrived during 'classic' autumn fall conditions, with south-east winds over the North Sea, rain and the occluded front of an Atlantic depression lying over the Northern Isles. It was not seen the following day. There has been one subsequent Fair Isle record, in 2003, and two more on Shetland – they are the only British records.

Southern Grey Shrike – Found by Ken Williamson on 21 September 1956, at Haa, and trapped later when the identity was confirmed as Great Grey Shrike of the desert race from Central Asia. At the time, Southern Grey Shrike was considered to be conspecific with Great Grey Shrike and has only been considered as a separate species by the BOURC since 1994. British records have concerned the Central-Asian race *Lanius meridionalis pallidirostris*, usually known as Steppe Grey Shrike.

Song Sparrow – Found by Roy Dennis at Ward Hill on 27 April 1959 and subsequently trapped. It remained around the observatory after its release and was occasionally heard in song until 10 May.

Sykes's Warbler – Trapped in the Gully on 29 August 1959 by Roy Dennis and J. Bazey and identified with Peter Davis in the ringing room. The bird was then recorded as a Booted Warbler of the race *Hippolais caligata rama* as the two species were considered conspecific at the time. It remained until the 31st.

River Warbler – The first was caught in the Warbler Ditch, Lower Leogh, on 24 September 1961. The bird was found and trapped by Gordon Barnes, Peter Davis, R.M. Nedderman and Peter Slater and was identified as a first-winter. It was released in Gilsetter and was seen the following day at Lower Stonybreck.

Cretzschmar's Bunting – First discovered when flushed by Roy Dennis, Bill Landells and Mikael Kristersson while trying to record Corncrakes at Gaila on 10 June 1967. It was not seen for four days until it was relocated and trapped in the same area by Roy Dennis on the 14th. The bird was aged as a first-summer male and released near the observatory the next day. It remained until the 20th.

Hermit Thrush – Found in a newly-ploughed field at Field by Stephen Rumsey and Harold Nash on 2 June 1975. After carefully noting the bird's features, they attracted the attention of other observers. The bird remained approachable for the rest of the day but was not seen again.

Tennessee Warbler – Amazingly, the first and second British records of this species were on Fair Isle in the same autumn. The first was seen briefly by Chris Heard and Grahame Walbridge at Finniquoy on 6 September 1975. It was relocated the next day in a crop at the south of the island. It was trapped on the 18th when it was aged as a first-winter bird and remained until the 20th. The second bird was found calling loudly at the mouth of the Observatory trap by Roger Broad on 24 September but was found to be unringed.

Siberian Rubythroat – Found around the North Grind trap by Simon Cook, Andy Lowe and Pete Roberts on 9 October 1975. After the arrival of the warden, Roger Broad, it was caught at the Plantation. The bird was originally sexed as a male due to traces of red in its white throat-patch but is now considered to have been a first-winter female.

American Kestrel – On 25 May 1976, an adult male was seen by several observers who reported an 'odd-looking kestrel' before it was finally identified by A. M. Taylor. It was last seen on the 27th. This bird remains the only Scottish record and one of only two British records – the other arriving in Cornwall just a few weeks after the Fair Isle bird.

Pallas' Reed Bunting – First found on 29 September 1976 near Skerryholm, by Roger Broad, it was seen by only one other observer that day and remained unidentified. It was not until the following day that Pallas' Reed Bunting was suggested by Bill Oddie and Andy

Lowe, although the identity proved difficult to confirm in the field as the bird was an adult female. It was finally trapped on 10 October when its identity was verified. It remained for one further day.

White-crowned Sparrow – Initially trapped in Double Dyke trap by John Potter on 15 May 1977, its identity was confirmed by Roger Broad and Mike Peacock. Although it was a first for Britain, a second followed several days later in East Yorkshire.

Asian Brown Flycatcher – On 1 July 1992, Paul Harvey discovered a plain-looking flycatcher in the Plantation. The bird was seen to move into the trap when its identification as this species was suspected. This was confirmed back in the ringing room with other observers, including Roger Riddington, Roy Taylor, Steve Votier and Nick Dymond.

Chestnut-eared Bunting – On 15 October 2004, an 'odd-looking Little-type Bunting' was reported in the Skadan bird-crop by Hywel Maggs. It was still present the following day but not showing well. It was trapped by the warden, Deryk Shaw, and after some head-scratching was identified in the ringing room by a combined effort from Deryk Shaw, Alan Bull, Rebecca Nason and Phil Harris. It stayed until the 20th and remains the only Western Palearctic record.

Rufous-tailed Robin – On 23 October 2004, a small chat resembling a young European Robin was found near the road in Johnny Arcus' Park by FIBO Director, Mike Wood. It was trapped, ringed and aged as described in the Fair Isle chapter.

Filey

Harlequin Duck – A male was found dead in 1862 by Mr Whitaker and is now in Mansfield Museum.

Rufous-tailed Robin on Fair Isle in October 2004. This first for the Western Palearctic was found just a week after another first: Chestnut-eared Bunting (see p. 560) (Rebecca Nason – www.rebeccanason.com).

Spectacled Warbler – Craig Thomas and Richard Harbird found a small *Sylvia* warbler on 24 May 1992 along the Long Hedge. The bird was trapped and identification was confirmed in the hand. Several earlier British claims of this species have been subsequently re-identified as Subalpine Warblers.

Flamborough

Taiga Flycatcher – Early on 26 April 2003 Andrew Lassey found an apparent male Red-breasted Flycatcher, but could not immediately work out why the red on the throat was so restricted and the bird had a brown-looking cap. Whilst he was photographing the bird, Ian Marshal arrived and between them they decided the bird was probably a Taiga Flycatcher. Mike Pearson was alerted and the bird was quickly trapped and identification confirmed in the hand. It remained at South Landing until 29 April.

Isle of May

Pied Wheatear – A first-winter male, shot on 19 October 1909, belonged to the nominate race *Oenanthe pleschanka pleschanka*, is now at the National Museum of Scotland (NMSZ 1910.9).

Isabelline Shrike – On 26 September 1950, W. U. Flower and M. I. Kinnear found a pale shrike near the Lighthouse. Identification was confirmed as this species when their descriptions were compared with skins in the National Museum of Scotland in Edinburgh. The bird was an adult male.

Siberian Thrush – A male was glimpsed at dusk on 1 October 1954, but not positively identified. It was trapped the following day by D. G. Andrew, J. A. Nelder and Mary Hawkes and was still present on 4 October when they left the island.

The Chestnut-eared Bunting on Fair Isle in October 2004 (Rebecca Nason – www.rebeccanason.com).

Eastern Olivaceous Warbler – One was found by D. A. I. Baty, W. M. Morrison and A. D. K. Ramsay on 24 September 1967, when it was trapped and ringed. It remained until the 27th when it was killed by a Great Grey Shrike. The specimen was preserved and subsequently attributed by K. Williamson and others to the south-east European and south-west Asiatic race *Hippolais pallida elaeica*.

Landguard

Lark Sparrow – One was discovered by Trevor Charlton and his wife, Lesley, on 30 June 1981. The bird remained until 8 July.

Portland

Orphean Warbler – On 20 September 1955, one was trapped by K. B. Rooke and J. F. Monk and wasn't seen in the field except on release. At the time it was considered to be the fifth or sixth record for Britain and Ireland, though, following a review of the 'Hastings' and 'Tadcaster' rarities this record became the first for Britain and Ireland.

Calandra Lark – J. S. Ash found the bird on 2 April 1961 and it was seen by a further 22 observers. It was present for the whole day and left with Skylarks at dusk.

Asian Desert Warbler – On the morning of 16 December 1970, Grahame Walbridge found an umber-coloured *Sylvia* warbler. He returned with Frank Clafton and, having relocated the bird, it was trapped and roosted overnight. It was identified as a Desert Warbler when its description was compared with the literature. It spent the next two weeks around the observatory and was last seen on 2 January 1971.

Savannah Sparrow – On 11 April 1982, Gary Edwards saw a small bird 15 metres away. Although he and three other observers watched it for about one minute before it disappeared beneath a rock, none was able to identify it. About 10 minutes later, a group of observers, which included Keith L. Fox and Ron King, noticed a small, streaky passerine on some nearby rocks. Their views too, were brief, as the bird quickly disappeared. Some suggested that it was a Little Bunting. In the afternoon, S. J. Broyd saw the bird and immediately identified it as a Savannah Sparrow. The bird was thought to belong to the race *Passerculus sandwichensis princeps*, also known as Ipswich Sparrow. It was last seen on 16 April.

Lesser Short-toed Lark – On 2 May 1992, Ian Dickie found a small passerine that he thought was a small lark, as he was leading a YOC group round Portland. The bird flew off and was lost from view. Ian returned later and relocated the bird. Eventually, excellent views were obtained and a 'half-inch' primary projection was seen by about 20 observers, confirming this to be the first acceptable Lesser Short-toed Lark for Britain and Ireland.

Spurn

Penduline Tit – R. J. Raines (RJR) and A. A. Bell located a small bird that was alarm-calling at a Fox on 22 October 1966. The bird was identified immediately by RJR. When the observers returned to the area with others, the bird could not be relocated. On 28 October, what was presumably the same individual was found about three kilometres to the north, near Kilnsea.

Black Lark – On 27 April 1984, Barry Spence (BRS) and Nick Bell (NAB) saw a bird in the Parade Ground that they could not identify. An attempt to trap the bird in a single-shelf net was unsuccessful. The bird then flew over the River Humber towards the Lincolnshire coast and was not seen again. The observers thought the bird was an escaped cage bird. In 1990, NAB saw a plate depicting Black Lark in volume 5 of The Birds of the Western Palearctic (Cramp 1988) which revived memories of the Spurn bird, but he could not locate his own notes. In 1996, he discovered his note book in the attic of his mother's house, which included a description and sketch of the bird. BRS had discarded his notes in the meantime. Despite suspecting that the bird had to be a Black Lark, they decided that NAB's notes alone would not stand up to modern-day scrutiny by BBRC. However, in 2000, the hand-written bird logs that had been in the possession of John Cudworth were returned to Spurn and the then observatory warden, Dave Boyle, was surprised to find further notes from NAB in the log. The record was submitted to BBRC in 2000, but pended on first circulation and further details requested. Following a conversation with NAB, another observer, Alex Cruickshanks, submitted his own notes, having independently identified the bird as a Black Lark. By now, BBRC had three sets of notes to work with and the record was eventually accepted.

APPENDIX 3: NON-AVIAN SPECIES MENTIONED IN THE TEXT

The following lists give common names in the standardised form used throughout the text of the book, followed by the scientific names. The names of mammals follow Harris & Yalden (2008), the names of moths follow Bradley (2000) and the names of plants follow Stace, C. (1997).

Mammals

American Mink	*Mustela vison*
Atlantic White-sided Dolphin	*Leucopleurus acutus*
Badger	*Meles meles*
Bank Vole	*Myodes glareolus*
Barbastelle	*Barbastella barbastellus*
Bottlenose Dolphin	*Tursiops truncatus*
Brown Hare	*Lepus europaeus*
Brown Long-eared Bat	*Plecotus auritus*
Chinese Water Deer	*Hydropotes inermis*
Common Dolphin	*Delphinus delphis*
Common Pipistrelle	*Pipistrellus pipistrellus*
Common Rat	*Rattus norvegicus*
Common Seal	*Phoca vitulina*
Common Shrew	*Sorex araneus*
Daubenton's Bat	*Myotis daubentonii*
Eurasian Beaver	*Castor fiber*
European Roe Deer	*Capreolus capreolus*
False Killer Whale	*Pseudorca crassidens*
Feral Cat	*Felis catus*
Field Vole	*Microtus agrestis*
Fin Whale	*Balaenoptera physalus*
Fox	*Vulpes vulpes*
Greater Horseshoe Bat	*Rhinolophus ferrumequinum*
Grey Long-eared Bat	*Plecotus austriacus*
Grey Seal	*Halichoerus grypus*
Grey Squirrel	*Sciurus carolinensis*
Harbour Porpoise	*Phocoena phocoena*
Harp Seal	*Pagophilus groenlandica*
Harvest Mouse	*Micromys minutus*
Hedgehog	*Erinaceus europaeus*
House Mouse	*Mus domesticus*
Humpback Whale	*Megaptera novaeangliae*
Killer Whale	*Orcinus orca*
Loghtan Sheep	*Ovis aries*
Long-finned Pilot Whale	*Globicephala melas*
Minke Whale	*Balaenoptera acutorostrata*
Mole	*Talpa europaea*
Nathusius' Pipistrelle	*Pipistrellus nathusii*
Natterer's Bat	*Myotis nattereri*
Noctule	*Nyctalus noctula*
Northern Bottlenose Whale	*Hyperoodon ampullatus*
Otter	*Lutra lutra*
Pygmy Shrew	*Sorex minutus*
Rabbit	*Oryctolagus cuniculus*

Red Deer	*Cervus elaphus*
Reeves' Muntjac	*Muntiacus reevesi*
Risso's Dolphin	*Grampus griseus*
Sei Whale	*Balaenoptera borealis*
Serotine	*Eptesicus serotinus*
Soprano Pipistrelle	*Pipistrellus pygmaeus*
Sperm Whale	*Physeter macrocephalus*
Stoat	*Mustela erminea*
Water Shrew	*Neomys fodiens*
Water Vole	*Arvicola terrestris*
Weasel	*Mustela nivalis*
Whiskered Bat	*Myotis mystacinus*
White-beaked Dolphin	*Lagenorhynchus albirostris*
Wood Mouse	*Apodemus sylvaticus*
Yellow-necked Mouse	*Apodemus flavicollis*

Fish

Basking Shark	*Cetorhinus maximus*
Butterfish	*Pholis gunnellus*
Herring	*Clupea harengus*
Small or Lesser Sand Eel	*Ammodytes tobianus*
Sunfish	*Mola mola*

Reptiles and amphibians

Adder	*Vipera berus*
Common Frog	*Rana temporaria*
Common Lizard	*Zootoca vivipara*
Common (Smooth) Newt	*Triturus vulgaris*
Common Toad	*Bufo bufo*
Common Wall Lizard	*Podarcis muralis*
Grass Snake	*Natrix natrix*
Great Crested Newt	*Triturus cristatus*
Leatherback Turtle	*Dermochelys coriacea*
Marsh Frog	*Rana ridibunda*
Natterjack Toad	*Bufo calamita*
Ocellated Lizard	*Timon lepidus*
Palmate Newt	*Triturus helveticus*
Slow-worm	*Anguis fragilis*

Insects

Adonis Blue	*Polyommatus bellargus*
Annulet	*Charissa obscurata*
Antler Moth	*Cerapteryx graminis*
Ant-lion	*Eurolean nostras*
Azure Damselfly	*Coenagrion puella*
Banded Demoiselle	*Calopteryx splendens*
Bath White	*Pontia daplidice*
Bedstraw Hawkmoth	*Hyles gallii*
Birch Shield-bug	*Elasmostelthus interstinctus*
Black Darter	*Sympetrum danae*

Black-tailed Skimmer	*Orthetrum cancellatum*
Blue-tailed Damselfly	*Ischnura elegans*
Bordered Straw	*Heliothis peltigera*
Brimstone	*Gonepteryx rhamni*
Brindled Ochre	*Dasypolia templi*
Broad-bodied Chaser	*Libellula depressa*
Brown Argus	*Aricia agestis*
Brown Hawker	*Aeshna grandis*
Brown-tail	*Euproctis chrysorrhoea*
Camberwell Beauty	*Nymphalis antiopa*
Cepero's Groundhopper	*Tetrix ceperoi*
Chalk Carpet	*Scotopteryx bipunctaria cretata*
Chalkhill Blue	*Polyomattus coridon*
Chimney Sweeper	*Odezia atrata*
Cinnabar	*Tyria jacobaeae*
Clouded Magpie	*Abraxas sylvata*
Clouded Yellow	*Colias croceus*
Coast Dart	*Euxoa cursoria*
Comma	*Polygonia c-album*
Common Blue	*Polyommatus icarus*
Common Blue Damselfly	*Enallagma cyathigerum*
Common Darter	*Sympetrum striolatum*
Common Groundhopper	*Tetrix undulata*
Common Hawker	*Aeshna juncea*
Confused	*Apamea furva britannica*
Convolvulus Hawkmoth	*Agrius convolvuli*
Crescent Dart	*Agrotis trux*
Crescent Striped	*Apamea oblonga*
Dark Green Fritillary	*Argynnis aglaja*
Dark Sword-grass	*Agrotis ipsilon*
Death's Head Hawkmoth	*Acherontia atropos*
Delicate	*Mythimna vitellina*
Dewick's Plusia	*Macdunnoughia confusa*
Dog's Tooth	*Lacanobia suasa*
Downy Emerald	*Cordulia aenea*
Drinker	*Euthrix potatoria*
Dusky Peacock	*Macaria signaria*
Elephant Hawkmoth	*Deilephila elpenor*
Emerald Damselfly	*Lestes sponsa*
Emperor Dragonfly	*Anax imperator*
Emperor Moth	*Saturnia pavonia*
Essex Skipper	*Thymelicus lineola*
Eyed Hawkmoth	*Smerinthus ocellata*
Feathered Ranunculus	*Polymixis lichenia*
Fern	*Horisme tersata*
Flame Wainscot	*Mythimna flammea*
Four-spotted	*Tyta luctuosa*
Four-spotted Chaser	*Libellula quadrimaculata*
Fox Moth	*Macrothylacia rubi*
Gatekeeper	*Pyronia britanniae*
Gem	*Orthonama obstipata*
Golden Twin-spot	*Chrysodeixis chalcites*
Golden-ringed Dragonfly	*Cordulegaster boltonii*
Grayling	*Hipparchia semele*
Great Brocade	*Eurois occulta*

Great Dart	*Agrotis crassa*
Green Arches	*Anaplectoides prasina*
Green Hairstreak	*Callophrys rubi*
Green Tiger Beetle	*Cicindela campestris*
Green-veined White	*Pieris napi*
Grey	*Hadena caesia* ssp. *mananii*
Grey Bush Cricket	*Platycleis albopunctata*
Grizzled Skipper	*Pyrgus malvae*
Gypsy Moth	*Lymantria dispar*
Hairy Dragonfly	*Brachytron pratense*
Harlequin Ladybird	*Harmonia axyridis*
Holly Blue	*Celastrina argiolus*
Hornet	*Vespa crabro*
Hoverfly species	*Eupeodes lundbecki*
Hummingbird Hawkmoth	*Macroglossum stellatarum*
Kent Black Arches	*Meganola albula*
Large Red Damselfly	*Pyrrhosoma nymphula*
Large Skipper	*Ochlodes sylvanus*
Large Tortoiseshell	*Nymphalis polychloros*
Large White	*Pieris brassicae*
Leaf-miner species	*Stigmella repentiella*
Lesser Emperor	*Anax parthenope*
Long-winged Conehead	*Conocephalus discolor*
Lulworth Skipper	*Thymelicus action*
Lunar Hornet Moth	*Sesia bembeciformis*
Lyme Grass	*Chortodes elymi*
Magpie	*Abraxas grossulariata*
Mallow	*Larentia clavaria*
Many-lined	*Costaconvexa polygrammata*
Marbled Clover	*Heliothis viriplaca*
Marbled White	*Melanargia galathea*
Marsh Moth	*Athetis pallustris*
Marsh Pug	*Eupithecia pygmaeata*
Meadow Brown	*Maniola jurtina*
Micromoth species	*Cydia amplana*
Micromoth species	*Ethmia bipunctella*
Micromoth species	*Melissoblaptes zelleri*
Micromoth species	*Gelechia hippophaella*
Migrant Hawker	*Aeshna mixta*
Minotaur Beetle	*Typhaeus typheous*
Monarch	*Danaus plexippus*
Moth species	*Pima boisduvaliella*
Moth species	*Agonopterix curvipunctosa*
Mottled Grasshopper	*Myrmeleotettix maculates*
Narrow-bordered Five-spot Burnet	*Zygaena lonicerae*
Netted Pug	*Eupithecia venosata*
Ni Moth	*Trichoplusia ni*
Norfolk Hawker	*Aeshna isosceles*
Norwegian Wasp	*Dolichovespula norvegica*
Oak Eggar	*Lasiocampa quercus*
Oak Processionary	*Thaumetopoea processionea*
Orache Moth	*Trachea atriplicis*
Orange Footman	*Eilema sororcula*
Orange-tip	*Anthocharis cardamines*
Ornate Shield-bug	*Eurydema ornatum*

Painted Lady	*Vanessa cardui*
Pale Clouded Yellow	*Colias hyale*
Pale Grass Eggar	*Lasiocampa trifolii f. flava*
Pale Pinion	*Lithophane hepatica*
Pale-shouldered Cloud	*Actinotia hyperici*
Peacock	*Inachis io*
Pearly Underwing	*Peridroma saucia*
Pigmy Footman	*Eilema pygmaeola pallifrons*
Pine Beauty	*Panolis flammea*
Pine Hawkmoth	*Hyloicus pinastri*
Poplar Hawkmoth	*Laothoe populi*
Portland Moth	*Actebia praecox*
Portland Ribbon Wave	*Idaea degeneraria*
Privet Hawkmoth	*Sphinx ligustri*
Pseudoscorpion	*Dinocheirus* spp.
Pyralid moth	*Gymnancyla canella*
Red Admiral	*Vanessa atalanta*
Red Sword-grass	*Xylena vetusta*
Red-eyed Damselfly	*Erythromma najas*
Red-necked Footman	*Atolmis rubricollis*
Red-tailed Sand Wasp	*Ammophila sabulosa*
Red-veined Darter	*Sympetrum fonscolombii*
Ringlet	*Alphantopus hyperantus*
Roesel's Bush Cricket	*Metrioptera roeselii*
Ruddy Darter	*Sympetrum sanguineum*
Rush Veneer	*Nomophila noctuella*
Rusty-dot Pearl	*Udea ferrugalis*
Sand Dart	*Agrotis ripae*
Sandhopper	*Gammarus* spp.
Sandy Carpet	*Perizoma flavofasciata*
Scaly Cricket	*Pseudomogoplistes vincentae*
Scarce Bordered Straw	*Helicoverpa armigera*
Scarce Chaser	*Libellula fulva*
Scarce Merveille du Jour	*Moma alpium*
Scarce Pug	*Eupithecia extensaria*
Scarce Silver Y	*Syngrapha interrogationis*
Scarlet Tiger	*Callimorpha dominula*
Sexton Beetle	*Nicrophorus humator*
Shore Wainscot	*Mythimna litoralis*
Short-winged Conehead	*Conocephalus dorsalis*
Silver Y	*Autographa gamma*
Silver-studded Blue	*Plebeius argus*
Six-spot Burnet	*Zygaena filipendulae*
Slender Groundhopper	*Tetrix subulata*
Small Blue	*Cupido minimus*
Small Copper	*Lycaena phlaeas*
Small Elephant Hawkmoth	*Deilephila porcellus*
Small Heath	*Coenonympha pamphilus*
Small Mottled Willow	*Spodoptera exigua*
Small Ranunculus	*Hecatera dysodea*
Small Red-eyed Damselfly	*Erythromma viridulum*
Small Skipper	*Thymelicus sylvestris*
Small Tortoiseshell	*Aglais urticae*
Small White	*Pieris rapae*
Southern Emerald Damselfly	*Lestes barbarus*

Southern Hawker	*Aeshna cyanaea*
Speckled Wood	*Pararge aegeria*
Spurge Hawkmoth	*Hyles euphorbiae*
Square-spot Dart	*Euxoa obelisca*
Star-wort	*Cucullia asteris*
Striped Hawkmoth	*Hyles livornica*
Sussex Emerald	*Thalera fimbrialis*
Swallowtail	*Papilio machaon*
Thistle Ermine	*Myelois cribrella*
Thrift Clearwing	*Synansphecia muscaeformis*
Toadflax Brocade	*Calophasia lunula*
Rusty Oak moth	*Cydia amplana*
True Lover's Knot	*Lycophotia porphyrea*
Vagrant Darter	*Sympetrum vulgatum*
Variable Damselfly	*Ceonagrion pulchellum*
Vestal	*Rhodometra sacraria*
Violet Carpenter Bee	*Xylocopa violacea*
Wall	*Lasiommata megera*
Wasp Spider	*Argiope bruennichi*
Water Boatman (bug) species	*Corixa iberica*
White Admiral	*Limenitis Camilla*
White Colon	*Sideridis albicolon*
White Spot	*Hadena albimacula*
White-letter Hairstreak	*Satyrium w-album*
White-line Dart	*Euxoa tritici*
White-point	*Mythimna albipuncta*
White-speck	*Mythimna unipuncta*
Yellow-winged Darter	*Sympetrum flaveolum*

Other Invertebrates

Portuguese (or Pacific) Oyster	*Crassostrea gigas*
Ross Coral	*Pentapora foliacea*

Plants

Fungus species	*Lepiota medullata*
Fungus species	*Lactarius lanceolatus*
Lichen species	*Anaptychia ciliaris subsp. mammillata*
Lichen species	*Lecanora straminea*
Lichen species	*Ramalina siliquosa*
Seaweed species	*Pterosiphonia complanata*
Seaweed species	*Grateloupia filicina*
Adder's-tongue	*Ophioglossum vulgatum*
Alder	*Alnus glutinosa*
Alexanders	*Smyrnium olusatrum*
Allseed	*Radiola linoides*
Alpine Bistort	*Polygonum viviparum*
Altar Lily	*Zantedeschia aethiopica*
Annual Sea-blite	*Suaeda maritima*
Ash	*Fraxinus excelsior*
Autumn Gentian	*Gentianella amarella*
Autumn Hawkbit	*Leontodon autumnalis*
Autumn Lady's-tresses	*Spiranthes spiralis*

Barometer Earthstar	*Astraeus hygrometricus*
Barren Strawberry	*Potentilla sterilis*
Beaked Tasselweed	*Ruppia maritima*
Bedstraw Broomrape	*Orobanche caryophyllacea*
Bee Orchid	*Ophrys apifera*
Beech	*Fagus sylvatica*
Bell Heather	*Erica cinerea*
Bird's-foot	*Ornithopus perpusillus*
Bittersweet	*Solanum dulcamara*
Blackening Waxcap	*Hygrocybe conica*
Bladderwrack	*Fucus vesiculosus*
Blinks	*Montia fontana*
Bloody Crane's-bill	*Geranium sanguineum*
Bluebell	*Hyacinthoides non-scripta*
Bog Pimpernel	*Anagallis tenella*
Bracken	*Pteridium aquilinum*
Brackish Water-crowfoot	*Ranunculus baudotii*
Bramble	*Rubus* sp.
Brookweed	*Samolus valerandi*
Broom	*Cytisus scoparius*
Buck's-horn Plantain	*Plantago coronopus*
Buddleja	*Buddleja* sp
Bur Medick	*Medicago minima*
Cat's-ear	*Hypochaeris radicata*
Chaffweed	*Anagallis minima*
Ciliate Strap-lichen	*Heterodermia leuchomelos*
Claytonia	*Claytonia* sp.
Common Bird's-foot-trefoil	*Lotus corniculatus*
Common Broomrape	*Orobanche minor*
Common Centaury	*Centaurium erythraea*
Common Chickweed	*Stellaria media*
Common Cord-grass	*Spartina anglica*
Common Cornsalad	*Valerianella locusta*
Common Fleabane	*Pulicaria dysenterica*
Common Knapweed	*Centaurea nigra*
Common Reed	*Phragmites australis*
Common Restharrow	*Ononis repens*
Common Saltmarsh-grass	*Puccinellia maritima*
Common Sea-lavender	*Limonium vulgare*
Common Sorrel	*Rumex acetosa*
Common Spotted-orchid	*Dactylorhiza fuchsii*
Common Stork's-bill	*Erodium cicutarium*
Common Water-starwort	*Callitriche stagnalis*
Coralroot Orchid	*Corallorrhiza trifida*
Corn Marigold	*Chrysanthemum segetum*
Corn Spurrey	*Spergula arvensis*
Corncockle	*Agrostemma githago*
Corsican Pine	*Pinus nigra* sp.
Cotoneaster	*Cotoneaster* sp.
Creeping Buttercup	*Ranunculus repens*
Creeping Thistle	*Cirsium arvense*
Creeping Willow	*Salix repens*
Cuckooflower	*Cardamine pratensis*
Curled Dock	*Rumex crispus*
Dame's-violet	*Hesperis matronalis*

Damson	*Prunus domestica ssp. insititia*
Danish Scurvygrass	*Cochlearia danica*
Dewberry	*Rubus caesius*
Dittander	*Lepidium latifolium*
Dodder	*Cuscuta epithymum*
Dog-rose	*Rosa canina*
Dove's-foot Crane's-bill	*Geranium molle*
Dune Fescue	*Vulpia fasciculata*
Dune Helleborine	*Epipactis leptochila var. dunensis*
Dwarf Willow	*Salix herbacea*
Early Forget-me-not	*Myosotis ramosissima*
Early Gentian	*Gentianella anglica*
Early Marsh-orchid	*Dactylorhiza incarnata*
Early Spider-orchid	*Ophrys sphegodes*
Elder	*Sambucus nigra*
Elecampane	*Inula helenium*
Elm	*Ulmus* spp.
English Scurvygrass	*Cochlearia anglica*
English Stonecrop	*Sedum anglicum*
Escallonia	*Escallonia macrantha*
Evening-primrose	*Oenothera* spp.
Evergreen Oak	*Quercus ilex*
Eyebright	*Euphrasia* spp.
Fairy Flax	*Linum catharticum*
Fairy Inkcap	*Coprinellus disseminatus*
False Oat-grass	*Arrhenatherum elatius*
Few-flowered Spike-rush	*Eleocharis quinqueflora*
Field Maple	*Acer campestre*
Field Mouse-ear	*Cerastium arvense*
Field Woundwort	*Stachys arvensis*
Floating Club-rush	*Eleogiton fluitans*
Foxglove	*Digitalis purpurea*
Fragrant Orchid	*Gymnadenia conopsea*
Frog Orchid	*Coeloglossum viride*
Fuchsia	*Fuchsia magellanica*
Fumitories	*Fumaria* spp.
Germander Speedwell	*Veronica chamaedrys*
Glassworts	*Salicornia* spp.
Glaucous Sedge	*Carex flacca*
Goat Willow	*Salix caprea*
Golden Hair Lichen	*Teloschistes flavicans*
Golden-samphire	*Inula crithmoides*
Gorse	*Ulex* sp.
Grass-of-Parnassus	*Parnassia palustris*
Great Mullein	*Verbascum thapsus*
Great Willowherb	*Epilobium hirsutum*
Greater Pond-sedge	*Carex riparia*
Greater Sea-spurrey	*Spurgularia media*
Greater Spearwort	*Ranunculus lingua*
Green-flowered Helleborine	*Epipactis phyllanthes*
Green-winged Orchid	*Orchis morio*
Grey Poplar	*Populus x canescens*
Hairy Bird's-foot-trefoil	*Lotus subbiflorus*
Hairy-fruited Cornsalad	*Valerianella eriocarpa*
Harebell	*Campanula rotundifolia*

Hare's-foot Clover	*Trifolium arvense*
Hawthorn	*Crataegus monogyna*
Hazel	*Corylus avellana*
Heath Bedstraw	*Galium saxatile*
Heather	*Calluna vulgaris*
Henbane	*Hyoscyamus niger*
Hoary Cress	*Lepidium draba*
Hogweed	*Heracleum sphondylium*
Holly	*Ilex aquifolium*
Hooker's Hebe	*Hebe brachysiphon*
Hop	*Humulus lupulus*
Hornwrack	*Flustra foliacea*
Horseshoe Vetch	*Hippocrepis comosa*
Hound's-tongue	*Cynoglossum officinale*
Indian Balsam	*Impatiens glandulifera*
Irish Spurge	*Euphorbia hyberna*
Isle of Man Cabbage	*Coincya monensis*
Ivy-leaved Crowfoot	*Ranunculus hederaceus*
Japanese Rose	*Rosa rugosa*
Jelly Ear	*Auricularia auricula - judae*
Kidney Vetch	*Anthyllis vulneraria*
Lady's Bedstraw	*Galium verum*
Lesser Burdock	*Arctium minus*
Lesser Celandine	*Ranunculus ficaria*
Lesser Marshwort	*Apium inundatum*
Lesser Sea-spurrey	*Spergularia marina*
Lesser Spearwort	*Ranunculus flammula*
Lesser Twayblade	*Listera cordata*
Lesser Water-parsnip	*Berula erecta*
Lesser Water-plantain	*Baldellia ranunculoides*
Little-Robin	*Geranium purpureum*
Lizard Orchid	*Himantoglossum hircinum*
Lodgepole Pine	*Pinus contorta*
Lousewort	*Pedicularis sylvatica*
Lyme-grass	*Leymus arenarius*
Marram	*Ammophila arenaria*
Marsh Cudweed	*Gnaphalium uliginosum*
Marsh Helleborines	*Epipactis palustris*
Marsh Pennywort	*Hydrocotyle vulgaris*
Marsh St John's-wort	*Hypericum elodes*
Marsh-mallow	*Althaea officinalis*
Marsh-marigold	*Caltha palustris*
Marsh-orchids	*Dactylorhiza* sp.
Meadowsweet	*Filipendula ulmaria*
Monbretia	*Crocosmia x crocosmiiflora*
Moonwort	*Botrychium lunaria*
Mountain Everlasting	*Antennaria dioica*
Mouse-ear-hawkweed	*Pilosella officinarum*
Mouse–ears	*Cerastium* spp.
Navelwort	*Umbilicus rupestris*
Nettle	*Urtica dioica*
New Zealand Flax	*Phormium tenax*
Nodding Bur-marigold	*Bidens cernua*
Northern Marsh-orchid	*Dactylorhiza purpurella*
Nottingham Catchfly	*Silene nutans*

Oak	*Quercus* sp.
Oraches	*Atriplex* spp.
Oysterplant	*Mertensia maritima*
Pale Butterwort	*Pinguicula lusitanica*
Parrot Waxcap	*Hygrocybe psittacina*
Parsley-piert	*Aphanes arvensis*
Pellitory-of-the-wall	*Parietaria judaica*
Pheasant's-eye	*Adonis annua*
Pink-sorrel	*Oxalis articulata*
Portland Hawkweed	*Hieracium portlandicum*
Portland Spurge	*Euphorbia portlandica*
Prickly Saltwort	*Salsola kali kali*
Procumbent Pearlwort	*Sagina procumbens*
Pyramidal Orchid	*Anacamptis pyramidalis*
Ragged-Robin	*Lychnis flos-cuculi*
Ragwort	*Senecio* spp.
Ray's Knotgrass	*Polygonoum oxyspermum*
Red Campion	*Silene dioica*
Red Fescue	*Festuca rubra*
Red Hemp-nettle	*Galeopsis angustifolia*
Red Valerian	*Centranthus ruber*
Rock Samphire	*Crithmum maritimum*
Rock Sea-lavender	*Limonium binervosum*
Rock Sea-lavender	*Limonium britannicum subsp. celticum var. pharense*
Rock Sea-spurrey	*Spergula rupicola*
Rosebay Willowherb	*Chamerion angustifolium*
Round-leaved Fluellen	*Kickxia spuria*
Round-leaved Crowfoot	*Batrachium omiophyllus*
Round-leaved Sundew	*Drosera rotundifolia*
Rowan	*Sorbus aucuparia*
Royal Fern	*Osmunda regalis*
Rue-leaved Saxifrage	*Saxifraga tridactylites*
Sand Couch	*Elytrigia juncea*
Scarlet Pimpernel	*Anagallis arvensis arvensis*
Scarlet Waxcap	*Hygrocybe coccinea*
Scots Lovage	*Ligusticum scoticum*
Scots Pine	*Pinus sylvestris*
Scottish Primrose	*Primula scotica*
Scurvygrass	*Cochlearia* spp.
Sea Aster	*Aster tripolium*
Sea Beet	*Beta vulgaris maritima*
Sea Bindweed	*Calystegia soldanella*
Sea Campion	*Silene uniflora*
Sea Club-rush	*Bolboschoenus maritimus*
Sea Couch	*Elytrigia atherica*
Sea Fern-grass	*Catapodium marinum*
Sea Pea	*Lathyrus japonicus*
Sea Plantain	*Plantago maritima*
Sea Rocket	*Cakile maritima*
Sea Sandwort	*Honckenya peploides*
Sea Spleenwort	*Asplenium marinum*
Sea Spurge	*Euphorbia paralias*
Sea Stork's-bill	*Erodium maritimum*
Sea Wormwood	*Artemisia maritima.*

Sea-buckthorn	*Hippophae rhamnoides*
Sea-heath	*Frankenia laevis*
Sea-holly	*Eryngium maritimum*
Sea-kale	*Crambe maritima*
Sea-lavender	*Limonium recurvum* subsp. *recurvum*
Sea-milkwort	*Glaux maritima*
Sea-purslane	*Atriplex portulacoides*
Seaside Centaury	*Centaurium littorale*
Sea-spurreys	*Spergularia* spp.
Selfheal	*Prunella vulgaris*
Sharp Rush	*Juncus acutus*
Sharp-leaved Fluellen	*Kickxia elatine*
Sheep's Sorrel	*Rumex acetosella*
Sheep's-bit	*Jasione montana*
Shepherd's Cress	*Teesdalia nudicaulis*
Shepherd's-needle	*Scandix pecten-veneris*
Shoreweed	*Littorella uniflora*
Shrubby Sea-blite	*Suaeda vera*
Silver Birch	*Betula pendula*
Silverweed	*Potentilla anserina*
Sitka Spruce	*Picea sitchensis*
Slender Trefoil	*Trifolium micranthum*
Small Adder's-tongue	*Ophioglossum azoricum*
Small Sweet-grass	*Glyceria declinata*
Small-flowered Buttercup	*Ranunculus parviflorus*
Southern Marsh-orchid	*Dactylorhiza praetermissa*
Spear-leaved Orache	*Atriplex prostrata*
Spindle	*Euonymus europaeus*
Spring Squill	*Scilla verna*
Spring Vetch	*Vicia lathyroides*
Springbeauty	*Claytonia perfoliata*
Stiff Sedge	*Carex bigelowii*
Stinking Goosefoot	*Chenopodium vulvaria*
Stinking Hawk's-beard	*Crepis foetida*
Stonecrop sp.	*Sedum* sp.
Suffocated Clover	*Trifolium suffocatum*
Sulphur Tufts	*Hypholoma fasciculare*
Swine-cress	*Coronopus squamatus*
Sycamore	*Acer pseudoplatanus*
Tamarisk	*Tamarix gallica*
Tassel Hyacinth	*Muscari comosum*
Thrift	*Armeria maritima*
Tormentil	*Potentilla erecta*
Traveller's-joy	*Clematis vitalba*
Tree-mallow	*Lavatera arborea*
Upright Chickweed	*Moenchia erecta*
Variegated Horsetail	*Equisetum variegatum*
Velvet Shank	*Flammulina velutipes*
Verdigris Agaric	*Stropharia aeruginosa*
Viper's-bugloss	*Echium vulgare*
Walney Geranium	*Geranium sanguineum* var. *lancastriense*
Wasp Orchid	*Ophrys apifera* var *trollii*
Weld	*Reseda luteola*
Western Clover	*Trifolium occidentale*
Western Gorse	*Ulex gallii*

Western Marsh-orchid	*Dactylorhiza majalis ssp. occidentalis*
White Heather	*Calluna vulgaris*
White Water-lily	*Nymphaea alba*
Whitebeam spp.	*Sorbus* spp.
Wild Asparagus	*Asparagus prostratus*
Wild Cabbage	*Brassica oleracea var. oleracea*
Wild Gooseberry	*Rubra* sp.
Wild Mignonette	*Reseda lutea*
Wild Onion	*Allium vineale*
Wild Pansy	*Viola tricolor*
Wild Privet	*Ligustrum vulgare*
Wild Thyme	*Thymus polytrichus*
Willow	*Salix* sp.
Wilson's Filmy-fern	*Hymenophyllum wilsonii*
Wood Blewit	*Lepista nuda*
Wood Sage	*Teucrium scorodonia*
Wood Small-reed	*Calamagrostis epigejos*
Woody Fleabane	*Dittrichia viscosa*
Wormwood	*Artemisia absinthium*
Yellow Bartsia	*Parentucellia viscosa*
Yellow Centaury	*Cicendia filiformis*
Yellow Horned-poppy	*Glaucium flavum*
Yellow Iris	*Iris pseudacorus*
Yellow Water-lily	*Nuphar lutea*
Yellow-rattle	*Rhinanthus minor*
Yellow-vetch	*Vicea lutea*
Yorkshire-fog	*Holcus lanatus*

APPENDIX 4: CURRENT AND FORMER
ACCREDITED BIRD OBSERVATORIES

Thirty bird observatories have been accredited since the Bird Observatories Sub-committee first started the process of accreditation back in 1946, of which the 18 described in this book are still operating. However, as can be seen below, only two have ceased to be accredited in the past 30 years. All 30 are listed below in order of accreditation with the year of closure (or loss of accredited status) for those no longer running. Some, such as Great Saltee, Sanda and Malin Head, had relatively short lives as accredited observatories. Others, such as Hilbre, had been running for decades before they sought accredited status.

The reasons for loss of accredited status are varied. Some ceased operating because essential people moved elsewhere and others, sadly of a rather frequent occurrence, due to lack of support from the next generation. A few have been affected by issues with land owners, which has stopped operations.

Observatory	Year of accreditation
Skokholm (founded 1933)	1946–1976
Isle of May (founded 1934)	1946–
Spurn (founded 1945)	1946–
Lundy (founded 1946)	1946–1975
Fair Isle (founded 1945)	1948–
Gibraltar Point (founded 1948)	1949–
Cley (founded 1949)	1950–1963
New Grounds* (founded 1946)	1950–1971
Monks' House (founded 1950)	1951–1961
Dungeness (founded 1950)	1952–
Jersey (St Ouen's Pond) (founded 1951)	1952–1971
Bardsey (founded 1953)	1954–
Copeland (founded 1954)	1956–
Saltee (founded 1951)	1958–1964
Cape Clear (founded 1959)	1959–
Tory Island (founded 1961)	1961–1971
Bradwell (founded 1961)	1961–1983
Sandwich Bay (founded 1952)	1962–
Portland (founded 1955)	1962–
Calf of Man (founded 1959)	1962–
St Agnes (founded 1961)	1962–1971
Walney (founded 1964)	1965–
Malin Head	1965 (one year only)
Holme (founded 1962)	1971–1979, 1995–
North Ronaldsay (founded 1985)	1987–
Landguard (founded 1982)	1997–
Filey (founded 1976)	1999–
Flamborough (founded 2000)	2000–
Sanda (founded 1990)	2003–2009
Hilbre (founded 1957)	2008–

*New Grounds was operated on the site of the Wildfowl & Wetlands Trust Centre at Slimbridge.
The accredited observatories do not have exclusive use of the title 'bird observatory'. There are quite a few well-known migration stations which call themselves a 'bird observatory' even though they do not have accredited status. This is no reflection on the activities which take place there, but merely suggests that they have not sought, or perhaps

considered, accredited status, or they may not meet all the requirements. The following is by no means an exhaustive list and there may well be many others:

Bodmin Moor
Bradwell
Heysham
Knaresborough
Selsey Bill
Sheringham
Welney
Whitburn

APPENDIX 5: OBSERVATORY WARDENS, ASSISTANT WARDENS, OTHER ASSISTANTS AND OFFICERS UP TO APRIL 2010

Bardsey

Wardens

Alan Till	1953	Viv and John Phillips	1983–1984
Roy Thearle	1954–1955	Tim Collins	1985–1988
Reg Arthur	1956–1960	Paddy Jenks	1988–1989
Frank Clafton	1961–1962	Simon Walker	1990–1991
Carolyn Pratt	1963	Paddy Jenks	1992
George Evans	1964–1970	Richard Humpidge	1993
David Henshilwood	1973–1975	Andrew Silcocks	1994–1997
Peter Roberts	1976–1982	Steve Stansfield	1998–2010
Martin Sutherland	1983		

Assistant Wardens

Mike Harris	1957	Ian Rendall	1993
Martin Richards	1957	Kester Wilson	1994
Alan Morley	1959	Ian Fisher	1995–1996
Trevor Lloyd-Evans	1965	Paul Massey	1997
Malcolm Wright	1966–1967	Dave Anning	1998–1999
Keith Redshaw	1968–1969	Ross McGregor	2000 (part)
Mike Peacock	1978–1979	Malte Iden	2000 (part)
Chester Rowley	1980	Rhys Dandy	2001–2002
Dave Suddaby	1981–1982	Julia Davies	2003–2004
Steve Anderson	1985–1987	Adrian George	2005
Dave Okines	1988–1989	David Wright	2006–2007
Richard Hesketh	1990	Richard Brown	2008–2010
Alan Leitch	1991–1992	Richard Else	2009–2010

Calf of Man

Wardens/Ornithological Wardens

Einar Brun	1959–1960	Aron Sapsford	1989–1990
Alan H. Morley	1962–1964	Norman McCanch	1991–1994
Peter Bennett	1965–1966	Jason Bishop	1994–1995
Michael Alexander	1967	Tim Bagworth	1996–2004
Malcolm Wright	1968–1974	Richard Cope	2005
Bob Haycock	1975–1977	Stephen Reeves	2006
Pete Jennings	1978–1981	Richard Cope	2006–2008
Adrian del Nevo	1982–1983	Oliver Slessor	2007
David Walker	1984–1988	Sarah Harris	2009–2010

Assistant Wardens/Estate Wardens/Countryside Wardens

Peter Evans	1960	Peter Howlett	1984–1985
Gordon Craine	1961–1962	Colin Davison	1986
Rodney Rayment	1963–1964	Paul Leader	1987
Roderick Thorne	1965	Aron Sapsford	1988
John Walmsley	1965	Ian Fisher	1989
Richard Lorand	1967	Paul Naylor	1990
Barrie Harding	1967	Jeff Stenning	1990

Russell Leavett	1968–1969	Kevin Scott	1991
Tim Jorgensen	1970	Monica McCanch	1992–1994
Bob Smith	1971	Nik Aspey	1995 & 1997
Steve Madge	1972	Jonathan Fairhurst	1995–1996
Bob Haycock	1973–1974	Andrew Coates	1997
Paul Pratley	1975	Des Robinson	2000–2002
Martin Sutherland	1976	Ben Jones	2002–2003
Mike Harris	1977	Belinda Lloyd	2004
Graham Elliott	1978	Sarah Pimm	2005
Jim Redwood	1979 & 1981	Ben McCallum	2006
Steve Davies	1980	Ian Lycett	2007–2008
Julian Thomas	1982	Tom Clark	2008
Christopher Briggs	1982	Sarah Harris	2008
John Calladine	1983	Gavin Devaney	2009–2010
Mark Watson	1983		

Cape Clear

Wardens

Various	1959–1962	Colin Rhind	1978–1982
P. A. Wright	1963	Tim Collins	1983
Various	1964–1966	Dave Borton	1984–1988
Tom Green	1967–1969	Dave Bird	1989–1991
Brian Fagg	1969	Dave Okines	1991–1992
Paul McCartney	1970–1971	Richard Humpidge	1992
Various	1972	Various	1993
R. P. Russell	1973	Alan D'Alton	1994
Various	1974	Dave Boyle	1995–1996
Ian Burrows	1975–1976	Nick Robinson	1997
Laurence Davenport	1977	Steve Wing	1998–2010

NB 'Various' denotes no employed warden when the observatory was run by a succession of temporary wardens – usually the birders themselves!

Copeland

Copeland has been managed and run by numerous willing and hard-working volunteers, of whom many are of long standing, but has never employed a warden.

Dungeness

Wardens

H. E. Axell	1954–1959	D. Buffery	1981–1982
R. E. Scott	1960–1976	S. McMinn	1982–1989
N. Riddiford	1976–1981	D. Walker	1989–2010

Fair Isle

Wardens

Ken Williamson	1948–1956	Paul Harvey	1989–1992
Peter Davis	1957–1963	Paddy Jenks	1993
Roy Dennis	1964–1970	Roger Riddington	1994–1997
Roger Broad	1971–1977	Paul Baker	1998

Iain Robertson	1978–1980	Deryk Shaw	1999–2010
Nick Riddiford	1981–1988		

Assistant Wardens

Peter Hope Jones	1957–1958	Paul Harvey	1984–1985
Roy Dennis	1959	Kevin Osborn	1984
Gordon Barnes	1960–1961	Kevin Shepherd	1985
Barry Spence	1962–1963	Mike Pennington	1986
Eddie Wiseman	1964–1965	Andy Whittaker	1986
Nick Dymond	1966	Dave Bird	1986
Bill Landells	1967	John Allan	1987
Tony Mainwood	1968	Simon Aspinall	1987
Kevin Armstrong	1969	Peter Howlett	1988–1989
Brian Marshall	1970	Peter Potts	1988
Iain Robertson	1970–1971	Chris Donald	1990
Eric Meek	1972	Arfon Williams	1991
Nick Riddiford	1973	Roger Riddington	1992
Ian Black	1974	Steve Votier	1992
David Frost (died)	1975	Alan Leitch	1993
Peter Roberts	1975	Nick Ward	1994
Tony Taylor	1976	Kester Wilson	1995
Mark Peacock	1977	Mark Newell	1996
Martin Sutherland	1977	Jane Reid	1997
Pete Ewins	1978	Charlie Holt	1998
Tony Williams	1978	Steve Turner	1999
Dorian Buffery	1979	Hywel Maggs	2000
Nigel Jones	1979	Paul French	2001–2002
Pete Ewins	1980	Torcuil Grant	2003
Adrian del Nevo	1980	Alan Bull	2004
David Borton	1981–1983	Mark Warren	2005–2006
Chester Rowley	1981	Mark Breaks	2007–2008
James Dickson	1982	Jack Ashton-Booth	2009–2010
Dave Suddaby	1983		

Seabird Assistants

Cliff Waller	1964	Bob Proctor	1990
John Davies	1966	Chris Orsman	1991
Anders Tengelin	1966	Ben Stammers	1993
John Ginnever	1969	Guy Thompson	1994
Digby Cyrus	1973	Chris Hewson	1995
John Davies	1973–1975	Steve Votier	1996
Jan Petterson	1976	Jenny Bull	1997
Dan Law	1978	Steve Turner	1998
Pete Ewins	1979	Charlie Holt	1999–2000
Frances White	1979–1980	Hywel Maggs	2001
Adrian del Nevo	1981	Simon Pinder	2002
Glen Tyler	1982–1983	Rebecca Nason	2003–2004
Dave Carter	1984	Rael Butcher	2005
Dave Suddaby	1985	Will Miles	2006
Kevin Osborn	1986–1987	Simon Davies	2007–2010
Andy Silcocks	1988–1989		

Rangers

Alan Bull	1999	Phil Knott	2006
Diana de Palacio	2000	Ben McCallum	2007

Chris Rodger	2001	Paul King	2008
Alan Bull	2002–2003	Rob Hughes	2008
Claire Bailly	2004	Carrie Marell Gunn	2010
Rory Tallack	2005		

Filey

Bird Recorders

Andrew M. Paterson	1977–1980	Lez Gillard	1995–2005
Peter J. Dunn	1980–1990	Craig C Thomas	2005–2008
Paul M. Scanlan	1990–1992	Peter J. Dunn	2008–2010
David J. Williams	1992–1995		

Ringing Officer

| Peter J. Dunn | 1983–2010 |

Flamborough

Flamborough has been managed and run by various willing and hard-working volunteers, many of long standing, and has never employed a warden.

Gibraltar Point

Ringer-in-charge

Lenton Ottaway	1949–1952	Bill Paul	1986–1996
F. R. Bean	1952–1954	Robin Cosgrove	1997–1999
Barrie Wilkinson	1955–1958 &	Adrian Blackburn	2000–2004
	1964–1976	Mark Grantham	2005–2007
Marson Peet	1958–1963	George Gregory	2008
Dick Lambert	1976–1986	Mick Briggs	2009–2010

Resident warden

A. Lodge	1961–1971	Phil Davey	1988–1991
K. Payne	1973–1976	Carl Hawke	1991–1994
Dick Lambert	1976–1986	Kevin Wilson	1995–2010
Martin Curry	1986–1987		

Assistant warden

Dave Bromwich	1986–1989	Sarah Evans	1999–2003
Carl Hawke	1989–1991	Paul Troake	2003–2007
Kevin Wilson	1991–1994	Dave Miller	2007–2010
Mick Lawrence	1995–1998		

Hilbre

Whilst Hilbre has never employed a warden, Chris Williams has been ringing secretary and ringer-in-charge and Steve Williams has been observatory secretary, both over many years.

Holme

Wardens

Peter Clarke	1962–1994	Jed Andrews	1995–2010
Malcolm Cox	1995		

Assistant Wardens

Jed Andrews	1995	Sophie Barker	2001–2010
Rhys Dandy	2000		

Isle of May

Isle of May has been managed and run by numerous willing and hard-working volunteers, many of long standing, and has never employed a warden.

Landguard

Wardens

Rik Smith	1987	James Lees	2000
Dave Butterfield	1987–1988	Mike Reed	2001
Nigel Odin	1989–1995	Paul Collins	2001–2002
Mike Reed	1995	Richard Cope	2003–2004
Mark Grantham	1996	Oliver Slessor	2005–2006
Andy Mitchell	1997	Roger Skeen	2007–2008
Darrell Stevens	1998–1999	George Gregory	2009–2010
Ian Johnson	1999		

North Ronaldsay

Wardens

Kevin Woodbridge	1985–1986	Alison Duncan	1988–2010
Mike Pennington	1987		

Assistant Wardens/Volunteers

Alison Duncan	1987	Josh Nove	1996
Peter Donnelly	1988–1989	Dave Anning	1997
Phil Bloor	1989	Ross McGregor	1997 &
Andy Mitchell	1990–1993 &		1999–2000
	1995	Paul Brown	1998–2010
Bob Simpson	1990–1991	Peter Burston	2000
Ian Fisher	1990	Rob Swann	2000
David Patterson	1991–1992	Alastair Pout	2001
Kevin Scott	1991–1992	Torcuil Grant	2001
Steve Stansfield	1993–1997	James Lees	2002
Nick Ward	1993	Andy Simkins	2002
Louise Barker	1993	Hugh Bell	2003
Jason Bishop	1994 & 1996	Neal Gates	2003–2004
Tim Outlaw	1994	Jen Smith	2005
Alan Leitch	1994	Phil Knott	2005
Dafydd Roberts	1994	Ed Bennett	2006
Lyn Wells	1995	Rael Butcher	2008–2010

Portland

Wardens

Peter Morgan	1961–1962	Michael Rogers	1979–1995
Frank Clafton	1963–1975	Martin Cade	1996–2010
Iain Robertson	1975–1978		

Assistant Wardens

Peter Jennings	1977	Mike Lawn	1984
Simon Delaney	1978	Dave Beadle	1985
Bob Ford	1979	Peter Howlett	1986–1987
Sean McMinn	1980	Adrian Gardiner	1988
David Walker	1981–1982	Martin Cade	1989–1995
Paul Prior	1983		

Sandwich Bay

Wardens

John van der Dol	1977	Mike Pollard	1988
Norman McCanch	1977	Tony Davis	1988–1989
Ian Hunter	1984–1985	Rab Morton	1990–1999
Rik Smith	1985–1986	Kevin Webb	1999–2004
Eddie Maguire	1986	Ian Hodgson	2007–2010
Aron Sapsford	1987		

Ringing and records officers

John Websper	1962–1969	Keith Ellis and Dave Weaver	1978
Maurice Davenport	1970–1972	Keith Ellis	1979–1980
Pete Findley and		Pete Findley	1981
Martin Sutherland	1973–1974	Roger Lawrence	1982–1983
Dennis Batchelor	1975	Keith Ellis	2005–2010
Dennis Batchelor and			
John Walder	1976		

Assistant wardens

Mike Pennington	1985	Louise Barker	1991–1992
Eddie Maguire	1985	Colin Everett	1992
Aron Sapsford	1985–1986	Keith Gillon	1993–1994
Andy Whittaker	1985	Andy Johnson	1993–1996
Richard Newham	1986	Tim Bagworth	1993–1999
Nigel Odin	1986	Ian Fisher	1993
Andy McKay	1986–1987	Ian Williamson	1993
Clive Evans	1986	Rex Dunwoody	1993
Mike Pollard	1987–1988	Rob Wolstenholme	1993
Richard Newton	1987	Dave Gilbert	1993–1994
Colin Davidson	1987–1988	Alison Smithies	1993
Patrick Worsley	1987–1988	Wesley Attridge	1994–1995
Mark Chapman	1987	Nigel Baskerville	1994
Ian Kelly	1987–1988	Duncan Watson	1995–1996
Bill Fletcher	1987–1991	Christine Hawkins	1996–1997
Deryk Shaw	1989–1992	Tim Outlaw	1996–1997
Paul Brown	1989–1998	Andy Young	1997
Paul Naylor	1989	Mike Raven	1997
Neil Willis	1989–1991	Ian Lycett	1997
Steve Stansfield	1990–1992	Mark Game	1997

Simon Mander	1990	Paul Grigsby	1997
Mark Darling	1991	Vinnie Simson	1997
John Walton	1991	George Tordof	1998
Bill Makin	1991–1992	Andy Pierce	1998–1999
Pete Leonard	1991–1993	Mark Gash	2001–2003
David Anning	1991–1993	Mike Lambert	2002
Dave Beadle	1991		

Spurn

Yorkshire Naturalists' Trust Warden with voluntary responsibilities for the observatory
Barry Spence   1963–1996

Seasonal Wardens

Dave Boyle	1996	Mike Pilsworth	1997

Full-time Warden

Dave Boyle	1998–2001	Martin Stoyle	2002
Paul Massey	2001–2002	Paul Collins	2003–2010

Walney

Ringer-in-Charge

Howard Tickle	1964–1965	Keith Parkes	1966–2010

Walney Recorder (from 1970)

Keith Parkes	1970–1978	Colin Raven	1992–2010
Tim Dean	1979–1991		

All the information contained in this appendix has been supplied and checked by the observatories and every effort has been made to ensure its accuracy.

References

Akeroyd, J. (ed.). 1996. *The Wild Plants of Sherkin, Cape Clear and Adjacent Islands of West Cork.* Sherkin Island Marine Station, Sherkin.

Alexander, W. B. 1934. The Heligoland Bird Observatory. *British Birds* 27: 284–289.

Allis, T. 1844. Report on the birds of Yorkshire. Prepared for the York meeting of the British Association in 1844. Unpublished but deposited at the Yorkshire Museum in York.

Anderson, R. 2001. 'JCG' John Gittins, 1928–2001. *Hilbre Bird Observatory Annual Report 2001*: 76–78.

Anon. 1954. *Copeland Bird Observatory Annual Report 1954.*

Aplin, O. V. 1910. Summer in Lleyn, with some other notes on the birds of the district. *Zoologist* 4: 41–50, 99–108.

Arthur, R. W. Bardsey Bird and Field Observatory log file 1957. Unpublished manuscript.

Arthur, R. W. 1963. Summer Tanager on Bardsey, Caernarvonshire (1957). *British Birds* 56: 49–51.

Aspey, N. & Fairhurst, J. A. 1995. Preliminary review of the Calf of Man flora. *The Calf of Man Bird Observatory Annual Report 1995.*

Atkinson, N. K. A., Summers, R. W., Nicoll, M. & Greenwood, J. J. D. 1981. Population, movements and biometrics of the Purple Sandpiper *Calidris maritima* in eastern Scotland. *Ornis Scandinavica* 12: 18–27.

Bagworth, T. 2000. Rare and unusual birds on the Calf of Man 1996–1999. *Peregrine* 8: 47–50.

Bagworth, T. 2003. Rare and unusual birds on the Calf of Man 2000–2002. *Peregrine* 8: 227–230.

Bazin, F. (ed.) 1984. *The Manx Loghtan Sheep: the breed that refused to die.* Manx Loghtan Sheep Breed Society. Published privately, Douglas, Isle of Man.

Bearhop, S., Fiedler, W., Furness, R. W., Votier, S. C., Waldron, S., Newton, J., Bowen, G. J., Berthold, P. & Farnsworth, K. 2005. Assortative mating as a mechanism of rapid evolution of a migratory divide. *Science* 310: 502–504.

Bishop, J. 2000. Rare and unusual birds on the Calf of Man 1994–1995. *Peregrine* 8: 43–46.

Blathwayt, F. L. 1915. Birds of Lincolnshire. *Transactions of the Lincoln Naturalists Union* 3: 178–211.

Bonner, I. R. & Jones, P. H. 2002. *Contribution to the flora of Bardsey: flowering plants and ferns 1956–2000.* Countryside Council for Wales Report, Bangor.

Boyd, A. W. 1946. *The Country Diary of a Cheshire Man.* Collins, London.

Boys, William. 1792. *Collections of an history of Sandwich in Kent. With notices of the other Cinque Ports and members, and of Richborough.* Canterbury, printed for the author.

Bradley, J. 2000. *Checklist of Lepidoptera Recorded from the British Isles, (2nd ed.)* D. Bradley, Fordingbridge.

Briggs, A. 1893. Bird notes from North Ronaldsay. *Annals of Scottish Natural History*. 1893: 67–79.

Briggs, A. 1894. Some further bird notes from North Ronaldsay. *Annals of Scottish Natural History*. 1894: 82–87.

Brockie, K. 1984. *One Man's Island.* Dent, London.

Brooke, M. 1990. *The Manx Shearwater.* T. & A. D. Poyser, Academic Press Limited, London.

Brown, A. & Grice, P. 2004. *Birds in England.* T. & A. D. Poyser, London.

Brownbill, J. 1928. *West Kirby & Hilbre: a parochial history.* Henry Young & Sons Ltd, Liverpool.

Browne, S. J. & Aebischer, J. 2003. Temporal changes in the migration phenology of Turtle Dove *Streptopelia turtur* in Britain, based on sightings from coastal observatories. *Journal of Avian Biology* 34: 65–71.

Buckley, A., Dawson, A., Moss, S. R., Hinsley, S. A., Bellamy, P. E. & Gould, E. A. 2003. Serological evidence of West Nile virus, Usutu virus and Sindbis virus infection of birds in the UK. *Journal of General Virology* 84: 2807–2817.

Buckley, T. E. & Harvie-Brown, J. A. 1891. *A Vertebrate Fauna of the Orkney Islands.* David Douglas, Edinburgh.

Bullock, I. & del-Nevo, A. 1983. The Choughs of the Calf. *Peregrine* 5: 226–229.

Cannell, M. G. R., Palutikof, J. P. & Sparks, T. H. 1999. (eds) *Indicators of Climate Change in the UK.* London: Department of the Environment, Transport and the Regions.

Chadwick, T. & Raven, C. 2006. *South Walney Nature Reserve gull census 2006.* Walney Bird Observatory.

Chamberlain, D. F. 2006. Bryophyte records on the Isle of May, 2–5 September 2006. *Isle of May Bird Observatory Annual Report 2006.* Isle of May Bird Observatory and Field Station Trust.

Charlton, T. D. 1995. Lark Sparrow in Suffolk: new to the Western Palearctic. *British Birds,* 88: 395–400.

Chiverrell, R., Innes, J., Blackford, J., Roberts, D., Thomas, G., Tomlinson, P., Pooley, E., Fullen, M., Hallett, M. & Harris, J. 2006. The Holocene. In: Chiverrell, R. & Thomas, G. (eds) *A New History of the Isle of Man, Volume 1, Evolution of the natural landscape.* Liverpool University Press, Liverpool.

Coiffait, L., Clark, J.A., Robinson, R. A., Blackburn, J. R., Grantham, M. J., Leech, D. I., Marchant, J. H., Barber, L. J., de Palacio, D., Griffin, B. M., Moss, D. & Shephard, M. 2009. Bird ringing in Britain and Ireland in 2008. *Ringing and Migration* 24: 281–320.

Cope, R. & Pimm, S. 2006. A report on Manx Shearwaters *Puffinus puffinus* on the Calf of Man, 2005. *The Calf of Man Bird Observatory, Annual Report 2005.*

Cordeaux, J. 1865a. Ornithological notes from Flamborough. *The Zoologist* 23: 9567.

Cordeaux, J. 1865b. Ornithological notes from Flamborough. *The Zoologist* 23: 9566.

Cordeaux, J. 1865c. Ornithological notes from Flamborough. *The Zoologist.* Second series, volume 1, 1865 (January): 22

Cornwallis, R. K. & Smith, A. E. 1960. *The Bird in the Hand.* BTO Field Guide No 6. British Trust for Ornithology, Tring.

Coulson, J. & Odin, N. 2007. Continental Great Spotted Woodpeckers in mainland Britain – fact or fiction? *Ringing and Migration* 2007. 23: 217–222.

Coward, T. A. (ed.) 1910. *The Vertebrate Fauna of Cheshire & Liverpool Bay.* H. F & G. Witherby Ltd, London.

Craggs, J. D. & Ellison, N. F. 1955. *Birds of the Hilbre Islands, Cheshire.* Reprinted from *The North Western Naturalist* 1944.

Craggs, J. D. (ed.) 1982. *Hilbre – the Cheshire Island: its history and natural history.* Liverpool University Press, Liverpool.

Craggs, J. D. 1967. Population studies of an isolated colony of House Sparrows *Passer domesticus. Bird Study* 14: 53–60.

Craggs, J. D. 1976. An isolated colony of House Sparrows. *Bird Study* 23: 281–284.

Cramp, S. & Simmons, K. E. L. (eds) 1983. *The Birds of the Western Palearctic.* vol. 3. Oxford University Press, Oxford.

Cramp, S. 1988. *The Birds of the Western Palearctic.* vol. 5. Oxford University Press, Oxford.

Cramp, S. & Perrins, C. M. (eds) 1993. *The Birds of the Western Palearctic.* vol. 7. Oxford University Press, Oxford.

Cullen, J. P. & Jennings, P. P. 1986. *Birds of the Isle of Man.* Bridgeen Publications, Douglas, Isle of Man.

Dawson, T., Edmonds, M. & Johnson, R. 2002. Discovery of a Later Mesolithic assemblage on Ynys Enlli. *Report of Bardsey Bird and Field Observatory.* 46: 97–98.

Dean, T. 1990. *The Natural History of Walney Island.* Faust Publications, Burnley.

Dennis, R. L. H. & Shreeve, T. G. 1996. *Butterflies on British and Irish Offshore Islands: ecology and biogeography.* Gem Publishing Company, Wallingford, Oxfordshire.

Duncan, U. K. 1963. A list of Fair Isle lichens. *The Lichenologist* 2: 171–178.

Durman, R. 1976. *Bird Observatories of Britain and Ireland.* T. & A. D. Poyser, Berkhamsted.

Eaton M A., Brown, A. F., Noble, D.G., Musgrove, A.J., Hearn, R.D., Aebischer, N.J.,

Gibbons, D.W., Evans, A & Gregory, R. D. 2009. Birds of Conservation Concern 3: the population status of birds in the United Kingdom, Channel Islands and Isle of Man. *British Birds* 102: 296–341.

Eggeling, W. J. 1960, revised 1985. *The Isle of May: A Scottish nature reserve.* Oliver & Boyd, Edinburgh and London.

Evans, G. H. Bardsey Bird and Field Observatory log file 1964. Unpublished manuscript.

Evans, G. H. 1965. Yellow Warbler on Bardsey: a bird new to Great Britain and Ireland. *British Birds* 58: 457–461.

Evans, M & Edmondson, R. J. 2005. *A Photographic Guide to the Shieldbugs and Squashbugs of the British Isles.* WGUK, Bristol.

Evans, P. R. & Baggott, G. K. 1970. Fat levels and potential flight ranges of some passerine migrants killed at Bardsey lighthouse. *Report of Bardsey Bird and Field Observatory* 17: 45–47.

Farrar, G. B. 1938. *The Feathered Folk of an Estuary.* Country Life Ltd, London.

Feare, C. J. 2007. The role of wild birds in the spread of HPAI H5N1. *Avian Diseases* 51: 440–447.

Fisher, J. 1939. Map to show breeding-colonies in the British Islands of the Fulmar Petrel in 1939. In: Witherby, H. F., Jourdain, F. C. R., Ticehurst, N. F. & Tucker, B. W. *The Handbook of British Birds, Volume 4.* H. F. & G. Witherby Ltd, London.

Fox, A. D., Christensen, T. K., Bearhop, S. & Newton, J. 2007. Using stable isotope analysis of multiple feather tracts to identify moulting provenance of vagrant birds: a case study of Baikal Teal *Anas formosa* in Denmark. *Ibis* 149: 622–625.

Fullagar, P. J. 1963. A survey of the field mice of Bardsey. *Report of Bardsey Bird and Field Observatory* 10: 39–43.

Garrad, L. S. 1986. The countryside in trust. In: *100 Years of heritage; the work of the Manx Museum and National Trust.* Manx Museum and National Trust, Douglas, Isle of Man.

Garrad, L. S. 1990. Nature conservation. In: Robinson, V. & McCarroll, D. (eds). *The Isle of Man: celebrating a sense of place.* Liverpool University Press, Liverpool.

Gauthier-Clerc, N., Lebarbenchon, C. & Thomas, F. 2007. Recent expansion of highly pathenogenic avian influenza H5N1: a critical review. *Ibis* 149: 202–214.

Gibbons, W. & McCarroll, D. 1993. *Geology of the country around Aberdaron, including Bardsey Island.* HMSO, London.

Gittins, J. C., McFarland, V., Cleeves, A. & Barnacal, B. 1999. Professor John Craggs. *Hilbre Bird Observatory Annual Report 1999:* 62–63.

Glenday, C. 2006. *Guinness World Records 2007.* Guinness World Records Ltd.

Gray, C. M. 1995. Feeding ecology of Choughs on Bardsey. *Report of Bardsey Bird and Field Observatory* 39: 75–86.

Griffiths & Wilson. 1945. *The birds of North Wirral.* Informal booklet.

Guilford, T., Meade, J., Willis, J., Phillips, R. A., Boyle, D., Roberts, S., Collett, M., Freeman, R. & Perrins, C. M. 2009. Migration and stopover in a small pelagic seabird, the Manx Shearwater *Puffinus puffinus*: insights from machine learning. *Proceedings of the Royal Society B: Biological Sciences* 276: 1215–1223.

Hardy, E. 1941. *The birds of the Liverpool area.* T. Buncle & Co, Arbroath.

Hardy, T. 1897. *The Well-Beloved.* (original publisher Osgood, McIlvaine.)

Harris, S. & Yalden, D. W. 2008. *Mammals of the British Isles: Handbook, 4th Edition,* The Mammal Society.

Harrison, J. M. 1953. *The Birds of Kent.* H. F. & G. Witherby Ltd, London.

Harvie-Brown, J. A. & Cordeaux, J. 1880. Report on the migration of birds in the autumn of 1879. *Zoologist,* third series, vol. 4, May 1880, no.41: 161–204.

Hayman, P. J., Marchant, J. H. & Prater, A. J. 1986. *Shorebirds – An identification guide to the waders of the world.* Croom Helm Ltd, Beckenham, Kent.

Hellowell, J. 1998. *A Tour of Manx Lighthouses.* Peter Williams Associates, Milford Haven, Pembrokeshire.

Hussell, D. J. T. & Ralph, J. C. 2005. Recommended methods for monitoring change in landbird populations by counting and capturing migrants. *North American Bird Bander* 30: 6–20.

Jennings, P. 1983. The recent status of the Manx Shearwater on the Calf of Man. *Peregrine* 5: 225.

Jones, L. (under the pseudonym 'Islander') *c*.1888–1923. Ornithological records from Hilbre. *The Mersey*, Liverpool.

Jones, L. 1939. *Atgofion Ynyswr.* Hugh Evans, New Brighton.

Jones, P. H. 1988. *The Natural History of Bardsey.* National Museum of Wales, Cardiff.

Jones, P. H. 1993. Agricultural patterns at Bardsey, 1920 and 1990. *Report of Bardsey Bird and Field Observatory* 36: 86–88.

Jones, R. G. & Arnold, C. J. (eds). 1996. *Enlli.* University of Wales Press, Cardiff. (in Welsh.)

Kim, S. Y. & Monaghan, P. 2005. Interacting effects of nest shelter and breeder quality on behaviour and breeding performance of Herring Gulls. *Animal Behaviour* 69: 301–306.

Knox, A. G., Mendel, H. & Odin, N. 1994. Red-billed Tropicbird in Suffolk. *British Birds*, 87: 488–491.

Kruuk, H. 2003. *Niko's Nature.* Oxford University Press. Oxford.

Lassey, A. 1996. Paraphrased from: Record passage of Red-throated Divers in February 1996. *Flamborough Ornithological Group Report 1996*: 67–68.

Lassey, P. A. 1993. A site guide to Flamborough: No. 1 the Fog Station (Sea-watching). *Flamborough Wildlife Group 1993 Report* 72–74.

Law, S. 2008. *Seasonality in the North Atlantic oscillation and its control over bird migration in North Ronaldsay, Scotland.* BSc dissertation, Coventry University.

Leaper, G., Stansfield, S. & Mitchell, P. I. 2005. *Census of the breeding population of Manx Shearwaters* Puffinus p. puffinus *on Ynys Enlli (Bardsey Island), Wales, 2001.* Rep. Joint Nature Conservation Committee, Peterborough.

Ling, S. 1996. 'Eastern' Stonechat – First of race '*variegata*' for Suffolk. *Suffolk Birds*, 45: 166–168.

Lockington Marshall, W. 1978. *The Calf of Man.* Shearwater Press. Ramsey.

Lockley, R. M. 1931. An article about Skokholm, title unknown. *The Countryman*. 78 et seq.

Lockley, R. M. 1938. *I Know an Island.* Harrap, London.

Loxton, D., Kittle, T. & Jones, P. H. 1999. *Atlas of recoveries of birds ringed by Bardsey Bird and Field Observatory, 1953–1996.* Bardsey Bird and Field Observatory, Gwynedd.

Loxton, R. G. & Silcocks A. 1997. The rise and fall of Bardsey Blackbirds. *Report of Bardsey Bird and Field Observatory* 40: 76–99.

Loxton, R. G. 2000. *An annotated list of the freshwater and terrestrial invertebrates of Bardsey.* Privately published. Bangor.

MacGregor, A. 1972. The broch of Burrian, North Ronaldsay, Orkney. *Proceedings of the Society of Antiquaries of Scotland* 105: 63–118.

Mainwood, A. R. 1976. The movement of Storm Petrels as shown by ringing. *Ringing & Migration* 1, 98–104.

Makin, B. 1996. Birding Walney. *Cumbria Bird Club Newsletter* 17: 15–20.

Manx National Heritage. 2002. The Sound and Calf of Man, *Yn Chellys as Yn Cholloo* Guide booklet. Douglas.

Marra, P. P., Hobson, K. A. & Holmes, R. T. 1998. Linking winter and summer events in a migratory bird by using stable-carbon isotopes. *Science* 282: 1884–1886.

Marsh, M. & Odin, N. 1994. The Blyth's Pipit in Suffolk. *Birding World*, 7: 473–475.

Marsh, M. 1987. Great Grey Shrike – showing characteristics of the race *pallidirostris* colloquially known as the Steppe Shrike. Race new to Suffolk and only the third for Britain. *Suffolk Birds*, 44: 154–155.

Marshall, I. 2002. Adapted from monthly highlights. *Flamborough Bird Observatory Report 2002*: 12.

Marshall, I. 2004. Paraphrased from the Systematic list 2004. *Flamborough Bird Observatory Report 2004*: 54–55.

Marshall, I. 2005. Adapted from monthly highlights. *Flamborough Bird Observatory Report 2005*: 13–14.

Mather, J. R. 1986. *The Birds of Yorkshire.* Christopher Helm. London.

McKee, N. D. 1982. *Factors relevant to the estimation of colony size of the Storm Petrel* Hydrobates pelagicus. MSc Dissertation. New University of Ulster.

McKee, N. D. 2001. History of the long-term study of the Manx Shearwater *(Puffinus puffinus)* colony on the Copeland Bird Observatory. In: Zonfrillo, B., Camara, D. B., Bolton, M. & Perrins, C. M. (eds). 2001. *Proceedings of the First Manx Shearwater Conference, Funchal, Madeira 2000.* 59–67 S.P.E.A. Madeira.

Messenger, D. 1993. Spring passage of Little Gulls across Northern England. *British Birds* 86: 397–406.

Mitchell, P. I., Newton, S. F., Ratcliffe, N. & Dunn, T. E. 2004. *Seabird Populations of Britain and Ireland Results of the Seabird 2000 Census (1998–2002).* Christopher Helm. London.

Moore, A. 2004. Choughs in the Isle of Man in 2002, the year of the International Census. *Peregrine 2004*: 8.

Morgan, R. A. 1978. Changes in the breeding bird community at Gibraltar Point, Lincolnshire, between 1965 and 1974. *Bird Study* 25: 51–58.

Morris, the Reverend F.O. 29.10.1874. In a letter to *The Times*, London.

Neal, G. 1996. *The birds of Spurn – a comprehensive checklist.* Spurn Bird Observatory.

Neal, G. 2007. *Birds of the Spurn Peninsula.* Spurn Bird Observatory.

Neto, J. M., Newton, J., Gosler, A. G. & Perrins, C. M. 2006. Using stable isotope analysis to determine the winter moult extent in migratory birds: the complex moult of Savi's Warblers *Locustella luscinioides. Journal of Avian Biology* 37: 117–124.

Newsome, M. & Willoughby, P. J. 1993. Extract from monthly highlights. 1993. *Flamborough Ornithological Group Report 1993*: 4.

Newsome, M. 1995. A site guide to Flamborough: No. 3 South Landing. *Flamborough Wildlife Group 1995 Report* 80–82.

Newsome, M. 1996. A site guide to Flamborough: No. 4 Danes Dyke. *Flamborough Wildlife Group 1996 Report* 80–82.

Nicoll, M., Summers, R. W., Underhill, L. G., Brockie, K. & Rae, R. 1988. Regional, seasonal and annual variations in the structure of Purple Sandpiper *Calidris maritima* populations in Britain. *Ibis* 130: 221–233.

Norman, D. (ed.) 2008. *Birds in Cheshire and Wirral – a breeding and wintering atlas.* Liverpool University Press. Liverpool.

Odin, N. & Cope, R. 2005. Spring Redpolls. *Ringers Bulletin* 11: 71.

Odin, N. 1996. An analysis of the occurrence of Wren, Dunnock, and Reed Bunting at Landguard Point, Suffolk. *Suffolk Birds*, 45: 16–21.

Odin, N. 2003a. Racial, age and sex composition of Snow Buntings wintering in the Felixstowe area of Suffolk. *Suffolk Birds*, 52: 24–25.

Odin, N. 2003b. Red data book moths at Landguard Point. *White Admiral*, 55: 24–26.

Odin, N. 2003c. Pale-shouldered Cloud at Landguard, Suffolk. *Atropos*, 20: 58.

Odin, N. 2004. More notes on red data book moths at Landguard Point. *White Admiral*, 57: 28–29.

Ogilvie-Grant, W. R. (ed.) 1909–1914. Report on the immigrations of summer residents […], also notes on the migratory movements and records received from lighthouses and light-vessels during the autumn […] *Bulletin of the British Ornithologists' Club, 1909–1914*: 24, 26, 28, 30, 32 & 34.

Olsen, K. M. & Larsson, H. 2003. *Gulls of Europe, Asia and North America.* Christopher Helm, London.

Pain, D. J., Green, R. E., Giessling, B., Kozulin, A., Poluda, A., Ottosson, U., Flade, M. & Hilton, G. M. 2004. Using stable isotopes to investigate migratory connectivity in the globally threatened Aquatic Warbler *Acrocephalus paludicola. Oecologia* 138: 168–174.

Pashby, B. 1988. *A list of the birds of Spurn 1946–1985.* Spurn Bird Observatory.

Pennant, T. 1810. *Tours in Wales.* Wilkie and Robinson. London.

Pennington, M., Osborn, K., Harvey, P., Riddington, R., Okill, D., Ellis, P. & Heubeck, M. 2004. *The Birds of Shetland.* Christopher Helm (Publishers) Ltd, London.

Perrins, C. M., Harris, M. P. & Britton, C. K. 1973. Survival of Manx Shearwaters *(Puffinus puffinus). Ibis* 115: 535–548.

Peterson, R., Mountfort, G. & Hollom, P. A. D. 1954. *A Field Guide to the Birds of Britain and Europe.* Collins, London.

Pickett, E. 2001. *Isle of Man, foundations of a landscape*. British Geological Survey, Keyworth.

Pierce, M. A. 1981. Distribution and host-parasite checklist of the hematozoa of birds in Western Europe. *Journal of Natural History* 15, 419–458.

Polunin, O. 1950. Notes and additions to the flora of S.W. Cork. *Watsonia* 1:359–363.

Rae, R., Nicoll, M. & Summers, R. W. 1986. The distribution of Hardangervidda Purple Sandpipers outwith the breeding season. *Scottish Birds* 14: 68–73.

Ratcliffe, D. (ed.) 1977. *A Nature Conservation Review*. Cambridge University Press. Cambridge.

Raven, C. 2005. *The Breeding Birds of Walney Island – a status review*. Walney Bird Observatory.

Raven, C. E. 1942. *John Ray, Naturalist, his Life and Works*. Cambridge University Press. Cambridge.

Ray, J. 1676. *Francisci Willughbeii Ornithologiae*. Royal Society. London.

Ray, J. 1678. *The ornithology of Francis Willughby*. Royal Society. London.

Redfern, C. P. F., Slough, A. E. J., Dean, B., Brice, J. L & Jones, P. H. 2000. Fat and body condition in migrating Redwings *Turdus iliacus*. *Journal of Avian Biology* 31: 197–205.

Rees, J. 1928. A preliminary survey of the rough pastures of the Llŷn peninsula. MSc thesis Wales. Bangor.

Riddiford, N. J. 1991. Migration strategy and population fluctuations: an explanation of the occurrence of birds at Dungeness Bird Observatory during the 25-year period 1953–1977. MPhil thesis.

Roberts, P. 1983. Feeding habitats of the Chough on Bardsey Island, Gwynedd. *Bird Study* 30: 67–72.

Roberts, P. 1985. *The Birds of Bardsey*. Bardsey Bird and Field Observatory.

Salmon, D. G. & Moser M. E. 1984. Wildfowl and Wader Counts 1983–1984 – the results of the National Wildfowl Counts and Birds of Estuaries Enquiry.

Sanderson, B., McGregor, B. & Brierley, A. 1994. *Dive Sites and Marine Life of the Calf of Man and Neighbouring Area*. Immel Publishing Ltd, London.

Scott, D. A. 1970. *The breeding biology of the Storm Petrel* Hydrobates pelagicus. DPhil thesis. University of Oxford.

Scott, M. 1967. *Island Saga – the Story of North Ronaldsay*. Alex P. Reid & Son, Aberdeen.

Scott, W. 1972. *A Check-list of the Flora of Fair Isle*. Fair Isle Bird Observatory Trust.

Sharpe, C. M. (ed.) 2007. *Manx bird atlas*. Liverpool University Press, Liverpool.

Sharrock, J. T. R. (ed.) 1973. *The natural history of Cape Clear Island*. Comharchumann Chléire Teo, Cork.

Shaw, D. 2004. The Chestnut-eared Bunting on Fair Isle - a new Western Palearctic bird. *Birding World* 17 : 415–419.

Shirt, D. B. (ed.) 1987. *British Red Data Books 2: Insects*. Nature Conservancy Council, Peterborough.

Smith, A. E. & Cornwallis, R. K. 1955. *The Birds of Lincolnshire*. Lincolnshire Naturalists' Union, Lincoln.

Smith, Ted. 2007. *Trustees for Nature – a memoir*. Lincolnshire Wildlife Trust, Horncastle.

Sparks, T. H. (1999). Phenology and the changing pattern of bird migration in Britain. *International Journal of Biometeorology* 42: 134–138.

Sparks, T. H., Collinson, N., Crick, H., Croxton, P., Edwards, M., Huber, K., Jenkins, D., Johns, D., Last, F., Maberly, S., Marquiss, M., Pickup, J., Roy, D., Sims, D., Shaw, D., Turner, A., Watson, A., Woiwod, I. & Woodbridge, K. 2006. *Natural Heritage Trends of Scotland: phenological indicators of climate change*. Scottish Natural Heritage Commissioned Report 167 (ROAME No. F01NB01).

Stace, C. 1997. *New Flora of the British Isles*. Cambridge University Press. Cambridge.

Stansfield, S. 2003. Non-avian animals. *Report of Bardsey Bird and Field Observatory* 46: 84–85.

Stewart, J. 2001. Some results from an analysis of ringing and recapture data from the Manx Shearwater colony on Light House Island, Co. Down, Northern Ireland. In: Zonfrillo, B., Camara, D. B., Bolton, M. & Perrins, C. M. (eds). 2001. *Proceedings of the first Manx Shearwater Conference, Funchal, Madeira 2000*. 22–30 S.P.E.A. Madeira.

Storey, A. E. & Lien, J. 1985. Development of the first North American colony of Manx Shearwaters. *Auk* 102: 395–402.

Summers, R. W. 1995. Diurnal and tidal activity patterns of Purple Sandpipers on the Isle of May, Fife. *Scottish Birds* 18: 51–54.

Summers, R. W., Underhill, L. G., Nicoll, M., Strann, K-B. & Nilsen, S. O. 2004 Timing and duration of moult in three populations of Purple Sandpipers *Calidris maritima* with different moult/migration patterns. *Ibis* 146: 394–403.

Ticehurst, N. F. 1919–1920. The birds of Bardsey Island. *British Birds* 13: 42–51, 66–75, 101–106, 129–134, 182–193 and 214–216.

Tulloch, P. A. 1974. *A Window on North Ronaldsay.* Kirkwall Press, Kirkwall.

Vaughan, R. 1998. Seabird city a guide to the breeding seabirds of the Flamborough Headland. Smith Settle, Otley.

Vinicombe, K. & Cottridge, D. 1996. *Rare Birds in Britain and Ireland: a photographic record.* HarperCollins, London.

Wade-Martins, P. 1990. *The Manx Loghtan Story: The decline and revival of a primitive breed.* Geerings of Ashford Ltd, Ashford, Kent.

Wallace, Ian. 1979. Discover birds. Whizzard Press/Andrè Deutsch, London.

Wallace, D. I. M. & Bourne, W. R. P. 1981. Seabird movements along the east coast of England. *British Birds.* 74: 417–426.

Wallis, A. J. 1956. *The Natural History of the Scarborough District.* Vol. 2. Scarborough Natural History Society, Scarborough.

Wanless, S., Harris, M. P., Murray, S. & Wilson, L. J. 2003. Status of the Atlantic Puffin *Fratercula arctica* on the Isle of May National Nature Reserve, Craigleith and Fidra, Forth Islands Special Protection Area. Rep. to Scottish Natural Heritage, Cupar.

Watling, R. 1992. *The Fungus Flora of Shetland.* Royal Botanic Garden, Edinburgh.

Watling, R., King, R. & Riddiford, N. 2001. New and interesting records of fungi from Shetland. *Botanical Journal of Scotland* 53: 57–64.

Wernham, C. V., Toms, M. P., Marchant, J. H., Clark, J. A., Siriwardena, G. M. & Baillie, S. R. (eds). 2002. *The Migration Atlas: movements of the birds of Britain and Ireland.* T. & A. D. Poyser. London.

Whitfield, D. P. 2002. Eurasian Dotterel (Dotterel) *Charadrius morinellus.* In: Wernham, C. V., Toms, M. P., Marchant, J. H., Clark J. A., Siriwardena G. M. & Baillie S. R. (eds), *The Migration Atlas: movements of the birds of Britain and Ireland,* 281–283. T. & A. D. Poyser, London.

Williams, D. 1996 *Bird-watching in Filey.* Akalat Publishing, Bedford.

Williamson, K. 1955. Migrational drift. In *Acta X1 Congressus Internationalis Ornithologici* (eds A. Portmann & E. Sutter), 179–186. Birkhauser Verlag, Basel and Stuttgart.

Williamson, K. 1965. *Fair Isle and its Birds.* Oliver & Boyd, Edinburgh.

Williamson, K. 1967. A bird community of accreting sand dunes and salt marsh. *British Birds* 60: 4: 145–157.

Williamson, K., Rankin, D., Rankin, N & Jones, H.C. 1941. Survey of Copeland Islands 1941. Unpublished report.

Willoughby, P. J. 1994. A site guide to Flamborough: No. 2 the Outer Head. *Flamborough Wildlife Group 1994 Report* 73–76.

Willoughby, P. J. 1994. Where to watch birds at Flamborough. *Flamborough Ornithological Group 1994 Report* 75–76. Reprinted 1995. *Flamborough Ornithological Group 1995 Report* 83–84.

Winstanley, D., Spencer, R. & Williamson, K. 1974. Where have all the Whitethroats gone? *Bird Study* 21: 1–14.

Witherby, H. F., Jourdain, F. C. R., Ticehurst, N. F. & Tucker, B. W. 1938–1941. *The Handbook of British Birds.* H. F. & G. Witherby, London.

Woodbridge, K. F. & Duncan, A. E. 1998. Condition of passerine vagrants on North Ronaldsay at first capture using fat score. *Ringing & Migration* 19: 5–6.

Woodbridge, K. F. & Duncan, A. E. 1999. Condition of passerine vagrants on North Ronaldsay: reply. *Ringing & Migration* 19: 214.

Woodbridge, K. F. 1996. *Population monitoring using migration count data from British and Irish bird observatories.* Report to Bird Observatories Council, January 1996.

Wright, M. 1976. The Calf of Man. In: Durman, R. (ed.) *Bird observatories in Britain and Ireland.* T. & A. D. Poyser, Berkhamsted.

Zonfrillo, B. 2001. Manx Shearwater ecology and diet. In: Zonfrillo, B., Camara, D. B., Bolton, M. & Perrins, C. M. (eds). *Proceedings of the first Manx Shearwater Conference, Funchal, Madeira 2000* 11–13 S.P.E.A. Madeira.